U-BOATS IN NEW ENGLAND

U-BOATS IN NEW ENGLAND

SUBMARINE PATROLS, SURVIVORS AND SABOTEURS, 1942–1945

ERIC WIBERG

FONTHILL

for Cameron B. Clark, New Englander, friend

Fonthill Media Language Policy

Fonthill Media publishes in the international English language market. One language edition is published worldwide. As there are minor differences in spelling and presentation, especially with regard to American English and British English, a policy is necessary to define which form of English to use. The Fonthill Policy is to use the form of English native to the author. Eric Wiberg was born and educated in the U.S.A; therefore, American English has been adopted in this publication.

Fonthill Media Limited
Fonthill Media LLC
www.fonthillmedia.com
office@fonthillmedia.com

First published in the United Kingdom and the United States of America 2019

British Library Cataloguing in Publication Data:
A catalogue record for this book is available from the British Library

ISBN 978-1-78155-720-4

Typeset in 10pt on 13pt Sabon
Printed and bound in England

Foreword

The number of published books with themes relating to World War II by far surpasses all other historical topics. Of these, those that scrutinize naval operations comprise a considerably smaller subset. Yet, it was the war at sea, fought on a global scale, that is arguably the most important single component of this worldwide conflict. Command of the oceans allowed the Allies not only to strike the Axis powers in Europe and to carry the war to the Japanese throughout the Pacific, but it also allowed the merchant fleets to keep the American and Allied armies supplied during the war. The U-boat campaign off the New England coast, examined by this book, was one of the more important battlefields of the global naval war.

It is significant that just over a month after the Japanese attacked the naval base at Pearl Harbor, Germany was able to wage a submarine campaign against the United States within eyesight of the coast. The Germans, operating on the doorstep of our shore, undeniably caught the U.S. Navy off guard. The Navy was hard-pressed to meaningfully protect coastal commerce for many months. The psychological impact of the German attacks was extremely important. The forays on shipping off the New England coast rattled the populace, not only in this region but nationally. After the German successes, many wondered if the U.S. Government was capable of protecting our shores.

There are only a few naval historians that are currently digging into primary sources to find new material and interpretations in World War II naval topics. Eric Wiberg is one of these historians. In his earlier studies, he performed the "spadework" needed to relate details of U-boat operations in the Bahamas and around Bermuda during the war. These operations have been under-investigated by historians, who, for the most part, viewed these actions as obscure and did not study them with vigor. Wiberg helped remedy this failing.

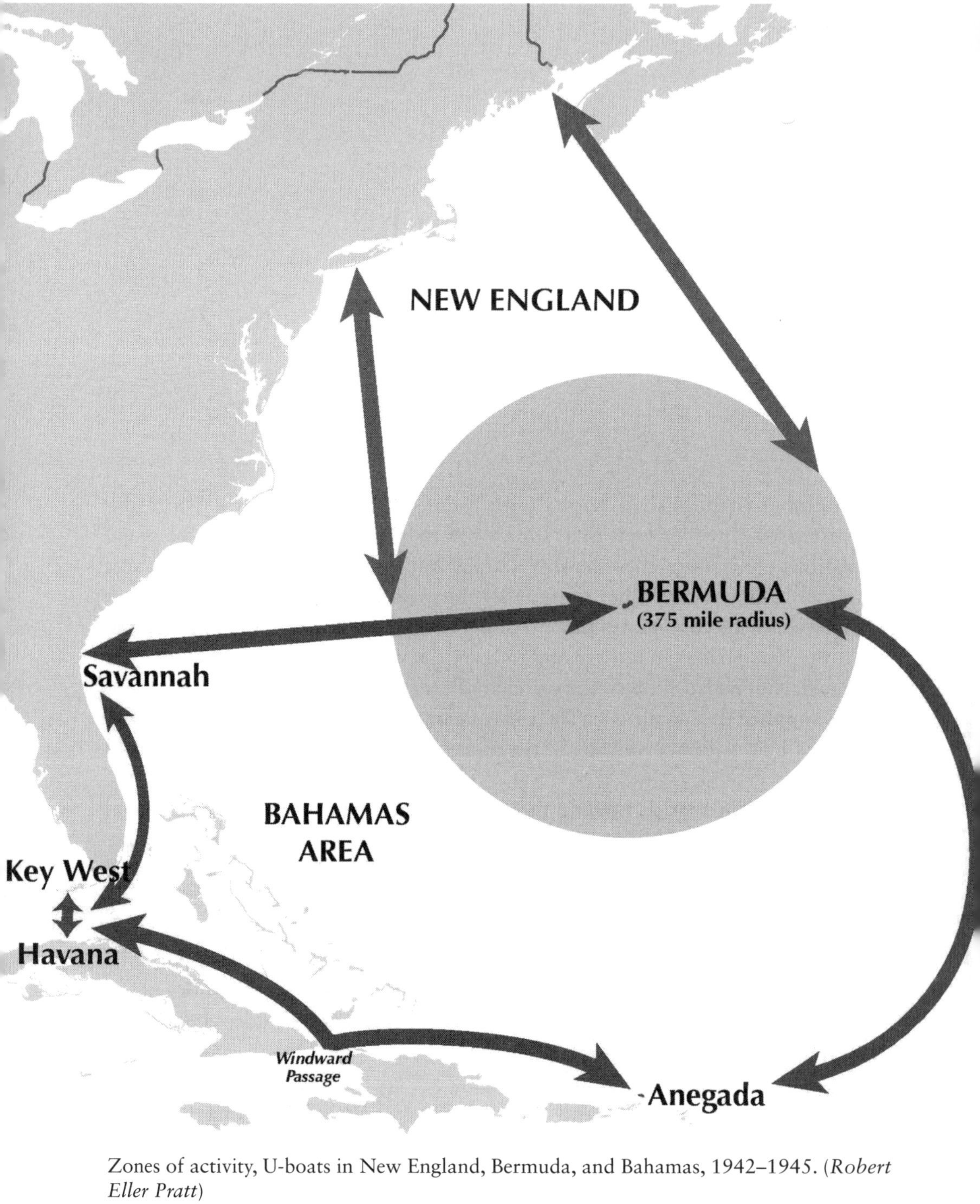

Zones of activity, U-boats in New England, Bermuda, and Bahamas, 1942–1945. (*Robert Eller Pratt*)

U-Boats in New England is a study of the coastal war that follows the path of his earlier works. Within the pages, he provides new details and material to this particular story of World War II. He looks at the regional impact of the naval war and the components affected by the attacks. With great detail, he looks at the U-boat patrols as they unfolded. This format allows the readers to absorb quickly the German exertions, boat by boat, to decimate the merchant fleet sailing off New England. In many of the attacks covered within the pages, he gives an account of the action in intimate detail that virtually places the reader at the event. The author treats the readers with information on both the Germans participants and the merchant crews and their responses during these exploits.

As part of the theatre of operations, he also covers the Nazi landings designed to strike terror into the hearts of the public as well as to slow down American industry that crucially bolstered the war effort. While these covert operations were unsuccessful, they are an important part of the story. He moreover discusses the account of the "Corsair Fleet," the flotilla of private yachts thrown into the war as a stop-gap measure to detect and deter the U-boats prior to the U.S. Navy being able to fully patrol the coast with purpose-built warships. Wiberg also relates the story of the Coast Guard cutters that operated along the coast. Usually, their story is missing or their role minimized in the text. These warships were incredibly important to the early anti-submarine efforts. They significantly made up much of the early coastal presence that combated the U-boats. Additionally, they also performed many daring acts to rescue hundreds of merchant mariners from torpedoed vessels.

Those who read this book will come away with several things. Importantly, they will garner a greater understanding of each U-boat patrol in the region, and how this fits into the overall tapestry of the naval war off the coast of New England. Furthermore, it should give one a greater grasp and appreciation of the participants of this segment of the naval war. Lastly, the reader will obtain a greater perception of the overarching efforts by both the United States and Germany to control the ocean off this nation's northeastern coastline, then the most important maritime commercial sector.

Robert M. Browning, Jr.
Chief Historian, U.S. Coast Guard (Ret.)

Acknowledgments

I thank Guðmundur Helgason and Rainer Kolbicz of the site Uboat.net, as well as stalwart Capt. Jerry Mason of Uboatarchive.net, for their inestimable help, particularly parsing data, cheerfully sharing it, and translating every U-boat patrol to the Americas. Dr. Axel Niestlé solved riddles of U-boat losses, sorting fact from fiction. Michael Constandy of Westmoreland Research and Robert Eller Pratt, cartographer, both in D.C., continue to do excellent work on archival research and map-making respectively. In the U.K., archival researcher Simon Fowler proved his cheerful mettle once again. My agent Alan Morell of Creative Management Partners provided invaluable guidance. John Rousmaniere, Vanessa Cameron, Mark Gabrielson, and Tim James at the NYYC are always supportive. I thank Matt Schulte, Astrid Drew, Bryan Lucier, and fellow board members at the Steamship Historical Society, and Scott Steward, editor-in-chief of the New England Historic Genealogical Society. Other archival researchers include Nathanial Patch, Kevin Leonard, and Kevin Morrow in D.C. and Kevin Reilly at NARA in New York.

I thank Dr. Joshua Smith of the U.S. Merchant Marine Academy; Dr. William H. Thiesen, Atlantic Area Historian, United States Coast Guard; Maurice Gibbs, President Emeritus, Nantucket Shipwreck and Lifesaving Museum; the teams at Nantucket Atheneum; and the Nantucket Historical Association. In Newport, I thank Professor Emeritus John B. Hattendorf; Commander David Kohnen, Ph.D.; and their teams at the Naval War College. Though the conclusions reached in this book may be thorny, this in no way diminishes my personal appreciation for the women and men who serve, and my gratitude that despite publishing critical material, my family is safe due to their sacrifices. My mentors Paul Aranha and David Northrup deserve recognition, as do publishers Alan Sutton and Jay Slater for sticking with me until I publish on a topic where more than 60,000 readers live.

Derek Waller is an authority over the disposition of submarines post-war, and without him, an entire section of eighteen U-boats would be either missing or riddled with errors. I thank Dr. Robert Browning for graciously contributing the foreword, and for his support over the years. Annemarie Bredow, Kai Steenbuck, and Peter Monte and at *Deutsches U-Boot Museum* were very helpful and kind hosts in Germany. Tony Cooper, host in the U.K., and Mike Holdoway of Convoyweb helped immensely, as did Platon Alexiades, host in Montreal, who with Mark Jones traced Italian and French submarine movements. The family of several participants submitted first-person accounts and colorful details, for which I am grateful. I hope to have done their loved-one's stories justice. One eyewitness, Captain Louis Albert Coley, Jr., passed away on May 8, 2018. His family wrote that "it really made a difference in his life to have his experience validated. If you could have seen the relief on his face."

One cannot write a trilogy of this breadth without taking time away from relationships. I recognize that and offer deep gratitude to our son and fellow author Felix, and our family for their continued support. Special thanks to M. C. G. for bearing many all-nighters. Tremendous gratitude to my employers, the McAllister family of New York. K. P. took all of my calls, as have Cam, John, Ann, M&D, Gustaf, Rymes, Paul, and Ian D. Many people supported me in myriad ways: the team at Royal Palm on Harbour Island, at the YC in NY and RI: Emilio, Philip, Alex, Roman, Ricardo, Donna, Ina, Jim, Peter, Catherine, and Peter, and at Doma: Sasha, Becky, Bonnie, Seran, Melinda, Ewa, and Nima. Certain of my immediate circle will be relieved that after a decade this will be the final of my trilogy on U-boat attacks in the Americas.

A note on words: Tons are all gross registered (GRT); miles are nautical (nm); dollars are U.S.$ unless otherwise stated. German U-boats in World War II had both electric and diesel motors, so they never sailed or steamed; rather, they motored. Sydney refers to Nova Scotia, and Nantucket to the island, town, and harbor. Navy generally refers to the U.S. Navy. As for vessels (a term for anything that floats), once often referred to as U.S.S. *Rowan*, DD 405, the same ship may be called simply the *Rowan*. While ship names are italicized, names of foreign shipyards are not, even if the language is foreign.

Since every ship must have a master (*de facto* leader), whether she or he is a licensed captain, Captain Smith is also master of the ship (i.e.: the *Whisper*). S.S. or M.T. before a ship name indicate "steamship," or "motor tanker." Once sunk, the captain could obviously only be in one lifeboat (or dead), yet there might be many boats or rafts. Who became master of each boat was determined by rank but also by merit. If the senior officer on a sailing lifeboat was an engineer but one of the men was an expert sailor, the sailor generally ran the boat, with the officer overseeing rationing and discipline. Often the practice of naming the senior officer present (SOP) to command was enforced by navies and not the merchant marine. By long tradition, ships are known in English by the feminine, as in "she sank," and men alone in boats are never described as acting solo, as in "he did," but rather "they did." A simple way to remember that "port" means "left" is that both have four letters.

The ship's bridge is like the cockpit of an airliner: where leadership decisions are made, data received and transmitted, and courses altered. By necessity, they are often the most central, elevated, and widest rooms and decks of a ship. Think of a drogue as a parachute in the water trailed behind a lifeboat to slow it, and pemmican as a bland protein paste of lard, pork or fruit paste designed to inject energy into depleted bodies. The words "enemy," "American," "us," or "our" are imprecise, and thus are used as rarely as possible. All times are local (Zulu in military parlance), at the site of action whether on land or at sea, not fixed to U.S., Canadian, U.K., or German time. An SSS signal is just an SOS specific to submarine attack. A KTB is simply the daily diary German U-boats kept—literally "war day book" in German, and this is the first book where every available KTB for attacks on New England is readily available in English. The 700 endnotes are provided to be helpful back-stories.

In 2009, Michael Gannon (author of *Operation Drumbeat*) told me via phone: "Eric, be sure to tell all sides of your story." Seventy-five years after the events, we all must be prepared to study what really happened in those dark days. This author's role is a modest one: to let the facts tell a story that is interesting and informative.

E. T. W.
West Village, NYC
November 2018

By the Same Author

U-boats off Bermuda
U-boats in the Bahamas
Bahamas in World War II
Swan Sinks
Mailboats of the Bahamas
Tanker Disasters
Round the World in the Wrong Season
Published Writing
Juvenilia
Åke Wiberg (with Mats Larsson)
Napoleon's Battles (with Felix Wiberg)
Drifting to the Duchess (script with Paolo Pilladi)
Travel Diaries and Voyage Logs

CONTENTS

Introduction

There are some 350 miles between Montauk, eastern Long Island, New York, and Sable Island Light, on the southeastern tip of Nova Scotia, Canada. The route takes ships around Nantucket Island and through the waters of New England, namely Connecticut, Rhode Island, Massachusetts, New Hampshire, and Maine. These waters were vital in World War II, as over 10,000 Allied ships transited the coast in order to join up with the massive column of convoys bridging the Atlantic east to the U.K. The United States government tasked the U.S. Navy with protecting their ships and the ships of dozens of other Allied nations, along this narrow strip. They failed—at least, at first.

When the dust settled, an Allied ship had been sunk for every 10 miles of that short voyage, one lost every month. The attacks began just thirty-four days after Germany declared war on the U.S., and the British warned the Americans with increasingly urgency about the track of U-boats to their coast, but nothing was done. Despite there being U.S. Navy bases in New London, Newport, Boston, Portsmouth, and Portland, with Coast Guard stations scattered liberally along the shores, it took the Royal Canadian Navy to initiate convoys through the area in March 1942.

By then, the British were pitching in, too; their Royal Navy contributed and manned twenty-four trawlers fitted to fight U-boats, as well as ten corvettes, on March 24 then in July 1942, 53 Squadron from the Royal Air Force Coastal Command settled into Quonset Point, Rhode Island, at least for a month. The U.S. had a string of airfields and bases for coastal defense, including a special convoy air escort group at Naval Air Station Quonset Point, and the Northern Air Group under Rear Admiral Felix Gygax in Boston, with bases in Salem up to northern Maine, and the Narragansett Air Group under Rear Admiral E. C. Kalbfus, in Newport. Others operated from Bar Harbor Naval Air Field southward. U-boat

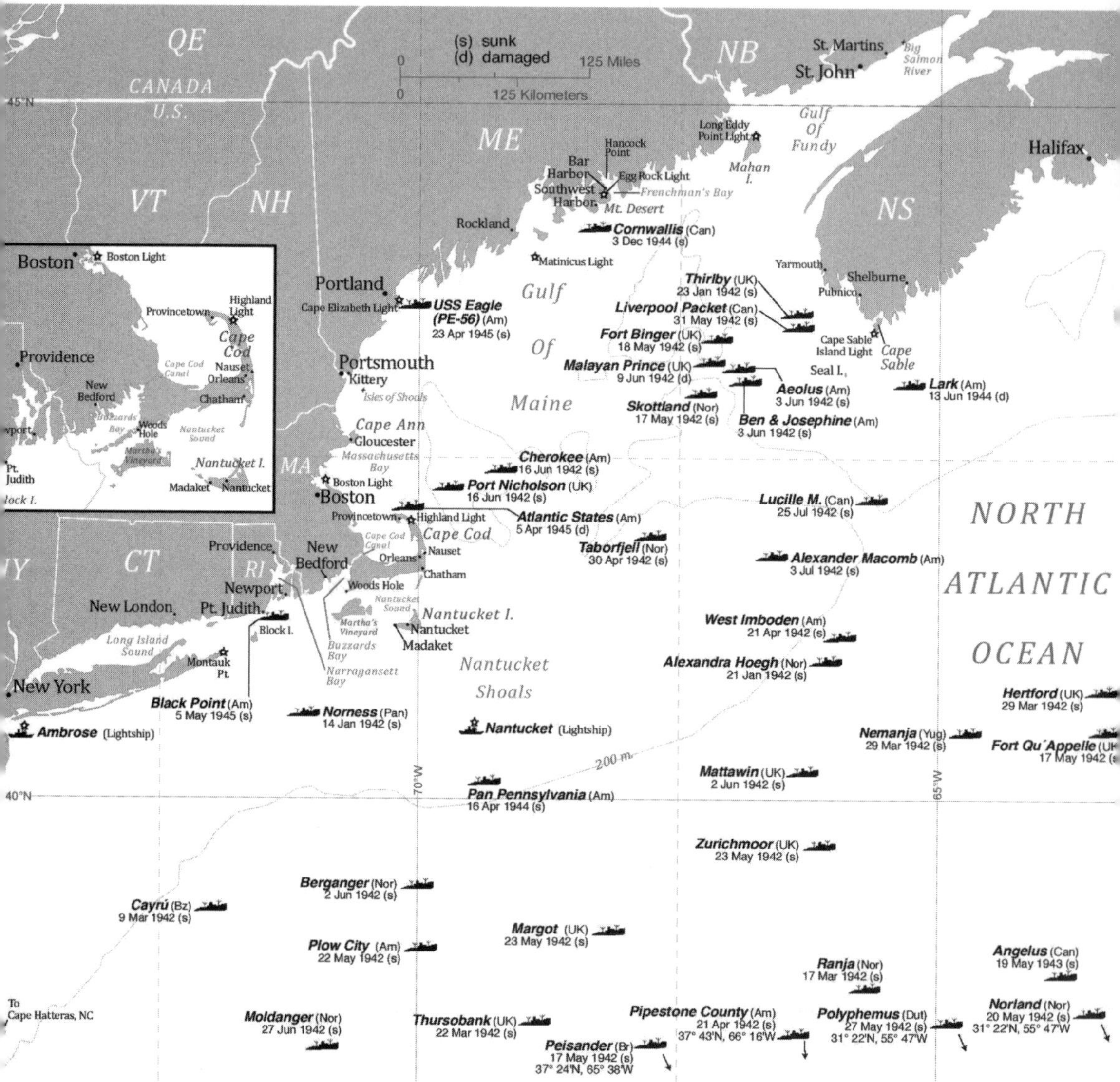

Merchant and naval ships sunk or attacked by German U-boats, 1942–1945 (thirty-eight). (*Robert Eller Pratt*)

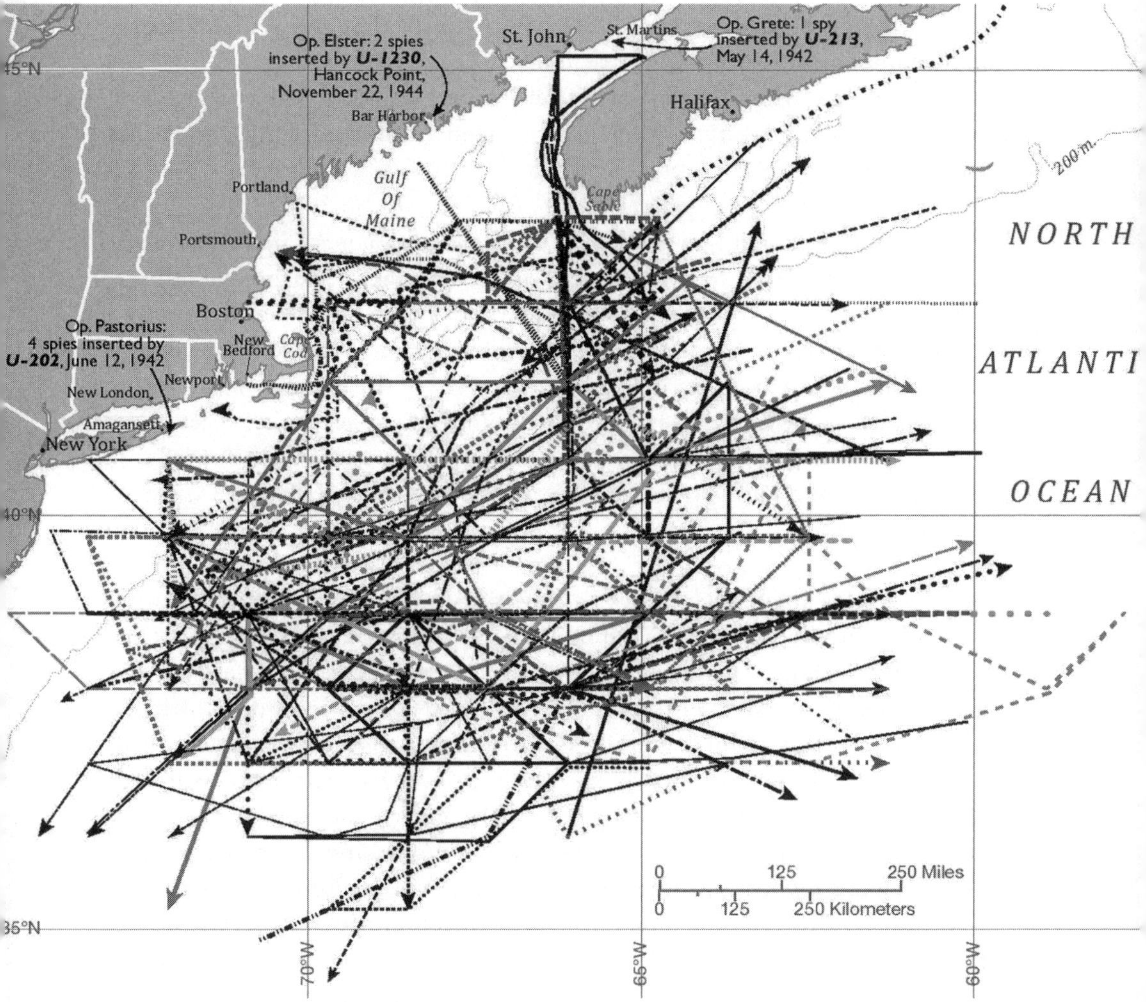

German U-boat patrols (seventy-three) and saboteur landings (three) in New England, 1942–1945. (*Robert Eller Pratt*)

war diaries (*Kriegstagbücher*, or KTBs) demonstrate that those aircraft did eventually harass most U-boats in the region.

In a secret memo after the initial blood-letting, senior U.S. naval leaders admitted this much, writing to their overall leader Admiral King about the Eastern Sea Frontier:

> As established, [it] did not fully meet war conditions.... Commandants of Naval Districts are so occupied with other district activities that they could give but little attention to military and Frontier matters.... U-boat activities along the coast showed clearly that the handling of combat forces required the full-time and immediate attention of local operating commanders [yet] ... the authority of District Commandants was delegated to subordinates—either retired or reserve officers—not fully experienced or competent to handle situations that arose, and not fully prepared to make decisions ... officers actually exercising command should be active officers of high rank.[1]

The memo went on about such basics as a fighting element which goes airborne to sea should "be divorced from the control," of non-combatant support or service personnel ashore. There was talk that the control of District Commanders "would cease at the harbor entrance net." Admiral King's tone-deaf officers suggested sending "additional flag officers" into a scenario clearly already clogged by desk staff. Their offer was rejected by Admiral Andrews' staff, who "believed that additional personnel would not 'meet fully the active conditions.'"

By the time these memos were flying about discussing lessons learned, the U-boats were mostly mopping up their glorious "second happy time," or Operation Drumbeat, and heading south on Operation *Neuland* to the Caribbean, Gulf of Mexico, Panama, Trinidad, the ore (bauxite) route, then Brazil and beyond, as opportunities presented themselves. In other words, the memos had no real effect on U-boats, at least not for some years. German submarines did not return to New England again in force until three years later, on an almost suicidal final assault. The historian Ed Offley wryly noted that "the top ranks of [U.S.] operations and ONI [Office of Naval Intelligence] engaged in their bitter turf struggles, in the midst of which Pearl Harbor might be described as a mere *contretemps*."

All of New England from Quoddy Head, Maine, to Fisher's Island in Long Island Sound (effectively Montauk) fell under the First Naval District, commanded by Rear Admiral W. T. Tarrant, who reported to Rear Admiral (Dolly) Andrews of the Eastern Sea Frontier; he, in turn, reported to Admiral Harold (Betty) Stark, Chief of Naval Operations (replaced March 26, 1942), and Fleet Admiral Ernest J. King, who replaced Admiral Husband Kimmel (who took the fall for Pearl Harbor) as Commander in Chief, United States Fleet on December 30, 1941, then replaced Stark as CNO in March 1942. King was the only U.S. Navy officer to fill both CNO and C-in-C roles concurrently. A flinty Ohioan of few words, one of his own daughters described him as "the most even-tempered person in the United States Navy: he is always in a rage." He served in the Spanish-American War and on U.S. and Royal Navy ships in World War I in the Atlantic, even affecting a handkerchief beneath his ribbons like Admiral Beatty, RN, though he was known to be an Anglophobe. When King told President Roosevelt late in 1942 that he had reached retirement age, the reply was "so what, old top?"[2]

> For purposes of planning and defense, each coastal frontier was divided into sectors and subsectors. For example, the North Atlantic Coastal Frontier originally included the First, Third, Fourth and Fifth Naval Districts, with coastal boundaries extending from the International Boundary ... This area was divided into three sectors: New England sector ... further subdivided into the Portland sub-sector, Boston sub-sector, Newport sub-sector, Long Island sub-sector.[3]

A tremendous amount of coordination between different U.S. land, air, and sea forces as well as among other Allies and other districts was demanded of this very fluid situation. To a U-boat patrolling the coast, of course, it mattered not what unit an enemy craft represented. Their victims in lifeboats, seeing the horizon from a foot or so above the surface, just wanted to be taken to the nearest land.

When the overlays of command and interpretation are removed, the reader is left with very human stories of young Germans probing for a chance at glory and the possibility of surviving to return to France, and Allied merchant sailors performing mostly workaday jobs with no glamor, also hoping to make it through the next line of submarines, over the next wave, through the next storm, and ultimately to a home that lay thousands of miles and years in the future. For the men who manned a thousand Norwegian commercial ships, they could only go home following the expulsion of German troops from their country, occupied in April 1940.

Every reader has heard of Pearl Harbor and 9/11. In the Japanese attacks on Hawaii of December 7, 1941, 2,403 Americans were killed. During the Al-Qaeda terror attacks of September 11, 2001, 2,996 people were killed in New York, D.C., and Pennsylvania. Although at least 5,000 Allied sailors were killed by German and Italian submarine attacks on 397 ships starting five weeks after Pearl Harbor; this fact is little-known and rarely discussed. Both the Pearl Harbor and 9/11 attacks were achieved from the air. The U-boat assault on the U.S. Atlantic coast in both world wars, as well as those on the Gulf of Mexico and Caribbean shores in World War II, were waged from beneath the seas, by an enemy whose very existence, intent, and location the victims could never be sure about. To look skyward alone to anticipate attack on a nation with coastline in the Atlantic and Pacific oceans, Great Lakes, the Gulf of Mexico, and Bering, Chukchi, and Beaufort seas would be to ignore the grim reality that in early 1942, a mortal enemy grabbed the U.S. by the nose, then spent an entire season kicking it along its own coast.

Today, innumerable foreign ships call on U.S. coasts daily, and an unknown fleet of submarines—a number of which have been captured whole by various militaries in recent decades—penetrate U.S. waters from narco-economies to consumers in America. Submarines pose a national security risk today, with some doubting the long-term viability of surface fleets, vulnerable as they were to attack from above and beneath the sea. Enemy and terrorist submarines, manned or unmanned, need to be closely studied.

There were no catchy names, no heroes charging up hills, and no enemy submarines dragged into busy harbors in the tragic seagoing battles described herein; the ocean left no traces of what was etched on its surface. The catchphrase "sighted sub, sank same" was invented by the press. Photos of New York City through a periscope were fabricated by Joseph Goebbels. Germans never recorded receiving aid from shore in the Americas, except when they arbitrarily stripped abandoned ships. No vast intelligence mechanism led them to Allied ships—rather it was down to half a dozen teenagers with binoculars sitting on top of a small tower gyrating in the ocean.

Even today, German U-boat attacks on the U.S. northeast are laced with false rumors of U-boats inside New York Harbor, German U-boat sailors watching movies, buying bread and newspapers ashore, or firing on Allied sailors floundering in the water. While several U-boats saw the lights of New York, they never had to enter the harbor—the ships they wanted to sink came right out. When Germans wanted to land in the U.S., it was not to watch movies but to blow up dams, train stations, and power plants, as well as assemble radios to transmit espionage; therefore, when they were ready, they simply inserted three groups of terrorists on Long Island, in Maine, and the Bay of Fundy (and Florida and St. Lawrence River). Over a period of years, they simply took advantage of the under-protected belly of the U.S. coast to land men, in the first instance simply bribing a U.S. Coast Guardsman, who quickly ran away. Their greatest danger came from Jewish clothiers who recognized the cut of their clothing as being of German and recent manufacture.

U-boat commander, author, and Florida retiree Herbert A. Warner confided in this author that young German sailors were not above bringing souvenirs, including movie tickets and newspapers, from men in lifeboats or the bridges of abandoned ships home to girlfriends, but that they were far too concerned for their safety to ever go ashore on enemy soil. The U.S. was given an extraordinary intelligence opportunity when *U-202* under Hans-Heinz Linder stranded and rolled over 40 degrees in the surf a mere 250 feet off Amagansett, Long Island. It was the final hour before sunrise on the morning of June 12, 1942, and the commander had ordered scuttling charges prepared and a message drafted to tell Germany they would surrender.

The sub's presence was heard by a team of U.S. Coast Guardsmen on shore nearby, as well as seen and smelled by locals on shore. The invasion was interrupted but not prevented by a series of odd delays, starting when a young United States Coast Guardsman accepted as credible a bizarre explanation that a group of armed Germans in different stages of undress were clam fishermen. The soldier sworn to protect the beach then accepted $280 in cash and ran into the night. Though he did beckon assistance, they fared no better, allowing the onset of fog to both sit on their haunches to wait it out, and then, when they heard and smelled a German submarine on its side helpless a few hundred feet away, they did nothing, allowing it, as well as the German soldiers nearby, to get away using conventional escape routes including the public rail system from a village. This prevented the alarm being raised or a vessel being launched from nearby Montauk (20 miles, or an hour away) or Hampton Bays (just 16 miles to the south) to investigate. The Germans were characteristically a step ahead, and at the last moments, the sub's engineers connected all the motors to one shaft and managed to force the beast clear of the sand and into deeper water. The capture of *U-202* would likely have saved countless lives by further enabling the U.S. Navy to crack their counterparts' codes and develop better countermeasures, as well as improve on designs for their own impressive and vastly more comfortable submarine fleet, which destroyed Japan's merchant, tanker, and passenger fleet (including, sadly, thousands of civilian Allied prisoners).

As for resupply, U-boat men did not need supplies from shore; they improvised, stripped vessels they sank or found, and had floating supply subs waiting on the way out and the way back. Often, they met with other U-boats in American waters, affectionately naming the boats by their commanders, as in U-Schultze rather than *U-432*. Where the parties interacted, U-boats provided the Allies with rum, bread, water, and directions—in the case of *U-593* under Kelbling, three times in one day. Where German commanders obtained details of their victim via radio messages sent from the sinking ships, the U-boats often motored away without interacting at all.

The German chief of U-boats only forbade his men from rescuing survivors and taking them back to Europe after his subs were attacked from the air while engaged in a humanitarian mission to rescue survivors of the *Laconia*. *Großadmiral* Dönitz lost both of his sons, Peter and Klaus, in the war, and his son-in-law, Günther Hessler, was asked by the Allies to compose *The U-Boat War in the Atlantic* after the war.[4] When Fleet Admiral Chester Nimitz admitted to a Nürnberg tribunal that the U.S. Navy and the Imperial Japanese Navy conducted unrestricted submarine warfare (including countless cases of men on both sides being shot while in the water), the legal doctrine of *tu quoque* (meaning "but you too") was invoked, essentially neutralizing the charges against the Germans.[5]

While all sides that fought committed atrocities in World War II, off the U.S. coast in 1942, the Germans controlled the surface and below the seas, with the

Canadians and Americans able to control the air with various craft, from airships (blimps) to seaplanes to Civilian Air Patrol planes. That meant that Allied sailors bobbing around in lifeboats were more likely to be found and helped by U-boats than by Allied ships, and friendly ships were wary of stopping to pick up survivors.

Under the 1939 Declaration of Panama, the Pan-American Security Zone, creeping from 300 miles to 1,000 then 2,300 miles from the U.S., essentially kept the war away from the Americas, although everyone recognized that convoys were being sent to the U.K. from Canada, and that the U.S. Navy was, indirectly or otherwise, assisting the Allies.[6] In six incidents from September 1939 to October 1941, 156 U.S. servicemen or citizens were killed by German U-boats, with U.S.S. *Reuben James* sunk.[7] The U.S. answered the Danish Ambassador's request and destroyed a German weather station on Greenland in September 1941, and though U.S.S. *Niblack* claimed to have attacked *U-52* on 10 April 1941, no U-boat reported such an attack.[8] The zone was nullified after Germany became a belligerent of the U.S.'s on December 11, 1941.

The man charged with the security of the entire U.S. eastern seaboard, Vice Admiral Adolphus (Dolly) Andrews, knew what was coming. Presciently, he wrote Admiral Stark from 90 Church Street downtown New York, on the day before *U-123* left France to attack that city, that the Navy did not have "a vessel available that an enemy submarine could not out-distance when operating on the surface [and] the guns ... would be out-ranged by those of the submarine."[9]

Andrews and the U.S. had forty-five ships off Canada and Iceland. There were a dozen destroyers in the Gulf of Mexico and the Caribbean, as well as five destroyers each around Bermuda and the South Atlantic. That left nineteen destroyers ranged from Portland to Norfolk. Then, as they had been warned, *U-123* sank the *Cyclops* off Nova Scotia on the night of January 11–12, exactly a month after Germany waged war on the U.S., then headed for New York via Nantucket. On January 14, Hardegen sank the tanker *Norness* off Newport and the following day, the morning of January 15, the *Coimbra* just 80 miles outside the entrance to New York. Before thirty-six men died, one of them managed to send a distress message by radio. People in the Hamptons saw the flames over the horizon 25 miles south. New Yorkers knew. The Navy knew.

Then the U.S. Navy did something that beggars comprehension to this day: they ordered the last thirty-two warships at their disposal into Task Group 15 to escort each other as well as six Allied merchant ships in Convoy AT 10. This vacuum created a thirty-six-ship force dubbed Operation Magnet, which when it sailed on January 15, steamed over the site of the sinking of the *Coimbra*, even dispatching U.S.S. *Rowan*, DD 405, and U.S.S. *Mayrant*, DD 402, to pick up survivors. Despite many conflicting reports and obfuscations, we know now that ten of those were whisked away from the scrutiny of U.S. journalists and landed in Placentia Bay, Canada on January 22–23. Historian Ed Offley describes the ensuring days as "a panic-driven cover-up by the Eastern Sea Frontier and Admiral Ernest King's headquarters in Washington."[10] So began a vicious cycle by the Navy: deny, defer, misinform, obfuscate, deny more, deny what other officials declare. When all else failed, they blamed the victims by citing intentionally nebulous Fifth Column activity and suggesting that the enemy could not succeed without local help. Was there a method to the Navy's response—a strategy or apparent recipe? Soak these reactive outburts in the blood of thousands of Allied sailors over a period of years, then repeat.

A wall of denial and official silence was to prove most unhelpful to those who were trying to learn what became of their loved ones along shores presumed, naively, to be safe—particularly as tankers could be seen burning from shore: when the *Gulfland* and the *Gulfbelle* collided in October 1943 due to a U-boat-caused-blackout, the *Gulfland* struck the wreck of a U-boat victim named the *Republic*, then beached and burned off Hobe Sound, Florida, for fifty-two days. The failure to protect shipping through U.S. waters was most unhelpful to the factories in the U.K. operating on fumes while the tankers sent from the Caribbean were decimated in the Americas. The losses were embittering to the men, including vocally critical Norwegians, who carried their material to the doorstep of their ally, only to have it shot from under them.

The British soldiers in North Africa were awaiting resupply at the same time, yet helplessly watched the delivery of fifty-five German tanks to Rommel on January 5, 1942, which he used to destroy twice as many Allied tanks (110) at Benghazi. The Germans thus retook Benghazi on January 29, leaving Wavell and his men to fall back on Alexandria. A ship sunk off New England had very real, life-and-death consequences, not just for the men on that ship but the men and women at other battlefields, home and abroad.[11]

Then, rather than hunt and destroy the submarines at their doorstep, the fleet left the coast, left their country, and carried on to Iceland and Ireland, not only abandoning the merchant marine and the U.S., but also knowingly putting the troops in the convoy (thousands, followed a few days later by 22,000 more in Task Group 16 to the Pacific) in the direct path of U-boats. They delivered two ships—the *Chateau Thierry* and the *Strathaird*—in Convoy AT 10 to Belfast, arriving January 26. These two slow troopships, carrying a detachment of a medical battalion, a quartermaster battalion (accountants), military police, engineers, signals, and a hospital station were moving non-urgent behind-the-lines support logistics, which took priority over countering a full-fledged and fully anticipated assault on American shores. In contrast, the arrival of Task Group 15 was heralded as follows:

> Initial increment of MAGNET Force docks at Dufferin Quay, Belfast … Contingent strength is 4,058, Medical personnel in contingent total 41 officers, 42 nurses, and 322 enlisted men. [Commander] M. G. Hartle steps ashore at 12.15 hours in Belfast

> and is met by a delegation including the Governor General (the Duke of Abercorn), the Prime Minister of Northern Ireland (John W. Andrews), the Commander of British Troops in Ulster (General G. E. W. Franklyn), and the Secretary of State for Air (Sir Archibald Sinclair). Officially the first man to step ashore is Private William H. Henke of Hutchinson, Minnesota (although he is actually preceded ashore by approximately 500 others).[12]

The diary goes on to record that "Public Relations Officer in the first MAGNET Force convoy is LTC Theodore Arter ... Initial postal service for American forces.... Six field post offices are established ... Temporary mortuary and graves registration services." Thirty-six sailors on the British ship *Coimbra* probably died unnecessarily so that Billy Henke could be photographed landing with his feet dry and backed by forty-two nurses from the British ship *Strathaird* "first" (only behind 500 others) in a publicity stunt attended by aristocrats and politicians.

Many (especially divers and fishermen) know about the *Coimbra* wreck off New York. Who recalls the momentous time the Allies were making a show of their locking hands far from a battlefield? That very day, the Imperial Japanese Army under General Yamashita was crushing the British and colonial troops at Endau in Malaya (literally overnight), others landed on the Anambas Islands, the British lost H.M.S. *Thanet*, and a tanker named the *Harpa* off Singapore, a *Luftwaffe* fighter ace named Wilhelm Speis was shot down on the eastern front, his boss Hermann Göring was meeting with Mussolini's leadership, the Imperial Japanese Navy submarine *I-73* was sunk by U.S.S. *Gudgeon* off Midway, and Japanese troops on Borneo were probing Singkawang. Meanwhile, back in Northern Ireland, "the enlisted contingent ... purchased civilian clothing at Glasgow retailers Austin Reed."

Blair defended this re-allocation of assets to Europe for "the political and symbolic value of the troops." Clearly, the Navy agreed that preceding General MacArthur's oft-rehearsed "I have returned" Philippines landing to tout Mr. Arter's arrival with a photographic unit was of higher importance than preventing the largest U-boat assault on U.S. shores ever. That same day, off the coast they were supposed to be protecting, 107 British and U.S. merchant sailors were killed by U-boats: ten from the British *Refast* (sunk by *U-582*); fifty-two from *Traveller*, also British (sunk by *U-106*); and forty-five from *West Ivis*, U.S.-flagged (sunk by *U-125*). All the while, *U-123* continued its spree, sinking the *Culebra* with forty-five killed on the 25th and *Pan Norway*, with no casualties, on January 27. Hardegen sank or damaged a dozen ships of 58,000 tons in the Americas on this forty-nine-day patrol.[13]

For years, the standard practice was for Allies to move troops by unescorted, high-speed liners: the *Queen Mary* (which left Boston alone the following day with 8,398 troops for Australia) and the *Queen Elizabeth* alone moved 1,250,000 Allied troops across 930,000 miles, not stopping for friend or foe, lifeboat or in one case an escort ship (the H.M.S. *Curacao*) cut in half by the liner. Three others peeled off for Iceland, and some destroyers made for Newfoundland.[14] In January 1942, four destroyers were retained in New York but sailed six days later for the Pacific; two others were spun off locally: U.S.S. *Bristol* to Casco Bay, Maine, and U.S.S. *Ellyson* for New London to train.[15] Blair, a World War II veteran in the exemplary U.S. Navy submarine service, was in many ways an apologist for King, and staunch defender of U.S. accomplishments.[16] If Blair's "symbolic value of the troops" sent was justification, it has eerie echoes of British Prime Minister Winston Churchill sending green British troops from Durban and Bombay to Singapore, only to have them arrive just ten days before that bastion fell to the Japanese. Was he perhaps leavening the mix of PoWs with more British and Indian soldiers, in order to placate Australians and New Zealanders, thick in Singapore at the time, who, as First Lord of the Admiralty from 1911 to 1915, had sent ANZAC troops to slaughter at Gallipoli in the previous war?[17] Is there a chance that Task Group 15 deserted the world's largest port for political, rather than military purposes? It certainly gave the appearance of form over substance, the deliverables of just over 100 people per thirty-six ships, were, by contrast with other theaters of the time, marginal at best.

Germany took full advantage. The first five U-boats during their "second happy time" (*die glückliche Zeit*) sank twenty-three ships in U.S. waters. The U.S. Navy group left to defend the U.S. East Coast simply left, in its country's time of greatest need since 1812. Meanwhile, the U-boat skipper they left the spoils to had been to New York as a young naval cadet. Hardegen waxed nostalgic while viewing the country's largest port through *U-123*'s periscope (his Italian comrades did the same off San Salvador, the Bahamas, weeks later). The twenty-eight-year-old taunted the Americans in the U-boat's log, writing, "these are some pretty buoys we are leaving for the Yankees in the harbor approaches as replacement for the lightships." [18]

U-123 then ambled away, and on the same patrol sank a total of nine ships of 57,627 tons. On his next patrol, on 27 March 1942, off Hatteras, the same commander was surprised, tricked, and attacked by the U.S. Navy's decoy ship, U.S.S. *Atik* (AK-101). In a savage counterattack, the sub that had made its location known twice at the feet of twenty-three American warships six weeks before sank the disguised warship and all 141 U.S. Navy personnel were killed.

When they realized their defenses were useless, the U.S. Navy at first lied (directly to *The New York Times*, no less), saying they had sunk twenty-eight German submarines in the Americas up to March 11 (not even that many U-boats had arrived) and lost twenty-eight Allied ships. In fact, the Germans had already sunk ninety-one ships, at a cost of *U-85*.[19] Then they decided that any information on sinkings would be "limited." While Germans relayed details and names of ships sunk, often including whether there were survivors, and the German public was then informed via propaganda radio (at times exaggerated, often surprisingly accurate), American families were not informed of ship names and details until after the war. Terms like "an Allied ship" and "an eastern port" sprinkle news articles of the time. The situation was so dire that diplomacy took a back seat to blunt talk: General George Marshall told Admiral King, the highest naval officer in the U.S., "the losses by submarines off our Atlantic seaboard, and in the Caribbean now threaten our entire war effort."[20]

The inertia of the U.S. Navy during this critical time is known as the Battle of Washington, as bureaucrats dove for cover, during which Andrews had to be bailed out by FDR for the *Normandie* fiasco: the invaluable French liner caught fire on February 9, 1942, at Pier 88, New York City, then rolled over and sank. This study is concerned with action rather than inaction. The *eminence grise* of American naval history (after Alfred Thayer Mahan), historian, rear admiral, Oxford and Harvard professor Samuel Eliot Morison, wrote: "the United States Navy was woefully unprepared, materially and mentally, for the U-boat blitz. On the Atlantic Coast ... it had no plans ready for a reasonable protection to shipping ... and were unable to improvise them for several months." Canadian oral historian Mike Parker put it more bluntly:

> not only were defenses lacking, but so was common sense.... The carnage could have been avoided [quoting the British] "it is remarkable that no plans had been made for coastal convoys." ... Admiral King ... steadfastly pursued the outmoded concept of roaming aimlessly in search of U-boats, a tactic which provided no kills in [the first] five months. Direct intervention by Roosevelt was finally necessary to have convoys organized.[21]

Writing in the journal of the New England Historic Genealogical Society, Offley opines that "the U.S. Navy lied to the public about the terrifying U-boat attacks. The news media agreed to government censorship, which helped to hide the military's incompetence in protecting shipping and the lives of merchant seamen." The same writer attributed 5,000 Allied deaths in the Americas in 1942 alone, claiming that with the loss of a quarter of the tankers from the U.S. Gulf, where 95 percent of New England's oil originated, "fuel shortages slowed wartime production and forced gasoline rationing, one of the most unpopular restrictions of the war."[22] An example of outright lies must include Secretary Knox's absurd public claim that the U.S. Navy sank fourteen German submarines before a single U-boat arrived off the American coast, by "making the recent statement that in the North Atlantic the Navy either sunk or damaged fourteen undersea raiders."[23]

The article quotes heavily from a U.S. Navy communique:

> In a statement edged with grim irony, a Navy spokesman disclosed tonight that an unspecified number of enemy submarines had been liquidated off the Atlantic coast but that details on these "excursionists" were being kept secret to deal a blow to Nazi

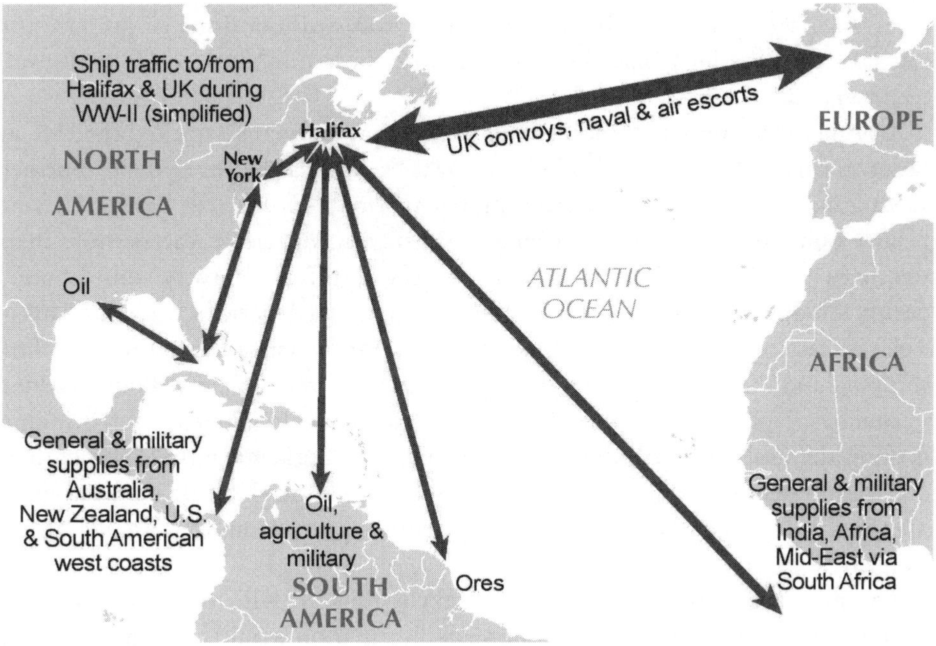

Allied merchant marine supply routes globally to New England and Halifax in World War II. (*Robert Eller Pratt*)

> morale. The Navy Statement [reads] "the percentage of one-way traffic is increasing, while that of two-way traffic is satisfactorily on the decline.... This is a phase of the game of war secrecy into which every American should enter enthusiastically ... from the viewpoint of psychological counteroffensive.... The Navy will 'take care' of enemy submarines, and the people can help the Navy and the country by keeping quiet about what they see or hear ... If you hear something, stop its circulation with you—don't pass it on."[24]

Knox's view of a strategy of silence was perplexing to many, including *The New York Times* authors, and certainly jars against the "see something, say something" approach employed more recently. Would that pens were truly mightier than swords; the U.S. would have fared much better on the eastern seaboard in early 1942, as words filled the air.

Not all leaders were on the same page, with Andrews, FDR, Churchill, and New York Mayor Fiorello La Guardia contradicting each other publicly. While the Navy's Secretary Knox crowed about self-censorship by the press, La Guardia said that the U-boat attacks "certainly bring the war very close. If the people will only realize how close, and what a dangerous and critical situation it is, it will be very helpful." In the same article, FDR stated that "he had been warned three weeks or a month ago that submarines soon would be off our coasts." While true, that statement begs the question: why was nothing done to prepare for the attacks? Like La Guardia's call to action, these quotes were rarely, if ever, re-circulated.

An American-fabricated red herring theory that Germans attacked the U.S. in order to sink a ship with Churchill on it was "scoffed at by the British." Further sewing doubt and fear, the article quotes a British spokesman saying "it was believed unlikely that any submarine could stay in American waters more than ten or twelve days, unless there was a supply ship hidden away somewhere," darkly alluding to a Fifth Column or shore support in American waters.[25] This is a classic case of blaming the victim. If an organization has failed to protect Allied shipping and the general public from predation and remains unwilling to admit it, one desperate fallback or obfuscation is to blame the citizenry for bringing it upon themselves by supplying the enemy. This might have the (predictable) collateral effect of forcing your own populace to start accusing each other of abetting the invaders, further drawing attention away from the organization's shortcomings.

The greatest irony came from Roosevelt himself, who told weekly press conference attendees that "publishing such information would be akin to inviting everyone to inspect a map showing the location of every United States naval vessel."[26] Of course, that is exactly what the naval and Washington establishment dreaded most: a chance for the citizens they were sworn to protect to learn that almost all of the military force intended to save them from U-boat attacks were simply not there. They had been sent to Europe and the Pacific. FDR did not wish his citizens to learn the Navy essentially abandoned them in their hour of need, though they did eventually learn. No one was blameless: FDR went to huge exertions to appease isolationist voters and not alarm them with pre-war naval build-up, which largely created the mess: a lag between the demand for naval ships big enough to effectively defend the U.S. coast and the time it would take to supply them. Meanwhile, the country limped by, using merchant and naval craft built during and for the last war.

Secretary Knox then claimed that "the release of information of attacks on our shipping unaccompanied by information as to what we are doing to protect it, must not be construed by the public as an indication that the Navy has done nothing."[27] In a nation known for its vibrant freedom of speech, enshrined in traditions as well as the constitution, who did Knox and the U.S. government think they were fooling? Their job, after all, was to protect and defend the exercise of freedom of speech by the citizenry in the fight against fascism and totalitarianism. The editors of the *Lowell Sun* wryly observed:

> The Nazi submarine pack has been able to operate so successfully off the Atlantic and Gulf coasts means one of two things, either the United States was taken by surprise and has been unable to cope with this menace, or there is laxity somewhere

> in official channels. Survivors of torpedoed merchantmen and tankers are being landed at eastern ports every day of the week, it seems, while there is yet to be published any report which would denote positive progress in freeing the coastal sea lanes of these lurking engines of death and destruction. Many survivors have complained bitterly of the inadequacy of the patrol system.... Shipyards from Maine to Florida are building merchantmen with breakneck speed—but what is the use if the U-boat menace is not brought under control? We have yet to hear any favorable and authenticated reports on progress.[28]

Take, for example, the contortions which *The New York Times* reporters were forced to make in order, after three days, to get even a vague confirmation of the sinking of a ship 35 miles east of lightship *Ambrose* early on January 15, 1942. Even though fishermen, witnesses on shore, Navy personnel, and pilots observed the wreck, the naval headquarters in New York not only played dumb, but misidentified themselves, and when directly contradicted by their superiors in Washington, where they had sent the reporter for information, still remained silent. Rather than say the ship was sunk, the Navy said she "had been observed 'in a sinking condition.'" Unwilling to say she was British, all they said was she was "flying the flag of a United States ally."[29]

After U.S.S. *Rowan* rescued three survivors, they cast adrift the bodies of three others, including possibly Captain John Patrick Barnard without bothering to identify them; an extremely insensitive practice not seen in 250 other sinkings from Cuba to Canada. The British chief mate, William L. Pinder, aged thirty-one, related how a naval doctor simply "came down into our boat, certified as being dead the bodies, which were not picked up." U.S.S. *Mayrant* bravely launched a whaleboat, managed to bring four survivors to the *Rowan*, and rescued and retained three more before they peeled out after roughly three hours on the scene. Vice Admiral Alfred Eugene Montgomery, Commander Aircraft, Atlantic Fleet, sent out the memo on "Rescue of Survivors from the British Tanker *Coimbra*", from the aircraft carrier U.S.S. *Ranger*, CV 4, to all concerned, from the Commander of the Atlantic Fleet to Commander of Destroyers, Atlantic Fleet.[30]

The Navy knew full well from survivors that a U-boat had sunk the merchant ship. Yet to the press, they said only that *Coimbra* was "presumably the victim of a submarine-launched torpedo," and it took three days for the public to learn that much. About twenty hours after the sinking, "the Navy Department insisted there was no confirmation of the sinking." Then, "even after official word from Washington, Third Naval District headquarters in New York continued to report that it had 'no information' on the *Coimbra*." The site of the sinking was said to be "approximately 100 miles east of New York," which is 25 miles further east than the actual spot 75 miles from Sandy Hook. In any event, the figure is inaccurate, and placed the *Coimbra* attack closer to that of the *Norness*, sunk the day before. *Norness* survivors landed in New York, permitting the press to get the facts directly from the participants, something not repeated for the *Coimbra*, for whatever motive.

Within a day, the press learned that Southampton's hospital was placed by the Navy at the ready at 3 p.m. on the 15th for "survivors of a maritime disaster," however the injured never arrived: many had frozen to death waiting critical hours for rescue by then. The journalists then shared granular details on the German yard which had built the *Coimbra*, and consulted "shipping men," who were skeptical of the Navy's versions of events which said the attack took place "well out of sight of shore." Initially, Long Island police and the U.S. Coast Guard confirmed that "a patrol plane had sighted the sinking ship, and also seen survivors floating in a dory and on a raft. The Navy steadfastly refused to give confirmation to these reports" until Washington had already done so over twenty-four hours later, at 4 p.m. on January 16. Then the cover-up began, with Vice Admiral Andrew's aide saying "there would be no statement," then "a Coast Guard station in the neighborhood of the submarine attack reported it has been instructed by the Third Naval District not to disclose any information."[31]

Meanwhile, members of the shipping industry had been informed "that the derelict of the torpedoed ship [*Coimbra*] still was afloat, and constituted a menace to navigation," with "some reports" locating the wreck just "twenty miles out," as it was that distance south of Long Island. Of course, the Navy and coast guard would neither confirm nor deny at that point for the balance of the war. There was, throughout this protracted struggle to either convey or withhold details of the demise of the *Coimbra*, one party who called it as they saw it: Captain Harald Hansen, aged forty-five, of Vestfold, Norway. As master of the *Norness*, he left no one in no doubt, in New York or beyond, stating that "a third torpedo from a plainly visible submarine sent the *Norness* to the bottom." He had thirty-four other witnesses to back him up. Sadly, this kind of speaking truth to power probably caused the Navy to resent the very men they were duty-bound to protect.

Thanks to the prompt decisive action of a pilot and the destroyer crews, only one of the living sailors perished *en route* to shore, and ten were landed in Placentia Bay, Newfoundland. The *Mayrant* landed their four survivors at 4.30 p.m. on January 22 probably to U.S.S. *Santee*, which was alongside; the following day at 10 a.m., Lieutenant Commander Beverley Randolph Harrison, Jr. of the *Rowan* logged "Transferred six survivors of the S.S. *Coimbra* to NOB [Naval Operating Base] Argentia, N.F., in accordance with orders of SOPA [Senior Officer Present Afloat]." Two went to a hospital on shore and four to a "receiving ship," possibly U.S.S. *Trippe* (which was alongside). Yet this directly contradicts Harrison's message named "Serial 01" of January 20 in which he stated, "Seven survivors rescued and taken to New York."

Since *Coimbra* Fireman and Trimmer Michael Byrne, aged twenty-four, had gone mad in the raft and died on board U.S.S. *Rowan* at 3.30 p.m. the day he

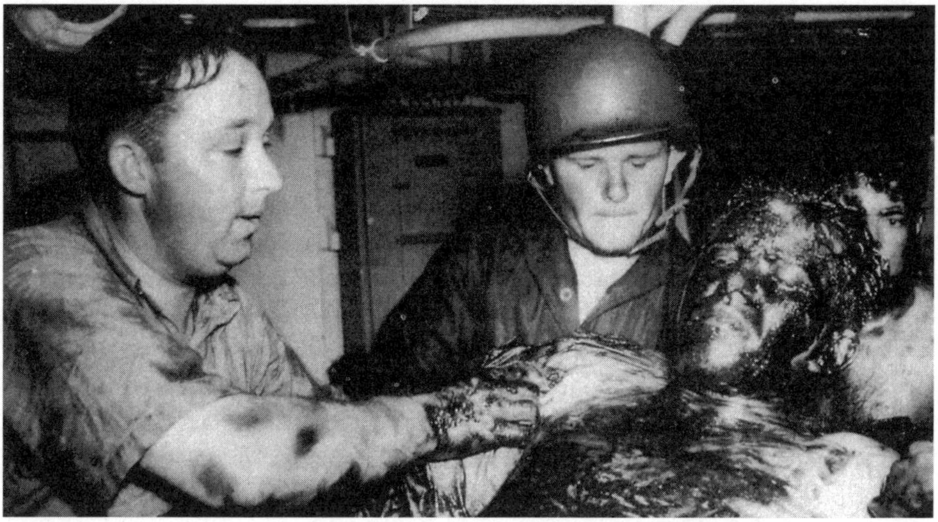

The effects of oil from ruptured tanks and sinking ships on the human body exposed to it, indeed immersed in in, can be seen in this U.S. Coast Guard image of a survivor of German U-boat attack on the U.S. east coast in 1942. Men aboard the *Norness*, the *Pan Penn*, the *Coimbra*, and numerous other tankers on the U.S. shores suffered the toxicity of their cargoes in their eyes and on their skin. (*U.S. Coast Guard, Public domain*)

was rescued, and was buried at sea between 1.01 and 2 p.m. on the 16th (the next day), Harrison clearly knew that he only had six survivors to transfer anywhere, and not the figure of "seven" he informed his superiors. Furthermore, the men were still on board his ship on January 20, on the high seas *en route* for Newfoundland, at the time he sent the message, so it was impossible for them to have also been "taken to New York," which they were steadily going away from, the same day, as he claimed. The six *Coimbra* survivors on the *Rowan* did not, in fact, leave his ship (or the *Mayrant* for that matter) until two days later, after they made landfall.

Furthermore, there is no evidence, or even a likelihood, that the British survivors were taken to New York. Why would they go there? They were much closer to the U.K. and the Halifax convoys in Newfoundland, and clearly, as demonstrated by the contortions they made to obfuscate or hide the truth, the U.S. Navy did not want this particular set of survivors being interviewed by the likes of *The New York Times*, least of all in New York City. Clearly, Harrison glaringly contradicted himself in official correspondence. Yet why would an officer, a graduate of the U.S. Naval Academy in Annapolis, do that and risk his career for a matter that was, effectively, over (after all, the *Coimbra* had sunk a week ago)? He perjured himself and for what? Who ordered Harrison to do it, and why didn't his colleague Edwin Ashby Taylor of the *Mayrant* do the same to his ship's logs? We will never know. Like many other industries and traditions, mariners around the globe live by certain sacrosanct rules, including aiding fellow mariners in distress. One hard and fast rule is that the official ship's log is not to be doctored; it must be clear-eyed, accurate, and never politicized.[32]

The loss of the *Coimbra* and the first half a dozen ships off the east coast was the kind of failure followed by obfuscation which characterized the Key West minefield fiasco, in which the U.S. Navy's Mine Squadron Seven (U.S.S. *Monadnock*, U.S.S. *Miantonomah*, and U.S.S. *Keokuk*, supported by U.S.S. *PC 449*) arrived from Trinidad, laid over in Key West near U.S.S. *Sturtevant*, a four-stack, Clemson-class destroyer escorting Allied convoys and rescuing sailors (118 of them in recent weeks alone). On April 20, 1942, the mine-laying squadron headed to nearby Boca Grande, Florida, and by the 24th, they had sewn a minefield west of Key West meant to protect a convoy anchorage. That day, the three ships lay 1,113 mines, of which two floated free and sixteen detonated prematurely. No one saw fit to warn any naval or merchant ships about the field, with the result that on the afternoon of April 26, U.S.S. *Sturtevant* sped right into it and detonated one; this caused Lieutenant Claude Lee Weigle to reverse to face an attacker, drop depth charges, blow up more mines, drop more depth charges, and split the ship into three pieces. Thirteen sailors were killed in the carnage, two corpses were taken ashore from a sea of 90,000 gallons of spilled fuel, and four more died on the shore. Thankfully, an aviator on an unrelated mission happened upon the scene, since the ship was *en route* toward New Orleans and out of main channels.

The silent treatment continued. The following day, U.S.S. *Monadnock* made no mention of the *Sturtevant*'s loss and they continued mining, on April 28 sewing 1,131 more mines, with two more floaters and thirty premature explosions among them. In the weeks ahead, three more Allied sailors were needlessly killed, since British naval authorities were also kept in the dark and sent convoys into the minefield. On June 14, the Norwegian ship *Gunvor* was lost with cars, tractors, and mail. Five days later, the Yugoslavian ship *Bosiljka* with medical supplies succumbed to the mines. Then the U.S.-flagged steamer *Edward Luckenbach* was sunk while carrying roughly 10,000 tons of tungsten, a cargo of manufacturing metal so valuable that it was said to represent 15 percent of the world's supply. Overall, twenty men and 15,271 tons of Allied ships, plus irreplaceable cargoes, were lost due to a misguided and horribly misapplied sense of naval secrecy.[33]

Inevitably mistakes are made and odd things happen during war. Before the U.S. entered World War II, a German convoy of merchant ships attempted a dash from the Dutch Antilles to Germany via neutral Mexico and the U.S.; the pilot of an U.S. Air Corps B-18 *Bolo* Douglas light bomber witnessed H.M.S. *Orion* firing into U.S. territorial waters on December 19, 1939, in an effort to prevent the German freighter *Arauca* from reaching sanctuary in Miami. The U.S. fired back. The incident began in late October 1939, when the fast German passenger liner *Columbus*, tanker *Emmy Friedrich*, and other Axis ships tried to evade multiple British warships by dashing from Veracruz, then through Florida, where they were only allowed a twenty-four-hour transit, to break out for the North Atlantic and Germany.

For a time, they were shadowed by U.S. Navy ships, leading to angry telegrams from Washington to London demanding the British not fire on U.S. waters. British commanders wondered aloud whose side the Americans were on, when really the answer was their own. The final outcome was perhaps predictable: the U.S. confiscated the *Arauca*, and the British forced the *Columbus* and the *Emmy Friedrich* to scuttle themselves in deep water. Then, the U.S. Navy took the German sailors ashore as emigrants rather than prisoners of war. This status enabled many of the Germans to emigrate back to Germany.[34] In World War I, the U.S. Navy had taken British sailors and passengers off Allied ships being sunk by a German U-boat off Nantucket.

Based on roughly 397 Allied ships being sunk in U.S. waters, and an average of forty-eight men per ship (later in the war there were more likely ten extra gunners; the term "men and women" is rarely used as just one survivor was female), a rough estimate of sailors thrown into American waters would be 19,000, and an extrapolation of 5,000 killed is consistent with other theaters, but little more than an informed estimate. Helgason and Kolbicz cite the following on Uboat.net:

> 339 U-boat attacks resulted in the loss of 4,999 lives (2,366 were aboard U.S.-flagged vessels). The most casualties occurred in the sinking of *Lady Hawkins* (251), USS *Atik* (141), USS *Jacob Jones* (138), *Tacoma Star* (97) and USS *Plymouth* (95). There were no casualties in 77 of the attacks.

None of the attacks in New England were so significant that they took on a *Titanic*-like aura to enter local or regional legend: the largest loss of life was eight-six, from the *Cherokee*.[35] It seems extraordinary that the numbers have not been tallied and made more public, even seventy-five years on.

The authority on the topic and a master at gathering and portraying data, Blair assessed that in the "Americas" overall (excluding the South Atlantic or west coasts, but including Canada and the Caribbean), there were 771 Allied ships sunk by German U-boats. This would convert to roughly 37,000 mariners who would have lost 9,250 persons at an attrition rate of 25 percent—clearly, this is on the higher side.[36] Due to the Herculean efforts of researchers and historians, many of them volunteers, it is possible to name most, if not all, of the 1,761 individuals sunk by U-boats off New England.[37]

The U.S. effectively controlled ASW (anti-submarine warfare) activities from Fundy to Brazil, including around their bases in Guantanamo, Panama, Puerto Rico, Trinidad, Aruba, and the waters adjacent to other major U.S. military facilities (Bermuda, Antigua, and so forth). They and British Admiralty routing officers were largely responsible for much of the western hemisphere's merchant traffic. To add another element, five Italian submarines (the *Enrico Tazzoli*, the *Giuseppe Finzi*, the *Pietro Calvi*, the *Morosini*, and the *Reginaldo Giuliani*) performed war patrols south of New England, between Bermuda and the Caribbean, and sank fifteen Allied ships in 1942. Those attacks resulted in 625 persons thrown into the sea, ninety-four of whom died, with 531 surviving.[38]

In New England, the mortality rate for 1,761 people attacked was 25 percent; in Bermuda, 3,366 sailors and passengers experienced death rates of 29 percent; and in the Bahamas area, 5,299 men and women thrown into the ocean died at the rate of 19 percent. Based on this author's research of the aquatic U-boat battlegrounds from Key West to Canada, the number of Allies killed in action from 397 ships would be 4,250, compared with 5,000. These regions accounted for roughly 200 Allied ships sunk but do not include the area from Montauk to Savannah, out to sea 300 or so miles, or the Gulf of Mexico.

The largest ship lost in New England waters, the *Pan Pennsylvania*, of 11,017 tons, a massive tanker less than half-a-year old, was set ablaze not by Germans, but by friendly fire from a swarm of U.S. Navy destroyer escorts (the *Gandy*, the *Joyce*, and the *Peterson*) aiming for *U-550*. Even though their shells set it ablaze, it stayed afloat until sunk—this time intentionally, and after numerous ships had tried and failed—two days later. In the spring of 1942, lifeboats filled with Allies (whose ships were sunk between Bermuda and New England) were more likely to be met by and provided with bread, rum, directions, blankets, water, and cigarettes by German U-boats rather than friendly navies. One U-boat, *U-593*, encountered three sets of lifeboats in one day; men in the *Empire Dryden*'s lifeboat watched three German subs signaling each other immediately after being sunk. Some survivors of the Norwegian ship *Norland* were sunk from not one but two ships and encountered several others before making shore so traumatized that they could not recall. Survivors of the *Pipestone County* were acutely anxious when, within sight of shore aboard the rescue ship *Tropic Star*, they were attacked again by the exact same sub (*U-402*) off Nantucket.

New England was blessed with the Cape Cod Canal, designed to protect Allied shipping from German U-boats in World War I and completed by a private firm in 1916. Yet after the coal ship *Stephen R. Jones* ran aground and sank in the canal on June 28, 1942, it was allowed to effectively block traffic. For thirty-four days, Allied ships had to round the U-boat-riddled waters off Nantucket and the Outer Cape, adding at least 62 miles to their voyages. One ship, the Liberty *Alexander Macomb*, was sunk by *U-215* on July 3 as a result, and ten men were killed. Finally, the government blew the *Stephen R. Jones* up with 17 tons of dynamite.[39]

There were other alternatives to the sea route: Canadian Railways ran an important cargo railroad across Maine to St. John, New Brunswick, intended to avoid U-boats. Yet trucking was a poor resort, as the trip between New York and Halifax by road is 900 miles, which took too long for too small a cargo, and was just not as effective. As for pipelines, the region was then (as it is still) underserved, but after April 1942, insurers were refusing to underwrite tankers due to the staggering losses, so emergency measures were taken. Wartime pipelines named Big Inch and Little Big Inch were constructed from Texas to New Jersey across between 1,200 and 1,500 miles but did not open until August 1943 and mid-1944. In the interim, efforts to increase oil movements by rail tenfold were constrained by a lack of tank cars. Still, the oil stopped short of New England, which geographically begins on the western borders of Connecticut, Massachusetts, and Vermont.[40]

In 1941, the Canadians envisioned fuel shortages resulting from the Battle of the Atlantic, in which they were actively engaged, so they commissioned the Portland–Montreal Pipeline from Maine to Quebec to ensure safe oil delivery in such a cold climate. Three pipes on the same right of way were opened in 1941 before the supply situation became critical. In the ensuing months, all of Canada's eastern coast, including the St. Lawrence River, came under U-boat attack, as did New England, with U.S.S. *Eagle 56* being sunk just 3 miles south of Cape Elizabeth, Portland in the last week of the war (the U.S. Navy blamed it on a boiler explosion until sixty-five years later). These measures were necessary since there was no coastwise canal system to fall back on such as the Inter-Coastal Waterway. Canada thus lead the way over the U.S. in preparing their rail and oil supplies, their pipelines and their convoy system. Because so many Germans used it to attract and attack victims in both world wars, U.S. authorities finally shut off the lightship *Nantucket*; however, the captains of British and other ships who had not been informed of the measure complained bitterly to the British Admiralty in July 1942.[41]

The Battle of the Atlantic is the longest continuous conflict in the war: it began with the loss of the *Athenia* on September 3, 1939, and lasted to the sinking of the *Black Point* off Point Judith, Rhode Island, on May 5, 1945. It never let up. A reliable database can name 88,067 Allied and neutral sailors from over seventy nations who gave their lives on merchant ships.[42] Over the same period, at least 87,767 Allied naval sailors perished.[43] The same database shows 3,474 attacks by German U-boats alone (before factoring those by Italian and Japanese navies and in other oceans). The U.K. lost 1,660 ships, the U.S. lost over 550, and Norway over 300. In American waters, there are believed to have been 609 ships sunk between January 14, 1942, and May 5, 1945; that would be roughly fifteen a month, or an average of one every two days. Some 348 were sunk between February and May 1942 alone, for an average of four ships a day. Hundreds more were sunk in the Caribbean, from Panama to Trinidad. Roughly 200 Allied merchant ships were sunk off Canada.

Ships that sailed from Calcutta or Bombay sailed over fifty days and covered 12,000 miles around Africa, since Germans made the Suez and Mediterranean too dangerous. They carried ores and other raw materials. From Australia and New Zealand, other ships carted meats and grains nearly 10,000 miles over forty days.

The men operating these ships and the guns on them braved Japanese submarines and surface ships as well as U-boats in the South Pacific (U-862 invaded Gisborne New Zealand on January 15, 1945) to get to Panama.[44] Then, if fortunate, they dodged U-boats from both Operation Drumbeat and Operation *Neuland* to reach New York via the Caribbean and U.S. eastern seaboard.

Allied ships voyaging from India, western Australia, East Africa, and the Middle East faced myriad threats in the Indian Ocean: a fleet of highly effective German commerce raiders like the *Atlantis* early in the war, then Italian, German, and Japanese submarines. Once in the South Atlantic, the German U-boat threat persisted unabated to the doorstep of New York, which *U-123*'s film-maker and propagandist Alwin H. Tölle photographed and filmed in January 1942. If these ships, proceeding mostly alone and without protection, were to avoid becoming one of over 3,500 Allied merchant ships of over 18 million tons (which were sunk by enemy action) and arrive safely in New York, they still had one final dash to get to the comparative safety of Halifax. If the sailors thought they would be safe along the U.S. shores, they were wrong. Some 439 of them would pay for the lapse in protection with their lives. Fortunately, over 70 percent would survive, with half landed in New England ports. Once in Halifax the Royal Navy, the Royal Canadian Navy, and the U.S. Navy combined forces to escort over 25,000 merchant ships carrying more than 165 million tons of cargo to beleaguered Britain and other Allies.

To sail between New York and Halifax at 10 knots took two-and-a-half days. To transit New England waters from Montauk to round the lightship *Nantucket* then north to Cape Sable Lighthouse in Canada took just over a day, or thirty hours. Yet in that relatively short distance, German submarines found and sank thirty-eight Allied ships (merchant and Navy) in the space of forty-one months. Seventy-four U-boats attacked New England; seven others surrendered or were brought there post-war, and thirteen friendly Italian and French submarines were moved along the region's coast during and after the war. All ninety-four submarine voyages are detailed herein.

On that small thread between the U.S. and Canada's most important hubs hung the balance of victory for the British in early 1942, and the Germans under Hitler and Grand Admiral (*Großadmiral*) Karl Dönitz, a veteran of Germany's little known but highly successful U-boat war against the U.S. in World War I, knew it. The seeds for Germany's second U-boat invasion of America were sewn in 1899, according to which "three battalions of infantry would invade New York Harbor, and a battalion of engineers would establish a beach-head on Long Island ... the Navy and army would spread north to Boston." Plan "B" called for 100,000 soldiers to then land on Cape Cod. Much more of an immediate threat was Hitler's 1941 demand for a battle plan for "a submarine assault on ... Boston, New London, Newport ... New York." Although the naval staff considered a submerged assault "untenable" due to strains on the batteries as well as the U-boats and the men, Dönitz did not share the planner's faith in American anti-submarine capabilities. When they did insert Germans ashore months later, it would be in small groups from New York to Maine to New Brunswick and all of them would get through.[45]

In 1941, the Germans calculated correctly that the Americans would leave their flank undefended in the rush to avenge Pearl Harbor, and that they gave many destroyers to Britain in what can only be called a thinly veiled breach of neutrality: the Lend-Lease Act of March 1941, which enabled the U.S. to fortify Bermuda with air bases. Hitler, however, preferred to hold back; he felt the British were planning an invasion of occupied Norway (they did infiltrate in Operation Grouse in October 1942 and then Operation Gunnerside in February 1943 to prevent the cultivation of heavy water for development of atomic weapons).[46] He was particularly wary of the Royal Navy completely bottling up the Mediterranean Sea to German U-boats, something which they came very close to achieving.

The Germans waged a tonnage war: a campaign of attrition through which they worked to strangle the U.S. manufacturing base by depriving it of raw products with which to make airplanes, tanks, bombs, then sink what the U.S. factories were able to manufacture and export. Put more simply, their goal was to sink Allied ships faster than they could be replaced. As Albrecht Achilles of *U-161* explained to the ten men and a dog cast adrift from the barque *Angelus*, "we're out for tonnage, sorry to have to sink her." Five days later, the *Angelus*'s mate, Art Holmans, cradled his son Sandy's frozen body until his crewmates Walter Boudreau and James Boyd forced him to cast him adrift. Many of the stories are gut-wrenching—far from glamorous. While the press played up the rescue by the fastest woman on water, Marion (Joe) Carstairs, of forty-seven sailors from the *Potlatch* steamer after a month in a boat, and their delivery to Wallis Simpson, Duchess of Windsor and head of the Bahamas Red Cross, in Nassau, the men were rolling around the rescue boat in their own vomit and excrement—details the press left out.

Most of the Germans, who lost 87 percent of their boats and about two-thirds of their men, were killed during the war. Many of the Allies died too. Yet naval servicemen resented the higher pay merchant sailors received along with higher mortality rates, and even to this day, merchant mariners have not been granted official World War II veteran status. Since documenting non-English-speaking foreigners working as civilians on foreign ships cast ashore is incomplete, the fate of each sailor lost the region may never be known. Though both Italian and French submarines were used to train the U.S. Navy in anti-submarine warfare, their subs had to be dry-docked in different New England ports, the French and Italian crews disliked each other so much.

One German commander stated bluntly that he worked in the largest ship-scrapping effort in the world, and he was making a valid point. While they sank an average of a tanker every ten hours off the U.S. coast in the spring of 1942, it looked like the Germans might succeed. A major vulnerability for both the British and U.S. war machines, which the U.S. recognized in the Japanese and ruthlessly attacked, was the supply of oil, particularly high-octane aviation fuel, but also the oil needed for factories, machines, tanks, and Naval ships. After Britain effectively lost reliable contact with Middle-East oil due to battles for naval supremacy in the Mediterranean, they and the U.S. had two choices: the refineries at the Aruba, Bonaire, and Curaçao (ABC) islands off Venezuela, where the oil originated in shallow Lake Maracaibo, and the U.S. Gulf, specifically the Houston, Port Arthur, and Galveston areas.

These supply lines had to first reach Halifax in order to make it to the U.K. and to supply the northeast they had to make it to New England, or at least New York. However, the Germans took advantage of several key chokepoints: as tankers rounded Florida and headed north in the Straits of Florida, they were savaged off Cape Canaveral (ships like the *Gulfland* hit another Allied tanker, the *Gulfbelle*, then hit the wreck of a U-boat victim, the *Republic* then burned for fifty-two days, a boatload of sailors stumbled into the home of Mrs. Scranton, whose husband's family named the city in Pennsylvania, in Hobe Sound as she finished a memoir at 2 a.m.). Then they had to get around Cape Hatteras, the dreaded Torpedo Junction. In mid-April 1942, a clearly terrified young Canadian galley-boy named Ralph Kelly aboard the *Vineland*, which was sunk within days, described the following:

> We went down along the American coast without convoy, without lights.... you knew you were goin' to get it, you could sense it. Down around the Diamond Shoals off the Carolinas, you could see where the submarines had chased ships right up onto the shoals and they were sinking. They were afire, there were a lot of bodies around. We seen bodies pretty near every day. Then we said, "Well, it's goin' to be our turn."

When the *Vineland* was sunk by Walther Kölle in *U-154* off the Turks and Caicos on Hitler's birthday, oil-soaked young J. Lawrence Hanson was crushed by debris in the water, yet the thirty-three others made it ashore after four days; one was hospitalized after being bitten by a shark, another, "just a boy, really, was a nervous wreck, having been torpedoed three times," and they were forced to cross the Caribbean then voyage on a Dutch ammunition ship from Curaçao to Halifax, though "they were scared stiff," and were finally entitled to eat at the "Reserved: Survivors Only" table there.[47]

The Germans were even more systematic off Venezuela: knowing that if they sank the shuttle- tankers from Venezuela to the refineries, each would take over a year to rebuild, they attacked and sank enough of them that the mostly Chinese sailors refused to work. On February 16, 1942, *U-156* under Hartenstein shelled a refinery on Aruba, but first, they left the plug in the deck gun and it exploded, then, on hearing hundreds of shouting children from a boarding school, they feared a counterattack and retreated. Yet they hit three tankers (the *Pedernales*, the *Oranjestad*, and the *Arkansas*) in San Nicolas, Aruba. Contrary to a report by the U.S. governor of Puerto Rico, who heard it from the Boy Scouts, the Germans did not shell Mona Island; they made effective use of channels like the Mona Passage and Windward Passage and several others through the Bahamas and Turks and Caicos and along the north Cuban coast to sink ships forced to avoid shallower waters.

Since essentially all of New England's oil came from the Gulf and the ABC group, and the U.K. also relied on the same supply chain, the fact that the U.S. allowed this pillar of survival to be chopped almost to the tipping point is astounding. Only a series of odd events—including the failure to remove the plug from the muzzle and U-boat commanders who effectively disobeyed *Großadmiral* Dönitz' instructions to bomb shore installations because they did not believe it was the best utilization of their weapon—prevented further destruction of oil supply. Ultimately, it might be as simple as the German's strategic refusal to save their torpedoes for tankers. For obvious reasons U-boat commanders also disfavored the unwritten rule that, while refueling from U-tankers, it was better for an attack U-boat, rather than a resupply submarine, to be sunk.

Then, after a series of technological advances and counter-advances (from radar to encryption and decryption of Enigma wheels and signals, to Leigh Lights, Aphrodite, Metox, weather stations in Greenland and Iceland, ASV airborne centimetric radar, ASDIC, Fu.M.U., Hedgehogs, wolfpacks, *Sieglinde, Pillenwerfer*, *Alberich, Siegmund, Schnorchel*, BOLD bubble targets, and myriad other inventions), the Allies broke the back of the German wolfpacks in Black May of 1943, during which they sank forty-three U-boats, all but nine of them in the Atlantic, and *Großadmiral* Dönitz pulled all U-boats back to base to regroup.[48]

Instead of asking where German U-boats and raiders went in WWII, the better question would be where they did not go, because they traversed almost every ocean and sea except the Great Lakes. German, Italian and Japanese submarine operations were ambitious and expansive. The German auxiliary cruiser (commerce raider) *Komet,* HSK 7, crossed the Arctic north of the Soviet Union, from Poland to Japan between July and September 1940. She was escorted through the ice by the Soviet icebreakers named, appropriately, the *Lenin* and the *Stalin*. She then went to Japan and raided the Pacific Ocean, sinking ten Allied ships. She met with the supply ship *Kulmerland*, then the *Orion*, HSK 1, which sank six ships, laid mines, which sank four more, and sank another four ships working with the *Komet*.

The German auxiliary cruiser (disguised raider) *Pinguin*, HSK 5 sailed into Antarctic waters equipped with its own aircraft and managed, on 14 January 1941, to capture an entire whaling fleet, worth 36,000 tons of shipping, fourteen ships, and 20,000 tons of invaluable whale oil valued at over $4 million. The

Pinguin caught or sank twenty-eight ships, mined ports, and sent 52,000 tons of captured shipping back to Germany. The *Kormoran*, HSK 8, was caught ambling along as a wounded Dutch merchant ship by the mighty Australian light cruiser H.M.A.S. *Sydney*, which allowed itself to get within range of the decoy's guns. They sank each other on November 19, 1941, with only Germans making it to Western Australia. The *Atlantis*, HSK 2, sank or captured twenty-two ships of 144,384 tons over 622 days continuously at sea. Overall, nine German raiders sank 140 ships (averaging over fifteen each), for over 700,000 tons. They kept Allied defenses off balance and, once initially converted and supplied, were largely self-sufficient, scavenging off vessels they captured and sharing with their countrymen ashore as well as afloat (one ship carried so many eggs that the Germans and their prisoners ate almost nothing else for months).

On the west coast, the Japanese, who attacked roughly half a dozen other locales (Hong Kong, Singapore, Malaya, Dutch East Indies, Philippines, and Thailand) at the same moment as the attack on Pearl Harbor, had aircraft-carrying submarines ready to attack Panama as well, but decided they would be over-extended. Between November 1944 and April 1945, the Imperial Japanese Navy did launch over 9,000 fire-balloons toward the United States, killing five children and a woman in Bly, Oregon, and possibly setting the Tillamook Burn which killed a parachutist. The Japanese dropped incendiary bombs on Mount Emily in Oregon on September 9, 1942. On the night of June 21 and 22, 1942, their submarine I-25 fired shells at Fort Stevens at the mouth of the Columbia River, also in Oregon. The fort's gunners were denied permission to fire back; however, a U.S. bomber was able to. Ellwood Oil Field near Santa Barbara was attacked by shelling from *I-17* on February 23, 1942, damaging a catwalk, oil well, and pumphouse, with damages not reaching $1,000; however, the attack did trigger an invasion scare. Starting on June 3, 1942, the Japanese did invade and occupy some of the western Aleutian Islands for roughly a year.

The Italians entered the war in June 1940 with a fleet of 110 active submarines. The Germans, who started the war with just fifty-seven U-boats, quickly created the *Betasom* joint venture to harness Italian *sommergibili* for the *Kriegsmarine* and sent them to the Americas, Japan, and beyond by 1942. *Betasom* is a *portmanteau* of 'b' for Bordeaux and 's' for the Italian word for submarine. Axis submarines patrolled the Persian (or Arabian) Gulf, the Red Sea, Mediterranean Sea, Indian, South, and North Atlantic oceans. The Germans went on to build 1,100 more U-boats. They sent five of the Italian submarines to attack the Caribbean, Bahamas, and Florida, with R.Smg. *Giuseppe Finzi* making it between Jamaica and South America. When the flotilla's most successful commander, Carlo Fecia di Cossato in R.Smg. *Enrico Tazzoli*, rammed the tanker *Athelqueen*, bending the bow and torpedo tubes, he coasted the U.S. eastern seaboard in March 1942, taunting Allied shipping as well as confusing German U-boat skippers nearby.

Another Italian Commander, Junio Valerio Borghese of the 10th Light Flotilla (a special operations group), devised a plan to attack West Street, on Manhattan's Hudson River wharves, with explosives delivered by frogmen in a miniature submarine. The Italians had considerable expertise as frogmen in several daring and successful attacks. On September 9, 1942, the Italian submarine R.Smg *Leonardo da Vinci* loaded the midget sub on its deck as preparation for raids on New York and Freetown, Liberia. Though it was to have departed a few days later, the operation's leaders concluded that their intelligence about New York was not current, so the raid was postponed until December 1943; however, with changes in allegiance, it was never carried out. Interestingly, FDR proposed rounding up German-American and Italian-Americans and sending them to camps, as had happened with Japanese-Americans in the desert; however, his advisors—and strong voices in the Italian-American community, particularly in New York—dissuaded him.[49]

No analysis of U-boats in the Americas would be complete without recognizing the innovative contribution of three supply submarines called *Milchkühe* (milk cow), in reference to their large-capacity tanks filled with diesel. These three underwater tankers—*U-459*, *U-460*, and *U-461*—provided fuel and supplies thirteen times to U-boats in transit to and from the battlegrounds in the western Atlantic. As U-boats unleashed their fury on the coastlines of the U.S. and dozens of countries and island groups in the Atlantic, the hundreds of thousands who witnessed the carnage asked "how?" They had been misinformed that German submarines could not reach that far and attack for so long. They blamed traitors and saboteurs from within, playing right into German hands. What the American public did not know was that, beginning in March 1942, seven of these innovative craft supplied 437 Axis U-boats, for an average of sixty-two supplied each (three U-tankers were sunk on their maiden voyages).

As Napoleon said: "amateurs discuss tactics, professionals discuss logistics." The Germans introduced an ingenious feature to their supply chain: to make up for a lack of land bases (they did have weather-spotters in Greenland and Iceland), they created these floating bases. Not only were these huge Type XIV U-boats fitted with massive fuel tanks and pumps enough to feed many Type VII and Type IX attack subs, they also offered amenities such as a large bakery, surgical stations with physicians, extra torpedoes, workshops with skilled machinists, and numerous other conveniences (such as mail from home) for German sailors far from home. The boats even provided a psychological advantage, as they were commanded by veteran aces who could dispense fatherly advice to the young skippers heading west. These included *Kapitänleutnant* Georg von Wilamowitz-Möllendorf, aged forty-eight, on *U-459*; Leo Wolfbauer, forty-six, in *U-463*; and Ebe Schnoor, forty-seven, in *U-460*—all venerated, often older, even aristocratic commanders completely at ease in their roles as father figure and provider.

U-459 supplied *U-566* twice, then *U-571*, *U-135*, *U-432*, and *U-653*; *U-461* refilled *U-89* and *U-332* mid-Atlantic; and *U-460* rendezvoused with *U-202*,

U-608, *U-89*, *U-458*, and *U-132*. Though they could influence the battlefield without entering, it, the Achilles heel of the system was intense communications traffic, which the Allies broke into. Eventually, they were victims of their success:

> Their location 1,000 miles out of New York permitted the smaller VIIC Atlantic boats to operate in U.S. waters, and in the Caribbean during 1942, but vastly improved Allied radar and better air coverage of the Atlantic eliminated them during 1943, and fourteen other XIV were cancelled. The *Milchkühe* were of course a priority target for all Allied forces.[50]

One of the brilliant tactics that the U.S. Navy ultimately employed was hunter-killer groups: essentially floating airfields centered around U.S. and British aircraft-carriers that supplemented air bases in Bermuda and the Azores. The theory was simple: like turtles, dolphins, and whales, U-boats had to come up for air, and quite frequently. Combine signals intelligence with coverage of vast swathes of ocean, which the submarines had to traverse in order to return to base, and there was a good chance they could surprise and sink U-boats, particularly if aircraft had radar. Utilizing these tactics, Allied hunter-killer groups are believed to have sunk fifty-two German U-boats between April 1943 and May 1945.[51]

Some might say that, strategically, Hitler was over-cautious and the greater opportunity lay in the new world. Had the Germans thrown enough U-boats at the line connecting New York and Halifax in 1942, while the lights were blazing and only yachtsmen lay between the Germans and victory, they may well have succeeded in cutting it. The young U-boat commanders who were celebrated as national heroes following daring exploits like the raid on Scapa Flow, the sacrosanct British anchorage, by U-boat, and incursions into ports in Trinidad, St. Lucia, Honduras, and Barbados, called early 1942 the second happy time, recalling when they fought virtually unopposed. Merchant sailors accustomed to being defended coastwise in Europe expressed their dismay at their lack of protection in America. When Washington commanders told the governors and mayors of coastwise states and cities to shut their lights out, they were told "no," as there was money to be made in the tourism business. Astoundingly (from our perspective in a post-9/11 world), the federal government and the military backed down.

Even the bellicose, omnipotent British Bulldog was scared by how close the Germans came:

> Winston Churchill once wrote that, "the only thing that ever really frightened me during the war was the U-boat peril." In saying this, he correctly identified the importance of the threat posed during World War Two by German submarines (the *Unterseeboot*) to the Atlantic lifeline. This lifeline was Britain's "center of gravity"—the loss of which would probably have led to wholesale defeat in the war.[52]

The very definition "under sea" is an indicator of the fear factor these craft wielded; merely being sighted offshore could engage massive Allied resources for weeks or months, even if the submarine had left long before. Cases—like when U.S.S. *Roper* depth-charged the survivors of *U-85* off Hatteras, U.S. destroyers depth-charged around both the *Cherokee* and the *Port Nicholson*, and later several destroyer escorts abandoned forty-four German sailors from *U-550*—demonstrated the fear factor around the U-boat menace was a very powerful if intangible force.

As Robert Kurson (the author of book *Shadow Divers*) put it, U-boats "could appear and disappear in a moment's notice," like sharks, and with similarly terrifying effect. The "fact that U-boats were basically invisible made them psychologically even more terrifying."[53] All of this just underscores the point that while Britannia was said to rule the waves, the Germans dominated beneath them in both world wars, notwithstanding that the British held the surface, and the Americans were able to virtually destroy or at least cripple the Japanese merchant marine.

There was even discussion among the senior leadership of the Eastern Sea Frontier under Admiral Andrews in New York, of moving a picket line of U.S. Navy submarines from Bermuda to New London and having them fan out to protect New England from U-boat attack. One can only imagine the effect that mixing German with American submarines, Civil Air Patrols, blimps, amateur yachtsmen on patrol, and larger naval vessels as well as coast guard and merchant ships would have had. The U.S. lost their submarine (U.S.S. *Dorado*) between New London and Panama, and the French (their massive aircraft-carrying sub *Surcouf*) between Bermuda and Panama early in the war, almost certainly to friendly fire. In any event, by June 30, 1942, the Commander-in-Charge, Atlantic concluded that it would be "impracticable to shift the R-type submarines from Bermuda and St. Thomas to New London."[54]

The general reactions to Operation Drumbeat and Operation *Neuland* to the south were shock, followed by disbelief, then inertia. This was followed by defiant refusal, on mayoral and gubernational levels to have coastal, including navigational, lights, shut off. After having been defied, the federal government imposed censorship even though those close to the action already could learn many of the details of the attack. Finally, the government-imposed cessation of all coastal maritime traffic, first coast-wise, then sporadically, effectively achieved the German's aims without requiring the expenditure of torpedoes. When the government realized that no one was going to win a war by never leaving port, and that hundreds of ships were already on their way to the U.S. and could not be stopped or kept in port, they finally considered implementing the convoy system that they had employed in World War I from Canada to the U.S. Gulf and Caribbean, and which the U.K. and others were using to considerable effect coastwise and across blue water.[55]

The Canadians took the initiative to escort Allied ships in U.S. waters, by implementing a set of convoys called BX for Boston–Halifax on March 18 and XB for Halifax–Boston, starting on March 21, 1942, and lasting through the war. The Royal Canadian Navy force utilized to bridge the Gulf of Maine was called WLEF for Western Local Escort Force, because "the United States was slow to convoy coastal shipping." There was also a convoy named ARG between Boston and Argentia, Newfoundland. Canadian waters had been protected by a neutrality belt only up until the U.S. entered the war in December 1941, after which the whole American coast was vulnerable to U-boat attack. The concept was that by going as far as Boston, the Cape Cod Canal and Long Island Sound could be utilized to bring essential cargoes to New York. St. John, New Brunswick was the first port used, then Boston from April 3, and others from Portland joined from May 7. One of the cargoes was explosives from Searsport, Maine. The interval between convoys was ten days.

There were tweaks, as in when the BX system was extended all the way from Halifax to New York on September 11, 1942. Then, on March 25, 1943, the assembly point for ships crossing the Atlantic in SC (Slow Convoys) was moved away from New York to Sydney, where northern Nova Scotia and the Gulf of St. Lawrence meet. When convoys named HX stretched from New York to Halifax, a smaller group was sent out to a designated point on the open ocean called "'HOMP,' for Halifax Ocean Meeting Point," from which the ships were either merged, assembled, sent onward, parsed apart, or sent into port. These shuttle convoys were called HHX.

One dramatic convoy rescue was performed by H.M.C.S. *Regina*, whose crew pulled survivors of the *Alexander Macomb* out of the cold waters. Just as a well-built fort is so strong that it becomes a deterrent never to be attacked, as a rule, convoys did not suffer enemy losses while transiting New England waters. A total of 206 BX convoys with 3,464 ships in them ran north or east from Boston up till May 22, 1945, and coming the other way the Allies escorted 2,194 vessels in 196 XB convoys. That figure (5,658 ships just in convoys from Halifax and Boston) would allow one to extrapolate that more than 10,000 Allied vessels plied the routes New York to Halifax during World War II since many were not convoyed.[56]

While everyone has heard of West Point (the U.S. Military Academy for officer of the U.S. Army) and Annapolis (U.S. Naval Academy), or Fort Collins (U.S. Air Force Academy), few know of New London (Coast Guard Academy) or Kings Point (U.S. Merchant Marine Academy). The United States Coast Guard performed yeoman's duty rescuing hundreds of Allied sailors, Chinese, African, and American alike, in New England. Founded in 1790, this service came under the control of the U.S. Navy on November 1, 1941, due to an order from FDR, though it had been under naval control before. At the outbreak of war with Germany, the service had 168 ships over 100 feet long and by 1943 had a fleet of 7,960 boats smaller than 65 feet. During the war, the Coast Guard manned

1,444 U.S. vessels utilizing 171,493 personnel, and ultimately controlled 802 vessels over 100 feet. They were patrolling ice off Greenland after Denmark was occupied by Germany in 1940, long before the U.S. entered the fray, and its sailors were at the fronts in Guadalcanal, Sicily, North Africa, the Aleutians, and Normandie. They closely supported the U.S. Marines and U.S. Army as well as the Navy.

In New England, the Coast Guard accomplished a wide variety of tasks from bases from Montauk to Maine, including escort, rescue, reconnaissance, and communication. The nine different Coast Guard vessels and vehicles involved in rescues of survivors of U-boat attacks included trucks on the beaches of Cape Cod, the lightship *Nantucket* (the service maintained thirty-nine of them since 1939), the cutters *Escanaba* (sunk off Greenland), the *General Greene* (at least four rescues in New England), and the *Argo* (rescued survivors of the first ship), and smaller Coast Guard boats who landed men from the *Black Point*, last ship sunk in the Americas in the war. Further along the coast, the *Icarus* sank *U-352* in May 1942, taking the U.S.'s first German prisoners; the *Thetis* sank *U-157* off Florida; and guardsman John Cullen on foot patrol intercepted a team of German saboteurs on Long Island. To take the battle to the enemy, the Coast Guard operated seventy-five frigates, eight corvettes, twenty-two troopships, landing craft manned by coxswains, or helmsmen, and a number of other ships including tankers and amphibious craft. They also had a division staffed by women named Coast Guard Women's Reserve (SPARS), which began in 1942 and employed over 11,000 women.

The *Argo* was there for the first rescue (*Norness*), then mothballed for years, then pulled back into service to assist in the destruction of captured German U-boats off Provincetown in the years following the war. U.S.C.G.C. *Triton*, WPC 116, was sold in 1973 to Circle Line of New York, which operates her still as the *Circle Line XVII*. The *Argo* also joined the Circle Line fleet after 1955 and was renamed the *Sightseer XII*, to be joined by the former U.S.C.G.C. cutter *Nike*, sold in 1966 and renamed *Circle Line XVI*. These vessels were involved in the largest and fastest evacuation ever: half a million people in just nine hours, from Manhattan on 9/11, as well as the rescue of all 155 persons on board U.S. Airways Flight 1549 when it landed on the Hudson River on a frigid January day in 2009.[57]

Regarding the departure of Task Group 15 for Europe, for obvious reasons, strong measures must be taken to ensure troopships avoid destruction. Losses of troop transports account for the highest losses of life in maritime mishap ever, and political fallout is devastating.[58] The Belgian troopship *Léopoldville* was rushing to Cherbourg France with 2,223 U.S., U.K., and Belgian reinforcements for the Battle of the Bulge when it was hit and sunk by *U-486* near France on Christmas Eve 1944, killing at least 819 men (records were sealed until 1996). Survivors tell of hearing greenhorn teenagers on the *Léopoldville*, many of them new to the ocean, crying out for their mothers, and the sounds of guns popping rattled through the *Steuben* and the *Wilhelm Gustloff* as hardened German veterans of the Eastern Front, many of them injured, knew they would not survive the sinking and ended their own lives with sidearms.[59]

These tragedies were complicated. When the U.S.-built *Benjamin Contee* was hit by a German airborne bomb off Bone, Algeria, it was under British operation, carrying thousands of Italian PoWs. At least thirty-two were entombed when bulkheads were sealed in order to save the ship. After being carried 4,000 miles, their remains were buried in a mass grave in Long Island, New York. When the British ship *Laconia* was sunk by a U-boat (*U-156* under Hartenstein), German and Italian PoWs were picked up by subs and ships of those nations, but bombed off West Africa by American pilots, leading to German U-boat commanders being ordered not to rescue Allied sailors going forward, per the *Laconia* order prohibiting rescues.

This is the third of a trilogy detailing German and Italian submarine attacks on the Bahamas, Bermuda, and New England, mostly in the spring of 1942. These sustained and largely invisible attacks had a devastating effect on the integrity and reliability of Great Britain's essential waterborne supply of oil and other necessities, as well as on the security of the United States' eastern and gulf flanks. It also compromised the safety of the coasts of the United States' neighbors, north and south: Canada, Mexico, the Caribbean, and South and Central America.

During the period from early 1942 to Victory in Europe (VE) Day in mid-May 1945, roughly 300 German and half a dozen Italian submarines patrolled the waters of Bahamas, Bermuda, and New England, and sank some 250 often defenseless Allied merchant ships flying multiple flags and carrying a variety of cargoes, including passengers, bulk ore, aircraft and supplies for North Africa, edibles from Australia and New Zealand, and oil from Texas or Venezuela.

New England waters are defined by arbitrary lines projecting south from Montauk as well as southeast from Cape Sable, out to about 300 miles. On those waters, at least 649 men from twenty-two of the ships managed to make it ashore in Connecticut, Rhode Island, Massachusetts, and Maine. The vessels attacked included modest fishing schooners, large modern tankers, a U.S. Navy vessel, and a mix of other craft. Small as it was, New England cannot be dismissed as an insignificant battlefield; nearly 200,000 tons (194,240 gross registered tons) of shipping were attacked, and 1,850 Allied sailors and gunners were thrown into the cold seas, of whom at least 492 perished. More than half of the 1,358 managed to row or sail ashore or be rescued in sixteen ports in four states (none landed in New Hampshire).[60]

Nearly thirty different boats and ships—civilian, coast guard, and military—worked together to bring the men ashore. In several instances, men were sunk two or even three times, saw as many as five U-boats on just one voyage, and were transferred among several vessels before they could lay their heads down on *terra firma*, in such places as Madaket, Nauset, Brighton, Mt. Desert Rock,

Southwest Harbor, Point Judith, and New Bedford. Geographically, arbitrary lines from Montauk and Maine seaward are imperfect, as several ships fall on or near the line, starting with *Cyclops*, the first ship sunk in Operation Drumbeat, but in Canadian waters and the *Cayrú*, from which fifty-three souls lost their lives in New York waters. *U-84* under Otto Ites sank her on March 9, 1942, and when the American coastal minesweeper U.S.S. *AMc 202* discovered a lifeboat that had held twenty-one Brazilians, only six were alive. They were delivered, along with a frozen cadaver, to New London on the 12th. Some incidents thus may fall outside of the arbitrary lines; there may even be other ships sunk far away whose people were landed in New England, as hundreds of thousands of sailors served. While one goal was to include geographically New England waters, another has been simply to identify and carefully cover the U-boats activities in a strictly defined area not exclusively covered before, whereas the waters of Canada, New York, and the Carolinas have been well covered.

The fact the U.S. allowed German submarines to approach their shores near enough to land three teams of enemy saboteurs—in Amagansett, where they breezed through a Coast Guard picket to board a train to New York City, in Frenchman's Bay, Maine, and St. Martin's, Bay of Fundy—is a blemish on the country's national security record. It was pure luck that the young quasi-American perpetrators were, as a rule, more interested in profligately spending their troves of cash, then turned themselves, and their companions, in. That the Germans had done this to the U.S. before makes their second attacks more egregious. In World War I, the privately funded German cargo submarines *Deutschland* and *Bremen* traded in Baltimore and New London. The *Bremen* was *en route* to Norfolk in September 1916 with funds to start a submarine-building program in the U.S. She is believed sunk by H.M.S. *G 13* off the Shetland Islands. Hapag-Lloyd and Deutsche Bank funded the expeditions, designed to bypass the Royal Navy's blockade of German ports.

On the first voyage to America, the *Deutschland* carried a mixed cargo valued at $17.5 million—several times the cost of its manufacture. On the second voyage, she called at New London with $.25 billion worth of gems, securities, and medicines. Despite sinking the U.S. tugboat *T. A. Scott, Jr.*, killing all five officers and men, on November 16, 1916, and the fact that *U-53* had visited the U.S. Navy base in Newport on October 7, 1916, then sunk four Allied ships. SM (denoting World War I vintage) *U-53* stopped and searched other Allied ships, only ending when the British ship *Stephano* was stopped and searched and "the gathering American destroyers took off its crew and passengers," enabling the Germans to then sink her.[61] Despite all this, the *Deutschland* was repaired in New London and returned to Germany with at least 6.5 tons of silver bullion in November.[62] The *Deutschland* was then put to use by the Imperial German Navy and, as SM *U-155*, she sank forty-two Allied ships on three patrols. She survived the war after an expedition to cut telegraph cables at St. John's and a patrol off Nantucket in September 1918.

SM *U-53*'s commander Hans Rose visited Admirals Gleaves and Knights in Newport and the U.S.S. *Birmingham* on October 7, 1916, when the Newport harbor master started asking whether the submarine might be interned. SM *U-53* audaciously motored out to the lightship *Nantucket*, where it spared an American passenger ship then attacked and sank the Allied ships the *Christian Knutsen*, the *Strathdene*, the *West Point*, the *Blommersdyk*, and the *Stephano*. Seventeen U.S. Navy destroyers on scene stood by uselessly and watched the carnage. Less than two months later, the same sub, SM *U-53*, under the same commander, Rose, sank the U.S.S. *Jacob Jones* off France, killing sixty-six American sailors. Overall, 375 German U-boats sank 7,548 Allied ships, sail to steam, worth over 15.6 million tons in World War I. SM *U-53* alone sank eighty-eight of them, while SM *U-35* sank 226 vessels. The U.S. lost 174 ships in the war, 116 of them off North America.

The British, who urgently dispatched three Canadian destroyers from Canada to catch SM *U-53* without result, were not amused, nor were they again when the U.S. Navy failed to act upon Britain's hard-won lessons on the importance of convoys and other defensive strategies until their noses had been badly bloodied in World War II. The U.S. Navy's inertia spurred their neighbors to the north into action, and the U.S. allowed Canada to escort ships from Boston and Portland to New York. That may explain why this story of German attacks on the U.S. between 1916 and 1945 are rarely told; the details are an embarrassment to the extent that the Germans called early 1942 in the Americas the "second happy time." Teddy Suhren, who sank over 125,000 tons of Allied shipping from *U-564*, related how German U-boat officers and crew were regaled in French ports by Parisian and Berlin society, and even the elite *Waffen SS* bodyguards at Hitler's *Berchtesgaden* compound made exceptions for the mad mavericks of the U-boat arm who were grateful to be alive and fond of returning to the compound early in the morning and in their cups.[63]

The fact is that the U.S. Navy cannot credibly assert that they did not have direct timely warnings from the British about the World War II attacks, or that they were unaware of extensive World War I attacks, based on first-hand experience, either. On July 21, 1918, SM U-*156* under Richard Feldt approached and fired upon the town of Orleans, on the outer coast of Cape Cod. The shells landed on Nauset Beach (where *Mattawin* survivors landed on June 4, 1942) and in a marsh, prompting a local to fire back with a shotgun from a bluff, a surfboat to launch and row against enemy fire to rescue thirty-two sailors, and flying boats and R 9 bomber planes from nearby Chatham to counterattack with sacks of TNT explosives. SM *U-156* then used two deck guns to attack and sink four barges and chase off their tug, the *Perth Amboy*.[64] Mines laid by the same sub sank the U.S. Navy's 13,680-ton armored cruiser U.S.S. *San Diego en route* out of New York, killing six. At least six German U-boats attacked the U.S. from June to September 1918: SM *U-151*, SM *U-156*, SM *U-140*, SM *U-117*, SM *U-155*, and SM *U-152*.[65]

New England and Canadian lighthouses played an important part for both sides, as did lightships. The navigational aids most referenced by U-boats and their victims, starting in Canada, were Sable Island Light, Mt. Desert Rock Light, Thatcher Island Twin Lights on Cape Ann, Boston Light, Highland Light at Provincetown, Chatham Light, lightship *Nantucket*, and Montauk Point Light. U-boats that moved closer in-shore utilized smaller lights, such as Owls Head off Rockland, Maine; Cape Elizabeth off Portland; Nauset Light in Cape Cod; and so on. *U-552* on April 26, 1942 (and *U-556* two days later) utilized the lighthouse at Nauset to rest at the bottom, midway between Nantucket and Provincetown. Wreckage and bodies floated ashore at Cape Cod as they had in the World War I, and not just Allies: two German sailors are buried in Newport and others are buried in Fort Devens, Massachusetts, and on Long Island.[66]

The town fathers on Nantucket Island in the summer of 1942 were so concerned about losing their well-heeled visitors due to U-boat scares that the selectmen first threatened ("admonished") islanders not to spread U-boat rumors, then sagaciously sent a task force called the Nantucket Public Relations Committee to New York. One result was an article in *The New York Times* extolling the "charming" island and its safe ferry system.[67] In fact, ninety survivors of four Allied ships were taken to and tended on the island, which serves as a geographic fulcrum for aquatic New England. There was a blackout; the army, Navy, and air force all occupied the island; and two of their ferries were requisitioned by the Navy. Beaches were strewn with "wreckage, debris, and oil from sunken tankers and other targets of the U-boats were found along the shores, and many souvenirs were carried home by beachcombers."[68] So many ships utilized the Cape Cod Canal that Cape Cod was effectively cut off for many hours at a time until the drawbridges closed again.

Given later anti-submarine efforts, the lookouts who strained their eyes seaward, the brave sailors who plied the waves in small, inadequate amateur craft (the corsair fleet, or hooligan Navy), and the aviators and many servicemen who risked (and gave) their lives to protect America's shore, it is vitally important that the full details of these episodes be aired for future researchers while some of the survivors of these incidents are still alive. The merchant mariners remain an unheralded, often even unknown, branch of the nation's defense network, but nevertheless still a vital one, like that of the U.S. Coast Guard.

As we bear the responsibility of telling the details of World War II (the smaller, more intimate human-interest stories of survival, second-chances and untold acts of compassion and bravery), we learn of the volunteers who left Ivy League universities to sail to the battles of North Africa, Italy, and Burma, of Red Cross volunteers in small New England towns who went out of their way, and in strict secrecy, to aid freezing, starving mariners, many of them badly traumatized and often unable, by virtue of their international backgrounds, to speak English. We can imagine the sheer frustration of the Allies: for two weeks, Nantucket was abuzz with nearly 100 survivors, yet for the other 164 weeks, none arrived. The U.S.C.G. cutter *General Greene* had to spend most of its sea time patiently standing sentry duty on picket lines protecting Newport. Since U-boat tactics relied on surprising soft targets to minimize losses, they only struck hard in the first few (and then the last few) months of the war.

The battle was not entirely one-sided: Allies (U.S., Canadian, and British navies) managed to destroy three German U-boats—off Block Island, off Nantucket, and at the mouth of the Gulf of Maine. They captured a further seven from as far afield as Argentina (two subs) for utilization, research then destruction following the war. One of the skippers was so aghast at being thrown in a common jail in downtown Boston that he cut his wrists and was ignored by the American doctors until after he had bled to death (his brother was a scientist in Los Alamos, highly decorated by the U.S.).

A desperate but determined group attack on the region by the Germans in the final days of the war could have extracted much more damage if the Americans and Canadians were not vastly more prepared to repel it. Still, Allied sailors admitted to being surprised when, after *Großadmiral* Dönitz ordered the U-boats to surrender and all but three U-boats popped to the surface to give up, there were so many of them. They were also not far from Maine, Portsmouth, Boston, and New London.

We all know that the Americans and their Allies prevailed over the Germans in World War II. This book demonstrates—with source material, factual data, and analysis—just how close we came to leaving our northeast flank, the gateway to the *megalopolis* that stretches from Boston to Washington, D.C. and the hinterland beyond, exposed and compromised. The Germans mined Boston once and were less than a day from mining it a second time. As the mines did not explode, the public generally had no idea that *U-87* laid its bombs on June 12, 1942, and escaped to sink two ships off Cape Cod despite the U.S. finding a floating German mine off Stellwagen Bank soon thereafter.

Now documented (using mostly declassified national records from the U.S., U.K., Canada, and Germany), this story provides us the opportunity to more fully appraise the importance of New England to national and international strategy during the most all-encompassing conflict in human history. It paints a dire picture, not only of the consequences of compromised vigilance, a national distraction toward avenging Pearl Harbor, and misplaced faith in old, outdated, small vessels as a means of defense. This account also underscores and reaffirms the popular image of Yankee ingenuity and moxie, defined as "force of character, determination, or nerve" and often attributed to flinty, self-reliant New Englanders. Coastal dwellers of little means and in isolated communities pulled together to help those washed ashore as a consequence of a global conflagration. As the Gulf of Maine includes the southern tip of Nova Scotia, those communities are often cited herein.

Take, as an example, the relatively isolated island of Nantucket, whose heyday as a whaling port had come and gone with mass-extraction of petroleum, which supplanted whale oil in the mid-1800s. The former Quaker stronghold retained its rugged and independent ways. Given their global forays in search of whales, to the Azores, Polynesia, the Bering Sea, Australia, Japan, and beyond, their global exposure would suit them well in World War II. Here are how the islanders, with support of servicemen and volunteers from across the region, coped with nearly 100 survivors in just over two weeks, followed by three years of relative inactivity.

Ninety men in five lifeboats washed ashore or were rescued from four victims of U-boat attack, one of them sunk hundreds of miles east of Bermuda: the *Peisander,* the *Polyphemus,* the *Norland*, and the *Mattawin*. The rescue vessel, U.S. Coast Guard cutter *General Greene*, left Newport on May 24, 1942, heading for Nantucket Shoals. They found and saved the following groups:

61 *Peisander* men, British, 30 of them Chinese, May 25, 1942—three boats
7 *Polyphemus* men, Dutch, June 6, 1942—one boat
3 *Norland* men, all Scots, June 6, 1942 (shared boat with *Polyphemus* rescuers)
19 *Mattawin* men, British, 7 West Africans, 7 injured, June 8, 1942—one boat

All were male, aged from teens to sixties, were under the British umbrella:

49 from the U.K., six Scots, three Welsh, one Singaporean, others of Hong Kong
7 British West Africans
3 U.S. American Field Service volunteers (prep-school and Ivy League graduates)
23 Chinese nationals (possibly domiciled Hong Kong)
1 Canadian, 1 Australian, 3 Dutch, 3 Irish
Totals: 90 (56 U.K., 23 China, 3 U.S., 1 Canada, 1 Aust., 3 Neth., 3 Ireland)

Four aircraft (at least) focused/ordered just to these searches

1 U.S. Navy airplane for *Peisander*'s third boat rescued—ex-Boston May 24
1 other U.S. Navy planes for *Peisander* location duty May 24
1 U.S. Army Air Force plane for *Polyphemus* boat June 6
1 plane for *Mattawin* location June 6

U.S. Coast Guard auxiliary/reserve vessels—six of five types:

1 U.S.C.G. cutter *General Greene*—took part in all rescues, all dates
2 U.S.C.G. Reserve (auxiliary) vessels, names unknown, *Peisander* rescue May 24
1 *CGR 37*, *Madaket* (CG Reserve, ACOTP/Assistant-Captain-of-the-Port-type)
1 motor lifeboat #3828 (U.S.C.G. *Madaket*)
1 Dory No. 5009 (*Madaket*)

Overall, the rescues involved eight U.S. Coast Guard, U.S. Navy, U.S. Air Force, and U.S. Army Air Force bases in three states. On Nantucket, rescuers utilized Brant Point CG Station (north), Coskata CG Station (central south coast), Madaket CG Station (west), and Surfside CG Station (south). On Cape Cod, the Orleans (a.k.a. Nauset) CG Station coordinated the *Mattawin* rescue, and Boston coordinated the airplane relays and searches for the *Peisander*'s third boat under Captain Shaw. The Naval Operating Base Newport, and Commandant, Eastern Sea Frontier in New York oversaw the *General Greene* rescues. This is just a window into one island, and one rescue vessel, over half a month. Many other survivors landed in sixteen New England communities were fed a variety of meals and transported in myriad directions to enable them to get back to the front lines of the Battle of the Atlantic, however opaque and terrifying those lines were.[69]

This wedge of nautical history describing a vertebra in a globe-girthing, complex supply chain, has been largely unheralded despite New England's location at the cerebral cortex. Before any other tragic episodes of invasion are recorded, audiences have a duty to understand and appreciate the sacrifices made during those cold months of 1942 and beyond. In the pages ahead, planes will swoop down, U-boats will dash to the seafloor for cover, spies will clamber up bluffs with the Coast Guard close behind them, fishermen with pull men, rather than fish, from the sea, and boys from Scotland will be sunk by, and interact with, so many German U-boats in a month that they literally lose track and are written off by the U.S. Navy as incomprehensible.

The only ones that stayed long enough to be known were the dead, and almost all of those buried in the region are Germans, interred in Long Island, Rhode Island, and Massachusetts. Even some of those unfortunates had their paperwork sent to the Office of Naval Intelligence in Washington, and their remains another direction, arriving at the mortician with no papers, resulting in their gravesite reading "Unknown." Thanks to access to declassified files, their names—and this story—will be classified unknown no more.

1

Early 1942: The First Four U-boats Attack the *Thirlby*, the *Norness*, and the *Alexandra Hoegh*

U-123 under Reinhard Hardegen was the first German submarine to invade the United States under Operation *Paukenschlag*, or Drumbeat (literally "kettle drum roll"). Born in Bremen, Germany on March 13, 1913, Hardegen remarkably lived until June 2018. At the time of this patrol, he was *Kapitänleutnant*; however, at the end of his storied career, he was promoted to *Korvettenkapitän* and awarded the Knights Cross with Oak Leaves and the U-boat Badge with Diamonds. Hardegen has been the subject of a great number of books, interviews, films, and television treatments. This is understandable as he sank twenty-two Allied ships of 115,656 tons and damaged another five for 46,500 tons, including the H.M.S. *Aurania*, F 28, of 13,984 tons. He was fooled by the U.S. Navy Q-Ship, or decoy named U.S.S. *Atik,* AK 101, ex-*Carolyn*, and after losing a man to the U.S. counterattack, he destroyed the vessel with the subsequent loss in horrible weather of all 141 officers and men.

Hardegen was a member of the Crew of 1933 and began with the German naval air arm before an injury resulted in his joining U-boats in 1939, roughly two years before Germany declared war on the United States on December 11, 1941. He first served as skipper of *U-147*, then in May 1941, he took over *U-123* from Karl-Heinz Moehle. The boat was in the 2nd U-Boat Flotilla based in Lorient. Before he moved ashore in May 1942, Hardegen berthed at Blücher Bridge flying the pennants of all forty-five ships that *U-123* had sunk over its career. The word U-boat refers to an *untersee* ("under-sea") boat; it was essentially a fast-attack vessel that remained on the surface most of the time except to attack, avoid attack, or escape rough weather. It could not remain without oxygen for the motors and men for even a day.

On his patrol to New England, Hardegen was supported by 1st Watch Officer (sometimes 1WO) Rudolf Hoffmann, 2nd Watch Officer Horst von Schroeter,

U-123, Hardegen emerging from a bunker in France. (*James Payne, Through Their Eyes*)

and Bosun Walter Kaeding. They left Lorient two days before Christmas in 1941 and returned forty-nine days later on February 9, 1942. While approaching the sea border between Canada and the U.S., Hardegen sank the *Cyclops*, a British ship of 9,076 tons, on January 12 then entered the area south of Cape Sable. As he approached Cape Cod, the curled arm of sand jutting east from Massachusetts, around noon Hardegen "sighted drifting submerged wreck."[1]

The following day, they dodged a schooner using its motor and crash-dived to avoid Allied aircraft. Late that night, they passed Montauk Light to starboard, noticing a "glow from the direction of New York and the cities on Narragansett Bay. Seems that they are not darkened." On the 14th, *U-123* attacked and sank the Panamanian tanker *Norness*, which was amazingly "showing all lights," 75 miles south-southeast of Montauk. Then *U-123* headed toward the lightship *Ambrose*, off New York, and chased the *Isla de Tenerife*, until realizing it was a neutral Spanish ship. As the sun rose, the sub headed for the safety of deep water.

The following day (January 15), Hardegen sank the *Coimbra* south of Long Island, and then the *Norvana*, the *City of Atlanta*, the *Ciltvaira*, the *Culebra*, and the *Pan Norway* off the U.S. East Coast and north of Bermuda on the return voyage. They also damaged the *Malay*. Most of the casualties were inflicted at the killing zone, which came to be known as Torpedo Junction, off Cape Hatteras, North Carolina (along with Cape Canaveral, another sandy spit that forced ships to thread a rock and a hard place).[2] After damaging the *Malay* in very shallow water, *U-123* came within 250 feet of being rammed and run over by the Norwegian factory-whaling vessel *Kosmos II*, but managed to start a disabled engine at the last minute and, over a wrenching two-hour pursuit, slowly outpaced the merchant ship. The last two ships of the patrol were audaciously sunk by gunfire alone, since *U-123* was out of torpedoes. Though all the men on the *Culebra* perished, Hardegen vectored the Greek steamer *Mount Etna* to the rescue of the *Pan Norway* survivors, at risk to he and his crew's safety.[3]

One of the effects of sinking ships with fewer than a thousand men and women on them along a heavily populated shoreline is that urban populations in the millions can feel indirectly harried and fear attack themselves, however unrealistic. In that sense, U-boats were a psychological as well as physical weapon. On January 21, the U.S. Navy's Eastern Sea Frontier *Enemy Action Diary* recorded that the Mayor of Newport needed to confirm an International News Service story about "a captured submarine being escorted to New London or Newport." Also New York Harbor Police notified all its vessels to "be on lookout for sneak-attack by small submarines." The Navy, of course, went to pains to downplay both reports.

The *Norness* was a Panamanian motor tanker armed with a 4-inch, 50-caliber U.S. Navy gun manned by naval personnel. At 9,577 tons, she was built just before the outbreak of war in May 1939 by Deutsche Werft AG, Betrieb Finkenwärder, in Hamburg. She was 510 feet long, 66 feet wide, and 28 feet deep. The ship was propelled by a single diesel engine that pushed her at 12 knots. Originally the petroleum tanker was owned by Hamburger Walfang-Kontor GmbH, who sold her to Norwegians the same year, apparently in exchange for the Norwegian tanker *Vikingen*, which under German ownership was known as first the *Wikinger* then, after the war, the *Empire Venture* for U.K. owners. Her final owners were the Johan Rasmussen Tanker Corporation of Panama (a jurisdiction known to flag U.S.-controlled tankers), which in turn was a subsidiary of Viking Tankers, London. Her charterers were the U.S. Maritime Commission, which handed the ship over to the British Ministry of War Transport, based upon the terms of the Lend-Lease Act, by which the United States supported the United Kingdom during wartime while giving the appearance of remaining neutral.

In 1940, the *Norness* transited New York several times, arriving there on February 13, March 4, and July 31. Her master was Captain Harold Hansen, and there were forty-one persons on board for the trans-Atlantic voyage ahead. Thirty-seven of them were Norwegian, supplemented by two Danes, a Swede, and one Icelandic citizen. One of her crew informed the Norwegian-American maritime historian Siri Lawson that January 3, 1942, found the *Norness* in Newark, New Jersey, where workers were installing a gun on deck. Unfortunately, though, the ammunition for the weapon was not due to be loaded until they reached Halifax weeks later.[4] The ship then moved to the Esso Refinery in Constable Hook and loaded her cargo of Admiralty fuel oil there.

On January 13, the *Norness* set out into the cold winter night bound from New York for Liverpool via Halifax, where she was to join a trans-Atlantic convoy—her first. In her tanks was a valuable cargo of 12,222 tons of ship-ready fuel oil for the Royal Navy. The German U-boat menace had not unleashed itself on the U.S. northeast coast since World War I, over twenty years before. The British were warning their American counterparts that a fleet of German submarines was converging on the approaches to New York as well as Cape Hatteras, based on intercepted intelligence; however, the Americans were focused elsewhere. The stage was set for men aboard the *Norness* to die in the frigid northeast waters hours after leaving the largest harbor in the world.

The ship made it just beyond the length of Long Island, which protects the sound of the same name along the Connecticut shore. They were southeast of Montauk in roughly 200 or so feet of water heading east on a course of 87 degrees at 12 knots. She was not zigzagging as no ships had been sunk west of Halifax. The weather was fair; the skies were clear with a light breeze from the southwest pushing the ship along as the men settled into their routines. There was a significant swell rolling in from seaward. Two lookouts kept a vigil: the second mate from the starboard bridge-wing and a seaman on the port wing. Given the darkness, no ensign or nautical flag was flying. As a sign that they were not blacked out, the ship's navigational lights were only dimmed, so that the masthead light was visible to all vessels, including U-boats, for 2 miles.

On the night of the *Norness*'s departure, at 1.34 a.m., Hardegen sent a torpedo hurtling from *U-123*'s stern into the ship's port side. The missile struck about 15 feet below the 28-foot underside of the ship. The first struck at the number seven cargo tank on the port side, aft. The second, fired two minutes later, at 1.36 a.m., hit forward of that, in the number six tank on the same side. Immediately, the *Norness* took on a list (or heel) to port. There was no opportunity for the Allied sailors to bring their gun to bear on the submarine, which was not sighted until too late.

Two sailors and a dog mascot were killed: a Norwegian oiler named Egil Bremseth was standing on deck near the number six tank after the first torpedo struck beneath his feet, and he was thrown into the ocean to his death. Kaare Reinertsen, a cargo pump-man, was sitting in the port-side lifeboat, where the torpedoes hit. Due to the profusion of oil, the falls, or lines holding the lifeboat to the ship while the boats were being lowered by many pairs of young hands, were slippery, and they were released too quickly. As a result, Reinertsen was flung into the water and was not found or rescued. A white-furred mongrel puppy named Pete also perished.[5]

The first torpedo caused the *Norness* to list heavily to port. Able-Bodied Seaman Peder Andersen made it to deck nearly naked where he struggled with a "rain of black oil."[6] The dangling port-side lifeboat made him fear the worst for his ship-mates that had been in it. Although he struggled to help launch the starboard lifeboat, it was not possible at first. When it pulled clear with twenty men under the leadership of the third officer, those still aboard the ship were told the boat was filled to capacity and to seek salvation elsewhere.

The men on the ship then "saw a black shadow gliding slowly very close to *Norness*, coming all the way up to her stern, as if he knew we had no ammunition for the gun." At that moment, the second torpedo hit directly in the pump-room, causing a giant "sea of flames." Andersen tried to protect himself against the flying debris as best he could. The *Norness* then righted herself somewhat, enabling the remaining men to launch another, port-side, boat, and they rowed away as fast as they could before the *Norness* was hit by a third torpedo and sank. He stated that a strong, northwesterly wind was blowing, and it was freezing cold. He found a raincoat in the boat, as well as some sweaters, which he used as pants, but attributed being covered in oil to keeping him warm and saving his life. One of the survivors, an able seaman named Sande, was picked up from the water after falling out of the other lifeboat. His clothes froze to his body, but fortunately, there were more sweaters and raincoats in the boat, and he changed his deadly clothes.[7]

Everything moved at an accelerated pace. Captain Hansen said that the men behaved well and exhibited no signs of panic. Immediately, the radio officer managed to transmit the SSS signal indicating a submarine attack. No reply, however, was received aboard. Twelve minutes later, the officers and men abandoned their floating home. The survivors managed to launch and board two lifeboats and a raft. After they were clear and nineteen minutes following the attack, Hardegen and his men sent a third torpedo, a G7e-type, known as the *coup de grâce*, as in final touch of grace, or mercy killing, toward the tanker.

Unknown to the Norwegians, a third torpedo malfunctioned and never made contact with the *Norness*. The fourth and final one (called the third), however, hit on the starboard side beneath the ship's bridge. The *Norness* began to go down level; however, the port-side lifeboat nearly capsized before the ship stabilized. At 1.50 a.m., the *Norness* sank on a sandy bottom. The stern separated from the forward section and fully sank. Even when sunk, though, because of the 510-foot length of the ship and 200-foot water depth, the tanker's bow remained above the surface for several weeks. The front two-thirds of the ship simply grounded, with the jack-staff, or 20 feet of the foremost bow, still defiantly arcing into the air. The ship immediately became a "grounded derelict," and thus an alarming danger to its brethren, as well-disguised a hazard as most U-boats.

The Allied sailors had not yet seen the submerged U-boat or the torpedo. Then, at 1.56 a.m., *U-123* surfaced and motored from the starboard side of the ship, around its stern to the port side, no doubt confirming the name on the transom, or stern. It passed between the lifeboats and the raft; however, it did not slow or stop to interact. No one was seen in its conning tower or on deck. At that time, the Allies were able to observe their attacker. The U-boat was seen to be awash in the waves and heading east at about eighty degrees. The men vaguely said it was "apparently large" and dark grey, with a clipper bow. No guns or damage were observed. *U-123* was swallowed into the night soon after being sighted and did not open fire on the ship with deck guns. Hardegen's people heard the name of the ship from the SSS signal and could have learned its dimensions from an extensive reference book for the purpose called simply *Gröner*, for the German guide's author. The secret routing codes (Series 781) and all confidential papers were sunk with the *Norness* while in Captain Hansen's safe amidships.

The survivors were to remain in boats for over twelve brutally cold hours. Fortunately for them, a U.S. Navy airship, or blimp, flying out of Naval Air Station (NAS) Quonset Rhode Island, was attracted to the ship's bow and discovered the men in the lifeboats and raft. They called this intelligence to shore, and at 2.30 p.m. that day the fishing vessel *Malvina D.* out of New Bedford, Massachusetts, at the entrance to Buzzards Bay, managed to rescue nine of the Scandinavians and took them to her homeport, from whence they were taken that night to Newport by Navy truck or ambulance. Word was quickly circulated, and soon the U.S. Coast Guard cutter *Argo*, WPC 100, and the U.S. Navy destroyer U.S.S. *Ellyson*, DD 454, were able to arrive on the scene and rescue thirty of them and took them ashore at the U.S. Navy Operating Base (NOB) Newport. Several of the men were admitted to the naval hospital there. For many, it was the first they learned that they had lost two of their shipmates and countrymen. Within twenty-four hours, all thirty-nine survivors were reunited in Newport and ultimately returned to New York City, where Captain Hansen was interviewed by *The New York Times* and other news outlets and emphatically stated his ship was sunk by a German U-boat.

According to Lieutenant-Commander Walter M. Wynne (U.S.N. Ret.), Shipping Control Officer of the Third Naval District, the U.S. Coast Guard promulgated a formal Notice to Mariners for all vessels in the vicinity to take note of and act upon, with a copy to the Port Director of New York Harbor. It stated that on January 20, 1942, they established a lighted whistle buoy to identify a wreck or hazard to navigation off Block Island. The buoy that marked the *Norness*, like a grave marker for the ship, was a distinctive mix of red and white horizontal bands as well as a quick-flashing white light transmitting seventy-five times a minute for four seconds, then a dark period of another four seconds. At 390-candlepower strength, it was located 16 feet above water. A further postscript reads:

> The incident resulted in big, front-page headlines in *The New York Times* the next day, then later all over the U.S. The proximity to land, only sixty miles off Montauk, left the American population in a state of shock. This was only the second ship to be torpedoed on the east coast, the first one was the British steamship *Cyclops* on 12 January 1942, which lost ninety-four passengers and crew. Eighty-seven men, women and children spent twenty cold and windy hours in lifeboats before they were found.[8]

Kapitänleutnant Ulrich Folkers, aged twenty-six, took *U-125* to New England on the same day as Hardegen: January 12, 1942. Despite rough weather, he and the men worked hard switching tanks from fuel to ballast and repairing depth charge damage to the bow. His destination was the shipping lanes off Nantucket, where he spent from January 14–22, 1942, patrolling, with no result, though he saw small fishing boats and other craft. On the 14th, they crash-dived to escape aircraft and, like *U-123* chased after the *Isla de Tenerife*, a Spanish passenger ship of 5,115 tons built in 1921 which had been detained in New York on December 13 and sailed the day before. The next day another crash-dive, then Folkers reported their fuel reserves to Germany.

U-125 left Lorient on December 18, 1941, as one of five boats ordered to initiate Operation *Paukenschlag*. On December 22, the submarine encountered northbound convoy HG 76 but could not penetrate the task force protecting it. Between January 17 and 20, *U-125* lingered off the lightship *Nantucket*, noting that it "lies in peacetime position and burns as in peacetime." They waited for victims coming from or going to New York but evidently found no suitable targets. After another crash-dive, more fishermen were to be avoided. Then on the 21st, Folkers took his boat to the northeast, dangerously close to the Nantucket Shoals, still finding no victims.[9]

Exasperated, Folkers headed southwest at a fast clip. "It is pointless to remain here longer.... I have a choice between the area off Boston and the area south of Delaware Bay: I decide on the latter." On the 25th, he fired a torpedo at the U.S. tanker *Olney* off the entrance to Chesapeake Bay, missing the target, though the ship was aground and a detonation was heard. He had better luck off Cape Hatteras, where he sank the U.S. steamer *West Ivis* of 5,666 tons before returning to France, where she arrived on 23 February. "*BdU* [*Befehlshaber der Unterseeboote*, headquarters of *Großadmiral* Dönitz, overall U-boat commander of the *Kriegsmarine*'s submarine arm, or *Ubootwaffe*] was not very happy with Folkers' performance on his first patrol." He was able to redeem himself in subsequent actions.

Ulrich Folkers was born in 1915 in Kiel and was in the Crew of 1934. Early in his naval career, he served on the light cruiser *Emden* and as watch officer on the destroyer *Z8 Bruno Heinemann*. He was killed on May 6, 1943, when *U-125* was sunk between Greenland and Newfoundland by British destroyers. The submarine was scuttled after being rammed and suffering artillery fire from H.M.S. *Oribi* and H.M.S. *Snowflake*, leaving open the possibility that at least some of the men survived the sinking, but drowned in the North Atlantic.[10]

U-130 under *Korvettenkapitän* Ernst Kals was the second-to-last of five U-boats in the first wave of Operation Drumbeat attacks. It was a busy patrol for the submarine before it even arrived in New England. Having left Lorient on December 27, 1941, the boat was surprised by a Royal Canadian Air Force Bolingbroke bomber, which dropped two depth charges on it on January 12, 1942. On the 13th, Kals and crew sank the Norwegian ship *Frisco* and the Panamanian ship *Friar Rock*. Then on January 18, just before entering New England, the sub made two attacks on a ship off Cape Breton Island but was driven off by a U.S. Navy destroyer of the *Craven* class. Kals then brought *U-130* west from a point south of Cape Sable on January 20 then south of Montauk four days later, going mostly on the surface in good weather, with tank-cleaning and occasional test dives.[11]

In the middle of the Gulf of Maine on the 21st, *U-130* found and sank the Norwegian tanker *Alexandra Hoegh* of 8,248 tons. An initial torpedo strike on the port bow "ripped [it] open for its full length." Then Kals waited for the men to abandon ship before delivering a *coup de grâce*. The ship broke in two parts and sank, so Kals correctly surmised there was "no further action necessary." The twenty-eight survivors divided between two lifeboats, the motorized one towing the rowboat, until they were discovered by the Boston-based trawler *Grand Marshal* two days later and landed at Shelbourne, Nova Scotia the same afternoon.[12]

U-130 continued to the coastlines of New Jersey and Delaware, where it sank another Norwegian tanker, the *Vernanger* (January 25) and then the U.S.-flagged steamer *Francis E. Powell* (January 27). On the same day, *U-130* damaged the U.S. tanker *Halo* off Hatteras. It then bent its course eastward toward Europe, re-entering New England on January 28 and exiting south of Cape Sable on February 2. On the 4th, *U-130* and *U-109* under Heinrich Bleichrodt met mid-ocean while north of Bermuda, and *U-130* provided some fuel for the other sub. On February 18, *U-130* and *U-587* under Borcherdt rendezvoused, and Kals received five downed German fliers who had been rescued from the Bay of Biscay.[13] *U-130* then returned to Lorient on February 25 after a sixty-one-day patrol.

Ernst Kals was born in 1905 and was thirty-six during this patrol. Born in Saxony, he was in the Crew of 1924 and served as a gunnery officer aboard the cruiser *Leipzig*. Late in 1940 he joined U-boats and was ably mentored by Asmus Nicolai Clausen in *U-37*. On Kals' first voyage in command of *U-130*, he claimed three ships sunk. He later experienced destructive results in the Caribbean, West Africa and particularly against Operation Torch, during which he sank three American transport ships for the loss of 105 U.S. lives. Kals served as commanding officer of U-boat operations at Lorient from January 1943 until surrender and was badly injured by a land-mine in November 1944. Captured by the Allies on May 10, 1945, he was not released until January 20, 1948. He died in Emden in 1979 at age seventy-four, having sunk or damaged twenty-one ships.

The motorized tanker *Alexandra Hoegh* was built in Gothenburg, Sweden, by Eriksberg Mekaniske Verkstad in 1935. The ship was 8,248 tons, 469 feet long, and 61 feet wide. A six-cycle, two-stroke diesel engine propelled her at 12 knots. She had an eventful war, with multiple trans-Atlantic voyages from the Mediterranean to Canada, South America, the Caribbean, New York, and Halifax. Then, on January 2, 1942, she began a voyage from Portland to Caripito in Venezuela, where she arrived on the 12th. The following day, the tanker turned around for Halifax.[14]

The master of the *Alexandra Hoegh* was Anton Bredo Heian of Norway, and his first officer was Franz Speich. Most of the crew were Norwegian; however, the cook Sven Hudin was Swedish, as was Able-Bodied Seaman Kaare Karlsen. Mess Boy Anthony Zahardis was American and the electrician, Knud Lund, was Danish. The original owners were Leif Høegh of Oslo; however, during the war, she fell under the control of Nortraship, the ship-operating entity of the exiled Norwegian government. The new owners were Skibs-A/S Arcadia. The *Alexandra Hoegh* could carry 12,600 tons of oil, and in Venezuela, she loaded roughly 12,000 tons of crude. After leaving Caripito just after dawn on the 13th, the voyage proceeded uneventfully until the afternoon of Wednesday, January 21. That afternoon at 4.21 p.m., Able-Bodied Seaman Kristoffersen witnessed a torpedo streaking toward the tanker's port side, but it was already too late. The projectile, from the submarine *U-130* under Ernst Kals, struck the port bow of the *Alexandra Hoegh* while the ship was several hundred miles east-southeast of Cape Cod.

Captain Heian and Second Officer Bjarne Eftang opted to remain on board while their twenty-six crew mates abandoned ship, the main engine having been promptly stopped. Eftang sent out radio distress messages that were received and acknowledged by stations in Halifax, Canso, and Seal Rock, Nova Scotia. At 4.35 p.m., the skipper and mate abandoned ship in the starboard motorboat and were getting away from the ship when they saw a submarine periscope closing on the ship from port. At 4.54 p.m., *U-130*, after determining that all the men had gotten away in three boats, fired another torpedo into the *Alexandra Hoegh*.

The effect of the second torpedo was immediate: it struck in the middle of the ship and snapped the massive tanker into two parts as a result of an explosion. Both halves of the ship drifted away from each other, with the bow portion sinking quicker than the aft. Soon, darkness loomed, and to all concerned, the fate of both portions of the Norwegian ship seemed sealed. The three lifeboats with twenty-eight sailors and the U-boat left the *Alexandra Hoegh* to sink alone.

By midnight, the men rationalized the lifeboat distribution and climbed into one of the non-motorized boats, casting a third boat adrift. With dawn came a possible periscope sighting, and then in mid-morning, they heard and saw strong detonations or explosions to the east; however, they could not verify whether any ship was being attacked there. At 1 a.m. the following morning, they learned that the motorboat had consumed all but three gallons of the petrol, so they conserved it and set sail. At 3 a.m., they sighted a light to the northeast and tried to attract attention with flares, with no success at first. Then they noted a boat coming toward them, and indeed it was a fishing schooner out of Boston named the *Grand Marshal*. The survivors had been motoring and sailing towards land for thirty-eight hours and over 100 miles.

The skipper and crew of the *Grand Marshal* took the twenty-eight Allied sailors to Shelburne that afternoon. The *Grand Marshal*, owned by United Fisheries of Gloucester, had a history of its own.[15] In 1935, she was sailing from Provincetown under Captain Simon Theriault and was fishing Nova Scotia. Another of her skippers was named Albert Grimes, who fished the Grand Banks with her. Maritime archives in Provincetown have images of her docked there for fuel, supplies, and repairs.[16]

The Swedish cook and American mess boy were hospitalized for non-life-threatening conditions. The other twenty-six men traveled to Halifax the next day, Saturday 24. There, the Norwegian consul as well as emissaries from Nortraship met them and provided the sailors with clothes and accommodation. That Friday (January 30, 1942), hearings were held at which Captain Heian and a number of officers and crew were questioned. Survivors credited the rubber Varco Suit, designed in 1939 by Norwegian Carl Dybberg, with saving a number of lives and making the otherwise miserable and freezing cold passage in an open boat survivable. The suits were required by Nortraship, which ordered roughly 30,000 of them aboard their thousand or so ships.[17]

Kapitänleutnant Heinrich (Ajax) Bleichrodt brought *U-109* into a complex twelve-day patrol off Cape Sable and into the Gulf of Maine between January 17 and 28, 1942. He was one of the first five U-boat skippers to attack the Americas (*U-123*, *U-66*, and *U-125* went to the U.S., and *U-130* to the Gulf of St. Lawrence). The patrol was a qualified success. The boat arrived in such "driving snow" that it "again iced up," and was forced to dive. This was followed by the sounds of eight depth charges. The Canadians were evidently hunting for *U-130* or *U-123* closer in-shore. While surfaced, watch-standers had to strap themselves in to avoid being washed overboard.

The first intended victim, a freighter of about 4,500 tons, avoided all six torpedoes fired at it on January 19 when nearly in sight of Nova Scotia's southeastern tip. The vessel chatted away with Yarmouth Radio throughout the attack. On the 21st, Bleichrodt's men chased a large, 6,000-ton freighter toward Shelburne and shallow waters they could no longer pursue it into. Neither vessel has been identified. Two days later, Bleichrodt had more success, sinking the *Thirlby* in the same general area, despite having the attack interrupted by aircraft, destroyers, and a schooner. The Germans could clearly see the crew "abandoning ship in lifeboats; their lights are clearly visible on the water." Due to confusing radio traffic and the proximity of Convoy SC 66, from which the *Thirlby* straggled, the target was misidentified by the Germans as the Greek ship *Andreas*.[18]

After rounding Cape Sable several times, the U-boat headed south in the direction of Bermuda and sank the steamer *Tacoma Star* (7,924 tons) closer to there on February 1. Three days later, *U-130* provided fuel for *U-109*, which on the following day sank the British tanker *Montrolite*. The next day, they sank *Halcyon* by gunfire alone, also north of Bermuda. Then Bleichrodt bent a course back to Lorient, where the sub arrived on February 23 after fifty-nine days. His 1st Watch Officer, Friedrich-Wilhelm Wissman became a commander in his own right, as did Siegfried Keller.

Born in 1909, Bleichrodt lived until 1977 and passed away in Munich. He began his career on the sail training vessel *Gorch Fock*, as well as the heavy cruiser *Admiral Hipper*. He served on *U-8* as well as *U-34*, in which, as 1st Watch

Officer, he sank eight ships. Aboard *U-40*, his 1st Watch Officer was future ace Reinhardt (Teddy) Suhren. Bleichrodt commissioned *U-67* in 1941 and went on to become an instructor and flotilla chief. He was heavily decorated by both the Germans and Italians, earning the Knights Cross with Oak Leaves, U-boat Badge with Diamonds, and War Merit Cross 2nd Class with Swords.

The British steamship *Thirlby* was completed in February 1928 by William Gray shipbuilding in Hartlepool, Sunderland. Her owners were Sir R. Ropner of the same city. At 4,887 tons, she was 405 feet long, 54 feet wide, and 27 feet deep. A 505-hp engine drove her at 10.5 knots when built. The *Thirlby* loaded her cargo in New York, as well as 850 tons of mixed coal for fuel from Brooklyn and sailed for Halifax on Monday, January 19, 1942. From Halifax, she was to rendezvous with Convoy SC 66 for Loch Ewe, Scotland. The convoy sailed on January 23 and arrived in the U.K. on February 9 without the *Thirlby*.

On the final voyage, the *Thirlby*'s master was Captain Philip Edmund Birch, who had been her skipper when the ship was attacked by two German U-boats and an Axis aircraft in early April 1941, limping into Canada with two dead. On this voyage, the *Thirlby* carried 8,400 tons of maize, a corn-like vegetable, also described as 7,600 tons of corn. Military personnel on board included nine gunners—two Royal Army and seven Royal Navy—as well as a U.S. Air Force pilot. They manned a 4-inch gun, seven machine guns (including Hotchkiss, Marlins, and Lewis), and two airborne rocket parachutes. There were a total of forty-five men on board, thirty-five of them merchant mariners.[19]

By 2 a.m. on January 23, while sailing independently, the *Thirlby* was about to round Cape Sable with its navigation lights dimmed. She was not zigzagging, nor had she been told to, though the tanker *Norness* had been sunk by *U-123* off New York's Long Island that very week. The night was very dark, the sea calm, with just a light breeze. Captain Birch noted significant traffic: two ships were ahead, one of which had just passed the *Thirlby*, as well as several local fishing vessels.

U-109 under Bleichrodt sent a stern torpedo hurtling toward the *Thirlby*. At fifty minutes after midnight, a dozen miles from Seal Island bearing 50 degrees, the torpedo slammed into the starboard stokehold, used to store coal. The explosion impacted the bunker and destroyed much of the ship's accommodation as well, resulting in the loss of three men. The ventilator serving the starboard stokehold was blown off.

Captain Birch was woken by the very loud explosion. As he arrived on the bridge, debris was cascading onto the deck. He saw that the port-side hull plating was pushed outward, and on starboard, it was bent inward by the explosion, and that cargo hatches were blown off. Neither sub nor torpedo track were ever seen. Birch believed the torpedo ignited the bunkers and caused the hatches to be blown off. An aroma of cordite (torpedo gunpowder) permeated, but there was no fire or smoke. Birch and his officers succeeded in closing the door for the vulnerable propeller shaft, and another door connecting the cross bunkers and stokehold.

The *Thirlby* began sinking level with the sea at first. Chief Engineer Thomas Cecil Barff plunged into the flooded engine room and rescued the third assistant engineer, who was unable to swim. Birch searched for other men, found none, and, when water was flush with main deck, ordered abandon ship. Birch noted that his crew "behaved very well indeed," noting that "there was no sign of complaint or panic." No one tried to pre-emptively meddle with the boats, rather they all waited in an orderly fashion to be instructed. The vessels surrounding the stricken ship immediately went into blackout mode and vanished.

As the starboard boat was destroyed and lost on impact, they lowered both the lifeboat and jolly boat from the port side. Forty-two men got away from the doomed ship in those two boats. Three men, presumed killed or drowned, were left behind: Irish Fireman Charles T. O'Reilly (aged thirty-four), Greaser Albert Frederick Huish (seventeen), and James Gillespie (forty-one). Roughly an hour later, the second officer and Captain Birch reboarded the *Thirlby* and fired a flake-type rocket to draw attention. The ship seemed to be sinking so imminently that both men quickly retreated back to the boats.[20]

At 3.15 a.m., the *Thirlby* rolled over on its port side, yet remained afloat, bottom-up, until 4 a.m. The attack occurred very close to land—only 10 miles southwest of Big Tusket Island, which is nudged against mainland Nova Scotia; 7 miles northwest of Seal Island, even closer to its northern neighbor; and 16 miles west of West Pubnico. In short, it was within easy reach of the skilled local mariners and fishermen. The depth was about 200 feet: too deep for a lifeboat to drop anchor.

The boats were well-equipped with food, pumps, and colored sails; however, there was no radio with which to relay their position to ships or shore. The men remained in the boats for over six hours, until 9 a.m., when they were spotted and retrieved by the U.S.-flagged steamship *Belle Isle*, which took the forty-five men to Halifax. Buses took the merchant mariners to one place, and the gunners to another. However, on arrival at the Royal Navy base, the gunners were arrested for lacking proper uniforms (a misunderstanding that was quickly diffused). As other merchant captains during World War II did in ports like Guantanamo, Captain Birch decried the overcrowding of survivor facilities in Halifax. He stated that conditions were difficult and the men had trouble organizing return voyages to the U.K. through highly dangerous waters. Birch noted that authorities in Ottawa, Canada's capital, had prepared repatriation for survivors from foreign ports, but not from within Canada.

Birch also faulted the deficiency of the 850 tons of bunker coal loaded in Brooklyn, prior to their departure. This coal was craned aboard from barges. Though described as "mixed, good looking" coal, it did not burn well in the ship's furnaces. Although the stokers and firemen added ninety minutes each to the watch in order to produce more steam, it was barely enough, and Birch had intended to replace the coal in Halifax. On February 5, *U-109* bent a course back to Lorient.[21]

2

Five U-boats Follow Up: *U-654*, *U-106*, *U-103*, *U-107*, and *U-578*

Oberleutnant zur See Ludwig Forster, aged twenty-six, was the next U-boat commander to attack New England, for five days. The primary mission of *U-654* was to patrol the waters off Newfoundland and Nova Scotia. The track of the patrol goes westward from Cape Sable to inside the Gulf of Maine from January 24–25, then southward to the 27th, and finally southeast of Sable and away on the 28th. On January 24, Forster almost ran into a barrier island unmarked on his chart. The following day, he chased two steamers fruitlessly. He found that many fishing vessels in the area got in the U-boat's way. The night of the 25th was spent on the bottom only 8 miles off the lightship *Yarmouth*.

On the morning of the 26th, Forster fired several torpedoes at a steamer, which then stopped, with a "lamp illuminat[ing] several times" on the stern. The Allies fired a white star rocket and then raised steam to escape. Believing it to be a "U-boat trap," or decoy ship (Q-ships, which the British used more than Americans or Canadians), and having heard nothing via radio, he left the quarry. After hearing more aircraft and learning from "the homeland" that his attack on the ship off Nova Scotia was reported widely and the element of surprise lost, Forster wrote, "I am convinced that now there is no longer much opportunity for success in my existing operations area."[1] Aside from participating in the *Ziethen* wolfpack from January 6–22 and tracking Convoy ONS 61, 700 miles east of Cape Race, not much was accomplished by *U-654* during this patrol. It did, however, hit the Free French Flower-Class Corvette *Alysse*, K 100, on February 9 in the convoy, and it foundered the following day, with the loss of thirty-six lives.

Born in 1915 near Dillingen, Forster was a member of the Crew of 1936. His career total was three merchant ships sunk and one naval ship destroyed. Before serving aboard *U-654*, he was 2nd Watch Officer of *U-29* and 1st Watch Officer of *U-62*. Most of Forster's successes would find him on the next patrol to the

Americas, when he orchestrated the destruction of the *Empire Prairie*, the *Steel Maker*, and the *Agra* near Bermuda in April. In the Caribbean, *U-654* made it to Panama without sinking any ships, then was sunk east of Nicaragua on 22 August 1942 by bombs dropped from a B 18 Digby of U.S. Army Bomber Squadron 45. Forster and all forty-four men aboard were killed.

Oberleutnant zur See Hermann Rasch, aged twenty-seven, took *U-106* on a seven-day incursion across New England at the end of January. Starting on the 26th, he passed west across the Gulf of Maine for the next three days. *U-106* exited west of Montauk on January 29. Then, after several days looking for targets off New York, the submarine returned on February 4 via roughly the same route, far to the south. He sank no ships while off New England, yet after moving south Rasch and his men sank five Allied merchant ships.[2]

U-106 was active along the rest of the U.S. coast, sinking the British *Empire Wildebeeste* two days before entering the area, then on the day it transited out of Canadian waters, the "loaded and armed" ship *Traveller* of 3,963 tons. This British vessel was sunk in a matter of minutes in the early hours, and a secondary detonation was heard by the U-boat. None of the ship's fifty-two officers and men survived. In New England, on the night of January 26–27, they fired two torpedoes at a large northbound tanker. A click was heard, and the ship stopped. The tanker slowly resumed its course and dropped depth charges. Rasch is convinced the pistol mechanism of the torpedo failed, despite hitting the ship. Then the men found torn metal in the torpedo tube and realized that "the torpedo retaining pin was not completely moved clear of the stop. Otherwise the ejection was normal." They had to let the tanker go, mostly due to foul weather. Later that day, they also abandoned a chase for a "large fast approaching steamer," as it was faster than the submarine—possibly a passenger ship. After passing Montauk, *U-106* sank the American ship *Rochester* on January 3; then the Swedish *Amerikaland* on February 3; and finally on the 6th, the *Opawa*, a British motor vessel of 10,354 tons, northeast of Bermuda.

Born in 1914 in Wilhelmshaven, Rasch joined the Navy in the Crew of 1934. Over six patrols, he led *U-106* on 308 patrol days and earned the Knights Cross on December 19, 1942, for destroying two large vessels in as many days that month. After leaving *U-106* in April 1943, Rasch moved to officer, command, and administrative roles ashore, including admiral staff officer and head of the midget submarine program. As a *Kommando* group commander, he developed the *Seehund*- and *Biber*-class midget subs. The Allies imprisoned him for over a year, following which Rasch was a journalist in Berlin, Hamburg, and Düsseldorf. He died in 1974 in Hamburg, aged fifty-nine.

Kapitänleutnant Werner Winter took *U-103* along the far southern boundaries off New England, along the continental shelf, starting on January 28, 1942. For five days until February 2, the boat made a straight westward path till it exited south of Montauk. On the 29th, it recognized the neutral Portuguese freighter

Guine and gave it free passage. The next day the men were inspired by listening to a speech by Hitler. Then Winter stalked what he believed was the *Tacoma Star*, and fired three torpedoes at her, all of them misses. Another sub, *U-130*, then tracked and sank the same ship.[3]

On February 2, *U-103* cleared Montauk then sank the *W. L. Steed* off Delaware, followed by the *San Gil* off Maryland on the 4th. The following day, *U-103* sank the U.S. tanker *India Arrow* off New York then another tanker, the *China Arrow*, off Delaware Bay the same evening. *U-103* returned on an eastward track for four days until it exited. Off New England on February 6, Winter had to let a steamer go due to lack of torpedoes. Then he tried to accommodate a supply request from Teddy Suhren in *U-564* but the weather was very foul and so *U-103* used much more fuel and could not transfer in those seas. Hunting off Nantucket was said to be poor: "nothing going on." On leaving, he noted the "same regular [flying boat] reconnaissance from Bermuda as observed on the outbound transit." The patrol began as the second wave of Operation Drumbeat U-boats consisting of *U-103*, *U-106* (Rasch), and *U-107*. It ended on March 1 in St. Nazaire, having begun in Lorient on January 3, 1942.

Born in 1912 in Hamburg, Winter was a member of the Crew of 1930, aged twenty-nine. He served on the *Schlesien* and light cruiser *Emden*, then joined U-boats in 1935. He performed training and two fruitless patrols in *U-22* in 1939. His three successful patrols in *U-103* in 1941 and 1942 earned him the Knights Cross in June 1942. Winter was in command of the 1st U-Boat Flotilla in Brest from July 1942 to its capitulation, after which he was held captive from 1945 to November 1947. He returned to the *Bundesmarine* until retiring in 1970. He died in Kiel in 1972 at age sixty.

Oberleutnant zur See Harald Gelhaus, aged twenty-seven, brought *U-107* south of New England between January 30 and February 4, 1942. It was a simple trajectory from east to west, but started out in very rough weather, such that Gelhaus wrote: "no weapons use possible due to weather conditions." During a dip south, marginally closer to Bermuda than New England, on January 31, Gelhaus exclaimed "thank God the wind and sea are less," then sank the British tanker *San Arcadio*. On the afternoon of March 3, Gelhaus tried to keep up with a steamer that had two masts and the shape of a passenger ship, but could not and gave up.[4] In the same bad weather, the U.S.-flagged merchant ship *Dixie Sword* had run aground off Monomoy Lighthouse, at the very southern tip of Cape Cod, on February 11, 1942.[5] On heading for Cape Hatteras, *U-107* sank the U.S. steamer *Major Wheeler* on February 6; later, on the 21st, it damaged the Norwegian motor vessel *Egda* before returning to Lorient on March 7, two months after setting out.

Harald Gelhaus was born in Göttingen in 1915, and survived the war, living until the age of eighty-two. Beginning in the Crew of 1935, he served on the light cruiser *Karlsruhe* and then the battleship *Gneisenau* before joining U-boats in 1939. Gelhaus served on *U-103* as 1st Watch Officer on three patrols before taking command of *U-143* in March 1941. It was aboard the already established *U-107* that Gelhaus earned his reputation and, by sinking or damaging twenty ships of over 110,000 tons, the Knights Cross in March 1943. This was supplemented by the U-boat Front Clasp in October 1944. After a number of training and staff roles in 1944 and 1945, Gelhaus was captured and held by the Allies for three months.

Korvettenkapitän Ernst-August Rehwinkel, aged forty, brought *U-578* westward from France past Montauk from February 22–25. 1942. They sank no ships in New England and were hampered by such foul weather that Rehwinkel noted. "I had not expected such delays due to weather." On February 23, a flying boat was seen heading north, and 1st Watch Officer Raimund Tiesler immediately crash-dived. Although the sub went to maximum depth, the plane apparently had not seen them on the surface. Rehwinkel found that his estimated position was 17 miles off after crossing the Atlantic. On the 24th, they calibrated their position using radio signals from Chatham on Cape Cod, Amagansett, Long Island, and Tuckerton, New Jersey.[7]

In frustration, the commander noted that "we have been underway for exactly three weeks and have still not sighted a ship. Up to now, two aircraft." Two days after clearing the region, *U-578* sank the U.S. freighter *R. P. Resor* and the following day the destroyer U.S.S. *Jacob Jones*, DD 130, off Delaware with 138 killed; only eleven survived. He noted: "we have stirred up a hornet's nest." On February 28, it let the Swedish ship *Gulmaren* pass. On March 12, while on their way back to France, the submariners sank the Norwegian steamer *Ingerto*, a straggler from Convoy ON 70, from which there were no survivors out of a crew of thirty-two men. The patrol began in St. Nazaire on February 3 and ended there, fifty-one days later, on March 25. Rehwinkel was born in 1901 and went missing with the rest of *U-578*'s crew on August 6, 1942, in the Bay of Biscay. Over his career, he sank four merchant ships of 23,635 tons and the U.S.S. *Jacob Jones* of 1,090 tons.

3

The Coastal Picket Forms (1942–1943)

Counter-measures that had no effect on U-boats should not belong in a book cataloging U-boat attacks. However, between the onslaught of Operation Drumbeat in early 1942 and autumn of 1943 (when it was wisely called off), some 35,500 well-meaning mostly amateur sailors manned a defense fleet, meriting themselves inclusion in this study. Officially known as the Coastal Picket Patrol but nicknamed the corsair fleet or hooligan navy, their intent was to interrupt or deter U-boat attacks on America's vulnerable shores. Through no lack of effort, they achieved neither.

A quick chronology is appropriate. The Cruising Club of America under Commodore Alfred Stamford and his colleagues voted to submit thirty-six privately owned yachts to the U.S. Navy for conversion on March 24, 1942. Fellow yachtsman Commodore Vincent Astor (U.S.N.R.) assumed overall supervision of this fleet. Admiral King accepted their offer and ordered a Coast Guard Auxiliary formed on May 4. Then on May 23, King ordered them moved to the Navy's Eastern Sea Frontier. The Coastal Picket Patrol was organized into patrol areas designated Northern (to the Canadian border), Narragansett (south of Cape Cod to Long Island), and New York on July 14. The entire effort was disbanded on October 1, 1943, after roughly a year-and-a-half. One positive effect was to recruit seafarers and engineers from diverse backgrounds aboard yachts, tugs, and fishing vessels, and give them military training, discipline, and skills. This also led some to join the Navy or coast guard.[1]

The exercise stands as an example of effort not equating to result. It can only be seen in the context of the U.S. Navy—and thus the government's—failure to protect its own shipping, as well as that of its allies during this period. A lieutenant in the U.S. Navy reserves who penned an account of rescuing one of the coastal picket boats observed that, early in 1942, "with increasing vehemence, American citizens along the coast voiced their indignation against the government for not doing something to blast all the submarines out of American waters ... the oft-repeated question [was] 'Where was our much-vaunted Navy?'"[2]

He went on to explain how the U.S. had over-committed, or given away, many of their destroyers to the British via Lend-Lease and found themselves with a one-ocean Navy yet in a two-ocean war. He noted that "more than promises were needed to build a 'bridge of ships' across the North Atlantic,"[3] just as nations cannot win even a "splendid little war" (Secretary of State John Hay's term for the Spanish-American War) with press clippings and feel-good stories alone, particularly in a nation with a vibrant tradition of freedom of speech. The U.S. needed new ships, technology, and training to effectively stop the U-boats, yet they had none of those in sufficient quantities on the east coast at the time. New ships (both naval and merchant) would not roll out of shipyards in sufficient numbers for at least another year, meaning that Germany would continue to win the tonnage war. While the U.S. military fixated on avenging the Japanese attack on Pearl Harbor, starting with the Battle of Midway and the Doolittle Raid (whose purpose was not just to send bombs over Japan but a psychological message to both sides), thousands of Allied merchant mariners were thrown into the wintry ocean just off the coasts of the U.S.'s capital and major eastern ports.

FDR, who had been assistant secretary to the Navy from 1913 to 1920, and whose family were experienced yachtsmen, had a soft spot for the chivalry of small craft, coupled with an overblown sense of what they could accomplish. Against their better instincts, Admirals Andrews and King approved the plan. It can be seen as a desperate publicity measure, with participants being used as such. Tales of grit and derring-do, however, did not match the cold steel of U-boats. The U.S. East Coast from January to end-May 1942 generally lacked naval vessels and aircraft capable of thwarting U-boats, even by an active corps of volunteer Civil Air Patrol pilots and planes. They lacked tools in sufficient quantities like destroyers, radar, Leigh lights, sonar techniques, and the latest anti-submarine warfare techniques, including hedgehog anti-submarine projector and anti-mine defenses.

Instead of attacking random U-boat sightings, the British had learned that protecting convoys and pinpointing then destroying U-boats was more effective, even if it led to some merchant ship losses, the ratio as well as a number of losses was lower overall, and men could be rescued quickly. Yet their rare successful search and destroy attacks like those on *U-85* by U.S.S. *Roper* off Hatteras in April 1942, and on *U-157* by U.S.C.G.C. *Thetis* off Key West in June 1942 (in which all ninety-eight Germans were killed in action, thus providing no intelligence), encouraged the U.S. planners to believe in their methods. Moreover, when the government requested coastal ports to douse their lights, mayors of tourist towns in Miami and Virginia Beach (backed by governors interested in profit over patriotism) refused, citing tourism and an unwillingness to upset the populace,.However, the ships burning within sight of shore could be called worst-kept secrets: they were not a secret at all, really—only the government seemed to think they were. The leaders of both the U.S. government and military (FDR himself, a master of big government) backed down from December 11, 1941, to May 19, 1942, allowing innumerable more sailors to drown.

In at least one instance (*U-123* shelling the *Gulfamerica* off Mayport, Florida on April 10, 1942), U-boat commanders were concerned about hitting spectators lit up by shore lights, and maneuvered between the shore and their victims, at great peril to themselves.[4] The survivors of the *Norland* and the *Polyphemus* and many other U-boat victims received more comfort and aid from U-boats than from Allied ships; often, U-boats were more aware of the disposition of survivors than the Allies themselves. All of these are symptoms of the alarming fact that the enemy controlled the waters of America's doorsteps on two of the nations' three coasts and continued to do so for a long time, arguably until the Germans voluntarily moved on in July 1942. Almost all their damage in New England was inflicted in the first six-and-a-half months: thirty-two out of thirty-eight attacks occurred between January 14 and July 23, 1942, after which no ships were sunk until 1943 (one), 1944 (two), and a final, near-suicidal wave of attacks in spring 1945 (three).

The losses were galling and particularly unacceptable as they flew in the face of the roughly eight years of German U-boat warfare, which the United States had been allowed to study and prepare from, yet effectively ignored (1914–1918 and then 1939–1941). New York was a fulcrum for essential bulk as well as manufactured and refined products to reach beleaguered Great Britain from the Indian Ocean, Australia, and New Zealand, the entire East and West coasts of the Americas, via New England and Halifax. Whether losses on the eastern seaboard amounted to a tanker every ten hours in the spring of 1942 (as is generally accepted), the fact is that strategists on both sides believed it to be the case and were shocked at how effectively the Germans were strangling the U.K.'s supply lines as they passed unprotected through U.S. waters. Neither the Germans nor Americans were throwing their full fighting effectiveness at the battle during that time.

As Allied defenses effectively failed on that critical final leg to mid-1942, Churchill was nearly apoplectic. Yet for political reasons, he had to bite his lip since the U.K. desperately needed U.S. support. For the U.S. Navy to place unevenly and unevenly manned private craft into a quasi-disciplined force, with each vessel only able to perform a week or so of patrols before being recalled was a leap of faith. The Coastal Picket Patrol required careful oversight of small craft operating in extreme weather conditions. To believe that these mostly wooden boats would be an effective deterrent against an enemy that had largely controlled the battle in numerous oceans in both wars would be optimistic, desperate, delusional, or all three. Perhaps naval leaders knew as much, yet were still willing to roll the die with so many people's safety. For commanders on the east coast, learning daily of the exploits of their brethren in the Pacific, and setting up administrative layers while both watching their charges being sunk and waiting for ships of their own to be built, perhaps it is understandable that they threw themselves into such a distraction.

A leader of the Cruising Club of America, whose members contributed greatly to the effort, observed that from their base in Greenport, northeastern Long Island, "in wintertime aboard those little, practically unheated yachts, it was a grim business ... jogging under sail [with] a simple, non-directional sonar listening device which was lowered over-side, a couple of small machine guns, and twenty-five-pound depth charges which could only alarm submarines." Writing nearly twenty years later, he makes the unsubstantiated claim (a fabrication really) that "their radio reports of U-boat positions are said to have been responsible for several submarine sinkings by the Navy," going on to claim that Admiral Andrews of the Third Naval District in New York commended them "for most efficient work."[5]

There is no disputing the good intentions, bravery, and often skill of the thousands of volunteer mariners who went to sea in small craft in deplorable winter conditions and put their lives in direct peril for the defense of their country at a time of critical need, the likes of which has not been seen before or since. The Coast Guard candidly professed that "in the early days of the war, the Navy was in desperate need of vessels to patrol the coastal waters, to look for subs and rescue survivors from attacks."[6] Desperate times are known to call for desperate—be that as it may, from the cold, analytical view of strategic utility, and given the safe distance of seventy-five years from the events, it must be recognized that what started as the "offshore ... listening patrol," was not even a pest to German U-boat commanders or strategists.[7] The U.S. side's intent was for the small boats to listen undetected to approaching U-boats; however, if the yachts then transmitted their intelligence to shore, they could then be detected (and destroyed) by the same U-boats. In any event, despite over 17,000 boats giving it a try, there do not appear to have been any interactions between the two groups, which led to any military outcome; rather, there were a couple of clumsy, amateur exchanges: a collision and a reprimand by a U-boat commander—exactly what might have been predicted.

Author Ernest Hemingway's biographer in *The Hemingway Patrols* demonstrates as much, describing him in his diminutive 38-foot fishing yacht *Pilar* scrambling up and down the Cuban coast and Old Bahama Channel seeking an opportunity for heroism, often in his cups and scrawling illegibly in an overused logbook. Hemingway (a civilian equipped with radio equipment by the U.S. Embassy in Havana) convinced himself and the U.S. government that a German submarine would allow his small vessel to approach close enough for its armed crew to drop a grenade down the U-boat's open hatch. Despite such Quixotic fantasies and delusional thinking, the hen-pecked Navy ended up assigning a junior officer in Key West the task of manning a phone to make Hemingway feel appreciated, while at the same time trying to keep him from hurting himself or others.

No doubt, the Navy considered the famous swashbuckler's activities of possible publicity value (Hemingway's fictional work, *Islands in the Stream* depicts aspects of U-boat hunting in the war and has been conflated with fact). Hemingway's grandiose yet naïve plans of attack are metaphors, really, for the entire amateur effort. While it may have made them feel good, the only party that was supposed to notice—namely, the enemy—failed to do so, unless (really) the only party supposed to have noticed was the U.S. reading public.[8] The Germans were too busy making real progress, carrying their war to American shores. They were the realists. They were not fighting with pens, but with projectiles.

To believe that a German U-boat—manned on average by fifty men, many of whom who had experienced three years of warfare, armed with torpedoes fired fore and aft as well as guns of varying caliber on deck, plus machine guns, anti-aircraft weaponry, and mines—would be intimidated or delayed by a half a dozen men aboard a wooden sailing or motor craft less than 60 feet long armed with a few Tommy guns and 25-pound depth charges that were more likely to blow up the boat rather than the U-boat is ludicrous. Yet many professionals appear to have believed just that, and so they put their plans into action.

Rather than destroy German subs and lives, the entire effort cost immeasurable Allied resources, including indirectly causing attacks on four fishing vessels off Massachusetts and Maine. In a single gale of December 1942, the Coastal Picket Patrol yacht *Rose* was lost ashore near Provincetown, and the former yacht *Zaida* was blown from off Montauk to Nantucket Shoals and ultimately 3,100 miles for over twenty-three days. It landed at Ocracoke Inlet, North Carolina with all original nine men, several of them injured.

The fact that *Zaida* (renamed *CGR 3070*) incident is about the best-known of the coastal picket experience was the highly informative, if only for the massive vacuum of resources it absorbed. Chroniclers of these events virtually crow about how "more than twenty-five planes and ships of the U.S. Army and Canadian Air Forces, the U.S. Coast Guard and the U.S. and British navies searched for the sturdy craft." Is it a good thing that all those resources were diverted, and effectively wasted? Had those resources followed a German U-boat for 3,100 miles, they would abut against Europe and virtually ensure the submarine's destruction, and that of several others to boot. Yet all of those resources failed to rescue the sailboat.

While publicists wrote of the uncontestable bravery of the survivors, the fact is that tremendous resources were drawn away from the core battle against U-boats to search for this crew. A Royal Navy destroyer diverted to tow her; she interrupted a convoy, innumerable aircraft, a blimp that dropped food, and other fixed-wing craft that communicated with them, which were all allocated to what was touted as "one of the greatest searches in maritime history," and "the largest search-and- rescue operation in the Atlantic by Allied Forces during World War II." Firstly, the search failed: the men essentially rescued themselves. Secondly, all of those military resources were diverted from the protection of Allied shipping, as in actually saving lives. From a strategic and practical point of view, it was an unmitigated disaster.

The only known instance of physical contact with the enemy by the coastal picket fleet was when a German U-boat surfaced beneath the motor picket boat *Jay-Tee* off Fort Lauderdale, forcing the 38-footer (the same size as Hemingway's *Pilar*) to roll off of the sub's deck and spring some planking.[9] From the U.S. point of view, skipper Willard Lewis and Uncle Bill avoided detection, tried to ram the U-boat twice with a re-purposed Buick engine, and were caught on the deck of *U-333* in the morning of May 6, 1942. Then "Cremer and is crew, below, looked up with knitted brows. What the hell was that?"[10] Except that Cremer did not even mention any motorboat, because he was engaged in fighting a war, and was focused on his men's survival.[11] There is no mention in his war diary to a picket boat, and in his memoir, he focuses instead on Captain Henrik K. Johnson of his victim the merchant ship *Halsey* (sunk May 6, 1942, in sight of Florida) as a searing indictment of the U.S. Navy before the Marine Investigation Board in New York. Johnson decried:

> His ship had been regularly lit up by the rotating searchlight at Jupiter Inlet airfield, so that the U-boats had a good look at him. He himself had been blinded by the light and seen neither the enemy, nor a torpedo track.... Again, and again, like all other captains, he had also suggested the convoy system should be improved, but so far nothing had been done.[12]

So, while the U.S. historians, even one whose cover text includes the words "slaughter at sea," recite feel-good stories of swashbuckling eccentrics, the enemy was busy at work, recording only relevant details, observant of the enemy's weaknesses and exploiting them. Cremer noted that he and his colleagues had sunk or damaged a dozen ships in the same area in three days, leaving fourteen lifeboats in his region alone and only a scattered defense. Though navies on all sides were duty-bound to activities that could, and often did, cause loss of life, Cremer noted that "if we tried indeed to destroy tonnage, we were never indifferent to the fate of the ship-wrecked crews; their rescue always took a weight off our minds."[13]

In one apocryphal encounter, blurred and conflated in more than one locale, a German U-boat commander is said to have approached yachtsmen on picket patrol and told them "get the hell out of here, you guys! Do you want to get hurt? Now scram!"[14] This legend of an encounter between a hardened veteran and amateurs in the battlefield surfaced and is kept alive by the U.S.; the Germans make no mention of it—would that the yachtsmen had listened. By blurring the lines between harmless bystanders and armed belligerents, the mix of yachting and fishing enthusiasts indirectly obliged the Germans to view any (and all) vessels along the U.S. coast as capable of relaying their position, and thus as a threat that would be best silenced or eliminated. As a result, they went on to sink innocent fishing boats in New England. The U.S. Navy outfitted hundreds of fishing boats with radios as well as carrier pigeons but also decried U-boat attacks on fishing vessels like the *Lark* off Boston later in the war as unjustified attacks on civilians.

Optics matter. The Navy scrambled to clamp down on news about myriad sinkings; however, editors along the coast let them know that the truth was common knowledge coastwise, and advised the government that owning the story would prevent wild rumors or even panic. Regarding *CGR 3070*'s failed mission, Thompson claimed he depicted "the diverse and complicated activities which thwarted the Axis submarine campaign and thus assured the vital flow of American supplies and troops from the United States to the beleaguered Allies throughout the world."[15] Yet it is disingenuous, and factually unsupported, to say that any aspect of the Coastal Picket Patrol "thwarted the Axis submarine campaign." There are no known sinkings of, or even effective attacks upon, German U-boats who patrolled New England (or the Americas) by these picket boats, though, as one might expect, myriad accounts of the "one that got away," oil slicks, and the placement of fiction in for fact.[16] It is not surprising that participants wished to account for, an justify, the outlay of what grew from 2,600 men and 2,300 vessels in the Coast Guard Reserve in 1940 to a Coast Guard Auxiliary that had processed and trained over 50,000 Auxiliarists and 50,000 temporary Reservists by war's end.[17]

Brown concluded that "as an anti-submarine force the Coastal Picket Patrol proved ineffective as a deterrent." He went on to describe the boats used as "uniformly too slow and fragile to attack a U-boat." Notwithstanding this stark reality, by mid-1943, the force had swelled to 35,484 people aboard an astounding 17,474 boats organized into 584 flotillas that assigned 15-mile squares within the 50-fathom (300-foot depth) line to individual boats. It is said that when ice accumulated too thickly, skippers would take their vessels away offshore and into the Gulf Stream to melt it away.[18] Like so much written about this fleet, this claim is probably apocryphal, as patrols generally lasted one week—a very tight schedule to leave your patrol area in New England, make it to the Gulf Stream (some 200 miles each way, or two-and-a-half-days round-trip at 6 knots), melt the ice, and return while still performing a patrol. These tales defy common sense, leading one to wonder what assumptions the authors made about the intelligence of their audience.

It was as though having had a German U-boat shell U.S. vessels and mainland in World War I, and their sinking numerous Allied ships off American shores, had never happened. The British could barely disguise their dismay, horror, then anger at just how little the U.S. was doing to protect British and other Allied ships through American waters. It took until 19 May 1942 (over five months after Hardegen in *U-123* began the carnage) before lights on the coast were dimmed and the, albeit toothless, picket patrol took their stations. By then over one hundred ships had been sunk off the U.S. In two months, the Germans pulled away to other targets, marginalizing the utility of whatever defenses were subsequently put in place. They had snookered the U.S. Navy on their own coast, though the Germans were subsequently overwhelmed by the Allies in the mid-Atlantic from May 1943 onward.

One (understandably little-publicized) example of ineptitude during the initiation of U.S. defenses is the case of a tern sailing schooner *Irene Forsyte*, fitted by enthusiastic new naval officers in New London. The ship began its career as the *MacLean Clan*, launched in Mahone Bay, Canada in 1920. She was 144 feet long, 283 tons, built of wood with a beam of 27 feet, and was capable, at one point, of 13 knots. During the Great Depression, her upkeep was not maintained, and she "was in poor condition by the end of the decade," relegated to the punishing coastal coal trade.[19] Under the name *Irene Myrtle*, her captain, Thomas Antle, died in New London in mid-1942. For a variety of reasons, most of them financial, the ship rotted in port. Wooden hulls do not hold up well to exposure and the collection of pools of fresh water.

In November 1942, ambitious officers of the U.S. Navy (un-named) purchased her. So began a predictable tale of gradual destruction. Due to a rush to convert an essentially condemned and rotting hull, the newly renamed *Irene Forsyte* was permitted by the U.S. Navy to go to sea in the fall of 1943, fitted with a 4-inch deck gun, a 40-mm gun, twin 22-mm guns and an "anti-submarine rocket." By October 4, she was discovered northeast of Bermuda, flailing around in deplorable condition, hove-to, stalled and leaking. She requested (and was provided with) a tow into Bermuda, where repairs were effectuated. The scathing naval post mortem to this well-intentioned but regrettable incident reads:

> The conversion of U.S.S. *Irene Forsyte* is an instance of misguided conception and misdirected zeal, which, coupled with inefficiency resulting from lack of supervision by competent authority, has cost the government nearly half a million dollars ... and a serious waste of effort. In addition, much valuable material that can ultimately be used has been frozen for the better part of one year ... the failure to ascertain, prior to or during conversion, that the vessel was unseaworthy, is an indication of professional incompetence on the part of the officers concerned ... some of the officers took advantage of the broad authority that was granted in the interests of secrecy to obtain equipment that did not contribute to the military value of the vessel.[20]

The *Irene Forsyte* was able to limp to New York in November, and by December 16, 1943, was stricken out from the naval register of vessels. In response, the U.S. Navy declared "the practice of granting to Frontier Commanders and District Commandants uncontrolled authority to implement projects of this nature has been discontinued." That same week, they also canceled the Coastal Picket Patrol program as the new 83-foot Coast Guard cutters began entering service quantifiably.

It had also become clear to organizers how easy it was for watch-standers aboard coastal pickets to mistake "whales or sharks or blackfish or porpoises" for the enemy.[21] Many veteran boat skippers and aircraft pilots learned that the thrill of a submarine sighting was often quickly allayed by the realization that they had in fact seen surfacing creatures, wreckage, flotsam, sunken wrecks. Even cormorants, the voracious black water-fowl, were reported as periscopes from onlookers standing on Ocean Drive in Newport. U.S. Navy pilot Captain Jerry Mason adds:

> First, there were very few attacks by aircraft on U-boats off the U.S. East Coast, because when they were operating close to shore (within 100 miles) they were almost always submerged by day. They only surfaced at night to recharge their batteries and attack shipping. There was no need to risk the boat by being on the surface by day. In that period [1942], the aircraft were not equipped with radar or a searchlight to detect or attack a U-boat at night. Second [as] a retired U.S. Navy anti-submarine pilot, I can say from experience that there are many things that look like a surfaced submarine or a periscope when you are flying over the water: certain wave formations, debris in the water and probably the most common submarine-like phenomena, a pod of whales or dolphins. These were often attacked by aircraft. For every actual attack on a U-boat, there were dozens of attacks on non-submarine targets. At this point in the war [1942], when the aircraft were not specially equipped, and aircrews were not specially trained, the advantage lay entirely with the U-boats. A year later, things would be much different and the aircraft became a deadly foe.[22]

The loss of the Q-ship, or decoy, U.S.S. *Atik* (AK-101) on March 27, 1942, demonstrates the horrific human toll that failed experiments can take. She was sunk with all 141 hands by Hardegen in *U-123* after the U.S. sailors managed to lure the U-boat close enough with concocted abandon ship and radio activities. Then, in a brazen, pre-planned counterattack, U.S. Navy gunners managed to hit the sub's conning tower with bullets, killing German sailor *Fähnrich zur See* Rudi Holzer.

Rather than damage or destroy the submarine, however, they merely enraged the commander, the same who had been ignored by Task Group 15 as it left New York past his victim *Coimbra* in January 1942 and who outlived most of his adversaries.

Hardegen's retribution was swift and fatal to all aboard. In part because of confusion over whether the U.S.S. *Atik* was still pretending to be S.S. *Carolyn* (her *nom de guerre*), and despite the fact U.S. sailors were seen to abandon ship before the *Atik* was blown up by more torpedoes, all of the Allies drowned when the destroyer U.S.S. *Noa*, DD 343; tug U.S.S. *Sagamore*, AT 20; and fellow-decoy U.S.S. *Asterion*, AK 100 were delayed from rescuring them by gale conditions.

Historian Lowrey concludes that during World War I in U.S. and Canadian waters, 116 Allied ships were attacked or sunk by German submarines. Of those, roughly one third were fishing vessels. Perhaps for that reason, the fishing fleets on the northeast were reluctant to volunteer themselves as listening posts against U-boats, for fear of being sunk *en masse* again, as they had been on the Grand Banks in the previous war. Nevertheless, when the U.S. Navy asked the fishermen to carry radio transmitters and report U-boat sightings after 1942, they did so. U-boat commanders could hear transmissions from fishing vessels just as clearly as the Allies ashore could. They thus naturally distrusted fishermen, taking them to be enemy spies, or worse, Navy decoys, and sank them when possible. Thus, the attacks on the *Ben and Josephine,* the *Aeolus,* the *Lark*, and the *Lucille M.* in New England waters in World War II were predictable.

It is no fault of the volunteer mariners that the effort to interrupt the German invasion of their waters was ineffectual. Their duty was to throw whatever they had at the enemy, and they had at their disposal hardy yachts and fishing boats and arguably even hardier men to operate them, even those deemed too old or unfit to serve in regular services. Like the Doolittle Raid and other military ventures with a greater psychological than actual outcome, there is great value in what they did, and how they made themselves and others feel. However important, those benefits should not be confused with results. Rhetorically, if the *Jay-Tee* charged and then made contact with *U-333*, yet Ali Cremer, the commander never noticed, does it count as an attack? If Hemingway spent hundreds of hours puttering about looking for glory in the form of a U-boat to attack, yet no U-boat sailor afloat, or German officer ashore, ever noticed, does it count as a disruption?

Picket patrols were nothing but an easily ignored nuisance to U-boat skippers. Certainly, these little vessels and the brave men who manned them neither altered the German's strategy, damaged their equipment, nor injured their people. Rather the records are replete with instances where personnel, equipment, and innumerable hours and countless dollars were invested in creating, training, maintaining, then rescuing a fleet of vessels numbering nearly 17,500 that returned no discernable result, except perhaps as a training exercise while the military prepared and equipped itself to tackle the adversary in an effective manner.

As if further evidence were needed, almost the entire bibliography of this epoch in U.S. national maritime defense has been researched, written, funded, and published either by U.S. government agencies such as the U.S. Navy, U.S.

Coast Guard, U.S. Coast Guard Auxiliary, or yachting clubs, associations, and magazines who contributed to it and thus had (and have) a vested interest in its favorable portrayal. Gabe Christy points out some residual benefits to Allied vessels:

> Picket ships often assisted with rescues and retrieving lost cargo. *CGRT 2267*, the *Pioneer*, a fishing yawl, was able to rescue all [44] survivors from the tanker *R. M. Parker Jr.* when she was torpedoed [on 13 August] 1942. And *CGR 355* was able to recover much of the ordnance from the freighter *Benjamin Brewster* around the same time.[23]

Indeed, the *Pioneer* did great work, but CGR would have been destroyed removing ordnance from the *Benjamin Brewster*, which lay in 37 feet of water burning for nine days until even the hull had melted. The same article lent credence to the wild supposition that "John Kimball, a carpenter on the *Actaea*" and his colleagues vectored in "our picket ships, five Civil Air Patrol Planes, four U.S. Navy Planes, two U.S. Navy vessels and a U.S. Navy blimp," to sink a U-boat. Seen through the prism of reality, what a massive investment in resources for a phantom sighting this demonstrates. Kimball and his cohorts hurt, rather than helped the real war against U-boats by depleting scarce resources. The author then tags on the following fiction: "this proved to be a psychological shift for the German submariners on the east coast: it was no longer open season; they were being watched."[24]

Evidently, even more than seventy-five years after the fact, it is permissible to amplify rumor and legend when it comes to the corsair fleet or hooligan navy (call it what you may), and this will probably never change. Wishful thinking is warmer than the truth. A patriotic riff is a far sweeter sound than the shriek of steam whistles as Allied ships sank within sight of major cities, torn to pieces and set afire by the enemy below, as hundreds of merchant mariners struggled in cold, deadly waters that first winter of war on U.S. shores.

4

Five U-boats Attack the *Norland*, the *Polyphemus*, the *Berganger*, and the *Cayrú*

Korvettenkapitän Klaus Scholtz entered New England in command of *U-108* on February 2, 1942, south of Cape Race, proceeded to a point about 50 miles south of Nantucket, then headed southwest and out of the region on the 6th. Scholtz complained of the harsh weather and its effect on his fuel supply, noting "despite most economical transit speed (one diesel engine at 250 rpm), due to the continuous stormy headwinds and high counter sea, consumption is about twice as high." On the 4th, he noted land-based aircraft off Nantucket. He saw searchlights and bright glowing lights off Newport but noticed the absence of the lightship *Nantucket*. He wryly noted that "hope of meeting traffic here is not fulfilled. The withdrawal of the lightship suggests that the traffic is routed only intermittently under escort to North American or Canadian ports."[1]

If the goal of U-boats was to disrupt their adversary's supply chain, it seemed it was working after just over two weeks. Starting on February 8 off Maryland, *U-108* sank the *Ocean Venture* and off Hatteras the *Tolosa* and the *Blink*, followed by the *Ramapo* and the *Somme* off Bermuda in just ten days. *U-108* was part of the second wave sent to maintain Operation Drumbeat, though some purists consider only the first wave to be Drumbeat U-boats. The patrol began in Lorient on January 8 and ended there on March 4, 1942. Klaus Scholtz was born in Magdeburg in 1908 and was thirty-three at the time. He was a highly successful U-boat commander, with twenty-five ships sunk or damaged for over 128,190 tons. This earned him the Knights Cross with Oak Leaves in September 1942. Overall, Scholtz led eight patrols, all in *U-108*, between February 1941 and July 1942, for a total of 361 days. He began his career on the torpedo boats G 8, G 11 and *Jaguar* before moving to U-boats in 1939. In April 1941, he sank the British Armed Cruiser AMC *Rajputana* of 16,644 tons, in the Straits of Denmark, earning him a "Well done!" message from *Großadmiral* Dönitz.

Klaus Scholtz of *U-108* being greeted on return to Wilhelmshaven in February 1941. (*Willy Wilke, U-108*)

Scholtz became commander of the 12th Front U-boat Flotilla in Bordeaux. When it was overrun in August 1944, he and 220 men tried to break out and trek overland to Germany but were captured by Americans in the Loire Valley. He was imprisoned for eighteen months as a PoW. After the war, he joined the *Bundesmarine* and was base commander of Kiel and Wilhelmshaven. By 1966, he was *Kapitän zur See,* and he passed away at age seventy-nine in 1987.

The Norwegian motor tanker *Norland* was built by Blythswood Shipbuilding of Scotstoun, near Glasgow, and launched in September 1941. Commissioned by the U.K. Ministry of War Transport, her original name was the *Empire Pict*. On May 6, 1942, she was transferred to Nortraship and given a new name: the *Norland*. Built of steel, she was 8,134 tons, 463 feet long, 61 feet wide, and 33 feet deep. Her motor was built by John G. Kincaid of Greenock and developed 490 hp, which pushed the ship at 12 knots. The ship's 4-inch gun and machine guns were manned by four military gunners: Hedve Davis, Harry Meek, Gilbert Burron, and Thomas Sullivan. The mostly Norwegian and British merchant officers and crew totaled forty-eight.[2]

The *Norland*'s first and final master was Captain Eugen Cristoffersen of Norway. There were several teenagers aboard, including mess-room boys William Morris Cohen, Ronald John Wilson (both fifteen), engine-room boys John Hannah, Thomas Miller (sixteen), deck boy Victor Annesley Haggith, and Francis J. Agnew. Aside from Norwegians, there were two South Africans and a Swede in the crew. The chief officer was Gilbert R. Schmidt, a Dane; the second officer was Andreas Bjelde; and Knut Kristiansen, twenty-nine, was third officer. The chief radio operator was Daniel McNeil, aged thirty-five.[3]

The *Norland* sailed the day following her delivery in Glasgow. On Thursday, May 7, she left Gourock for Liverpool. There, she joined Convoy ON 93 with twenty-six merchant ships and five escorts. Her destination was Corpus Christi to load aviation fuel destined for the U.K., possibly topping up on Port Arthur or Galveston. Captain Christoffersen loaded 5,000 tons of water ballast. To stabilize the ship for the voyage, he and Chief Officer Schmidt filled center tanks two, four, six, and eight all the way, then also allowed sea water up to sea level in wing tanks from one to nine on either side. The ship's draft afterward was 23 feet—a deep enough target for torpedoes.

The convoy dispersed on Sunday, May 17 northeast of Bermuda. By the early afternoon of May 20, the *Norland* was 925 miles southeast of Nantucket motoring at 236 degrees southwest and making over 12 knots. She was not zigzagging. There were four lookouts: Second Officer Bjelde along with two watch-standers on the bridge and one on the monkey island, above the wheelhouse. Swedish Ordinary Seaman Rolf Inage Danielsson, aged eighteen, was at the wheel. Three of the four gun-crew were on duty aft. The weather was clear, the seas moderate, with a wind from the southeast at about 10–15 knots. Visibility was excellent.

Nothing was seen until at 12.57 p.m., when there was a "tremendous blow" on the starboard side in the number eight tank, which was just forward of the bridge. From 10 feet below the water up to the ship's side and even bulging the deck plates upward, there was a large hole in the ship's side, roughly 50–60 feet long. Mess boy Cohen recalled:

> A loud bang was heard throughout the ship, there was a slight shudder. I heard one of the men shout out "torpedo!" The men came running out of the mess-rooms, and I went over to [Mess-boy] Ronnie's pantry. He had slipped, and was sitting on deck. I shouted "torpedo!" He replied, "No kidding."[4]

Though the engines were immediately stopped for five minutes, by 1.02 p.m., Captain Christoffersen defiantly raised the Norwegian ensign, stabilized the ship somewhat by allowing sea-water into the tanks on the opposite side, and ordered full speed for Bermuda. Rushing from his cabin to the bridge, he saw men preparing to launch the lifeboats and ordered them to stop. Cohen said, "We went on deck. The crew was all active on different tasks."

The *Norland* motored away, but due to the damage, it was unable to gain full speed. While scanning the horizon for their foe, the gunners sighted a periscope roughly ten minutes later and fired at it. The submarine (*U-108* under Scholtz) immediately submerged. Half an hour later, the U-boat re-emerged from the depths and began shelling the ship. At that point, the *Norland*'s gunners opened up in earnest, firing fifteen to twenty shells. Cohen records that, "Ronnie and I helped to carry the shells up to the gun platform. The first shot our crew fired deafened us. We had nothing to cover our ears with. Our shots did not reach the enemy, but their shots were landing on us." What the sixteen-year-old may not have known was that the submarine, with superior artillery, wisely remained some 6 miles away, out of range of the merchant ship's single gun, leaving the ship a sitting target.

All this time, the *Norland*'s radio operators had been sending SSS or "submarine sighted surfaced" messages on the emergency frequencies for half an hour. These were picked up in Halifax and the U.S. and passed on to the British Admiralty, which relayed them to Bermuda. The Eastern Sea Frontier *Enemy Action Diary* for May 20 notes that the *Norland* was attacked east of Bermuda. Between 2.30 p.m. and 3 p.m., roughly two hours after the U-boat initiated the attack, the bridge and the aerials were hit. According to Cohen, a fire broke out on the bridge; this is substantiated by photographs that *U-108* crewman Willi Wilke took, which show smoke spewing from the *Norland*, which was also heeled over.[5] Conceding to reality and focusing on the safety of his men, Captain Christoffersen stopped the engines, threw the confidential codes overboard, and ordered *Norland* abandoned. The forty-eight men succeeded in launching three lifeboats. None of them was severely injured by the shells.

As the *Norland* slowed down, the submarine caught up with the ship, and the German's artillery became more accurate. The men rowed the boats away from the hulk to avoid being hit by errant shells. Scholtz focused on destroying the *Norland*, which finally rolled over and sank at about 8 p.m. By then, his men had expended all of their 37-mm ammunition, hitting the wing tanks, which were filled with seawater. Only fourteen of the hundred shells from the deck gun hit the ship. According to a U.S. Navy post mortem, the "submarine was last seen circling the ship and firing shells." Cohen wrote that "the submarine continued to fire shells at the *Norland* as we rowed further away from the ship." Scholtz never bothered to ask the survivors its name or destination, as he already obtained that intelligence from the radio signals and observing the *Norland* up-close.

While the *U-108*'s officers and crew dealt death-blows to the ship—expending between 150 and 200 shells on her demise—the three lifeboats went alongside each other. Two boys from one of the lifeboats were transferred to Captain Christoffersen's boat in which Cohen, his friend Ronnie, and Chief Radio Officer McNeil sat. The final disposition of the boats was: boat one: Captain Christoffersen and fourteen others; boat two: Chief Officer Schmidt and eighteen others; and boat three: Second Officer Bjelde and thirteen others—overall total forty-eight. Boat one was rescued by U.S.C.G. cutters *CGC 453* and *CGC 473*, then taken to Morehead City, NC on June 7. Boat two was rescued by Dutch ship *Melampus*, which landed in Halifax on May 31. Boat three was rescued by Dutch ship *Polyphemus* on May 25 only to be sunk by *U-578* on May 27; the crew dispersed.

Cohen's narrative of the open boat voyage is of special significance since the boats soon became separated. One of them lost contact with the other boats on Saturday, May 23 and the other late on Monday the 25th. Their shared destination at the outset was Bermuda, the nearest land. On board Christoffersen's boat was a water-storage tank under the seat and in other spaces were pemmican meat paste, chocolate, and hard biscuits. Among the supplies found were a battery-operated radio (which did not function well), flares, some blankets, a compass, and a first aid kit.

Since the boat was equipped with eight oars, a mast and sails, they were able to utilize a good breeze on the first few days to sail westward. Yet when the wind died, they were obliged to row for it, and the boy's tender hands quickly blistered. Their rations were "one square of chocolate, a biscuit with a cube of pemmican about the size of a thumbnail, and a very small drop of water." The weather was mostly clear, except for a terrible storm that lasted a whole night. Most of their energy was focused on scanning the horizon for rescue. While some of the men swam, one of them unwisely tangled with a Portuguese man o' war jellyfish and suffered from its poisonous toxins later. The men did not fish; however, they collected moisture on a tarpaulin and were very thirsty. They did manage to capture and eat flying fish, which landed on the sail and in the boat.

As an indication of how active the waters off Bermuda were for Axis submarines that spring, on the tenth day in the boat (May 30), the *Norland* men came across an abandoned life raft. They boarded it and scoured compartments for provisions but found none. Christoffersen noted which ship it had come from; it was most likely from the *Culebra*, under Captain George Bonner who with forty-four of his men perished after being sunk January 25, 1942, by *U-123* under Hardegen. Over time, the *Norland* men became sunburnt, and their legs ached, despite the refreshing dips in the water, during which non-swimmers tied a rope around their waist. Each day one of the officers or crew was convinced they saw a rescue craft. On around June 2, they were surrounded by a pod of whales, which swam past harmlessly.

The boat overshot Bermuda and was making for the American mainland under sail when they spotted another empty life raft, lowered the sail and rowed over to it. This was from an American ship, most likely from the *Steel Maker*, sunk April 20 by *U-654* under Forster 350 miles east of Hatteras. Though she sank in fifteen minutes, two lifeboats and at least one raft got away, with Radio Operator Harley A. Olson left behind to fend for himself. The poor fellow survived a month aboard a makeshift raft before being rescued by a passing ship. Alternately, the raft might have come from the *Pipestone County*, sunk by *U-576* on April 30 some 340 miles north of Bermuda, and on which eleven survivors may have tried to escape, or possibly from the rafts known to have floated from the *Robin Hood* (sunk April 16 by *U-575* some 400 miles north of Bermuda), or the tragic *Muskogee* (sunk by *U-123* on March 22 some 350 miles north of Bermuda, from which there were no survivors after ten men on a raft were photographed but left behind in stormy conditions). The raft provided the *Norland* survivors with "a small container of water and a container with several little bottles of vitamin tablets. This was a gift from heaven, as [their] water supply was very low." A few days later, on Friday, June 5, they were in the Gulf Stream and were able to digest seaweed and the little crabs which drifted with it.

The following day brought another false alarm when the men thought they saw a rescue ship which turned out to be an Allied vessel sunk by enemy submarines in such shallow water that its mast and funnel were above water. This would have been the 2,609-ton U.S.-flagged ship *Caribsea*, which had been sunk up to its masts in shallow waters just east of Morehead City and remained there since 11 March 1942 when Erwin Rostin of *U-158* sank her in three minutes off Cape Lookout. The captain pointed out that it must mean land was not far away. Because of their transmissions and the captain's encouragement, the men believed that rescue was imminent. However, they would have to sail, drift and row over 1,000 miles nearly three weeks (eighteen days) before they were spotted by aircraft 25 miles from Cape Lookout on June 7. Cohen recorded:

> At noon on the eighteenth day, an airplane was spotted some distance from our position. A flare was fired and we saw the plane turn and come in our direction. He flew in low and circled round us several times. We knew that he would signal his sighting and our position to his base. An hour or so later, at 3.55 p.m., a U.S. Navy PT-Boat [actually *CGC 453*] was sighted. It pulled alongside and we all clambered aboard. With the lifeboat towed astern [by *CGC 473*], the rescue boat headed toward their base ashore.[6]

This was Morehead City, North Caroline, where the men landed at 5.45 p.m. Their lifeboat followed, arriving at 6.30 p.m., sparing the men a nineteenth day on the open water. Cohen records that "The sailors offered us coffee or buttermilk. I only sipped the milk and the taste was awful ... I was offered an orange, and this I gulped down without any bother."[7]

Those rescued on the captain's boat included Advisory Engineer Sidney Clifford Paige, Welsh, aged forty-four, engine boys Miller and Hannah, Ronnie Wilson, and Fireman Arthur Hardy Ballard, of South Africa. The U.S. Navy sailors retrieved two sweaters, six blankets, twelve lifejackets, a flare, four gallons of oil, the first aid kit, a "distress outfit," radio transmitter and receiver, and three lights from the boat. The fifteen men were very well looked after by U.S. Navy doctors. The American Red Cross fitted them with a complete set of civilian clothes.[8]

Then, after about three days of recuperation, a representative of Nortraship arrived and provided transportation by bus, ferry, and rail to New York City.[9] During the trip, strangers offered the men and boys, who didn't yet have money, food, drink and conversation. They were put up in a hotel on Atlantic Avenue in the Cobble Hill section of Brooklyn. During their stay, young Cohen and Wilson befriended Harry Garber, whose father outfitted them with merchant mariner uniforms. Ultimately, they were paid $150, most of which was rationed out to them by Mr. Garber, so they did not spend it all at once. They moved to the Soldiers and Sailors Club on Lexington Avenue in Murray Hill, on Manhattan. They were able to meet some of their shipmates in Brooklyn and to hear of their trials that had enabled them too to reach shore safely. The boys went sightseeing, then caught another ship back to the U.K.

Boat two under First Officer Schmidt was rescued by the Dutch ship *Melampus*, built in 1924 by Palmer, and owned by the Dutch firm Oceaan in Amsterdam. She was 5,280 tons, 452 feet long, 55 feet wide, and 30 feet deep. Her two steam turbines developed 4,350 hp that propelled the ship at 13 knots. All nineteen men were landed in Halifax on Sunday, May 31, eleven days after the attack. Most likely the survivors then caught passage on some of the many Allied ships leaving Halifax for the U.K. in convoys that spring. There were only seven ships in the Oceaan fleet, and one of the other vessels, the *Polyphemus*, played an instrumental role in the rescue of the fourteen remaining men in *Norland*'s boat three under Second Officer Bjelde on May 25, some 25 miles northeast of Bermuda. This was testament to the strong navigational skills of Bjelde, as the boats had set out for Bermuda five days before.

Korvettenkapitän Ernst-August Rehwinkel brought *U-578* for its second patrol to New England on May 27, 1942, the same day he sank the *Polyphemus*. The attack took roughly seven hours, starting with a fan of two torpedoes, which after waiting for the target to go in and out of squalls, struck behind the aft mast, forcing the crew into five boats. A single *coup de grâce* did not hit the ship, following which an exasperated Rehwinkel refused to fire another "dead man" torpedo. Rather, he surfaced to sink the ship with gunnery, only to learn that even "sinking by artillery is no longer possible." Rehwinkel cattily described his adversary as "a typical corpulent Netherlander. [The captain] sits impassively throughout. The crew consists for the most part of coloreds, mostly Chinese."[10]

The *Polyphemus* was a 6,269-ton Dutch ship *en route* from Sydney, Australia, to Halifax. On 25 May she rescued fourteen survivors of the *Norland*. Rehwinkel destroyed the ship's stern, killing fifteen Chinese crew there, and leaving sixty-five persons on board, who were rescued by a variety of vessels. The next day, Rehwinkel determined to stay in deep water looking for targets, then patrol east and north of Nantucket with better moonlight. A plane noise caused a crash dive. On May 29 and 30, the boat made several crash dives to avoid flying boats and other planes. From then through June 1, the men were on the defensive, replacing cylinders, repairing the diesels, avoiding aircraft, and listening carefully. That evening, they were the third U-boat in a row to consider an attack on the neutral Swedish ship *Drottningholm* before they could verify its nationality and let it pass.

Dutch motor cargo-passenger ship *Polyphemus*, involved in complex lifeboat survival voyages and U-boat attacks in New England in 1942 along with half a dozen other vessels, including the *Norland*, whose men it rescued. Sunk by *U-578* under August Rehwinkel on May 17, 1942. Note the high number of lifeboats amidships. (*Courtesy of Guðmundur Helgason, Uboat.net/allies/merchants/ ship/1711, crediting Arendnet.net*)

Rehwinkel sank the Norwegian *Berganger* south of Nantucket on June 2 before exiting the region on the 9th. It was raining when *U-578*'s men caught up with the twin-mast ship. Of the three torpedoes fired, one hits amidships with a "heavy detonation [and] large smoke cloud." Rehwinkel saw a cannon, but he wrote; "by my observation [it was] unmanned. Boats were being prepared." Then, after they surfaced and he and 1st Watch Officer Emil Claussen climbed to the bridge, the ship "sho[t] at me with his cannon (impacts must be in the immediate vicinity)." The Germans crash-dived and Rehwinkel "drew the conclusion their ship will float. Therefore, I decide to shoot a *coup de grâce* ... so as not to let an aircraft snatch the prey from me." He seems satisfied when explosions astern caused it to "break upward" and render the cannons out of action. The Norwegians could take some consolation from Rehwinkel's inspection of his U-boat on surfacing: "On the boat an artillery hit is found astern to port in the metal plating. The starboard net deflector is broken astern. I have it disconnected and put overboard." He gave the Norwegians time to rescue their shipmates from the water.[11]

Characteristically of the siege underway, the *Berganger* had just escaped a determined but unsuccessful attack by *U-213* under von Varendorff.[12] That same day, while about 150 miles south-southeast of Nantucket, the ship was then fatally hit by *U-578*. Four of the merchant sailors were killed and forty-three managed to get away. Of those, seventeen were rescued by the Norwegian ship *Bañaderos* and taken to New York, thirteen of them by the diesel-powered fishing vessel *Mary J. Landry* and landed at New Bedford, and thirteen by U.S.S. *Madison,* DD 425, and taken to Norfolk.[13, 14] Built of wood in 1928, the *Mary J. Landry* survived a 1957 collision that sank the other boat. Up to at least October 1975, she was owned by Stephen F. Lozinak of Plymouth, Massachusetts.

On June 4, the submariners in *U-578* crash-dived to avoid a flying boat, then loaded new torpedoes that night. On the night of the 7th, a plane roared in from port amidships, dropping three depth charges that exploded less than 150 feet away, roughly 30 feet deep. The damage report included repairs necessitated:

> Both motors stopped by the failure of the motor circuit-breaker. Rudder, both diving planes, rudder angle indicator, hydraulic oil pump, gyrocompass installation, speed measurement installation, depth gauge, control tower and control room, both engine telegraphs, 23 incandescent bulbs, 42 fuses.[15]

A crash dive the following day made Rehwinkel suspect the periscope may also have been damaged, made him doubt the ability of the conning tower hatch to close, and the boat's self-defense system generally. However, he stayed in the way of traffic to and from New York and Boston. Given the freedom to choose his next move, the commander opted for open waters and surface attacks in daytime rather than the foggy coast, with just a few hours a night to attack, with airplanes lurking.

The patrol began in St. Nazaire on May 7 and ended there on July 3. The day the sub entered, it motored to a point southeast of Nantucket. *U-578* remained in the general vicinity, tacking back and forth until June 9. Then it motored south, avoiding airplanes. Forced to pass on "a brightly illuminated Swede," it then lost a steamer with several masts. Most of June 9 and 10 was spent outside New England waters tracking a British steamer of the *Eurymedon*-type, which roused so many of Rehwinkel's suspicions of a decoy that he refused a deck gun attack with half his men exposed, and let it pass. *U-578* also participated in the seven-sub patrol lines called *Padfinder* and *Hecht* from May 9 to 11. After its patrol off New England, the U-boat went to Cape Hatteras, then back to France, having sunk two ships. Rehwinkel was born in 1901 and went missing with the rest of *U-578*'s crew on August 6, 1942, in the Bay of Biscay.

The *Polyphemus* was a diesel-motor ship of 6,269 tons built by Scott's Shipbuilding and Engineering of Greenock in 1930. She could carry 7,950 tons of cargo as well as passengers and was fitted with at least five lifeboats. The *Polyphemus* was 430 feet long, 56 feet wide, and 26 feet deep; she could motor at just over 14 knots, propelled by two 687-hp engines turning double propellers. She was a large, fast ship manned by forty-eight personnel including Captain Cornelius Koningstein: twenty-seven Chinese, three British, and the balance eighteen were Dutch. Among those were two passengers—a Mr. Stewart of Singapore and R. G. Lock of Weymouth—plus Chinese sailors, stewards, greasers, and a quartermaster (Lung Tai) from Canton. After rescuing fourteen *Norland* men, the number of persons on board was seventy-seven.[16]

The ship was on its way from Sydney, Australia, via Panama to Halifax and Liverpool carrying wheat and wool. After picking up survivors of the *Norland*, the *Polyphemus* was able to cover 335 miles northward from the rescue site during the next thirty or so hours, before it was itself sunk, starting at 6.18 p.m. on Tuesday, May 26. Some 350 miles southeast of Nantucket, two torpedoes from *U-578* under Rehwinkel tore the stern accommodation off, killing fifteen of the Chinese sailors who lived there. An SSS signal was sent; however, no reply or confirmation was received. From that point, there were thirty-three *Polyphemus* men, including passengers, plus all fourteen *Norland* men, for a total of sixty-two persons requiring rescue. As with the *Norland*'s survivors, these men would be scattered further afield in different lifeboats meeting differing fates.

The German attackers moved their submarine in among the survivors and asked for details of the ship, cargo, and destination. The Allies observed two stripes and a swastika on one of the German's uniforms and that they spoke English well. The commander gave them standard German cigarettes of the Reemsa brand, his crew took photos, then they motored off, wishing them *bon voyage*. The Allies noticed the logo of a snorting bull on the conning tower. The sixty-two survivors boarded five lifeboats, and were rescued in New England or New York by six vessels: D/S *Maria Amelia* (to New York); S.S. *Torvanger* (then to F/V *Elva and Estelle,* to New Bedford); F/V *Elva and Estelle* (to New Bedford); F/V *Huntington Sanford* (to New Bedford); D/S *Mirandella* (to New York); and U.S.C.G.C. *General Greene* (to Nantucket, then Newport).

Twenty-six *Polyphemus* survivors landed in four New England ports (not counting those to NY): on boat one: eight from the *Polyphemus* and two from the *Norland* were rescued by the *Huntington Sanford*, New Bedford; on boat three: seven from the *Polyphemus* and three from the *Norland* were rescued by the *General Greene*, landing in Nantucket; and on boat five: eleven from the *Polyphemus* and two from the *Norland* were rescued by the *Torvanger* and the *Elva and Estelle*, heading to New Bedford.[17]

Twenty-two *Polyphemus* survivors landed outside New England: on boat two, twelve from *Polyphemus*, along with three *Norland* men, were rescued by the *Mirandella*, and landed in New York; and on boat four, ten from the *Polyphemus*, along with four *Norland* men, were rescued by the *Maria Amelia* and landed New York.

Boat one, a motor lifeboat, was led by Captain Koningstein and held eight *Polyphemus* and two *Norland* men. It was found by the fishing boat *Huntington Sanford* commanded by Joshua W. Murphy, Jr., roughly 50 miles northeast of the lightship *Nantucket* at 3 a.m. on Monday, June 1. They had sailed 315 miles since the loss of the *Polyphemus*. These men were landed in New Bedford the following day. Boat two was under the command of the *Polyphemus*'s second officer, L. J.

Burger. This is also described as the surgeon's boat, as most of the injured were in it, along with the ship's surgeon. On board were twelve *Polyphemus* and three *Norland* survivors, or fifteen total.

Boat three under Third Officer Jan Dykdrenth (or Dijkdrenth) of Katwyksee held ten men. Seven were *Polyphemus* sailors (three Dutch, one Welsh, and three Chinese), and three ordinary seamen from the *Norland*, all from Scotland: Angus J. Campbell from Inverness, Donald Campbell from Stornoway, and Able Seaman William P. McAllan from Peterculter. Being boys, their next of kin were their parents. Since the Germans seemed to control this bit of ocean, the men in the lifeboat were fortunate, as two U-boats approached them, and both Dykrenth and Fourth Engineer Molenaar spoke German with them.

First, *U-566* under *Kapitänleutnant* Dietrich Borchert approached their boat. He and the crew were friendly and engaging, even giving them his last name, allowing them to walk the deck, and telling them he was able to get intelligence from Europe and planned to be back in Europe in three weeks. The encounter occurred on Monday, May 29, four days after the *Polyphemus* had been sunk, and ten days after the *Norland* was lost. Borchert gave the men water and a course to the nearest land, which was Nantucket, 350 miles to the northwest. He logged: "encountered a lifeboat of the steamer *Polyphemus*, sunk by U-Rehwinkel. Supplied with water and gave a navigation fix. On board were crew members of the Norwegian *Norland*, sunk one week earlier."[18] Young "helper" James Glover told his daughters that "when the German captain came up he gave them chocolate along with the cigarettes."[19] Indeed, the seas of New England were thick with German submarines.

The following day, at 7.30 a.m. on the 30th, boat three under Dykdrenth was again approached by a U-boat, this time *U-593* under *Kapitänleutnant* Gerd Kelbling. Due to the rough weather, with winds about 15 knots and 6-foot seas, they were barely able to come alongside. Although invited to do so, no one from the boat boarded the submarine's deck. They were asked the customary questions and provided with directions as well as a tin of German bread and a bottle of rum. Kelbling affirmed the encounter, logging that a "lifeboat cutter with sail from Dutch *Polyphemus* passed. A can of bread and a flask of rum handed over."[20] The emblem on the U-boat was a "jumping steer," really the snorting bull logo of the Bull of Scapa Flow, also on the conning tower of the sub that had sunk the *Polyphemus*. They were southeast of Nantucket. Perhaps because they were so far from land, Kelbling provided the men with bread from the U-boat's bakery as well as the rum. The boat had made it 325 miles northwest of the *Polyphemus* sinking, and to within 35 miles of Siasconset.

Coastal authorities were scrambling to stay ahead of numerous reports of ships being attacked and sinking, sending men drifting in lifeboats up and down the east coast that poured into the frontier diarist. On June 4, the First Naval District dispatched the U.S. Coast Guard cutter *General Greene* from Newport to

Nantucket Shoals at 8.25 p.m.[21] They were looking specifically for *Polyphemus* survivors, and equipped themselves with a pharmacist's mate. At 5.45 p.m. the following day, Lieutenant Shea and his men discovered the ten Dutch and British sailors in boat three, assisting them aboard. Then they tied the lifeboat astern and towed the boat to Nantucket Harbor. The survivors were landed the same day (Friday, June 5) at the Brant Point U.S. Coast Guard base guarding the island's main harbor. Nantucket historian Robert Mooney noted:

> The first human casualties of the war arrived in Nantucket [when] two boatloads of survivors of a ship torpedoed off Bermuda were brought into Nantucket after drifting at sea for several days.... The Red Cross called for volunteers, and scores of nurses and volunteers responded to help out. All the men survived and left the island in a few days. This ... left a lasting memory with all who attended them.[22]

Overall, Nantucket absorbed ninety Allied survivors of U-boat attack in the war, from the *Peisander*, the *Norland*, the *Polyphemus* and later the *Mattawin*, then repatriated them and their lifeboats to the Navy base in Newport. The seven *Polyphemus* and three *Norland* survivors spent seventeen hours on the island during part of the night of June 7–8. Only Leonard Woyle from the *Peisander* spent several days on Nantucket in hospital for his teeth.[23] Of all these rescues, that of the men from the *Polyphemus* and the *Norland* stood out, as the local paper, *The Inquirer and Mirror*, points out, relating that they arrived at midnight and were housed in the local theater, Bennett Hall, which is also, conveniently, adjacent to a church.

> The next day, being Sunday, all ten men filed into the Congregational Church to morning service through the door connecting with Bennett Hall, thus keeping within bounds. In the afternoon they were taken, still carefully guarded, to a baseball game which they thoroughly enjoyed. These wet, tired and hungry men were refreshed and restored by the same friendly hands and hearts that has [*sic.*] ministered to the first arrivals and they were equally grateful and appreciative.... we are fortunate that our shoal waters permit so few of these disasters to come to us. But if and when they come, we are ready to meet them.

One eyewitness, a curious boy with relatives in the Coast Guard, tried to see more of the survivors; however, they were kept quite sequestered, perhaps for reasons of security. "Although townspeople were asked, and did, respond quickly with clothing and bedding, the survivors were kept somewhat isolated. I do remember my mother taking what little we could give [to them]. However, she only went to the door of Bennett Hall."[24]

U.S.C.G.C. *General Greene* was a 125-foot patrol boat built by American Brown Boveri Electric of Camden, opposite Philadelphia, in 1927. She was 24 feet wide and 7.5 feet deep with twin engines giving her 13 knots. The *Norland*'s survivors were interviewed by U.S. Navy officials, but the men were so confused over both submarine attacks that a number of the facts were muddled and deemed unreliable by their interrogators. In words of the First Naval District intelligence officers, the men and boys "were a little confused as to facts, often mixing the details of the torpedoing of the S.S. *Norland* and the S.S. *Polyphemus*." Today, this might be attributed to post-traumatic stress disorder (PTSD).[25]

By Wednesday, June 3, the men in boat two under Second Officer Burger were 250 miles east-southeast of Nantucket when discovered by the Portuguese ship *Mirandella, en route* to New York. The *Mirandella* was formerly named the *Fernao Veloso* (to 1925) and the *Khalif* (to 1916). Built in 1906 by Bremer Vulkan in Germany, she was 5,179 tons, 409 feet long, 53 feet wide, 26 feet deep, and capable of 14 knots. The ship's owners were the same as those of the *Maria Amelia* in Lisbon. The *Mirandella* picked up a total of fifteen men from the lifeboat—twelve from *Polyphemus* and three from *Norland*—all of them landed in New York on June 5.

Boat four was in charge of the chief officer of the *Polyphemus*, Herman Brandenburg of Utrecht. It held ten of his and four of the *Norland*'s men. On

Survivors of several nationalities from the *Polyphemus* (ten, including four Chinese) and the *Norland* (four). This group reunited with other shipmates in New York before, ultimately shipping back out to the front lines of the Battle of the Atlantic. (*Photo shared by James Glover's daughters: Patricia C. McCormack, Jeannie T. C. Kilgour, Catherine Ann Roodhouse, and Joan Deanna Angel. Posted by Siri Holm Lawson at warsailors.com/singleships/norland*)

Friday, May 29, three days after the sinking and the day after being separated from the other boats, the lifeboat was approached by *U-593* just after dawn (at 7.15 a.m.). The Allied sailors saw two puffs of smoke from the U-boat's diesels and set off flares. Rather than a reply, they were approached by the U-boat, whose officer asked in English about cargo, invited the chief officer on board, and offered aid. There were no logos, marks, or crests on this boat. The Germans wished the survivors *bon voyage* and motored off. The commander of the boat, Gerd Kelbling, is less descriptive about the encounter, writing simply, "passed lifeboat cutter with sail course 300°" Raised in coastal Salzbrunn, Silesia, Kelbling must have been a sailor to have recognized the cutter rig of a sailboat. It is basically a sloop configuration with an inner foresail, or staysail.

Less than an hour later, at 7.30 a.m., the Portuguese ship *Maria Amelia* under the command of Captain de Mirande picked up the four *Norland* and ten *Polyphemus* survivors. Just over two hours after passing the lifeboat, at 9.20 a.m., Kelbling saw smoke from the *Maria Amelia*'s funnel 315 miles southeast of Nantucket. At 10.30 a.m., he dove to attack. At 11.50 a.m., the ship unwittingly steamed into the U-boat's crosshairs half a mile away. Thankfully, Kelbling saw that the ship was clearly marked a Portuguese neutral and broke off the attack. The submarine approached the ship so closely that the men on the neutral vessel could clearly see the emblem of Ferdinand the Bull on the conning tower. Kelbling noted: "Surfaced. Steamer stopped, sets identification signal, is not armed. Moved off on the surface." The *Polyphemus* and *Norland* men thus very narrowly avoided a third sinking.

The *Maria Amelia* (previously the *Gaia* and the *Girgenti*) was built by Neptun Werft in Germany in 1913. Her owners in 1942 were the Societa Geral de Comercio, Industria e Transportes Limitada of Lisbon. The ship was 1,766 tons, 302 feet long, 41 feet wide, and 18 feet deep. She was capable of 10 knots when built, probably less twenty-nine years later. Captain di Mirande brought his vessel to New York, where he deposited the four *Norland* survivors. These included Deck Boy Victor Annesley Haggith, only fifteen, of Wembley; and Saloon Boy Frank McMillan of Greenock, Scotland, age seventeen. The boys encountered young William Cohen and Ronnie Wilson at their Atlantic Avenue Hotel in Cobble Hill, Brooklyn, when the latter group arrived from North Carolina the second week of June 1942.

Haggith and McMillan caught the attention of the press, with the *Fitchburg (MA) Sentinel* pointing out on 5 June (before the other four British teenagers from the *Norland* had landed) that "two teenage British survivors of the latest sinking said their Norwegian ship was sunk in the Atlantic 20 May, and they spent five days in open boats until they were rescued by a Dutch merchantman."[26]

> Victor Haggith of Wembley had run off at the age of 14 and joined the Merchant Navy instead of going to school one day. Shortly after his 15th birthday he

> experienced two sinkings within a week, surviving the sinking of *Polyphemus* in the lifeboat in charge of the chief officer and being rescued by the *Maria Amelia*. The authorities eventually discovered that he had lied about his age and later sent him around the world as "the boy hero" to sell war bonds.[27]

The men rescued by *Maria Amelia* were able to obtain passage to the U.K. from ships leaving New York.

Boat five was under the charge of the chief engineer of the *Polyphemus* and the second officer of the *Norland* (Bjelde), with a total of eleven *Polyphemus* and two *Norland* men. They were rescued 130 miles east of Nantucket in the evening of Tuesday, June 2. The rescue ship, for a brief time only, was the Norwegian ship *Torvanger*. She was a 6,568-ton steamship built in 1920 by William Doxford and Sons of Sunderland. The ship was 420 feet long, 54 feet wide, and 34 feet deep. Her owners were the Westfal-Larsen Company of Bergen, and her skipper was Captain Leif Danielsen.

Captain Danielsen did not keep his charges for long. She was *en route* from New York to Halifax then Cape Town and Alexandria with a cargo of 8,000 tons of war material including tanks, beer, gliders in crates on deck, and ammunition. Rather than take the *Norland* and the *Polyphemus* men to Halifax, Danielsen transferred them to a local fishing vessel, the *Elva and Estelle* (*Elva* given as *Alpha* in other accounts), when about 60 miles east of Pollock Rip, which separates Nantucket from Cape Cod. This was itself a risky operation, given the required stoppage and known proximity of U-boats in the area, but Danielsen felt it was worth the risk, and the survivors probably did not want to risk another trans-ocean passage with land so near.

The *Elva and Estelle* landed the thirteen men in New Bedford on Wednesday, June 3. They were the last of the forty-eight men aboard the *Norland* to set foot ashore, all of them having survived. As a group, the *Polyphemus* men had had to withstand two U-boat attacks (*U-578* versus *Polyphemus* and *U-593* versus *Maria Amelia*) as well as being approached by three U-boats while in lifeboats (*U-566* under Borchert, *U-593* under Kelbling, then *U-593* again). This is clarified by the following list:

1. *U-578*/Rehwinkel sank *Polyphemus* on Tuesday, May 26
2. *U-593*/Kelbling saw *Polyphemus* boat four on Friday, May 29
3. *U-593*/Kelbling stalked and lined up to attack *Maria Amelia* with boat four, men aboard, Friday, May 29
4. *U-566*/Borchert, provided *Polyphemus* boat two with water, directions, Friday, May 29
5. *U-593*/Kelbling, provided *Polyphemus* boat two with bread and rum, Saturday, May 30

An Allied merchant ship retrieving sailors from a lifeboat from a ship torpedoed by a U-boat off the U.S. east coast in early 1942. Taken from a U.S. military plane, this photo is what the *Torvanger*, the *Polyphemus*, and many other Allied merchant ships did to rescue fellow sailors at peril to themselves. (*U.S. Coast Guard, Public domain*)

The rescue took three merchant, two fishing vessels, an aircraft, and three U.S. Coast Guard craft: U.S.C.G.C. *General Greene* (June 5, Newport, Nantucket); *CGC 453* (June 7, Madaket, Nantucket); *CGC 473* (June 7, Madaket); F/V *Huntington Sanford* (June 1); F/V *Elva and Estelle* (June 2); the *Maria Amelia* (May 29); the *Torvanger* (June 2); and the *Mirandella* (June 3). They were heading to five ports of first arrival: Halifax (May 31); New York (June 5); New Bedford (June 2–3) Nantucket, then Newport (June 7); and Morehead City, North Carolina (June 7).

Few U-boat attacks in World War II could have had as diverse, drawn-out, and successful rescues, particularly given that they also came across evidence of the many mariners who never made it: an abandoned life raft (ex-*Culebra*?) around May 30; an abandoned American life raft (ex-*Steel Maker*?) on June 2; and a partially sunken ship (off the Carolinas) on June 6.[28]

The thirteen men transferred from the *Torvanger* were fortunate. After she arrived in Halifax to top up cargo, the *Torvanger* sailed for Cape Town on June 14, 1942. She was sunk by *U-84* under Horst Uphoff roughly a week later, on June 23, less than 500 miles west of the Azores. Four men out of her complement of thirty-seven perished. Captain Danielsen survived. The *Maria Amelia* survived the war and lasted until 1949. The *Mirandella* also survived the conflict and lasted until 1955, when it was sold for scrap in La Spezia, Italy. The *General*

Greene was decommissioned in 1968 and sold in 1976 to become a museum ship in Newburyport, Massachusetts. When that plan failed, she was flagged to Guatemala in 1979, sold, and renamed *Belmont*. The hunter became the hunted when the U.S. Coast Guard seized her former brethren for smuggling drugs. On May 24, 1941, off Greenland, she had almost been run over by the German goliath battleship KMS *Bismarck*.

After censorship was eased in 1945, an article appeared in the *Newport Mercury* claimed that four survivors were brought to Newport to be cared for by the American Red Cross. This must have been only the injured. The article, which could only name ships after censorship had been lifted, was entitled "Red Cross Here Aided 130 Sub Survivors Here, Disaster Relief Committee Revealed. Outfitted Crews of Six Ships Torpedoed Off this Area by U-boats in 1942." According to the article, one of the men had been injured (no doubt by the boom) and two had swollen feet, and the three were taken to the Marine Hospital in Brighton, near Boston. Presumably, those three and one other were taken care of by the Newport Red Cross.[29] In fact, the Red Cross under-estimated their good deeds: there were 160 Allied survivors landed in Newport: fifteen from the *Black Point*, thirty-nine from the *Norness* (nine of them initially taken to New Bedford by the *Malvina*), sixty-one from the *Peisander* (one left behind on Nantucket), twenty-six from the *Polyphemus* (with three *Norland* men mixed in), and nineteen from the *Mattawin*.[30] Added to these were the remains of two German U-boat sailors, from *U-550* during and *U-853* following the war.

While the *Polyphemus* and the *Norland* men struggled toward shore and safety, Rehwinkel continued his swathe of destruction. The Norwegian cargo ship *Berganger* was ordered in February 1931 for Westfal-Larsen of Bergen. She was built by Netherlands Dock and Ship Building in Amsterdam and completed in August 1932. Weighing 6,826 tons, she could carry 9,824 tons of dry cargo. The steel ship was 456 feet long, 61 feet wide, and 31 feet deep, and was powered by an 8,200-hp engine, which propelled it at an impressive 15 knots. On her final voyage, the *Berganger* was on charter to the Nortraship, having spent most of the war shuttling cargoes between the east coast of South America (Brazil, Argentina, and Uruguay) and the U.S. East Coast (Baltimore, Philadelphia, New York, and Boston). Then, late in 1941, the ship switched to the west coast, from Vancouver and California to Chile and beyond. By May 1942, she was back on the east coast run, under the command of Norwegian Captain Alm Normann Nymann.[31]

There were forty-seven persons on board who included nationals of the U.S., Poland, Britain, Denmark, Sweden, and Argentina. At least two of the Norwegians—Johan Vidnes and Olav Brevik—doubled as gunners as well as able-bodied seamen. The young Argentinian saloon girl Consuela Gonzales served as a rare female crew, along with a Danish saloon boy and American and British galley boys. The *Berganger* originally loaded 5,320 tons of dry cargo in Buenos Aires and then sailed to Santos, Brazil, where she topped up with 3,623 more tons, including 48,000 bags of coffee, 1,138 liters of sunflower seed oil, animal hides, and 1,000 bales of lintners, or malt extracts for brewing enzymes.[32] They left Santos on May 16.

The voyage northward to Boston proceeded uneventfully until the night of Monday, June 1, 1942, when *U-213* (under *Oberleutnant zur See* Amelung von Varendorff) sent five torpedoes streaking toward the ship and its unsuspecting crew. Amazingly, none of them struck the target, and the ship continued along, its officers, crew, gunners, and girl unaware of how close they had come to being sunk. Von Varendorff broke off his attack, primarily due to lack of sufficient speed. The next day, however, the Norwegians were not so fortunate. At 2.30 p.m., the *Berganger* was struck by a torpedo fired by *U-578* under Rehwinkel. It penetrated the port side ahead of the engine room and the number three cargo hold. Four engineers were killed: Assistant Engineer Lennart Larsson of Sweden and Norwegian mechanics Einar Nilsen and Søren Schjelderup, and electrician Arne Bedringsås.

Conditions at the time of attack were fairly mild, with a wind of roughly 15 knots from the northeast, good daylight visibility, and no other ships on the horizon. For two weeks, the ship had been zigzagging on the British plan number thirty. There were five lookouts: two on the bridge, another pair at the gun aft, and a fifth in the crow's nest equipped with binoculars. Seas were moderate as the *Berganger* headed northwest 283 degrees at 15 knots, having reached a point roughly 130 miles southeast of Block Island. Immediately on being struck an emergency message was broadcast on the radio, and the gun readied. The ship's port motor lifeboat was smashed, she began to list to port, and the bow swung in that direction as well. The engines stopped, lights went out, and the vessel began to sink. Captain Nymann raced from his cabin to the bridge, but his efforts to bring the vessel back on course were fruitless. He was informed by surviving engine-room staff that the spaces there were flooded or flooding.

Just two minutes after the torpedo struck, a submarine surfaced 1.5 miles off the port side, proving too tempting a target for gunners Vidnes and Bevik, who, under instructions from the master, managed to fire half a dozen rounds from their 4-inch gun aft, with a shot every five seconds, and "it is believed that the second shot hit the aft jumping wire of the submarine which immediately crash-dived." The first two shots probably missed, and the subsequent four shots were fired at the surfaced submarine which submerged before they detonated.[33]

Though Nymann threw the confidential codes overboard in a weighted bag, he kept the routing instructions with him when he abandoned ship, which was a somewhat chaotic process. The remaining forty-three mariners (there was one uncorroborated report of three passengers from Santos to Boston: Swedish mechanic Victor Johansson confirmed as much when he stated on June 4 that there were two passengers on board) abandoned ship roughly fifteen minutes after the attack, starting around 2.45 p.m. There were three lifeboats, one of which capsized and was bailed out by two mariners who jumped into the sea and swam to it. Three life rafts were also launched.

Eighteen minutes after the first torpedo struck, a second one plowed into the *Berganger*. The impact overturned a lifeboat which had just been launched and flung the twenty-one occupants into the water. As a result, the men (and possibly the saloon girl Consuela) clambered aboard one life raft, though eight people later moved to a boat, leaving thirteen on the overcrowded raft. Most of the survivors climbed into the starboard amidships and port aft lifeboats; the latter was overturned when a torpedo struck the number two cargo hold. Four men managed to right this boat, and while the seventeen others hung to the side, they set about bailing it.

At that awkward time, Rehwinkel and his men paid the lifeboat a visit to inquire about the tonnage of the ship, destination, cargo, flag, and whether an SOS was sent. The Norwegians answered correctly, except regarding tonnage and the SOS signal. They observed that Rehwinkel, who first asked in German whether anyone spoke that language, had a "movie type" beard or goatee. The *Berganger*'s survivors observed the lack of uniforms, and that all the men seemed to wear caps of some sort.

The Allied sailors also noticed a Ferdinand-the-Bull-type insignia on the side of the conning tower, and that a crew was repairing a jumping wire, used to hold up the radio antennae (they hoped this indicated a hit on the jumping wire by their shells). Indeed, *U-578* had the Snorting Bull emblem from *U-47* in which Gunther Prien penetrated Scapa Flow, Scotland earlier in the war. The conning tower also had a dent that was covered by red "lead" paint. The Germans photographed the desperate survivors. Then, at about 3 p.m., the submarine headed off, still surfaced, northwest toward New York.

It turned out the boat that was overturned by the second torpedo explosion was too damaged and had to be abandoned after its twenty-one occupants were rescued. The starboard boat deposited some men into the boat that had been overturned and bailed out by two men, so that it would have enough men to row two hours back to the raft and the overturned lifeboat in order to rescue the men there. After the *Berganger* sank, thirteen men including the girl were distributed among three life rafts and tied to a badly damaged lifeboat, and the two useable lifeboats with thirty-one sailors in them set sail for land.

Fortuitously, on June 4, all the men and the girl in various vessels were rescued by various other vessels. The most vulnerable group of thirteen under First Officer Sverre Hovik in a boat and rafts were picked up by U.S.S. *Madison* in league with U.S.S. *Plunkett*. These U.S. Navy destroyers were in a group of ships named Destroyer Squadron 7 proceeding from Boston to Cape Henlopen. At 12.55 p.m., they discovered wreckage from the *Berganger* and reduced speed from 22 knots. At 1 p.m., they saw two rafts and a boat with men on them. At 1.33 p.m., the *Madison* retrieved thirteen men and the girl from the rafts, and the *Plunkett* discovered an empty and overturned lifeboat. It is possible the lifeboat came from either the U.S. freighter *Plow City* (sunk May 22) or British ship *Margot* (sunk the following day), both by *U-588* under Vogel. The *Plow City* left two lifeboats at the scene and another where rescued on May 27; the *Margot* left a large boat at the scene, and a jolly boat and smaller lifeboat when rescued, also on May 27, or eight days before U.S.S. *Plunkett* found the boat. The *Madison* sailors fired at the rafts and boats with 20-mm guns.

The condition of the men was good, with only the third officer having his feet badly sun-burnt. At 2.45 p.m., they discovered an empty lifeboat and determined it had belonged to their crew mates, with sails and the red and yellow bunting Captain Nymann had instructed them to fly. The first officer said the boat was "undoubtedly" from the *Berganger*, and indeed the occupants had recently been rescued by the Norwegian ship *Bañaderos*. The American sailors were very solicitous of the Norwegians and Brazilians, and "the crew of the *Madison* donated articles of clothing to the survivors with an insufficient amount. The ship's laundry was used to wash, clean and press the clothing worn … soap, a toothbrush, and a package of cigarettes for each survivor were issued from the Ship's Service Store." They were taken to Norfolk and landed at 7 p.m. on Saturday the 6th.

Second Mate Finn Jenssen's boat with a total of seventeen persons in it was rescued by a fellow Norwegian ship, the *Bañaderos*, on June 4 and landed in New York the following day. Their lifeboat was the one discovered empty by U.S.S. *Madison* and destroyed the same day. Nymann's lifeboat made it to within 14 miles of Block Island before the fishing vessel *Mary J. Landry* rescued him and his men on the evening of the 4th.[34] The fishermen took the thirteen survivors with them to New Bedford the following day, Friday, June 5.[35] By Monday the 8th, all forty-three survivors, passengers and saloon girl Consuela were reunited in New York, where naval hearings were held.

The *Bañaderos* survived the war and was broken up in La Spezia in December 1965. The *Mary J. Landry* survived being thrown ashore in Fairhaven in Hurricane Carol and may still by fishing out of Plymouth, where the *Mayflower* anchored in 1629. U.S.S. *Madison* was sunk off southeastern Florida for target practice on October 14, 1969, a few months after being decommissioned from the U.S. Navy. *U-578* was lost about two months later, between August 7 and 8. It left St. Nazaire for a patrol in the North Atlantic and was posted missing on the 11th, having presumably been sunk by Allied forces in the Bay of Biscay, precise fate unknown.[36]

Kapitänleutnant Heinrich Lehmann-Willenbrock brought *U-96* into New England for a comparatively long patrol of nine days from February 24 to March 5, 1942. The patrol carried west across the Gulf of Maine to a point off Cape Cod, south to Nantucket, then southeast, before closing a box-like route to return to the waters of Nova Scotia. Lehman-Willenbrock and his men were highly successful before and after their incursion to New England, yet sank nothing there. The night *U-96* entered New England south of Cape Sable, it encountered a destroyer, and in its effort to submerge and get away from "very loud sound gear, hammering fast impulses," the submarine actually bumped into the seafloor in about 150 feet of depth. The Germans later heard a depth charge exploding. The commander decided that since "operations area stirred up [to] transit to Gulf of Maine. Intend to search for traffic for Boston at Cape Cod." That night, they dove to avoid a flying boat and cleaned guns and repaired a rattling noise. Early on the 25th, the men saw a patrol vessel, and a fishing trawler the next day, followed by a formation of patrol vessels. On February 27, "Cape Cod lighthouse in sight. Burns as in peacetime"—this must have been Highland Light, Provincetown. Then more fishermen, patrol vessels, and airplanes. The commander reported four battery cells knocked out by aerial bombing, then headed over the Georges Bank and toward Nova Scotia blanketed by foul weather.[37]

Between February 19 and 22, *U-96* sank the *Empire Seal*, the *Lake Osweya*, the *Turengen*, and the *Kars*, followed on March 9 by the *Tyr* outside New England waters. Overall, Lehmann-Willenbrock was a very effective skipper who was decorated commensurate with his achievements. He sank or damaged twenty-seven ships of 195,000 tons and was awarded the Knights Cross with Oak Leaves on the final day of 1941, before this patrol. Born in 1911 in Bremen, Lehmann-Willenbrock lived until 1986 and age seventy-four. A member of the Crew of 1931, he served on the light cruiser *Karlsruhe* as well as the *Horst Wessel*, a sail-training ship. His early U-boats were *U-8*, as 1st Watch Officer, and *U-5*, which he commanded. He managed to flee Brest aboard *U-256* before the city fell in September 1944, and arrived in Norway, where he was captured and held for a year.

The U-boat commander enjoyed a colorful post-war career, when he and another U-boat skipper, Karl-Friedrich Merten, cleared shipwrecks from the River Rhine. Then he helped build a sailboat, the *Magellan,* and sailed it to Argentina, where they founded a racing regatta. As a merchant marine captain in 1959, he and his men rescued survivors of the burning ship *Commandante Lyra*. He went on to skipper the *Otto Hahn*, a nuclear research ship, for a decade to 1979. Lehmann-Willenbrock chaired the U-boat comrades' association in Bremen for several years. He also served as a consultant with the gritty German film *Das Boot*.

Oberleutnant zur See Otto Ites brought *U-94* into New England from south of Cape Sable on March 5 westbound then past Montauk on the 9th. The submarine sank no shipping there. On February 24, *U-94* sank the *Empire Hail*. Ites was frustrated by the heavy seas and wind from dead ahead encountered in New England, as these forced *U-94* to submerge. In the same area just before sunset, the destroyer U.S.S. *Noa* collided with lightship *110*, which it had been towing, 3 miles east of Cape Ann, and both returned to Boston.[38]

On March 6, *U-94* exchanged recognition signals with *U-404* under von Bülow, and that night, Ites followed a steamer but could not see it even from 3,300 feet away. He fired a G7e torpedo from Tube I and it struck the ship after thirty-three seconds. The target then turned its beam to the ocean swell, and men holding lights began running to the stern, as though to launch lifeboats. Ites estimated the ship was 6,000 tons and could carry fourteen passengers. Arrogantly, he was so convinced that it sank after two minutes that *U-94* simply kept going. Oddly, no ship reported an attack in that area at that time, nor has a ship been reported missing or sunk there since. That night, *U-94* dove to avoid an "antiquated type, slow" airplane. After Ites passed Montauk to starboard, he sank the Brazilian ship *Cayrú* on the night of March 8–9. This led to the tragic loss of fifty-three persons out of eighty-nine passengers and crew. Six survivors and the body of another were found by the U.S. Navy coastal minesweeper U.S.S. *Amc 202* on the 11th and taken to New London at 3 a.m. on the 12th.[39] Ites followed by sinking the Norwegian *Hvoslef* on March 11 and damaging the *Imperial Transport* on the 25th.

Otto Ites was born in 1918 in Norden and lived until 1982 aged sixty-three. This was despite the fact that *U-94* was bombed by aircraft and rammed by the Canadian corvette H.M.C.S. *Oakville* in the Windward Passage, which killed twenty-six Germans and left only nineteen German sailors alive. Ites was a member of the Crew of 1936, serving aboard the torpedo boats *Albatros* and *Kondor*, then joining U-boats in 1938. He served aboard *U-51*, then as 2nd Watch Officer on *U-48* along with Teddy Suhren. From March to August 1941, Ites commanded *U-146*, then took over *U-94* from Herbert Kuppisch. Captured after the sinking of *U-94* in the Caribbean, Ites was released in 1946, became a dentist, then joined the new German Navy (the NATO force called *Bundesmarine*) a decade later, commanding the destroyer *Z2* (D 171, ex-U.S.S. *Ringgold*, DD 500). He retired as counter admiral in 1977.

Kapitänleutnant Otto von Bülow in *U-404* entered New England heading westward on March 6, 1942. The boat past southeast of Nantucket on the 10th and left south of Montauk on the 11th. The sub did not sink any Allied ships while there. On the 6th, *U-404* exchanged recognition signals with *U-94* under Ites. That afternoon, *U-404* chased a passenger ship and fired from Tube V, but missed due to having undercalculated the ship's speed. The sub first gave up on the ship (the *Newfoundland* type, 6,791 tons), then on Cape Sable itself, heading southward, it encountered numerous fishing and patrol vessels as well as aircraft.[40]

At 10.05 a.m. on March 10, the *Enemy Action Diary* recorded:

> A bombardier of the First Bomber Command reported sighting three submarine conning towers awash. The submarines were 60 yards [180 feet] apart on course 90 degrees [east]. This position is about 15 miles due south of Martha's Vineyard. A bomber plane and a Navy patrol plane were sent out to investigate the area.[41]

Only *U-404* was in the area at that time, yet it was 75 miles to the southeast, and *U-588* under Vogel was sinking the U.S. tanker *Gulftrade* 150 miles away off New Jersey at the same time. On that basis, the sightings must be written off as erroneous; in any event, U-boats generally had either just a periscope or the full deck awash, rarely just "conning towers awash."

U-404's patrol began in Lorient on February 14 and ended in Brest on April 4. While off Halifax, von Bülow managed to sink the American freighter *Collamer* of Convoy HX 178 on March 5, and after leaving New England they sank the *Tolten* on the 13th, the *Lemuel Burrows* a day later, and on the 17th the *San Demetrio*, for a total of 22,653 tons. Otto von Bülow was born in Wilhelmshaven in 1911 and lived until 2006 at the age of ninety-four. In April 1943, he was awarded the Knights Cross with Oak Leaves and a year later the War Merit Cross 2nd Class with Swords. A member of the Crew of 1930, he served aboard the cruiser *Deutschland* and battleship SMS *Schleswig-Holstein* as well as in naval anti-aircraft detachments. He joined U-boats in 1940, commanding the training boat *U-3*.

In August 1941, von Bülow commissioned *U-404*, on which he was to stake his reputation until he handed over command to his erstwhile 1st Watch Officer *Oberleutnant zur See* Adolf Schönberg, who was born in Babylon, New York in 1918. The boat was lost on July 28, 1943, during its first patrol under the new commander. Overall, von Bülow sank or damaged seventeen Allied merchant and naval ships of roughly 89,000 tons. After some months in British captivity following command of the *Elektro* boat *U-2545*, von Bülow joined the new German Navy in 1956, and retired from it in 1970. Since it ties in with New England history, while Otto von Bülow is related to fighter aces Harry and Walter von Bülow, another person by that name, socialite Claus von Bülow (born Borberg), was in 1982 accused of poisoning his wife Sunny in Newport, with the trial forming the basis of the 1990 film *Reversal of Fortune*.[42]

5

A Dozen U-boats Attack the *Ranja*, the *Thursobank*, the *Hertford*, and the *Nemanja*

Kapitänleutnant Victor Vogel brought *U-588* eastward from sinking the *Gulftrade* off New Jersey to a point south of Montauk starting on March 10, 1942. On the 7th, Vogel attacked a large passenger steamer named *Cordania* but could not force it to stop. At dawn, a motor-sailing boat appeared, which turned out to be a patrol vessel, so the submarine submerged to the bottom. On the surface, a sound-based, or sonar pursuit of the sub continued for twenty-four hours in north-south then east-west directions.[1] The patrol along the continental shelf lasted four days, until *U-588* exited the area south of Cape Sable on March 13. No ships were sunk, though before entering New England, he sank the *Caperby* of Convoy ON 66 in the North Atlantic on March 1. The following day, Vogel claimed to have damaged then sunk a large tanker, likely the *Consuelo*, of 4,847 tons, which sent out an SOS on the 1st, and reached New York on the 3rd.[2] At 10.06 a.m. on March 1, U.S. forces logged: "SSS from S.S. *Consuelo*, 4,700-ton British tanker, sub sighted on surface." The position was 35 miles southeast of Halifax.[3]

On March 10, Vogel attacked a large tanker of the *Canadolite* type, using a fan shot from both Tube II and Tube III. As he under-estimated the speed, both missed, and while setting up another shot, the attack was interrupted by a second steamer from the opposite direction, plus a patrol vessel. Low on fuel, a frustrated Vogel broke off further attacks and headed for home. The next day, he had to pass on the Swiss ship *Helene Kulukundis* after initiating the attack, then a tanker with two destroyers escorting it. The patrol began in Lorient on February 12 and ended in St. Nazaire on March 27. Vogel, twenty-nine, was born in Tübingen in 1912. He was in the Crew of 1932 and served in minesweeping and anti-submarine fleets before joining U-boats in March 1941. In Hamburg that September, he assumed command of *U-588*. Vogel sank seven ships and damaged two of roughly 34,500 tons. He received no decorations. He returned to the region in May 1942 to remedy the lack of targets on his first patrol there.

Kapitänleutnant Walter Flachsenberg, aged thirty-three, brought *U-71* into New England for two transits, inbound and outbound, between March 16 and April 2, 1942. The inbound leg headed southwest out of the region on March 21. The patrol began in St. Nazaire on February 23 and ended in La Pallice on April 20. On March 17, Flachsenberg found and destroyed the Norwegian motor tanker *Ranja*, which he hit with a pair of torpedoes near the bridge. A *coup de grâce* started a fire the length of the vessel. Captain Andreas Mossin and all thirty-four officers, men, and gunners of the *Ranja* were killed. Mistaking the name for *British Fidelity*, the German commander noted that the tanker was armed and that as it burned it turned slowly and settled deeper. A final torpedo created a 700-foot-high explosive column, which was unsurvivable.[4]

On March 20, *U-71* encountered and sank the U.S.-flagged steamer *Oakmar* south of Nantucket. The Germans continued to have trouble with their hydroplanes, making attacks more challenging, particularly in heavy seas. When the *Oakmar* overtook *U-71*, the Germans could see an ensign at her stern, and when spotted, the ship tried aggressive maneuvers to escape. Out of thirty-six men, two were drowned, four from the port lifeboat were never found, and thirty survivors were rescued by the *Stavros* and landed in Bermuda.[5] Captain Nolan Eugene Fleming was one of those lost.

On the 21st, an airplane forced *U-71* to crash-dive, and the following day it was too rough to surface. On March 26, while off Hatteras Flachsenberg found and sank the U.S. ship *Dixie Arrow*, but was fought off by the destroyer U.S.S. *Tarbell*, which attacked with depth charges, then broke off the attack to rescue survivors of the *Dixie Arrow*.[6] On March 30, *U-71* avoided aircraft and the skipper decided to hunt "independent traffic to and from New York." The next day, they sank the 12,915-ton British ship *San Gerardo* between Nantucket and Bermuda, coldly observing that "a part of the crew still swims in the oil slick. I attempt to ask the name of the tanker, however, was not understood. Cargo was heavy oil."[7]

The second leg to New England began south of Montauk on March 30 and ended on April 2 when the boat headed south toward Bermuda. Flachsenberg sank the British steamer *Eastmoor* of 5,812 tons north of Bermuda on April 1. The first two torpedoes missed, then, at 4.03 a.m., a third torpedo sank the ship in twelve minutes. Captain James Basil Rodgers and fifteen officers and crew were killed; however, thirty-six men were picked up by another British steamer, the *Calgary*, and they were landed in Cape Town. The ship was bound from Savannah to Halifax, then the U.K. with 7,500 tons of general cargo. On April 3, *U-71*'s men saw a fast-moving passenger ship but could not attack as poor weather prevented them reloading the torpedo tubes quickly enough. The following day, they attacked another ship with a partially loaded torpedo and it, predictably, failed.

Walter Flachsenberg was born in Mönchengladbach. He was in the Crew of 1929 and served in naval flak, or artillery, before joining U-boats in April 1940. He served under Schepke in *U-100*, doing very well, until gaining command of *U-71* in December 1940. All of the five ships of 39,000 tons that he sank were on this patrol. Then Flachsenberg moved ashore to administrative roles, emphasizing torpedo testing. He joined the new German Navy following the war and retired from it as rear admiral. He received no decorations but lived until 1994 and the age eighty-six.

The Norwegian motor tanker *Ranja* had a colorful history and a sudden tragic end. As all thirty-four men on board her perished when she was sunk off New England, we rely entirely on the perspective of her German attackers in detailing her demise. The ship was built by Götaverken in Gothenburg, Sweden, in April 1928. She was 6,355 tons and owned by the Norwegian firm Rederi Ruth, which in turn entrusted management of the tanker to Hagb. Waage of Oslo. At the end of January 1941, the ship, under a British commander and with some 150 British, Swedish and Norwegian passengers (one of them female) escaped the earlier Nazi occupation of Norway. Managing to survive aerial bombardment, they made it to Kirkwall, Scotland, intact. The *Ranja* then participated in numerous voyages and convoys, including to Curaçao, Bermuda, New York, Providence, and Halifax, mostly bringing petroleum cargos to the U.K. via Canada.[8]

On its last voyage, the *Ranja* was under the command of Norwegian Captain Andreas Catrinus Backer Mossin, aged forty-eight, directed by Nortraships. There were thirty-four souls on board, all Norwegian, except for Jens Kristensen (a Danish able seaman), Karl Erikson (a Swedish cook), and Robert Halliday Cairns (age twenty-one) and George Arthur Craske (age twenty) (both British gunners), as well as a Royal Army gunner. The ship arrived from Loch Ewe to begin loading petroleum in Galveston on March 7, 1942, and sailed for Houston later the same day. After completing loading, she left Houston two days later bound for Halifax, where she was to join Convoy HX 181 leaving Halifax on March 21 for Liverpool.

Just over a week later, on the afternoon of March 17, the *Ranja* and her men were 290 miles southeast of Nantucket. At 5.40 p.m., *U-71* began stalking the ship, which was armed but unescorted and far from land or aerial protection. *U-71* spent nearly ninety minutes setting up its torpedo shots. At 6.58 p.m., her commander, Flachsenberg, fired a pair of projectiles set at a depth of 8 feet, from a distance of 4,620 feet. They found their mark; one striking the bridge, and the other ahead of the *Ranja*'s only funnel, which was located aft, the bridge being situated on a so-called island amidships. There was a large explosion and a column of flame, followed by smoke, shot 1,300-feet high. Nine minutes later, Flachsenberg and his men identified her as an armed tanker. By then, the fire had spread to the forward parts of the ship.[9]

Under reduced speed, the mortally stricken *Ranja* veered to port, sinking by the bow and listing to port ever more dangerously. At 7.54 p.m., a third and final

A good commander always made room for the crew's entertainment and diversion. This scene is aboard *U-108* as she returns from patrol, judging from relaxed poses and facial hair. (*Willy Wilke, U-108*)

torpedo was fired, which skipped over the surface, porpoising, from about 2,500 feet. This *coup de grâce* struck between the bridge and the bow, at the forward mast, and caused another explosion. Shortly thereafter, the foredeck appeared to break off as it submerged, the forward mast and bridge collapsed, and what remained of the *Ranja* above water was burning from head to stern. The ship was stationary. Concluding that the vessel was doomed, and not having observed any survivors, Flachsenberg and his men pointed *U-71* toward Cape Hatteras at 8.06 p.m. and motored away. No one survived the attack on *Ranja*. Her merchant seamen are commemorated at the Stavern Memorial in the U.K., and the two British naval gunners at the Chatham Naval Memorial.

Oberleutnant zur See Paul-Karl Loeser brought *U-373* on a two-way incursion into New England between March 19 and 30, 1942, during which he sank the *Thursobank* on the 22nd, southeast of Nantucket. *U-373* was one of eleven boats on the fourth wave of Operation Drumbeat and sank the *Mount Lycabettus* on March 17 south of Nova Scotia. She left Lorient on March 1 and returned to La Pallice on April 17. *U-373* initially headed from Cape Sable to a point south of Nantucket. On March 19, Loeser fired a torpedo at a 9,600-ton Norwegian tanker of the *Basilea* type, however, it remained in the submarine's Tube V for sixteen seconds: an anomaly called "tube runner." Not being able to know if the tube (like a gun barrel) was empty or full left Loeser confused, and took up time, during which the boat sank over 75 feet from the ocean surface. Although they chased the valuable target into the night, it escaped. On the 21st, *U-71* tracked another ship, then, on realizing that it was neutral, the Germans broke off the attack.[10]

The *Thursobank* was a British motor ship of 5,575 tons heading from New York to Cape Town and Alexandria when at 5.09 a.m. it was caught by *U-373* southeast of Nantucket. The attack killed thirty men; however, twenty-six were rescued after a tumultuous lifeboat voyage during which Chinese crew stripped the British officers of equipment and authority. They were rescued by the *Havsten* and arrived Halifax on March 28. *U-373* then submerged to reload and service the diesels, headed northwest off Buzzards Bay, which guards the Cape Cod Canal, and finally west of Montauk on March 24. Coming back eastward on March 27, *U-373* headed along the continental shelf and exited south of Cape Sable on the 30th after a ten-day incursion.

On the 27th, Loeser observed a vessel emitting a lot of smoke and moving erratically. Originally, he considered attacking, but then believed it was a trap by a patrol boat or Q-ship decoy, and in light of his low fuel, he let the opportunity pass. For the next few days, the only observations were of patrol boats, Allied aircraft, and sub-sea detonations. Loeser sank most of his three ships of 10,263 tons on this patrol. A member of the Crew of 1935, he was born in 1915 in Berlin and lived until 1987 and age seventy-one. His first U-boat was *U-30*. He received no decorations during his career.

The British motor vessel *Thursobank* was built by J. Readhead and Sons in South Shields in 1940. The ship's owners were Andrew Weir and Company of London (other iterations included Inver Tankers, which lost all seven of its ships in World War II, British-Mexican Petroleum, Lago Shipping, and Compagnie Venture). The *Thursobank* was 452 feet long, 57 feet wide, and 26 feet deep. Her single screw was turned by a 542-hp diesel engine that pushed the ship at 12 knots.[11]

On her final voyage, the *Thursobank* was under the command of Captain Ralph Bryan Ellis, age forty-one, whose father Edwin was also a master mariner. She was bound from New York to Alexandria via Cape Town and the Red Sea carrying 11,839 tons of general cargo in support of Allied armies in North Africa. The ship's armament included a 4-inch gun, a 12-pound gun, and several machine guns, namely two Marlins and two Hotchkiss, as well as four rocket flares on kites. The total complement of sixty-four men included a dozen gunners (five Royal Navy, seven Royal Army). The balance of fifty-two men were merchant mariners, including fourteen British, or European officers and men, and the majority (thirty-eight) ratings, or junior engine room and deck crew, from China.

The *Thursobank* departed New York on Friday, March 20 independently, with no warnings about submarines from official channels, though Captain Ellis heard that two ships had been sunk in the area recently. Two days later, the sky was cloudy and overcast, though visibility was good. There was a very boisterous sea, with a strong southwesterly wind. *Thursobank* completed its zigzag routine and was plodding at 10 knots on a course of 141 degrees. Third Mate Reginald Johnson ascended to the bridge at 10 p.m., and forty minutes later he saw the wake of a torpedo pass in front of the bow, from right to left, about 50 feet from the ship.[12]

Johnson immediately called Captain Ellis, who had the course changed thirty-nine degrees to 102 degrees. At 11.30 p.m., with nothing more observed, Ellis changed the course back to 141 degrees, then went below half an hour later. Ten minutes later, one of the gunners serving as a lookout observed a torpedo zeroing in on the port beam. Just at that time, a grating explosion erupted against the side of the engine room. This caused the ship to tremble and take a small list to port. It was very dark, leaving Johnson unable to ascertain the extent of the damage from the bridge. He did confirm that the after-rigged port lifeboat was shattered. Captain Ellis ordered all men to assemble on the boat deck, and that the remaining boats be lowered. Engines were stopped by a valve located on the deck just for that purpose.

Both the starboard and port (forward) boats were put into the water, and the men quickly filled them and got clear of the stricken *Thursobank*. Second Officer Douglas Masson Davidson, age twenty-three, was in charge of a starboard boat, but was not seen again; presumably, he managed to launch a raft and got clear in that. Johnson was in command of Captain Ellis's starboard boat, but the skipper refused to leave this ship before all the crew were safely off. Ellis was last observed shining a flashlight onto his boat.

Twenty minutes after the first torpedo was fired by Loeser in *U-373*, he sent a second projectile into the *Thursobank*, dooming it and those on board. Johnson described the impact as a "much more violent explosion." It was the last anyone saw of the ship, which was struck near the engine room a second time. Johnson threw off a sea anchor, or drogue (a way to slow or stall a small vessel in heavy seas by launching a water-parachute attached to a line from the bow), to ride out a storm. He also had the men hold up red flares, in the hopes that other survivors would swim or row to them. None did. Survivors saw much wreckage and debris drift by.

The men were 200 miles southeast of Nantucket, even further east of the Chesapeake, and well northwest of Bermuda. The lifeboat was well equipped and supplied with water, enabling the senior officer on board to dispense a dipper for each man daily. His boat was occupied by most of the ship's complement, namely thirty-three persons, with the third engineer, one apprentice, five gunners (two Navy, two army), as well as twenty-six Chinese ratings. The engineer complained that the water-sensitive magnetos enabling the Morris motor to be started were situated near the bottom of the boat, where they became wet in over a foot of water and were thus made useless until and unless dried out.

The men pumped out water with a semi-rotary pump, but the constant cold water and exposure limited their effectiveness and affected their morale. Since all the men lacked dry or warm boots they were disabled, to the extent that one of the Chinese ratings later had both feet amputated (it was March in the North Atlantic). Many men also suffered from sea-sickness in varying degrees, not being used to the sudden movements of a small boat. On top of all these concerns, the Chinese crew, by far the majority, were convinced that the Anglo-Saxon men would horde all the food, and thus they threatened to eject the white men into the water. Fortunately, there were no weapons handy, and the situation was tamped down with diplomacy rather than blows. The distrust, however, lingered for the duration of their open boat voyage. Johnson reported their mutinous behavior naval officials in Halifax but believes no action was taken. According to another account, the Chinese ratings were all arrested on arrival in Halifax. They were accused of having placed British officers "in the front of the lifeboat, throwing the oars away and refusing to share the food and warm clothing in the boat with them."

On Tuesday, March 24, having drifted on the sea anchor, the storm abated to the point that Johnson could hoist sail and make progress westward, toward North America. The Gulf Stream, however, was setting them to the northward. He commended the sailing capabilities of the boat's rig. Then at 11 p.m. on 25th, after almost five days adrift in cold seas, Johnson espied a ship off the boat's port bow, roughly half a mile ahead. The men anxiously burned what was left of the flares and flashed a torch. Every crewman was ordered to turn on the lights on their life jackets. Gratifyingly, the ship, a Norwegian motor ship named *Havsten*, altered course to them. At the time of rescue, the lifeboat was 165 miles due west of where the *Thursobank* was sunk.

The *Havsten* was a 10,040-ton tanker under the command of Captain Gjert Sofus Olsen. In the service of the British Admiralty, she had loaded a cargo of diesel in Curaçao and left on March 15 bound for Halifax, thence bound to fill the fuel tanks of convoy-escort ships based in Iceland. Johnson was effusive in his gratitude for his Norwegian rescuers, whom he said, "treated us with every consideration." They were 430 miles south of Halifax when retrieved.

They arrived in Halifax on Saturday, March 28. Sixteen of the twenty-six Chinese ratings suffered from exposure. Johnson regretted that due to the fierce weather, he did not distribute massage oil until the third or fourth day. He, too, was hospitalized for exposure. Everyone but Johnson and the third engineer wore insulated suits; however, Johnson's suit was stolen from him right after he entered the boat. He felt that the other boat and raft "must have capsized during the gale." He did protest that, although they were never able to start the motor to turn the propeller, still the screw was only a fraction of an inch from the stern-post, and the metal and wooden components often jammed against each other.

Those missing and presumed lost included three Navy and four Army gunners. Captain Ellis, twenty-two crew members, and seven gunners were lost (possibly three more, as thirty are commemorated on various memorials). One of the Royal Navy gunners, Walter Davison Wallace, was thirty-one at the time and married to Elsie. Their little son George was two years old when his father drowned. The *Havsten* was attacked by torpedoes and gunfire from *U-160* under Lassen on August 4, 1942. Two were killed, with Captain Olsen and the radio operator taken prisoner on the sub. The other men managed to make it to shore twelve days later. The burning hulk of their ship was sunk by the Italian submarine *Enrico Tazzoli* on the 6th, after the Italians rescued the ship's cat, which had been abandoned.[13, 14]

At 2.32 p.m. on April 27—some five weeks after the sinking—the destroyer U.S.S. *Greer*, DD 145, found an empty lifeboat "bearing name of S.S. *Thursobank*, painted on its bow." Whether the boat was upright or overturned is not stated, but the name could only have been easily read if it was floating. This can be taken as definitive proof that the thirty men who failed to escape in Johnson's lifeboat perished at sea in the storm which enveloped the area of the attack for days afterward.

Kapitänleutnant Erich Topp brought *U-552* into New England on a six-day incursion between March 25 and 30, 1942. On the 24th, Topp found a convoy of five or six steamers, protected by a large Allied naval ship and several destroyers. He believed it was the same convoy that *U-404* was chasing, but because of head seas could not keep up and broke off. He spent the rest of the day tracking a tanker, but it zigzagged too much during daylight. At night in moonlight, the ship seemed to mimic the U-boat, making Topp more cautious, and indeed the submarine only avoided being run over by the ship by the emergency reverse of both engines and was missed by a mere 20 feet. On the 25th, *U-552* counterattacked and set the tanker *Ocana* on fire. The hulk drifted until April 15 when the H.M.C.S. *Burlington* sank it. On March 25, *U-552* crossed the Gulf of Maine from Cape Sable toward Provincetown.

U-552 then headed for Nantucket, encountering motor sailors and fishing vessels along the way. On the 26th, they crash-dived from an airplane, and the next day passed the lightship *Pollock*, then "closed [hugged], and drove parallel to the coast from buoy to buoy … all lighthouses are lit." They rested on the bottom at Nauset Light. For the next few days, to the 29th, they would surface to periscope depth to track propeller noises then be forced under by aircraft or vessels until well outside New England.[15] After leaving Cape Cod, *U-552* also left the area south of Montauk on the 30th. The patrol began in St. Nazaire on March 7 and ended there on April 27. Topp sank seven ships of 45,731 tons between April 3 and 10 off Hatteras: the *David H. Atwater*, the *Byron D. Benson*, the *British Splendour*, the whale factory ship *Lancing*, the *Atlas*, and the *Tamaulipas*.[16]

Topp was born in Hannover in 1914 and lived until 2005 and the age of ninety-one. A member of the Crew of 1934, he served on the *Karlsruhe* then joined

U-boats in October 1937. After serving as watch officer on *U-46*, he assumed command of *U-57* from Korth. He accomplished most of his total of forty ships sunk or damaged, totaling over 230,000 tons, while aboard *U-552*, and was highly decorated, ultimately with the Knights Cross with Oak Leaves and Crossed Swords in August 1942. He wrote the manual on operating the new Type XXI *Elektro* U-boats and commanded *U-2513* up until its surrender in Norway in May 1945. After a stint as a fisherman, Topp became an architect before rejoining the new German Navy, spending time in the U.S. with NATO. He retired in 1969 and until the mid-1980s was a shipyard consultant.

Kapitänleutnant Johannes (Hans) Oestermann brought *U-754* across the waters south of New England from east to west between March 27 and 30, 1942. He sank the *British Prudence* off Newfoundland from convoy HX 181 on the 23rd and entered New England in heavy rain on the 27th. The next day the Germans avoided a destroyer sweep in the Gulf of Maine. On the 30th, sailing craft and airplanes were seen, making Oestermann believe there were patrols on the 700-foot-depth mark. *U-754* damaged the *Ontario* off Maryland on the 31st and sank the tug and its barges the *Barnegat* and the *Alleghany* on the same day. Then he sank the ship *Tiger* on 1 April, the *Otho* two days later, and the Norwegian tanker *Kollskegg* on the 6th. The patrol began in Brest on March 7 and ended there on April 25.[17]

Born in 1913, Oestermann was a member of the Crew of 1933. He lived until July 31, 1942, when *U-754* was sunk east of Boston—he was twenty-nine years of age. The boat was sunk by a Canadian Hudson airplane with the loss of all forty-three officers and men. Over three patrols of 135 days, Oestermann sank thirteen ships and damaged another for over 56,000 tons. Early in his naval career, he served aboard the destroyer *Z7 Hermann Schoemann*. He joined U-boats in July 1940. His first U-boat command was *U-151* before he commissioned *U-754* at Wilhelmshaven.

Kapitänleutnant Helmut Möhlmann took *U-571* on a five-day incursion of New England, beginning on March 29 and ending on April 2, 1942. On the 27th, Möhlmann ducked a Bermuda-based aircraft. On the day that *U-571* entered the area, it sank the British ship *Hertford*, a large, 10,923-ton freighter steaming for FedNav of Montreal between Sydney, Australia, and Halifax. As the sub was racing for the cover of a cloud-bank, its port diesel engine failed, so they proceeded with one diesel and one electric motor. Möhlmann was stubborn after missing with one torpedo, musing "who knows if we will meet as valuable a target again? ... a hard nut against wind and sea." Then the attack periscope fogged up, so 1st Watch Officer Gerhard Linder took it over while Möhlmann moved to the one in the control room.[18]

The Germans sent torpedoes into the ship and noticed a large gun and machine guns on the bridge, so they dove. On approaching the lifeboats, he noted: "they reject my offer of rum and hard bread. They make a pretty disciplined and calm impression for those that had just fallen into the water." The Germans motored "through a vast field of butter cases, half pigs, calves, cattle, and sheep. The fourteen hours hunting down this fat roast was worth it and was not too expensive at just under six cubic meters of fuel." Four men out of sixty-two were killed, with fifty-eight making it ashore in Nova Scotia.[19]

Following the *Hertford* attack, *U-571* ducked away from a large flying boat which circled around at the direction of the *Hertford*'s lifeboats. Möhlmann wrote: "I blame myself that I remained on the surface so long at the sinking point," provoking the plane. On April 1, his colleague *Kapitänleutnant* Linder in *U-202* called attention to a warship, thought to be as large as a cruiser. Möhlmann thought it was a U.S. Coast Guard cutter of the *G. W. Campbell* class. The vessel dropped charges and was supported by aircraft, but some of *U-571*'s detection equipment was out of service, so they moved off. In the ensuing days, several fishing vessels were sighted, and on April 5, *U-571* signaled Hans-Heinz Linder, whose younger brother Gerhard was the 1st Watch Officer aboard *U-571*, so they could all wish each other happy Easter, "unfortunately without the Easter eggs" (Gerhard survived the war, his older brother did not). *U-571* passed south of Nantucket on April 1 and west of Montauk the following day.

U-571 sank the Norwegian tanker *Koll* off Bermuda on April 6, with Möhlmann observing that after the oil tanker spewed "a thick stream of oil," which burned inside the ship, "the men lift up their hands anxiously" as they U-boat approached. The Germans gave the thirty-three survivors bread; three perished. After the surface oil caught fire, sending smoke over 1,500 feet into the sky, he remarked, "that was something for our P.R. [public relations] man." On the 14th, they sank the steamer *Margaret* off Hatteras. In order to return to La Pallice, which it left on March 10, *U-571* took fuel from the U-tanker *U-459* roughly 500 miles northeast of Bermuda. She returned to La Pallice on May 7, 1942.

Möhlmann was born in 1913 in Kiel and lived until 1977 and age sixty-three. A member of the Crew of 1933, he started out on the torpedo boat *Luchs* then the light cruiser *Nürnberg*, before joining U-boats in April 1940. He served aboard *U-52* and commanded the training boat *U-143*, then assumed command of *U-571* from May 1941 until May 1943, patrolling eight times. After that, he moved to U-boat staff headquarters (*BdU*) and then the 14th U-Boat Flotilla in Narvik. He was a PoW for four months following the war, after which he joined the modern *Bundesmarine*.

The steamship *Hertford* was launched in 1917 in Germany as a general cargo ship of 10,923 tons. Her builder was Bremer Vulkan of Vegesack, and her original name was *Rheinland*; however, due to the exigencies of World War I, she was not completed for the Hamburg-Amerika Linie (Hapag) until 1920, when she was renamed *Friesland*. Two years later, the British claimed her as a war reparation and renamed the ship *Hertford*, putting it into the New Zealand and Australian trades carrying frozen carcasses of meat. It was in those trades, on December 7, 1940, that *Hertford* ran into a mine laid by a German deep-sea raider named *Pinguin* in Australia's Spencer Gulf, off Melbourne. The ship was laid up and in repair until January 20, 1942. Weeks later she loaded a full cargo of 11,000 tons of Australian and New Zealand produce—including sides of lamb and mutton.

The *Hertford* sailed from Sydney in late February. Her master, Captain John Tuckett Collier, complained that the authorities seemed unaware or new regulations for safety and provisioning of lifeboats. He therefore took the initiative to have a number of water tanks welded into the bottoms of his ship's four lifeboats. After Sydney, the *Hertford* topped up cargo in Wellington New Zealand and sailed across the Pacific for the entrance of the Panama Canal in Balboa. They left the Caribbean, or western side of the canal from Colon on March 21, 1942. At first, the voyage proceeded uneventfully, in part via the Straits of Florida and then, further north, on March 27, the ship was routed to seaward on instructions from Bermuda. Her final destination was the U.K., via convoy from Halifax.[20]

On March 29, 1942, the *Hertford* was approximately 240 miles from Halifax and 190 miles from Cape Sable. They were heading northeast at 11.5 knots. The winds were roughly 18 knots from the southeast at the time, only a slight swell prevailed, and visibility was "very good." The ship was armed with a 4-inch gun and a pair of Vickers machine guns, which were manned by a British and an Australian gunner. In total there were sixty-one persons on board. Degaussing (a system of booms and electrically charged cables which never prevented a torpedo attack in the waters from Cuba to Canada) was turned off at the time.

Captain Collier was in the bridge at 2.40 p.m. with three lookouts and the second officer when there was an explosion behind them, on the starboard side of the number four hatch. Although no water-column was seen, there was a strong smell of cordite burning. The *Hertford* stopped moving immediately and began to sink on an even keel. The number four hold filled with seawater, and the engine room became inundated. Soon, the entire aft deck was awash. The ship was doomed. The radio officer transmitted that the ship had been attacked and they were abandoning ship.[21]

Captain Collier anticipated just this set of circumstances. He threw the codes in the ocean and ordered all lifeboats readied for lowering. As the number three boat was destroyed by the torpedo, lifeboats number one, number two, and number four were launched by 2.50 p.m., ten minutes after the attack began. Ten minutes later, a second torpedo slammed into the middle of *Hertford* on the starboard side, blowing the hatches off number three hold and badly damaging the bridge wings. Had Captain Collier and others still been on the bridge, they most likely would have been killed. The *Hertford* quickly sank by 3.10 p.m., disgorging her cargo into the cold water.

In a dramatic twist, an enemy submarine was seen by the mostly British crew to round the bow of the sinking ship. It was heading to the northward when, roughly half a mile from them, it emerged to the surface. When the U-boat approached the boats, Captain Collier went alongside the sub in his boat. A German officer asked the ship's name and whether the Allied sailors required water, food, medicine, medical treatment, or a course to land. Then the sub broke away to cruise among the debris for fifteen or twenty minutes, trophy-hunting. Collier watched as Germans pulled mutton carcasses from the water. Then the U-boat motored off, still on the surface, as though unafraid of reprisal, in a southwesterly direction.

While alongside *U-571*, Captain Collier noticed a net-cutter as well as an emblem of a white shield and red cross on the side of the conning tower. This is similar to the symbol of a red cross on a white background with a blue rectangle that the *Hertford* had on its funnel for FedNav, or the Federal Navigation Company of Montreal. Apparently, on the German cross, a dagger, protruded into the right side of the shield. To Collier, the submarine looked freshly painted. He was very specific in describing the German officer who interacted with him as a "short, stocky man aged about 36-to-38. He was clean shaven and was not wearing a hat and walked with a jerky step." Probably, if this was Möhlmann (then aged thirty-nine), his legs stiff from the cramped conditions of the U-boat.

At 4.45 p.m., roughly two hours following the initial torpedo, the occupants of the three lifeboats agreed to head north together. Just an hour later an Allied flying boat circled them, indicating that they had been seen. Then two more amphibious planes appeared, one of them communicating that a ship was being vectored to the boats. The planes continued to circle them until about dusk, when they flew off, after advising the boats to stick together. At 10 p.m. that night, they burned red flares repeatedly until dawn and continued northward.[22]

The next day (March 30), the boats continued together; however, that night foul weather sprung up, visibility plummeted, and all three of them were separated. Captain Collier sailed onward and in a remarkable feat of seamanship, arrived at the sea buoy off Liverpool, Nova Scotia, on April 3. A local tug guided them into the harbor, and the men in the boat tied up at 10.30 a.m., after six cold days and nights. Only Captain Collier was able to walk out of the lifeboat; all the eighteen others had such swollen feet from the cold and immersion that they had to be carried or at least assisted. The chief steward, thirty-two-year-old Benjamin McMahon, was in such a bad way that he contracted pneumonia in hospital and perished. All the men suffered from exposure and the effects of swelling of the feet. The same day that Collier's boat made it ashore, the third officer's lifeboat with eighteen men was rescued by a ship named *Fort Townsend* and taken to Halifax. Meanwhile, the chief officer's boat (with a total of twenty-one men) was rescued by the British steamer *Glen Strae* on the 31st, after nearly three days. No explanation was proffered for the false hope and failure to land on the sea surface that the three flying boats represented to the dispirited survivors.

Captain Collier spoke of manufacturing extra water tanks in his lifeboats during long months of repairs in Sydney, and how he laid on extra portions of pemmican paste as well as Horlicks. He did not give the men their first ration of water until the day following the attack. He complained that though the boats were said to accommodate over forty men, his was crowded with more than twenty. When men huddled under the cover in the bow to escape the cold, and the rudder lifted out of the sea and it became difficult to steer. Collier also felt that the boats should have had a small heating stove with which to cook a morale and health-boosting hot drink daily. Overall, while fifty-seven men survived the sinking of the *Hertford*, four men, including the chief steward, were killed. The other three were forty-year-old C. Bick, fireman; Hugh McGinnity, sixty-three-year-old greaser; and twenty-two-year-old Seventh Engineer Timothy Gunn Stratton.[23]

Kapitänleutnant Rolf Mützelburg took *U-203* on a four-day patrol of New England from east to west between April 3 and 6, 1942. On the 1st, the crew missed a Dutch tanker of some 7,000 tons due to weather, thunderstorms, and squalls, after fourteen hours of observing it. In the same vicinity on the 2nd, the U.S. Navy tug *Y 17* rescued a seaplane 35 miles east of Portland, and towed it to that port, arriving at 7.30 p.m., with the North-Carolina-based pilot safe.[24] Nothing of note took place till the 5th, when a plane forced *U-203* to crash dive. The next day, they heard a faint sound but could not find it afterward, despite rising and sinking to track it. On the 7th, they saw a tanker burning off the shore. A plane swooped overhead just 175 feet above sea level. Then several aircraft, including one which dropped a bomb, and destroyers forced the sub to lay on the seafloor about 100 feet deep. They went to Cape Hatteras, where on the 10th, Mützelburg sank the *San Delfino*. In the next four days, the Germans also damaged the *Harry F. Sinclair Jr.* and the *Stanvac Melbourne* and sank the *Empire Thrush* off Cape Hatteras.

U-203 left Brest on March 12 as part of the fourth wave of Operation Drumbeat boats. About two weeks into the patrol, she was refueled by the tanker submarine U-A, west of the Azores and returned to Brest on April 30. Mützelburg was born in 1913 and died while diving from the conning tower near the Azores on September 11, 1942. When the submarine lurched, he struck the saddle tank, killing him and forcing *Oberleutnant zur See* Hans Seidel to take over. Earlier that year, Mützelburg was awarded the Knights Cross with Oak Leaves for the twenty-two ships he sank or damaged for nearly 100,000 tons.

Oberleutnant zur See Eberhard Greger brought *U-85* on a short patrol through New England between April 8 and 10, 1942. He sank the Norwegian tanker *Chr. Knudsen* off New Jersey on the 10th. As nothing was heard from either the U-boat or the ship after the 9th, it is possible that the *Chr. Knudsen* was sunk inside New England waters; however, the ship was on its way to Cape Town, requiring a more southerly rather than easterly course, and all thirty-three men perished. Until the wreck is found, it will remain a mystery.[25]

Three days later, *U-85* was caught on the surface by the U.S. Navy destroyer U.S.S. *Roper* whose crew, having witnessed tens of thousands of tons of Allied shipping and hundreds of Allied sailors being killed off Cape Hatteras, were keen to exact revenge. *U-85* fought it out on the surface until it was a lost cause, then roughly half of the forty-six men aboard abandoned the submarine. Desperate to confirm sinking the U-boat, the officers and men of the *Roper* pressed on the attack without pause, while the Germans in the water could be heard calling out "comrade." Eleven depth charges were dropped on the site, killing all of the sailors in the water.[26] This was the first German submarine from Operation Drumbeat sunk off the U.S. East coast. The propeller of the U.S.S. *Roper* is on display at the entrance of the Naval Construction and Engineering Museum on Massachusetts Avenue at MIT in Cambridge.

Twenty-nine German sailors' bodies were retrieved; two others were too badly mangled. Those retrieved were buried in the National Cemetery at Hampton Roads.[27] Eberhard Greger was not one of those whose bodies were identified. He went down with the sub, which is now an accessible diving site. He was born in 1915 in the Netherlands and was twenty-six when lost. He sank three ships for 15,060 tons, and he was not decorated. Greger was a member of the Crew of 1935. He obtained early experience aboard the destroyer *Z9 Wolfgang Zenker* up to October 1939, when he joined U-boats, serving as 1st Watch Officer of *U-110* up to April 1941. He commanded *U-85* from June 1941.

Oberleutnant zur See Horst Uphoff brought *U-84* on a six-day incursion into New England, beginning April 8, 1942. After nearly a week of zigzagging north and south while motoring west, the submarine exited south of Montauk on April 13. On the 7th, Uphoff gave up on a steamer due to fog. The day *U-84* entered the region it sank the Yugoslavian ship *Nemanja* of 5,226 tons 180 miles south of Cape Sable. It cost Uphoff ten hours to pursue the *Nemanja*, which was zigzagging, plus four torpedoes. The merchant captain was killed, along with a dozen others. Thirty-four men were rescued by a ship named the *Franche Comte* the following day and landed in Halifax. That night another ship, indistinct and out of sight, escaped the Germans' grasp.[28]

On the 9th, a destroyer sped toward them, so *U-84* submerged. As the boat headed out of New England *U-84* surfaced to ventilate and expel heavy air. The only other ship sunk by Uphoff on this patrol was the *Chenango*, Panamanian flagged, off Hatteras on April 21: thirty-seven sailors were killed, with only one survivor. The patrol began in Brest on March 16 and ended on May 16. On April 2, *U-84* was refueled off Newfoundland by the submarine tanker U-A. Perhaps one of the reasons that *U-84* did not sink more ships is that they moved about 350 miles east of Hatteras looking for ships to sink yet found none there.

Uphoff joined the *Kriegsmarine* as a member of the Crew of 1935. After experience aboard the U-boat supply ship *Donau*, he joined U-boats in October

1940. As 1st Watch Officer under Endrass in *U-46*, Uphoff helped to sink seventeen ships of nearly 100,000 tons. In April 1941, he commissioned *U-84* and began patrolling from Norway in August 1941. He performed eight patrols in her, sinking or damaging seven ships of over 37,000 tons. Uphoff was born in 1916 and was sunk, with all hands, off Bermuda by U.S. Navy aviators under Lieutenant Thomas Rudolph Evert on August 7, 1943. During his life, he was awarded the Iron Cross 1st Class, then posthumously granted the German Cross in Gold.[29]

The steamship *Nemanja* was built in 1918 as the *War Perch* by Bertram and Sons of Sunderland. Ordered by the U.K. Shipping Controller for World War I, she had a colorful twenty-four-year career with four names, including the *Trojan Prince* for the Prince Line (Furness Withy), between 1919 and 1924, then the *Hoosac* for the White Diamond (Warren) Line, of same parent firm, until 1926 when ship owners Atlanska Plovidba Ivo Racic firm of Dubrovnik purchased her. Her final owners were Jugoslavenski Lloyd Akcionarsko Drustvo of Zagreb. The ship was a B-class steam cargo vessel, 5,226 tons, 412 feet long, 52 feet wide, and 29 feet deep. Her 517-hp engine turned a single screw to provide 11 knots.

Between mid-1941 and 1942, the ship participated in a half a dozen convoys which took her from Liverpool to Halifax several times and to West Africa at others. On her final voyage, *Nemanja* was under the command of Captain Karlo Loser supported by Chief Officer Jacob Mardesic, both Yugoslavian. There were at least four British citizens on board; two Defensively Equipped Merchant Ship (DEMS) gunners named Benjamin Parry, age twenty-one, and twenty-four-year-old Sidney John Lawrence, both Royal Navy, to man the 3-inch gun aft, as well as Royal Army gunner Anthony Connor, age twenty-seven, and twenty-one-year-old Galley Boy Sidney Evans. There were forty-seven men aboard for the voyage from San Pedro de Macoris in the Dominican Republic to Halifax. The cargo was 7,207 tons of sugar in bulk. The *Nemanja* left on March 30, 1942, on charter for the British Ministry of War Transport (MoWT).[30]

Just over a week later, at 10.25 p.m. on April 7, *Nemanja* was 250 miles south of Halifax. She was only thirty hours from her destination and was zigzagging around a base course of 25 degrees north-northeast. No lights were showing, and though the wind was between 15 and 20 knots, there was a rough sea running and the night was very dark. Taking no chances, Captain Loser posted five lookouts: one aft by the gun platform, three in the bridge, and an extra lookout between the two beside the engine room.

Uphoff had been trailing *Nemanja* for roughly ten hours, and at 7.57 a.m. on April 8, he fired a pair of torpedoes from *U-84* at the ship. Both missed but were undetected by the lookouts. Uphoff then maneuvered ahead to take more shots. Two hours later, at 10.25 a.m., *U-84* fired another torpedo which caused a significant explosion on the *Nemanja*'s starboard side between number three cargo hold and another hold containing bunker coal. The impact caused the radio aerials to collapse along with one of the masts, meaning that distress signals could not be sent, though efforts were made to send them. Worse yet, the ship's steering was disabled. The gunners could not make a bead on the enemy, as *U-84* remained out of sight in the darkness.[31]

With the ship sinking, thirty-four of her complement launched and boarded a lifeboat which was damaged. Neither the captain nor the chief officer was able to board in time or to launch the other lifeboat or rafts. Thirteen out of forty-seven men were never seen again. *U-84* fired a shell at the doomed ship from a quarter of a mile away. Those men who were getting away in the lifeboat saw *U-84* in the distance. Uphoff fired a fourth torpedo, and the *coup de grâce* sent *Nemanja* to the bottom, 14,000 feet down. Though there was no radio message to tell him the ship name, and darkness prevented his learning it, Uphoff chose not to interact with the survivors, and *U-84* motored off into the choppy seas.

After roughly a day-and-a-half in the hostile cold waters off Canada, the thirty-four men in the crowded and damaged boat were discovered by the British tanker *Franche Comte*, which picked them up at 10 a.m. on April 9. The *Franche Comte* participated in over thirty convoys in World War II and was on its way to join Convoy HX 185 in Halifax, which was due to depart for Liverpool on April 14. She was a 9,314-ton tanker built in 1936. The men on the British ship took care of the thirty-four men for two days before disembarking them in Halifax, where they arrived on the morning of April 11. News of their arrival was transmitted to, and then by, the U.S. Navy at 12.55 p.m. that day.

Oberleutnant zur See Ludwig Forster took *U-654* both eastbound and westbound through New England between April 10 and May 2, 1942. They entered westbound south of Cape Sable and motored five days, exiting south of Montauk on April 14 in such foul weather that only one diesel was used, and no weapons could be brought to bear. Then Forster returned briefly from Bermuda northbound on May 1, going south of Cape Sable on the 2nd. Forster and his men sank the *Empire Prairie* off Canada on 10 April. The men tracked the freighter with three masts and a crane on the stern. She was a British ship of 7,010 tons under Captain Richard Townsend Payne. When struck after a six-hour pursuit, the ship immediately broke apart and sank, leaving only men floating in the water with debris. None of the forty-nine Allied sailors survived. *U-654* approached the lifeboats and relayed how "everywhere on the wreckage people sit and call for help. Asked for the name of the steamer. … Continued transit."[32]

The *Empire Prairie* attack came back to haunt the men when on 3 May they came upon the following:

> The location of a steamer (apparently sunk by me on 10 April). A case of soap and a bale of raw rubber were taken on board. Drove in a large circle at the sinking location, to search for items, [then a] submerged enemy U-boat, [whose]

> *Kommandant* seemed to work the periscope badly [as] occasionally the periscope is extended over one meter above the surface. Ran off at high speed.[33]

After leaving New England to patrol hundreds of miles east of Hatteras, *U-654* sank the *Steel Maker* and the *Agra*. Between April 13 and 14, the boat encountered a kind of U-boat trap made of barrels and cables off Hatteras and was snarled on the bottom desperately trying to blow its tanks to survive. It was almost continuously pinned down and depth-charged. On May 2, Forster returned and signaled Dietrich Hoffmann in *U-594* well southeast of Nantucket, closer to Bermuda. They came close enough to speak and "report experiences." The patrol began in Brest on March 21 and ended there on May 18. A week into the patrol, one of the German sailors broke his arm. This was Forster's second patrol to the U.S. coast, the first being off New England between January 24 and 28, 1942. On his next patrol, Forster and all forty-four men aboard were killed when a B-18 Bolo bomber from the U.S.A.A.F. sank it without depth charges north of Colon, Panama.

Kapitänleutnant Heinrich Zimmermann operated *U-136* across New England for eight days between April 12 and May 6, 1942. At first, he headed southwest and exited south of Montauk on April 15. Then on May 3, *U-136* returned, exiting south of Cape Sable on the 6th. On the 11th, *U-136* sought to find and destroy the drifting wreck of the *Ocana* or the *Fleur de Lis*, but fog prevented them. Heavy seas then enemy aircraft further hindered offensive operations. Seaplanes (biplanes) forced them below on the 13th and 14th. They failed to attack a tanker off Hatteras on the 16th. On May 2, the sub was repairing the port diesel, which would not reverse, while at the same time dodging aircraft and a "schooner trap that works together with aircraft." Thick fog set in, and Zimmermann heard from Hoffmann in *U-594* on May 3. A target that night (named *Rageland* or similar) turned out to be neutral. On the 7th, *U-136* and U-boats under Heydemann (*U-575*) and Mohr (*U-124*) submitted weather information to Germany. Then Zimmermann headed home.[34]

Though Zimmermann sank no ships off New England, he destroyed the three-mast Canadian schooner *Mildred Pauline* off Newfoundland on May 8 after missing with a torpedo. It took 102 shots to set the schooner, which was *en route* from Barbados to St. John's laden with rum or molasses when it was sunk, ablaze. All seven officers and men perished in the cold water. Zimmermann damaged the *Axtell J. Byles* on April 19 off Hatteras, followed by sinking the *Empire Drum* on the 24th and the *Arundo* on the 28th, also in U.S. waters.

Heinrich Zimmermann was born in 1907 and a member of the Crew of 1933. He served in minesweeping flotillas up to March 1941 when he joined U-boats.[35] After commissioning *U-136* in Bremen in August 1941, he began patrolling in January 1942. Overall, he sank or damaged eight ships of nearly 36,000 tons. He was killed when *U-136* was sunk west of Madeira on July 11, 1942, by the Free French destroyer *Leopard*, H.M.S. *Pelican*, and H.M.S. *Spey*. Out of a crew of forty-five, there were no survivors. Zimmermann was thirty-five.[36] He received no decorations in his naval career.

Kapitänleutnant Siegfried Freiherr von Forstner brought *U-402* into New England on a westbound trajectory on April 16, 1942, and exited south of Montauk on the 19th. On this patrol, he sank *Empire Progress* off Nova Scotia three days before entering New England. On the same day, he had to pass up on attacking a ship with "well lighted Swiss neutrality markings," of 10,000 tons "in the vicinity of the Swedish route." On the 18th, von Forstner was given freedom to patrol in New England southward after several days of confusion between Forster and von Forstner. The submariners identified a Vought-Sikorsky OS2U 1 float-plane about 20,000 feet away heading north, then another plane which suddenly shone red lights on them on the 19th. Late that night, *U-402* exchanged signals with *U-571* under Möhlmann, which was heading home, and *U-572* under Hirsacker. Extraordinarily, *U-571*'s men witnessed the *Harpagon* being blown up by *U-109*, with Möhlmann writing: "detonation with bright glow, probably a munitions freighter sunk by Bleichrodt." At the same moment, Bleichrodt was jotting down "two high-explosion columns, especially with the second hit. Heavy explosion from munitions or explosives," adding that "except for two calcium-light life buoys from lifeboats or rafts, nothing is seen." Forty-nine men were killed in the explosion; there were eight survivors.[37]

Late on the 19th, Möhlmann in *U-571* noted: "recognition signals exchanged with *U-572*. Experiences exchanged and took over recognition settings for month of May." Just nine minutes later he adds "recognition signals exchanged with *U-402* and experiences exchanged." Then *U-572* under Hirsacker joined *U-571* and confirmed delivering May code documents to Möhlmann of *U-571* and meeting with *U-402* under von Forstner (whom he misnamed Forster). By extraordinary coincidence, these exchanges were witnessed by all fifty-one survivors of the *Empire Dryden*, perched in three boats, two of which Hirsacker had ignored (he did note "on the stern there is work by floodlight, [and] two boats with anchor lanterns remain."

The witnesses were sitting in lifeboats just after the attack.

> Two submarines were seen immediately after the torpedoing, one off the starboard bow, and second off the port quarter. They were approximately a half-mile apart. The submarines were signaling to each other by torch and signal guns, but the survivors could not read the messages exchanged.[38]

Within an hour, Allied merchant sailors witnessed four enemy submarines: first *U-572* under Hirsacker sank them, then they saw *U-571* under Möhlmann communicating and physically exchanging documents with *U-402* under von Forstner, then exchanging signals with *U-572* under Hirsacker, followed shortly thereafter by *U-109* which sank the *Harpagon* nearby. Though they did not see the sub, it was near enough for *U-571* to see it. All the while there was no sign of Allied counterattack, indicating the extent to which the Germans controlled the battlefield at that time.

The next day, von Forstner sighted "three lifeboats with sails," 4 miles away, between Bermuda and Hatteras; they may have been from half a dozen Allied ships, including four rafts and a lifeboat carrying eight men from the *Harpagon*, sunk that morning by Bleichrodt in *U-109*. In fact, they were the twenty-five survivors of the *Empire Dryden*, left floating in the starboard lifeboat, port motorboat and jollyboat at that time after having been sunk by Heinz Hirsacker in *U-572* at 8.55 p.m. on the previous night. Twenty-five men including the captain in one of the lifeboats were never heard from again, presumed lost in a gale. The remaining men were rescued by the *City of Birmingham* and taken to Bermuda, before that ship, too, was sunk by *U-202* under Linder on July 1, 1942, severing one of the key supply lines to Bermuda.[39]

To illustrate how thick the seas off America were with the jetsam of war that spring, a further forty-seven survivors of the *Steel Maker*, sunk nearby at the same time by *U-654* under Ludwig Forster, managed to escape in two lifeboats; the twenty-four survivors of the *Robin Hood* sunk April 16 by *U-575* under Heydemann shared just one boat, and were further north; and the thirty-three men from the *Agra*, sunk that night by *U-654* under Forster, had just one boat as well.

On the 29th, von Forstner pursued freighters and a tanker being protected by a destroyer. He estimated the tanker to be 8,000 tons, of the *British Confidence*, or the *North Atlantic* class, and the destroyer of the *Barney* class. Von Forstner sank the *Ashkhabad* (mistakenly called *Kapelnos*) and missed a 100-foot patrol boat on April 30. The same day, his men avoided an airship and chased a convoy of three merchant ships and a four-stack destroyer. Then, on May 2, he attacked and sank U.S.S. *Cythera*, PY 26, off Hatteras, while it was *en route* from Norfolk to Panama. Although sixty-nine of the patrol yacht's crew were killed in the final attack, von Forstner disobeyed the *Laconia* order to pick up the two survivors, observing "while searching for clues for identification, we see a raft with two men whom we get aboard. It is unlikely that many more survivors exist.[40]

Then, "most unfortunately," they began the "return transit due to fuel inventory," headed back to St. Nazaire, where *U-402* arrived on May 20 having set out on March 26, 1942.[41] On May 9, *U-402* fired a torpedo at a 3,500-ton steamer which behaved oddly, so that when the sun rose the sub continued eastward. On the 14th, he passed on a report from *U-128* under Ulrich Heyse to shore. For the final approach, *U-402* was joined by *U-136* (Zimmermann), *U-773* (Baldus), and *U-752* (Schroeter). In convoy, they motored from Buoy Nanni 1 to St. Nazaire lock, ending a 8,912-mile patrol. *U-402* was in the fifth wave of Operation Drumbeat boats.

Born in Hannover in 1910, von Forstner was killed by aircraft launched from U.S.S. *Card*, CVE 11, on October 13, 1943, when he and all members of the *U-402*'s crew were sunk. Aged thirty-three when killed, he received the Knights Cross earlier that year and was promoted to *Korvettenkapitän* in April. Von Forstner and his younger brother Wolfgang-Friedrich were both U-boat skippers (the younger brother survived the war).[42] A member of the Crew of 1930, he served aboard the light cruiser *Nürnberg*. After joining U-boats in April 1940, he sailed on *U-99* under Otto Kretschmer before moving to *U-59* for further training. He commissioned *U-402* and was her only commander from October 1941 on. Overall, von Forstner accounted for eighteen Allied ships sunk or damaged, comprising roughly 100,000 tons.

6

Two Boats Sink Three Ships: the *West Imboden*, the *Pipestone County*, and the *Taborfjell*

Kapitänleutnant Karl-Ernst Schroeter brought *U-752* on a seven-day incursion into New England during which he sank the freighter *West Imboden* on his second day. After entering on April 20, he headed west past Montauk on the 23rd. The *West Imboden* was a U.S. steamer *en route* from Cape Town to Boston via Trinidad. Early on the morning of April 21, *U-752* struck the ship with a torpedo well east of Nantucket. The first two missiles passed ahead of the ship, creating much phosphorescence. The third shot went behind due to a gyrocompass failure, and a fourth ahead of it. The fifth missile struck under the bridge, and the final one about 100 feet further ahead. The ship's back was broken so quickly that propellers showed out of the water. Schroeter brought *U-752* to the surface and began shelling the *West Imboden* before all thirty-five officers and men were clear. Thirty-five shells later, all the merchant sailors managed to get free from the burning vessel.[1]

That same day, Schroeter evaded twin-engine airplanes sent from shore, followed later by sea-planes. Nevertheless, they managed to download new torpedoes during the night, and on the 23rd damaged the Norwegian ship *Reinholt* with gunfire, which managed to return fire fourteen times and suffered one injured and another killed. Schroeter noted: "enemy answers with two small cannons. After a few shots, hits on the bridge and after [part of] ship. Large spurts of flame at the level of his cannons – probably munitions hit." Though the ship caught fire, the destroyer U.S.S. *Rhind*, DD 404, came to the rescue and helped her limp to New York. Schroeter heard the *Rhind* approaching and crash-dived to avoid two destroyers; however, the "boat was exactly run over," followed by six depth charges.

The Germans counted "masses of depth-charges" and "detonation series of up to twenty," believed to be from the *Reinholt*, knocking out their G.H.G.-type sensors and partly disabling the attack periscope. Captain Hans Nielsen, and fifteen of his men received the War Cross and other medals from the Norwegian government. Schroeter gave up on the *Reinholt*, despite initially planning to follow whatever ship towed her to the coast. On the 24th, another destroyer ran right over the submerged sub, which then lay on the bottom to allow eleven of the crew suffering from food poisoning to recover.

U-752 returned on May 5 heading east past Montauk in a straight line south of Nantucket to exit two days later. On May 1, 1942, *U-752* had sunk the Norwegian ship *Bidevind* in roughly the same position as the *Reinholt*. All thirty-six men managed to get away and made it to the U.S. Coast Guard station at Toms River, New Jersey. On the 5th, the German commander observed that "despite the most economical consumption, cannot stretch [fuel] more than 55 days" of patrolling. He believed the depth charges caused a fuel tank to leak, noting that fuel oil made it into the battery room. They rounded the lightship *Nantucket* while investigating and repairing for the long voyage to Europe, making more crash dives to evade airplanes. On the 7th, a petty officer came down with syphilis, leading everything to be disinfected. They exchanged recognition signals with *U-213* (von Varendorff) two days later. *U-752* returned to St. Nazaire on May 21, having left La Pallice on March 28.

Born in 1912, Schroeter's total number of Allied ships sunk or damaged was ten for over 38,000 tons. He joined the German Navy in the Crew of 1934 and saw experience aboard *U-9*. Then he was 1st Watch Officer of *U-38* under Leibe and later on the training boat *U-121*. He commissioned *U-752* in May 1941 and was her only commander until she was sunk by British Swordfish aircraft from H.M.S. *Archer* in the North Atlantic while going after Convoy HX 239 on May 19, 1943. Schroeter was struck in the head by gunfire from aircraft as he climbed the conning tower. Seventeen men were rescued by Allied escorts and *U-91*. Schroeter, however, was killed at age thirty.

The American steamship *West Imboden* was built in 1919 by Columbia River Shipbuilding of Portland, Oregon. She was 5,751 tons. Her owners were the Seas Shipping of New York; however, the ship remained registered to Portland, then later to Wilmington, Delaware. Originally commissioned by the United States Maritime Commission, she was laid up after World War I and relegated to the government's reserve fleet. On February 6, 1942, the *West Imboden* reported sighting a flare roughly 12 miles from its position while in the South Atlantic. According to Cape Town Radio, nothing further was learned.

The *West Imboden* sailed from New York on December 6, 1939, and on other voyages arrived there in April, August, and December 1940. In 1941, she also called in September, May, August, and December before sailing for India to load various dry cargoes. On its final voyage, the *West Imboden* sailed via Durban, Port Elizabeth, and Cape Town, then departed Trinidad on Saturday, April 11, 1942, bound north for Boston. Her 7,357-ton cargo included chrome ore, asbestos, and hides. The draft was 24.5 feet, providing a plentiful target for a U-boat skipper to strike. The ship was unarmed. Captain Anton Anderson (American, aged sixty) served as master. William Gibbons was an able seaman, and Frank M. Jasper, aged forty-six, was the first officer. Although thirty-three of the crew were American, one was Swiss and another Danish. There were eight officers and twenty-seven men.

Routing instructions provided five different waypoints for them to steer for. Late on the night of Monday, April 20, 1942, just over thirty minutes following the changing of the watch at 10 p.m., the *West Imboden* was making 9.5 knots and heading a shade west of north. The wind was mild from the direction they were heading at about 10 knots. Visibility that night was about 1 mile: dark, but clear. Though all portholes and lights were extinguished, for about a quarter of an hour preceding the attack (from 10.33 p.m.), the ship's stack emitted sparks visible to any vigilant enemy in the area. Out of concern for sparks flying into the open ventilators and below, Anderson, a wizened mariner, altered course to the northeast. Though the first change of course threw off the attacker, the sparks also increased the visibility of the ship from 1 mile to 12 miles.[2]

The ship resumed its course after about ten minutes, at 10.43 p.m. There were two lookouts, one each on the bridge wings, without binoculars, though there was a pair in the bridge. At 10.48 p.m., Captain Anderson spotted a torpedo 150 feet from the starboard side at a 90-degree angle and closing fast. It left a phosphorescent, glowing wake with bubbles. It was too late for the men to turn the *West Imboden*, so the missile struck seconds later, roughly a quarter of the length aft from the bow. The mud-like chrome ore in the cargo hold cushioned the impact, resulting in only a dull thud, with no debris thrown up on deck.

The radio officer was able to send out SOS and SSS messages on 500 kilohertz, giving the nature of distress and ship's position, 185 miles east of Nantucket. This was confirmed received by the WIM station in Chatham, on Cape Cod. It was the first time the radio was used since leaving Trinidad a week before. Captain Anderson had confidential routing codes from the British and Americans, some issued in New York six months before. He threw them all overboard in a weighted box.

Overall, Schroeter in *U-752* sent six torpedoes toward the *West Imboden*, but only the final one burst into the starboard side of the number one cargo hold, forward. It was not a clean kill. Schroeter recorded the hours leading up to the attack thus:

> Smoke cloud bearing 310°. Turned towards it, maneuvered ahead. Steamer steers in zigzags. General course 350°, 11 knots … At the beginning of darkness, the boat is positioned to starboard ahead of the steamer. Angled in, steamer runs on a straight course. Two-fan Tubes I and III, range = 1,000 meters. Torpedoes are followed by marine phosphorescence until passing by. Both passed ahead. Matched

> speed. Steamer runs about 10 knots. Want to shoot from a short distance, because the possibility exists that shots will be noticed early, due to marine phosphorescence.[3]

The flustered commander then added:

> Two fan, Tube II and Tube IV, range = 500 meters, target speed = 11 knots, target angle 95°, because target optic was loose, target angle 0° ... enemy speed seemed to be set too high. Second torpedo went behind the stern of the steamer. The second torpedo is a gyrocompass failure and crosses the running track ahead of the first torpedo. The first torpedo passes by just ahead. While reloading, ran along ahead of the steamer. The steamer runs a straight course with fluctuating speed settings.

He was right: the U-boat commander overcalculated *West Imboden*'s speed by 1.5 knots, at 11 instead of 9.5. An hour and a quarter later, Schroeter concluded:

> Two single shots one after the other. Range = 1,000 meters, target speed 9 knots, target angle 90°. Ran on with one diesel, so as not to be noticed. Hit forward 10 meters (under the bridge) forward 40 meters. Fore ship settles intermediately. Steamer is broken in two, propellers jut far out of the water. 30 seconds after the hits, the steamer transmits on the 600-meter wave name and position: *West Imboden,* 5,751 GRT, home port, Portland. Crew goes to the boats. The stern of the ship floats on the cargo. Shot on fire with artillery, after a few minutes burns brightly. Total loss.

Within ten minutes of the torpedo strike, all thirty-five men evacuated their ship and boarded two lifeboats, one from each side, as it was still level and going down by the bow. After the torpedo hit, Schroeter and his men spent two hours pumping shells into the hulk to sink the vessel. In fact, the Germans opened fire before the starboard lifeboat was fully lowered. They fired five shots, four of which were seen to strike. The sub was about 500 yards away, and the ship was illuminated by the sparks from the stack. Then men in both boats rowed astern of the ship. While the starboard boat was scrambling away, the men in the port lifeboat saw *U-752* rounding the bow of their ship, from right to left, from a distance of about 400 yards away. By then, the *West Imboden* was aflame from the shells and dead in the water.

The attack lasted three hours and twenty-three minutes from 10.48 p.m. on Monday to 2.11 a.m. on Tuesday from initial contact to the time of sinking. The Germans began to shell the ship at 11 p.m., firing at a slow rate and focusing more on making each shot hit the target. They managed to set the vessel afire, which doomed it. It was seen to sink by the Allied sailors at 2.11 a.m. First the bow settled, then while sinking the ship turned over on its starboard side. At 11.08 p.m., half an hour after the sixth torpedo struck, *U-752* broke the surface abeam of the ship on the port side, about 1,500 feet off, and was seen by the men in the port lifeboat. Its bow was pointed at the ship. The Germans asked whether anyone had been killed, and the name of the ship. Specifically, "the chief mate [Jasper] replied 'No, none in our boat,' to which a German officer replied That's good, what ship?" The Americans felt that the German officer spoke "excellent English with no accent;" however, his pronunciation of the word "killed" was rather like "kilt." One of the Americans spoke German and observed that the German was clearly well educated. Schroeter observed that "during the bombardment the lifeboats came close, crew partly German." There were six Germans on the forward deck and two men aft of the conning tower. Between two and three men could be seen in the tower itself.

After interviewing the Allies, the Germans, unafraid of counteroffensive, fired roughly eight parachute rockets over the starboard side of the ship, illuminating it with a red glow. Then they pumped over five more shells into the port side, amidships. Anderson believed that thirty-three out of thirty-five shots hit the ship: an excellent ratio. When *U-752* motored off on the surface, at about fifteen minutes after midnight on April 21, her course was to the northeast. The survivors admired how the submarine, estimated at 700 tons, was able to maneuver with apparently no exhaust or noise; this was probably due to the sub using its electric, not diesel motor at the time. They also observed that the sub's deck was roughly 4 feet above the water-line, and the conning tower around 12 feet. Their overall impression was that *U-752* was "small with two guns and painted black or dark grey." The bow was higher than the stern, and the conning tower was flat-topped, with no rake.

U.S. Navy Lieutenant (junior grade) David Cone opined that the sub was advised ahead of time of the ship's expected position and time, and that the sinking was a simple matter of firing a single torpedo, and that the thirty-five shells were merely "excellent target practice ... for it was apparent that the ship would have gone down with one torpedo hit." None of this is substantiated by the combined Axis and Allied accounts, and thus can be dismissed as conjecture.

The Allied crew found themselves alone on the open sea, hundreds of miles from the nearest shore. Then, two days later, the thirty-five American seamen had the good fortune to be discovered by the officers and crew of the destroyer U.S.S. *Bristol*, DD 453. After concluding its mandated exercises, the naval ship delivered all survivors of the *West Imboden* to Portland, from whence they went to Boston, their original destination. The *Bristol* was less than a year old, having been commissioned on October 22, 1942. She was a *Gleaves*-class destroyer built at the Federal Shipbuilding and Drydock of Kearny, New Jersey. Capable of 37 knots, she was 348 feet long, weighed 2,395 loaded tons, and manned by 276 sailors. Lieutenant-Commander Chester Clark Wood led her while performing escort and patrol duties with U.S.S. *Edison* and crossing the Atlantic to and from Ireland. U.S.S. *Bristol* was torpedoed by *U-371* under Waldemar Mehl on October 13, 1943, broke in two and sank. Fifty-two of her complement were killed. The *West Imboden*'s First Officer Jasper was killed months later when *U-175* sank the *West Chetac* on which he was serving as captain.

Kapitänleutnant Hans-Dieter Heinicke brought *U-576* on a thirteen-day patrol to New England between April 20 and May 2, 1942, heading west from Cape Race then to Nantucket. *U-576* then began a slow patrol northward ending off Provincetown a week later. The boat then regained speed eastward toward Halifax on May 2, 1942. *U-576* sank two Allied vessels: the American *Pipestone County* on April 21 halfway between New England and Bermuda, and the Norwegian *Taborfjell* on the 30th, east of Provincetown. The *Pipestone County* of 5,102 tons and commanded by Captain Richard E. Hocken, was sunk by two torpedoes. Until the final blow was delivered, the engine room bulkheads remained intact, enabling the ship to keep the propeller in the water and steam ready. The crew told Heinicke that they were bound to Southampton, U.K. All forty-six of her sailors managed to survive the attack and were given provisions by the Germans.[5]

The same afternoon, another steamship, a U.S.-built C 2-type steamer, emerged from a rain squall. After a chase of an hour without gaining, Heinicke broke off the hunt. On April 22, the men on *U-576* saw "a lifeboat with set sails ... twelve miles away." This was most likely one of the three boats from the *Pipestone County*, sunk a day before; however, lifeboats from several ships including the *Derryheen*, the *Bris*, the *Steel Maker*, the *Agra*, the *Empire Dryden*, and the *Alcoa Guide* were struggling in the vicinity at the time. Since the U-boat evaded being seen, it was not reported by Allied sailors.

On April 23, a destroyer was detected; the following day, a large ship with five hatches and roughly 375 feet long of 5,000 tons was attacked on a "mirror flat sea." Heinicke bitterly reported a pistol failure on his first torpedo, then a miss, then the British freighter counterattacked with "a cannon disguised by wood planking." The ship was actually the *Tropic Star*, which sent an SSS using the call sign "MOKJ" at the exact same time from, reporting it was "being followed by a suspicious craft that disappeared when a plane came over," and that the submarine surfaced dead astern then submerged.[6] Amazingly, twenty-three survivors of the *Pipestone County*, which *U-576* sank, were on board. Those men, representing half of the forty-six survivors, were understandably skittish about being sunk by the same (or any) submarine before they even reached land from the first attack. Nantucket was 43 miles to the west at the time.

Ensign Frank N. Keathley (U.S.N.R.) was in charge of the gun crew aboard the *Pipestone County* and was allowed by Captain Anderson to oversee the gun crew on board the *Tropic Star* as well. As soon as the *Pipestone County*'s Chief Officer Gibson D. Hillary saw the periscope he blew the ship's whistle and ordered the guns manned. Keathley relates:

> At 8.10 a.m. the periscope of a submarine was first sighted about seventy-five feet away from the port side of the *Tropic Star*. The sub apparently crash-dived and

> passed a few yards astern of the ship. We could see the bow wave. The alert was sounded and panic occurred among the survivors from the *Pipestone County*. The crew of the *Tropic Star* acted better. At the request of Captain Anderson, the armed guard unit of the *Pipestone County* manned the 3-inch gun. The periscope of the sub was next sighted at 8.45 a.m. ... on the starboard side at a distance of 12,000 feet. We trained the gun to starboard and the conning tower came up about 6,000 feet away (on the port side). The gun had no slewing gear and we could not train it quickly enough to port. About two minutes later we saw the feather from the periscope and opened fire. The first shot was well over; the second appeared to be right on, exploding and throwing up black smoke; the third shot was over. The periscope was not seen after the second shot.[7]

Hillary corroborated Keathley's statements, adding that he saw 2 feet of periscope about 450 feet away. Able-Bodied Seaman Roland E. Foster said the periscope was 3 feet in the air and turned toward the ship, and when *U-576* dove, he "judged that the periscope hit the keel." He thinks the second shot hit the U-boat as well, since "smoke came up and there was a resounding sound." Carpenter Anselm Snow said the periscope moved at about 3 knots and turned away from the *Tropic Star* at about 60 feet. Then the submarine approached the ship's stern from about a 38-degree angle. He was so convinced that the periscope hit the ship that he later pointed out a rusted scratch on his vessel's hull.

Heinicke conceded that "the intended surfacing for artillery combat was broken off due to shelling of the periscope, no damage." Following this encounter, he took *U-576* to the seafloor to repair the forward diving plane. On the 25th, a plane forced them to crash dive after bombing the sub with "poorly placed" missiles. The boat evaded more planes that day, and the following day found itself up against the U.S.C.G.C. *Argo*, "unpleasantly close," which forced them to crash dive. Often the boat found the sanctuary of the bottom in about 250 feet of water. On the 28th, it rested just off Nauset Beach among "many small fishing vessels, possibly patrol vessels." The following day, they tried to creep silently up on a destroyer and "large patrol vessel," but could not. The next day, *U-576*'s pursuit of a different steamer was interrupted by an *Argo*-type Coast Guard cutter.

The men on the *Taborfjell*, sunk by *U-576* 100 miles east of Cape Cod on April 30 were not so fortunate as the *Pipestone County* crew in that seventeen out of the officers and men on the 1,339-ton ship perished, leaving only three survivors. Despite the moon being from behind him, Heinicke missed her with two torpedoes. Then *U-576* surfaced to get ahead of the Norwegian ship, which evaded twice, requiring a submerged attack. The *Taborfjell* was not just altering course, but speed as well. A second fan of torpedoes struck after a run of forty-six seconds, sinking her within a minute. The three survivors made it to a raft and witnessed three others in the water. Heinicke noted: "steamer sinks immediately with the usual sounds. Surfaced. Two survivors." Twenty hours later, H.M.S. *P 552* rescued three of the men and took them to St. John's.

That night, the Germans heard more of the cutter *Argo* passing overhead as they worked on diesels and torpedoes below the sea. Then a four-stack (vintage) destroyer-escorting ten steamships with another two destroyers passed over them. That evening Heinicke excitedly hunted the convoy, an early version of the BX series from Boston to Halifax begun weeks before, on April 3, 1942. The four ships which arrived in Boston on May 1 were the *Trolla* and the *Bonde* sailing independently, and the *Bur* and the *Empire Spey*, voyaging in Convoy ON 86 from Liverpool to Cape Cod.[8] The first shot was made with an enemy escort following right behind the U-boat, and detonated after a run of six minutes and forty seconds. Heinicke fired from nearly 1,750 feet away, observing that a ship fell astern to the protection of destroyers. Thereafter poor weather prevented confirmation of anything except "steamer and destroyer lying stopped, [and] because of worsening visibility, the arrival of aircraft can hardly be expected and there is still room to maneuver ahead. The broken steamer can never escape." Yet after many hours of harassment by destroyers, float planes, aircraft bombs, and the sudden appearance of "vessel with large bow wave at low range ... an armed fishing trawler," probably H.M.S. *Le Tigre*, he observed that "due to air and sea, operating on reported convoy hopeless. One hit probable."

On May 1, *U-576* matched the speed of a 700-ton submarine believed to be American, as no other German subs were near, with no response from the other sub. Heinicke attacked another steamer with two torpedoes, but the G 7a surfaced and missed astern, and the sub's gyrocompass jammed. On sighting the U-boat, the merchant ship escaped. As the boat left the region on May 2, it continued to be harried from the air and also large U.S. Navy vessels like a *Ranger*-type aircraft carrier, a *Texas*-type battleship, and steamers *West Point* and *Mount Vernon*.

Heinicke was born in 1913 and was in the Crew of 1933. Early in his naval career, he served as 1st Watch Officer of the U-boat tender *Weichsel,* then aboard *U-73* in 1940 and 1941. He commanded *U-576* from September 1941 until July 15, 1942, when he and the boat were destroyed by two Kingfisher aircraft and the MV *Unicoi*'s gunfire off Cape Hatteras on the 15th.[9] His career tally was six ships sunk or damaged for some 35,000 tons. He received no decorations, and perished at age twenty-nine, along with forty-four crewmates.

The U.S.-flagged steamship *Pipestone County* was built by American International Shipbuilding, better known as the Hog Island Shipyard, in Philadelphia. Her original name was *Shawano*; however, when completed in July 1919, her name was *Pipestone County*. She was built for the United States Shipping Board. The name is derived from a county in Minnesota in which fewer than 10,000 people reside. The ship was 5,102 tons, 401 feet long, 54 feet wide, and 32 feet deep. A single steam turbine powered by three boilers turned a single shaft, which turned a four-bladed propeller to achieve 11.5 knots. The General Electric and Babcock and Wilcox machinery developed 2,500 hp.

From 1923 until 1942, the Seas Shipping Company of New York (known as the Robin Line) owned *Pipestone County*. At the time of her loss, she was on charter to the U.S. War Shipping Administration. The ship had an active war. In 1939, she called in New York in September, October, and November and in 1941 called again in March, April, July, and November. On January 8, 1942, the ship sailed for the Middle East and Africa. In Lourenço Marques (then in Portuguese East Africa, now Mozambique), she loaded 3,500 tons of manganese ore, 1,200 tons of wattle extract (a vegetable tanning material originating in wattle, or acacia tree, bark), asbestos, skins, hides, and 100 kegs of brandy.[10]

On the way to Cape Town, on March 16, 1942, the *Pipestone County* men came across survivors of the recently sunk Dutch ship *Alcyone*, which had struck a mine laid by the captured British ship *Speybank*, which the Germans used as a decoy to deploy mines off Cape Town. The sixty-five other crew rowed ashore. Yet the state of the survivors in boats brought the war to the men in the American ship, some of whom vowed to be prepared for whatever lifeboat situation might await them in the long voyage to Trinidad and Boston.

The *Pipestone County* left Trinidad, where it had called for fuel, on Monday, April 13 at 4 p.m. Her total cargo consisted of roughly 6,700 tons, which is said by some sources to have included gold worth £17,600. While approaching Trinidad, they had been warned by a ship from the same company, *Robin Hood*, about the presence of an enemy submarine east of Barbados. Then, on Sunday 19 April they received word via wireless radio to be on the alert for enemy U-boats, and to zigzag around the clock, which they immediately began to do. The same day, the men noticed a strong smell of petroleum on the ocean's surface, and "in scanning the horizon could see through binoculars a small red spot to the eastward," that may (or may not) have been a lifeboat with the red sails standard on British ships. This was 400 miles south-southeast of Bermuda; sadly, they did not divert to rescue their fellow mariners in distress.

The *Pipestone County*'s captain was a naturalized American raised in England named Captain Richard E. Hocken. The second officer was Gabriel Covas Reina. Most of the crew were Americans or naturalized; however, two of them came from the Philippines. Overall, there were thirty-seven merchant mariners and nine members of U.S. Navy Gun Crew 28E of Brooklyn, led by a U.S. Navy ensign in charge, with seven seamen and a coxswain. The vessel was armed with a 4-inch gun located aft below the bridge, four .50-caliber machine guns and four .30-caliber machine guns.

On the afternoon of Tuesday, April 21, there was an able-bodied seaman and a Navy seaman on the upper bridge, roughly 45 feet above the sea, Second Officer Reina and a merchant sailor on the lower bridge, and a Navy seaman at the aft gun. The ensign, Frank M. Keathley (U.S.N.R.), said that Kirchmer was on the flat bridge and another gunner was in the machine gun turret at the time. Engineers complained that the bunker fuel taken in Trinidad was of an inferior quality and produced too much smoke or sparks from the exhaust stacks, making the ship particularly vulnerable to being seen by lurking U-boats.

The ship was in the Gulf Stream, and the weather was moderate. Though they had experienced a storm in the morning, by afternoon the seas were settled, wind was about 20 knots from the north, and visibility was good. The zigzagging pattern employed at the time was from diagrams nine and thirty-seven, but the base course was 310 degrees, or roughly north-northwest. The ship was 325 miles north of Bermuda and 275 miles southeast of Nantucket.

At 1.05 p.m., Able-Bodied Seaman John J. Culeton was the helmsman. Culeton contradicts Reina by saying that the following occured at 12.54 p.m.:

> Berg, the lookout on the bridge, called out *Torpedo*. I looked and saw the torpedo about a half mile away. I've always been told that torpedoes run under the water, but this one was on top, and I saw it plainly. I then saw about four feet of the periscope bearing about one point forward of our starboard beam at a distance of three-quarters-of-a-mile. As soon as Berg shouted, I threw the helm hard a starboard. It seemed to be a full minute before the torpedo struck the forward part of Number One hold. It blew the hatch covers off and I narrowly missed being hit by flying cargo.[11]

The captain was not on the bridge at the time. On arrival, he assessed that the ship had lost 10 feet of draft and was down by the bow, and sinking, that the engines had stopped, and a submarine had been sighted in the vicinity. He then ordered abandon ship within ten minutes. According to some witnesses, Captain Hocken was "nervous" and the men abandoning ship were "panicky."

Hocken did manage to throw overboard the secret signals and collect the ship's papers in a satchel. He ordered the radio operator to send an SOS message, which was acknowledged from shore. At 1.05 p.m. the U.S. Navy's Eastern Sea Frontier *Enemy Action and Distress Diary* records "SOS from S.S. *Pipestone County* … torpedoed … 300 miles North of Bermuda. Bermuda sent patrol plane to scene." Culeton wrote, "The boats didn't wait and the Bos'n and I got on the raft which was on the port quarter." The U.S. Navy Coxswain, I. R. K. Culley, wrote, "We didn't have any orders from our Ensign, in fact I never saw him at any time. I just followed my orders." The ensign says he was busy conveying the captain's orders to abandon ship to his and other men.[12]

Once the *Pipestone County* sailors and gunners had all abandoned ship in four lifeboats and at least one raft, Heinicke sent the final torpedo into her side about twenty-five minutes after the first, or at about 3.15 p.m., Carpenter Anselm Snow was quite close to where the torpedo whizzed past:

> I was about 200' off the starboard side, almost astern, when I saw what looked like the prow of a fast motor-boat coming through the water, followed by a heavy concussion which hurt my eardrums for one hour afterward. The ship sank in less than one minute. I had not seen the sub previously. A couple minutes later the sub came to the surface about three-quarters-of-a-mile away. It approached slowly—it took about a half-hour to approach—went directly to the captain's boat.[13]

With the threat of counterattack gone, Heinicke identified Captain Hocken as he transferred from boat to boat carrying a satchel and wearing a cap.

The submarine approached the captain's boat and Heinicke held a conversation with Hocken in poor English. He said he was sorry to have to sink their ship and asked after the cargo, destination, and ship name. Eight men lined the conning tower, with Heinicke described as being in his early thirties and clean shaven. He asked a younger officer to do the questioning, and this officer was in his mid-twenties. A lot of the men were described as being boys in the seventeen-year-old range, with about ten-to-twelve days' worth of facial hair.[14]

The conversation lasted roughly fifteen minutes. Heinicke then said he hoped they reached land, but that they were far away from it. He asked if anyone was wounded and was told they were not. Heinicke was described as 5 feet, 10 inches tall and 160 pounds with light brown hair. He had on "what looked like an aviator's helmet—wool or fur lined." The other sailors were casually dressed, not in any discernible uniform. The Germans provided two 8-kg tins of bread marked "KLEVe 8 kilograms," apparently Danish, and 1 kg of Danish butter.

Allied sailors described *U-576*'s insignia as a "snorting bull," or "either a laughing cow or laughing jackass stenciled in white on the dark grey conning tower"—this was the famous "snorting bull" emblem from Günther Prien's 1939 Scapa Flow attack that became the emblem of the 7th U-Boat Flotilla in St. Nazaire. An inscription along the barrel of the large gun read "Piermole," others saying it was "Tripoli." The U-boats' crest showed a lion holding a key, which is the coat of arms for Radevormwald, a sub-region of the North Rhine.[15]

By the following day, all four lifeboats had separated, indicating a lack of centralized control, given that many other lifeboats had managed to stay together in far worse weather, using a painter and signals from flashlights. The majority of the survivors were found by the Norwegian motor ship *Tropic Star* the next day, on April 22. At 5 p.m., Captain G. Anderson of the rescue ship came alongside to rescue the men, and an hour later, they found the second lifeboat and picked those men up as well. Together, twenty-three out of a total complement of thirty-seven were plucked from the seas and an uncertain fate. That left one lifeboat of thirteen men in it, plus ten men in the fourth lifeboat at sea. The *Tropic Star* headed to Boston where it arrived at noon on Friday the 24th.

The steel motor ship *Tropic Star* was 5,088-tons and owned by Alf Jakhelln of Oslo, whose fleet was involved in the general tramping and petroleum trades globally.

She was built by William Denny and Brothers at Dumbarton, near Glasgow in 1926. Up to 1927, she was the *Yomah*, then for the next decade the *Ashburton*. She could carry 8,455 tons of cargo, was 415 feet long, 52 feet wide, and 25 feet deep and capable of 12.5 knots. On this voyage, she was carrying 7,890 tons of cargo from Beira, Portuguese East Africa, including 5,600 tons of chrome ore in bulk, of which 1,500 was for Boston, sisal, and wool. Her agents were Peabody and Lane and she had a total of twenty-nine men on board. Captain Anderson commended Captain Hocken, noting that he "was sitting up in the boat looking around and had refused to take cover down in the boat, although he was wet and cold."

As noted, during the voyage to Boston they fired on *U-576* on April 24 at 8.10 a.m., east of Nantucket. U.S.S. *PC 461* was in pursuit of the U-boat half an hour later. There is no mention in the local press about the survivors' arrival or integration into Boston and repatriation. Such disclosures are inconsistent: when the Navy press office found an attack of publicity value, they would invite reporters and photographers, as they did with the stricken fishing boat *Lark*. In this case, at 7.30 a.m. the following day (April 25), a highly observant and pro-active naval officer boarded *Tropic Star* and quickly deduced what had happened. U.S. Navy Reservist Lieutenant Gordon B. Hebb noted:

> Two lifeboats on the deck of [*Tropic Star*], as well as more than usual number of crew members standing around. Upon inquiry ... was informed that there were survivors aboard from the torpedoed steamship SS *Pipestone County* (U.S.). DIO, 1-ND was immediately notified.

Hebb and his team then interviewed not just the *Tropic Star* officers and men, but those from Pipestone County as well.[16]

It would be over two long weeks (sixteen days) before the next group of *Pipestone County* survivors was rescued. At 10.17 a.m. on Thursday, May 7, the U.S. Coast Guard cutter *Calypso* recorded in its deck log that "Coast Guard patrol plane sighted lifeboats with occupants 30 miles east of Oregon Inlet. From Elizabeth City [NC] Coast Guard Station by dispatch. *Calypso* directed to scene." By 3.20 p.m. that day, she was on the scene, reporting "picked up thirteen survivors from torpedoed American steamship *Pipestone County*. Boat at sea sixteen days and separated from three other boats with the remainder of crew from first day. Condition of survivors good except for two possible mental cases." The *Calypso* landed her charges at the U.S. Navy base in Norfolk the same day. Built at Bath Iron Works in Maine and launched in January 1932, the *Calypso,* WPC 104, was commissioned two weeks later, on January 16 and served the Coast Guard. She rescued many mariners before, during and after World War II, until being decommissioned in July 1947. Sold in 1955, she went into service ferrying passengers around Manhattan for the Circle Line, which she continued to do as *Circle Line XI*, until late 2008.[17]

The last group of ten survivors had the longest to wait until rescue: seventeen days, until Friday, May 8. The boat, led by Second Officer Reina, discovered an abandoned raft from a Panamanian ship at sea four days into their ordeal, on April 26. This must have been a boat from the Panamanian-flagged *Ramapo*, sunk by *U-108*, Scholtz in that vicinity on February 26. Though the *Ramapo* sank in just eleven minutes, thirty-four of the forty men under Captain Johan Magnus Ørn Lorentzen got away in lifeboats and were interviewed by Scholtz and his men. Tragically, none of the forty men were seen alive again. Like a hand from the dead, their lifeboat provided the *Pipestone County* survivors with water and food in their hour of need exactly two months later.

Reina was not happy with his boat, however, stating that he actually put his thumb through its rotten hull, and the men had to patch it with rags. Then on April 30 at about 7.15 p.m., a PBY Mariner airplane spotted the survivors off Cape Hatteras. The plane signaled that help was on its way, and the men ate more of the rations than they usually would in expectation of imminent rescue. The following day, a second PBY from Elizabeth City dropped them a U.S. Navy parachute at the end of which was water and food. When the realization set in that no immediate rescue was on the horizon, the men's morale fell. One officer even stated that it would have been better not to have the false hopes raised at all. Yet the new water helped to offset the loss of water consumed in the expectation of imminent rescue.

Meanwhile, the Gulf Stream pushed the boat further north for a week. Then at 4 a.m. on May 8, they fired flares to attract the attention of a 94-foot Canadian fishing schooner with an auxiliary motor, the *Irene and May*. At the time they were off McCries Shoals, roughly 8 miles from Cape May, New Jersey, near Hereford Inlet. At first, the captain and crew of the *Irene and May* were concerned that the men in the boat represented some kind of Axis trap and called the Coast Guard for advice. However, by 5.30 a.m., they went alongside the lifeboat. By then, there was a U.S. Navy blimp circling overhead as well. The *Irene and May* men interrupted their fishing to take the ten survivors ashore at the Cape May Naval Air Station. By 1.30 p.m., efforts were made to repatriate the two Navy gunners, J. L. Giannotti and L. D. Greene; however, they were told to remain in Cape May.

The *Irene and May* was built in Essex Massachusetts in 1901 as a schooner. By 1920, she was owned by Maude E. Morris of Nassau, Bahamas. In 1926, she was sold to Mark Sheppard of St. John's Newfoundland. By 1940, it was still owned by Mark Sheppard and was registered at ninety tons with an auxiliary engine installed. The *Robin Hood*, which had warned *Pipestone County* men about U-boats, was itself sunk days earlier, on April 16, 1942, by *U-575* under Günther Heydemann, also north of Bermuda. After Boston, the *Tropic Star*'s next port was New York, and she survived the war to be scrapped by her Finnish owners in Valencia, Spain, in 1961.

There was inevitably other overlap between the northwestern quadrant of the 375-mile circle around Bermuda and the southeastern extent of what are considered New England waters. Only the *Pipestone County* qualifies for coverage in both studies, as survivors were landed in Boston. Among other ships sunk between Bermuda and Nantucket, the *San Gerardo*'s survivors were landed in Halifax, the *Robin Hood*'s in Bermuda, the *Alcoa Shipper*'s in New York, and *Empire Wildebeeste*'s survivors were taken to Bermuda. All ninety-seven men of the *Tacoma Star* sadly perished.

The Norwegian steamship *Taborfjell* was 1,339 tons and could carry 2,600 tons of dry cargo. She was built in Oslo in 1938 by Nylands Mekaniske Verksted and her owners were A/S Rudolf, whose managers were Olsen and Ugelstad of Oslo, who in turn chartered the ship to Nortraship in New York. Her final master was Captain Erling Nilsen, age thirty-two. Supporting him were nineteen mariners, all of them Norwegian except for William A. Hood and George Michael Parsons, age eighteen, both of Britain (one of them from British Honduras), as well as Thomas J. Berrigan, a twenty-nine-year-old ordinary seaman from Canada.

Between 1940 and mid-1942, most of the ship's voyages were in the U.K. and Europe, with others to Montreal, Halifax, Sydney, St. John's, and Quebec. In January 1942, the ship traded several times with Manzanillo, Cuba. On April 17, she left New Orleans for Matanzas and left the latter port on the 22nd with 2,320 tons of sugar in roughly 16,000 bags. She is also said to have stopped in Havana on April 23 on a draft of 18 feet. Her destination was New York, which she reached on April 28. The *Taborfjell* left the following day on its final voyage.[18] The ship proceeded via Long Island Sound and through the Cape Cod Canal, which it transited on April 29 for Montreal. That day at 3 p.m. Radio Operator Olaf Alfsen noted a U-boat sighting in the area they intended to transit. By the following day, the ship was some 95 miles east of the north tip of Cape Cod, and 125 miles southwest of Cape Sable. There were two lookouts: one on the bow, the other on the bridge. The radio had not been used to transmit since leaving Cape Cod Canal. The ship was armed with a 3-inch gun mounted aft, five machine guns: a pair of Hotchkiss, a Marlin, and two Lewis-type, and a Colt 50-mm pistol.

On her last evening under way, the *Taborfjell* was making her maximum speed of 10.5 knots and had been zigzagging eastward for roughly eleven hours. Conditions were calm, with a slight westerly breeze of about 10 knots. The moon was bright and visibility was good. There was no ensign flying. At 1.37 a.m. on April 30, Heinicke in *U-576* sent a single torpedo into the side of the *Taborfjell*. The results were as catastrophic as they were immediate. To quote from official reports, the "starboard side, from number three hatch to stern, entire side of the ship ripped out from just below the waterline to deck plates … 40 to 50 feet long, 10 feet deep."

Within one and two minutes, the ship sank by the stern, with its bow sticking out of the water at an angle of 60 degrees. The cargo holds were filled to the brim with sea water. There was no time for the sailors aboard to send any SOS message, launch a boat, or fire guns in retort. The gaping hole torn in the starboard side extended upward to the deck and allowed water to fill the ship with stunning rapidity, against which the men below were helpless to flee. Alfsen, the "Sparks" or radio operator, was one of the lucky ones who managed to run from his cabin to the radio shack, which was out of power. He then leapt overboard from the bridge. Swimming around for some twenty minutes, he sought a lifeboat but never found one. Rather, he found a life raft, which had popped free. He was joined by Second Officer Erling Arnesen. Together, they found Third Engineer Ole Karlsen Svartangen floating in the water.[19]

As they were pulling Svartangen out of the water, *U-576* surfaced 60 feet away for just two to three minutes, then motored by. The third engineer was on deck when the torpedo struck, not in the engine room, whose occupants perished. The men witnessed two of their crewmates floating dead in the water, without recognizing—or retrieving–them. In the dry tone of official reports, it was observed that "many [were] trapped in cabins; others died in water after jumping overboard."

Unusually for such a remote sinking in ideal conditions (and no SSS being sent, giving the Germans the ship's name), Heinicke preferred not to interact with the three survivors on the raft, alongside whom he motored. The Norwegians estimated the sub was 900 to 1,000 tons. Then, after just a few minutes, *U-576* submerged and motored off. For over twenty-two hours, the three men floated in the vicinity. In another stroke of luck, at 11.30 p.m. on that day, they were spotted by the British submarine H.M.S. *P 552*. Until ten days earlier, the friendly sub was known as U.S.S. *1* before it was transferred to the Royal Navy in New London. Her commander was Lieutenant Anthony Robert Daniell, R.N.

The British submarine spent two hours searching—in vain—for any more survivors among the seventeen remaining *Taborfjell* men. On May 7, they diverted to St. John's to drop the three survivors ashore. The Norwegians arrived in New York on May 24 and were interviewed by Lieutenant (junior grade) R. D. Warden, Jr. (U.S.N.R.), on June 30. The submarine H.M.S. *P 552* arrived in the U.K. in July but was found by the British to be inefficient, and was scrapped in Durban in 1946.[20]

7

Five U-boats Attack the *Skottland*, the *Fort Binger*, the *Plow City*, and the *Margot*

Kapitänleutnant Dietrich Borchert brought *U-566* deep into New England, including off Long Island, Block Island, Nantucket, Cape Cod, the Gulf of Maine, and Massachusetts Bay, between May 1 and 23, 1942. The incursion began inauspiciously, heading west from Cape Sable for five days to south of Block Island. By the night of the 2nd, Borchert was planning to attack "independents to and from New York in the eastern approaches area." Seeing no targets, he hugged the coast. On the 6th, the Germans withstood three crash dives due to aggressive airplane attacks from astern and submerged. By the 7th, they were resting in 100 feet of water off Block Island.

Borchert headed to the northwest toward Montauk, arriving May 8. The next day, they saw steamer lights, but it was just a small fishing boat. *U-566* turned southeast then north on the 10th, and back to within 200 miles of Block Island on the 12th. During the day, the boat would listen, emerge, see fishing and sailing boats or airships, and dive. When a pair of flying boats and a blimp interrupted him, Borchert complained, "operating on target is not possible due to heavy air escort." They then motored southeast to patrol the approaches to the Cape Cod Canal on the 13th, and northeast to a point about 150 miles from the lightship *Nantucket* on the 15th. Borchert noted that "heavy air surveillance extends to the 650-foot line, making proceeding on the surface impossible by day." He decided to head toward the "suspected steamer route."[1]

From off Nantucket, *U-566* headed past Provincetown on May 16 and heard a steamer's fog whistle, followed by aircraft, then two bombs dropped "close" from the air. This attack is corroborated in Allied war diaries which note "Navy planes attacked sub ... 35 miles northeast of Cape Cod ... Several attacks made ... Surface vessels ordered to scene." Borchert noted a sailing boat, a steamer, and more fishermen. On the 17th, he heard a German U-boat nearby; a Type

VIIC heading west 1,500 feet away. However, the nearest U-boats were *U-588* (under Vogel) attacking the *Fort Bringer* in the central Gulf of Maine at the time, and *U-213* (under von Varendorff) much further to the east, and neither of them record hearing *U-566*. Borchert then attacked a steamer with two torpedoes, which both impacted the side of the ship but did not detonate. "The target was a 3,000-ton size freighter with a stern cannon." No such ship reported an attack to the Eastern Sea Frontier at that time.

Then, despite having been just 1,500 feet from an Allied submarine which he mistook for a German U-boat, Borchert headed north to "operate on" an American submarine of the "520" type, motoring at 8 knots. Thick fog meant the search was called off, as a sudden sound contact necessitated a crash dive. Borchert then headed into the Gulf of Maine for four days to the 19th. At that point, *U-566* reversed course and headed southwest to a point off Chatham. Along the way, he encountered the U.S.C.G.C. *Northland* and a pair of *Somers*-class U.S. Navy destroyers. Visibility remaining poor, the Germans lay on the bottom, then left the area, heading south. While lining up an attack, Borchert "recognized [his target] perfectly as Swiss," and broke off. Then they chased a destroyer until the port engine valve developed a constricted intake line, slowing them down.

Starting off Nantucket on the 21st, *U-566* began its exit voyage southeast until clear of the region on the 23rd. Though unsuccessful, this was the most extensive enemy patrol of New England to that date. The only ship which they sank on this patrol, which began in Brest on April 8 and ended there on June 30 was the 8,967-ton British freighter *Westmoreland*, on June 1 off Bermuda. On June 2, U.S.S. *Gannet*, AVP 8 and H.M.S. *Sumar* were ordered to rescue *Westmoreland* survivors, as a result of which *U-653* under Feiler sank the *Gannet* on June 7 with the loss of fourteen U.S. Navy sailors.

U-566 was provided with extra provisions by *U-459* some 500 miles northeast of Bermuda. She and seven other U-boats composed the *Padfinder* group on May 21 roughly 400 miles east of New York.[2] After trying to determine how far east ships were operating between New York, South America, and Central America, the boats dispersed on about May 25 and *U-566* moved southward. On its return voyage, *U-566* received fuel from *U-459* once more, this time west of the Azores.

Borchert was born in 1909 and lived until 1990 and the age of eighty-one. He was thirty-three at the time of this patrol and a member of the Crew of 1933–34. He began his naval career in sea aircraft weapons school and joined U-boats in November 1939. After serving as commander on *U-24*, he commissioned *U-566* in March 1941. During five patrols of 196 days, he sank two ships (the *Meropi* on February 15, 1942, then the *Westmoreland*), and received the Iron Cross 1st Class in July 1942. That month, he moved ashore with the 1st U-Boat Flotilla, then the 24th U-boat Flotilla, then to Danzig and Kiel, where he ended the war in detention, being freed in November 1945. He was promoted to *Korvettenkapitän* in April 1945. *U-566* was scuttled off northwest Portugal on October 24, 1943, after being damaged by six depth charges from a British Wellington bomber. All forty-nine German sailors survived.[3]

Kapitänleutnant Werner Schulte brought *U-582*, on a four-day incursion into New England, from May 7 to 10, 1942. It was an eastbound crossing from south of Montauk to east of Cape Sable. The patrol began on March 19 and ended on May 24 in Brest. Originally, *U-582* was to escort the blockade-runner *Rio Grande* from Japan into France; however, the orders were changed when the ship broke the rendezvous. On April 24, *U-582* received fuel and eighteen days' worth of provisions from *Kapitänleutnant* Georg von Wilamowitz-Möllendorf, age forty-eight, in *U-459* and interacted with other commanders, Rathke in *U-352*, Möhlmann in *U-571*, Teddy Suhren in *U-564*, and Ali Cremer in *U-333*.

On April 28, the U-boat passed only 17 miles from Bermuda, observing "a white light house" on Gibbs Hill. On May 6, the submarine was bombed by Allied aircraft and pestered by several planes. On the 9th, a Lockheed Hudson bore down on them close to the surface. On the 12th, Schulte considered attacking a fishing schooner on the Newfoundland Banks, but it was clearly of neutral Portuguese registry. *U-582* sank no ships on this patrol. They encountered the friendly Italian submarine *Reginaldo Giuliani* under Giovanni Bruno on May 20. *U-582* was escorted into Brest with *U-152* under Hildebrandt.[4]

Werner Schulte was born in Kiel in 1912 and died on October 5, 1942, at the age of twenty-nine, when *U-582* was sunk southwest of Iceland. He joined the Crew of 1937, and early in his career served in gunnery aboard the light cruiser *Konigsberg*. Until 1940, he served joined naval command in Bergen before moving to U-boats in October. He served under Gysae on a patrol aboard *U-98* before commissioning *U-582* in August 1941. Schulte and all forty-six mariners aboard *U-582* were killed during an attack by a U.S. Catalina plane off Iceland.[5] He received no decorations but was posthumously given a promotion with seniority. Schulte sank six merchant ships and one warship, for a total of just under 39,000 tons.

Kapitänleutnant Gerd Kelbling brought *U-593* into New England for just under two weeks between May 8 and June 7, 1942. There were three separate incursions: from May 8 to 11, the boat entered just south of Cape Sable, motoring southwest south of Nantucket. Then it motored west of Montauk. On the 8th, it was chasing a steamer; however, when it turned out to be a 600-ton fishing trawler, Kelbling broke off. The following day, *U-593* followed another trawler, then course set for New York. On the 11th, searchlights and airplanes caused a crash dive, then a three-stack destroyer covered by an airship placed the boat further on the defensive. The next few days were spent in fog off New Jersey. During an attack by depth charges, some of the torpedo canisters were crushed by the pressure, the compass was thrown off a few degrees, and the periscope became foggy.

On the 13th, *U-593* made for Fire Island past the lightship *Ambrose*, hearing more sounds but nothing to hit except trawlers. After damaging the Greek freighter *Stavros* on May 14 (it was marked Swiss but indistinctly and had to be let go), Kelbling returned to New York and chased a Coast Guard cutter of the *George Campbell* type. Then on the 19th, the Germans fired two torpedoes at a passenger ship of 7,000 tons. The torpedoes took 5.5 minutes to detonate on the sea floor at the end of their run, meaning Kelbling did not time the shots correctly. The next day, an air-intake valve jammed shut, despite which they pursued another ship, thought to be a destroyer, which escaped. On the 23rd, they calibrated their position using Allied lighthouses.[6]

After sinking the *Persephone* of Panama on the 25th, *U-593* returned eastbound. In the war diary, Kelbling bemoaned a miss on a tanker group "due to failure of fire control system." On May 27, *U-593* passed south of Montauk, and on the 29th, Kelbling frightened the *Norland* and the *Polyphemus* survivors by attacking the *Marie Amelia* of Portugal, which he called it off on realizing she was neutral. As noted, the next day, he found a lifeboat from *Polyphemus* and provided a "can of bread and a flask of rum." On May 30, Kelbling dog-legged northwest and exited south of Cape Sable. The third and final incursion occurred a few days later between June 5 and 7, *U-593* and was just a foray south of Cape Sable. On the 6th, Kelbling let the Swedish steamer *Drottningholm*, named for a royal palace outside Stockholm, pass. No ships were sunk or attacked in New England on this patrol.

During the first week of May, *U-576* under Heinicke directed *U-593* and three other boats toward a convoy located 80 miles southwest of Cape Sable; however, they never locked into an attack, as the convoy was "hugging the coast," so the U-boats dispersed between Halifax and New York.[7] After sinking the *Persephone*, Kelbling and his men were subject to an attack by convoy-escorts but escaped undamaged. The patrol began on April 20 in St. Nazaire and ended there on June 18, 1942.

Gerd Kelbling was born in 1915 in Silesia and lived until 2005 aged eighty-nine. His career total was eighteen ships sunk or damaged including seven warships of roughly 57,000 tons. In August 1943, he was awarded the Knights Cross. He was a member of the Crew of 1934, following which he served aboard minesweepers.[8] Kelbling joined *U-557* in 1941 before commissioning *U-593* in October. After extensive experience in the North Atlantic, he brought the submarine through the blockade of Gibraltar and into the Mediterranean in October 1942. The boat survived a dozen patrols there, before being pinned down for over a day by two Allied destroyers then forced to surrender. Kelbling and all his men were taken prisoner and sent to Canada until September 1947.

Korvettenkapitän Hans-Heinrich Giessler in *U-455* patrolled New England for eleven days between May 10 and 21, 1942. Like *U-593*, *U-455* encountered the *Drottningholm*, causing Giessler to wryly comment "attack broken off and remained submerged so as not to disturb the diplomats." From the 10th, the U-boat headed west and exited west of Montauk. Between May 19 and 21, she returned, briefly ducking south of Montauk. On May 30, *U-455* patrolled south of Nantucket then headed east of Cape Sable the following day.[9]

Giessler and his crew sank two Allied ships on this patrol: the *British Workman* on May 3 and the *Geo. H. Jones*, on June 11. The boat left St. Nazaire as part of a group of thirteen heading for Canada and the U.S. on April 16 and returned there on June 16. On May 1, Giessler learned of a convoy, 80 miles southwest of Cape Sable, but was too far east at the time and did not make contact. Though *U-455* teamed up with *U-553* under Thurmann, *U-588* under Vogel, and *U-593* under Kelbling, the convoy was too close to shore and the group dispersed.[10] While *U-455* was off New York on May 18, it attacked a large passenger ship without result. On the 21st, she joined seven other boats to create the *Padfinder* group. A member of the Crew of 1931, Giessler was born in Berlin in 1911 and survived the war. He sank two ships (both on this patrol) of nearly 14,000 tons and was decorated with the Iron Cross 1st Class. After four patrols, Giessler moved into armaments until February 1945, when he served as 1st Watch Officer of the destroyer *Z20 Karl Galster* to May.

Kapitänleutnant Victor Vogel brought *U-588* back to the region on a complex and highly destructive nineteen-day patrol from May 10 to 28, 1942. On the day that he entered the area, he sank the British ship *Kitty's Brook* of 4,031 tons, with trucks on its deck, in Canadian waters. The day before he had damaged the 7,460-ton U.S.-flagged *Greylock* off the lightship *Sambro*, near Halifax, which provoked a counterattack and cost him two torpedoes. His attacks were to continue. First, *U-588* lay on the sea-bed to repair a cylinder-head, listening to a motorized sailboat hunting for them with an ASDIC (a sub-detecting pinging device named after the Royal Navy's anti-submarine division). Then they surfaced to load more torpedoes.[11]

Just as they cleared Cape Sable, *U-588*'s men had to dive to avoid air attack, then dog-legged back northeast for several days into the Gulf of Maine. On May 13, Vogel fired at a 4,989-ton steamer named *Egba* approaching Halifax and though it missed, the *Egba*'s officers raised the alarm and fired rockets. The following day off Cape Sable, the submarine was setting up an attack on a steamer in thick fog when it was very nearly rammed. At the last minute, Vogel managed to turn down and along "the starboard side of the steamer." The ship headed southward in the thick fog. On the 16th, an Allied plane surprised the U-boat at low altitude and sent two bombs which caused three or four fuses to blow. Then another plane and a destroyer attacked *U-588*, keeping her men on edge.

On May 17, *U-588* surprised the Norwegian tanker *Skottland* of 2,117 tons. Vogel observed: "flush-decker raked mast, and smokestack, protected by flying boat ahead." Undeterred, Vogel fired a fan of three torpedoes from about 1,200 feet, causing two heavy explosions after thirty-five seconds. Ten minutes later, the ship rolled over and sank, with the flying boat circling overhead. One man of the *Skottland*'s twenty-four perished.

Clearly an aggressive commander Vogel attacked and damaged the *Fort Binger*, a 5,671-ton British steamer west of Cape Sable the following day. *Fort Binger* was originally in Convoy ONS 92. It was an unusual attack since the lookouts spotted the two torpedoes from *U-588* and the ship swerved to avoid one projectile and was grazed by another. Vogel calculated that his first two shots missed "because steamer lay very high out. May have undershot ... was seen by the steamer." Then Captain Andre Jean Jacques Joly turned to ram the U-boat, which opened up fire twenty minutes later with its deck gun. After another attempt to ram the sub, a merchant crew member was killed and four others wounded. Vogel records:

> Steamer drives in wild zigzags, after a hit in the boiler stops it briefly, however it soon gets underway again, steamer returns fire. Impacts fall short. After hits in the bridge and waterline the steamer goes on opposite course smoking heavily ... ceased fire because the crew cannot see. Steamer lost in fog. Because there are several patrol vessels ahead and flares to starboard, [we] set off to the north. Five hits observed.[12]

The *Fort Binger* boldly made a run for Yarmouth Harbor which it reached safely, sending a boat ashore for medical assistance. The Royal Canadian Air Force sent out their crash boat the *Arresteur*, which picked up those crew who had abandoned the *Fort Binger*, and the Free French crew of sixty-one reboarded their ship. They barely escaped sinking, saved in part by a heavy fog. Indeed, on the 20th, a clearly exasperated Vogel logged: "return transit due to fuel, because in operations area continual fog. Moving off to the south. Finally, good visibility, weather with a clear horizon."

Vogel headed south until May 20 then southwest until the 22nd, where they encountered the U.S.-flagged, 3,282-ton *Plow City en route* from Trinidad to New York. *U-588* sank her at night with a single torpedo. The *Plow City* was in the process of fleeing a lifeboat and suspected U-boat (the *Peisander*'s lifeboat, their ship having been sunk by *U-653* under Feiler), and Vogel zeroed in on the resultant smoke from the stack. He fired an ETA-type torpedo from Tube IV, followed by an ATO-type torpedo from Tube III, and was surprised when "the ATO caught up with the ETO" to create a "huge explosion column," after thirty-five seconds. A *coup de grâce* brought down the after mast and transformed the *Plow City* from floating gracefully on an even keel to "sunk."

Though the ship's second mate was killed, thirty survivors managed to scramble into lifeboats. Vogel took one of the survivors aboard *U-588* then placed him in a lifeboat along with rum and cigarettes, noting "one man taken and transferred to a lifeboat." Even though there was only one ship named *Plow City*, Vogel was puzzled by different descriptions of whether the engines were coal or fuel-fired. On the 27th, the U.S. Navy patrol yacht U.S.S. *Sapphire*, PYc 2, rescued the men in the boats. When the U.S.C.G. cutter *General Greene* rescued the lifeboat of survivors from the *Peisander* (which had been approached by the *Plow City* before the ship fled into the periscope sites of Vogel), the *Greene* attacked a suspected U-boat contact. This could not have been *U-588*, as Vogel makes no mention of such an attack in the sub's log, and in fact the water was so shallow that the lifeboat anchored, meaning a U-boat could not have been submerged there and avoided grounding or being detected.

U-588 then headed southeast and the following day encountered the hapless British steamer *Margot* of 4,545 tons, bound from New York (Vogel was told Boston) to Trinidad, Cape Town, and ultimately Alexandria. Her general cargo included "aircraft parts," and explosives intended to help oust Field Marshal Rommel from North Africa. Vogel observed: "steamer armed with one 10.5-cm, one 4-cm astern and one 2-cm [gun] on bridge." The torpedo which Vogel fired hit *Margot*'s boilers amidships after thirty-nine seconds. She was sunk by artillery and gunfire early the next day. Out of forty-five men under Captain Henry Bell Collins, all but one survived. They were given rum by Vogel and his men, picked up four days later by the Swedish ship *Sagoland* and taken to New York.[13]

Following the attack on the *Margot* and three other ships, Vogel headed toward Cape Sable on the 26th and left the area about 300 miles south of Sable on May 28. The patrol began in St. Nazaire on April 19 and ended there on June 7. *U-588* was part of a group of other boats (*U-455*, *U-553*, and *U-593*) vectored to Cape Sable to intercept a convoy, but by May 4, the line was disbanded.

Vogel was born in Tübingen in 1912 and was twenty-nine. A member of the Crew of 1932, he served in minesweeping and anti-submarine fleets up to 1941 before joining U-boats in March 1941. In Hamburg that September, he took over command of *U-588*. His attacks resulted in seven ships sunk and two damaged of roughly 34,500 tons. Despite his audacity, Vogel received no decorations.

The 2,117-ton steamship *Skottland* was built in 1920 as the Dutch ship *Stad Zwolle* by Meyer and Company's Scheepsbouw Mij of Zalt-Bommel, near Amsterdam. Her original owners up to 1939 were the Halcyon Lijn of Rotterdam, which sold the ship to the Norwegian firm F. N. Nordbø in Haugesund. Thus, in 1942, Haugesund was her home port, and her master the Norwegian Captain Lauritz Jensen. The owners were Dampsk. A/S *Skottland*, or 'Shipowner, *Skottland*,' a single-ship firm not uncommon in ship-owning.[14] On April 25, the *Skottland* arrived in Halifax and on the 29th, she then sailed to St. John and Philadelphia. On May 12, she completed loading a full cargo of 1,575,467 feet of lumber and voyaged to New York, where she lay at anchor until May 1, awaiting instruction.

In New York, the ship was to pick up a pilot for Sydney then cross the ocean for London. As there is no record of a pilot being among the twenty-four men aboard the ship at the time of the subsequent attack, the pilot likely disembarked after transiting the Cape Cod Canal. The officers and crew were all Norwegians except for Norbin Folke, a Swedish engine-room stoker, Sven A. Lindell, another stoker from Sweden, Philip Seils, a British mess-room "boy," and Edward F. Simard, a Canadian ordinary seaman.

The *Skottland* headed up the East River, through Hell Gate and Long Island Sound, the navigators obtaining position fixes despite the fog by using the Radio Direction Finder (RDF) to triangulate shore features. They sailed through the Cape Cod Canal noting "nothing of Naval interest" until the morning of Sunday, May 17. Around midday, they were in a position roughly 170 miles east-northeast of Boston, in roughly the center of the Gulf of Maine.

Captain Jensen and his men were defensively equipped with two sets of machine guns; one each on either side of the after boat-deck, and one each on either wing of the navigating bridge. There was also a 3-inch gun mounted on the stern of the ship. The vessel is described as a "three-island" type, with "houses" located aft, midships and forward, and also had ten smoke floats of the cylindrical type, filled with oil. Also, on board were Merchant Signals (MERSIGS) and code books from the Royal Navy. Though operated by Nortraship, the *Skottland* was chartered to the British Ministry of War Transport.

Sunday morning began calm and clear, with a breeze of fewer than 10 knots from the southeast. The ship steamed on a straight course of 82 degrees eastward, without zigzagging, at 9 knots. Around the middle of the morning, the men were accompanied by the reassuring presence of a Royal Canadian Air Force plane out on patrol. At around 11 a.m., after flying overhead several times, the plane flew off and Captain Jensen and the officers initiated a lifeboat drill and gun practice. They left Folke Norbin at work in the engine room and three lookouts posted on the bow, stern and bridge amidships.

Twenty men were drilling when at 11.40 a.m. Second Mate Nils M. Ugstad saw "a break in waves with a flash of white water that lasted two seconds." He immediately called First Officer Konrad Naess over to corroborate the sighting, which was roughly 600 feet off the ship's port side. Other sailors saw a brief splash which they dismissed as a fish of some sort. They had just finished firing practice shots from the 3-inch gun aft. Then there was a "terrific explosion and everything was covered with steam. Lumber flew in all directions." The *Skottland* had been hit by two torpedoes fired by Victor Vogel in *U-588*. One struck between the number three and number four cargo holds, near the after mast. The other penetrated the fire room on the port side, killing Norbin, the stoker working there, then continued right through the space, bulging out the bulkhead on the starboard side over 4 feet.

The ship rolled to port, submerging and destroying all lifeboats and rafts on that side, and spilled vast quantities of dangerous timber into the ocean, so quickly that the men had to push the starboard lifeboats over that side of the ship and along the nearly horizontal ship to reach the water. They did the same with rafts. Captain Jensen was on the starboard bridge wing on impact and he ensured the secret codes were destroyed, grabbed other important papers from his cabin, and ran to help launch the boat. Third Engineer Olav Berg was below long enough to see steam fill the engine room, the power cut off, and the engines stop, before he raced for the deck. If they were not almost all on deck at the time, many more would have doubtlessly perished, as within four minutes, the *Skottland* broke in two, rolled over on its port side, and sank. There was no time to issue a mayday or swing the guns and fire, even though they were manned, as *U-588* was never seen.

Captain Jensen and twenty-two of his men found themselves in two life rafts and a lifeboat. He ordered them to look around the extensive wreckage for the missing fireman, in vain. During their search, and in the last moments that the ship teetered at a 90-degree angle, they observed a "prominent bulge, approximately 5 feet in diameter" below the bridge on the starboard side, opposite which the torpedo had struck. After half an hour of searching for Norbin, a friendly airplane returned. After circling the men, ascertaining that their ship had been sunk, and that they were at the mercy of the elements, the pilot flew off.

About seven minutes of steaming away, the airplane's pilot encountered a Canadian lobster boat named *O. K. Service IV* under Captain S. E. Himmelman. At 1.15 p.m., the fishermen were approached by the plane, which repeatedly flashed red lights, using a method of signaling with which the mystified fishermen were unfamiliar. Since signals failed to elicit the desired response, the pilot then opened fire with a machine gun off the bow of the *O. K. Service IV*. That caught their attention. The pilot then waved to them and they followed his plane for seven minutes until they could see the *Skottland*'s lifeboat and rafts.

Although the sea was covered for nearly 1 mile in timber and other wreckage, Himmelman and his men managed to pull all twenty-three survivors aboard their craft by 1.30 p.m. At that time, they were 60 miles from Seal Island Lighthouse. Two of the men were badly injured and four lightly hurt. For whatever reason, they decided to head to Boston, where they reached Pier One in South Boston. The pilot circled overhead until all the men were landed aboard the Canadian vessel, then signaled again and flew off. During the passage, everyone who could keep a very sharp lookout.

The *O. K. Service IV* made impressive time and docked the same day, the 17th, though another report has them arriving the following morning. Two ambulances from the Medical Corps arrived to take six of the men to the Boston Navy Yard Annex, across the channel from Charleston, in Chelsea Naval Hospital. Second Engineer Harold Ludvigsen and Second Mate Nils Ugstad had contusions and abrasions, and Ugstad had a fractured left wrist. Karl Myrsseth and Nils F. Olsen had fractured skulls and a leg respectively. British sailor Philip Seils fractured his left shoulder, and Canadian Edward Simard fractured his left ankle. Whereas Ugstad and Ludvigsen returned to their crew-mates and were "turned over" to the Norwegian Consul in Boston, the other four remained in hospital for a few more days.[15] U.S. Navy Reserve Lieutenant P. G. Tague and Ensign P. H. Skuse interviewed Captains Jensen, Himmelman, and other witnesses in Boston.

Two elements of the attack stand out. Captain Jensen and others expressed to interviewers their frustration at not having been able to strike back at the enemy, particularly as they were literally manning guns and ideally prepared to do so during the actual attack. Jensen said, "the whole thing happened so quickly that we were unable to do anything about it, particularly the one thing we wanted to do most, which was to get a few shots, at least, at our attacker." The naval interviewers added that "the survivors all expressed a strong desire to go to sea again as soon as billets could be found and appeared particularly incensed by the fact that they were unable at no time during this attack to fight back."

Another odd (and really amazing) fact is that as the men scrambled for their lives, one of them managed to find and keep hold of a fragment of one of the torpedoes that struck the *Skottland*. As the Navy reported, "a small fragment of what was determined by the 1 ND Demolition Officer to be the warhead of a torpedo was submitted by the survivors and subsequently sent to the Bureau of Ordinance." Before joining other ships, the men were taken to New York, where senior officers were interviewed by more U.S. Navy officials, on May 27.

Vogel's swathe of destruction in New England waters was far from over. The steamship *Fort Binger* was ordered in July 1917 and delivered by the Craig Taylor shipyard of Stockton-On-Tees in June 1919. In mid-1942, she was owned by William Thompson and Company and was on charter to the Ministry of War Transport (MoWT). The ship was 5,250 tons and her officers and crew were all Free French, meaning those Frenchmen who had resisted the German occupation in 1940 and fled France to continue the fight against Fascism from exile globally, including from Africa, the U.K., the Caribbean, and at sea. The *Fort Binger* had a colorful history: the British Shipping Controller named her the *War Ferret*; however, by the time construction was completed, World War I was over and her name was changed to the *Cornish City* with the St. Just Steamship Company (Sir William Reardon Smith and Sons, Cardiff) as owners. In 1929, the ship was sold to French owners named Française de Navigation à Vapeur Chargeurs Réunis in Paris. On August 29, 1940, the MoWT seized her at Douala, Cameroon, French West Africa. Between December 1940 and May 1941, the Free French Navy used her to bring troops to Port Sudan in the Red Sea, and in 1944, she was returned to Chargeurs Réunis.[16]

Approaching Canada in May 1942, the *Fort Binger*'s master was Captain Andre Jean Jacques Joly, supported by sixty other Free French sailors. The ship left Liverpool on May 6 and stopped in Belfast the following day in order to land an ill crew member. On May 8, she sailed for New York in ballast. As a result of her high-freeboard (which made the ship crankier to handle in heavy weather), she fell out of Convoy ONS 92 and carried on unescorted and alone. By the night of May 17, the *Fort Binger* was less than a third of the way across the Gulf of Maine and roughly 60 miles south of Yarmouth. For two days, she had been steaming at 11 knots and zigzagging. There were five lookouts spread from the bridge to the aft gun. The French were armed with a 4-inch gun and several smaller machine guns. The wind was very light at 3 knots, visibility was considered fair, though also described as "pitch darkness." There were no other ships visible, perhaps because the *Skottland* had been sunk in the general area less than ten hours before. The *Fort Binger* was heading nearly due west, at 251 degrees, and there was a slight swell.

Though it was very dark, a battle between lookouts began just after 10.05 p.m., with the eager eyes of *U-588*'s watchkeepers detecting the ship. Vogel quickly sent two well-aimed torpedoes toward the *Fort Binger*. The Germans, however, were quickly outwitted by the French, whose lookouts both saw and anticipated the torpedoes off the port bow. With sharp communication and action, the French helmsman jammed the rudder left to turn sharply to port. As a result, one torpedo passed harmlessly astern, and another caused just a glancing blow off the port bow. The torpedo that missed passed roughly 60 feet astern, and the one that struck the port bow dealt the vessel merely caused a "bumping" sensation among the crew. Having been detected 1,200 feet away, giving the helmsman time to evade, it did not even explode.

Captain Joly decided to use the *Fort Binger* as a weapon, so when twenty minutes later *U-588* surfaced roughly half a mile away, the ship twice attempted to ram it, throwing Vogel off-guard and disrupting the U-boat's follow-up attack. This did not prevent the Germans from pumping seven 3-inch shells and fifty rounds of machine gun fire at the *Fort Binger*, making their malice abundantly clear. Some of these found their mark at the bridge and side of the ship, and one crew member (forty-two-year-old cook Maurice Poba) was killed. Two were seriously and another slightly wounded. Blood was spilt and the battle was on.

The gunners on the *Fort Binger* were able to avenge their crewmates by sending four rounds of 4-inch shells at the sub when the two craft were only half a mile apart. They believed the U-boat was hit at least once, though the Germans claim they all fell short of the mark. The French also used a half a dozen machine guns. They had to pause when one of the German shells nearly disabled their boiler, then resumed the attack after sending emergency signals. The transmissions were successfully received by stations in Chatham (U.S.), Valentia and Camperdown (Canada), and Portishead Radio (U.K.). The stations all noted that the *Fort Binger* was being shelled and abandoned. This led to at least one report listing her as sunk. Captain Joly's second attempt to ram was hampered by severed steam pipes that reduced the ship's speed. He then headed into nearby fog banks and lay a course toward Nova Scotia and assistance. This tactic worked, as Vogel was unable to rediscover his quarry in the fog.

Meanwhile, Eastern Air Command received the ship's mayday and sent aircraft out to search for the *Fort Binger* and its antagonist, but they were unable to locate either. To inform the *Fort Binger* of their presence as well as warn off U-boats, the plane dropped pyrotechnics consisting of red Very lights and parachute flares. These were seen by the dueling vessels. The Allies believed the lights contributed to Vogel's belief that an air attack was imminent and hastened his retreat, and they were right. The RCAF noted that "it is believed ship and sub sighted flares dropped by plane, and sub submerged, fearing aircraft might be equipped with ASV," referring to anti-submarine vessel-detecting radar capabilities.[17] The situation was highly fluid and confusing to all involved. At roughly 11 p.m., *U-588* sauntered off, having been unable to sink the defiant ship or outwit its clever master. As a precaution, Captain Joly threw the British routing instructions and codes into the sea in a weighted box. Impressively, none of the mariners abandoned their ship, which other understandably terrified sailors had done on numerous similar occasions.

Joly and the *Fort Binger* made it to the entrance of Yarmouth, but because of the fog, they decided to anchor and repair the damaged steam pipes themselves. The radio set had been knocked out in the action against the submarine. The second officer was dispatched ashore with five men to obtain medical aid. Then the RCAF sent its crash (or rescue) boat the RCAF *M 305 Arresteur*, which delivered a physician on board. He tended to the wounded. The *Arresteur* was built in 1937 by Ditchburn Boats of Gravenhurst, Ontario for the Royal Canadian Mounted Police. She was 41 tons, had two 300-hp gasoline engines, was 67 feet long, 14 feet wide, and 5.5 feet deep.

The *Fort Binger* docked in Yarmouth at 11.30 p.m. on May 18. The following day at 12.33 p.m., the merchant ship *Ocean Honour* sighted *U-588* and proceeded unharmed into Halifax. On the 19th, the sailors upped their claim of hits on the sub to three. The *Fort Binger* arrived in New York on June 22. By the 24th, she was aground in the approaches the New York but worked herself free.

Vogel and all forty-six officers and crew were killed south of Greenland on their next patrol when the corvette H.M.C.S. *Wetaskiwin* and destroyer H.M.C.S. *Skeena* sank her with depth charges off Newfoundland on July 31. The *Fort Binger* was scrapped in 1950 by Briton Ferry. The *Arresteur* was sold in 1947 and renamed the *Linda Belle*. That year, she was wrecked and then written off by the owner's insurers.

The U.S.-flagged motor vessel *Plow City* of 3,282 tons was sunk off the New England coast on May 22, 1942. She was built by the Hedger Steamship Company in Newark in 1920. Her original name was the *Yapam* up to completion in March of that year, then the United States Shipping Board (U.S.SB) renamed her the *Plow City*. The ship was 336 feet long, 46 feet wide, and 25 feet deep. Twin steam-turbine engines of 386 horsepower moved her at 10.5 knots. Her owners between 1938 and 1942 were also Hedger Steamship of New York. The Charles Nelson Company of San Francisco were her owners from 1920 when the U.S.SB sold her to 1938.[18]

The *Plow City* was flagged to Wilmington and was carrying 4,971 tons of bulk bauxite ore from South America, destined for New York via Trinidad. The cargo owners and charterers were the Alcor Steamship Company in the aluminum smelting business, for which iron ore was a key component. There were thirty-one men aboard, led by Captain George Hazeleaf, a naturalized Swedish-American based in Oakland, where his wife lived. Born in 1882, he was sixty years at the time. Two other crew were naturalized Americans; a Norwegian and a Filipino. The *Plow City* departed Trinidad on May 10, with the 2,000-mile voyage projected to take eleven days. Routing orders were provided by British Naval Control officials on Port of Spain.

On the 20th, the men on the *Plow City* witnessed what they say was a vessel supplying a U-boat, which proceeded slowly alongside a ship, heading in a westerly direction. They specifically said they saw a tender of about 7,000 tons that had lights on the starboard side and a submarine on the other. The Americans claim to have passed far enough to the east of the other vessels that they were unseen. In fact, they saw the lifeboats of the ship *Peisander*, which was sunk by *U-653* under Gerhard Feiler on May 17 roughly 350 miles from Nantucket. Captain Angus Shaw and sixty-four officers, men, gunners, and passengers were cast adrift and undiscovered until the *Plow City* loomed over the horizon promising reprieve—or so they thought.

After dawn on Thursday, May 21 (their fourth day in the boats), the *Peisander* survivors sighted the *Plow City*. At 7.30 a.m., the ship was 4 miles away, but they were able to row 2 miles toward it. They tried to transmit a mayday message by the small wireless set, but it was not received. Half an hour later, the lifeboat and ship were only 2 miles apart when suddenly the *Plow City* changed course away from the boat and sent an SSS message along with their position. Captain Shaw recorded his position and determined they were 220 miles west-northwest of where the *Peisander* sank. Then, 140 miles south of Nantucket, they were picked up by U.S.C.G.C. *General Greene* and landed at Nantucket, then taken to Newport.

In the morning of May 21, the lookouts aboard *U-588* saw the smoke from the *Plow City*'s stack and began a four-hour pursuit of the ship. The Allied sailors soon spotted the submarine chasing them, as visual conditions were 12 miles, with no other ships in sight. At 9.30 a.m., the radio officer sent an SSS message on 500 kilocycles. Replies came from Tuckerton, New Jersey, and Nova Scotia. The ship was heading north-northwest, at 8 knots, with three lookouts: the second officer was on the bridge, one on deck, and a third forward on the forecastle. At between Force One and Force Two, there was only a very gentle breeze and flat seas.

Immediately, Captain Hazeleaf started to zigzag his ship, with a base course of 200 degrees and varying by 45 degrees each side of that course every ten minutes until 10.30 a.m., when *U-588* appeared to have abandoned the chase. Soon thereafter, the zigzagging was dropped. Then at 1.30 p.m., the submarine fired two torpedoes at the ship. The initial projectile passed ahead by a mere 5 feet, but the next torpedo penetrated the hull toward the stern at the waterline on the port side, just behind the number two cargo hold. The damage was "tremendous." The second officer, Fred C. Martin, was blown off the ship and never seen again; he was presumably killed on impact or drowned. The same torpedo cut off communications between the bridge and engine room; however, they were stopped manually when the team in the engine room managed to secure the engines.[19]

Very promptly, almost all of the men assembled and boarded two lifeboats. There was "some panic" by the crew in lowering the first lifeboat; however, rather than becoming infectious, the situation was "easily controlled by [the] captain." The radio officer remained behind to send SSS messages to shore. Twelve minutes later, Vogel sent a third torpedo at the starboard side of the engine room which sank the ship in three minutes. The crew, though they did not see any of the torpedoes, actually heard the third missile being fired from the nearby submarine, less than half a mile away. All of the captain's confidential papers were seen to sink with the ship in 1,100 feet.

Vogel then maneuvered among the two boats. The ship and its men were unarmed. The Germans took one of the Americans aboard to be questioned. When they returned the man fifteen minutes later, he was laden with rum and cigarettes. Vogel's English was described as "very good." The label on the cigarettes was in German and read "*Zigarettenfabrik, Hans Neuerburg, Kolna Rhein, Trierad Mosd, Hamburg Munchen Fugendicht, Verpackt, 25 Zigaretten, Barem Nidst*," meaning they were made by the Neuerburg firm in Hamburg and each pack contained twenty-five cigarettes. The rum label read "*Feiner Rum-Verschnett, Marke Plesse-Beruh D, Plesse-Wesermunde-Gegrundet 1870-Fernruf 138*," indicating the rum was blended in Wesermunde at a firm founded in 1870.

Vogel noticed that one of the "mess-boys," a Filipino, had a bleeding head wound and so he had the German crew provide bandages to him. This was actually Chief Cook Inocencio D. Sabido, the only Filipino on board. Two of the Germans (believed to be the gunnery officer and Vogel) inquired about the ship, cargo, destination, and departure ports. The Axis sailors then voluntarily turned a capsized lifeboat back upright for their victims. After men in both vessels heard "heavy caliber gunfire" coming from the southeast, the Germans motored off on the surface in that direction. It was 9.55 a.m., or about twenty-five minutes after the initial attack, and four-and-a-half hours after pursuit began.

Survivors described the U-boat as 200 feet long with an emblem of two colorful roosters fighting affixed to the conning tower in rainbow colors. The hull was grey, and the conning tower flanged and oblong. The bow was bulbous, and a cable ran from the conning tower to the stern. They estimated *U-588* at 550 tons and observed a smallish gun mounted 10 feet in front of the tower, with another about 7 feet behind it. Due to the fresh paint, they felt that the U-boat was quite new. The Americans believed the it was manned by a blend of German and Italian sailors, describing them all as "big husky young fellows."

The U.S. Coast Guard and U.S. Navy initiated a strident search for *Plow City* survivors. On May 22, a coast guard aircraft flew 248 miles in support of a destroyer and a patrol craft looking for them. Though a *PH 3* seaplane found "two empty life rafts and some wreckage," the survivors were probably already rescued by that time.[20] Once two lifeboats with occupants were reported by various sources heading northward, Headquarters of the Commander, Montauk Section, Third Naval District, ordered U.S.S. *YP 388*, U.S.S. *YP 389*, and U.S.S. *Sapphire*, PYc 2, to search exhaustively in designated squares for "two lifeboats adrift."[21] On May 26 at 11.01 a.m., the three vessels reported that they were on-station and searching. Less than six hours later, at 4.36 p.m., after five days adrift, the thirty survivors were found and rescued by the U.S.S. *Sapphire*, PYc 2, under Lieutenant (junior grade) F. C. Riley, Jr. (U.S.N.R.).[22] Almost immediately, the naval vessel came alongside the lifeboats.[23] They were taken to New London, where the large patrol yacht was based, arriving at 9.30 p.m. that evening.[24]

The *Sapphire* was built in 1929 as the *Margo* at George Lawley and Sons' well-known yacht yard in Neponset, Massachusetts for a Mr. B. A. Masse. Then Leon Mandel of Quonset, Rhode Island bought and renamed her the *Buccaneer*. As an exigency of war, the U.S. Navy purchased her in November 1940 and renamed it the *Sapphire*, with commissioning taking place in June 1941 in Boston. Her first naval commander was Lieutenant A. N. Daniels, and one of her crew was Ed Hickey.[25] Following the war, she was decommissioned in Charleston in October 1945, sold as the *Kirkland*, and sank in 1957. The vessel was 165 feet long, 25 feet wide, 12 feet deep, and could make 13 knots. It was propelled by twin 850-hp Cooper-Bessemer diesel engines.[26] Capable of carrying fifty-nine sailors, the little ship was armed with depth charges with a projector as well as a 3-inch gun.

The British steamship *Margot* of 4,545 tons was built by Lithgows of Glasgow in December 1926. Her owners in 1942 were Kaye, Son of London. During World War II, she sailed from New York once, on May 21, 1942. Her cargo was 5,500 tons of airplane parts, tanks, explosives, and other military stores intended to support the Allied armies in North Africa. Her charterers were Elliman Bucknell, whose agents were a firm named French Edy. The shipowner's agents in New York were Furness Withy. Her initial voyage was to Trinidad to refuel, then Cape Town and Suez via the Red Sea. She was only fated to make it a day out from port.[27]

On the final voyage, the *Margot* 's master was Henry Bell Collins, aged thirty-six. Duncan Stuart Miller, aged twenty-one, was radio operator, and one of the firemen was Mohamed Aham Hassan, aged twenty; they were all British citizens. There were thirty-nine men on board, seven of them from the subcontinent. At 3.30 p.m. on May 22, the *Margot* was several hundred miles southeast of

Nantucket when she was struck by a torpedo from *U-588*. The ship's defensive armament consisted of a 4-inch gun, Twin-Marlin, Hotchkiss and Lewis machine guns, a 12-pound gun, Oerlikon, and PAC rockets and kites. The two Royal Army and three Royal Navy gunners on board to man them were never used in the subsequent fight. Captain Collins sailed per British routing instructions. He was given no forewarning of enemy submarines in the area.[28]

At the time, Collins and his men had the ship going 9.75 knots to the southeast. They were not zigzagging, and four lookouts scanned the horizon: two aft and one on either side of the monkey deck above the bridge. Though all of them were equipped with strong binoculars, none of them sighted the torpedo streaking toward them until it was too late. That could be due to a considerable swell and a roughly 15-knot easterly breeze; however, visibility is described as excellent. Degaussing was active but ineffective.

Vogel's torpedo slammed into the coal stokehold on the starboard side, causing a dull explosion and a smell of burning cordite, or torpedo fuses. Fireman and trimmer Hassan was killed on impact. The accommodations cabins on the starboard side were flooded by a high geyser of water. The impact caused the ship's exhaust funnel to crash down, bringing with it the aerials, so no distress message could be sent. Despite all this, the actual detonation caused just a dull thud, with some of the men not even realizing right away that the ship had been torpedoed. Even though the men closed the watertight doors between the holds, or partitions of the ship, as a precaution before the attack, both the engine room and stokehold quickly flooded with seawater, and the engines died. The *Margot* was then a sitting-duck for *U-588*'s gunners.

The merchant ship was equipped with a pair of small jolly boats for harbor work, as well as two larger lifeboats, the starboard of which was destroyed by the torpedo attack. Collins threw the confidential codes and wireless books into the sea in a weighted, perforated box. Three of the men were injured and one (Hassan) missing. Ten minutes after the attack, the three boats were ordered to be lowered and the ship abandoned. At 3.40 p.m., *U-588* surfaced about a half-mile off the port side and hastened the abandonment by firing six or more machine gun bursts. Since the ship was rapidly swinging around, the machine gun volleys mostly landed off the starboard side "as a warning to us," Collins wryly observed.[29]

Soon, the crippled ship had pivoted to port, so that the starboard side was exposed to the sub. Just as the abandonment was completed, *U-588* began shelling her. It was roughly 3.45 p.m., and by then, Collins had the thirty-eight survivors distributed in three boats and clear of the ship. The Allied sailors counted twenty explosive shells fired at the *Margot*. Only nine, or less than half of them, were observed to hit the hull; however, these had the effect of collapsing the bridge and setting the ship ablaze from stem to stern, with ammunition exploding.

Vogel first brought his submarine to Second Officer J. Robinson's boat and asked standard questions about cargo and destination. Eight German sailors were seen on the conning tower and manning 50-caliber-looking machine guns. Two officers addressed them: one named Muller, about twenty-nine years, dark complexioned and clean-shaven; and the other with a naval insignia on his uniform, a dark mustache and goatee, who was described as "Latin-looking." The latter did not speak but stood on deck with his arms folded across his chest. They know Vogel remained on the conning tower, since when Muller gave the Brits the commander's name, he pointed at the conning tower. After questioning the second mate, Muller offered them a bottle of rum. However, this bottle was not easy to transfer, as the waves, piling up around, push the boat out from the side of the sub and made it dangerous for a frail lifeboat to approach. Muller then tied a line around the neck of the bottle and tossed the line to men in the boat, who untied it and returned the line.[30]

Next, the U-boat sailors motored over to Captain Collins' boat. Vogel was described as "a dark man with a black beard, slim and about 5 feet, 10 inches in height." Vogel did not address the Allies directly; rather, he again deferred to Muller, who asked Collins lots of questions about his family, why he went to sea, and demonstrated Vogel's name by flapping his arms to imitate a bird, for which Vogel stands in English. The Allies said they were sailing for South Africa, which was only partly true. The Germans, of course, would have known the likely destination was Egypt.

Collins and his men were also offered, and accepted, a bottle of rum, a sample of which he saved for Navy officials to analyze. Muller ordered a sailor below to retrieve the second bottle. Since they didn't have an opener in the jolly boat, Collins asked Muller to pull to cork for him, to which the German replied, "Oh yes, excuse me. This will do you for Saturday afternoon." Collins could not resist asking him, "Well, why the hell did you sink me on a Saturday?" to which Muller retorted "Oh well, the fortunes of war." Collins feels he would have been offered cigarettes, except that his personal packet was visible to Muller at the time, giving the impression that the Allies had enough already. After the rum had been opened, Muller recorked it lightly and threw it across the water to Collins, who caught it.

Muller refused to tow the *Margot*'s survivors toward land, saying the U-boat was "too busy and in a hurry." However, he promised to send an SOS on their behalf. Collins then wagered that he would not, and in fact, Muller did not. Collins observed that a pair of white roosters "with heads erect, wings furled, facing each other," sparring off were painted on the conning tower. This description aligns very closely with the actual emblem painted on *U-588*'s tower at the time.[31] The conversation having played itself out, Muller wished the Brits good luck and motored over to the *Margot*'s burning hulk. Then they poured twenty-four more shells into the bow section while circling it from a distance of roughly two ship's lengths. The stricken vessel was seen to sink at 6 p.m. that evening. Roughly half an hour later, after taking film footage of the attack and meandering around the wreckage looking for items of interest, *U-588* motored off "leisurely to the southward, apparently quite confident of not being spotted by aircraft or by surface vessels."

Without a mother ship or anyone ashore knowing of their fate, Collins had to choose their next moves carefully, and he did. First, he divided the men equitably according to the size of their boats: Collin's jolly boat had eight men, Chief Officer F. W. Gardiner's boat had nine, and the balance of twenty-two occupied the larger lifeboat. Collins rationed water to half a dipper four times a day. A dipper was an essential symbol of efficiency and authority: it was a small rust-proof tube holding from one to six ounces of liquid. Utilizing a chain or twine lanyard of around twenty inches, it would be lowered into a wooden cask of fresh water with which lifeboats were required to be equipped, allowing distribution of water to take place with minimal spillage and maximum fairness. Collins also doled out ample rations, including chocolate and the less popular, thirst-inducing Horlicks tablets, and determined that whether they had wind or not, the men would keep busy. That meant that after the breeze died, ending a night of sailing some 40 miles, Collins put the sailors to rowing in shifts of half an hour, followed by two hours of rest.

Most importantly, Collins insisted that the boats stay together and that they retrace their route from New York in the hopes of meeting traffic outbound from that port. His strategy paid off. Morale and health remained high in the lifeboats, and the three injured men remained alive. The night of the 23rd, around midnight, Collins saw a blue flare resembling a star-shell which went high in the air but did not come down. It originated in the direction of the attack. Could it have been Hassan on some flotsam, signaling for help? On the 24th, planes were heard overhead but not seen—probably traffic to Bermuda or the Caribbean. For over three days, until May 26, all boats remained in sight of one another; however, on that date, fog set in and the lifeboat was separated from the two jolly boats.

The following day, Collins used a portable wireless set to try to reunite with the lifeboat, but to no effect. Then, in the evening, Third Officer G. F. Eaton in command of the lifeboat managed to attract the attention of the Swedish refrigerated ship *Sagoland*. According to Collins, they were roughly 85 miles from the U-boat attack and 165 miles from the U.S. coast when found. Eaton prevailed upon the captain of the *Sagoland* to look for the men in the two jolly boats; however, the Swede was understandably concerned for the vulnerability of his ship while stopped to retrieve survivors, particularly as the British sailors had recently been torpedoed in the area. Good fortune continued to shine on the *Margot*'s survivors, favoring the prepared. The *Sagoland* posted extra vigilant lookouts, who spotted the jolly boats twenty-five minutes later, at 6 p.m.; Collins and Gardiner and their men lit off smoke floats that attracted attention, and by 6.40 p.m., all the *Margot*'s survivors were safely aboard the *Sagoland*. To save time the three boats were stripped of equipment, their plugs were pulled, and they were scuttled, rather than risk retrieving them.

As luck would have it, the survivors were taken directly to New York on May 28 (the following day). The three injured men were hospitalized and the British consular officials supplied them all with "a complete new set of clothes and all toilet necessities." The *Sagoland* was a refrigerated cargo ship of 3,243 tons, which departed New York seven times in 1940 and 1941, and three times in 1942, sailing on May 23, 1942, roughly three weeks after delivering the *Margot*'s officers and men.[32] She was built in 1939, and owned by Svenska Orient Linien, Swedish Levant and Swedish Orient Line. She was built by Eriksbergs Mekaniska Verkstad of Göteborg and survived the war. In 1963, she was sold to Zafir of Panama, renamed *Cyclades*, then again in 1971 sold to Marmarine Shipping and renamed the *Apostolos M*. Finally, in 1975, the ship was sold to Marimar of Panama, then, in 1978, it was grounded and wrecked.

Interrogation by naval officers in the U.S. and the U.K. revealed that the Allied sailors felt that the submarine was exceptionally small (less than 100 feet long) and just out of drydock. The sailors also deduced that, since the submariners had little facial hair and lots of rum and cigarettes, they must have resupplied from a base in the Caribbean or elsewhere. Finally, the fact that aircraft were heard by the men in the boats at the same time every day indicated to them that the enemy could predict and anticipate their arrival, and thus avoid them.

Radio Operator Miller was sunk on another ship, the *City of Athens*, that October and survived again. Captain Collins was not so fortunate: when his ship the *Empire Turnstone* was hit and sunk by *U-261* on October 23, 1942, he perished in the cold waters south of Iceland. So, too, did his shipmate from *Margot*, Bosun Reginald Lloyd Edwards, age thirty-five.[33] No doubt, the survivors of the *Margot* benefited with their lives from Collins' level-headedness, discipline, and care for his men. Though he was criticized in subsequent reports for abandoning ship too quickly and not firing back, had he fired on the approaching submarine, which remained at least half a mile away and had far greater range with their guns, more of his men would likely have joined Mohamad Aham Hassan in death.

Two months later, on July 31, 1942, *U-588* was caught south of Greenland and sunk by H.M.C.S. *Wetaskiwin* and H.M.C.S. *Skeena* using depth charges. There were no survivors out of forty-six men.[34]

8

U-213 Inserts the First German Saboteur into the Bay of Fundy

Oberleutnant zur See Amelung von Varendorff took *U-213*, a type VIID minelayer, into a complex twenty-three-day patrol of New England in May 1942. He as the first U-boat to probe the Bay of Fundy. The boat was nicknamed the *Star of Scapa Flow* since von Varendorff had been 2nd Watch Officer aboard Gunther Prien's *U-47*.[1] The original plan was to load *U-213* with mines; however, because of problems with dockside cranes and the pressure to get a secret agent (known to the crew only as a propaganda officer) aboard, they were never loaded.

On leaving Biscay around Cape Finisterre, the boat was attacked with seven depth charges from the air. The spy, Alfred Langbein, observed first-hand that morale aboard *U-213* was deplorable: during the attack, von Varendorff lay inert in his bunk with a loaded pistol by his side to kill himself with. Young crewmen cried and banged their heads against chains and the hull while officers slapped them around. Later on, a fight between a radioman and a senior officer regarding showing pictures of loved ones escalated into a shouting match, the smashing of the radioman's photo of his mother, and a go-slow work protest that may have included sabotage of the sub's equipment. As a consequence, von Varendorff deprived the men of treasured cigarette breaks on the conning tower, which can only have spiked stress levels. Langbein describes another case when an officer learned of the birth of his son, then fell into a despair of homesickness.[2] In the enclosed, informal confines of a submarine, such negativity spreads and infects crewmates with particular speed. Von Varendorff later commended the same officer, noting "the behavior of the Second Watch Officer was sure and assertive and contributed to the success of the landing."

No ships were sunk on this patrol, in part due to dense fog off Canada. On May 12, von Varendorff motored northwest from into the Gulf of Maine, passing west of Yarmouth and entering the Bay of Fundy, infamous for its massive tides and currents, the next day. He was already planning "afterwards possibly cracking a steamer off St. John." On the west, or New Brunswick, side of the bay, von Varendorff affected Langbein's landing near Saint Martins, northeast of St. John. The purpose of Operation Grete was to have Langbein provide German handlers with information on convoys to and from Halifax.

While re-emerging from the Bay of Fundy on the 15th, *U-213* was surprised on the surface in fog by an Allied four-stack destroyer painted white, which slightly damaged the U-boat with over "ten heavy detonation again in the direct vicinity of the boat." This resulted in cracked battery cells and a torpedo that went rogue as a "runner" in the casing. Since "the entire bow room filled with smoke and hydrogen odor," they were forced to surface and ventilate the boat. The submarine managed to escape to the south and exited the area southeast of Cape Sable on May 18 but was not to be so fortunate ten weeks later. On the 19th, the Germans made crash-dives several times to avoid flying boats. *U-213* then returned to the waters off Cape Sable, where it performed circular patrols between May 22 and June 6 in a dense cluster southeast of Nantucket. This was part of Operation Padfinder. On May 26, von Varendorff expended the entire day stalking and firing three torpedoes at an Allied steamer, all of which missed due to errors in data feeds between instruments. The search was abandoned as the steamer clawed away.[3]

On the 30th, the men underwent more crash dives from flying boats, then *U-213* entered the steamer lane to find prey. The opening day of June brought more frustrating errors: the commander fired another three-torpedo fan at what he took to be a destroyer, but all missed. This time the depth-settings had been set incorrectly, costing him "a unique opportunity that will not offer itself again." The young skipper coached himself, writing "exact data, be calm, take time, do not rush." He then added his opinion, based on the recent example, of an American destroyer:

> [It] rarely constitutes a danger when, as in this case, one is paying such close attention. He saw nothing. That I was not seen by the enemy is beyond me. Since visibility and distance for him represented the best conditions. I am not sure what a single destroyer is doing in this area. While proceeding independently there is more danger than prospects for him to successfully perform U-boat hunting.[4]

Von Varendorff was referring to the visibility advantages which the destroyer had: his enemies were positioned at a greater elevation above sea-level on the bridge of a destroyer and thus had a better height-of-eye, than submariners. They also had more men, and perhaps even radar, plus also the advantage of being on home territory with more assets—waterborne and airborne—at their request. Again, on June 2, a full day and five torpedoes were expended on a ship that outpaced the U-boat and therefore should have been ignored much sooner. Tube I was a miss from 4,500 feet. Later, Tube III a runner, "pushing a water column ahead of it ...

passed behind [the ship]. Now the freighter runs at high speed." Tube IV fired yet missed, crossing behind the ship and to its other side. Sub accelerated to 16 knots to overtake the ship. Tube III was a surface runner in smooth seas, also behind the ship. Stern shot attempted from Tube V, resulting in a miss. Bitterly, the attack was then broken off.

Although the first few prospective victims did not inform the Eastern Sea Frontier of *U-213*'s attempts to sink them, the U-boat attack on "a large freighter of about 7,000 GRT with a brown superstructure ... general course about 300" degrees was the Norwegian ship *Bañaderos*. The vessel was heading toward New York from Para, Brazil, at the same time and place, on a course of roughly 300 degrees. She left Para on May 24 and arrived in New York on June 4, 1942. The captain reported: "sighted periscope ... about 345 miles East of Winter Quarter Shoals." That position corresponds roughly with that of *U-213*. In fact, they are 29 miles apart, and given the area covered in the attack, that the chase lasted over six hours and covered roughly 60 miles, with both vessels going off dead reckoning and sporadic sun sights during a time of high stress, it had to have been them, though the estimated tonnage for the *Bañaderos* was off, the color of the superstructure was unknown, and not all times align. The only other boat in the area at that time was *U-578* under Rehwinkel; however, he was busy sinking another Norwegian ship, the *Berganger*, at that time.[5]

On the way back, von Varendorff, ever observant and critical, points out that "in wind and sea, speed is sharply reduced and at the same time greatly increased fuel consumption. This is a very big disadvantage of the Type VIId boats." They began to limp back to France with "a beating shaft and a failed supercharger ... no longer fully operational." On the 3rd and 4th, they crash-dived to avoid flying boats. Then they avoided destroyers on the 4th and steamer noises on the 5th, but too much rain for visual fixes. On June 6, after dodging several flying boats, and in poor weather, *U-213* began its homeward voyage, with von Varendorff deciding to take his sub into the warm waters of the Gulf Stream in order to get a boost from the current.

Von Varendorff was born in 1913 in Kiel and sank no ships as a commander, which upset *Großadmiral* Dönitz. He was a member of the Crew of 1935. According to his passenger, Langbein, in April and May 1942, "morale ... was shaky—beginning with the captain ... who had kidney problems, and suffered from rheumatism, was clearly homesick and lonely for his wife." Furthermore, von Varendorff is said to have belittled Gunther Prien, loathed Nazi propaganda based on his religious convictions, and "was extremely nervous and in moments of tension his skin would tighten over his cheekbones and the pupils of his eyes expand and contract rapidly."[6] Nine days into their next patrol, *U-213* was tracking Convoy OS 35 when it was attacked west of the Azores and sunk by depth charges from H.M.S. *Erne*, H.M.S. *Sandwich*, and H.M.S. *Rochester*, L 50, on July 31, 1942. All fifty submariners perished. Von Varendorff was twenty-eight.

Operation Grete, named for the sole agent's wife, was the first of half a dozen landings by German spies planned for the U.S. and Canada, of which four initially succeeded. The effort—long anticipated by Hitler as a vital first strike against America akin to their bold, preemptive, Doolittle Raid on Japan—can be read as a predictor for the others, as they initially succeeded thanks to the skills of U-boat commanders, then failed due to the shortcomings (and surrender) of the teams ashore. The only saboteur in this mission was *Kriegsmarine leutnant* (*Abwehr*) M. Alfred Langbein. He wore a Navy sailor's standard-issue leather pants rather than officer's uniform aboard *U-213* and was introduced to the men as a "naval lieutenant attached to the Ministry of Propaganda and People's Enlightenment." Within three hours of his arrival in Lorient with heavy packages on April 23, the sub whisked him into the Atlantic. Lovely weather encouraged Allied aircraft to attack, and the U-boat to submerge repeatedly.[7]

The trans-Atlantic voyage proceeded as planned, though heavy winter seas reduced headway and increased fuel consumption. At first, the idea was for Langbein to be landed on Cape Breton Island, north of Nova Scotia; however, Langbein did not like having to take a ferry to his destination. Using British Admiralty charts, he and von Varendorff decided instead to use the indented coast of St. Martins, in the Bay of Fundy, because of its proximity to both a road and a rail line. Von Varendorff was understandably cautious, and crept passed the beaming lights of St. John, New Brunswick, at night in order to spend the following day on the seabed. Despite the sub being caught several times in the beams of a lighthouse, its commander pressed on unperturbed. From 6.30 a.m. to 10.30 p.m. on May 13, *U-213* lay submerged in 165 feet of water 2 miles from the St. Martin's Light. The immense tides swung the boat like a compass needle.

On surfacing in darkness to recharge the batteries and refill its bottles of compressed air, the sub headed east to the mouth of the Big Salmon River the following day. It was a wise choice as there were no significant roads or communities for 35 miles from St. Martins to Alma, further up the coast, thus a minimal chance of detection. As they approached to within 1,000 feet of the shore, the sailors found themselves "hemmed in by an opaque grey curtain" of fog.[8]

At twenty minutes after midnight on May 14, Langbein provided a pistol and letters as well as his naval uniform to von Varendorff and was given cash, radio equipment, a shovel, blanket and identification papers. Second Watch Officer Kueltz and two sailors rowed Langbein toward shore, hearing the clang of a navigational buoy along the way. It took twenty minutes before they were out of sight. High, steep cliffs and strong winds prevented a smooth landing until Keultz decided on a beach situated 1.25 miles southwest of the river mouth. Kueltz, Langbein, and a sailor toting the radio trudged up 250 feet of rock face to a plateau. Thereafter Langbein was left to fend for himself. They had lost the blanket. The first thing Langbein did to fulfill his mission was attempt to carry the radio. After a few yards, he gave up and buried it shallowly, throwing the shovel down a gully. Then he fell asleep under a tree, wearing U.S.-made clothing provided to the *Abwehr* earlier by Nazis arriving in Germany from America.[9]

Aboard *U-213*, von Varendorff was becoming anxious, motoring vulnerably back and forth off the Big Salmon River and an enemy shore on a windy night. The incredibly strong Fundy currents were clawing his submarine both from shore and the men in the dinghy trying to find them. After more than two-and-a-half hours, at 3 a.m., the men on the submarine sent a light signal as arranged, to which there was no reply. Finally, at 4.30 a.m., Kueltz and the two German sailors were sighted struggling toward *U-213* in the gloom. Fortunately, four hours and ten exhausting minutes after they left, the duo were quickly retrieved. *U-213* then headed southwest in the dark until off of St. John, where they submerged for the day again. The next day, von Varendorff transmitted to German headquarters "have carried out task." *U-213* was shortly thereafter attacked by an Allied destroyer in the fog, probably having intercepted the signal.

Ashore, Langbein's job was to head east to Halifax and report back to Germany on the incredible assemblages of convoys there. Instead, he walked and hitchhiked south to St. Martins, where he shopped and made a small donation to the Red Cross outside the store, receiving in exchange a receipt.[10] Contrary to his expectation, there was no railway line from St. Martins to Sussex and the outside world, so he hitch-hiked on logging trucks to St. John, saying that a cold prevented him from speaking beyond a whisper, though he had lived in Canada before and spoke English well.

Though his original instructions were for him to bury most of the cash along with the radio equipment until he could establish a base in Halifax, then retrieve both, Langbein kept the cash and ditched the radio, burying it where it was easily found by him and Canadians later. Furthermore, when he came to the critical railway junction in Moncton, he was supposed to go right, or east, toward Halifax, but instead headed left, west, and inland for Montreal. He later admitted his plan to find work in mines in northern Ottawa and ended up leading a largely reclusive, self-indulgent life for two-and-a-half years. Langbein never offered a credible reason for why he abandoned his mission—for which fifty of his countrymen aboard *U-231* had risked their lives—essentially at its inception. It was the beginning of a pattern in which the Germans invested a tremendous amount in men, all of them American or Americanized, who failed to even approach delivering on them, and whose loyalty and commitment proved largely baseless. One lingering question is whether the *Abwehr* itself, led by Admiral Canaris, who went on to betray Hitler (and was killed by him) sent men on missions it deemed doomed to fail, though this is conjecture.

As planned, Langbein became Alfred Haskins of Edmonton. He could not find work without Canadian selective-service papers and used instead the receipt from the Red Cross to help establish his identity. Moving with impunity, he rode a train to Montreal, where the police released him on his own recognizance following a raid on a brothel, where he claimed to have been waiting to change currency. Langbein then made for Ottawa, Canada's capital, further north. There, he became so comfortable and spent his U.S.-dollar cash with such abandon that he earned the nickname "Mr. Fifty-Dollar Bill." He had been issued 140 $50 bills, worth $7,000—a very considerable sum at the time—as well as twelve Canadian $1 bills that turned out to be outdated and physically too large.

Ironically, when a Canadian military officer, the brother of a young lady (Eva Rose) Langbein was courting, declared in a taxi that Langbein was a spy and lunged for him, the Canadian (not the German) was ejected from the cab for his antics. Fortunately for Langbein, the issue never arose again.[11] He spent most of his time playing cards with polyglot staff of his guest house—the lonely banding together. On a springtime outing with them to a park, he chose a snow-covered crevice under a rock to hide a large portion of his cash; however, despite frequently returning to look for it, he never found it again. This error significantly reduced his survivability, yet he never took up employ or undertook the espionage he was sent to Canada to perform.

After twenty-nine months of living the high life, as well as the anxiety of being caught behind enemy lines, Langbein ran out of money and turned himself in to Canadian authorities in October 1944. At first, the Royal Canadian Mounted Police and British M15 interrogator Cyril Mills did not believe him; however, he led police to where his radio and uniform had been buried near St. Martins. Unable or unwilling to press charges against him, they interviewed him at length, trying to make up for obvious intelligence failings early in the war. His inactivity may have saved him after all: without having contacted his handlers, Lanbgein was not a good prospect to turn into a double-agent. He was interned in Fredericton, New Brunswick until after VE Day. Ultimately, the Canadians simply sent him back to Germany and to Mrs. Grete Langbein. After all, his father had correctly predicted that going to America as a spy was probably safer for his son than playing cannon-fodder for politicians on the Eastern Front.[12]

9

Two U-boats Attack the *Peisander*, the *Mattawin*, and the *Fort Qu'Appelle*

Kapitänleutnant Gerhard Feiler brought *U-653* for a three-day patrol through southwestern New England between June 4 and 6, 1942. Entering south of Montauk, the submarine headed east for a day and out of the region. Though no ships were sunk during this incursion, *U-653* sank the *Peisander* on May 17. During an attack of June 2, the sub was bombed by aircraft and patrol craft, and was leaving a stain of leaking diesel, what Feiler called "a quite heavy oil trace," which they determined to repair. On June 3, Feiler and his men detected a Navy patrol boat nearby but ran off, and they heard other destroyers' noises too, but only faint steamer sounds.[1] By June 6, they had pumped the diesel from a tank in order to store saltwater there for ballast purposes. In that way, they "fixed" the leaking oil issue, as the tank just leaked salt water. A destroyer and tender passed, then *U-653* motored toward New York and away from New England, passing on attacking the Portuguese neutral *Lobito*. On the 7th, Feiler was extremely disappointed to waste four torpedoes set too deep on a shallow patrol vessel.

This patrol began in Brest on April 25 and ended there on July 6. On May 21, *U-653* was part of an eight-boat line called *Padfinder* looking for Allied ships east of Hatteras that disbanded soon after. On June 7, *U-653* sank U.S.S. *Gannet* north of Bermuda. On the way back to France, *U-653* refueled from U-tanker *U-459* west of the Azores around June 22. Feiler was born in Breslau in 1909 and lived until 1990, aged eighty. A member of the Crew of 1933, he first served aboard the destroyer *Z20 Karl Galster* before joining U-boats in 1940. He commissioned *U-653* in May 1941. After two years and seven patrols, he moved ashore to the 1st U-boat Flotilla, 20th U-boat Flotilla, and 19th U-boat Flotilla, mostly in training capacities. He sank or damaged five ships of over 25,000 tons and was awarded the German Cross in Gold.

The British motor ship *Peisander* was on a voyage from Australia to Liverpool via Panama when she was torpedoed and sunk by Feiler. The *Peisander* was completed in April 1925 by Caledon Shipbuilding and Engineering in Dundee, Scotland. Weighing 6,225 tons, she was 432 feet long and 55 feet wide. Twin-diesel engines propelled the ship at 13.5 knots when built. In 1942, the ship was owned by Alfred Holt and Company, which was known as the Blue Funnel Line, or Ocean Steamship Company, of Liverpool.[2] The ship traded mostly in the Far East and Pacific at the outset of World War II. On December 20, 1937, the *Singapore Free Press and Mercantile Advertiser* promoted the *Peisander*'s voyage from there to New York via Cape Town, leaving January 8, 1938.[3] On January 31, 1942, the British Admiralty noted that *Peisander* was not in Convoy MS 1, which arrived in Singapore the day before, and just weeks before that base fell to the Japanese. When built, the ship was fitted with eight boats to carry Chinese passengers; she would need them.

On her final voyage, the *Peisander* departed Newcastle, Australia, on March 15, 1942. Her cargo consisted of 6,590 tons of wheat and 97 tons of wool and tungsten, bound for her home port, Liverpool, via the Panama Canal. In Panama, the ship loaded consular mail for London and other bags of ordinary general post office mails. On Wednesday, May 13, the destroyer U.S.S. *Davis*, DD 395, came upon the *Peisander* 125 miles north of Puerto Rico at 9.49 a.m., 12 miles apart. Thinking the *Peisander* might be a U-boat supply ship, the U.S. Navy men went to battle-stations until they could verify otherwise. Then, *Peisander* men did not sight any other ships, only Allied aircraft.[4]

Captain Angus Shaw was responsible for sixty other persons aboard the *Peisander*: three gunners and fifty-seven merchant mariners. The chief officer was F. C. Brown of Smiths Cottage, Latham, Lancashire. Second Mate W. Thomas hailed from Childwell, Liverpool, and Third Mate I. H. Browning was from Weston-super-Mare, Somersetshire. The ship was armed with a 4-inch gun, two Lewis machine guns, two Hotchkiss machine guns, three depth charges, four parachute flares, and kites.[5] On Sunday, May 17, at midday, the *Peisander* was 300 miles southeast of Nantucket. Captain Shaw had obeyed his Admiralty routing instructions by passing through the Mona Passage, then at least 25 miles east of Bermuda. The ship was zigzagging continuously during the day, varying between three different patterns.

Before 1 p.m., Shaw was just enjoying a midday lunch below the bridge. There were two lookouts on the bridge, another aft by the gun and a fourth in the crow's nest up forward. The weather was "fine and clear, the sea was moderately rough with a heavy swell, and there was a southeasterly wind" of about 20 knots. Unbeknown to Shaw, *U-653* has been following his ship for several hours, thrown off by the constant zigzagging (then in Admiralty pattern eleven). Feiler refused to be entirely deterred, and he had plenty of sea room and no opposition. He first sighted the *Peisander* at 10.20 a.m., observing that she was armed with a gun, anti-aircraft weaponry, and was painted dark grey; he estimated her tonnage at 4,500.

At 1.01 p.m., Feiler fired two torpedoes, with the first seen by Able-Bodied Seaman W. M. Galor of London in the crow's nest up forward. It passed some 17 feet ahead of the ship, but before an alarm could be sounded or anything done about it, the second torpedo struck the starboard side, after a fifty-nine-second run. According to Feiler, this resulted in a large water-column erupting on the side of the ship. He noticed that, at first, the crew remained on board, and because of their guns, he remained submerged.

Captain Shaw was quite a descriptive skipper, relating how "the noise was jarring, as if the vessel had grounded on a hard rock. There was no flash, but a column of water shot up mast-high." This must have caused quite a fright to young Galor in the crow's nest. Two of the boats on the starboard side, which had been swung out in the event of an emergency, were immediately destroyed. Shaw noted that "the after deck was flooded and littered with lifeboat debris and concrete blocks from the starboard wing of the bridge." Those blocks and other *ad hoc* materials were used by jittery mariners to shore up defenses of the bridge and other sensitive areas, knowing that U-boat or German raider gunners often targeted the radio shacks and bridges for quick destruction.

The damage reports reaching Shaw were quite dire: the wireless apparatus was a tangled mess, so that no SSS message could be sent, the engine room was flooded to the platform plates, probably because the engine room plates had been stoved in by the explosion. Hold two and hold three forward were flooded. The *Peisander* was already listing 5–10 degrees to starboard. The engines had stopped and the ship was losing headway. Shaw decided to order abandon ship and turned the wheel hard to port in order to do so.

The *Peisander* was originally equipped with eight lifeboats to accommodate 400 passengers and crew. On the starboard side, boat one and boat three were smashed, and boat five was swung inboard, meaning that it was both harder to launch and on the same side as an enemy U-boat that could fire another torpedo at any time. Boat five was thus never launched. Three lifeboats on the port side were undamaged, and thus were the only ones launched. Shaw destroyed the secret code books then threw the ship's log and some navigational equipment into a suitcase and into one of the boats; the three boats cast off with all sixty-one persons in them.

They rowed 600 feet and waited to see what would happen next. Then, twenty-seven minutes after the first attack, at 1.28 p.m., Feiler fired a single G7e, high-precision torpedo at the ship. Sixty-seven seconds later, this projectile found its mark. The submarine commander recorded hearing six explosions after seeing another high water-column. Attributing the residual explosions to boilers, he watched the ship slowly sink after sixteen minutes (Shaw's timings differ from Feiler's by about fifteen minutes). Feiler complained that he could not read the name of the ship on the hull, and since no SSS message had been sent, he never did learn his victim's name. Why the submariners never approached the lifeboats for this information is not known, perhaps because Feiler was cautious. Also, he was in hot pursuit of another ship two-and-three-quarter hours later.

From his new vantage point, Shaw saw a hole in the starboard side of his ship between hold two and hold three that was 10 feet wide and 20 feet above the water line. He saw that "suddenly the ship straightened up and appeared as if she would remain afloat." They were just going to row back to her in order to retrieve warm clothes and a chronometer when a second torpedo struck (not counting the first miss). It also hit the starboard side, this time further aft and in the engine room.

Shaw said it took only five minutes for the *Peisander* to sink by the bow. There were two lifeboats on the poop deck which floated away from the hull as she sank. Shaw saw *U-653*'s conning tower breakwater, but only for a few minutes before submerging. According to a crew member, the periscope followed the boats for up to an hour. Shaw's boat (boat two) held eighteen men, boat four twenty-three under First Officer Brown and Second Officer Thomas, and boat six twenty men under Second Engineer Wilson. They all assembled and agreed to sail west in order to counter the easterly effects of the Gulf Stream currents. They ultimately made for Nantucket, over 300 miles to the northwest. The 35 gallons of fresh water was rationed to about 3 ounces per day per man. For food, there was pemmican, Horlicks, raisins, peanuts, and prunes, as well as chocolate and biscuits.

Shaw described the biscuits as "hard as bell-metal, and after three or four days of trying to chew them with my false teeth, my gums became so tender that I finally had to pound them into powder before I could masticate them at all." Shaw saved a biscuit and gave it to his dog, a Scottish Terrier, who preferred to bury, rather than eat it. The pemmican "tasted somewhat like Stockholm tar and sawdust." At 2 p.m., they raised sails. By 4 p.m., assuming the submarine had left them, they set up the emergency wireless radio set. At 11 p.m., there was a heavy rain squall, and Shaw's boat was separated from the two other boats, which were under the command of First Mate Brown (Shaw believed Second Officer William Thomas, age thirty was in charge) and Second Engineer John W. Wilson. The rain continued the next day and the men in Shaw's boat were wet and unhappy. Shaw had a change of clothes and warm layers, but most of the men did not. When the rain stopped and the sun came out, they were more cheerful. He devised a makeshift platform in the boat for the men to take turns lying on to sleep.

On Tuesday the 19th, the wind died and Shaw took a dip in the sea, followed by some of the crew. The wind filled in during the evening. On Wednesday the 20th, the wind lightened, yet they made headway. At 9 p.m. that night, they obtained a time-signal via wireless radio, which vastly assisted Shaw's navigation. After dawn on Thursday, May 21, the men sighted the 3,282-ton American steamer *Plow City*. The ship was *en route* from Trinidad to New York with 4,971 tons of bauxite ore. At 7.30 a.m., she was 4 miles away, but the *Peisander* men were able to row 2 miles toward it. They tried to transmit an SSS message by the small wireless set, but it was not received.[6]

Half an hour later, the lifeboat and ship were only 2 miles apart when suddenly the *Plow City* changed course away from them and sent an SSS message saying they had seen an enemy submarine, giving their position. Shaw was thus able to record his position and verify navigation. Shaw determined that they were 220 miles west-northwest of where the sank, and 140 miles south of Nantucket. Given the dangers of Nantucket Shoals, he opted to navigate toward Cape Cod instead. The *Plow City* was sunk at 2 p.m. that day by *U-588* under Vogel.

On Wednesday, May 20, the 4,573-ton British steamship *Baron Semple* came across the two *Peisander*'s lifeboats, which were still together, and offered to take the men aboard, even though it would have been a challenge to feed, house, and clothe the forty-three men. The *Baron Semple* was built in 1939 by C. Connell of Glasgow. Her skipper was Captain Philip Jarvis Carnie, a "rather bemused master ... [who gave them] some hot tea, magazines, and blankets." The vessel's owners were H. Hogarth and Sons (known as the "Hungry Hogarths"), also of Glasgow. After giving the offer some thought, the *Peisander*'s men weighed that "*Baron Semple* was bound for Cape Town, and if they accepted rescue it would have been a slow voyage in cramped conditions and another forty-three mouths to feed. The survivors were fit and well, and the weather was very good, and the possibility of being seen very soon. They told the *Baron Semple*: "Thank you, but we stay where we are."[7] It was, according to Stilgoe, "a decision which surprised everyone aboard the steamship."[8]

The night of May 20 and the morning of the 21st, they again broadcast their position with no reply. The weather became very rough, and they were forced to ride out the gale with a sea anchor. On May 22, morale was low due to continually soakings from rain and spray. The chief steward came up with a bottle of rum, which was shared around. They kept trying to send a distress message, but Shaw said, "by this time I could have shouted ashore with a megaphone more successfully." As he had predicted, after they passed north of the Gulf Steam, fog and heavy seas set in. On May 23, Shaw decided that, given their proximity to land, he would share out the food by "giving them as much of the boat's rations as they could eat and consoled them again with a small quantity of rum."

All three boats heard surf breaking ahead on the morning of May 24, and two of them landed on the beach before being towed away by small Coast Guard Auxiliary motorboats. Boat four with twenty-three survivors under First Mate Frank Anthony Brown (age thirty-seven) reached shore first and spent from dawn to just after midday slowly being pushed along the coast westward until they arrived off the tip of Nantucket at Madaket and landed at about 1 p.m. At 3 a.m., the following occurred:

> An able-bodied seaman in [a lifeboat] of the torpedoed British freighter *Peisander* heard what he thought might be a cow mooing. He woke F. Brown, first officer of the steamship, and commanding the boat, who soon discovered the sound to be that of

> surf breaking on Nantucket Island beaches. A few hours later, trailing a pail astern on a line to slow their progress through the surf, the castaways aboard the double-ended life-boat arrived on the sand unharmed after six days, fourteen hours at sea, having navigated some 340 miles.[9]

Boat six with twenty men under Second Engineering Officer John William Wilson, age forty, followed close behind. They were picked up at 1.30 p.m. and towed by the U.S. Coast Guard reserve vessel *CGR 37*, then quickly handed over to the U.S.C.G. motor-lifeboat *CGR 3828* based at Madaket Lifeboat Station. Boat two with Shaw and eighteen men landed over shoals rather than land, so the captain wisely sailed away then anchored until they were able to get their bearings and send signals.

Together, the rescue boats towed the first two *Peisander* lifeboats with the forty-three survivors, to Nantucket Harbor, where they arrived at 5.40 p.m. on May 24 and spent the night, leaving just under twenty-four hours later.[10] All sixty-one *Peisander* survivors assembled at the U.S. Coast Guard station at Brant Point, Nantucket. The coast guard noted that twenty of them were Chinese. The local Red Cross, who were already busy with injuries sustained by a large influx of servicemen, reported that the *Peisander* survivors "were taken to Bennett Hall, where they received medical attention, food and clothing. Most of them were suffering from exhaustion, and needed rest and refreshment only, but three were taken to Nantucket Hospital for special care, x-rays, etc."

The *Nantucket Inquirer and Mirror* went on to describe how only one man was held behind for further medical treatment and observation when the sixty others left the following day. The poor fellow has lost his false teeth overboard in the attack, and after being provided a complete set of new teeth by the Red Cross, he wrote them a grateful letter from New York. Red Cross Headquarters in New York commended the island sub-station for their hard work.[11]

On May 24 at 9 a.m., the men in boat two under Shaw saw and heard breakers on the port bow, to the northwest. Deducing correctly that they had drifted south onto Nantucket Shoals, Shaw shaped a course to the northeast for 8 miles. At 5 p.m., two planes saw them and circled around the lifeboat. The fog set in thickly, then darkness enveloped them, so Shaw decided to anchor and await rescue. Indeed, help was on the way. At 1.40 p.m., the Coast Guard cutter *General Greene* under Lieutenant (junior grade) P. F. Shea[12] was ordered from NOB Newport to find and bring back the *Peisander* boats.[13] That night the cutter pulled into Nantucket Harbor, but only until 3 a.m. the following day, when she left port heading southeast.[14] At 7.30 a.m. the *Greene* headed east. By 8.20 a.m., the men were at general quarters, fully alert.[15]

At daylight on May 25, the planes returned and advised the *Peisander* men to remain anchored. They also dropped supplies in two packets, which were retrieved. They contained first aid and eight cans of tomato juice which proved very popular, American pemmican which was vastly preferred over the British variety, and chocolate. By now, liquids were all that the second steward could swallow, his teeth had become so painfully bad. Finally, the fog cleared enough for the patient survivors to be rescued. When they were discovered by *General Greene* at 9.45. a.m., the boat had made it to within 30 or so miles of Siasconset. *En route*, the rescuers attacked a suspected U-boat and Lieutenant Shea, believing they had seen a wake trailing into a fog bank, decided to ram:

> [He] responded to a call for assistance from the torpedoed British freighter SS *Peisander* in a dense fog off Nantucket Shoals. As the cutter approached a lifeboat with the freighter's survivors aboard, a lookout sighted a U-boat crash diving across the cutter's bow. The cutter first tried to ram the submarine but did not arrive before the submarine slipped beneath the waves. The *General Greene* then acquired the U-boat on sonar and closed. She dropped three depth-charges on the contact which produced an oil slick, some 400 feet in diameter. The cutter was unable to regain sonar contact and returned to rescue the eighteen survivors.[16]

According to Eric Phillips, a crewman who was struggling to free up the cutter's motor lifeboat and could thus see from the bridge, the double-detonations caused the *General Greene*'s stern to fly 10 feet above the surface of the sea. Though Shea ordered Phillips to prepare the boats for abandon ship, the hull plates were not staved in. Phillips states that whereas the depth charges were ordered set for 150 feet, in fact, they detonated merely 50 feet from the surface, and one is believed to have triggered the other. At 9.55 a.m., the *General Greene*'s people were convinced they sighted a submarine 32 miles east of Nantucket and at 10.13 a.m., they engaged. Three depth charges were dropped, but two did not explode initially. After one exploded, it is believed however to have set off another of the depth charges. The report concludes that "oil came to the surface, and a sub may have been sunk." Most likely they saw a blackfish (small whale) or porpoise and attacked an old wreck. Given that the water was so shallow the lifeboat was anchored, U-boats could not operate there, and since no U-boats were there then, the coast guard did not, in fact, attack a U-boat.

The eighteen *Peisander* men were picked up at 10.45 a.m. At 11 a.m., "the fog cleared and all the crew were taken on board a U.S. Coast Guard vessel, *General Greene*, about 20 miles E.N.E. of Nantucket Island. We were treated very well on board the coast guard vessel, and those who required medical treatment were attended to." Phillips records that "some of them were in poor condition and had to be assisted from the lifeboat." After all the men were aboard, Shea and his men towed the empty lifeboat into Nantucket Harbor. He had anticipated wounded sailors and had a physician's mate, or medic, on board.

Nantucket Coast Guard reported the arrival of a lifeboat with "mostly Chinese," from the *Peisander* landed on that island. The lifeboat was described as 45 feet, which may explain why it was later towed 70 miles to Newport. Lieutenant Shea logged at 4.06 p.m. on May 25 that he "put L. Doyle [*sic.*] 2nd Steward, seriously ill, ashore for hospitalization. Forty-one survivors came aboard for further transportation to Newport." Less than an hour later, at 5 p.m. the *Greene* "unmoored and stood away from dock. Received two lifeboats for transportation." So, the *General Greene* men and Shaw's eighteen survivors from boat two only spent fifty-four minutes at Nantucket and took forty-three new men on top of seventeen remaining aboard after Woyle landed for dentistry.

The *General Greene* docked at the Coast Guard Pier in Newport at 2 a.m. on the 26th. Fifteen minutes later, all sixty Allied sailors were "turned over to the captain of the port." This highly efficient dispersal of the entire ship's crew and its boat has been verified by the deck logs.[17] Shaw was proud of the derring-do exhibited by the men in the other boats:

> The crew of the other two boats, which had kept together, could have been rescued much earlier by the *Baron Semple*, which was going to South Africa. They decided, however, that it would be much more unpleasant being landed in South Africa than having an adventure in a lifeboat in the open sea with the hope of ultimately landing on the American Coast.

In November 1942, Captain Shaw was honored with a King's Commendation for "brave conduct when their ships encountered enemy ships, submarines, aircraft, or mines."[18]

Feiler in *U-653* refueled from *U-459* northeast of Bermuda before returning to Brest, where he and the men were based with the 1st U-boat Flotilla. The patrol began on 25 April and ended on July 6. Over seven patrols and 412 patrol days, he attacked five ships of 9,382 tons, which were less-than-stellar results when compared with his colleagues in the same timeframe. He was awarded the German Cross in Gold in 1944 and lived until 1990.

The 6,919-ton diesel-motored ship *Mattawin* was originally built in 1923 as the *Ediba* at Harland and Wolff's storied shipyard in Govan, Glasgow. Ediba is a rural hamlet northeast of Port Harcourt, Nigeria. The ship's owners, the Elder Dempster Lines of Liverpool, traded to West Africa regularly and named many of their ships for African locations. Six years later, the same owners renamed the ship the *Mattawin*, a mutation of the Matawin River that empties into the St. Lawrence at Trois-Rivières, Quebec. In May 1942, the ship was chartered to the Kerr Silver Line and provided with routing instructions by British Naval Control based in New York.[19]

During World War II, the *Mattawin* participated in at least two ocean-going convoys: SL/MKS 100 from Freetown, West Africa to Liverpool in February 1942, and ON 89 from Liverpool to Halifax in April 1942, from which she was a straggler. Then she sailed to New York and loaded 7,786 tons of military cargo that included thirteen airplanes, steel, guns and ammunition, and motorized vehicles. The ship loaded for Alexandria via Cape Town and Durban, where she was to take on more fuel.

A dozen mostly prep school and Ivy League-educated volunteers in the American Field Service were passengers on their way to operate ambulances in the Middle East and beyond. The group putting their idealism to work included Richard Edwards (who graduated from Princeton in 1939), Nicholas Madeira Jr. (Harvard '43), Edward Fenton (Amherst '37), James Morrisey, Edward LeBoutillier, Ronald Gubelman (MIT '22), Coffin Wilson III (Pennsylvania Museum School of Industrial Art), Harry Blackwell, Charles Fagan, Robert Nelson, William Shoemaker, and Marshall Phelps (Yale '35).[20] Seven of the AFS volunteers' colleagues had been sunk aboard the Swedish steamer *Agra* by *U-654* under Forster in waters between New England and Bermuda on April 20, 1942. All had survived. The AFS unit, called ME Eleven, for Middle-East, arrived at the New York State Terminal Pier in Brooklyn on May 28. At that time, *Mattawin* was berthed in Staten Island, so the dozen volunteers were ferried to her aboard the tug *Revere*.[21]

British Captain Charles Herbert Sweeny, aged forty-seven, led the *Mattawin*'s seventy-one persons: fifty-two British merchant marine officers and crew, including three from British West Africa, three British naval gunners, and four British military gunners from the Royal Army. The *Mattawin* was armed with a large 4-inch gun and nine machine guns (four stripped-Lewis type, four Hotchkiss, one Oerlikon), a pair of illumination rockets as well as kites, and a degaussing system that was switched on. Among the merchant crew was Second Engineer Officer John Alan Wilson, aged forty. The *Mattawin* left New York on Friday, May 29 at 8 p.m. and anchored off City Island, Bronx, for the night, most likely waiting for a favorable tide. They adjusted compasses the following morning from 6 a.m. to noon. Then they headed east through the sheltered waters of Long Island Sound off the Connecticut coast. However, they were compelled to stop just three hours later due to engine trouble, which delayed them for a day until Sunday, May 31.

"Naval Control Authorities" instructed Captain Sweeny to pass the lightship *Nantucket* at dawn the following day, and they passed the light at 6 a.m. the following day, dropped the pilot off, and developed 9.5 knots toward South Africa. That evening at 7 p.m., a U.S. military plane circled overhead.[22] Their first night on the open Atlantic began uneventfully. It was a dark and cloudy night penetrated by occasional moonlight, with a rough sea, with the wind coming from the northeast at about 20 knots. The ship was steering southeast, the wind coming over the port bow. Unbeknown to the seventy-one souls aboard, the *Mattawin* was being stalked by *U-553* under *Kapitänleutnant* Karl Thurmann. Though Allied accounts claim Sweeny was not zigzagging, the German logbook indicates that the ship "steers in legs about 30° around general course 110.°" The base course was actually 124 degrees southeast.

At 10.48 p.m., *U-553* fired two torpedoes, with one of them a surface-runner that porpoised harmlessly past the *Mattawin*. The other was a dud, to the extent that even without earphones the Germans heard it hit the ship. Apparently, the many men aboard the *Mattawin* did not hear the clang, as no torpedoes were seen or heard, and no alarm was sounded. At 1.18 a.m., Thurmann fired two torpedoes, one of which hit roughly 100 feet from the bow on the starboard side. The Germans saw boats being launched and heard an SSS message being sent by the *Mattawin*'s radio operator, giving the name of their victim.

Captain Sweeny noted that at 1.19 a.m., a minute after the third and fourth torpedoes were fired, his ship was hit in the forepeak on the starboard side. AFS volunteer Nicholas Madeira was a lookout on the starboard bridge-wing and wrote, "I am not positive, but I'm pretty sure I saw the wake of the torpedo just before it hit. I was in the gun turret, and the tremendous spray came over me from the torpedo holes." Sweeny said that "The explosion was very loud and violent … a huge column of water was thrown up both from the forepeak hatch and alongside, as far as I could see." Though there were three gunners at the 4-inch gun aft, two AFS volunteers supplementing an apprentice and a sailor as lookouts at the bridge, and a sailor on the forecastle head, the moon was often obscured by clouds, and visibility was poor. The lookout on the bow was blown overboard by the explosion and as the *Mattawin* began sinking by the bow, "the forefoot having been blown away, the fo'castle head deck was lifted, jamming the doors making it very difficult for some of the men to get out, and the starboard anchor was blown away."

Sweeny ensured that an emergency radio signal was sent, and was told it was received by Halifax. Then he instructed the chief officer to launch the lifeboats while he shut off the engines. In doing so he noticed that the collision bulkhead had collapsed and that his vessel was going down by the head quickly. He threw the secret codes overboard and had a sailor collect his sextant and chronometer for navigating. AFS volunteer Marshall Phelps wrote that a "submarine was pointed out to me, in a position about 600 feet off the starboard quarter. No time to look at the sub much." He and his roommate slept fully clothed in preparation for an attack and noted: "there was no confusion or panic." Edward Fenton wrote that "the decks were wet, and cold.... Everything was very much under control … we shoved off, rowing." With four boats mostly loaded and ready to push off, Sweeny signaled the engine-room team to abandon their posts. Then the second torpedo hit, this one near the number four cargo hold, behind the engine room and about 100 feet from the stern:

> There was a tremendous explosion, a huge column of water was thrown up, there was no flash, but an exceedingly strong smell of burnt cordite, which made several of the men very sick. All watertight doors were closed.[23]

At that point, three of the boats pulled away from the doomed ship, whose back was broken by the eruption. Phelps claims that "the lifeboat was still in the falls when the second torpedo struck, about 15 feet astern of the boat. We got off, down the tidal wave it caused. The ship sank about three minutes after that. Five men remained on board: Sweeny, the chief mate, second mate, carpenter. and an apprentice. The captain yelled 'every man for himself' and hastened to the number one lifeboat, which gratefully remained along the starboard side."

Only two minutes after the blast, after everyone was aboard the boats, the *Mattawin* sank vertically by the stern, showing the horrified men the extent of damage to her bows. Richard Edwards, who had worked on motor yachts, observed that the chief mate "came down the ladder, hardly touching a rung. Then we were able to push off and watch the ship go down. She buckled in the middle as she went down. We could see the gash in the bow, where the first one had hit." The sailor who had been serving lookout duty on the bow was Jonah Peter, a twenty-five-year-old steward's boy from Liberia, described as British West African.

Edward LeBoutillier, using language deemed acceptable at the time, observed that "the only missing man was a negro deck-hand, and we picked him up. He had two leg injuries and a gashed eye." There were later comments about the African crew not pulling their weight; however, if this disparagement was meant for Peter, clearly he was too injured to pull much of anything. Although Sweeny said "everyone behaved very well indeed, and there was no sign of panic or confusion," there were moments of acute danger when number one lifeboat was snagged by the line from the ship's log boom, and in danger of being pulled under by the sinking ship. Finally, the chief steward used a knife to cut the line, and the boat moved clear of the doomed vessel.

The third officer, in charge of lifeboat number three, "thought he saw a submarine surface on the port side ... then submerge, but there was a considerable amount of floating wreckage about." He added that two of the gunners in the chief officer's boat (number two) from the port side, "reported that they saw the submarine surface, but the chief officer did not see anything." In fact, Thurmann does not report surfacing, as he already had the name and tonnage of the ship, so to do so would have unnecessarily endangered his U-boat. Besides, he saw from his periscope that four boats filled with men got clear, and thus it was thus unlikely that his men could be of much service. He noted the fifth torpedo struck at 1.30 a.m., and that the *Mattawin* sank four minutes later.

Then, at 2 a.m., the U-boat men picked up an emergency signal from one of the lifeboats; Captain Sweeny had instructed his men to send SOS messages every fifteen minutes for an hour. The Germans were not the only ones to hear them: the U.S. Navy logged that *Mattawin* was torpedoed 200 miles east-southeast of Nantucket, citing a "radio message from one of this vessel's lifeboats," along with a position. *U-553* motored off northward, where it sank two Allied ships in the Gulf of St. Lawrence. Then Thurmann turned back to France, arriving there on June 24.

Sweeny assembled all the boats together, calibrated compasses, and arranged for all boats to stick together and steer northwest toward Cape Cod. Bout Four, under the leadership of Second Engineer Wilson, had a motor in it. The motor was immersed in salt water upon launching and would not work; however, they lubricated it with massaging oil (intended for sunburn), in the crank case and Vaseline on the plugs, which worked satisfactorily to enable them to start the motor. The disposition in the boats was as follows:

> Boat One: fifteen under Captain Sweeny, aged forty-seven, starboard boat
>
> Boat Two: seventeen under the Chief Officer Robert W. Philip, aged thirty-seven, port boat
>
> Boat Three: nineteen under the Third Officer, Geoffrey H. Griffiths, aged twenty, port boat
>
> Boat Four: twenty under Second Engineer John Alan Wilson, aged forty, starboard motorboat

During the four hours between the *Mattawin* sinking and the first streaks of dawn across the eastern sky, the men rowed northwest, averaging over 2 knots. Given what many would consider rather bleak prospects, those in boat two (including AFS volunteers Fenton, Edwards, and Madeira) were cheerful. Fenton relates what it was like for him and sixteen others in boat two with the chief officer:

> We didn't put up the sail until about dawn. I'll never forget how beautiful it was—the great red sail unfurling, and the sun upon it, and the men in their yellow suits against it. We sailed on all day, the other three boats following. We had an extremely good time in our boat, laughing, telling jokes; and the British engineers taught us a number of songs to which we have words. We were very pleased by the way the seamen accepted us and liked us. They called me Tubby. Edwards was a good sailor, and Madeira was outstanding in his stoicism. We slept in the lifeboat, uncomfortably, but with good cheer, and with occasional songs and jokes.[24]

Pay for the merchant sailors ended at the time of sinking, making their ordeal doubly difficult on them and their families ashore.

Captain Sweeny in charge of boat one was ever-attentive to his men's needs. At noon, he and the chief took good noon sights and shared their position with the other boats. By 2 p.m., the third officer's boat fell behind, so Sweeny ordered the motorboat to go ahead and look for a rescue ship, using their fuel sparingly. Edwards, who was an experienced small-boat sailor, wrote that "we took pride in the fact that we were the best sailors, and were able to outdistance all the others. We lost sight of boat number three about six in the evening." Sweeny observed that "one of the passengers, an American Field Serviceman, gave valuable assistance, having had a good deal of experience in motor yachts." A graduate of Deerfield Academy, Princeton and Harvard, Edwards grew up in the yachting community of Rye, New York, and lived until 2016 (aged ninety-nine). Sweeny highly commended Second Engineer Wilson for his ingenuity and leadership.

That evening, Canadians logged that "a Yarmouth-based Canso flying boat from 162 BR Squadron sighted the lifeboats ... dropped food and distress flares and vectored the Norwegian freighter *Torvanger* to the rescue. Nine hours later, they picked up thirty-two survivors from two lifeboats."[25] The *Mattawin* survivors were rescued but did not report receiving food and flares from the air. The *Torvanger* had had a short but very eventful voyage since leaving New York on Sunday, May 31, bound (as the *Mattawin* had been) for Egypt via South Africa laden with war supplies.

By sunset at 7 p.m., Sweeny and Chief Officer Philip's boats were still together. They could barely discern the third officer's boat astern and the motorboat ahead. It was the last they would see of each other. Although for the first twenty hours they had averaged 2.5 knots, the wind died that evening and they were forced to row. That night, it also rained quite a lot. The men were wet and cold, huddled under the canopies at the bow.

Further east, *Mattawin*'s erstwhile adversary noted Allied aircraft twice, within fifteen minutes. Then they stumbled upon a ghostly Allied lifeboat adrift on the open sea. At around dusk on Wednesday, June 3, Thurmann wrote: "empty lifeboat without name taken. Obtained enough good hard bread and chocolate for two full meals, and also condensed milk, flavored vitamin lozenges of outrageous satiating effect." By that time, the Germans had been on patrol for nearly a month and a half and cherished the change of diet.

On the false assumption that seven boats were launched (which Thurmann and author Michael Hadley recorded), this boat has been ascribed to the *Mattawin*; however, all four of the *Mattawin*'s lifeboats are accounted for, so the boat was from another unfortunate ship. The most likely candidates are the *Berganger* (sunk by *U-578* under Rehwinkel the day before on June 2, 1942), the *Plow City* (by *U-588* under Vogel on May 22), the *Thursobank* (by *U-373* under Loeser on March 22), the *Pipestone County* (sunk by *U-567* under Heinicke on April 21), and further to the east the *Margot* (by *U-588* under Vogel on May 23), the *Peisander* (by *U-653* under Feiler on May 17), and the *Ranja* (sunk by *U-71* under Flachsenberg on March 17). In fact, this was the *Berganger*'s port boat, damaged beyond repair in the attack the day before, as the other two boats had occupants until the following day, when in the same position U.S.S. *Plunkett*, CDS 7, which was rescuing the *Berganger* survivors with U.S.S. *Madison*, CDD 14, came across the overturned port boat.

Back on the occupied *Mattawin* boats, Madeira, in lifeboat number two, recorded:

> That night was fairly uncomfortable for everyone, since it was raw and cold. But we all huddled under tarpaulins and rubber suits, with six blankets among us. Often, we bailed out water from the bottom of the boat. We all woke up soon after 5 a.m. and had something to eat. The wind had died down considerably, and we were going much slower than the previous day. We couldn't see the third mate's boat at all. The launch had gone way ahead of us. The captain's boat was some distance to the rear. Between 7 and 8 [a.m.], we sighted a ship on the horizon and, after a lot of conjecture, we decided that the ship was approaching us. Finally, it drew within about a quarter of a mile, and we rowed over to it.[26]

The ship, of course, was the *Torvanger*, busy rescuing its third batch of Allied survivors in as many days. At dawn on June 3, boat number two was ahead and to the west of Sweeny's. Unbeknown to these men, the *Torvanger* was vectored to the motorboat by a Canadian plane, and the motorboat had sent the ship to the two boats. At about 6 a.m., the *Torvanger* discovered the second engineer's motorboat. It stopped in calm conditions about a quarter of a mile away, and the survivors rowed to the ship.

When Captain Danielsen offered to take them to South Africa, all the men in the boat demurred, preferring instead to strike out for nearby Cape Cod, which they were told was 120 miles or so ahead, course 302 degrees. The Norwegians then provided between ten and fifteen gallons of petrol for the petrol engine, plus cigarettes, then motored off in search of the other three boats. Then Danielsen told the relieved the *Mattawin* men that he could see the other two boats from high up on his bridge.

Fenton, in boat three, wrote, "about six in the morning we saw a smokestack on the horizon. We got near it and recognized a similarity of cargoes between it and our own sunken ship; and we figured that their destinations were probably the same. Chief Officer Philip, therefore, asked only for positions and cigarettes (which were given); and we shoved off." Sweeny noted the following at 9.15 a.m.:

> He lowered the sail, we pulled alongside, and I asked the captain where he was bound. He told me that he was going to Cape Town, so I said I would not come on board, but would try and make land with my boat. He offered me any supplies I might require, so I asked him for some bread and cigarettes, which he gave me.[27]

The two parted about 9.30 a.m. Then the rescue versus self-rescue conundrum became more acute, as *Torvanger*'s men entertained serious doubts about their safety across a stretch of ocean littered with U-boat victims. Sweeny explained the following happened about 9.45 a.m.:

> When we were roughly 600 feet away, the captain hailed me to return alongside, when he told me that his officers and crew had insisted on picking us up and returning to New York, as they refused to proceed further on their voyage without an escort. Apparently, we were the second lot of survivors he had rescued in forty-eight hours, his vessel having already returned once with the other men.[28]

By 10 a.m., the *Torvanger*'s officers and crew had "very quickly and efficiently" retrieved all men from Sweeny's boat (as well as the boat itself) and moved on toward the chief officer's boat, which they caught up with a quarter of an hour later. Fenton related:

> We had gone half an hour when we noticed that the ship was steaming towards us again ... we also were taken aboard. It was a Norwegian ship, and there was coffee and cheese in the salon, and a general reunion. For the first time since the torpedoing, I found myself trembling. The coffee slopped all over from my shaking hand. We had a good time with the crew. Edwards and I shared bunks with the men aft.[29]

Between 10.30 a.m. and noon, they searched for the motorboat that had been motoring away from them for several hours. Due to hazy and foggy conditions, they could not locate it or the third officer's boat, and soon gave up. As there was imminent danger from U-boat attack, the Norwegians showed exemplary bravery in stopping not only to rescue the men, but to salvage their boats. During numerous operations (the *Torvanger* stopped five times just for the *Mattawin* survivors and at least twice for those of the other ships), Captain Danielsen exposed his vessel (as well as its men and cargo) to danger, so it is not surprising that they turned for shore. Although Sweeny called upon him to drop the *Mattawin* men and their boats near the coast of Cape Cod, the *Torvanger*'s chief engineer, Ernst Lindstrand, reported at about noon that there were problems with the ship's main engines. Captain Danielsen decided to sail to Halifax to assemble in a convoy per his men's wishes.

At the same time, the men in the motorboat "sighted two fishing boats approximately 35 feet in length with two masts, one of which carried a storm trysail. Flares were used to signal these boats, but these were either not observed, or the fishermen were afraid to approach, as both boats veered off and shortly disappeared." Undiscouraged and equipped with the oddly lubricated motor, the men continued on toward Cape Cod.

At noon the following day (June 4), the men aboard the *Torvanger* met Convoy BX 22 from Boston to Halifax, which welcomed them to join; the merchantman took the lead. By 3 p.m., they were motoring in foggy weather, despite which they arrived in Halifax at 7 p.m. An hour later, Sweeny, along with thirty-one other men, disembarked, with their two lifeboats. It is unusual that Danielsen released the boats along with the men, since in most other similar circumstances, the rescued would surrender them to the rescuing ship, or the Good Samaritan could claim them as his property under salvage law. Once again, Danielsen was generous. Among the men landed in Canada, five were AFS volunteers, and the U.S. Navy gratefully recorded "none injured." Fenton recorded:

> After arrangements were made, [and we] were landed we were rushed in a bus to the Allied Seaman's Institute, where tables had been roped off, with signs on them that read "Reserved—For Survivors Only." We had eaten so well on the Norwegian ship that we weren't particularly hungry, but we did want a pie à *la mode* and milk, which we hadn't been able to get on shipboard. The expression on the waitress's face was wonderful to behold when we gave our order. I refused the hot soup. The Red Cross women brought us chintz bags filled with the necessary toiletries; and we shoved off to the Halifax Hotel.
>
> We spent our time—after going to the [U.S.] Consulate—being interviewed by naval authorities. The next day there was a bang-up farewell party, and all of us and the crew had our pictures taken. There was an exchange of addresses, wise-cracks, and they saw us off on the train [to AFS headquarters in New York]. The thing that impressed me most about the entire business was the spirit of the crew. For the first time, they gave me a real sense of what the war was about. When we waved goodbye to them, we felt that we were saying goodbye to some of our best friends.[30]

The same day, boat four, the motorboat under Second Engineer Wilson, supported in navigational duties by the wireless operator, and in sailing by some of the four AFS volunteers, landed about halfway up the outer arm of Cape Cod, propelled by the fuel they had been given by the *Torvanger*'s men. After being spotted by a lookout at 4.45 p.m., U.S.C.G. *Truck 1043* was loaded with medical equipment and blankets and sent to their aid. Within ten minutes, the coast guard sent U.S.C.G. *Truck 1719* with U.S.C.G. *Surfboat 4590* to look for the lifeboat, along with U.S.C.G. *Truck 1263*. They found the twenty survivors on the outside beach, with "wind-burn and strained muscles from two days' exposure."[31]

They were taken via the hamlet at Eastham to nearby Nauset Light Coast Guard Station, near Orleans, arriving at 6.20 p.m. They had to be shuttled by truck. The boat was taken as far inland as it would go. There were at least two men that required medical attention: "one punctured ear drum from block blow, one recovering from exposure." The man hit in the head by the ship's block was young lookout Jonah Peter, who was then pulled from the water. The Red Cross provided clothing and other wants.

> [The survivors] were given immediate attention by four local doctors for face burns and other minor injuries. They were then provided with hot coffee and sandwiches, after which they were taken to the station and given an opportunity to take showers and get some much-needed sleep.[32]

Civilian calls to the station seeking information were blocked or diverted. Coast Guard officers from Provincetown, then Lieutenant W. E. Ireland, the officer-in-charge at Hyannis, and local Red Cross volunteers who offered some forty-five blankets and an ambulance, were praised for keeping civilians and the press away from the survivors in order for them to recuperate. The Red Cross then transported them by boat from Provincetown to Boston.[33]

The last remaining batch of survivors in boat three, which included Edward LeBoutillier and two other AFS volunteers, were not having an easy time of it. Having become stragglers, they were left behind by boat four with the motor, as well as by boat one and boat two, and were left out of the *Torvanger* rescue. Third Officer Geoffrey Hollis Griffiths, age twenty, and his shipmates "had a more difficult passage," the company historian wryly observed.[34] At 4.50 p.m. on June 6, U.S.C.G.C. *General Greene* was ordered to the scene where an U.S. Army Air Force plane had dropped food to about twenty men in a lifeboat off Nantucket. At 3.55 p.m., U.S. Navy Airship K 3 contacted *General Greene* to "explain negative results" of their efforts to find a lifeboat off Orion Shoals. The previous day, K 3 was also unable to find survivors, lifeboat, or the *Greene* due to fog. The fog enshrouded all, and the nights were cold. LeBoutillier records a boat voyage punctuated more by heavy downpours than the outpourings of camaraderie that Fenton described:

> It rained for three nights, and about 6 a.m. Saturday morning [6 June] we were sighted by a Navy Patrol plane. They circled the lifeboat and dropped supplies, and that evening they repeated the procedure, this time enclosing a note saying that the Navy was coming to the rescue.

The final batch of nineteen *Mattawin* survivors was discovered southeast of Georges Bank by the *General Greene* on Sunday, June 7. Canadian historian Hadley and the U.S. Navy's *Enemy Action Diary* at 12.35 p.m. that day confirm that "*General Greene* (CG) picked up lifeboat with ... survivors of the *Mattawin*." The *Greene*'s deck log provides even more precision:

> 6 June, *General Greene* searched for U-boats and lifeboats off Nantucket
>
> 10.09 a.m., *Greene* crew first sighted *Mattawin* lifeboat 60 miles east of Siasconset
>
> 10:35 a.m., lifeboat alongside cutter; "men came on board." Shea listed all men, ranks
>
> 10.45 a.m., lifeboat in tow, under way for Nantucket with ninteen *Mattawin* men aboard
>
> 8 June, 00.25 a.m., docked Steamship Wharf, *Mattawin* men not permitted to disembark
>
> 5.25 a.m., embarked seven *Polyphemus* and three *Norland* men, plus a new lifeboat, for RI.

Shea noted with satisfaction that "this accounts for all the *Mattawin* lifeboats known to have been launched." They never set foot on the island; rather, they were in transit to Newport. It was a sleepless night for the survivors, though they were very pleased to learn that all of their shipmates also made it. Third Officer Griffiths was ever solicitous of his eighteen charges, and grateful for the professionalism and discipline of the medic aboard *General Greene*:

> After two cups of coffee we all felt fine. A meal was prepared for us. Some people ate rather a lot and were heartily sick. I ate just a little, slowly, as the ship's doctor recommended, and felt highly refreshed and my stomach was not in the least upset. During the time I was in the boat I did not pass a motion.... After the meal on the

Captain Robert Penney Robertson and thirty-three men of the British ship *Effna,* sunk by *U-108* under Scholtz on February 28, 1941, south of Iceland. With the exception of the German sailor on the right, everyone in this photograph died within a day or so. (*Willy Wilke, torpedo mechanic on U-108*)

> rescue ship my bowels worked normally immediately ... though I believe that some members of the crew had difficulty at first.[35]

As there was no "ship's doctor" on the *Mattawin*, he was referring to the naval hospital corpsman, or medic, on the *General Greene*. Although the Eastern Sea Frontier enumerates that the *Greene* carried one on both voyages in order to tend various survivors, the abbreviated rank HM1 or HM for Hospital Corpsman does not appear in the logbook and articles, so his name is not clear from the log.

LeBoutillier penned a letter to the Elder Dempster Lines commending Griffiths "for his splendid leadership and the order he kept, also for keeping morale up." The *Greene*'s commander showed resourcefulness by boarding ten other U-boat survivors landed from the *Polyphemus* and *Norland* three days previously, and then towing one lifeboat from each vessel to Newport. Shea relates the following occurring on June 8:

> 12.05 p.m., Buzzards Bay, "spoke Yawl *Morning Star*, IH 52, Mt. Desert Maine-Connecticut"
>
> 2.05 p.m., docked at Newport, U.S. Navy dock, landed twenty-nine men
>
> 4 p.m., granted [*Greene*] sailors liberty [shore leave] until 8 a.m.
>
> 9 June, 6.30 a.m. *Greene* shifted from the Navy dock to U.S.C.G. Station, Castle Hill, Newport.

By that evening, the *Greene* was on to its next assignment, standing by to assist the steamer *Empire Woodcock*, disabled off Brenton Reef. There would be no more Nantucket rescues for her during the balance of the war. The following day, Lieutenant Shea was sent for in-patient treatment at the Naval Hospital, Newport, reasons not given. He had done stellar duty.

The Eastern Sea Frontier *Enemy Action Diary*, Narragansett Force reported how "*General Greene* arrived at Newport with survivors and turned them over to the Coast Guard." Kolbicz added that "one crew member had been injured during the sinking, and two had swollen feet by exposure in lifeboat, so they were taken to the U.S. Marine Hospital at Brighton, Massachusetts." Brighton is a western suburb of Boston, less than 100 miles from Newport.[36]

LeBoutillier relates that "on Sunday morning, about 9 or 10, a coast guard cutter came out and we were taken aboard. We reached Nantucket about 2 a.m., [and] a naval intelligence officer came on board to question the third mate. Then we proceeded to Newport, where we were met by Mr. Warren." This was George Henry Warren, Jr., until very recently an AFS volunteer assigned to the organization's headquarters. By sheer coincidence, he both sent them off on behalf of the AFS from New York and welcomed them to Newport for the local Disaster Relief Committee. The *Newport Mercury* related:

> Prior to becoming chairman of the Disaster Relief Committee, Mr. Warren was engaged with the American Field Service in New York. There he said goodbye to a group of young men who were sailing for England [*sic.*]. He returned to Newport a short time later and accepted an invitation to become chairman of the local [disaster relief] committee. Among the first group of survivors brought in here were three of the AFS boys he had said farewell to in New York. They and the others had been picked up after bobbing about on the Atlantic Ocean for six days in a lifeboat.[37]

AFS volunteer Marshall Phelps was in the motorboat and described his crewmates thus: "swellest bunch you would want to meet. Everybody did everything he could. Credit should go to the English boys. There was no whimpering among them. They were always ready to help." Perhaps amazingly, since an injured man was blown off the forecastle, five men remained on board when the second torpedo struck, and the boats were mostly separated by distance and fog, all seventy-one men aboard the *Mattawin* survived.

Most of the AFS men went on to serve in the Middle East (AFS Unit ME Sixteen), and many went further. Richard Edwards served in Burma and China, became fluent in Chinese, married Yale Professor Vee Ling, and became a distinguished academic specializing in Asiatic studies. Things did not end so well for Captain Danielsen and the men of the *Torvanger*. On June 23, 1942, just three weeks after rescuing so many sailors, and after dispersing from a convoy in mid-Atlantic, the ship was sunk west of the Azores by *U-84* under Horst Uphoff. Although four were killed, thirty-three survived, among them the generous Captain Danielsen. On November 24, 1942, John Alan Wilson, second engineer and *de facto* skipper of the motorboat, was awarded the King's Commendation for restarting his boat's soaked engine and helping to navigate it to Cape Cod, saving himself and nineteen other men.

Kapitänleutnant Friedrich-Hermann Praetorius brought *U-135* into New England for seven days starting on May 17 when he sank *Fort Qu'Appelle*, putting the first torpedo into its midriff after a minute. Men with lights were seen scrambling into boats, and a *coup de grâce* hit behind the funnel in the engine room. Since she did not sink, a third shot was fired after a wait of twenty-five minutes. Yet a fourth and final shot was required, as Praetorius declared "this giant ship must be brought down now." The Germans noticed "in the fiery glow it was seen that the king-posts are goal-post masts, just like the big ones on the Blue Funnel Line."[38]

Fort Qu'Appelle was a 7,127-ton British steamer *en route* from Vancouver to Halifax via Panama and Jamaica, when it was surprised by *U-135* on her maiden voyage, southeast of Nantucket.[39] Later that day, another steamer, this one brown in color and about 5,000 tons, came into site and Praetorius again declared "we must have him." It was not so easy, as the first and second torpedoes missed. Then a third shot missed as both vessels ran north. The Germans considered it pointless to continue. With a tinge of admiration, Praetorius noted that the merchant captain dodged the torpedo using trickery: "at the moment of the shot, the steamer had stopped, we saw his propeller water whip up, at the same moment he turned away hard and showed us his stern." Oddly, no ship called in an attack to the Eastern Sea Frontier at that time and location.[40]

On May 18, *U-135* re-loaded torpedoes, and the following day crash-dived to avoid airplanes, just as they began a pursuit of a tanker heading west which also got away. On the 20th, the sighting of another steamer materialized into two tankers, accompanied by aircraft. By surfacing and racing at the same speed as the ships, Praetorius hoped to catch them, and constantly checked the relative bearing between the ships to ascertain who was overtaking who. Alas, there was no change, so "it is not to be, therefore with a heavy heart [we] broke off the pursuit after six hours." The incursion ended on the 23rd, when the submarine motored west of Montauk after its foray south of Nantucket.

After participating in the *Padfinder* group, Praetorius brought his sub to Cape Hatteras via New York before heading back to Brest. *En route*, they found and sank the Norwegian motor vessel *Pleasantville* north of Bermuda. The patrol began as one of thirteen U-boats in the sixth wave of Operation Drumbeat on April 26. *U-135* refueled from the *Milchkuh,* or U-tanker *U-459* under von Wilamowitz-Möllendorf west of the Azores about June 19. She repositioned to St. Nazaire on July 5, 1942.[41] Praetorius was born in 1904 and was a member of the Crew of 1934. He became a captain in the German merchant marine before passing away at age fifty-two in Lübeck. Early in his naval career, he served as 1st Watch Officer of *U-98*. He commissioned *U-135*, then left her in November 1942. He earned the U-boat War Badge 1939 for three ships sunk for 21,302 tons. *U-135* was sunk under Otto Luther near the Canary Islands on July 15, 1943, by the H.M.S. *Rochester,* L 50, H.M.S. *Mignonette*, H.M.S. *Balsam*, and U.S. Navy aircraft VP 92, a Catalina P 6. Though five German mariners perished, forty-one were rescued.[42]

The British steamship *Fort Qu'Appelle* was built by Burrard Dry Dock Company in North Vancouver for the U.S. War Shipping Administration (WSA). Her owners were William Thompson and Company, known as the Ben Line, of Leith, who chartered the ship back to the MoWT. Completed in March 1942 and homeported in London, she was 7,121 tons, 441 feet long, 57 feet wide, and 35 feet deep. Her triple-cycle steam engines developed 505 hp, driving the ship at 11 knots with a single propeller.[43]

On her maiden and final cargo-carrying voyage, the *Fort Qu'Appelle* was under the command of Captain Wilfred Alexander Murray, age thirty-eight, seconded by First Officer John Gair. The ship's only voyage was a long and eventful one, routed from Vancouver to Panama via Seattle, then to the U.K. via Halifax. On May 7, the *Fort Qu'Appelle* radio operators heard an SOS message in the Caribbean north of Panama, but on arriving at the scene of distress, they learned that another vessel had already retrieved the survivors. The following day, though, they picked up twenty-four survivors of the merchant ship *Green Island* of the Ford Motor Company and brought them to Kingston, Jamaica as instructed. The *Green Island* was sunk by *U-125* under Folkers on May 6. After a few hours, the *Fort Qu'Appelle* resumed course for Halifax on May 9, zigzagging during the night.[44]

The ship carried a general cargo of between 7,000 and 9,200 tons and included 1,000 tons of the chemical Acetone stowed in the number one and number three holds forward, below decks. This included 104 bags of parcels in the number two hold, four bags of special mail, and one bag of consular mail from Jamaica to the U.K., stowed in Captain Murray's cabin. *Fort Qu'Appelle* was armed with a 4-inch gun, one Oerlikon machine gun, four parachute rockets with kites, and two .5-caliber Colt hand-guns. There were two naval gunners on the 4-inch gun and forty-five merchant marine officers and men operating the ship and engines. The vessel was equipped with degaussing equipment strung around it, though it played no part in the subsequent attack, whether on or off.[45]

At 10 p.m. on Saturday, May 16, the *Fort Qu'Appelle* was heading north at 11 knots 250 miles south of Cape Sable. The seas were moderate and the winds were about 20 knots from the west. Chief Officer Gair described it as "a very dark night, but the weather was fine and visibility good." In the bridge, Captain Murray, Gunner John McLaren (aged thirty-five) and Third Officer James Stanley Chapman (aged twenty-one) were on watch. At 10.54 p.m., a torpedo fired from *U-135* under Praetorius slammed into the aft end of the number two cargo hold forward, on the starboard side, just forward of the bridge. Gair, who had been off watch and sleeping, recalled two distinct thuds followed by a muffled explosion.

Immediately, Murray, Gair and the chief engineer inspected the *Fort Qu'Appelle*, not finding damage to the deck. As the ship began settling by the bow, though, so Murray ordered abandon ship at 11.10 p.m. He instructed the boats to stay nearby and, if the condition of the ship was stable in the morning, to reboard and salvage her. He then sank the confidential codes and mail in weighted bags. The impact of the first torpedo shattered the two lifeboats on the starboard side; however, the number four lifeboat was launched with thirty men, leaving thirteen on board and Gair, the second officer and two cadets engaged in letting the boat free. Five minutes later, at 11.15 p.m., the number two lifeboat was lowered on the port side, just forward of the bridge. During this process, a second explosion slammed into the ship in the vicinity of the lifeboat, almost cutting the young ship in two, and exploding the Acetone cargo loaded up forward.

The effect of the second torpedo on the second lifeboat was devastating: it "destroyed," the boat, killing all its occupants, including Captain Murray, a gunner, the third officer, two stewards, the fourth engineer, and a radio operator. The effects on the remaining crew, who saw the carnage, can be imagined. According to Gair, there was a "tremendous flash," followed by a "huge column of water thrown up, and beams and hatches were also thrown high into the air." Boat number four was tied to the ship but was blown away by the blast, with several men thrown into the water due to the concussion. Those men swam back to the boat and reboarded it. Gair and the three other men let go one of the rafts situated aft. As the *Fort Qu'Appelle* was sinking quickly by the head, they jumped into the water after it. They stayed on the raft and signaled with lights to the men in the lifeboat that they were to remain near the ship until dawn. Praetorius never approached the survivors for information and *U-135* remained out of sight.

Fifteen minutes after midnight on Sunday, May 17, a "violent explosion," presumably from the Acetone up forward, "lit up the whole horizon." At that time, the forecastle head was at sea level. When the ship sank twenty-three minutes later, the lights were still burning, meaning the generator was still functioning. By 7 a.m., Gair and his shipmates swam from his raft to the lifeboat. Gair said: "the water being quite warm, I thoroughly enjoyed the swim." The ship was still in the warm Gulf Stream current. Before leaving the *Fort Qu'Appelle,* her radio operators managed to send a distress signal to shore, which was received by New York and replied to from Halifax.

Early on Sunday, Eastern Air Command intercepted the distress message and a patrol plane named *Canso 9750* was sent toward the signal. The plane located the lifeboat at 7.03 a.m., based on its being "able to transmit on 500 KC's" (kilocycles). Though the same war diary recorded "RCAF planes searched and found thirty-four men in the lifeboat at 2.25 p.m., on westerly course at 3.5 knots," due to poor visibility, the would-be-rescuers were unable to rediscover the survivors right away. The following day (the 18th) was deemed "unsuitable for aircraft operation" due to the weather.

As a result of the Canadian portable wireless set on board (the ship was built in British Columbia), the men were in contact with Halifax continually. The set "worked splendidly," although the signal faded somewhat during rainfalls. Their emergency food supplies held up, and since it rained all but a few hours, they had plenty of water to drink. Compared with most other lifeboat ordeals, where the men craved water, the ocean was freezing, and no one was aware of their plight, theirs seems especially blessed.

Airplanes were sent to their aid again on Tuesday the 19th. The *Canso 9748*, "in spite of very adverse weather conditions, proceeded on patrol for the lifeboat and finally sighted it at dusk." The pilot then worked on vectoring a surface vessel to the survivors, who saw one of the planes. Due to a 60-mile position error, the plane was some distance off. Amazingly, the *Fort Qu'Appelle* survivors radioed Halifax, whose operators instructed the plane to alter course toward the boat's position, so that the plane discovered them. The pilot then dropped food as well as four rockets, explaining they would be instructed when to fire them.

That evening, the Canadian minesweeper H.M.C.S. *Melville,* J 263 (under Lieutenant-Commander Ralph Thomas Ingram, Royal Canadian Naval Reserve) hove into sight. Without awaiting instructions, Gair fired two of the rockets, saying that "they were wonderful, each one sent up twelve bright white flares, which the corvette saw 30 miles away." As a double indemnity, the airplane remained on scene, bathing the lifeboat in a halo of light from floating flares. The survivors were blessed. H.M.C.S. *Melville*, guided to the survivors as a mother hen to her chicks, picked up the thirty-four survivors by 9 p.m. They managed to sail 100 miles closer to shore in two days. The wind has been steady to the westward and they had sailed close-hauled for all forty-eight hours. The *Melville*'s commander, Ingram and his officers and crew delivered the *Fort Qu'Appelle* survivors to Shelburne at noon the following day, May 19.[46] Gair commended Second Mate Mitchell for being particularly helpful in managing the sailing lifeboat, modestly admitting that he himself "had little experience in this direction," and that Mitchell was "a very good sailor and did most of the sailing." He recommended that Roman Candle-type rockets be carried in all Allied lifeboats.

An unusual and lasting friendship sprung from this rescue. Young James Carney Ferster was serving as a non-commissioned gunnery officer on H.M.C.S. *Melville,* and he pulled one of the *Fort Qu'Appelle* survivors on board the Canadian warship. The merchant mariner he pulled up wore an oil-covered leather aviator's jacket, reddish-brown in color. The grateful survivor gave that jacket to Ferster, who wore it proudly throughout World War II. Ferster's son emigrated to Brisbane, Australia, and while visiting him in 1972, the former Canadian Navy sailor stepped into a taxi-cab being driven by the very man who he had rescued from the *Fort Qu'Appelle* lifeboat thirty years before. They spent several days taking in the sights of Brisbane together. Three generations of Ferster have worn and cared for the jacket since, with the third generation receiving it in 2018.[47]

10

One Boat and Attacks on the *Zurichmoor*, the *Liverpool Packet*, the *Ben and Josephine*, the *Aeolus*, and the *Malayan Prince*

Kapitänleutnant Heinz-Otto Schultze brought *U-432* into New England for twenty-four days, the longest patrol to that date. It lasted from May 20 to June 16, during which Schultze sank the *Liverpool Packet* and the *Zurichmoor* near Cape Sable, then two fishing vessels, and attacked two others. Three days before, *U-432* sank the small ship *Foam*, a 324-ton Boston steam trawler off Halifax. Three days into the area, Schultze found and sank the British *Zurichmoor*, 4,455 tons, 150 miles south of the Gulf of Maine. She was bound from Halifax to St. Thomas in ballast, having left on May 21. A week after sinking the *Zurichmoor*, Schultze found and sank the Canadian 1,188-ton steamer *Liverpool Packet*. Three days later, on June 3, *U-432* found and destroyed two fishing vessels—the *Ben and Josephine* and the *Aeolus*—west of Cape Sable.[1]

Roughly a week later (on 9 June) and in a similar position, *U-432* came upon Convoy BX 23A east of the Gulf of Maine and attacked the *Kronprinsen* and the *Malayan Prince*, a German-built, British-flagged 8,593-ton motor ship hit by one of four torpedoes. Only slightly damaged, it was back in service the following month. The *Kronprinsen* was hit after a minute-and-a-half by *U-432*'s torpedo; however, the 7,073-ton Norwegian motor ship was towed to shore despite losing her stern and having her deck cargo catch afire. Ultimately the vessel was towed from Pubnico Fairway to Halifax on July 23 and to Boston on October 9 for further repairs. The ship was abandoned in the Yellow Sea, confiscated by the Chinese government; since 1969, her whereabouts have been unknown.[2]

After sinking five ships of 6,110 tons and damaging two others for 15,666 tons (all but one—the *Foam*—in New England), Schultze headed back to France, arriving at La Pallice on July 2. The patrol began on April 30. *U-432* took part in the *Padfinder* group between May 21 and 27 and proved the impetus behind the sortie correct, inasmuch as the submarine sank or damaged several targets.[3]

On the way to New England on May 2, *U-432* was attacked from the air near La Coruña and escaped six bombs with minor damage.[4] At the end of June, *U-432* was refueled by *U-459* west of the Azores.

Schultze joined Crew 1934, and then U-boats in May 1937. He was the 2nd Watch Officer of *U-31* to 1938 and participated in gunnery school in Kiel. He then commanded *U-4* in 1940 and *U-141* before commissioning *U-432* in April 1941. After *U-432*, he commanded *U-849*, aboard which he perished. Schultze sank twenty ships and damaged two others for over 83,000 tons and was awarded the Knights Cross on July 9, 1942. *U-432* was sunk without Schultze aboard, northeast of Newfoundland on March 11, 1943, by the Free French corvette *Aconit*. Twenty out of forty-six mariners survived.[5]

The British dry-cargo steamship *Zurichmoor* of 4,455 tons was completed in September 1925 by J. Readhead in South Shields. She was 386 feet long, 55 feet wide, and 26 feet deep; she was propelled by a three-cylinder triple-expansion 460-hp engine that turned a single screw to achieve 10.5 knots. Her owners were Runciman Walter, known as the Moor Line, in Newcastle upon Tyne. Moor Line ships were named for cities, with the appendage Moor affixed to it.[6] In 1928, she sailed under Captain B. Jenkins to Australia and beyond.

The publication *Marine Engineer and Naval Architect* announced the arrival of the ship thus:

> The vessel is of the improved single-deck type, and is built to Lloyd's highest class, [with] ... long extended bridge and topgallant forecastle, ... fitted throughout with shifting boards and feeders, in compliance with the requirements of the Grain Loading Act and is well-equipped with a large number of steam winches and derricks for the rapid handling of cargoes. She has a double bottom for water ballast, as well as a large after-peak tank.[7]

The *Zurichmoor* sailed from New York twice in November 1941, and on January 25, 1942, she dragged anchor nearly ashore on Stornoway in the Outer Hebrides. Her captain urgently requested tugs. The *Zurichmoor* departed Liverpool on April 28, 1942, in Convoy ON 90, bound for Halifax. Originally composed of fifty-one ships, it arrived in Halifax on May 15 missing four of them.[8] She remained in Canada for a week, discharging part-cargo in Montreal. On her final voyage, the *Zurichmoor* was under command of Captain Herbert Dixon Hodgson, with forty-five persons on board: thirty-nine merchant sailors and six military armed guards. They were on a voyage without escort from Halifax to St. Thomas, U.S. Virgin Islands. Leaving on Thursday, May 21, she proceeded south in ballast, which, given the boisterous weather in May Hodgson took on quite a lot of. The greater depth made the *Zurichmoor* an easier target to hit.[9]

Schultze lined up the *Zurichmoor* in *U-432*'s periscope at 5.24 a.m. on Saturday, May 23, then sent two torpedoes into its side. The ship sank in ninety seconds. In the unlikely event that anyone survived the sudden nighttime sinking, she was 200 miles southeast of Nantucket and far from rescue with little hope of boats or rafts getting free. Probably most of the men were off duty and resting below decks and were quickly trapped and drowned. Those who escaped from the doomed ship—and most watch-standers on deck would have—would not have found much to float on. They probably died prolonged deaths of exposure or drowning—lonely ways to go. In any event, all forty-five of *Zurichmoor*'s complement perished. No trace of them or the ship was ever found.[10]

Among the dead were six teenagers: Tom Bullock and Robert Dowie (seventeen), Leslie Fletcher (nineteen), Richard James (eighteen), Edward Scott (seventeen), and James Telfer (eighteen). Leslie Fletcher was awarded the British Empire Medal but perished before receiving it. He was "eighteen years of age at the time of being decorated—for his part in the very first of Commander Binney's clandestine operations out of Sweden (a.k.a. Operation Rubble)." His citation reads:

> Leslie Frederick Fletcher was decorated for his services in the tanker *Ranja*, one of five vessels selected to carry pig-iron, special steels, ball-bearings and machine tools from Sweden to the U.K. in January 1941, the whole manned by a total of 147 men and one woman, comprising 58 Englishmen, 57 Norwegians, 31 Swedes and one Latvian. From this daring enterprise, which was master-minded by Commander Sir George Binney (RNVR), then resident under a more innocent title at the British legation in Stockholm.

There were twenty sailors between ages twenty and twenty-nine, alongside the fifty-five-year-old Chief Officer Sidney Herbert Atkinson. After the casualty, the Allies intercepted Schultze's radio signal informing headquarters that the *Zurichmoor*, built 1928 and on course 165 degrees) was sunk. He was able to learn the ship's name by surfacing to motor around the wreckage, noting "among the wreckage a name shield." No distress messages were sent by the ship itself. Some commanders were detailed about interactions with survivors, but Schultze went into great detail about the Gulf Stream temperatures causing the periscope to fog up but did not say they saw any survivors in the water. On July 29, 1942, the *Zurichmoor* was listed as officially overdue and missing. The families of the deceased were informed of the tragic news.

Further north, the steam cargo ship *Liverpool Packet* was built in 1926 as the Norwegian *Nidarnes* by the Swan, Hunter and Wigham Richardson shipyard in Wallsend, Sunderland. She was 1,188 tons, 248 feet long, and 37 feet wide. For her first two years, George Hansen or A. L. Ombustvedt owned her as the *Nidaros* of Oslo, then from 1928 to 1930, the Delson Steamship Company of Montreal took ownership and called her the *Delson*. From 1930 to 1941, she was renamed the *Sonia* and owned by Sonia Shipping under F. K. Warren of Halifax.

In 1941, she was sold to Markland Shipping of Liverpool, Nova Scotia. That year, she was in and out of New York seven times: in September, October, November, (twice) and December (twice) as well as January and March 1942, making her final departure from there on May 28.[11, 12] The ship was not in convoy as it sailed toward Halifax in the late spring of 1942. The ship had recently sailed to the Virgin Islands, Bermuda, Cuba, Australia, and Virginia.

The firm that owned the *Liverpool Packet* was founded in 1928 by an understudy of Lord Beaverbrook, the Canadian newsprint tycoon named Max Aitken. Izaak Walton Killam purchased 150 square miles of timber on the Mersey River and founded the Mersey Paper Company. He built a large mill and loading port for the export of rolls of newspaper print. In 1930, the firm started the Mersey Shipping Company to move its product to global markets. This was renamed the Markland Shipping Company in 1937, for its first ship. The *Markland* served the *Washington Post* as well as the *New York Times* and papers in New Zealand and Australia. During World War II, Mersey Paper officials realized that were the *Markland* requisitioned they would be left without a ship.[13]

As a contingency, the firm purchased the *Sapinero* in March 1940 and renamed her the *Vineland*. They later purchased former Swede *Sonia*, renaming her the *Liverpool Packet* after a Nova Scotian privateer in the War of 1812, and the *Zenda*, which became the *Liverpool Loyalist*. These ships were envisioned to carry finished newsprint to Australia and New Zealand, with interim voyages carrying pulpwood and coal from Cape Breton to Liverpool. They registered the *Vineland* under shell companies like Scotia Shipping, flagging her to Panama though her home port was still Liverpool.[14] The *Vineland* was sunk early in 1942, before being flagged back to Canada, in the Bahamas.

On her final voyage, the *Liverpool Packet*'s master was Captain Norman (Norm) Emmons Smith, a diminutive man with an oversized personality. At age sixty-one, he was an admired and revered patriarch of Woods Harbor, Nova Scotia. The skipper had been at sea in cold water from a young age and risen to master fully rigged sail ships, rum-running speedboats, others smuggling revolutionaries into South America, and merchant vessels during both world wars. During World War I, he carried so many cargoes of TNT that his nickname was "Dynamite." Historian Evelyn M. Richardson described him as "a small, quick-moving man with sharp blue eyes and sea-weathered face."[15]

After taking newsprint from Nova Scotia to Virginia via the Chesapeake and Delaware Canal, Captain Smith brought the ship between the wreck of the *Normandie* and the *Queen Elizabeth* at Pier 97, 57th Street on the Hudson River. On their way into New York, they passed the wrecked carcass of a tanker in shallow waters (self-inflicted, collision or other, as no U-boat forced a tanker aground in New York Harbor), and "a dozen planes buzzing around outside, dropping depth-charges." The *Liverpool Packet* left New York at 5 p.m. on Thursday, May 28 with 1,945 tons of U.S. government stores and supplies for

U.S. bases in Newfoundland, one destination thought to be an airfield. The vessel was not armed, the chief engineer claiming that the Royal Navy had informed them after a voyage unescorted from Australia to London up the English Channel that "the guns were not made for that ship yet." The coal they loaded in Brooklyn was inferior, and the ship's boiler tubes "were leaking like sieves," causing coal trimmer Reginald Trott, sixteen, to be "worked nearly to exhaustion" in order to achieve 8 knots.

The cargo included "bales of blankets, a large quantity of potatoes, flour, copper pipe, two big dynamos, each weighing about eight or nine tons, and car tires. On deck were eight cars and six trucks."[16] To this were added, "copper plating, jugs of acid," with one crew adding "canned milk, prunes, onions, five thousand cases of American beer, steel plates for ships, barrels of oil, Packards, Pontiacs and Studebakers, and two Mack trucks—the Lord only knows what else."[17] The twenty-one men transited Long Island Sound, then the Cape Cod Canal and crossed the Gulf of Maine, planning to hug their native coast, into the Bay of Fundy and past Bon Portage.

Third Mate Albert Sears was senior officer on duty on the bridge. Those men that could were resting below, as the following day watches were to be doubled to increase vigilance. Just as they approached Cape Sable from 20 miles away she was discovered by *U-432* under Schultze. Seventeen hours after attacking a large passenger ship escorted by a destroyer but having to break off due to deep-running and surface-skipping torpedoes, *U-432* rounded Cape Sable in calm conditions and clear blue skies. At 5.50 p.m., the *Liverpool Packet* emerged quickly from fog, heading northeast. It took twenty-five minutes for the ship and the submerged sub to pass each other about 10,000 feet apart. At 6.37 p.m., Schultze surfaced to observe, then dove and moved ahead of the ship in fog which reduced visibility to 2 miles.

After submerging at 6.55 p.m., Schultze surfaced at 8.15 p.m. and saw the *Liverpool Packet* roughly 5 miles away. Two minutes later, the Germans dove again; at 8.40 p.m., they fired a torpedo from Tube V that struck the ship less than a minute later—in the engine room area about 65 feet from the stern. Third Mate Sears had just left the starboard (seaward) side, to check the port bridge-wing, and thus did not see the torpedo. In the moments that followed, the chief engineer checked the engine room for signs of Atwood or Williams; however, the torpedo "tore it completely out of the ship," indicating that the two men were killed instantly.[18]

At the time of the attack, the skipper and several officers were anticipating a large ham with cloves in it presented by chief steward, who had survived as many as nine previous enemy attacks, including one in the Med where the men had been fired upon in the water, and another where they tread water for thirty-six hours. Captain Smith was at the head of the table, coffee cup in hand, when "he was thrown against the wall on the opposite side of the room." As he headed for the bridge, he noted that both portside boats were missing. As he clawed away from his doomed ship, Captain Smith called over his shoulder at a young sailor named Vernon from Shag Harbor for him to bring the ship's ensign; when the boy demurred, the skipper is said to have grabbed it himself.[19]

Bob Watt was relieved by Fireman Norman Atwood and Oiler Burns Williams at 8 p.m., then he had two cigarettes with a sailor before going below to fill a pail with hot water for tea. At 8.45 p.m., "something seemed to knock me all ways at once.... the shock was terrible—seemed to daze us so that we could not move for a few seconds." By the time he reached a stairwell after grabbing his life jacket, "the sea was coming down them." The starboard lifeboat was "blown to bits" so he and others struggled to free the smaller dory and a life raft, by which time "the water was nearly to our knees on deck."

Frantic efforts by the bosun, steward, second mate, and Watt failed to get a jammed raft free, another drifted off without any men in it. The dory was too filled with water to lift, so they only succeeded in floating it free of the ship by waiting "another few seconds for the ship to go down, then five of us jumped in—did we row to get clear of the suction!" It was swamped, but terrified sailors moved it clear quickly.[20]

Many of the men were forced to swim in the debilitating cold water to rafts or the swamped dory. By the time they managed to find Chief Officer John Tobin crying out for help, he was comatose and unable to speak. He later said that his fear was dispelled by hearing Captain Smith launch into a salty tirade. He had been blown over 75 feet by a secondary explosion and found refuge on a floating potato bind. Nineteen sailors were able to get away in a small ship's dory and a damaged lifeboat. Seven minutes after the torpedo was fired, Schultze wrote:

> [He] surfaced.... boats questioned and sinking location searched. It was the freighter *Liverpool Packet* from Liverpool NS loaded, allegedly from New York to Newfoundland. Name cannot be found in any register. Estimated at about 3,000 GRT.[21]

He could not find her name in his pre-war *Gröner* guide since it was only just renamed from the *Sonia*.

After watching the sinking, in which the bow was the last to submerge, Schultze surfaced *U-432* and moved toward the raft and boats, seeking (then finding) Captain Smith. The Canadians believed that the Germans wore underwear, perhaps misconstruing the gym-type gear popular with them. "After a 'pleasant' exchange, Schultze asked the crew if they knew where they were. In broken English, he pointed and said, 'Nova Scotia is that way.'" Before they left, an inquisitive Smith asked Schultze if he was German? "They said 'yes,' waved their hands, and steamed off." According to Radio Operator Howard Burchill's son, Michael, "Schultze ordered his crew to give the lifeboat some food, water, and a small compass."

U-123 Under Reinhard Hardegen entering a French port in 1942. (*James Payne, Through Their Eyes*)

Friedrichs and 1st Watch Officer Paul Loeser on *U-108*. Loeser later attacked New England in command of *U-373*. (*Willy Wilke, U-108*)

Korvettenkapitän Klaus Scholtz of *U-108* in his commander's berth, or small cabin, during patrol. There was minimal privacy on a patrol and the men never lived on the boats back at base, however a commander had more space than anyone else. (*Willy Wilke, U-108*)

Korvettenkapitän Klaus Scholtz of *U-108* on the conning tower during patrol. (*Willy Wilke, U-108*)

Chief Engineer Warner is timing a practice alarm dive, and clocked this one at 25.5 seconds. (*Willy Wilke, U-108*)

So many shipmates were eager to wish *U-108* "*bon voyage*" for her second patrol from Lorient in May 1941 that the spectator ship heeled over on its side. (*Willy Wilke, U-108*)

Oberleutnant zur See Fenn at a machine gun aboard *U-108*. (*Willy Wilke, U-108*)

Opposite above: The seasoned crew of *U-108* relaxing on the conning tower on return to France with victory pennants flying, which along with the beards indicate their arrival from patrol. They sank the *Norland* on this patrol. (*Willy Wilke, U-108*)

Opposite below: The Norwegian steamer *Norland* being sunk by *U-108* under Klaus Scholtz south of New England on May 20, 1942. All forty-eight Allied sailors survived, but the attack set up a highly complex set of rescues. (*Willy Wilke, U-108*)

Above: U-108 and Allied vessels encountering heavy seas typical of those off New England and the North Atlantic in the winter, though U-boats had the advantage of diving to avoid them for periods. (*Willy Wilke, U-108*)

Opposite above: Even among complex machinery, on the successful and timely operation of which everyone's lives depend, there is time for a smile. (*Willy Wilke, U-108*)

Opposite below: Machinist's Mate Werner. The Todt Organization constructed much of the *Autobahn* system in Germany as well as the impenetrable U-boat bunkers in France. (*Willy Wilke, U-108*)

U-boat sailor Max Henke, a friend of Willy Wilke's on *U-108*. (*Willy Wilke, U-108*)

Typical watch-standing routine on the conning tower: the potential for tedium is evident, yet without Radar or their own air cover in the Americas, binoculars and Sonar were all the Germans had to find targets and avoid destruction. (*Willy Wilke, U-108*)

A bird, also far from land, captured—or sheltered—aboard *U-108*. (*Willy Wilke, U-108*)

For both sides, weather was a constant foe: *U-108* in seas. (*Willy Wilke, U-108*)

U-boat life was not glamorous. There were two toilets (known as *heads*) below, and they easily backed up or exploded. One was usually filled with food for the first month. Mixing the detritus from heads with fuel, fumes, and sweat created quite a heady mix. (*Willy Wilke, U-108*)

Recreational activities being organized on the deck of *U-108*. (*Willy Wilke, U-108*)

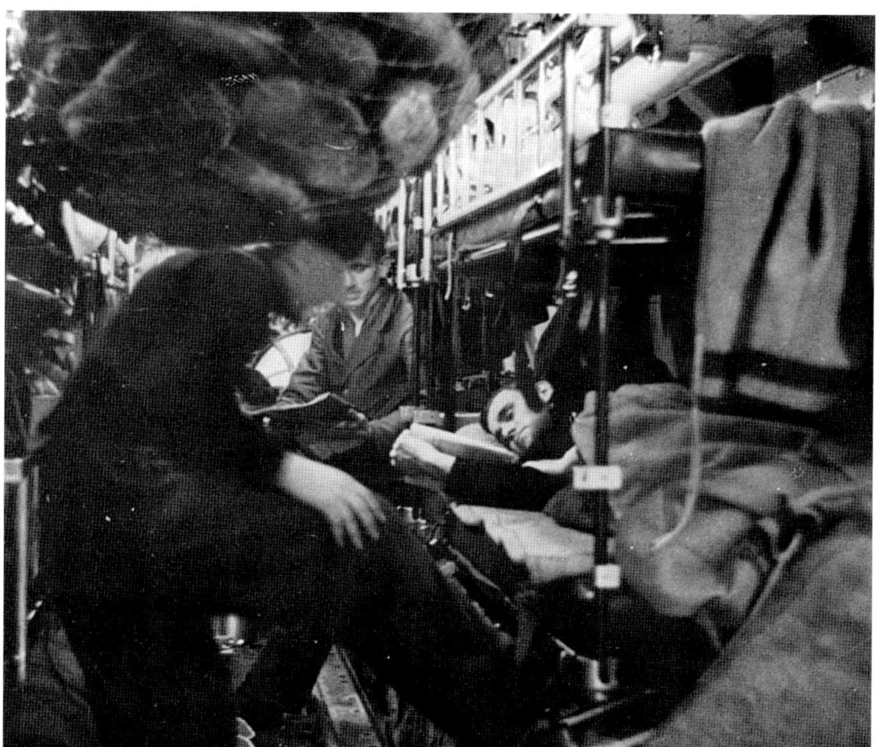

Above: Returning to Europe and safe harbor, *U-108* enters Wilhelmshaven in February 1941 from its first patrol. (*Willy Wilke, U-108*)

Opposite above: Eagerly returning to base: note the *Sperrbrecher* (minesweeper) behind in convoy escort, and the boom of a sailing craft tied alongside to the left. (*Willy Wilke, U-108*)

Opposite below: *U-108* bunks early in a patrol, as seen from the sacks of bread above the bunks: the clutter left little room to move around. (*Willy Wilke, U-108*)

Crew member of fishing vessel *Lark* showing an oar that had been shot up—Boston, June 15, 1944, after the boat was attacked by a frustrated *U-107* under Volker Simmermacher. (*NARA, U.S. Navy, Public domain, original in Author's collection*)

Opposite above: Another Allied ship being sunk by a U-boat in World War II: one of 3,474 sunk by Germans per Uboat.net. (*Public domain, Author's collection*)

Opposite below: The formerly French barquentine *Angelus*, operated entirely by hand, without even heat, just a stove. Built in 1912, it lasted thirty years until *Ajax* Achilles in *U-161* came upon her after a dry spell ad sent it to the bottom and the ten men to the boats, 80 percent of whom would freeze. (*Lou Boudreau, "Merchant Marines: Local tales of help and heroism in wartime," Halifax Herald News, November 9, 2017)*

10
10
10
10

These twelve sailors from the *Fort Qu'Appelle* seem justifiably elated after having just been rescued from the May waters of the Gulf of Maine by the friendly ship H.M.C.S. *Melville*, J 263, after two days in open boats. Thirteen of their shipmates perished in the ordeal; thirty-four made it. The photo must be on or after May 19, 1942 as the *Melville* under Commander Ingram pulled into Shelbourne. They had not seen land for about ten days, since leaving Jamaica after landing twenty-two survivors of the *Green Island* there. (*Helgason, Uboat.net/allies/warships/ship/2684, and uboat.net/allies/ merchants/ship/3516. Clearly taken by Royal Canadian Navy personnel and can be considered public domain*)

A new war order: U.S. Navy officers oversee the surrender by Germans and assumption of control over a U-boat in the mid-or-western-Atlantic in mid-May 1945. This scenario played itself a dozen times, with seven U-boats sunk in New England post-war and others repaired there. (*Courtesy of Derek Waller, U.S. Navy photo, NARA, Public domain*)

Survivors of the sinking of *U-550* on April 16, 1944, on the deck of U.S.S. *Joyce*. The relief of having survived, combined with the shock of what they just went through evident on their faces. (*uscg.mil/history/uscghist/U550.asp, public domain, c/o Munro, soundunderwatersurvey. com/wrecks/u-550/the-sinking-of-the-u-550*)

Charles Street Jail, now a hotel ironically named Liberty Hotel, celebrating its macabre past. (*nerconstruction.com/charlesstreetjail, now libertyhotel.com*)

U.S.S. *Guinevere*, IX 67, a former private yacht that patrolled Boston and Massachusetts Bay and rescued survivors of the stricken *Atlantic States*. (*Courtesy of Joe Radigan, Navsource.org/archives/09/46/46067, citing Hyper War, NARA, Public domain, U.S. Navy photo*)

The *Nemanja* working cargo in port as the *Trojan Prince* under the Prince Line (Furness, Withy & Co. Ltd.) between 1919 and 1942 (*wrecksite.eu/imgBrowser.aspx?20992, uboat.net/allies/merchants/ship/1510*)

U-234 being destroyed by U.S.S. *Greenfish*, U.S. Navy submarine, off Providence, in November 1947. (*courtesy of Derek Waller, U.S. Navy, NARA, Public domain, Wikipedia.org*)

The moment of discovery, foreshadowing rescue for Allied sailors adrift in a lifeboat on the North Atlantic after having been marooned by the loss of their ship to a U-boat in 1942–1945. The *Angelus* as well as the *Peisander* and many other sailors experienced the rush of relief from seeing a plane, though for the *Coimbra* survivors in January off New York, the plane did not bring rescue until it was too late for most of them. (*Robert Capa,* Disaster at Sea, Picture Story, Coronet, *May 1942, Vol. 12, No. 1, Whole No. 67, Author's collection*)

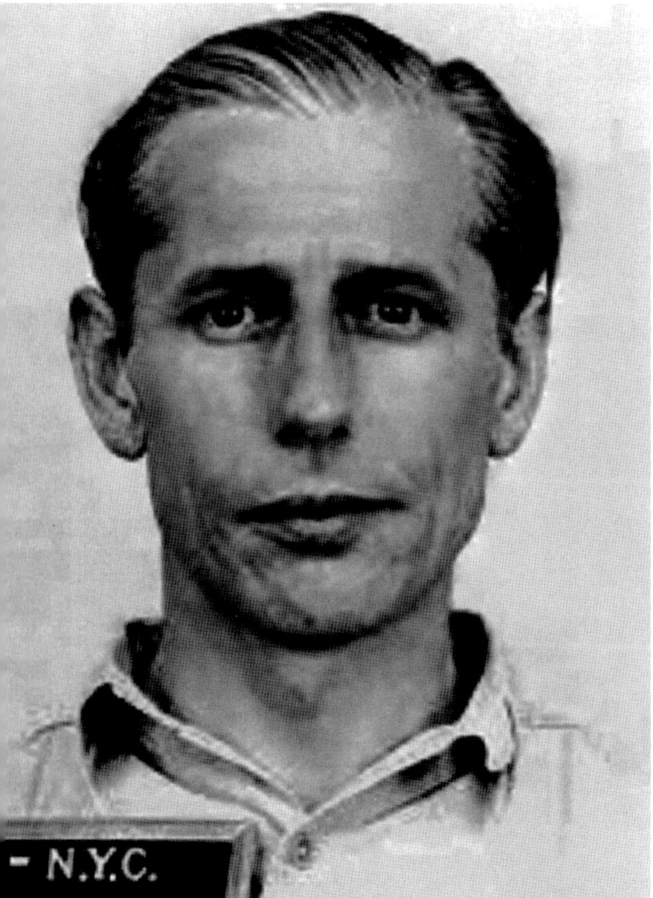

Above: An extraordinary image that must have been taken earlier in the war and in the "air gap" between where Allied planes could reach U-boats, showing a U-boat commander in white cap brazenly bringing his weapon (and no doubt other members of a wolf-pack) right among an Allied convoy, preparatory to opening fire and sinking ships laden with men and vital supplies. (*Public domain*)

Left: John Dasch, leader of *Operation Pastorius*, the failed plan to blow up infrastructure in the U.S. after an implausibly successful landing at Amagansett, Long Island in June 1942 in which *U-202* under Linder grounded itself at a 40-degree angle within earshot of armed American sentries, yet still managed to wriggle free after six hours. (*FBI mug-shot, NARA, Public domain*)

Friedrich (Fritz) Steinhoff, commander of *U-873* (which surrendered in Portsmouth), was then beaten while restrained, publicly taunted in the streets of Boston, jailed with common criminals opposite the main Boston hospital, cut his wrists, but was then allowed to bleed to death in transit (across the street) on May 19, 1945. His brother was a scientist highly decorated by the U.S. government. (*public domain*)

Otto von Bülow, commander of *U-404*, which patrolled actively in New England in World War II. (*Uboat.net/men/buelow*)

Above: U-977 and *U-530* departing Argentina for New England, summer 1945. (*Courtesy of Derek Waller*)

Opposite above: Burial of the "Unknown sailor" from *U-853* with military honors and dignitaries from the U.S. and Germany in 1960, fifteen years after the sailor perished. (*Adam Lynch, Naval History Magazine, "Kill and be Killed: the U-853 Mystery," June, 2018, Vol. 22, No. 3, Lusni.org/magazines*)

Opposite below: The burial at sea of German sailor Wenz from the deck of U.S.S. *Joyce* as it crossed the Gulf of Maine on April 17, 1944. (*U.S. Navy, NARA, Public domain*)

The spritely U.S.C.G. cutter *General Greene* which went to the aid of many ships during the war, notably men from the *Peisander*, the *Mattawin*, the *Norland*, the *Polyphemus*, the *Pan Pennsylvania*, and others. (*U.S. Coast Guard, Public domain*)

Three German U-boat sailors shivering and in shock after being pulled from a sinking or sunken submarine in the North Atlantic. It is believed to have been taken and distributed by the Royal Navy, further details unknown. (*Author's collection*)

Parade of Coastal Picket vessels, probably off Greenport, Long Island, late summer 1942. (*U.S. Coast Guard, Public domain*)

Propellers of *U-853* behind a security cordon at the Naval War College, Newport, Rhode Island, after having been moved from Castle Hill nearby, out of concern they may have been stolen during a spike in precious metals values. (*Google Images, Instagram, instarix.com/tag/u853, Tag: #u853, Instagram Pictures, InstaRix, image J8JyoZ, Medialar: image available in 2014, however link broken in 2018*)

Above: German propaganda photographer Tölle who rode along with Hardegen in *U-123* to record *Operation Drumbeat* in January 1942. Other amateurs like Willy Wilke took illicit photos for private albums aboard *U-108* under Scholtz, though officially not supposed to. U-boats were less formal than larger naval ships. (*Bundesarchiv Bild 101 II-MW-4006-20 Foto: Tölle 1942 Jan.–Feb.*)

Opposite above: The survivors of the *Gulfstate* sunk off the U.S. during 1942 improvised with material dropped from a U.S. Navy blimp to form this rough means of survival as seen from directly above. (*Kelly Bell, Operation Drumbeat: U-Boat Marauders on the American Coast, December 2016*)

Opposite below: German naval gunners preparing their weapon for action while on patrol in enemy territory in the Americas in 1942. (*Author's collection, Public domain*)

Rescue and retrieval of Allied survivors of U-boat attack on the U.S. eastern seaboard, early 1942, by a U.S. military vessel. Rescues were fraught with mortal perils; heavy work by the deck crew above, the seas were often rough, compounded communication barriers. Boats could be and were crushed against the sides, overturned, chopped by propellers, crushed by overhanging transoms at the stern, and men rolled into the sea where, even with rescue so tantalizingly close, they were overwhelmed. The rescuers worked in fear of being attacked. (*U.S. Coast Guard, Public domain*)

This tragic photo by Robert Capa shows men flung once again into the heart-stopping North Atlantic and losing their lives. Note the looks of shock on at least three of the men's faces, as seen in their eyes. These tragedies occurred aboard the *Pan Penn* and several other ships, which in the fear of a tanker about to explode, the dark of night, and a sense of a second torpedo imminent, men lost their heads, panicked, and launched boats while the ship was moving, or without clearing lines. (*Robert Capa,* Disaster at Sea, Picture Story, Coronet, *May 1942, Vol. 12, No. 1, Whole No. 67, Author's collection*)

A lifeboat of grateful survivors of a U-boat attack comes alongside an Allied ship and avoid being crushed or drowned in the critical transfer of personnel up a vertical wall of steel. The officer in brown cap, second from left at back, is in control of the boat. (*Capa, "Disaster at Sea,"* Picture Story, Coronet, *May 1942, Vol. 12, No. 1, Whole No. 67, Author's collection*)

Three Allied victims of German U-boat attack being rescued from a Carley Float raft off the U.S. eastern seaboard, early 1942. One is older the other seems on the verge of giving in to the cold. (*U.S. Coast Guard, Public domain*)

Rescue and retrieval of two injured Allied survivors of U-boat attack on the U.S. eastern seaboard, early 1942. (*U.S. Coast Guard, Public domain*)

Anti-American spy William Colepaugh. (*FBI files, Public domain*)

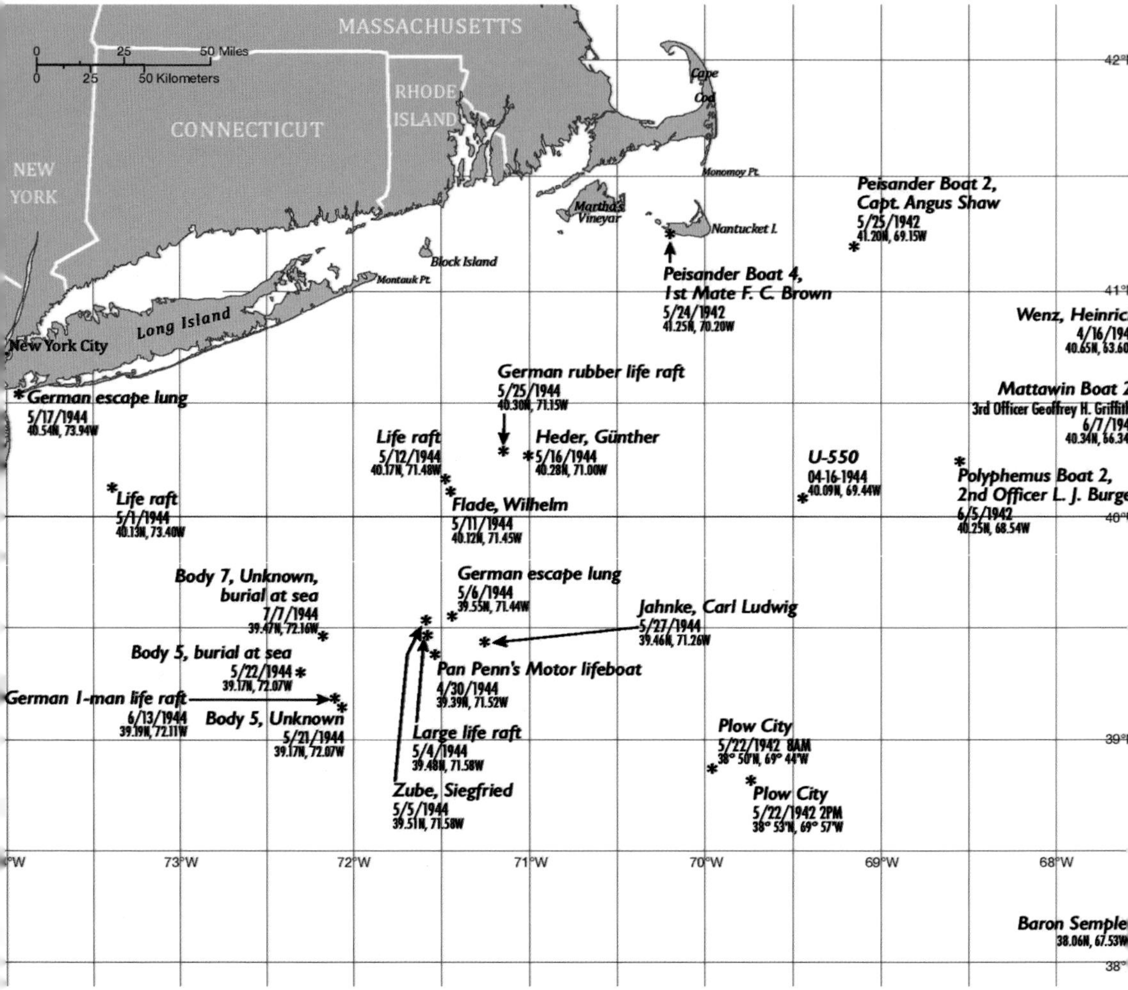

U-550 scatter debris field, shown to the left, or west, with other ships and lifeboats whose men landed on Nantucket by U.S.C.G.C. *General Greene* to the left. (*Robert Eller Pratt*)

Later, Smith was asked many times why he was not more defiant to the Germans. Pointing out that they had two large guns trained on him and his men at all times, he openly confessed to being kindlier than when he had been courting his wife. Then *U-432* headed off, and by 8 a.m. the next day was going after a schooner. Smith knew his way around the Atlantic, having crossed it forty-two times. A dozen of the sailors were from the Bay of Fundy and Nova Scotia—both very close-knit communities. The engine-room workers Atwood (aged thirty-five) and Williams perished. John Tobin was bruised in a bad way, James Hunt's hand was injured, Albert Sears had his head and shoulders injured, and others suffered from cuts and bruises.[22] By Bob Watt's account, they set off for land at 9.30 p.m. on Friday, May 30.

The attack was reported to the Eastern Sea Frontier as the *Sonia*, a Canadian fishing vessel of 1,188 tons, torpedoed 15 miles west of Seal Island. The nineteen men, including Burchill, managed to row for some twenty hours toward Seal Island. This was frustrating work, as they were brought close enough to see it, then the immense Fundy currents pulled and pushed them away until many hours later. The boats were originally lashed together, and in order to provide enough room for men to row, others had to hang their legs over the side. Their emergency supplies provided only squares of chocolate, some drinking water, and a first aid kit. Though the weather was settled, a night in May in those waters is a cold night. This was made worse by the few minutes most of the sleeping men had to grab clothes: the bosun and chief engineer were not wearing anything, and most of the other were "pretty scantily dressed," observed Watt, adding "I didn't think anyone could be so cold and live."[23]

At 5 a.m. on Sunday, eight hours after the attack, they first saw Seal Island, but despite rowing all day, they did not make it back there again until 3 p.m. At that point, they abandoned rowing and raised the lifeboat's sail. Being faster than the dory, the men in the lifeboat called back to the dory-men that they would send a motorboat to fetch them. Then the wind died, enabling those rowing in the dory to keep up with the lifeboat, as they inched toward the island from 2 miles out, dreading another cold night. Fortunately, it was unnecessary for the two groups to separate.

At 4 p.m., they were discovered by local lobstermen Captain Crowell Nickerson and his son. The inquisitive teenager kept insisting that his father stop pulling the string of traps that he had been the last to set that spring and look at the boats.[24] "We thought it was a can-buoy, and we'd salvage it," one of them said, "so we ran up on her."[25] When he realized it was a sail from a small lifeboat, Nickerson quickly sped over, and he and his son pulled the nearly naked men aboard. Some of them recognized each other. Then the Nickersons took the boats under tow for land.

As the twenty or so families eking a living from the sea on Seal Island had heard torpedo explosions the night before, they were on edge. When fourteen-year-old Sheldon Simmons saw nineteen strangers being landed on their island, he feared the worst—namely that Nazis had invaded. Once the misunderstanding was cleared up, their fellow-Canadians were "warmed up" and given seafood chowder, tobacco, dry clothes. Jamie Hunt, whose thumb was badly hurt, was so fond of the lobster chowder that he over-indulged, and during a three-hour voyage in a fast motorboat to Barrington Passage, on the mainland, he was sick, then passed out. The men were only on Seal Island from after 5 p.m. to 9 p.m., arriving in Barrington Passage at midnight, since Norm Smith commandeered the fastest boat on Seal Island.

Barrington Passage, on the mainland, is roughly 19 miles east of Seal Island and lies just shoreward of Sable Island. Captain Smith made his way home to nearby Woods Harbor, Milton Cranton to Doctor's Cove (without a fine suit he had bought in New York City to impress his wife), Edward Smith and John Sear to Clam Point, and Reginald Trott, Robert (Bob) Watt, and Jamie Hunt were from Barrington itself. Larry Townsend went a short distance east to Lockport, Ross Richards to LeHave, and Norman Penny to Liverpool. Other men stayed at the Victoria Hotel in Barrington Passage. From there, they found land transportation to Halifax, their original destination, the following day. Bob Watt concluded that "it was pretty tough at the time, but I guess I will be going again." Ruminating on the loss of his shipmates, he said, "I suppose the two didn't know what happened."[26]

Burchill's son, Mike, made a documentary about the episode; he still has his father's *Liverpool Packet* flashlight. Burchill is motivated not only to shed light on the events and unite family of survivors and the two men killed but also to reach out to Schultze's family and thank them for his having spared his father and the other men's lives. Captain Smith gave Crowell Nickerson of Stoney Island the compass Heinz-Otto Schultze had given him. Thus, the little compass was handed from the hands of three commanders—U-boat, merchant ship, and lobster boat—in less than a day. Smith intended to donate the lifeboat and dory to the lobsterman; however, the ship's owners would not permit it. Even though he did not receive formal recognition, Nickerson said he "had the personal satisfaction of knowing that I had saved nineteen men."

Smith said that the *Liverpool Packet* was the only ship he ever lost, as well as being the smallest he commanded.[27] He once took leave of a Royal Canadian Navy dockyard by telling the admiral in charge not to worry about policing the seas because Norm Smith had it under control.[28] He went on to a career in politics during his remaining twenty-eight years. Canadian folk historian Richardson noted that though "sunken and crippled ships had already given proof that the war was on our doorstep, the torpedoing of Cap'n Norm's ship, the death of two neighbors, and the narrow escape of many others, brought this home with terrible force."

The otter-dragger fishing schooner *Ben and Josephine* was built in 1941 by Morse Boatbuilding of Thomaston, Maine. Launched on March 15, her owners, agents, and godmother were the family of Captain Benjamin Curcuru. The master was Captain Giuseppe (a.k.a. Joseph or Joe) Ciaramitaro of Gloucester.[29] The wooden vessel was 102 tons, 92 feet long, had a 20-foot beam, and a 9.5-foot draft. She was capable of carrying 130,000 pounds of fish and was specifically designed for redfish. The schooner had cabins for ten persons and her deck was raised toward the stern. The *Ben and Josephine* was equipped with a 220-hp Atlas diesel engine capable of 335 rpm, as well as a smaller 7.5-hp diesel engine driving a pump, plus a 4-kilowatt generator. Her cordage was the Plymouth brand, nets by Grimbsy, and fish hoist by New England.[30]

The fishing vessel *Aeolus* was 41 tons, a dragger with a schooner rig and auxiliary motor. Her captain and owner was John O. Johnson, an unlimited-tonnage-licensed master. The vessel was built in 1922 in Friendship, Maine and

Family, ship's godmother, and owners of the *Ben and Josephine* at the large vessel's auspicious launch. (*Charles Dana Gibson, in an article about his grandfather's boat* Ben and Josephine, *republished 9 Jan. 2012, goodmorninggloucester.wordpress.com, also credits Douglas Norwood of Maine, who wrote an article for* "Sou'west Harbor" *Maine newsletter, Feb. 2010*)

was based in Gloucester. Everett Gallagher was her engineer, and there were four other men aboard—six in all. The *Aeolus* and her crew headed out of Gloucester on Cape Ann at 7 p.m. on Tuesday, June 2, 1942, in company with the *Ben and Josephine*, their destination the Seal Island fishing grounds. The two-vessel convoy traveled at about 9 knots until they were roughly 150 miles east-southeast of Thatcher's Island Light, east of Gloucester.[31]

At 3 p.m. the following day (3 June), the *Ben and Josephine* was 4 miles ahead of the *Aeolus*. The lead vessel had 1,500 pounds of redfish; the *Aeolus* had no fish yet. Although there was a slight haze on the horizon, the atmosphere was clear, there was no wind, and the sea was calm. Men on both boats observed an unmarked submarine on the surface nearby, on a parallel course about 2 miles to starboard, or to the east of the *Ben and Josephine*. Visibility was 6 miles, and the men on both vessels saw no reason for concern as they presumed the submarine was friendly. They studied the sub with binoculars, but, "finding nothing to indicate the craft was an enemy," held their course and speed for the next hour. The submarine did the exact same. Then, at 4 p.m., when the boats were all about 10 miles further east, the U-boat altered course abruptly to the west, or port, toward the *Ben and Josephine*. As it increased speed, it quickly became clear the sub planned to cut off the leading fishing boat.

U-432 under Schultze came to within just 600 feet of the *Ben and Josephine* before it again straightened course and ran parallel to its intended victim. Then the submariners fired a burst of machine gun fire behind the fisherman. The *Ben and Josephine*'s engineer was on deck and called for the captain, who was sleeping below.[32] Rousted to a shocking attack, Captain Ciaramitaro raced in the direction of the pilot house along the deck in order to use the radio and alert the authorities. Schultze anticipated his intent, and his men "fired a determined burst of machine gun or light cannon with tracer bullets through the pilot house." Ciaramitaro decided that discretion would be the better part of valor and ordered the fishing dories overboard and his vessel abandoned.

While the eight fishermen in a pair of dories rowed away from the doomed *Ben and Josephine*, the Germans fired into her from the forward gun using projectiles 3 inches in diameter. As the fishermen scrambled to get out of the line of fire, a pair of shells were landed near them. Once the men were clear, between thirty-eight and forty-eight shells were pumped into the wooden hull while *U-432* circled the stricken boat. Even at very close range, a number of the shots missed, though enough found their mark that after thirty minutes, at 4.30 p.m., the *Ben and Josephine* sank by the head Gulf of Maine.

Not far behind, the *Aeolus*'s Captain Johnson witnessed the attack and by 4.25 p.m. altered course to the north-northeast toward Canada. Schultze then fired a warning shell over the second fishing vessel. On recognizing the intent, Johnson ordered the engine stopped and dories launched. At that point, the sub started paralleling the *Aeolus*'s course to starboard about 750 feet distant, also going north-northeast. While the six men from the *Aeolus* were getting away in two dories, the submarine fired two shots from its deck gun, one of the shells hitting the fishing schooner's starboard bow. As the *Aeolus* men pulled astern, the submarine went around her bow and from the port side of the fisherman fired numerous times, making some eight hits on the hull. Johnson was concerned about navigating his dories without a compass, so he daringly rowed back to the starboard side, crawled aboard, yanked a compass out of the binnacle, or short stand, threw it into a dory, and followed it moments later. Unaware of his moves, seconds later, German gunners strafed the pilothouse where he had been.

The *Aeolus* was sinking, and *U-432* moved ahead of her and shot off two more rounds. The technique of firing the length rather than the width of a vessel maximizes destruction wrought by each shot but provides a much smaller target. One of the two shells did hit the hull, but the second missed and flew over both the schooner and the dories filled with survivors behind it. Engineer Gallagher related that he "hurt my hip when I fell into the dory from the rail of the boat and I had to do my turn at the oars." At 5 p.m., having devoted half an hour to the sinking, Schultze headed west at 15 knots, without having spoken audibly among themselves. The fishermen observed three Germans on the conning tower and three manning the gun and estimated they fired between sixteen rounds, of which eight were hits.

The fishermen did not have any valuable or classified information on board, though there were efforts by U.S. naval intelligence to place radio transmitters on fishing vessels, which were privy to enemy sub movements and a valuable resource. Clearly, there were fissures in the unspoken truce between submariners and fishermen. The Navy wishfully gloated about their utilization of fishermen and pigeons:

> Carrier pigeons were used to transmit messages from the fishing fleet to Naval authorities. [More than 500] fishermen observers also aided materially in rescue work and the recovery of floating materials from lost or damaged, ships … when the German sub commanders became aware [that] they were being reported, they were forced to move under-water instead of on the surface, slowing their progress into the areas through which Allied ships might pass.[33]

The fishermen described the sub as 250–300-foot long with no net-cutters, a dark, dull-grey hull, large conning tower, machine gun platform, and antenna. After the Germans left, the four dories of the *Aeolus* and the *Ben and Josephine* gathered together. They initially set off for nearby Seal Island; however, headwinds caused them to reappraise this decision, and they were forced to change course for Mount Desert Rock, which was further away but downwind. They rowed and sailed for the next thirty-six hours, from 5 p.m. Wednesday the 3rd to 5 a.m. Friday, June 5.

The *Ben and Josephine* men had no compass, yet arrived on isolated Mount Desert Rock at 4.30 a.m.

The *Aeolus* men, who had the compass, arrived about half an hour later on the same windswept rock. All fourteen men found shelter at the U.S. Coast Guard station there. During their voyage, the survivors heard gunfire twice: late on Wednesday and then at 3 a.m. on Friday. The *Aeolus* men heard seven shots fired at 6 p.m., an hour after the sub left them. When they arrived "all men suffered somewhat from exposure, but none were lost or injured." They were interviewed by Lieutenant (junior grade) Philip J. Deering, Jr. (U.S.N.R.), as well as a submariner aboard a U.S. Navy submarine in Canso Bay named Lieutenant (junior grade) W. M. Wilcox (U.S.N.R.), who helped other interviewers like Deering, particularly with illustrating the events.

The survivors were convinced they saw men in the conning tower taking film footage. Interviewers groused that many of the crew "spoke broken English, being of Italian and Portuguese stock, and their estimates of what they saw varied widely." The fishermen saw "considerable underwater exhaust smoke which they described as very yellow and very disagreeable in odor." Another observation seems odd, given that the fishermen were only 600 feet from an enemy vessel engaged in a wartime attack: "they could not recall hearing any words spoken by any person aboard the submarine."

Captain Ciaramitaro told his relatives, one of whom, Charles Dana Gibson, addressed the thorny issue of wartime morale in the Gloucester fishing community: "When the full news became known," Gibson relates, "enthusiasm for the offshore fisheries declined sharply. It would be some weeks before the men of Gloucester again extended their voyages east of Cape Porpoise, Maine." Douglas Norwood was a young Freshman in his first year at Pemetic High School in Southwest Harbor, near Bar Harbor. His father rushed home early from work chattering on the phone about making beds ready for fourteen freezing fishermen. Together with members of the American Red Cross and the Coast Guard, they set up cots in the high school gymnasium. Norwood said the men rowed through a twelve-hour rain storm.[34]

After they had recovered and been interviewed, the Coast Guard took the men to the Southwest Harbor Coast Guard Station, roughly 25 miles to the north. The survivors spent a night in the gym being offered "baskets of food" and "fish chowder and biscuits, hot coffee and dessert." Norwood's father was the chairman of the local American Red Cross and arranged for a bus to transport them home to Gloucester. Full of enthusiasm for revenge, Captain Johnson enrolled in the U.S. Navy, where he spent the balance of the war as a navigational instructor at Great Lakes Naval Training Station. After the war, one of his commands was the *Little Joe*, going for yellow-tail tuna out of New Bedford. Everett Gallagher, the *Aeolus* engineer, resented the Germans filming the sinking, and believing that his "boat was sunk just to get the pictures." He said that "one fellow pointed [the camera], and the other cranked it."[35]

The *Malayan Prince* was an 8,593-ton motorized merchant ship built in Germany in March 1926 by Deutsche Werft in Hamburg. Her owner at the time of attack off Canada was Furness Withy of Liverpool, and homeport London. At the time of the attack, the *Malayan Prince* was in Convoy BX 23A, voyaging New York to Halifax, then due to sail for Belfast Lough and Cardiff. She was laden with a general cargo consisting of war material.[36] At 8.01 a.m. on June 9, 1942, Schultze in *U-432* sent four torpedoes into the convoy as it approached Cape Sable. A minute and a half later, the ship *Kronsprinsen* was damaged by one of them. A different torpedo missed its target and after more than two minutes struck the *Malayan Prince*, damaging her, but only slightly. She was repaired in Halifax and returned to service in a matter of weeks, by July 1942. The *Malayan Prince* survived the war until July 1950, when she was broken up in Inverkeithing, Scotland.[37]

Heinz-Otto Schultze was born in 1915 and perished at age twenty-eight when *U-849* was found and sunk by a U.S. B-24 Liberator on November 25, 1943, at the mouth of the Congo River estuary off Africa. The depth charges doomed the boat with all hands. Schultze's father Otto commanded SM *U-63* in World War I, accounting for fifty-two ships of nearly 130,000 tons.[38]

11

The Boston Minefield and Five U-boats Attack the *Moldanger*, the *Port Nicholson*, and the *Cherokee*

Kapitänleutnant Karl Thurmann brought *U-553* on a two-week incursion into New England from May 25 to June 8, 1942. He rounded Cape Sable and headed northwest until the 27th, then entered the Bay of Fundy. On the 30th, *U-553* returned and motored southeast of Nantucket to June 2 then headed west for three days. Thurmann dog-legged back northeast for a day, then headed southeast and exited eastbound from Cape Sable.[1] The patrol began in St. Nazaire on April 19 and ended there on June 24, with more attacks on the submarine than by it. On May 3, the sub was driven away from a steamer by a corvette escort which damaged the periscope and other equipment with two depth charges. When Thurmann penetrated the Gulf of St. Lawrence an aircraft dropped three depth charges, and the minesweeper H.M.C.S. *Medicine Hat* followed up with an attack, requiring repairs to the submarine.[2]

Thurmann was being deliberately tracked by the Canadians, who reported a radio-direction-finding (RDF) fix at 11.33 p.m. on an enemy submarine "proceeding east-northeast.... 60 miles south of Cape Sable" on June 1. This was the same position and the same time as *U-553*, with no other U-boats there then.[3] At roughly the same time, *U-553* logged an aircraft at a low altitude heading west, "type not recognized," and (riskily) received and sent radio messages just before and after the plane's overflight. The sub's course was indeed "ENE" just as the Allies reported it.[4] It was a match: both sides were looking at each other.

Thurmann sank two ships—the British *Nicoya* and the Dutch *Leto*—on 12 May before entering the area, and the British *Mattawin* of 6,919 tons on June 2 while there. The *Mattawin* was hit at 7.18 a.m. and finished off only twelve minutes later by a *coup de grâce*.[5] Thurmann believed he hit another ship after his two successes, but it is unconfirmed. In the Bay of Fundy, the boat positioned itself to observe ship traffic in and out of St. John, for long enough to convince its commander that it was not a staging area for convoys. The boat had less than a month's provisions on June 2 when it sank the *Mattawin*, and so when the men found an empty lifeboat the following day they stripped it of supplies. Thurmann crowed about finding "lots of well-preserved bread and chocolate, for two complete meals, and condensed milk, too, and good-tasting vitamin tablets of enormously satiating effect, enough for fourteen days. All very welcome."[6] This was the *Berganger*'s port lifeboat which floated free after *U-578* under Rehwinkel sank the Norwegian ship on the night of June 1–2. While *en route* home, *U-553* dog-legged to find a convoy from Halifax, but the following day (June 11), *U-553* was caught by a flying boat while on the surface and forced to dive to evade and then withstood depth charges. Further damaged, *U-553* made for France.[7]

Thurmann was born 1909 and was a member of the Crew of 1928. He was lost four days after leaving France on about January 20, 1943, after sending the eerie message "periscope not clear," then all hands were never heard again.[8] His training included service aboard the light cruisers *Emden* and *Köln* until April 1940, when he joined U-boats. He was a commander-in-training of *U-29* before commissioning *U-553* in December 1940. Thurmann was the only commander of *U-553*, and together they accomplished 344 days over ten patrols. During that time, they sank thirteen ships for 62,315 tons and damaged two others for 15,273 tons. On August 24, 1942, he was awarded the Knights Cross.

Kapitänleutnant Otto von Bülow brought *U-404* on its second incursion of New England for eight days May 26 to June 29, 1942. *U-404* entered the region heading westward; then, on May 27, von Bülow turned north before backtracking south for the next two days. He exited the region on May 30. On May 26, he and Rehwinkel were warned to patrol "up to the fog limit," as many skippers complained that lack of visibility was stunting their success.[9] While away, *U-404*'s men sank six ships of some 25,000 tons: the *Alcoa Shipper* on May 30 closer to Bermuda, the *West Notus* on June 1, the *Anna* two days later, the *Ljubica Matkovic* on June 24, and the *Nordal* and the *Manuela* on the 25th, near Cape Hatteras. The next day, the Germans discovered a life vest from the Norwegian ship *Bris*, sunk to the south on April 21 by *U-201* under Adalbert Schnee. Four sailors lost their lives, and Captain Hansen's lifeboat was rolled over three times before the men were rescued. The life vest must have been torn free, along with "the loss of food and equipment."[10] On June 27, during his return leg, von Bülow brought *U-404* back through New England, sinking the *Moldanger* south of Block Island that day.

After *U-404* was attacked by an Allied aircraft and damaged, necessitating a return to base in France, it headed east on June 29.[11] On July 1, von Bülow and his men had the U-tanker *U-459* in sight and less than an hour later were connected to it with a fuel hose. Seventy minutes after sighting one another, they began transferring fifteen cubic meters of fuel oil. In three hours, the boats were separated. This patrol began in Brest on May 6 and ended in St. Nazaire on July

14. The laundry list of repairs for the shipyard included "new exhaust gas piping, port (pressure hull to muffler), two battery cells, rubber-bonded metal for drain pipes." *U-404* also took part in the *Padfinder* group with seven other boats, during which von Bülow sank the *West Notus* using scuttling charges set by a boarding party.

The Norwegian cargo motor ship *Moldanger* was completed in March 1933 by Netherlands Shipbuilding of Amsterdam. Her owners were Westfal-Larsen of Bergen, the ship's home port. She was a single-deck vessel of 6,827 tons, 496 feet long, 61 feet wide, and 31 feet deep. Her 8,200-hp oil-fired engine turned a single screw that propelled the *Moldanger* at 15.5 knots when built, and over 14 knots in 1942.[12] From March 1940, the ship ran dedicated runs hauling cargo from Atlantic South American ports to U.S. ports, Norfolk to New York. In 1941, the owners added Caribbean ports, then transited Panama for U.S. ports in the Pacific northwest as well as Vancouver. She left San Francisco for the last time in mid-April 1942 bound to Valparaiso, transited the Straits of Magellan with a call at Punta Arenas, and arrived in Buenos Aires on May 16 to load for New York.

Like nearly a thousand other merchant ships, the *Moldanger* was being operated by Nortraship—the Norwegians in exile in New York.[14] She was armed with a 4-inch gun located on the stern as well as a pair of .303-caliber machine guns positioned either side of the bridge manned by two Norwegian gunners and fitted for degaussing. Frode Bjørn Hansen of Bergen was in command of the forty-four men aboard the *Moldanger*. The only crew members not from Norway were a Swede, two Canadians, and three Danes.

For three weeks to June 8, the *Moldanger*'s crew loaded a diverse cargo weighing 8,700 tons in Buenos Aires. It included barrels of tallow (reduced animal fat), vegetable oil, sheep's wool, and salted hides destined for the markets of New York. The day before the ship sailed Captain Hansen asked his thirty-nine-year-old Bergen-born chief officer if he would like to telephone his wife and daughter in Norway. Ivar Bøe replied that he could never afford the $25 required for a three-minute phone conversation. Hansen generously proposed that if the mate put in some extra hours on painting projects, the cost would be covered. So Bøe was able to speak with both of them, and as chance would have it, this was to be the last time they would hear his voice. Later on, Hansen and his interviewers wondered whether German intelligence agents acted on information regarding the ship's movements provided in that call.

The *Moldanger* sailed up the South Atlantic and into northern waters per instructions provided by a British routing officer in Argentina. After crossing latitude 10 degrees south, Hansen zigzagged to throw off attackers. For nineteen days, nothing unusual occurred, until the ship was less than twenty-four hours from New York. Midday of Saturday, June 27, found the *Moldanger* 280 miles south of Nantucket, still in the mighty Gulf Stream, an in-ocean river flowing at 2–5 knots northeast, over ocean 10,000 feet deep. The weather was fair, with a smooth sea and light wind from the southwest, across the port beam. Visibility was good as the ship headed northwest.

Unbeknown to the crew until the last few seconds when a torpedo was sighted steaking toward them from 600 feet away by the lookout in the crow's nest, *U-404* under von Bülow was stalking them, trying to keep up with the fast-moving ship for almost six hours. The Germans finally struck at 4.57 p.m. There were four lookouts posted: one perched in the crow's nest attached to a mast high overhead, another at the 4-inch gun aft, and two deck officers on the bridge. The Norwegian ensign was not flying.

When the lookouts on *U-404* first sighted the *Moldanger* at 10.53 a.m., von Bülow described his quarry as a modern freighter with two large masts fore and aft, as well as two smaller ones, steering 325 degrees northwest at 14 knots and zigzagging. He kept track of her numerous course changes, at 1.20 p.m., 2 p.m., and 3.22 p.m. By 4.20 p.m., he was ready and "dove to attack," suggesting that the U-boat was surfaced when making its initial survey of the battle scene. *U-404*'s first torpedo left Tube V set for 10 feet depth and a speed of 40 knots. After a run of thirty-seven seconds, it a hit the center of the ship's port side, sending water as high as the funnels, but with a detonation which was barely audible.

The steamer stopped, but no boats were observed in the water yet. As the guns were manned and no boats were launched, von Bülow held his boat back, despite having seen the explosive column. To be sure they would be lured closer by a decoy, and as she did not seem to be sinking deeper, von Bülow sent a second torpedo from Tube III five minutes after the first and before waiting for the men to get clear in the boats. After twenty-seven-and-a-half seconds, von Bülow recorded "high explosion column, metal parts fly through the air, the cannon topples over. Surfaced. Steamer sinks quickly over the stern-post."[13]

Aboard the *Moldanger*, the first missile killed Second Engineer Ramsli and Motorman Tollefsen and knocked out the engines. There were frenetic efforts to gather life jackets, survival suits and gear, and quickly launch the boats and rafts in order to get clear of the ship. Since the first torpedo disabled the antennae, Canadian Radio Operator Charles Steward was unable to send a distress signal, meaning that von Bülow did not yet know the name of his quarry, and later felt compelled to ask survivors. Captain Hansen threw the Royal Navy code books overboard in weighted bags.

Since the torpedo struck to port, there was an emphasis on getting the boats and rafts on the starboard side free immediately, as they were undamaged and less unlike to be hit right away. Unfortunately, due to the *Moldanger*'s high speed when hit, the ship's forward momentum swamped the motorboat as it was lowered, immersing and putting its engine out of action for good. However, the men managed to salvage the motorboat, bail it out, and collect other survivors in it. The small gig, designed for running errands and repairs in harbor but fitted out by Hansen in Buenos Aires as an emergency survival craft for six men, was undamaged and occupied, as were three rafts, all of them manned by survivors.

Although there was no panic, the launching of survival craft did not go as planned. Twenty-two-year-old Motorman Einar Mendelev and seven other sailors were lowering a starboard lifeboat when the lines holding one end snagged, the other line ran free, and the boat dangled from one end, spilling two men into the sea. They clambered back aboard using nets strung for that purpose. When the boat was finally launched, the *Moldanger* made a sudden course change, with the result that the lifeboat was pulled under the stern of the ship and pressed into the water, flooding it.

Due to these failures to secure escape from the safer side, seven men were forced to run to the port side in order to board a lifeboat there. However, they arrived just as von Bülow sent a second torpedo aft, near the number five hatch, killing the group of seven new arrivals, as well as four others who were working furiously to free the lifeboat, meaning thirteen sailors, including Chief Officer Bøe who had called his family for the last time a few weeks before, were killed in the attack.

According to Hansen, "the whole stern ... seemed to be blown off with the striking of the second torpedo." He added that she flooded right away, and thus there were no fires aboard. The men who survived the carnage of the second torpedo suffered numerous wounds, broken legs and ribs, fractured jaws (which prevented them from chewing for weeks), concussions, headaches, and a dislocated shoulder from being banged around by the force of impact, sea water, cargo (like bales of wool), and numerous lines and wires associated with the chaos of a large sinking ship. The ship's stern was "practically demolished" by the second explosion and sank within three minutes.

Von Bülow dispassionately recorded how the explosion sent "iron wheels whirling through the air," and caused the ship's cannon to tilt at odd angles. At 5.30 p.m., he noted that "steamer sinks quickly by the stern ... from lifeboats, I learn she is the *Moldanger*, home port Oslo [Bergen, *sic.*]." The Norwegians gathered from their interactions with von Bülow that he was interested in the fate of another Norwegian ship named *Molda*, which had been in Buenos Aires at the same time as them. This, logically, led the Norwegians to believe that *U-404*'s men were acting on prior intelligence as to the movements of both the *Moldanger* and the *Molda*.

Since Captain Hansen was perched alone on a raft in the distance, von Bülow interviewed Boatswain (Bosun) Harry Monsen, who only spoke broken English, instead, saying "he was sorry," and "asking if the boys could pick [Hansen] up," as he saw Hansen on a raft by himself, together with a man hanging on to a smoke float in the water. The Norwegians told von Bülow that they would take care of their own, at which point "the commander saluted, in the old formal way ... and retired into the conning-tower. Shortly after this, the submarine submerged, and was not seen again." Assuming a formal manner would have been natural to von Bülow, the progeny of an aristocratic family in Schleswig-Holstein (a distant non-consanguineous von Bülow named Claus later settled in Newport with his wife Sunny). There were four Germans and a machine gun seen on the oval conning tower. While maneuvering among the men and wreckage, *U-404*'s engines were started and stopped a number of times, emitting a rumbling noise and smoky exhaust. This caused the Norwegians to believe she was an older submarine, although *U-404* was launched a year earlier, on June 4, 1941.

The Norwegians described the commander as a "short, dark complexioned individual with black pointed beard, wearing dark jacket, dark shorts and black naval officer's cap," and *U-404* as 250–300 feet long, dark gray with a 4-inch gun, machine gun on deck, and aerials strung from the conning tower. The crew was considered of a dark complexion and mostly shirtless. The Allies said the paint was "badly worn" and "grey with rusty patches," saying "sub believed to be old craft." Oddly, the Norwegians felt the submarine was Italian. *U-404* remained in the area for fifteen minutes before motoring off to the northwest and submerging roughly 1 mile away. This was just a typical U-boat ploy, as *U-404* was low on supplies after seventy-day patrol and quickly altered course to the east. It arrived in St. Nazaire more than two weeks later, on July 14. She was sunk on July 28, 1943, by three aircraft in the Bay of Biscay with the loss of all fifty-one officers and men. Von Bülow lived until 2006 and age ninety-four.

Both of the *Moldanger*'s port lifeboats and one starboard lifeboat were destroyed, with one starboard lifeboat, the small gig and three rafts getting clear. Out of forty-four men, two were killed by the first torpedo in the engine-room, eleven were killed by the second torpedo, and Motorman Johan Larsen was so badly burned that he would last just over a week in a lifeboat before expiring, no doubt creating a tortuous experience for the other men in the boat. Thirty-one men set off for land in (or on) five small craft, each of which was equipped with sails (the boats) or jury-rigged sails with oars (the rafts). The motor was a non-factor. At first, all of the craft raised sail and set off to the northwest and the U.S. coast. By the second day, a slow raft was stripped of equipment and people and cast adrift.[15]

On July 5, the British Admiralty inquired of Bermuda after the well-being of the *Moldanger*, in case the ship had called on the island *en route* to New York, with nothing learned. This demonstrates that authorities knew she was overdue. Hansen's boat, the biggest, stuck with the rafts and gig at first, until the line connecting them parted. After three days, the gig, though not equipped with a compass, went ahead hoping to find help. This was partly because no airplanes or ships had been seen. The remaining two rafts were ultimately swept east with the strong current. Without sufficient sails, oars, or a motor, the rafts were unable to make headway in the desired direction, and thus surrendered to winds and currents. After men shuffled to and from the various craft, there were seventeen men in Hansen's boat. Then, on July 4, Larsen perished from the burns he received in the attack, and he was buried at sea, leaving sixteen.

After an open-boat voyage of eleven days, the men were sighted by a convoy of Allied ships 16 miles southwest of Nantucket, almost in sight of that low-lying island. At 11 a.m. on July 7, they were picked up by H.M.C.S. *Buctouche*, K 179. The Canadians reported the *Moldanger*'s loss to headquarters and motored for Newport that afternoon, arriving shortly after midnight. It was customary naval practice to destroy Allied lifeboats with gunfire to remove hazards to navigation, practice gunnery, and save time. Hansen notes that H.M.C.S. *Buctouche*'s men "extended to us the most generous consideration and hospital treatment."

H.M.C.S. *Buctouche* was envisioned as H.M.C.S. *Bathurst* but was launched as the *Buctouche* in November 1940 by Davie Shipbuilding of Lauzon, Quebec. Commissioned on June 5, 1941, into the Royal Canadian Navy, a year later (right before meeting the *Moldanger* men), she was assigned the duty of Western Local Escort Force, helping protect shipping along the U.S. maritime frontier with Canada. Senior Lieutenant George Norval Downey (RCNR) assumed command the previous month.

H.M.C.S. *Buctouche* was escorting Convoy XB 28 into Newport with at least two other Canadian naval vessels. U.S. naval authorities, in their *Enemy Action Diary*, were surprised at the news, since they had no prior intelligence, and unlikely the British no presentiment, that the *Moldanger* had been lost, writing, "we have received no information of an attack on this vessel." The *Buctouche* arrived at Naval Operating Base Newport in company of H.M.S. *Montgomery* and H.M.C.S. *Regina* at 1.38 a.m. on July 8 and departed with the same two naval ships as well as H.M.C.S. *St. Clair* at 4.45 p.m. the same day. The sixteen Norwegians were transported to New York, where naval hearings were held on July 14.[16]

The six men under the third officer were still at sea in their little craft on the bosom of the tempestuous Gulf Stream, then they entered the colder waters of the continental shelf. Over nearly three weeks, they saw no ships or planes. They used sweaters to protect themselves from the sun during the day and rowed to keep warm during cold nights. Efforts to collect rain during a storm resulted with just salty water from the sail. They made it about 200 miles, to within 100 miles of New Jersey when an airplane of the U.S. Army Air Force found them southeast of the lightship *Ambrose*. Shortly after, U.S. Navy blimp *K 9* arrived on scene and took over husbandry duties for the distressed sailors. The Navy men dropped water and food to the Norwegians, remaining in the skies above them until patrol craft U.S.S. *PC 495* arrived at the gig at 6.09 p.m. on July 15.

Once the men were transferred to *PC 495*, they all headed for a naval section base in Cape May, arriving at 10.18 a.m. the next day. The daily *Enemy Action Diary* relates that the six survivors "were so dehydrated and weak from prolonged exposure that a week's rest would be necessary before they could be moved." Interviewing officer Lieutenant (junior grade) Fox (U.S.N.R.) said they "were in a state of semi-exhaustion due to the prolonged exposure and lack of food and water. Their pedal extremities [feet] were swollen and showed the effects of circulatory disturbances due to long exposure. None of the survivors spoke English fluently."[17] Based on the study of survivors of dozens of Norwegian ships in World War II, this is one of the rare cases where this group laid low.

U.S.S. *PC 495* was constructed by Dravo in Pittsburgh and launched on the last day of 1941. She displaced 280 tons, was 174 feet long, 23 feet wide, and 11 feet deep. Capable of 20 knots from twin 1,440-hp engines and manned by sixty-five Navy personnel, she was armed with a 3-inch gun, three 22-mm guns, and both rocket and depth charge launchers. Lieutenant (junior grade) Manley K. Fuller, Jr., commanded her in 1942.

The extraordinary lifeboat voyage for saloon boys Poul Andersen, Holger Aronsen, and eight other survivors lasted over 1,000 miles, all the way to west of the Azores, following the Gulf Stream. They endured three heavy storms (described as cyclones or hurricanes) and suffered most from thirst, cold nights, and the burning sun. Due to his skill at survival and ability to enforce discipline, the eight other men viewed Carpenter Olav Brekke, aged fifty-seven, as their natural leader, irrespective of rank.[18] Due to their ingenuity (turning pins into fish hooks), they caught many fish to stave off hunger. Some creatures, like sharks, threatened them during their swimming exercises, but also flushed turtles toward them, and they managed to catch three large reptiles of 50–60 lb, each of which provided life-sustaining nutrients for five days each. Holger Aronsen (aged thirty-four) faced a dilemma as he was a strict vegetarian. After considerable deliberations, though, and with his very survival at stake, he acquiesced and partook of the fish and turtle meat. Steward David Olai Holgersen was the oldest in the group at age sixty.

The rafts were roughly 7 feet by 10 feet. For a week, Brekke suffered from headaches resulting from injuries received in the attack. They rigged sails to head northwest but failed. A ship-shape rotating watch of four hours each was established. The men all had either full clothing or foul-weather gear to protect them, and the rafts had additional clothing. The storms they endured supplemented their water supply, which permitted them one cup each per day of the voyage. They had the usual food-type pills and tablets, but the bread, stored in tins, was ruined by water and insufficient. The rich Gulf Stream current carried Sargasso weed, under which fish and crabs sheltered. The men scaled fish with their fingernails and dried them along with their livers for a day-and-a-half before eating them. They rendered turtle fat in jars in the sun until it was palatable.

On the twenty-eighth day, the men espied a ship that continued on without seeing them. After about thirty-six days, another ship, this one a Liberty, steamed to within 1 mile of them. The men were so convinced that rescue was imminent that they begged to finish off their water supply, but Brekke warned them "we're not on board yet." He was right. Perhaps fearing that the rafts were decoys, the ship changed course and sped off. Despite this bitter setback, they kept morale up by singing, talking, and fantasizing about food. Once forty-five days had passed, they took to drinking small bits of seawater to ease constipation, which was effective. Each man lost 55 lb of body weight on average and wryly reported that "the barber shop was closed."

On August 14—their forty-eighth day on the rafts—the Norwegian motor ship *Washington Express* hauled over the horizon. At 3,643 tons, the ship was owned by Skibs-A/S Seattle on their Fruit Express Line and operated by Biørn Biørnstad of Oslo. Her master was Alf M. Bie. She left Liverpool on August 7 and was motoring for New York via Belfast, Lough independently when she came upon their countrymen on the vast expanses of the Sargasso Sea. Fortunately, the *Washington Express* was carrying two physicians. The senior of the two, Dr. Trygve Gjestland, was moved to tears and pride by watching all nine Norwegians climb up the rope ladder unassisted after seven weeks on rafts.[19]

Before they could reach thc men on the raft, the rescuers were forced to watch the scrawny men fight off the pod of whales with oars and whistles. Inexplicably, the whales threatened to overturn their raft, but dove beneath them at the last moment. A line was thrown from ship to rafts, and when it fell short, John Bakkemyr, a thirty-two-year-old able seaman from the *Moldanger*, leapt into the water to cross the intervening 100 feet, despite the omnipotent threat of sharks. On the *Washington Express*, the survivors savored luxuries like gruel, a soft-boiled egg, and bread, as well as fresh-water baths.

The *Washington Express* was a fruit carrier, and her unused owner's cabins were made available to the castaways for the four-day passage to their original destination: New York. A day after they were rescued, a mournful Captain Hansen in New York, unaware of the rescue thousands of miles away, ruefully reported the nine men "missing, probably dead." He and the other survivors were elated to learn of their rescue. Hansen and other shipmates were waiting on the dock with ambulances sent by the Red Cross when the *Washington Express* arrived in New York. The raft survivors walked off the ship unassisted, and the vehicles left empty. Dr. Gjestland treated some 22,000 Norwegian mariners in the U.K. and New York during WWII supported by small teams. The *Moldanger* survivors both inspired him and informed many others in the medical community.[20]

The *Moldanger* men's forty-eight-day survival feat is among the top three survival sagas of World War II. It will never be possible to know how long people survived on boats and rafts, as most died before rescue, and circumstances vary in each case. By comparison, though, the *Britannia*'s survivors spent twenty-six days adrift; Tapscott and Widdicombe of the *Anglo-Saxon* were seventy days in a lifeboat; C. P. O. Dixon (subject of *The Raft*) and two others were thirty-four days adrift in the Pacific; Louis Zamperini and a companion (subjects of the book and film *Unbroken*) were forty-seven days in an inflatable raft; and C. O. Jennings and a companion spent 127 days in a lifeboat escaping the capture of Singapore.

One reason the *Moldanger* survival story failed to reach a wider audience is that the rescuers were fellow Norwegians, and books written about, or covering, the episode were thus in a language with limited global readership.[21] Another factor is a cultural sense of modesty and a naturally taciturn nature of many Norwegian mariners. Captain Hansen told the U.S. Navy interrogators in Newport that he "would prefer not to talk to newspapermen," possibly out of a sense of respect for the fourteen dead and nine others believed to have perished on the rafts.

Had a non-Norwegian Allied ship discovered the men, more publicity would likely have been generated about the incident by U.S. and British press, resulting in books and articles about the men's feats. This was customary wartime behavior; however, as soon as peace descended, interest fell off as the 97 percent of Earth's population who survived tried to return to normalcy. A note in the *Moldanger*'s U.S. Navy file reads "pertinent information given public relations officer." Young Henry Jensen, a survivor of the American steamer *Potlatch*'s thirty-day life raft saga was immediately sent across the U.S. on a national speaking tour with publicist Earl Schenck, Jr.[22] Rather than being offered publicity tours ashore, most merchant mariners were pressed back into service, unheralded heroes, though in this case they did receive awards from the Norwegian government in exile.

Holm Lawson noted that the detailed medical examination of the nine *Moldanger* raft survivors by two doctors, as well as an analysis of their diet and equipment, enabled the Allies to improve on the equipment provided to shipwreck survivors in the lifeboats and rafts. This included more bread in better-sealed tins, more water, stricter enforcement that equipment be supplied, fishing equipment, and tools for scaling fish and cutting turtles.[23]

Kapitänleutnant Horst Degen brought *U-701* on an incursion of New England between June 7 and 10, 1942, only sinking ships outside of the region. On the way inbound, he also spotted the Swedish neutral *Drottningholm*, then passed on another steamer thought to be Uruguayan. Much traffic was sighted off Hatteras, but also *U-701* fired twin misses and withstood plane patrols and bombings. As its mines sank ships, traffic became more organized.[24] Mines that his men laid off the Virginia Capes accounted for five ships damaged (U.S.S. *Bainbridge*, DD 246; H.M.S. *Kingston Ceylonite*, FY 214; the *Robert C. Tuttle*; and the *Esso Augusta* all on June 15, 1942, and the *Santore* on the 17th). Then on the 19th, *U-701* sank U.S.S. *YP 389*, followed a week later by damage to the *Tamesis* and the following day (June 27), the *British Freedom*. On the 28th, the Germans sank the *William Rockefeller* of 14,054 tons.[25]

Revenge was decisive. A U.S. Army Bomber Squadron 396 Hudson aircraft delivered a three-depth charge attack on the submarine which sank it off Cape Hatteras. All but seven German sailors made it to the surface in two groups of eighteen; however, despite the aircraft dropping life vests and life rafts, only seven survivors were found more than two days later. At the time they were attacked, the submariners had not seen an Allied ship for eight days but were holding out for one more kill before returning to France, having departed Lorient on May 20, 1942.

Horst Degen was born in 1913 and survived the loss of his submarine to live until 1996 and age eighty-two. He was captured by the U.S. from the water and sent to PoW camp, then released in June 1946. Degen sank nine ships in his career for over 27,000 tons and damaged five more for over 38,000 tons, for which he was awarded the Iron Cross 1st Class. One of Degen's last messages stated "tightened sea and air patrol."[26] The German Chief of Operations (*Befehlshaber der Unterseeboote*) Dönitz, noted that "by message of the American government, the boat was sunk on 09.07.42 ... 39 sailors were lost." In a supplement, he added the postscript detailing "a direct hit from an aircraft bomb in the E-motor room in 100 feet of water. The crew escaped by the conning tower hatch and the forward torpedo hatch, some without *trauchnetter.* After 50 hours swimming, the survivors were rescued by a float plane." A *trauchnetter* is a life preserver or raft, and Degen complained "how they only had two *trauchnetter* and five life-belts [vests] between them. That the plane returned about an hour after the sinking, dropped smoke flares. Later the air-ship dropped them more life preservers and eventually the raft. The airplane also took pictures of them."[27]

Kapitänleutnant Joachim Berger brought *U-87* on a highly eventful fourteen-day patrol in New England, which included the mining of Boston Harbor, sinking of two ships off Cape Cod, and withstanding a damaging attack by aircraft off Cape Sable. The patrol entered far to the south on June 8, 1942. Immediately, the men had to stop to identify and repair a knocking sound in the bow, but it could not be identified even by surfacing. Then a sailor was diagnosed with syphilis. *U-87* motored west for two days until the 10th, and late on the 8th encountered "drifting automobile inner-tubes."[28] The inner-tubes were the remains of cargo from the *Mattawin*, which was sunk by Thurmann in *U-553* at the same spot less than a week earlier. The *Mattawin* carried 8,600 tons of "war cargo, planes, ammunition, guns steel, motor vehicles." Vehicles, particularly those destined for the desert combat, require spare tires, and so did the Allied armies the ship was sent to support in the desperate fight again Rommel's *Afrika Korps*.

On the 9th, Berger's men surfaced and loaded the mines for deployment, then doubled back from Montauk to the lightship *Nantucket*. Along the way, a U.S. destroyer raced toward *U-87* from the rising sun, causing a crash dive. That evening, the Germans found more detritus of war: "drifting rescue framework [raft] with red flag," and "drifting wreckage and rescue rafts."[29] This was detritus left from the sinking of the Norwegian ship *Berganger* in that location on June 2 by *U-578* under Rehwinkel (von Varendorff in *U-213* having failed with five torpedoes the very same day).[30] As the ship sank, one lifeboat was turned over and spilled its men into the water; some boarded a raft and then moved to one of three lifeboats. So the upturned boat and at least one raft were floating. Then, after pulling thirteen men aboard, "the abandoned rafts and lifeboats from which the men were rescued were fired at with 20-mm guns and are believed to have been left in a sinking condition," on June 4—five days before *U-87* passed through the debris field.

U-87 proceeded along Cape Cod, receiving instructions not to mine New York, but rather to mine the area northwest and southwest of the lightship *Boston* in waters less than 100 feet deep. If that failed, Berger was instructed to try planting his mines off the lightship *Barnegat*. In any event, he was to wait until *U-87* was 50 miles away before informing Germany via France. That night they dove to avoid aircraft, then passed the replacement for the lightship *Nantucket*, a whistle buoy, commenting that "there are always new fishing vessels." A land-based plane forced another crash.[31] On the 11th, *U-87* rounded Provincetown, saw a small sailing cargo ship, and avoided aircraft and a sailing boat. Berger noted that Nauset and Highland lights burned as though the people were still at peace (a ludicrous notion to those visiting from a Europe rent by continuous war), five months after *U-123* began the bloodletting. Not having a special chart of Boston, Berger improvised and drew one using the sailing instructions and list of lights that mariners on all sides relied on. After avoiding a patrol craft, *U-87* rose from the bottom in Massachusetts Bay. A speedy schooner with three masts ran above them, followed by three other fast boats and a launch. The sub lay on the seafloor near the lightship *Boston*. The Germans noticed a line of patrol ships between Provincetown and Gloucester, and much traffic in and out of Boston. In fact, the Cape Cod Canal was closed due to a vessel wrecked in it, so a lot more traffic than usual was going around the cape. A patrol boat must have detected them, as it dropped some bombs in the water, and aircraft passed over. Early on the 12th, another sailing vessel, possibly the 75-foot auxiliary schooner CGR *81*, along with three more boats went overhead. There were also numerous power yachts from fifty to 130 feet long; the *Wanderer,* the *Ida and Joseph*, the *Kelbele*, the *Onza*, the *Bobolink III*, the *Marionette II*, and the *Galaxy* operating in and around Boston at that time. The *Hawk* of 134 feet, and the *Queen of Peace*, 58 feet, are listed together with the *Disturbance II*, the *Holy Cross*, and the *Trinity*.

During the night of June 12–13, Berger observed that "the city of Boston is hardly darkened. The lighthouses burn as in peacetime." The sub spent two-and-a-quarter hours sowing six TMC-type mines. When a patrol boat was sighted at anchor, Berger simply submerged and kept laying the mines from underwater. There were issues, as when the third and fourth mines were released close to one another, due to Tube II ejecting the fourth mine too quickly. Then a fast pilot boat emerged from behind a nearby rock and quickly approached the sub, which managed to deploy its final mines as though a hen waddling away while still laying eggs. The boat submerged and made off in order to avoid several patrol craft.

Now liberated to attack ships, *U-87* headed beyond Cape Cod, where they found a convoy of fifteen merchant ships and four destroyers, but avoided attack due to very calm sea, and strong air defense. While motoring toward Cape Ann and Gloucester, Berger received a "well done" from headquarters. The Germans were flustered at the fog, reloaded torpedoes, checked zincs on the diving planes for sources of the knocking, and avoided aircraft and fishing boats. One twin-engine, double-tailed plane performed long loops to and from shore. On June 22, ten days after they were sewn, one of the mines was found floating over Stellwagen Bank north of Boston, and the U.S. Navy "reported suspected enemy mine," evidencing official knowledge that Boston may have been mined; however, no further action was taken.[32] The mines did not sink any ships and were never removed, neutralizing their effectiveness as a weapon of destruction or terror. On June 13, Berger headed 50 miles off Cape Cod.

On the 16th, the Germans encountered southbound Convoy XB 25 *en route* to Boston from Halifax. It started with their seeing a *Gleaves*-class destroyer within sight of Highland Light. Berger actually entered the convoy between the lead escort and the lead ship – audacious behavior not shown by many (or any) U-boats attacking New England till then. After firing from Tube I, he hit a 7,000-ton freighter, and then from Tube II, he hit a 4,500-ton freighter. In severe weather, *U-87* managed to pick off two vessels from the convoy without being sunk herself. They were the *Port Nicholson* and the *Cherokee*.[33] One of the ships sank, and he fired from Tube III and Tube IV, which ignited an internal explosion in one of the ships.

During the counterattack, Berger noted: "forward and flank escorts shoot heavily with star shells blocking both sides. I run to the rear of the convoy, because I suppose there is no escort there."[34] There followed flashlights flashing, artillery fire, and a crash dive which became worrisome when the bow was down twice as far as usual and had to be stabilized by blowing air into tanks. Berger surfaced for long enough to see the convoy head for the safety of Boston and then he ran east, observing many fishing vessels. The next day, he noted the same three-mast schooner, in poor condition, but with escorts. Headquarters informed the U-boats in U.S. waters that "no re-supply [was] possible." Then Berger discovered that, on top of the earlier syphilis case, five of his men were down with tuberculosis. He took *U-87* eastbound to a point southwest of Cape Sable. On the 19th, a steamer almost rammed the U-boat, then stopped. Berger fired from Tube V and missed, due to over-calculating the size at 6,000 tons, when in fact the ship was about 3,000 tons. The merchant ship's gunners opened fire, drawing the support of a destroyer, so *U-87* withdrew.

Berger and the men observed more aircraft and destroyers, then reloaded torpedoes. After the 20th, they moved close inshore near Seal Island before being attacked and damaged by Allied aircraft on the 25th. *U-87* arrived back in St. Nazaire on July 8, having left on May 19, 1942. Berger was born in 1913 in Berlin and lived until age twenty-nine when *U-87* was sunk off the Portuguese coast by depth charges from H.M.C.S. *Shediac* and H.M.C.S. *St. Croix* on March 4, 1943. All forty-nine officers and men perished.[35] Berger was responsible for sinking five

Allied ships of 38,014 tons, the others being the *Cardita*, the *Nyholt*, and the *Agapenor*. A member of the Crew of 1934, he started with the 2nd Torpedo-Boat Flotilla and the 24th U-boat Training Flotilla from May 1941. He commissioned *U-87* in August 1941 and was the boat's only commander.

The *Port Nicholson* was a British steamer of 8,402 tons *en route* from Avonmouth, U.K., to Wellington, NZ, via Panama with 5,600 tons of military stores and auto parts. At 11.30 a.m. on June 14, she sailed to New York in convoy XB 25, which assembled off Halifax's *Sambro* lightship and was underway by noon. Six hours later she was instructed to proceed to Boston, roughly half the distance away, instead of New York. The convoy commodore rode aboard the *Port Nicholson*, with ninety-one souls. Other vessels included *Pan York*, *Norlago*, and two other merchant ships totaling six. There were three corvettes and a destroyer-escort, among them H.M.C.S. *Nanaimo*, K 101 (under T. J. Bellas, (RCNR)); U.S.C.G.C. *Escanaba*, WPG 77; H.M.S. *Halifax*; and H.M.S. *Montgomery*.

The convoy held fourteen ships arranged from front row to back, left to right as follows: front row, H.M.S. *Halifax*, the *Millcrest*, the *Cherokee*, the *Port Nicholson*, the *Pan York*, the *Empire Franklin*, and escort H.M.S. *Veteran*. In the second row were H.M.S. *Montgomery*, the *Cathcart*, the *Norlago*, the *Empire Dabchick*, and H.M.C.S. *Nanaimo*. In the third and final row, U.S.C.G.C. *Escanaba* and the escort H.M.C.S. *Charlottetown*. At the time of attack, the *Cherokee* was behind and to starboard of the *Port Nicholson*. The order of merchant ships at the time of attack was row one, the *Halifax* and the *Veteran*; row two, the *Cathcart*, the *Port Nicholson*, and the *Pan York*; row three, the *Montgomery*, the *Millcrest*, the *Norlago*, the *Cherokee* and the *Nanaimo*; and row four, the *Escanaba*.[36]

Berger was waiting for ships to round Cape Cod or turn inbound for Boston, and this assemblage sailed right into his crosshairs. Though the rough weather made an attack more difficult, it also hid the periscope and torpedo tracks, and make escape easier. The bow lookout on *Port Nicholson* saw Highland Lighthouse at 10.15 p.m. At 10.18 p.m., the convoy was laboring in heavy weather and heading south when *U-87* fired a pair of torpedoes that hit and blew up the *Port Nicholson*. Although the casualty was clearly visible to all in the convoy, the captain of the merchant ship *Norlago* fired off a series of distress flares that illuminated the area around it, including of course the other ships in convoy. In the dry language of the U.S. Navy's post mortem report, the flares "rendered other vessels in convoy better targets" for the hungry U-boat already known to be nearby.

There was a fresh gale from the northwest, and though the seas were rough and it was partly cloudy, visibility was good. The other vessels in the convoy were "dimly visible." At 4.30 p.m. that afternoon, U.S.C.G.C. *Escanaba* "made a series of sound contacts," and "dropped numerous depth-charges," on the route subsequently taken by the convoy. Presumably, this was a submarine lying in wait, and the feeling, in retrospect, was that the convoy should have altered its course to avoid the contact. When the *Port Nicholson* was found to be still afloat at dawn, Captain Jeffrey, two ship's officers and three ratings from the Canadian corvette H.M.C.S. *Nanaimo* reboarded her. The ship then went down by the stern quickly—too quickly for the men in the lifeboat, who were overturned and sucked into a vortex. At 11.15 a.m., "an army plane saw her turn over and sink while in tow of H.M.S. *Charlottetown*. Four known dead—the captain, chief officer, and two seamen who had returned to the ship to attempt salvage." Only two men of the six who boarded her survived. They were taken with the others to Boston by the corvette. Altogether, six *Port Nicholson* men perished. Eighty-five of them made it ashore that terrible, stormy night.

The steamship *Cherokee* is the casualty with the most deaths in New England during World War II: eighty-six. The *Zurichmoor* had the second-highest loss of life at forty-five. Factors in this sad result were the high number of persons on board (169 souls) and the speed with which the ship sank (six minutes), as well as horrible weather, a fast convoy, and trigger-finger friendly fire depth charges. The *Cherokee* was a U.S.-flagged passenger ship of 5,986 tons on its first voyage for the U.S. Navy, from Iceland to New York via Halifax. She was 402 feet long, 55 feet wide, and 19 feet deep. Capable of 15 knots, the ship could steam 4,000 miles without refueling thanks to a pair of steam engines providing 981 hp to a single propeller.[37]

While in commercial service for the Clyde Mallory Lines (Agwilines) of New York, the *Cherokee* was fitted to accommodate 300 passengers; however, after being chartered to the U.S. Navy, her capacity was 1,373 troops. At the time of her loss, "her interior was still pretty much as she was in normal operation, and she had not yet been converted for troops."[38] Completed in June 1925 by Newport News Shipbuilding, her sister-ships were the *Seminole*, the *Mohawk*, the *Algonquin*, the *Iroquois*, and the *Shawnee*. The Mallory Line extended from the prominent ship-owning clan the Mallorys of Mystic, Connecticut. Subsidiaries included the New York and Texas Steamship Company. Agwilines served New York, Charleston, Jacksonville, Miami, and Galveston.[39]

For her final voyage, the *Cherokee* embarked troops to Iceland, where the U.S. Navy and U.S. Air Force maintained bases. She left New York for Providence on April 29, arrived the following day, loaded cargo and boarded passengers and sailed on May 4 for Boston via the Cape Cod Canal. Escorted by U.S.S. *Barnagat*, she arrived in Halifax on the 6th. The next day, she sailed in a convoy of fifty-six vessels. With the *Norlago*, she peeled off for Iceland, arriving at Reykjavik on May 20. After discharging and disembarking there and in Hvalfjörður, she sailed on the 29th, escorted by U.S.S. *Williamsburg*. She joined a small convoy going east, then a larger one of forty-three ships going west to Halifax, escorted in part by U.S.S. *Pleiades* and U.S.S. *Salinas*. It was slow going in fog, with an average speed of 3.5 knots, as a result of which they arrived in Halifax on June 10.

The *Cherokee*'s master was Captain Twiggs E. Brown, and the pilot was Captain Arthur E. Buck, British, who subsequently perished. There was a mix of merchant mariners (nine officers and 103 crew for 112 of various nationalities), as well as forty-one U.S. Army enlisted soldiers (including an Army Air Force pilot, four Russian naval officers, and eleven naval armed guard including ensigns). The *Cherokee* was not carrying cargo, rather she needed 350 tons of sand ballast and sailed to Halifax with a draft forward of 15 feet and aft of 18 feet. Captain Brown was entrusted with sixty-one miscellaneous bags of mail. At 11.30 a.m. on Sunday, June 14, 1942, she sailed in the same convoy as the *Port Nicholson*, between Halifax and (ultimately) Boston. There was considerable angst aboard *Cherokee*, which was capable of more than 15 knots of speed, at her being instructed to join a convoy where she was forced to go half of her rated speed.

When Captains Brown and Buck saw the *Port Nicholson* blow up only 3,000 feet away, they brought the *Cherokee* up to full speed and turned hard to starboard. Although armed with a 4-inch gun aft, as well as two .50-caliber Browning machine guns and other .30-caliber guns on each side of the bridge, there was neither time nor opportunity to find a target and take offensive action. The armed guard immediately reported to the bridge via radiophone that they were at their stations and ready for action. She was heading almost due west at 8 knots when struck. Being in convoy, she was having difficulty maintaining just half her usual speed as well as keeping maneuverability. They were not zigzagging, and both the portholes and the radio were blacked out. Altogether, the ship had seven men on lookout duty: a loner on the bow and pairs on the after deck, the flying bridge, and aft end of the bridge.

Despite the ship's efforts at escape, Berger's third torpedo hit the *Cherokee* port-side forward, beneath the bridge. The impact lifted the ship out of the water, destroyed the chart house, and caused an immediate list to port. Some ninety seconds later, the final torpedo hit the port forecastle-head. By 10.30 p.m. (between five and seven minutes following the first strike), the *Cherokee* assumed an extreme list of sixty (the third mate said seventy-five) degrees to port, then swiftly succumbed to the damage and sank beneath the waves.

Although the crew managed to cut seven emergency life rafts loose, because of the severe list, none of the boats could be launched. As a result of the wild angle of the deck, the guns could not be brought to bear. The ensign in charge of the gun crew, George B. Norro (U.S.N.R.), had his men work on freeing rafts, and reported that they "behaved calmly and expertly and without confusion." Norro got his men onto the rafts, looked for Captain Brown in the bridge, while the ship was almost on its beam ends, and then abandoned ship. The *Cherokee* was still moving forward, slowly. At 10.48 p.m., the *Cherokee* sank by the bow. Given the severe weather, speed of loss, and sheer number of 169 souls scrambling to survive in the cold, rough waters, evacuation was chaotic, as was rescue. Some of the men simply "ran down deck and jumped into water ... some climbed on rafts, others drowned."

The nearby U.S.-flagged merchant steamer *Norlago* carried forty-two survivors to Provincetown on Tuesday, June 16. The *San Bernadino* managed to save two men and land them in Provincetown as well. The U.S.S. *PYC 40* had the unenviable task of recovering twenty bodies and landing them in Provincetown by 3.30 a.m. "Early in the morning, a naval officer told the town's civilian defense leader that survivors were to be brought ashore."[40] Civilian defense officials including "the Red Cross, air raid wardens, auxiliary police, canteen workers ... doctors, nurses, housewives, businessmen, fishermen and others who in past years had answered seafaring men's calls of distress" made hotels as well as seven ambulances ready for the fourth-four survivors.

The same day, U.S.C.G.C. *Escanaba*, under the command of Lieutenant Commander Carl U. Peterson, assisted by Navigator Lieutenant (junior grade) R. H. Prause, took twenty-two other survivors to Boston, and H.M.S. *Halifax* and H.M.S. *Montgomery* took another sixteen between them. Altogether, eighty-six persons perished in the rough seas that night, of whom twenty-two bodies were recovered. A total of eighty-three, or roughly half of those on board, were rescued. There was an element of international intrigue when a cadaver from the *Cherokee*, that of Soviet Captain Affanasi Melechov, master of a Russian ice-breaker and a passenger on the *Cherokee*, washed ashore in the bucolic boat-building town of Southwest Harbor, Maine on July 25, some forty-five days after he drowned. Konstantin Volokov of the Soviet Consul-General in New York was sent to Maine and recovered the corpse, as well as Captain Melechov's Soviet passport and a letter of credit which he carried. The Soviet embassy in Washington assumed overall responsibility for the case, and it is unknown where Melechov was buried. There were two other Soviet Navy officers on the *Cherokee*: Anatoly Bolkov and Eugin Kohliacov.[41] Eleven of the crew identified themselves as Puerto Rican and one was Dutch.

One little-mentioned detail listed as a possible factor in the high mortality rates is the fact that "one of the destroyers screening the rescue dropped some depth-charges." Organs do not stand up well to having depth charges, or sub-sea bombs, dropped near them while treading water, and survivability in such circumstances is low, as many a German submariner discovered after they made it to the surface from stricken U-boats while still under attack. The Navy report, drenched in morbidity, records that "four [sailors] seen to drop into water from life raft; two severely injured; many suffering from shock and other minor injuries. Effect of torpedo, explosions [depth charges], falling debris, oil in water, and drowning." One of the survivors, Simon Bermudas, an able-bodied seaman from Brooklyn was listed as "alien," since he was born in Curaçao in 1894. One can only imagine the trauma which would have ensued had the rescue ships hit the mines which Berger had just been laid at the approaches to Boston Harbor.

Oberleutnant zur See Paul-Karl Loeser brought *U-373* on its second incursion into New England for three days from June 8–10, 1942, south of Montauk. The patrol began in La Pallice on May 18 and ended there on July 8. She was escorted into Biscay by *Sperrbrecher* (minesweeper escorts) and thought she encountered either *U-136* or *U-402* returning from the patrol; however, the other boat or boats did not answer. On May 20, *U-373* dodged a bomb from a plane, and on 31st, they exchanged signals with *U-701* under Horst Degen, which would later be sunk off Hatteras. On June 1, a westbound convoy was detected then lost, there being a bright moon and heavy swell. Due to the mining mission, *U-373* was ordered to spare the convoy and proceed west.[42]

On June 7, the Germans logged more activity, as a fast-moving steamer of either the *Clan MacArthur* or *Uruguay* type evaded *U-373* with fast zigzags, then did the same to Degen in *U-701*. Off Montauk, the sub surfaced on June 10 and loaded mines offshore, then rested on the seafloor. Before rising, the cautious Loeser prepared his U-boat for self-destruction, and took the Enigma coding machine apart, distributing the wheels around the boat. *U-373* laid fifteen TMB-type mines on June 11 off Virginia, using Oberfalls Radio Beacon as a shore reference.[43] After sowing the mines the sub quickly went to deeper water and loaded its torpedoes, using earlier reports by *U-552* to determine which navigation aids were active. The only vessel sunk was the U.S.-flag tug *John R. Williams*, 396 tons, which struck a mine at the entrance to Delaware Bay, with fourteen killed.

The U-boat struck a large patrol ship like the German's *Sperrbrecher* minesweepers, with a dud torpedo on June 14 and again on the 15th, stopping it, but only temporarily. Water in the U-boat's engine compartment shorted some of the torpedo mechanisms. After obtaining two hits on the 5,000-ton steamer and pursuing for a gun duel on the surface only to be outmaneuvered there, *U-373* "turned away … because all attempts go amiss."[44] The ship was camouflaged, and the submarine's starboard engine was out for repairs. Oddly, the vessel under attack was not identified in the *Enemy Action Diary*, even though at 5.47 p.m. on the 14th a radio-direction-finding fix on a sub at *U-373*'s position was reported to the Eastern Sea Frontier.

On May 16, four months after the opening of U-boats attacks, the Germans relayed that "Hatteras anchorage closed to navigation by all U.S.-Government vessels and merchant ships. Danger." It was a bit like closing the barn door after the horses fled. On June 26, Loeser was ordered to make for La Pallice. On June 30, he reported sighting an oil slick probably created by a wounded and submerged U-boat. On July 6, they were surprised with lights and a fast air attack from a RAF Wellington bomber in Biscay, but when they aimed the C 30 and 34-cm machine guns, both jammed. After bombs were dropped so close that their spray drenched the conning tower, the boat crash-dived and sought safety in the depths. The bombs stopped, yet when they resurfaced there was still an RAF smoke float visible. Half a dozen more bombs were heard and two sailboats seen. On July 7, they detected four shadows which became German patrol boats, and the following day docked at La Pallice lock's Bunker Two.

A member of the Crew of 1935, Loeser was born in 1915 in Berlin, and lived to 1987 and age seventy-one. His first U-boat was *U-33* in 1938, aboard which he served as 2nd Watch Officer, then in the same role aboard *U-40*, followed by a stint as 1st Watch Officer on *U-43* from 1939 to 1940. He joined *U-108* as 1st Watch Officer, and was acting commander of *U-30*, in which he did not patrol.[45] The other ships he sank were the *Thursobank* off New England and the *Mount Lycabettus* on March 17, 1942. His total tonnage destroyed was 10,263 tons, for which he received no decorations. At war's end, Loeser was in the Guard Battalion Dönitz, was captured, detained, and released in August 1945.

12

Second Saboteur Landing, Amagansett, Long Island by *U-202*

Kapitänleutnant Hans-Heinz Linder brought *U-202* on a complex patrol of New England between June 11 and 16, 1942. On April 28, Iron Crosses were awarded on *U-202*'s deck in Brest by the flotilla chief, *Kapitänleutnant* Heinz Buchholz. Then *U-202* entered dry dock until the 16th, provisioned on the 27th, was given a farewell from Buchholz, and finally an escort offshore by minesweeper unit *Sperrbrecher* 19. Seven hours later, having hand-steered with a broken rudder, she made her way around Penmarch Light House and then was escorted to back to the different base at Lorient. Linder entered 250 miles south of Cape Sable motoring west from Nantucket to Block Island.

On June 13, the men deposited a team of saboteurs at Amagansett, near Montauk, as part of highly secretive Operation Pastorius. *U-202* found itself aground and motored furiously to free itself; the sounds were heard and diesel smelled ashore. Ultimately, high tide and ingenuity freed the sub. The following day authorities in semi-rural Manchester-by-the-Sea and Beverly, Massachusetts, reported landings by enemy saboteurs "by two or three men in a small boat." The first landing is said to have occurred at 3.15. a.m. in Manchester, and the second at 5.10 a.m. at Beverly. It appears that word spread up the coastal defense system *vis-à-vis* the need for extra vigilance against German landings after the saboteurs escaped Amagansett.[1]

Following the grounding, Linder and the men rested for a day on the seafloor, then headed south of Nantucket, to exit the area toward Delaware. Off New Jersey on June 22, Linder sank the Argentinian ship *Rio Tercero*. The U-boat was counterattacked by aircraft and a U.S. Navy blimp, both of which dropped bombs on the it. On July 1, *U-202* sank the *City of Birmingham* between Hatteras and Bermuda, with Linder noting "at least six lifeboats on each side. The steamer makes a massive impression about 9,000–10,000" tons. There was a strong counterattack by its escort, which crushed some deck canisters aboard the U-boat. "At the sinking location nothing is seen, also no rescue lights." On July 3, Linder chased a steamer of the Dutch *Brastagi* design. Two torpedoes missed ahead, probably due to the ship zigzagging. An aircraft counterattacked, prompting uncharacteristic praise: "there are quite beautiful flight operations here!" The boat broke off the attack and submerged; the ship did not report an attack.[2]

On the 6th, Linder reported that a machinist named Petersen injured both shins at the periosteum, and that it had gone three weeks without healing. On July 10, *U-202* refueled from *U-460* under forty-nine-year-old Friedrich Schäfer west of the Azores.[3] Deecke in *U-584*, who had landed the terrorists in Florida, joined. When four of his men were washed over during refueling Linder's men rescued two of them from the water. Seas were rough so they obtained provisions by lines rather than rubber boats. The *Milchkuh* needed to lighten ship before ending a fifty-five-day patrol and gave Linder more than they needed. On July 17, *U-202* tried to penetrate the screen around Convoy OS 34 but corvettes prevented it. On July 24, Linder signaled three escorts, only to learn they were French fishing boats. The next day, he passed Penmarch Light again, this time with rudders working, and despite a plane in the distance found five German escorts and headed for Brest, where she returned on July 25.

Linder was born in 1913 and was a member of the Crew of 1933. Up to November 1939, he was with the Luftwaffe and then joined the U-boat arm. He was then commander of *U-18*, served as supernumerary aboard *U-96*, and in March 1941 commissioned *U-202*. In September 1942, he moved ashore with the 1st U-boat Flotilla, then served as a training leader with the 25th U-boat Flotilla. He was caught in an air raid by the Soviets in Libau, Latvia on September 10, 1944, and killed at age thirty-one. His total claim of Allied tonnage was eight ships of nearly 34,000 tons. Though Linder received no decorations, he was promoted posthumously with seniority.[4] No other commander and engineering team is known to have extracted the rpm from a U-boat that Linder did to work free from the sandbanks of Amagansett.

On June 13, *U-202* deposited a team of saboteurs at the eastern end of Long Island as part of Operation Pastorius. There were many aspects to the raid: preparation and training, two U-boat voyages to insert teams in New York and Florida, then the attackers' ten to fourteen days of freedom in the United States, followed by the betrayal and rounding up of all (and execution of most) of the saboteurs. Although the Germans chose sabotage over spying for this operation, basic security measures such as preventing any one member of the spy cell from knowing enough about the others to betray them all, were not taken.

This study is concerned mainly with one single aspect: the voyage from France to New York of *U-202* with the overall leader of both teams, John Dasch, and insertion of he and three others ashore at Amagansett. This effort came within minutes of costing the entire submarine and its crew. Even though the landing took place in New York and not New England, *U-202* transited New England, and the South Fork of Long Island is adjacent to Block Island, Rhode Island, as well as southeastern Connecticut and Long Island Sound. The error of omission would outweigh an error of inclusion.

Due to the inattention and distraction of those ashore, who might at the very least have dispatched a patrol vessel around Montauk or up the south shore to intercept the U-boat, the American military sat for two hours waiting for daylight, focusing inland on four men who they failed to capture. More could have been done to capture *U-202*, yet nothing was. In the course of World War II, the U.S. Coast Guard and U.S. Navy never came closer to a stranded U-boat on their shores than those hours. It would be two years, almost to the day, until they captured *U-505* off West Africa, and it was kept in Bermuda until after VE Day.[5]

Being given the chance to capture a German submarine on their shores at the outset of hostilities against the U.S. was the equivalent of having a baby floated to the U.S. military in a reed basket. The intelligence that could have been gleaned from an entire crew, the apparatus to support a terrorist raid, multiple unused torpedoes, and perhaps even an Enigma machine (however damaged) would have provided them with a unique opportunity to analyze and anticipate the enemy's plans, equipment, and personnel, thus enabling them to have anticipated the German's next moves and protect the United States. Even had Linder alerted Germany of the U-boats capture and destroyed vital equipment, the morale boost would have been immeasurable.

Had Linder blown up the boat, or U.S. soldiers and sailors attacked *U-202* and men were killed in machine gun duels, the submarine was only 100 miles from Brooklyn Navy Yard, where U.S. intelligence could have spent three years studying the carcass. The failure to even attempt to capture *U-202* was a catastrophic strategic blunder, the official response to which was not a single reprimand, due in part to FBI Director Hoover insisting on getting credit for the saboteur's capture. The official response, rather, was the issuance of a Legion of Merit Award to Seaman John Cullen for taking money from the enemy and then backing away, issued by Rear Admiral Stanley V. Parker.[6] Of course, when Cullen raised the alarm, his superiors reacted along similar lines: ineffectually, by failing to apprehend either the men drinking, arguing, digging and stumbling around in the dark before boarding the first train out of town, or the Germans stranded within earshot. The failure was clearly as systemic as it was pathetic.

Hitler planned the U-boat invasion of the United States before declaring war on them on December 11, 1941. An effort to infiltrate and sow terrorism by blowing up factories, dams, railroad junctions, bridges, canals, and even Jewish-owned department stores in major cities was also implemented through the *Abwehr*, a secret guerilla division within German Military Intelligence Corps. Admiral Wilhelm Canaris was in overall charge, and he was later executed by Hitler for an attempt on the *Führer*'s life. He appointed a thirty-seven-year-old lieutenant named Walter Kappe to lead training. The operation was named after a German settler in America, Francis Daniel Pastorius.

Kappe recruited a dozen prospective civilian invaders from the *Ausland* Institute, which had sent many Germans the other way (from America to Germany) and kept a number of their belongings, clothing, and paperwork to re-purpose. By April 1942, two groups of four each were in training. A total of $100,000, as well as caches of bombs, weapons, radio equipment, and uniforms were provided in their support.[7]

The overall leader of the New York team was George (John) Dasch, aged thirty-nine and the oldest. After serving in the German Army during World War I, he moved to the U.S., where he worked in the midtown area of New York City as a waiter until returning to Germany at the outbreak of the next war. A smooth talker and natural manipulator, he was chosen to lead. His second-in-command, Ernest Peter Burger, had been an *aide-de-camp* to the infamous leader of the Brown Shirts, Ernst Röhm, the scar-faced early storm-trooper also killed by Hitler. Having fled an assault charge in the U.S., Burger returned to Germany, criticized the Gestapo, and spent seventeen months in jail for it. He was sent to the infantry, following which he was selected for this mission—an odd choice given his disparaging the state's secret police.

From the outset, the men lacked discipline and focus: they drank each night after training, and while traveling from the base to Brest, they drank heavily, boasted loudly on the train. As a result, they left much of their super-secret equipment on the train and had to wait for it to be painstakingly replaced, during which time a member succumbed to a severe case of social disease and was withdrawn. According to Garrett, the French underground and British intelligence who learned of the ruckus felt it inconceivable that the Germans would be so reckless and foolish, so they dismissed the trove of material as a ruse.[8] When the saboteurs finally boarded the cramped *U-202*, the sailors were told that the newcomers were shipyard workers, bringing along heavy tools.[9]

The first mission, under Joachim Deecke in *U-584*, departed Brest on May 25, 1942, and arrived at Ponte Vedra Florida on June 17. Four terrorists were landed south of Jacksonville and proceeded to major U.S. cities undetected, leaving their weapons buried in the dunes. Following the failed departure from Brest and the rudder breakage, *U-202* followed Convoy L 2 to Lorient after 105 miles, but only stayed eleven hours to make repairs. Finally, on the night of May 28, they were under way again for the wide Atlantic, where Linder utilized the Great Circle Route to arrive off the sandy coast of Long Island fifteen days later, on the evening of Friday, June 12. Then Zimmermann, an *obergefreiter* (torpedo mechanic) began to have appendicitis. As the men were unable to cure him, even with radio support, he was given most of their supply of opium and morphine until the sepsis subsided several days later.[10]

Before dusk, Lindner took *U-202* up to the 100-foot-depth line, then lay the boat on the bottom awaiting darkness. At 11.06 p.m., the boat rose to the surface and headed for the insertion point, which was an area near where Dasch had stayed near Southampton. They used the more silent electric motors and kept a very low profile of deck above the water. There was a thick fog, reducing visibility to about 350 feet, the temperature was 63 degrees Fahrenheit, and seas and wind were calm. They nudged ashore on a sandbank quite far from the shore, but were able to back off of it. So they continued again toward the surf, protected by the fog.

At 11.52 p.m., while proceeding just enough off the surface of the sea to avoid getting one's shoes wet, *U-202* ground ashore on another sand bank. They could hear the surf breaking on the miles-long beach, but not see it. They inflated a large rubber boat using an air line from a compressor below. Then six men boarded it and rowed to shore, all of them in German military uniforms so as to comply with Geneva Conventions. They trailed a long line so that the boat could be retrieved from the U-boat and set out at five minutes after midnight on Saturday the 13th. Soon the sailors on the U-boat were distressed to see a stranger approaching their countrymen with a light, but then the light went out and the person carrying it "was apparently reassured by the people."[11]

What really happened was Dasch was approached by nineteen-year-old Coast Guard seaman named John Cullen of Queens, New York, who had volunteered less than six months before. Even though, unbeknown to the Germans, the area had been designated a high-security area, Cullen did not have backup, was not armed, and did not have a radio, dog, or horse. Though he initially grabbed Dasch by the elbow, the young American quickly became scared. During an increasing bizarre encounter, Cullen saw two uniformed men in the water holding a dinghy, then another man on the beach in swim shorts, having ditched the uniform.

Cullen asked if the men were stranded fishermen, inadvertently offering them an alibi. When Dasch said yes, Cullen asked what fish they were after. When told they were clamming, Cullen became understandably suspicious as clamming is generally not done at night in the surf-line from boats. It is mostly done by hand from shore, or via a commercial dredge. Cullen or Dasch might, or may not, have known that. Suddenly, Burger charged up, yelling in German that Dasch should kill Cullen on the spot. In response, Dasch slapped Burger, dismissed him, and clumsily offered Cullen a randomly pulled number of bills totaling $280 cash—a considerable bribe. The men bizarrely discussed Cullen's family and how he would spend it, an inference being that Cullen's family would miss him if he was killed.

Before Cullen ran off to tell his colleagues at the nearby Coast Guard station, Dasch stopped him, had Cullen shine a light on Dasch's face, and instructed him "you will hear from me in Washington." Backing into the darkness, the terrified seaman blurted out "thank you, sir." Dasch had disobeyed his orders to kill or capture witnesses and have them rowed to the U-boat for interrogation, capture or death. His own colleague, Quirin, threatened to kill him for failing to kill Cullen. When a flare was fired, the Germans were convinced they were doomed, only to realize when a corresponding signal was sent soon after that *U-202* was signaling the men in the dinghy.[12]

Fortunately for the Germans, the defenders bungled the morning as much as they did. When a coterie of Coast Guardsmen returned, apparently without any galvanizing leadership, the young sailors merely sat in the sand, waiting for sunrise. Astoundingly they appeared oblivious to the flares, increasingly desperate, loud maneuvers of *U-202* a few hundred feet out to sea, the cache of weapons buried nearby, and the four escaping Germans, who bumbled around the dunes without a flashlight, compass, or maps while swearing, smoking, digging, and drinking. In short, the Coast Guardsmen missed the exact clues they were trained to detect, recognize and act on. Before retrieving the dinghy, *U-202*'s men found themselves aground again, this time on a sandbank roughly 650 feet offshore. As the men struggled to free it, using both engines, the U-boat was heard by hundreds of people, including the Coast Guard, yet nothing was done. The men landed ashore were seen from a walkway above the bluff carrying equipment up the beach by twenty-two-year-old Farrar Teeple and her younger sister. One of the Germans even waved to her. She reported what she saw to her father, who patronizingly dismissed her.[13]

Just half an hour after it set off, at 12.35 a.m., the rubber boat with two German sailors rowing it returned to the U-boat. Then began a morning of hell for the submariners, as they fought desperately to save their ship from destruction, and themselves from capture. At its lowest point, Linder ordered the appendicitis case, Zimmermann, taken ashore by a sailor named Mühlhausen in order to save his life, then for a final radio signal to be sent to Germany, the men to abandon ship and surrender, and the submarine to be blown up—all of this while "no one on land seemed interested in the boat's presence," despite their literally lying helpless on the doorstep of the United States' largest port and population center.[14]

Linder's war diary was an exercise in fatalistic restraint. He observed in painful detail how his submarine was caught in the surf and ended up on its side, rolled over to an alarming 40 degrees, was pushed inward by waves, the men standing on one side of the pressure hull to balance her. They tried the electric motors to no avail. Then they were forced to flood the tanks in order to prevent being pushed further toward shore—surely a difficult, counter-intuitive decision to make. They were in the worst position imaginable, stranded on the enemy's shore within hours of daylight. Linder and his engineers decided to fill some tanks with air, clutch the diesel engines onto the same shaft as the electric motors, and engage both at full rpm. Though not successful, the effort changed the direction of U-boat's direction, so that *U-202* faced out to sea rather than along the shore. When the fog thinned they discovered they were beneath the gaze of the Amagansett radio tower. They saw a home, a beacon, and a radio station with two masts on a hill. Linder worried:

> It is gradually getting lively on land. Cars driving back and forth, but not stopping at the landing site. A dog barks loudly and persistently. At times, bursts of machine guns, but from quite far … lively spotlights play at the radio station, and at three other points on the island … ineffective because visibility in fog is still about 2,000 feet … starry sky. I suspect that either our maneuver with the diesels was heard, and was taken for aircraft noise, or that something seemed not right with the man with the light [Cullen], and he made a report to a [person or group on] watch.[15]

After preparing a coded message to Germany and telling his men to expect to become prisoners of war before daylight, they all attempted an engineering feat not known to have been tried before or since. When the tide finally crept back in and lifted the boat, however gently, Linder's team emptied water tanks with compressed air. The commander observed: "there is only a slight hope. Most grueling is the helpless feeling waiting for the accumulating water. All tanks are pumped except for fuel bunkers. Torpedoes are still in the boat."

At 3 a.m., Linder updated that "The water comes slowly—however in an hour it will be bright, then I must be away or carry out demolition. So now a final attempt. Blew all ballast tanks with the last air, both diesels ahead three X AK [main engine] with the E-motors switched on." Then, ten minutes later, success:

> The boat makes a little progress with each swell and is free of the bottom after about four tries! Hurrah!! Elation in the boat. But now must get away while it is still dark! On land … all the hustle and bustle is not taking place right on the coast, but in the background. The visibility is better, about [two-and-a-half miles]. That was the utmost and final time for us to get away, otherwise we could march along at tomorrow's Flag Day parade in New York! The diesel saved us, they achieved the previously unreached power of 520 rpm.[16]

By 3.50 a.m., the crisis had abated to the extent that Linder was able to submerge in order to give the men a rest and settle their highly taut nerves: "the crew needs some rest. The nervous strain of the last hours was too great! The attitude of the entire crew was outstanding!"[17] Double exclamation marks are not standard punctuation marks in German commander's war diaries.

Back on shore, the saboteurs turned their back on the sailors with the dinghy and dragged their crates into the dunes, throwing off German uniforms into the sand as they went. One left a packet of German cigarettes, and another swigged from a small bottle of Schnapps until it was empty, then threw it aside, as though the men were Hansel and Gretel leaving a trail. They dug a deep hole for the boxes, covering them with fresh grass, yet neglected to hide one of the shovels.

In fact, they left it with the handle standing upright like a cross on a grave, as though to lead authorities directly to it.[18]

After several hours of walking in civilian clothes, they avoided a boisterous trailer-camp and made it to railway tracks, which led to the small Amagansett railway station. After a short wait, pretending to be bumbling city slickers attempting to catch fish from the surf, they boarded the train to Queens, then went separately into New York City's Manhattan borough.[19] By the low-tech expedient of switching trains in Queens, they successfully bypassed whatever traps might be set for them in major New York City hubs like Grand Central or Pennsylvania Station. That was wise as they left their seating area littered with the butts of German cigarettes.

Within two weeks, the leaders—Dasch and Burger—had betrayed all of their colleagues, thus saving themselves from the electric chair.[20] Details of their capture are not germane, and are interwoven with rumor, falsehoods, and *braggadocio*. FBI Director J. Edgar Hoover desperately wanted to impress FDR by claiming credit for the capture of three teams of saboteurs, when in fact all had turned themselves in or been betrayed. The case of the two teams of saboteurs made it all the way to the U.S. Supreme Court, which found against the Germans. They were ordered to undergo a hastily convened military tribunal in Washington, D.C.[21]

On August 7, 1942, FDR's White House stated that "they had not completed review of the case."[22] However, the following day, six of them were executed. Hitler rebuked Admiral Canaris for the failure. Dasch and Burger were spared and eventually, in 1948, returned to Germany, despite having served only 10 percent of their sixty-year sentences.[23] There followed a blame game between them, with Burger naming and shaming Dasch, followed by Dasch publishing an account of his own a year later. Then both of them discretely slipped out of the public eye. Dasch died in 1992 and Burger in 1975 in American-occupied Germany; they were never welcomed back by their own people, who considered them traitors. Hoover had promised them pardons but never delivered.

On the way back to Brest, Linder sank the *Rio Tercero* on June 22 and the *City of Birmingham* on July 1, arriving in France on July 25. It had all turned out much better than anticipated, though Linder did not live long enough to learn of the success or failure of the mission. He was killed in the Baltic without any recognition for saving *U-202* that morning while the enemy smoked on the sand nearby. Deecke in *U-584* and his men also returned safely to Brest from inserting saboteurs in Florida, arriving July 22 without having sunk any ships on the patrol.[24]

13

Ten U-boats Attack; the *Lucille M.* and the *Alexander Macomb* Sunk

Kapitänleutnant Johannes Liebe brought *U-332* on an eleven-day patrol in New England across Long Island, Block Island, Martha's Vineyard, and Nantucket, between the June 12 and 22, 1942. On June 10, Liebe and Deecke in *U-584* greeted each other in passing. For two days, the sub motored west then, on the 16th, it dodged an aircraft, heard detonations, saw the plane, and then heard more bombs far off before moving south of Nantucket. On the 17th, a small ship was sighted off New Jersey which proved to be a Swedish neutral named *Industria*. The following day, the neutral Portuguese ship *Mirandella* was also given free passage.

A patrol craft was ignored, and the sub rested on the sea floor. The boat moved close inshore to the eastern point of Long Island on the 18th and 19th then patrolled the south coast of New England, its capes and islands, until it exited on the 22nd. Liebe decided on June 19 that they "must shift the operations area to the north via the lightship *Nantucket*, where traffic was reported by boats stationed there."[1] On the 20th, they chased an antiquated four-stack destroyer for four hours. The following day, they were told no resupply would be possible. At mid-afternoon on June 22, a strutted flying boat with twin-tandem motors swooped over them low and fast: 150 above sea-level. Two bombs were dropped and blew up 100 feet off the port stern. Liebe noted several clutch-related failures. Though their machine guns were readied, they were not fired. On the 24th, the same occurred. Liebe learned that hunting off Cape Hatteras was promising for U-boats and since *U-332* still had eleven torpedoes, decided to patrol there.

The patrol began in La Pallice on May 24 and ended there on August 1. After leaving New England, Liebe sank the U.S. freighter *Raphael Semmes* south of Bermuda (he was solicitous of the wounded), and on the way back to Europe the *Leonidas M.* of Greece on July 19. Liebe took two officers on board his submarine, something frowned upon after the *Laconia* order, issued after German and Italian submariners were attacked by U.S. aircraft during a rescue mission west of North Africa.[2]

On July 1, the men on *U-332* found "empty drifting rafts and buoys of the steamer *Everalda*," the last ship sunk by Erwin Rostin in *U-158* on June 29. Due to Rostin's persistent radio signals about his successes, the U.S. Navy was able to send a plane under Lieutenant Richard E. Schreder to sink the sub the following day. He did so, killing all on board including the *Everalda*'s Latvian captain and a Spanish neutral also taken aboard.

Toward the end of July, *U-332* received fuel from *U-461* under *Korvettenkapitän* Wolf-Harro Stiebler west of the Azores.[3] Liebe was born in 1913 in Saxony and lived until 1982 and the age of sixty-nine. A member of the Crew of 1933, *U-6* was one of his early commands. His earlier experience was with German naval airfields. After March 1941, he served under Schultze in *U-48*, then took command of *U-332* after work-up in June 1941. Liebe had eight ships of over 46,000 tons to his credit. The end of the war found him working on torpedo testing, and though he was made PoW, he was released in end July 1945.

Kapitänleutnant Dietrich Lohmann brought *U-89* on complex sixteen-day incursions into New England between July 1 and August 3, 1942. She cast off from the bomb-proof bunkers of Brest on the evening of June 5 and ran to Lorient in convoy, entering Biscay with *U-105* and *U-505*. Then 1st Watch Officer Hans-Gert Mahrholz fell ill with tonsillitis. *U-89* was one of several U-boats which came upon the Swedish neutral *Drottningholm* off Canada, letting it pass. On July 1, a biplane approached. Then on July 2, the submariners came upon an odd sight 200 miles south-southeast of Nantucket: a large cylindrical ship's boiler from the bowels of an Allied merchant ship. The young sailors could not resist firing machine guns at it for practice.

The boiler could have come from a dozen ships, but the strongest candidates were the *Mattawin* (sunk by *U-553* under Thurmann on June 2, with the G7a *coup de grâce* torpedo ripping the engine room apart 40 miles and a month apart), the *Zurichmoor* (sunk only 8 miles away but five weeks earlier and by hits to the bow not engine spaces on 23 May by Schultze in *U-432*) the *Nemanja* (sunk 90 miles east and eleven weeks before by *U-84* under Uphoff), or even the *Margot*, sunk the same distance away on the same day, by Vogel in *U-588*, but west.

On the 4th, the men in *U-89* chased a sound-bearing to no avail, the next day the "mirror flat sea" made the sub's interior "like a dripping cave" which fogged up lenses to periscope, binoculars, and sextant. The boat was off Delaware, New Jersey, and New York by then, experiencing sightings of planes, patrol craft and steamers. During the day, they mostly remained at bottom.[4] During the patrol, Lohmann sank the Canadian fishing schooner *Lucille M.* without loss of life on July 25. *U-89* crossed New England from Cape Sable to Montauk from August

1–3. On the 11th, U-boat command issued a directive which illuminates both their tactics and those of the Americans:

> Apparently, after the heavy merchant ship losses in June, the enemy has from the beginning of July arbitrarily stopped traffic in some areas. These measures can only be for a limited duration and will lead to a strong sudden glut of traffic. Seize this moment tenaciously, use every opportunity. Report immediately, so that other boats are not positioned in empty areas. Until then, search systematically but with economical fuel consumption.[5]

The boat was bombed by aircraft off Delaware on the 13th. The following day, Lohmann vented his exasperation at being followed by U.S. aircraft, even after being submerged; the skipper blamed phosphorescence. Then on the 18th, they returned to the region past Montauk heading northeast across the Georges Bank for two days from July 18–20. For nearly two weeks, Lohmann circled around southwest of Cape Sable, looking for prey. In the first week, they found the *Lucille M.* about 75 miles southwest of the cape. He noted that "about 10–12-man crew is found in three large rowboats." They were on the southern tip of Browns Bank when *U-89* caught up with them.

Just before dawn the fishermen heard the deep-throated thrum of the U-boat surfaced, charging its batteries. At 3 a.m., the *Lucille M.* loomed out of the mist, within sight of Lohmann, whose men opened fire on the defenseless fishermen, wounding four of them.[6] The Germans flung twenty flammable (incendiary) and fifteen high-explosive rounds from their deck-gun into the 75-foot long schooner. The first shells hit the sails and the top hamper of the schooner. The eleven men scrambled into a lifeboat and managed to row to Shelburne (possibly Clarke's Harbor), a voyage of some 70 miles. They said they could hear the Germans reloading their guns, the empty shell-casings hit the deck, and the submariners swore. Wynn writes that "Lohmann had expressed regret in good English, but they should understand that he was only carrying out orders."[7]

On the 22nd, *U-89* took bearings from Cape Sable, Seal Island, and Blonde Rock. On the 23rd, the Germans fired at a fast-approaching destroyer, then tracked a convoy of up to five steamers. Allied activity was so intense, with ASDIC probes and counter-fire in the distance, that the boat lay on the bottom. On July 24, they encountered a U.S. Coast Guard cutter of the *Comanche* design, and crash-dived with ASDIC impulses bouncing off the boat. Then *U-89* headed east and out of the region on the 27th. Citing the "unfavorable weather and hopelessness of the pursuit," Lohmann broke off attacks simply logging "sank fishing schooner between Georges and Browns Bank," as though he had been simply letting off steam at their expense. On the third incursion, *U-89* returned westward from Cape Sable for a day, up to August 3 then back southeast, heading for Europe.

On July 26, they crash-dived as a plane drove them off a potential schooner target. The following day they found a life-ring from a ship named *Donovania* sunk by *U-160* under Georg Lassen; however, the 8,149-ton British ship was sunk just five days and over 2,000 miles away, off Trinidad on July 21, 1942, nowhere near the Canadian Maritimes. U.S.S. *Livermore*, which rescued the survivors in the Caribbean, could not have transported it to Canada that quickly, so it was either flown then lost after the attack or lost overboard before. Though she was in Halifax three times (August 1941, February and April 1942), the life-ring must have entered the water during four days of repairs to lifeboats and engines in Halifax from April 16–19, 1942, or either side. She was also bombed and damaged off the U.K. Life-rings are kept loose for easy deployment and thus wash over in severe weather. The same day, several *Gleaves*-class destroyers were sighted. On July 30, Lohmann worked with Vogelsang in *U-132* to track a convoy, and *U-132* succeeded in sinking the *Pacific Pioneer* that day.

On July 31, a destroyer raced up from behind, with red glow from the smoke stacks. Aircraft sent *U-89* racing to the safety of deep water with four detonations close. Lohmann observed that several electrical pulses were used on his submarine, like gravel hitting the hull. By August 1, they were off the Georges Bank, and the following day off Nova Scotia. The next day, an aircraft was seen overhead off Cape Le Havre. Compared with those by his colleagues, this was not a very successful mission for Lohmann. The patrol began in Brest on June 6 and ended there on August 21. At the outset, *U-89* and seven other U-boats formed a line called Endrass off Spain to intercept Convoy HG 84 from June 14–15, with five ships were sunk, none by *U-89*. *U-460* then refueled *U-89* west of the Azores. On August 16, *U-89* was attacked near the Azores by a RAF Liberator under T. M. Bulloch from 120 Squadron but managed to escape.

Lohmann was born in 1909 and perished on May 12, 1943, at age thirty-three. On that day, *U-89* was lost with all forty-eight men to a combined attack by a RAF Swordfish, H.M.S. *Broadway*, H.M.S. *Lagan*, and H.M.S. *Biter*. A member of the Crew of 1930, Lohmann sailed on the training ship *Horst Wessel*, joining U-boats in April 1940. He was a watch officer on *U-99* then commissioned *U-554* in January 1941. He commanded *U-579* and ultimately *U-89* for a total of five patrols, sinking four ships of 13,815 tons. He received no decorations.

The *Lucille M.* was a 54-ton Canadian schooner of the *Bluenose* type built in Mateghan, Digby County, Nova Scotia in 1918. She was originally owned by the Swim Brothers of Lockeport, then Frederick W. Sutherland of Yarmouth. She was 75 feet long, 18 feet wide, and had a draft of 9 feet. In early June 1932, the *Lucille M.* was home-ported in Pubnico when the crew rescued the eighteen officers and crew of a Boston fishing schooner named *Azores*, under Captain Foam Spinney that had suffered a destructive fire. The *Lucille M.* men took the survivors to Yarmouth. In the summer of 1942 she was fitted out as a harpooner and based in Lockeport.[8]

The *Lucille M.*'s final master was Captain Percy Richardson. On Thursday, July 23, she set out to fish the comparatively shallow grounds of Georges Bank. Fatefully, the captain diverted to Browns Bank along the way. The calmness of the seas encouraged the fishermen to believe they would see swordfish fins easier. At noon on the 24th, the skipper heard some fifty rounds of gunfire nearby. The same day, he and the men also saw four aircraft. That night at dusk, at the southern tip of Browns Bank they decided to heave-to and drift until dawn. Then, around midnight and off to one side, they heard the distinct sound of "heavy diesel motors" and a vessel remaining stationary, behavior they knew to be atypical of a freighter or fellow-fisherman.

The vessels were out of sight of each other in a night mist until 3 a.m. on July 26, when Lohmann and his men aboard *U-89* sighted the *Lucille M.* slowly emerging from the fog. The only light on the schooner was a small binnacle light enabling the men to see their compass. The Germans were tautly standing by their guns, and opened fire immediately, striking the sails as well as the top of the deckhouse. This was followed by machine gun fire, as the fishermen scrambled to abandon ship alive. Four of the Canadians were wounded in the desperate scramble to launch a dory and tumble in, but all eleven men managed to escape in two small dories. They had all rowed clear in five minutes.

Twenty shells were used to destroy the schooner, though Richardson told a journalist the following day that "about thirty to forty of her biggest" shells were used—apparently one every two minutes for ten minutes. Also, a total of 200 machine gun rounds were fired. These included twenty semi-automatic rounds from one hundred yards away. The submarine circled the sailboat while pumping fire into it until she sank. The *Lucille M.*'s stern was shot clear off, its wheel-house destroyed, and rounds could be heard striking the ice intended for the fish. The auxiliary-motor vessel had no radio. The Canadians testified that the submarine was so close they could hear the gun's breeches being opened by German sailors, as well as empty shell casings hitting the sub's metal deck. The attack lasted half an hour, following which Lohmann said he was "sorry, but that he had to do it ... [and] bad luck boys, we cannot help it."

Some survivors said they were given time to provision the dories; however, the four injured fishermen contradict that. The last words in the log book were "abandoning, badly damaged, shelled by submarine." The fishermen then rowed themselves 100 miles to Shelburne over thirty-six hours. On landing and being interviewed by the Royal Canadian Navy, some of the sailors said they heard a German exclaim "the damned thing won't sink!" Though a number of Canadian fishing vessels had been sunk by German submarines, and a trawler captured by them during World War I, *Lucille M.* was their first victim since. According to the Associated Press, she was the 399th Allied ship sunk in the Western Atlantic. Captain Richardson ominously warned that, at the rate things were going, more would be sunk "sooner or later."

Kapitänleutnant Hans Oestermann brought *U-754* into New England from July 25–28, 1942. The submarine was sunk with all hands three days later. Oestermann sank the 260-ton U.S.-flag trawler *Ebb* on July 28. The U-boat left Brest on June 19 and ten days later sank the 12,435-ton *Waiwera* between Newfoundland and the Azores; ninety-seven survived while eight perished.[9] *U-754* refueled from *U-469* in the same general vicinity on July 7 and also received torpedoes. "*U-754* was one of the last seven U-boats operating off the U.S. East Coast." On June 24, Erich Schiller dislocated his shoulder and so he and another sailor were (fatefully) transferred off the doomed *U-754* to *U-566* under Borchert, homeward bound. From late June to mid-July, Oestermann and his men patrolled of the Carolinas but were disappointed. On July 24, they were ordered to disrupt the route between Boston and Cape Sable with Diggins in *U-458*. The following day, *U-754* radioed to France that he had missed a 4,000-ton freighter. On July 19, *U-754* joined *U-89* under Lohmann, *U-132* under Vogelsang and Diggins in *U-458* off Nova Scotia. On July 30, he and Vogelsang were told to seek out a convoy in the area, which Oestermann never found but Vogelsang did, sinking the *Pacific Pioneer* from Convoy ON 113.

On July 31, immediately after sinking the *Ebb* and reporting "light air and sea surveillance ... much fog," *U-754* was surprised on the surface by a Hudson aircraft from RCAF Squadron piloted by N. E. Small. Small utilized the advantage of surprise and dropped depth charges, then banked sharply to strafe the conning tower with machine guns. An explosion an hour later indicated that the submarine was destroyed, confirmed when oil and debris came to the surface. All forty-three submariners perished.[10] On August 2, U-boat headquarters (BdU) informed Oestermann, by now drowned, of Allied shooting practice in "Cape Cod Bay." The boat was declared missing on August 7, again on September 2, 1942, and officially, on January 28, 1943, *U-754* was conclusively "presumed missing ... [and] total loss assumed." Her sailors are on eternal patrol. Oestermann was born in 1913 and lived until age twenty-nine. He was a member of the Crew of 1933 and served as 1st Watch Officer of the destroyer *Z7 Hermann Schoemann*, up to June 1940. Then he joined U-boats, starting with *U-151*, which he commissioned, before assuming command of *U-754*. He sank thirteen ships worth over 55,000 tons yet was not decorated.[11]

Korvettenkapitän Fritz Hoeckner brought *U-215* into New England for a one-day incursion on July 3, 1942, during which the U-boat managed to find Convoy BX 27 (possibly BA 2),[12] and sink a Liberty ship. *U-215* was swiftly counterattacked by escorting corvettes and destroyed with the loss of all forty-eight men.[13] Hoeckner had been ordered to mine Boston Harbor, as Berger in *U-87* had already done without result. By striking at a convoy before laying the sensitive mines, Hoeckner would have endangered his mission and crew. The ship they sank was the *Alexander Macomb*, on her maiden voyage, just as this was *U-215*'s maiden patrol. The *Macomb* was carrying 9,000 tons of military stores and explosives from New York to Halifax via Woods Hole. Her ultimate destination was Archangel in the Soviet Union.[14] The first torpedo ignited the explosives, and fifty-six survivors out of sixty-six total scrambled to escape the burning ship, which was still moving. Some made it to three lifeboats and a raft, but another lifeboat was swamped. Other men just leapt overboard and grabbed debris. The attack was equidistant 175 miles between Cape Cod and Cape Sable, in the middle of the of the mouth of the Gulf of Maine. The British crew of the anti-submarine trawler H.M.S. *Le Tigre*, FY 243, quickly counterattacked with depth charges and sank *U-215*. They also picked up thirty-one of the Allied survivors and took them back to Woods Hole. H.M.C.S. *Regina*, K 234, rescued twenty-five other Allied sailors and took them to Halifax.

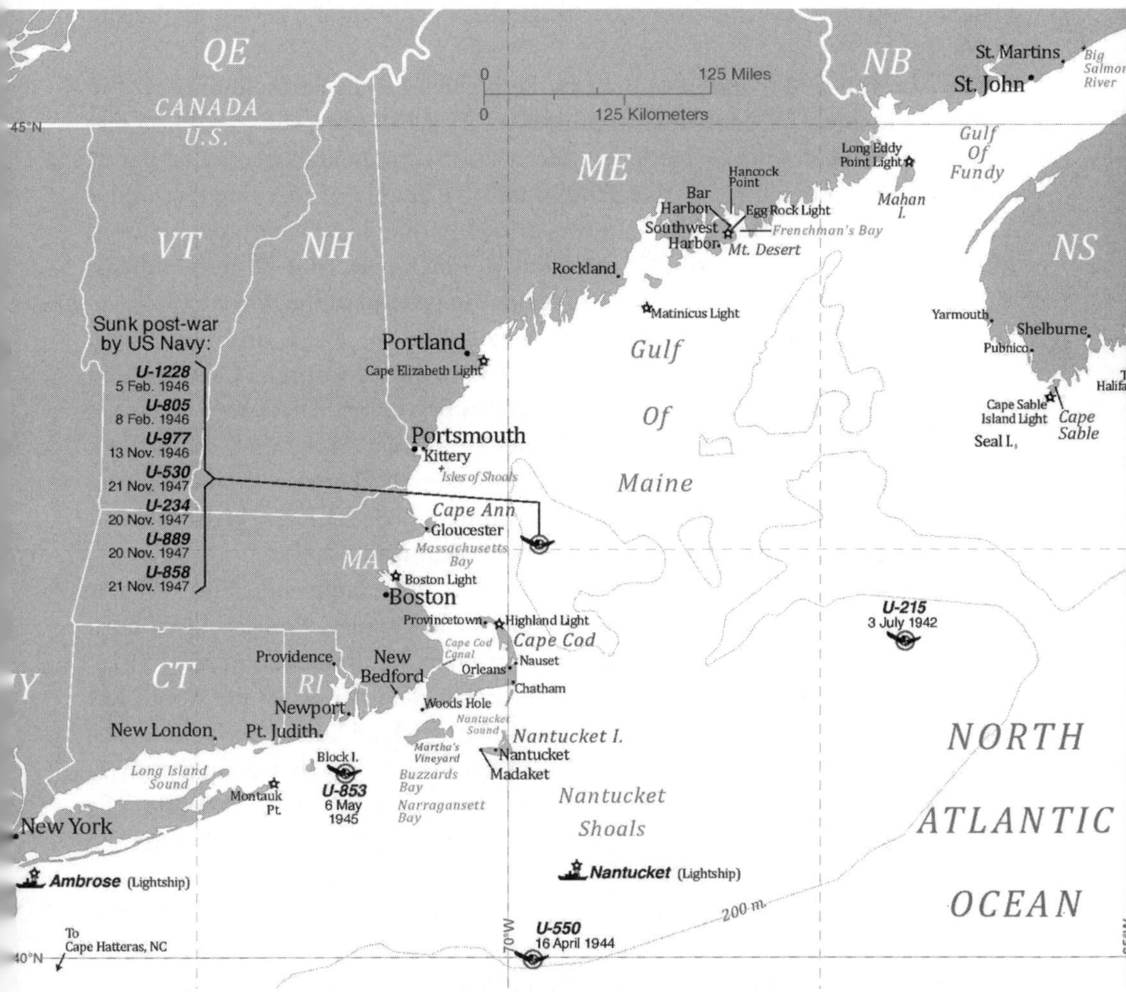

German U-boats sunk by Allies in New England: three during and seven after World War II. (*Robert Eller Pratt*)

U-215 left Kiel on 9 June 1942, and was in contact with shore on June 14, 18, 19, 23, 27, and 30: mostly about fuel, weather, and their colleague Horst Degen in *U-701*. By July 3, there were observations of aircraft out of Halifax. U-boat headquarters tried to contact the men of *U-215* on July 8–13, then again on August 28. Her men were officially declared lost on January 28, 1943, retroactive to July 8, 1942.[15] Hoeckner was born in 1912 in Berlin and was twenty-nine when killed. He was a member of the Crew of 1933 and was promoted to *Korvettenkapitän* with seniority posthumously. He served initially in the 5th Minesweeping Flotilla, joining U-boats in March 1941.[16] The final patrol originated in Kiel as a repositioning effort. The emblem of the U-boat was a rodent, similar to a rat.[17] *U-215* was discovered by a team of researchers called The Sea Hunters in July of 2004 inside Canadian waters. Leader Mike Fletcher said that weather and other difficulties prohibited a revisit to the site in 2017.[18]

The *Alexander Macomb* was built by Bethlehem Steel's Fairfield Shipyard in Baltimore for the U.S. Maritime Commission. At 7,179 tons, she was 441.5 feet long, 57 feet wide, and 29 feet deep. Her twin steam-engines propelled her at 11.5 knots for a distance of over 20,000 miles. Capable of carrying just under 11,000 long tons of cargo, the ship was armed with a 4-inch stern deck-gun as well as several anti-aircraft guns, including a 3-inch gun, four 20-mm and two .30-caliber guns. She was named for an American general in the War of 1812.

The *Alexander Macomb* was launched on May 6, 1942, and completed sea trials on June 2. Thereafter, under the command of Captain Carl Monsen Froisland, she steamed for New York to load her first cargo. That cargo consisted of urgent lend-lease supplies for the Soviet Union via Archangel: explosives, ammunition, P 38 airplanes whole and in parts, and Sherman tanks, totaling 9,000 tons. There were also sixty sacks of ordinary U.S. mail, and eight sacks of United-States-registered mail for the Soviet Union aboard.

Aboard the *Alexander Macomb* were sixty-six men; eight merchant officers, thirty-three merchant sailors, and twenty-five naval gunners. Froisland was born in Norway and became a naturalized U.S. citizen in San Francisco in May 1916. Less than two months after her launch, the captain and crew set off from New York on July 1. On the way from City Island, Long Island Sound, to Halifax, she stopped in Woods Hole, astride the Cape Cod Canal. She then joined convoy BX 27 of forty-one ships in thick fog and headed northeast for Nova Scotia. The convoy was zigzagging on the prescribed patterns of C40 and S11. Among the vessels escorted the merchant ships were H.M.S. *Le Tigre*, H.M.S. *Veteran* (which helped survivors of the *Port Nicholson* and the *Cherokee*), and H.M.C.S. *Regina*, K234. H.M.S. *Le Tigre*, FY243, was a former trawler converted to anti-submarine warfare, and was a thoroughbred in its hard-working class.[19] That March, the five-year-old vessel was loaned to the U.S. Navy to help defend convoys on the U.S. eastern seaboard, where its services were sorely needed.

On the night of Thursday, July 2 between 11 p.m. and 5 a.m., the *Alexander Macomb* fell behind the convoy, in part because of the fog, but primarily because of Captain Froisland's fear of collision. During that time, the engines were run at slow, sometimes with the steam, or propulsion completely cut off, or the ship stopped. Worse yet, as the ship lagged and fell out of the convoy, it flashed lights from its bridge to warn other vessels not to hit it, and the sailors were even told to tow a fog lamp astern, to warn other ships. Of course, the light would also alert and attract submarines, something for which the captain, who had extensive experience in the Atlantic, was roundly criticized. The spar at the masthead flew the Signal 23, the ship's convoy number.[20]

At 6 a.m. on Friday, July 3, Froisland and his lookouts thought that they saw the periscope of a submarine. Fifteen minutes later, they broke the seal of the emergency radio transmitter, but did not begin using it. There were twenty-five naval armed guards in position, an able-bodied, as well as an ordinary seaman looking out from the forecastle head, and on the bridge Captain Froisland, First Officer Lilly, another able-bodied seaman, and the naval-officer-in-charge of the gunners. At the time of the attack, the ship was heading north-northeast at 11 knots. The helmsman altered course occasionally, not strictly zigzagging. Visibility stretched to 2 miles, the seas were settled, a breeze filled in from the southeast, and in the distance half a dozen or so ships of the convoy could be seen less than 3 miles ahead. The vigilant watch aboard the *Alexander Macomb* was no match for the fog.

At 6.30 a.m., the men were trying eagerly to catch up with the convoy when a torpedo from *U-215* under Hoeckner hit her on the starboard quarter. Immediately, the SSS was transmitted, using the KEYE letters, with the alarm turned on. Hoeckner saw an opportunity that he felt he could not turn away from, despite being laden with mines for Boston Harbor. The U-boat's deadly missile hit the ship between the number four and number five cargo holds at the stern, igniting the ammunition stowed there. The area behind the bridge burst into flames. After impact, the engines continued to run, with the result that one of the lifeboats was swamped on launching.

One reason for a ten–fifteen-minute delay in stopping the engines was that First Officer Lilly abandoned ship in a boat with just five sailors in it, rather than oversee the engine stoppage. Captain Froisland disappeared for his stateroom, and neither he nor Lilly oversaw an orderly evacuation of the men. None of the men had sailed together before, and some of the naval recruits had never even been to sea. The gunners never formed a bead on the offending submarine, and none of the ship's guns were ever fired. Right away, the crew and gunners ran for the boats. The ship's codes were sealed up in the skipper's cabin or in the bridge, and all are presumed to have burned or gone down with the ship.

Many of the survivors, fearing that the explosives-laden ship might blow up beneath them, simply jumped into the freezing sea and clung to wreckage. Overall, three lifeboats and a life raft made it off the ship. In the next forty-five minutes, H.M.S. *Le Tigre* and H.M.S. *Veteran* lived up to their names and counterattacked, destroying *U-215* on the spot, men, mines and all. H.M.S. *Le Tigre* rescued thirty-one of the men by 7.15 a.m. H.M.C.S. *Regina* managed to pull twenty-five others from the cold waters. Some of the survivors are convinced that they saw *U-215* "come to the surface bottom up and sink again at 7 a.m." Although the officers and men on the British and Canadian warships were convinced that they sank the U-boat, none of them saw the sub surface bottom-up. The *Alexander Macomb* sank stern-first.

At 11 a.m. the following day, H.M.C.S. *Regina* landed twenty-five of the survivors in Halifax. H.M.S. *Le Tigre* deposited thirty-one sailors, including eight Navy gunners, at Woods Hole at 3.15 p.m. The British commander had some choice words to describe Captain Froisland, including "irresponsible and unqualified." Lilly was derided for abandoning ship before ensuring the engines were stopped, and for leaving the men, many of them inexperienced, to fend for themselves. Subsequent U.S. Navy interviewers concluded after interrogating Froisland that he was "incompetent and negligent, and it was very difficult to pin him down to details. He answered questions in a confused and contradictory manner." The rescuers generally felt that had the *Alexander Macomb* remained in the convoy the attack would not have taken place and she, her cargo and personnel would have survived the morning.[21] Lilly hardly fared better than Froisland, with his interviewers stating he "also made a very poor impression ... he was evasive and contradictory ... all the other forty vessels in the convoy kept together during the night, despite the fog, and there was no reason why subject vessel should have fallen astern." Conditions were, aside from the fog, calm and virtually windless.

After the war, H.M.S. *Le Tigre* was sold to the Hull Ice Company in the U.K., then renamed *Regal*, then *Othello,* and in 1962, she was scrapped in Ghent, Belgium. In the fall of 1964, salvors Risdon Beazley discovered the *Alexander Macomb* wreck in about 180 feet of water, and although they considered it dangerous to dive, by the following year a team based on the salvage ship *Droxford* managed to retrieve the bulk of metal from the wreck.

In 2004, a team filmed by the Canadian television program *The Sea Hunters* led by Mike Fletcher managed to find the wreck of *U-215*, guided to it by fishermen weary of snaring their nets on the metal carcass. The historians discovered that four out of the sub's five tubes were sealed, probably because its primary mission that day was as a minelayer, and also as evidence that the Germans did not have time to seal their torpedo tube before they were counterattacked and sunk.[22]

Kapitänleutnant Kurt Diggins brought *U-458* into New England from July 26–29, 1942. The incursion began southeast of Nantucket then moved northeast for four days, ending south of Cape Sable. On June 21, *U-458* left Germany, escorted by the *Munin* and the *Odin*. They refueled in Kristiansand, and by June

Drawing of how the sub-sea wreck of the *Alexander Macomb* looks today. (*Courtesy of Canadian diver Mike Fletcher, emails, 2017*).

23, the sub was free to patrol, evading various aircraft, including a Consolidated bomber. On June 26, they sighted a drifting mine, as mine-detection and evasion were Diggins' specialties. They encountered another mine north of the Faroes, followed later by a third.[23]

On the way across the Atlantic, Diggins found and sank the 2,714-ton *Mosfruit* on June 30. The attack required a fan of two torpedoes followed two hours later with thirty-one incendiary and twenty explosive shells. Diggins noted she was a "Norwegian banana carrier," armed with "one cannon, two machine guns on the bridge, two machine gun platforms astern with double-mounts, searchlight stand, and six depth-charges." On July 4, Diggins and Günther Pfeffer in *U-171* were told to refuel to the brim from Schäfer in *U-460. U-458* received its fuel, along with 1.45 tons of provisions, near the Azores on July 8. Operating between New England and Bermuda, Diggins gave up on a large steamer described as "a fat booty escaped ... a fast passenger-steamer with two smokestacks, around 15,000 tons," identity unknown. On July 18, the Spanish steamer *Marquis de Comillas, en route* to Bermuda, was given a pass. Then a plane came up astern and bombed them twice.[24]

To July 24, *U-458* was off Hatteras chasing or observing various Allied ships, a Swiss neutral, and Allied patrol craft. Then on the 25th, Diggins "gave up on search in the area and headed to operations at Cape Sable." The following day they chased another steamer as they headed north, well offshore. On July 27, they were on the Georges Bank and avoiding patrol vessels and planes. Exchanging messages with other boats, Diggins headed for Cape Sable to find convoys. On July 30, *U-458* found Convoy ON 113 southeast of Sable.[25] The ships had left the U.K. on July 17 and arrived in Halifax on the 31st, minus five ships lost to U-boats. The boat was harassed by destroyers and planes. The convoy was out to the east but had numerous escorts and was believed by the Germans to be bound to Boston. *U-754* under Oestermann came up to join *U-458* in an attack on the convoy but was unsuccessful and was sunk off Halifax the same day the convoy arrived there. The chase was broken off on August 1. Once clear of New England, *U-458* was also attacked, on August 2 by Hudsons from RCAF Squadron 113 and damaged.[26] On August 3, three detonations were heard.

On August 4, the boat was ordered to head northeast, off Canada. *U-458* was more effective in penetrating Convoy ON 115, as it found and sank the tanker *Arletta* of 4,870 tons on August 5 southwest of Cape Race. *U-458*'s maiden patrol began in Kiel on June 21 and ended in St. Nazaire on August 27 after crossing Biscay under a full moon. Numerous Allied aircraft, including a Sunderland, forced them to crash dive, and others which bombed, them, both heard and seen. They anchored in St. Nazaire with their fuel tanks empty—only 1.5 cubic meters remained.

> *U-458* ... was one of the last seven boats to operate off the U.S. East Coast. By this time, an efficient convoy system was in place and anti-submarine defenses were formidable. *U-458* patrolled south of Hatteras until 19 July when U-boats were withdrawn because of lack of success and the loss of *U-215* and *U-576*.[27]

To this, the loss of *U-754* might be added.

Kurt Diggins was born in 1912, and lived to 2007 and age ninety-four. A member of the Crew of 1934, he initially trained aboard the sail-training ship *Gorch Fock*, then the light cruiser *Karslruhe*. He was an officer aboard the *Admiral Graf Spree,* scuttled off Montevideo on December 17, 1939, after which he made his way back to Europe, starting as a stowaway on a ferry to Argentina.[28] Up to April 1940, Diggins led the 5th Minesweeping Flotilla as well as the 6th Minesweeping Flotilla, then he joined U-boats in April 1940. He commissioned *U-458* in December 1941. Less than a month after being commissioned in Kiel in December 1941, the U-boat collided with the ship *Elbmarschen*, damaging about 2 feet of the submarine's starboard side.

U-458 was sunk in the Mediterranean off Italy in August 1943. Eight perished and thirty-nine lived, including Diggins, who until late 1947 was held captive in the U.K. at Camp 18, Featherstone Park, Haltwhistle. Diggins joined the new German Navy a decade later and retired from it. He went on to become president of the German Submarine Veterans Association, or VDU. Over the course of his career, Diggins sank two Allied ships, both on this patrol, for 7,584 tons. He received the Iron Cross 1st Class and an Italian Bronze Medal for Military Valor.

Kapitänleutnant Ernst Vogelsang brought *U-132* into New England on July 31, 1942, merely cutting westward off Cape Sable, then turned eastward to exit. Although Vogelsang sank five ships during this patrol and *Pacific Pioneer* was sunk on July 30 all of them were sunk outside New England. The *Anastassios Pateras*, the *Hainaut*, and the *Dinaric* were sunk on July 6 from Convoy QS 15, and the *Frederika Lensen* from Convoy QS 19 on the 20th. The *Frederika Lensen* was towed by the corvette H.M.C.S. *Weyburn* and ended up breaking apart. During this patrol, Vogelsang daringly probed far into the St. Lawrence River, the Strait of Belle Isle, and the Gulf of St. Lawrence.

This patrol began in La Pallice on June 10, ending there on August 16. The year began with challenges for the men as in February 1942 the boat was heavily damaged, as a result of which she was dry-docked and the men given time off. Repairs continued haltingly until the end of May and the beginning of June, when she was provisioned on the 6th. They entered Biscay after a *Sperrbrecher* released them and saw a Luftwaffe Condor. They began in the *Endrass* line in mid-June, trying to catch Convoy HG 84. On June 13, the boat was surprised by a corvette, and her periscope damaged from 106 explosions. She was refueled by *U-460* mid-Atlantic. On June 16, they tried to follow a convoy while avoiding a destroyer. After its attack on Convoy QS 15 in the St. Lawrence River, the minesweeper H.M.C.S. *Drummondville* tried to ram *U-132*.[29] The boat submerged to the then-bone-crushing depth of nearly 600 feet to avoid further damage. After attacking the *Pacific Pioneer,* the sub was counterattacked by escorting warships with depth charges.

On July 15, Vogelsang dodged planes, noted lit navigational aids, and practiced crash dives all the time. Then they made six sightings of flying-boats in just an afternoon and evening. They sighted fishing boats over the next few days. On August 16, the boat was met by an escort and ultimately made La Pallice. Vogelsang's superiors were impressed with the patrol, claiming five Allied ships and over 27,000 tons, writing: "a well-executed patrol ... His toughness in the operations area of the St. Lawrence Seaway paid off and led to a beautiful success."[30]

Vogelsang was born in 1911 in Frankfurt, and perished in November 1942 at the age of thirty-one, when *U-132* was sunk near Cape Farewell. A member of the Crew of 1931, he participated in the Spanish Civil War and the invasion of Norway aboard the destroyer *Z5 Paul Jacobi*. Vogelsang joined U-boats in June 1940 and commanded the training boat *U-18* for six months. Then he took command of *U-132* in May 1942 for four patrols. *U-132*'s complement was likely all killed when the *Hatimura*, a British ammunition ship, blew up after being hit by torpedoes from *U-132* and *U-442* under Hesse, as she "was probably within the lethal radius."[31] Vogelsang destroyed ten ships over his career for 39,496 tons and damaged another for 6,690 tons. He was awarded the Spanish Cross in Bronze with Swords, as well as the Iron Cross 1st and Iron Cross 2nd Class.

Kapitänleutnant Walter Schug patrolled New England for nine cumulative days in August 1942. *U-86* entered heading west from August 10–11, turned southwest and exited south of Block Island on the 13th. *U-86* returned off Nantucket on the 21st, headed west for three days exit a second time on the 25th off Montauk. *U-86* sank no ships on its first patrol to the U.S. from March 25 to May 26; the only vessel sunk on this patrol was the 342-ton schooner *Wawaloam* under Captain Louis Kenedy on August 6, 460 miles south of Cape Race. This patrol began and ended in Brest between July 2 to September 18. *U-86* originally joined a wolfpack named, appropriately, Wolf toward Newfoundland Bank. They missed one convoy but trailed ON 113 from July 23, during which two ships were sunk for the loss of one boat, *U-90*.[32] *U-86* and other Wolf boats dispersed and were refueled by *U-461* under Stiebler from July 29–30 near the Azores.

On her final approach to France, the boat was attacked by an airplane of 58 Squadron. Schug was cautious and wary of approaching the American coastline because at "sometime during the patrol she had sustained some damage." Born in 1910, he was a member of the Crew of 1934. Before joining U-boats in February 1940, he served in reserve naval artillery, and was a commanding officer of a naval assault troop division. He then served as 1st Watch Officer of *U-74* from October 1940 to April 1941. He took command of *U-86* after its commissioning, in July 1941. Schug perished at age thirty-three east of the Azores when *U-86* was sunk by depth charges from H.M.S. *Rocket* and H.M.S. *Tumult* on November 29, 1943. He and his forty-nine crewmates were lost.[33] Schug's total was three ships sunk for 9,614 tons and one ship damaged for 8,627 tons. He received no decorations.

Korvettenkapitän Hans-Heinrich Giessler brought *U-455* on a four-day incursion into New England from September 26–29, 1942. The boat motored east from Montauk, exiting south of Cape Sable. This patrol began on August 22 in St. Nazaire and ended there on October 27. On August 12, facing a long shipyard layover and treatment of six sailors for diphtheria the crew "turned over the watch to a skeleton crew from the 7th U-boat Flotilla and drove the crew to the La Baule Hotel known as *Clemantites*," but after British troops attacked Dieppe, the boat was urgently readied to sail on the 19th. On August 22, *U-455* pulled ahead of the *Sperrbrecher* convoys, passed several sailing vessels and headed to sea.

Worried about sabotage, Giessler made a cryptic reference to "guards before the boat" planting bombs set to explode when a U-boat reached over 230 feet deep, and how "unfortunately it was not possible to inspect the boat with a diver before putting to sea ... if one knows that the enemy works by such means, more effective measures against this must be taken." On the 25th, they saw a sailing boat lit up, and thus probably neutral, and the following day they heard nine detonations, probably anti-sub activity by Allied naval ships. They realized that in the rush, no

Crewmates Kanonen Heini and Pulver Jonni on *U-108*'s Winter Garden, or gun platform, which was primarily added to fend off aircract. While merchant ships rarely struck fatal blows to U-boats, and even enemy naval vessels were forced to keep out of deadly range of them, a diving submarine with its guns abandoned and hatches sealed was particularly vulnerable to dexterous aircraft armed with well-placed depth-charges. (*Willy Wilke, U-108*)

one had placed an address book, or code interpretation device, on board, and that they would have to obtain one from an inbound U-boat. Giessler sang praise for the new Fu.M.B. device, designed to improve early detection of enemy craft.

On the 28th, three destroyers were sighted near where *U-455* was to rendezvous with Löwe in *U-256* from Kiel, twenty-eight days out and bound for France. The same day, they recognized *U-183*, under Schäfer not Löwe, and made the rendezvous and exchange with *U-256* after all. By September 6, Giessler was concerned at the heat and humidity on the boat and it sapping the strength of his men, softening their alertness. To cheer them up, he held a fundraising concert for the Red Cross in the German cities of Forst, or Lausitz, which raised 500 *Reichsmark*; seagoing leaders from Shackleton to von Luckner have recognized the value of group entertainment to morale and cohesion. On the 8th, they held target practice. Giessler took a slightly longer route to avoid fog off Newfoundland. On the 15th, news of a new child from headquarters: "for Giessler, strong boy arrived Sunday. Naturally great joy." As they headed for Charleston, the commander worried about being set south in the Gulf Stream.[34]

The primary purpose of the patrol was mining the entrances to Charleston. Though Giessler sowed the minefield, no ships struck them. He noticed the lights of the city, a pilot boat, and a tanker, as well as a wreck buoy. Steering by the North Star as the gyrocompass was off, they lay six mines outside then went closer to lay six more. When a 3,500-ton steamer with four cargo hatches passed nearby, an attack was withheld due to poor light conditions, and *U-455* lay on the seafloor. Giessler was enthused by the prospects of hunting along the 130-foot depth line, and the next day dove to avoid an airship. After looking for traffic patterns to Bermuda and southward, he was told to complete the "secondary task;" however, for him to understand what that meant was "a guessing game."

Giessler motored toward New England, dodging a land-based airplane along the way on September 24. The next day, a twin-engine, then a four-engine plane drove the sub for cover, the latter dropping four bombs. Giessler called this experience "beneficial to the future attention of the lookouts." On October 1, they chased a steamer with two masts and a single smoke-stack with very little smoke but had to give up the chase when the ship was "lost to sight." In the Gulf of St. Lawrence and Cape Race, Giessler found no targets and returned to France. On October 6, they could not line up on a twin-mast, gaff-rigged schooner, and observed several lighthouses as well as fishing and sailing boats. The following day they watched a Canadian naval corvette, then a tanker and a schooner, but they presented "no shooting possibility." More planes, a destroyer, and steamers showed themselves, but aside from the mines, *U-455* never deployed a weapon during 8,820 miles in sixty-seven days, of which twenty-two were without the gyrocompass.[35]

Giessler was born in 1911 in Berlin and was a member of the Crew of 1931. In 1938–1939, he served as 1st Watch Officer of the destroyer *Z16 Friedrich Eckholdt*, followed by a stint in torpedo inspectorate until joining U-boats in March 1941. Giessler served as commander of *U-455* for four patrols from August 1941 to November 1942 and sank two ships for 13,908 tons. He was awarded the Iron Cross 1st Class, then went back to torpedo inspectorate. In February 1945, Giessler became 1st Watch Officer of the destroyer *Z20 Karl Galster*, before being taken PoW. He was released in March 1946.[36]

Kapitänleutnant Rolf Struckmeier brought *U-608* into New England for eight days from November 6–15, 1942. At first, *U-608* headed in a straight line west past Cape Sable, loading mines along the way. After avoiding a destroyer on the 7th, the sub exited past Montauk on the 8th while dodging a patrol boat, then rested the boat on the seafloor, rising on the 9th to see a patrol boat and creep away on electric motors. On the night of November 10–11, *U-608* passed Fire Island and noticed that "all lighthouses burn as in peacetime. New York itself is apparently not dimmed."

Struckmeier then laid a minefield of ten TMA-type mines off New York Harbor, moving around and taking bearings from the lightship *Ambrose*, Navesink, Rockaway Bell Buoy, and John's Inlet. The mines never found their mark, unless U.S.S. *Turner*, DD 648, sunk by unknown explosions on January 3, 1944, with the loss of 164 Navy sailors off Sandy Hook was sunk by a German mine. The others were detected and removed. The next day, Struckmeier had the men reload torpedoes and *U-608* headed to the Gulf of Maine "intending to catch traffic between New York–Philadelphia–Halifax." After observing a "fishing trawler with cannon," they moved again, southeast and east on the 14th and 15th, to exit south of Cape Sable. A day later, east of Halifax, *U-608* caught the 5,621-ton Irish steamer *Irish Pine* and sank her with a second torpedo. It was a devastating attack with no survivors out of thirty-three men. On November 27, *U-608* exhausted its fuel supply and was adrift until *U-521* under Bargsten in mid-Atlantic, then the U-tanker *U-460*, rendezvoused and replenished *U-608*'s fuel northwest of the Azores.[37]

This patrol began in St. Nazaire and ended there on December 9. Struckmeier was born in 1916 and was a member of the Crew of 1935, then a range-finder aboard the *Admiral Hipper* to April 1940. He joined the 1st Torpedo-Boat Flotilla until October 1940, then U-boats. Struckmeier served as 1st Watch Officer on *U-205* for three patrols including to the Mediterranean. He took command of *U-608* from February 1942 until January 1944, then served as a training officer until the surrender.[38] Struckmeier sank four ships for 35,539 tons and a warship (which was cargo aboard a merchant ship), of 291 tons. He was awarded the German Cross in Gold, U-boat Front Clasp, and War Merit Cross 2nd Class with Swords.

Fregattenkapitän Heinrich Schäfer brought *U-183* into New England between November 13 and 16, 1942, heading southwest then southeast and away. The patrol began in Kiel on September 19 and ended in Lorient on December 23. One ship, the British *Empire Dabchick*, was sunk southeast of Cape Breton from Convoy ONS 146 on December 3. This was the U-boat's first patrol. *U-183* took part in two wolfpack patrol lines, starting with *Luchs* in early October west of Ireland, which was to hunt down westbound convoy HX 209. On October 1, *U-183* let a well-lit neutral, or hospital-ship pass. On October 5, *U-183* was detected and bombed by four depth charges from a U.S. Navy Catalina of Squadron VP 73 under Lieutenant G. F. Swanson.

The sub also participated in the *Panther* group between October 7 and 11. Once in Canadian waters, they joined up with *U-518* under Brachmann to investigate the Belle Isle Strait, north of Newfoundland. On November 11, they stalked a convoy, then fired two torpedoes at a tanker and heard two explosions. In the depth charge attack that followed, an unnamed *Unteroffizier* was badly injured with "testicles banged, greatly swollen ... cooled, seven days no decrease in swelling." The pain spread to the sailor's abdomen and both the right side and buttocks.[39]

Patrolling off Nova Scotia and Newfoundland *U-183* met Convoy ONS 146 and sank the *Empire Dabchick*. On November 12, east of Cape Sable, Schäfer dove to avoid an airplane with a white light on it. On the 15th, they cleared Seal Island Light to starboard and the next day a buoy also as *U-183* approached a fishing boat close enough to distinguish "set sails, white top-light, and several working lanterns. Probably not to be trusted. He had seen us in the moon, then later, after diving, an aircraft was seen in the periscope." The following day, they saw another aircraft. For nine days after November 10, Schäfer reported "nothing seen," except for sightings of and bombing by aircraft. The *Unteroffizier* patient who no longer required a transfer. After refueling from *U-460* under Schnoor north of the Azores on December 12, *U-183* returned to France two days before Christmas.

Schäfer was born in 1907 in Bremerhaven and was a member of the Crew of VII/1925. Early in his career he served on the gunnery target ship *Mars* up to June 1941, after which he joined U-boats. He trained in the 26th U-Boat Flotilla and 3rd U-Boat Flotilla from 1941 to 1942, then took over command of *U-183* from April 1942 until November 1943. He was in the 2nd U-Boat Flotilla at the end of 1943 and then commander of UIT-23 from December 1943 to January 1944. He died outside Tokyo of illness (paratyphoid and appendicitis) on January 7, 1944, at age thirty-six.[40] Schäfer sank two ships of 8,582 tons and received no decorations. UIT-23 was the formerly Italian submarine *Reginaldo Giuliani*, sunk in the Straits of Malacca on Valentine's Day 1944 by British submarine H.M.S. *Tallyho*; there were fourteen survivors. After nineteen months of operations in Southeast Asia, *U-183* was sunk on April 23, 1945 in the Java Sea north of Soerabaja, Indonesia (then the Dutch East Indies) by the submarine U.S.S. *Besugo*; one German survived, fifty-four perished.

14

The Tragic Saga of the Lifeboat of the Wind Ship *Angelus*

Kapitänleutnant Albrecht Achilles brought *U-161* into New England three times for thirty-three days between April 6 and May 19, 1943; by then, he was known both as "Ajax" among peers and as "the ferret" by his foes for his skills at entering ports like Castries, St. Lucia, Port of Spain, Trinidad, and Puerto Limón, Costa Rica to torpedo shipping and safely escape. It was the first patrol to New England in months (since *U-183* left in mid-November 1942) and the longest New England patrol yet. Achilles was delayed from combat by diverting outbound to rendezvous with *U-174* under Grandefeld and Axis blockade runners *Regensburg* (March 23), *Pietro Orseolo* (March 24), *Karin* (which was disguised with the name *U-915* even though *U-915* was never launched), and *Irene* (ex-*Silvaplana*). Approaching New England on April 4, the men in *U-161* heard four underwater explosions and two days later heard a fast destroyer heading northeast of Cape Sable. On the 8th, they eliminated a leak of more than three cubic meters of oil, then headed for Nantucket. They were detected by ASDIC and heard far-off detonations the next day. Off the lightship *Nantucket*, they again heard four detonations, then a patrol ship nearby, and a whistling sound on the radio, followed by a Douglass-type airplane dropping bombs.[1]

The next day, an airplane dropped a white flare over *U-161*, then a Northrup airplane (which the Fu.M.U. did not forewarn them of) attacked, sending them scurrying nearly 150 feet down. The boat was then hounded by three U-boat hunter-killer groups. It crept south, with bad weather roiling the surface. The next day a destroyer sent twenty-eight depth charges in the distance, followed by more ASDIC pings, and five more depth charges. On the 15th, *U-161* dove to avoid a land-based plane. After giving a radio report a pair of aircraft bombs were thrown at them, followed by a Consolidated bomber coming in low. Achilles reported air coverage and ASDIC 180 miles from shore. The coastal defenses had certainly improved since early 1942. On the 18th, they were ordered to resupply with *U-129* under Hans-Ludwig Witt, *U-161*'s previous commander and Grandefeld in *U-174* later on, in the central North Atlantic.[2]

U-161 held a position off the New York shipping lanes for three days, then moved southeast until April 20, then headed toward Canada for ten days after holding southeast of Nantucket for three days, waiting to use the lightship *Nantucket* as bait. Achilles's strategy was not working, and so, exasperated he turned east, leaving the area on the 30th. *U-161*'s return foray was a short three-day passage east-to-west, exiting May 8. On the 15th, *U-161* returned from Bermuda south of Nantucket, headed north for a day until the 17th, then turned southwest then east for four days, seeking targets and avoiding attack. On the 22nd, the Germans heard sixteen depth charges in the distance and remained submerged to avoid detection. The following day, Achilles tried to outsmart the Allies by throwing a "strong oil trace and boxes overboard in the direction of the convoy route." The same day, a tenacious single-stack destroyer pursued *U-161* three times, dropping four depth charges, then eight more, and seventeen more the following day.[3] Life was certainly a lot less comfortable for U-boat sailors than it had been when Achilles and his men seemed to reign supreme in the Caribbean during Operation *Neuland* the year before.

The 26th brought another destroyer and sixteen more depth charges. The next day, *U-161* required engine repairs, followed by sixteen more depth charges far off. A flying boat forced them to crash-dive, with many more depth charges and ASDIC impulses on the 29th. On May 3, more destroyers and depth charges off Halifax. On May 11, a crash-dive to avoid a flying boat, and yet another on the 14th. The next day, Achilles allowed the *Iciar* of Bilbao to pass, then *U-161* was almost run over by a neutral Swiss steamer. By the 17th they were northwest of Bermuda and on the 18th, *U-161*'s men began the return passage to France.

Despite all of Achilles' vigilance and efforts, he was only able to sink a single 255-ton ship between March 13 and June 7. On May 19, Achilles intercepted the Canadian sailing barque *Angelus*, which was *en route* from Barbados to Halifax with a cargo of rum and molasses. After dawn, they observed a "quickly growing larger vessel ... a brig on a northerly course, speed five knots ... maneuvered ahead by night. Surfaced. Because the vessel sets small lights, intend to order the vessel to halt with artillery in the morning." She was stopped by a warning shot and the ten officers and men, with a dog, abandoned ship in a lifeboat. *U-161*'s gunners sank her with gunfire, Achilles noting simply "after disembarking the crew, sank with artillery." When, five days later, U.S.S. *Turner* found what remained of Captain Edward Jensen and his men, eight had perished, and only two survived. They were landed in Portland after three days spent fruitlessly chasing *U-161*.[4]

On May 26, Achilles observed another U-boat which turned away without returning their signal then dived. On May 29, they met with *U-229* under Schetelig and received from them twenty-one cubic meters of fuel oil. The boats were ordered to transit Biscay together, but *U-229* only had half of her batteries, and *U-161* could only remain submerged for three hours at a time, despite a heavy risk of "aircraft bombs." Four detonations were heard on June 3. By the 5th, they heard over twenty-seven bombs going off and saw a drifting mine to port. Then *U-229* peeled off for Bordeaux. On May 6, another crash-dive due to planes. Then Achilles refused to submerge for the final plane, "due to large range," and on the 7th joined a convoy into Lorient.

Born in 1914, Achilles was a member of the Crew of 1934. He perished at age twenty-nine when *U-161* was attacked and sunk by a U.S. Navy Mariner aircraft northeast of Bahia, Brazil, on September 27, 1943. He had a reputation as a daring commander and is said to have thought like a merchant captain. He sank fourteen ships for 64,542 tons and damaged six for 41,122 tons earning him the Knights Cross and four other decorations. He started out on the training ship *Schleswig-Holstein*, then the battleship *Gneisenau*, following by officer's school. He joined U-boats in April 1940, patrolling under Zapp, another highly successful commander, on *U-66*. Achilles took over *U-161* in January 1942, leading missions to the Caribbean, Africa, and South America, and was promoted to *Korvettenkapitän* posthumously.[5]

The *Angelus* was a large sailing bark (short for *barkentine*, or *barque*) built in France and sporting three large masts and a bowsprit as long as most masts. Built in the Tranchemar yard in La Richardais, in 1912, she sailed under the tri-color for nineteen years, until May 11, 1942, when captured by H.M.C.S. *Prescott,* K 161, on the Grand Banks while under command of Felix Chevalier of Cancale, in Brittany. Used in very basic trades (such as collecting catches of dried cod and other bulk cargos), the *Angelus* was truly a throwback to times of yore inasmuch as she was propelled entirely by human sinew, and the only modern convenience on board was a stove. She relied on tugs to move the mother ship and oars to move the lifeboats, as there was simply no machinery on board.[6]

The *Angelus* was towed to Sydney by the Royal Canadian Navy and laid up until January 1943. During the interval, she was offered by the Free French to the Canadian Government. Between January 10 and 25, the *Angelus* was loading lumber in Louisbourg. On Friday 22 January her crew placed themselves repeatedly in extreme peril to rescue of eight of twenty-six U.S. Navy sailors shipwrecked off that port.[7] The men from the *Angelus*'s crew were Clarence Mullins and John Hillier of Fortune Bay, Joseph Chaiasson of New Waterford, and Walter Boudreau (twenty-five) of Moncton.

Later sought out for interviews as one of very few survivors, Boudreau related how when the sub-chaser U.S.S. *SC 709* grounded outside the harbor and iced over almost completely, it was clear to those ashore that her men would freeze to death unless rescued. Completely independently of each other, the motorboat *W. G.* with Louisbourg fishermen took a direct approach while the men of *Angelus*, fueled by cold potatoes and encouraged by their captain, carried two dories to Cemetery Point.

During two round-trips to the stranded sub-chaser, the Canadians banged on the ice to wake up the dying men. They were barely able to shuttle them ashore without tipping over the dories and killing all in them. While the local men and officials later basked in the success off their own rescue, by motorboat, those who had rowed out to the Navy ship were not allowed to meet those they rescued or even the fellow rescuers. Those who had burned up the most calories were not given a morsel to eat as a reward and were in fact treated very poorly, being ignored by their own countrymen, despite their obvious poverty and seamanship. Boudreau related:

> When we reached the beach, there was somebody there that took them over … [We] didn't go to the party or the gathering. we went [to] … one of those military places, or some kind of a building. We were not taken there in a truck or given any transportation. We walked out … in the snow. And when we got there, the Royal Canadian Navy was standing around; you know, tipping glasses. And we stood in the corner with our fur hats and ear muffs and mittens and rubber boots like dodos, and nobody paid any attention to us at all. I think somebody later came and gave us a drink, I seem to recall—or maybe it was coffee. And we said … "well, we may as well go home." Which is what we did. Now that was the last of the rescue as far as I was concerned. I never saw anything in print.[8]

The *Angelus* took on four fresh crew from Newfoundland after January 25 and sailed for the Montreal Shipping Company of Halifax, under the auspices of the Canadian Merchant Marine. From March to May she undertook Voyage Two of her new registry—a round trip between Halifax and Barbados, carrying lumber down and rum and molasses back.

The *Angelus*' master was Edward Jensen, married and a naturalized Scandinavian, short, likeable, and aged forty-two, from Lunenburg. He oversaw the safety of a crew of nine other men. Four of the new officers and crew hailed from the same tiny village clinging to the southeast shores of Newfoundland: Belleoram. In 1921, the population was 698 people in 140 households, and in 2011, it had dropped to 409 persons.[9] Having forty percent of the crew originate in the same tight-knit community meant their loss would be felt disproportionately. Head of household Arthur James (Art) Holmans worked in the cod fishery and reported CAD$100 income for all 1934. His wife Margaret emigrated to Newfoundland in 1919 and bore the family two sons: Alexander M. (Sandy) aged twenty, also on the *Angelus*, and Jeremiah, born three years earlier. Two childhood friends of Alexander's were entrusted to Art: Clarence Mullins, aged twenty-three, who came from a family of seven, and whose father Edward was also a cod fisherman, and John Thomas C. Hillier, twenty-four, son of a fisherman. John was also a laborer in the fishing room since age sixteen.[10]

They loaded a massive cargo of lumber below-decks, and a "big deck load … eleven feet high strapped, onto the deck." Though the "boat didn't have any machinery, no engine, the only machinery was the alarm clock. No refrigeration. Nothing like fresh eggs or fruit or anything like that. Just potatoes, potatoes, salt fish, salt beef, and potatoes," they set sail internationally in March. They needed a tow through the ice, as Boudreau related:

> [We] were towed out of Louisbourg in ice, in quite heavy ice, [to] maybe four or five miles outside. The old *Angelus* was not in very good shape. By this time, she was leaking, I mean right away, as soon as we were outside the harbor, she was leaking. And they come and say ... "well, get to the pumps." We never stopped pumping until they got to Barbados—and we had a very small crew. Watches were four hours on, and four hours off. Normal sailing today is four on, eight off. So, you have three watches. But this was an economy ship—two watches.[11]

They arrived in Barbados three weeks later and were towed through a torpedo-net strung across Carlisle Bay, Bridgetown. Barbados had been attacked by *U-514* under Aufferman seven months before, and though they missed the Norwegian *Betancuria,* the Canadian freighter *Cornwallis* was hit and beached. Later repaired, the *Cornwallis* was sunk by *U-1230* under Hilbig in the Gulf of Maine in December 1944.[12]

Though the stevedores were out of practice discharging such huge cargoes of lumber, they managed, and the Canadians had some respite in warmer climes. Local merchants convinced the harbor-master to prevail upon Captain Jensen to recaulk the *Angelus*, which was partially done. Boudreau says Jensen was "a very nice man. He was a little guy. But he was a good man." After loading 575 puncheons of molasses and barrels of rum on what was historically a leg of the triangle trade, the *Angelus* left Bridgetown on April 28, 1943. For three weeks, her people enjoyed the warm settled weather of the trade winds.

Being propelled by wind rather than noisy engines, plus having a shallow draft, lead Boudreau and other sailors to believe that sailing ships were less likely to be targeted by U-boats. Also, having less value than commercial cousins carrying petroleum seemed like an advantage to her sailors. At least seven schooners in the waters from Key West and Barbados to Halifax were sunk by U-boats in World War II, including the *Helen Forsey*, the *Wawaloam*, the *Vivian P. Smith*, the *James E. Newsom*, the *Carmen*, the *Cheerio*, and the *E. P. Theriault*, plus many more in the Caribbean and along the coasts of South America and Central America.[13] Over thirty schooners were sunk by U-boats in North American waters, and many hundreds were sunk globally, including the *Albert F. Paul* off Hatteras and others off Canada, the Gulf of Mexico, and the Caribbean, where they were a source of fresh provisions for Germans, to whom fresh meat, milk, eggs, and vegetables were rare.[14] In World War I, sinking wind-ships from U-boats was a matter of course.

On the morning of May 19, the *Angelus* had the misfortune of sailing into the crosshairs of *U-161* and her veteran commander, Albrecht Achilles, who was very frustrated with the prospect of returning to base empty-handed for the first time since his positioning patrol of thirteen days in January 1942. He had sunk over 58,000 tons of shipping on his most recent patrol, and 26,000 tons on the patrol before that, much of it in daring missions into enemy harbours, yet with the *Angelus*, he faced returning home with a mere 255 tons.[15]

Art Holmans was at the wheel at 4.40 a.m. when he spotted *U-161* roughly 4 miles off the starboard bow. He immediately sounded the alarm, and Captain Jensen and the eight others were quickly on deck. The *Angelus* was heading northeast by east at 4 knots. There were three men working the sails. The breeze was light from the southwest, seas moderate, and the conditions clear. Boudreau heard a shot and tumbled onto deck. The crew was unsure what they were looking for until another few shots were clearly intended to make them "stay there ... [*U-161*] motored in and there was the Swastika flying with the German flag."[16] The warning shot flew over the barque's port bow as the sub cruised on a converging course. Boudreau explained how, with his dog, the following occured:

> The captain got the code books in their steel box weighted with lead. Sextants, chronometer and charts were snatched up. The men gathered oil-skins and blankets. The crash of the U-boat's gun spoke again, and all hands rushed to the lifeboat. We had two provisioned dories also but decided to get away in the lifeboat before it was hit by a shell ... we drew away from the vessel as quickly as we could.[17]

U-161 then signaled the men in the lifeboat to row to the submarine, which they did. Achilles was already on his way toward the *Angelus* and came toward the boat. As they rowed to the sub, Boudreau noted two machine gun mounts on the conning tower as well as the following:

> Short staff flying the German ... red flag with a white circle in its center enclosing a black Swastika. The captain's hand, grasping the weighted steel box containing the code flags, had been held over the side. Now, his hand opened and the box sank into the depths of the ocean.

Once they were alongside, Achilles demanded that Jensen board the submarine and questioned him about the nature and route of his cargo for ten minutes. Achilles made an unusual offer: he said that Jensen was welcome to return to the *Angelus* for up to twenty-five minutes in order to "secure such personal effects and equipment as he might wish." After consideration, Jensen declined, thinking that just to return to his ship would consume all of the allotted time. He was also confident his men had all they needed. Achilles was described as thirty-five and had strong verbal English with a Cockney accent. There were six ratings in the conning tower scanning the horizon. Four men manned a deck-gun, two others a machine gun mounted in the conning tower, and three others also carried weapons (German sailors were wary lest their quarry conceal guns under sails in lifeboats and counterattack). Boudreau described Achilles' goatee, blue uniform with no decorations, the garrison caps with swastika devices, and leather pants some of the sailors wore.

Achilles inquired of his captor whether "any stores on the *Angelus* that were worth the time of the sub to procure," and was told no. Achilles considered rifling the barque, but Boudreau wryly observed that "I guess he didn't want a barrel of rum on that submarine, and you can see the point there." He asked Jensen about tonnage, explaining half-apologetically that "we're out for tonnage, sorry to have to sink her." Achilles instructed Jensen and his men to keep well clear of their ship due to the danger of shelling. After releasing Jensen back to the boat, the Germans began shelling the *Angelus*. Boudreau noted: "smoke and wood flying around ... one hit the crap-house on the stern [named the poop deck for that reason] and blew that up! Then the cook-house." The barque's sails were still defiantly set:

> The first [shell] went over, the second fell short, the third took away the foremast. Another blew the galley off the stern. Then the shells began to thud into the hull, and the rapid-fire gun joined in with a clatter. The old barkentine began to smoke. When we left her that morning, she had all sail on. Now, most of these were burning fiercely. It was a sad sight. Soon she took a list to starboard and slowly went down by the head. The last we saw of her was the Union Jack on the mizzen.

The Germans fired roughly twenty shells at the barque in a "leisurely manner, as though engaging in target practice." Although four shells missed the mark, the other sixteen splintered the masts and hull. The Germans did not board the *Angelus*, which had neither weapons or radio. It took roughly ten minutes for the sailors to destroy her, then *U-161* motored to the east at 6.10 a.m., not even bothering to submerge or assume a decoy route. Before leaving the ten Canadians to the elements, Achilles wished them "*bon voyage* to Canada."

The boat on which the survivors depended for their survival was a sloop-rigged (single-mast) lifeboat equipped with a pair of oars and provisions. Achilles has specifically asked Jensen "whether the lifeboat had adequate stores, water, and compass," and was told that it did. Jensen and his crew were of course experienced sailors, setting off northward toward Canada and home. Boudreau noted that "evening brought more wind, and a solid drizzle of cold rain which made us miserable." He added:

> [Even though they were in] a bathtub hundreds of miles from anything, with nothing but the strength in [their] arms to get home, [they] weren't going to try and row [as] the boat only had about two oars anyway ... meanwhile, we'll waddle along with

> this old sail as best we can ... any seaman is able to look at Polaris, the North Star, and figure that America's gotta be over there somewhere, you know. You can head there, or you can head there, you're going to get to America sooner or later.[18]

The lifeboat voyage proceeded admirably during three days of smooth sailing in conducive weather until May 22. Each day up to then it was "weather fine, crew in good spirits." Starting at 6 p.m. on the fourth day, a gale broke over them. The heavy seas caused them to lose the sea anchor as well as the sail. "A swell 40 feet high can look like a bloody mountain," from the perspective of a few inches above water. "Everybody was scared." They trailed the two oars behind to slow her down. Then they were at risk of losing all of the brakes dragged behind. A seabird coasted past, infuriating Boudreau by the ease with which it handled the weather; "the casual and complacent look in his eye seemed an insult" to the wizened mariners clinging tenuously to life.

As though just running helpless before the weather was not bad enough, their situation became exponentially graver. Jensen had been dozing off with his dog on his lap and was offered relief. Two hours later, at around 8 p.m., the storm capsized the boat and caused the loss of any survival equipment which had not been properly secured. All ten men managed to turn the boat back to level and bail it out. Even the "poor dog, which paddled and scratched, panic stricken, at the side," made it. Yet they only saved a single case of corned beef and another of condensed milk.

Half an hour later, at 8.30 p.m., the first of a series of horrible tragedies struck. When the boat was suddenly capsized for the second time, men scrambled for their lives back on board only to learn that their leader, Captain Jensen did not make it. He was lost, drowned, retrieval impossible.

> A big, big wave comes up under [us] and here she goes. Lifts the stern. She coasts down [the wave], digs her bow in the water, and over she goes [pitch-poled]. All men all over the place. Cold water—icy. The kind of water you die in, you know, in a few minutes. When the boat was there upside- down, we're all in the water, everybody's swimming back to clamber up on the boat or hold onto it. We were all hollering roll-call. Who's here and who isn't. Captain Jensen didn't show up, or his dog. He was missing.[19]

Art Holmans was now the captain of the lifeboat, leading its occupants, including his son and two neighbors. The terrible ordeal continued when the boat capsized again that night. Once more, it was righted. Boudreau cheerfully shouted the lyrics of a chanty named "Roll the Barrell" to encourage the men to roll the boat over. When the boat rolled a fourth and final time, because of the onset of hypothermia, it was only with "great difficulty" that it was righted by the exhausted and freezing men. They tied a line astern, so that men could grab it if they were swept off the boat. By 10 p.m., the waves were washing right over the boat, which was flooded, further sapping their bodies of warmth. They all began to experience severe muscular cramps.

Then the deaths began. Like their village, sailing ships tend to be extremely tight-knit communities, bonds especially close across bloodline, occupation, friendship, and community, as well as the hostility the outside world had shown the rural *Newfies* back in Louisbourg, Nova Scotia. As Boudreau said simply, "hypothermia started to come in … those guys just [drifted away]. Fell asleep, that's how hypothermia works. Just fell asleep and fell over." At 11 p.m., John Hillier died of exposure, and his body was quickly committed to the deep. Boudreau and the others began to die painfully of freezing and exposure. At midnight, Cecil Hardiman perished and also went overboard. Early the next morning, Clarence Mullens of Belleoram (the first villager to go) died. "Then Alexander Holmans passed away and was buried," his father laconically declared. Yet Boudreau saw events differently:

> We're down to maybe four or three men, something like that. And I remember two of them died. Two of the Newfoundlanders died very quickly, one after the other. In the boat. They just seemed to go to sleep. And one of them was Sandy, the son of the mate [Art]. The mate was holding him, trying to keep him warm—Sandy died in his arms, his son. And he wouldn't … holding him, and just wouldn't let go of the boy. Because when these people would die we had to put them over the side. We couldn't have the boat floating with dead bodies all over the place. So, the mate didn't want to release his son and he held onto him until the next day. Now, by this time, the cook was at one end of the boat, [Art] was at the other holding his son, and I was somewhere sitting around. And we went over to the mate and said, "You know, you have to let Sandy go." And he cried, and we put him over the side. So that [left] the mate, the cook, and myself.[20]

Though the wind and heavy seas abated the following day (May 23), the lifeboat was filled with freezing water. The constant exposure killed Francis Walsh at 5 a.m., then Jean Brunelle, and both were committed to the sea. The captain and then six young sailors had quickly perished. That left three others alive, in deplorable condition, barely hanging on to life. What little food they had made them terribly thirsty for water they did not have. Cans could not be opened except with a knife, which they did not have. They resorted to licking the benches in the mornings to obtain fresh mist. Boudreau cut a copper water tank in half and bailed the boat with it. Holmans was too grief-stricken to do much except join Boudreau in a warm, life-giving embrace in the bottom of the boat to stave off hypothermia. Boudreau noted:

> The boat was poorly stocked. It had some very inappropriate stuff. You don't want corned beef if you're dying of thirst. Had a few of those things. It didn't have any

> fishing equipment, no lights. It did have flares. Not a lifeboat stocked according to regulations at all ... we saw a couple of things floating one time—pieces of board—and scraped some little barnacles off and ate them. Oh, toothpaste we ate. I remember that. We ate a tube of toothpaste. Little barnacles, that's all. Nothing else. Had no water.[21]

At noon, cook James H. Boyd, aged thirty-seven, from Crescent Beach, British Columbia, the anointed provisions-provider, threw what food he could lay his hands on overboard. That left just two tins of corned beef and another of milk to sustain severely deprived bodies. Around ninety minutes later, a clearly raving Boyd jumped into the waves. Both remaining men were blinded by the constant exposure to salt spray. That gives an idea of the hostility of the conditions they faced. Holmans's body was turning numb, so he had Boudreau lash him to the bow of the boat.

Crossed fishing banks, they noticed a shark trailing and a whale broach nearby but could not catch either. "One of the last mornings we were there, we heard this tremendous fluttering and about fifty-thousand mackerel, or herring, went right over like a cloud, right over the top of us." When the weather calmed down a bit after 4 p.m., Boudreau began the exhausting task of bailing out innumerable gallons of salt water. By 7 p.m., they collapsed into each other's arms and slept. As they drifted off, they both heard an airplane passing overhead, but did not have the strength to signal it.

The next day (May 24), the men improvised a mast from a railing torn from the boat, a sail from a raincoat, and a jib-sail from pants. In order to navigate west, they kept the sun over their right shoulders, and during darkness used the North Star. At sunset, the dying men watched an airplane coming from southward, over them. They waved as much as they could and managed to send up the only flare not destroyed. To their immense relief, the plane circled the boat three times and tipped its wings. It signaled as well, but it was unintelligible to them. The men felt rescue was imminent but also recognized that life was ebbing from their wracked bodies inexorably.

The next day, the weather was clear and promising. At 9 a.m. on the 25th, another plane came, this one from the southwest. To their amazement and surprise, from the opposite direction, ahead of them to the north, a vessel came toward them. This was the destroyer U.S.S. *Turner*, DD 648, diverted to the scene by aircraft. The U.S. Navy sailors managed to retrieve the two men at 1.06 p.m., which they reported to shore at 2.46 p.m. The lifeboat which had carried them for a week was destroyed, its value was offset by the danger of retrieval.[22] U.S.S. *Turner* was on the second month of its eight-month existence. Commanded by Lieutenant Commander Henry S. Wygant, the *Gleaves*-class destroyer was commissioned on April 16, 1943. They came across Holmans and Boudreau during "shakedown and anti-submarine warfare training out of Caso Bay, Maine until early June."[23] Wygant met with Holmans and Boudreau and asked them to map out their ordeal, then promised them that he and his men would go after the sub which had killed Sandy and the other boys.

The Canadians were given medical aid and warm, dry clothing on the warship. Boudreau was upset when a plate heaping with eggs and sausages was taken from him before he could eat it, to be replaced with a more modest step-up dietary offering ordered by the ship's doctor. They were taken to Portland overnight, and arrived there the following day, landing at 6 a.m. on May 27, 1943. The *Turner*'s officers reported that the codes and ciphers were lost from the lifeboat, not the mother ship, though they were intentionally sunk by Jensen between the barque and the U-boat. In either event, they did not fall into enemy hands. On May 30, Holmans and Boudreau returned to Halifax via rail. What a horrible reunion it must have been for Arthur to return to Margaret and Sandy's older brother Jeremiah without him. Then he had to face the families of John Hiller and Clarence Mullins.

When he had recovered from their physical and emotional ordeal, Boudreau provided a list of recommendations for lifeboats which included medicine, spare sails, a stronger sea-anchor, brandy, lit compass, all securely lashed down, barreled or stowed. After the casualty, the tragic loss of crew, and the extraordinary tenacity involved in their survival, officials wrote that the *Angelus* "was believed to have been used as a fueling ship by French to aid German submarines during 1941, prior to her capture by the RCN. Accordingly, she may have been known to the German commander."

One of the intended recipients, or consignees, of the *Angelus*'s cargo was a longtime wholesale grocer in Halifax named James (Jim) Myrden, manager of R. B. Seaton and Company. As a courtesy, in 1948, the managing director of CHNS Maritime Broadcasting, William Coates Barrett, provided Myrden with a report on the casualty made by the consultancy Victory Transport and Salvage Company.[24] Based on this report and their purchase of H.M.C.S. *Calgary* in 1946, the Hamilton, Ontario firm appears to have specialized accounting for damaged and lost Canadian equipment, vessels and cargo from World War II.[25]

As part of an insurance settlement, a detailed account of the vessel's loss was provided to Myrden, whose descendants retained it.[26] The report is signed in Montreal by O. Johnson on June 8, 1943. The affidavits were signed by Holmans and Boudreau in Halifax and shared only on conditions of strict confidentiality, "as the publicity might be of assistance to the enemy." Newfoundland historian Robert C. Parsons documents that the three young friends from Belleoram lost from the *Angelus* were honored with a wake in their hometown that spring.[27] However, when this author reached out to a relative of the Holmans' in Belleoram who knew Sandy's brother Jeremiah, she demurred, explaining to a fellow-Newfoundlander that the community is still uncomfortable discussing the trauma with outsiders.[28]

Captain Walter Boudreau (left) and his trusted mate, Art Holmans of Belleoram, Newfoundland, reunited aboard the *Yankee* after their deadly lifeboat voyage from the *Angelus* in the war. (*Lou Boudreau, "Merchant Marines: Local tales of help and heroism in wartime," Halifax Herald News, November 9, 2017*)

Walter Boudreau admits that the *Angelus* gave him more adventure that he anticipated and credits his survival to the unshakeable conviction that he would live. He continued sailing and rose to captain, based in Cape Breton from 1946 to 1954. He commanded such wind-ships as the schooner *Yankee*, coastal trader *Keltic*, and seal-hunter *Inverleigh*.[29] U.S.S. *Turner* was sunk by several massive explosions, presumed to have been internal and caused by deactivation of depth charges deep in the ship, while anchored off the lightship *Ambrose* on January 4, 1944. Though "Commander Frank A. Erickson, U.S.C.G., struggled to keep his Sikorsky HNS 1 helicopter" airborne to deliver plasma to the wounded in a first-of-its-kind airborne rescue and aid delivery, and 163 men were saved, Commander Wygant and 136 officers and men perished.[30]

Thought the U.S. Navy investigation cited "anti-submarine munitions ... being defused around the time," no one seems to have considered the fact that *Kapitänleutnant* Rolf Struckmeier in *U-608* laid nine TMA-type mines using the lightship *Ambrose* as his primary reference just over six weeks earlier and the exact area:

> Bearing 277 degrees true on submerging, and 300 degrees true on surfacing, exactly two hours later, on the night of 10 to 11 November 1943, in depths from seventy-five to ninety-five feet, courses from 102 degrees to 325 degrees—mine number two did not eject.[31]

Despite numerous dives near the shore and shallow wreck, only four victims have been buried. Compounding the mystery, "according to 1944 interment records ... in Farmingdale [NY], the remains of four *Turner* sailors were buried in individual graves within a year of the disaster."[32] That is the same national cemetery that Siegfried Zube and Wilhelm Flade, German sailors abandoned alive by the U.S. Navy after *U-550* was sunk in April 1944 and buried in May the same year. There are "thirty-seven German and fifty-four Italian foreign nationals. Thirty-six of the Italian PoWs are interred in one group grave as unknowns; these men were [on] *Benjamin Contee* during an aerial torpedo strike on 16 August 1943." Furthermore, "there are thirty-nine group burials in Long Island National Cemetery containing the remains of 112 soldiers," as well as five French wartime sailors.[33]

Wilhelm Flade's gravesite next to Siegfried Zube ("Unknown"), also of *U-550*, Long Island National Cemetery, spring 1944, after their bodies were found by U.S. Navy and Coast Guard Reserve vessels. (*Findagrave.com*)

15

Six U-boats and the Battle to Attack and Save the Tanker *Pan Pennsylvania*

Oberleutnant zur See Wolfgang Grandefeld took *U-174* to New England briefly in April 1943 mostly back and forth south of Cape Sable. Earlier, *U-174* acted with *U-161* under Achilles to rendezvous with Axis blockade runners *Regensburg*, *Pietro Orseolo*, *Karin*, and *Irene* west of the Azores. On April 25, both U-boats encountered an eastbound convoy south of Cape Sable but were driven off by escorts. Then Grandefeld headed east to its destiny, as on the 27th the boat was caught on the surface by a Ventura of Squadron VP 125, B 6, piloted by Lieutenant T. Kinaszczuk. During the ensuing battle, the aircraft was hit but managed to send four depth charges at *U-174* from 25 feet above. Three detonated beneath *U-174* and one ahead of it. Initially, the sub's bow rose up, then she seemed to gain equilibrium before sinking by the stern, the bow turned almost vertical, and the boat sank. Canadian naval ships searched for survivors without success.[1]

U-174 left Lorient on March 18, 1943, after a stay of two-and-a-half months. Almost the entire patrol took place outside of New England, where no ships were sunk. On May 5, headquarters logged that *U-174* had not replied to signals since April 28. On December 3, 1943, the assessment was most grave, and the boat and her men were listed as irretrievably lost. Grandefeld was born in 1917 and was twenty-six when killed. He was 1st Watch Officer of *U-108* from April 1942. Before that, he was in the 2nd Minesweeping Flotilla, then the 5th Minesweeping Flotilla before serving in the 7th R-Boat Flotilla.[2] This was his only command patrol, as he took over *U-174* from Thilo in early March. He neither sank nor damaged Allied ships and was not decorated.

Kapitänleutnant Max Wintermeyer brought *U-190* south of Martha's Vineyard between May 31 and July 6, 1943. The first leg consisted of an incursion starting south of Montauk, heading east for two days until June 2. Then Wintermeyer

Emblem showing a polar bear standing on floating ice. *U-108* and other boats used this emblem on the conning tower; they were often used by Allied survivors to identify boats that did not carry their boat numbers in view. (*Willy Wilke, U-108*)

turned south for two days until June 4 then exited south of Montauk. They returned on June 28 south of Nantucket then jogged southwest for a week before heading toward Bermuda on July 6.[3] *U-190* found no targets during this long patrol. They became the target when discovered off Hatteras on May 28 by a U.S.A.F. Liberator piloted by Lieutenant J. M. Vivian and were damaged but survived. Wintermeyer noted "a marked increase in American air activity made U-boat operations extremely difficult and ship-sinkings were few."[4] On June 15, *U-190* fired torpedoes at a ship east of Hatteras.

On the way to the Americas, *U-190* participated in a wolfpack from May 5–10. *U-190* wound up the month of April being repaired in Lorient, then began the patrol on May 1, returning to France on August 19. Crossing Biscay, they encountered many aircraft and fishing vessels. Wintermeyer was born in Essen in 1914, living until 1990 and age seventy-six. He sank one ship of 7,015 tons and was decorated with the U-boat War Badge of 1939. A member of the Crew of 1934, he served as 1st Watch Officer of *U-105*, then skippered the training boat *U-62* before commissioning and assuming command of *U-190* in September 1942. After four patrols, Wintermeyer moved ashore in July 1944, serving in staff roles until war's end.[5]

Kapitänleutnant Paul Siegmann brought *U-230* to New England on two short two-day transits in 1943. The first was westbound past Montauk, and then eastbound from August 2–3 from Montauk to Cape Sable *en route* to Europe. The patrol began in Brest on July 5 and ending there on September 8. The primary mission to sow mines off the Chesapeake Bay was accomplished on July 21 when they planted eight TMC-type mines. These were neither discovered nor detonated accidentally. The boat was in repair at Brest for all of June 1943. It left Brest in a mine-avoidance convoy with Hornkohl in *U-566* and Weber in *U-677*, thought *U-506* under Würdemann did not join. By July 6, the others were out of contact. In Biscay, they encountered the customary aircraft, Sunderlands, followed by crash-diving and more bombs. They tested a new anti-ship decoy device named Aphrodite, determining that it worked seven out of twelve times.

On July 23 in the Central Atlantic, an Allied merchant making 20 knots to the west out-stripped the U-boat. It was a three-funnel passenger ship, possibly carrying troops. On July 24, they sighted another merchant ship; however, land-based airplanes interrupted an attack, plus a new propeller was reducing the boat's speed and flat-calm seas made the U-boat visible. On July 27, they sighted a convoy but were depth-charged twice, one of them "exactly over the boat," and Siegmann noted: "am run over by a vessel." While laying eight mines off Smith Island Shoal, Chesapeake Bay from July 30–31, they spotted fishermen and steamers.[6]

On August 3, they found "buoy with black flag and white diagonal cross. Apparently, the sinking location of a steamer. Oil slick, wreckage and life buoys seen," far south of Nantucket. A thorough check of any and all ships going back a month halfway between Bermuda and Nantucket turns up no likely candidate.

Such detritus of war was not uncommon during World War II. The next day and the following, carrier-borne aircraft kept *U-230* alert, particularly as the small size of the planes meant they were "only seen late [and thus] difficult enemies."

On its return voyage, *U-230* had grave refueling challenges. Siegmann was ordered to meet *U-117* under Neumann for fuel between Bermuda and Azores. When *U-117* did not rendezvous, *U-634* under Dahlhaus provided some fuel on August 17. Together, they were ordered to meet *U-847* under Kuppisch 800 miles southwest of the Azores. Out of fear for Allied aircraft carriers hunting for U-boats in mid-Atlantic, the Metox airplane-detection device was turned off. Then headquarters ordered its complete disassembly and placement under lock-and-key by the commander, in the belief that Allies could zero in on it.

On August 15, Siegmann was in contact with *U-333* under Cremer, *U-653* under Feiler (senior-commander-on-site), *U-847* under Kuppisch, Dahlhaus in *U-634*, Neide in *U-415*, Drewitz in *U-525*, Lüssow in *U-571*, and von Harpe in *U-129* in order for them to coordinate receiving fuel and exchanging ammunition, using radios sparingly, then they affected the refueling operations. On August 26, another well-lit neutral steamer passed, heading for Philadelphia. On August 27, an unseen U-boat headed past them toward battle, and *U-230*'s crew was able to see San Miguel and Santa Maria islands in the Azores.

When *U-847* radioed to base on August 27 to inform them that the rendezvous and refueling were complete she was promptly tracked down by Ventura aircraft from U.S.S. *Card*, CVE 11, and sunk with the loss of all sixty-two sailors. Siegmann decided to remain submerged most of the time to avoid being sunk and headed east due to low supplies and fuel. Headquarters confirmed as much on August 5 ordering "boats which are already short to return immediately ... without refueling or taking over provisions." *U-230* even turned off its short-wave radio receiver "to eliminate any enemy interference." During Black May in the Battle of the Atlantic that year, the Allies gained the upper hand over German U-boats, sinking forty-three of them, and causing a recall of Atlantic boats to France. *U-230*'s 1st Watch Officer of this patrol was Herbert A. Werner, author of the book *Iron Coffins*, who went on to command *U-415* and *U-953* and became rather bitter about the human cost of the war, particularly on his shipmates in the U-boat arm.[7]

On August 12, *U-230* passed up on sinking the neutral Portuguese ship *Gana* heading west in ballast. The next day, another well-lit neutral ship passed to the west. At the end of August, Siegmann was ordered to use the Piening Route, skirting the coast of neutral Spain to cross the increasingly dangerous Bay of Biscay. They could hear Dahlhaus in *U-634* taking a beating and saw an Allied corvette. On September 3, they were "overrun by a fast vessel ten minutes after diving." which were believed to have been three destroyers. Then more bombers, strong searchlights at night, bombers, mines, and a rendezvous with *U-415* under Neide as they approached France. On September 8, the commander noted with relief that he and the men were "taken in convoy [then] made fast, Brest U-boat bunker."[8] No bombs ever penetrated those bunkers, which stand today as monuments to the effectiveness of surprise and initiative.

Paul Siegmann was born in Hamburg in 1913 and lived until 1986 and age seventy-three. He was in the Crew of 1935 and began his naval career as 1st Watch Officer of the torpedo-boat *Greif* to March 1941, followed by U-boat training. He commanded *U-612* in May–June 1942, but on June 8, the submarine was sunk in a collision with *U-444* under Langfeld, from which both survived.[9] Siegmann then commissioned *U-230* in October 1942 and served aboard her until August 1944. From the following month, he commanded *U-2507* until the capitulation. He sank four ships for 6,453 tons, three of them naval ships and was awarded the German Cross in Gold and the Iron Cross 1st Class and Iron Cross 2nd Class.

Kapitänleutnant Hans Hornkohl brought *U-566* into New England for a punishing four-day patrol from August 7–10, 1943, beginning on the boat's return from mining the entrance to Chesapeake Bay on July 30. By July 28, they were off the U.S. coast dodging aircraft. The next day, a dozen mines were sewn off Cape Charles and Cape Henry, and the boat was prepared to self-destruct if caught. From July 28 to August 7, the war diary was filled with encounters with coastal patrols, aircraft, destroyers, escapes at high speed, deployment of Aphrodite device, and stymied attacks on Allied ships. On August 3, an attack by a flying boat which dropped bombs but "had not noticed the boat before shooting."

On the 7th and 8th, the boat was attacked by several airplanes, shot down two of them with fatalities, then accidentally submerged, washing many men off the deck, all southeast of the lightship *Nantucket*. Hornkohl held onto the periscope while the sub submerged and then resurfaced, sputtering for air.[10] On August 7, Lieutenant F. C. Cross in a U.S. Navy Ventura in VB 128 Squadron attacked *U-566*, but was counterattacked, damaged, and forced to crash-land. Cross, already injured, died in the water, but his crew was rescued by a flying boat. Hornkohl himself related the events of August 7–8:

> At 6.15 p.m. *U-566* was attacked by a second PV 1 from NAS New York, and again replied with AA [anti-aircraft] fire. One of four depth charges dropped actually hit *U-566*, and bounced off before exploding, but caused no damage. The Germans … scored several AA hits after [a plane] passed over the boat, causing the burning aircraft to crash at a distance of some 4,000 feet. All five air-crew were lost. *U-566* then made for the crash site, having sighted a rubber dinghy, but before it was reached, another Ventura [VB 126 U.S.N., pilot Lt. J. R. Smith] from NAS Quonset and a PBM Mariner flying boat [VB 211 U.S.N., pilot Lt. E. C. Scully] from Elizabeth City arrived at the scene.
>
> The U-boat fired at the aircraft [misidentified as a Mitchell and a Lerwick], and then dove at 6.29 p.m. The Ventura immediately dropped four depth charges [that]

> detonated without effect ... *U-566* was forced to surface by a malfunctioning diving tank and manned the AA guns again. The Mariner was hit as it made several passes while its eight depth charges hung up, until the emergency release was used. At the same time, the U-boat submerged accidentally, the commander closing the conning tower hatch from the bridge and clinging to the periscope standard until the 1st Watch Officer brought the boat to the surface again.
>
> The 2nd Watch Officer and seven crew were swept overboard, but were rescued within twenty minutes, during which the replacement crew on the AA guns fought off a strafing run by the Ventura at 7.08 p.m. *U-566* subsequently dived and escaped with only minor damage from gunfire, having shot down two aircraft and damaged two others in one day. One of the crew was wounded in the left hand during the last strafing attack while four men, including the commander and 1st Watch Officer, suffered burst eardrums from their involuntary dive.

The pilots overhead then tried to destroy their own colleagues' raft to prevent the seven swimming Germans from using it. At the same time, they resisted an opportunity to machine gun eight Germans floundering in the water:

> Both aircraft watched this maneuver, without flying toward the boat. During the rescue of the soldiers who were swimming in the water, one aircraft shot at the[m] with machine guns. No casualties. I myself observed, how the Mitchell shot at the life-boat of its own shot-down comrades with MG [machine guns], probably in the belief that it might be used in the rescue of the soldiers swimming in the water. The 1st Watch Officer believes he saw one of the shot-down airmen near the life-boats ... *Bootsmaat* Schier was shot through the left chest wall.[11]

Then on the morning of the 8th, a Halifax-based Catalina spotted *U-566* and vectored in three U.S. Navy destroyer escorts from Norfolk. Using the Aphrodite decoy device, the sub again managed to escape. Again the 8th, they managed to dodge a Mitchell bomber, by setting its starboard engine on fire after it bombed the U-boat with up to four bombs. One of the bombs in the next attack hit the stern of the U-boat and then bounced off. Four detonations close-by did not destroy the boat.

On August 9, a close attack by destroyer with floodlights. On the 11th, they avoided a Consolidated airplane and a Boeing on the 14th then the 19th an ASDIC attack. The Germans were subjected to a litany of attacks, with even the sole success, the mining of the Chesapeake using twelve MTB-type mines, producing no result. On August 4, Hornkohl found a convoy of twenty vessels, but an Allied naval vessel attacked then on August 5. The sinking of U.S.S. *Plymouth,* PG 57, while protecting a convoy off Hatteras (its commander, yachtsman Lieutenant Ormsby M. Mitchel, Jr., remained at his post despite losing a leg), brought renewed and intense anti-submarine activity onto the heads of the U-boat men in the area. *U-566* was attacked on August 2 by a Mariner, then tracked by aircraft and a blimp. Then the sub "held off the Mariner, two other aircraft, and two blimps until darkness came and it submerged." The boat was sighted under the moonlight by another Mariner southeast of Nantucket yet escaped.

This patrol began in Brest on July 5 and ended on September 1, 1943. *U-566* was in dry-dock all of May and June 1943, and left port in company with Siegmann in *U-230*. They practiced emergency breathing apparatus and withstood aerial attack by Liberators and others leaving France. On July 9, two destroyers and then Sunderland aircraft attacked the boat. On July 12, a "heavy battery explosion forward ... three serious casualties. 1st Watch Officer [Kurt Ahlers] life-threatening." A doctor was summoned urgently, and U-boat skipper Karl-Otto Weber in *U-709* was tasked with the handover southwest of Ireland. The boats passed each other twice, submerged, then sighted each other on October 13. A doctor was sent over in an inflatable boat, who then remained aboard *U-566*, where he was most needed.

Returning to France, he planned to use the Piening Route through Spain, though it would mean burning an extra 200 miles of fuel. On August 25, Hornkohl decided against the longer route in favor of crossing Biscay directly. On the 28th, the Germans observed bombs in the distance and a neutral Irish steamer on its way to Spain. On August 30 and 31, there were several air attacks. On September 1, *U-566* joined the *Sperrbrecher* convoy and entered Brest.

Großadmiral Dönitz praised Hornkohl highly, writing, "the very precarious and dangerous situation on August 7 was handled excellently by the cool-headedness and the full energetic operations of the *Kommandant*. The rescue of the bridge-crew under the eyes of the enemy air threat is a particularly fortunate and pleasing achievement." He commended the commander for sinking the gunboat, as well as two Mitchell bombers. Hornkohl was born in Hamburg in 1917 and lived beyond 2000. A member of the Crew of 1936, he was initially seconded to the Luftwaffe for long-range naval reconnaissance. He received commander sea-training in *U-753* from April to December 1942, then skippered six U-boats, more than any other commander that attacked New England. They were *U-566* to October 1943, *U-1007* to July 1944, *U-3509* to November 1944, *U-3512* to April 1945, *U-2502* to mid-April 1945, and *U-3041* up to the capitulation.

U-566 was sunk under Hornkohl's command 30 miles from Portugal on October 24, 1943, by a Wellington bomber piloted by Sergeant Donald Melvin Cornish, who disabled the sub but then ran out of fuel and had to leave the scene. Hornkohl had his men abandon ship in rafts and scuttled his boat. They were rescued soon thereafter by the Spanish trawler *Fina*. The men snuck into France aboard a train as civilians. Later, they took over a newer submarine, *U-1007*. Having evaded death and capture during the war, Hornkohl was held as a PoW until August 1945. U.S.S. *Plymouth* was his only ship sunk, and he received no decorations.[12]

Kapitänleutnant Hellmut Neuerburg and his crew aboard *U-869* spent their last days passing through New England on the way to meet their fate off the New Jersey days later. Although it is possible that on a sixty-six-day patrol, the U-boat spent more time in New England, at the very minimum it would have required four days. The uncertainty arises from the fact that from Christmas 1944 to January 6, 1945, to when it was sunk on February 11, there are no positions provided. Rather, it is estimated that Neuerburg took *U-869* on a straight course following the tracks of his predecessors from south of Cape Sable to south of Montauk, then southwest.

On February 11, 1945, *U-869* was caught by the destroyer escorts U.S.S. *Howard D. Crow* and U.S.S. *Koiner*, which dropped Hedgehogs and depth charges on the sound contact. It is thought that her own homing torpedoes may have come around to hit and sink the sub. In either event, all fifty-six submariners perished.[13] This submarine was the subject of intensive investigation when discovered on September 2, 1991, as covered in the best-selling book *Shadow Divers* by Robert Kurson.[14] At first, the official history had the boat sunk off Saharan Africa, then its final fate was corrected to New Jersey.

Neuerburg was born in 1917 in Strasbourg, became a member of the Crew of 1936, and was twenty-seven when killed. Between 1938 and 1943, he was seconded to the Luftwaffe, then joined U-boats in April, serving on the sub U-AA from October to November 1943. He commissioned *U-869* in January 1944 and went on three patrols in her, the first few being from Germany and within Norway. Neuerburg sank no ships, mined no harbors, and received no decorations. *U-869* and the remains of her crew lie east-northeast of Atlantic City, in 240 feet of water. Several recreational divers have perished at the site since.

Kapitänleutnant Klaus Hänert brought *U-550* on a dangerous patrol to New England between April 9 and 16, 1944. During that time, he torpedoed the large new tanker *Pan Pennsylvania*. For this brash move, his submarine was destroyed and most of his men were lost, cast adrift on the bosom of the North Atlantic. Unbeknown to Hänert and his men, several planes, flying from Canada to Quonset, and a number of U.S. Navy task groups, mostly from Canso, were tracking *U-550* and *U-856*, which set out for New York from Kiel on February 24 under Wittenberg. From March 29, *U-856* (nicknamed "Red Fox") was being tracked by the aircraft carrier U.S.S. *Croatan*, CVE 25, out of Canso, supported by four destroyers.

From April 4, task groups *TU 27.6.1* with the destroyers U.S.S. *Parker*, U.S.S. *Lanahan*, U.S.S. *Laub*, and *TU 27.6.2* with U.S.S. *Boyle*, U.S.S. *Champlin*, U.S.S. *Nields*, and U.S.S. *Ordoneaux*, supporting by TBM 18 planes from U.S.S. *Croatan* harried the boat. On the 7th, U.S.S. *Champlin*, supported by U.S.S. *Huse*, dropped eleven depth charges around the U-boat. Wittenberg had just risen to periscope-depth, as though he just watched the pin being pulled from a grenade and thrown into his pool. Despite the carnage, twenty-five sailors and three officers were rescued by the U.S. Navy. Twenty-two perished.

U-550, marked "Red George" by Allied forces, then became the primary target. U.S.S. *Croatan* was ordered to Bermuda, unless it could track the subs down and sink them. U.S.S. *Champlin* had to limp to shore due to damage from ramming Wittenberg's *U-856*, and task force *TU 27.6.2* returned to Canso. After April 15, this left the waters of southern New England, traveling Maine to Bermuda, to the six U.S. Navy destroyer escorts protecting Convoy CU 21, which assembled in Tompkinsville, Staten Island, for a trans-Atlantic voyage to Ireland. The destroyers were U.S.S. *Poole*, U.S.S. *Kirkpatrick*, U.S.S. *Harveson*, U.S.S. *Joyce*, U.S.S. *Gandy*, and U.S.S. *Peterson*. Many of them, including the *Gandy*, were manned by U.S. Coast Guard, rather than U.S. Navy, personnel, though they were both under Navy control at the time.

U-550 departed Kiel on February 6 and at first set out to perform weather-reporting duty off Iceland, Greenland and Newfoundland.[15] On February 22, a Catalina flying boat caught the *U-550* south of Iceland and two Germans were killed in a fire-fight, but the boat survived. By mid-April, she moved to the U.S. northeast coast and it was on its seventy-first day of the patrol when they encountered a disorganized outbound convoy with tempting tankers. *U-550* motored west of Cape Sable from April 9–13 then stopped near lightship *Nantucket* and motored north. From April 14–15, it was spent in the same area, then on the 16th Hänert headed north to find what he was looking for: a convoy. Convoy CU 21 did not begin well, with three ships lost to self-inflicted causes in just a few hours. They were late getting through the swept channel leading from New York Harbor with twenty-eight merchant ships, including the tanker *Pan Pennsylvania*.[16]

Routing was changed, but due to heavy fog, this intelligence had to be manually delivered and acknowledged by signals from destroyers down the line to each ship. It was dark by the time they left the cleared channel, so rather than assemble and wait till dawn, they just plodded onward. In the confusion, the small Honduran freighter *Aztec* and the huge U.S. tanker *Sag Harbor* collided. Worse yet, the destroyer U.S.S. *Peterson* was told to peel off and escort them back to New York. Twenty-six ships and five escorts were left before the convoy barely left the starting gate.

Eastern Sea Frontier headquarters (on nearby Manhattan) instructed the convoy commodore that *Red George* (*U-550*) was expected to be 175 miles south of Nantucket the next day, "within 200 miles" of its position the day before. On the day the convoy sailed, the sub's location was amended to "unlocated, general area within 600 miles east of Cape May" which is the rough equivalent of saying "off the east coast," or "near Europe."[17]

In the pre-dawn hours of April 16, *U-550* stalked the convoy southeast of Nantucket without the escorts knowing it. The destroyers were still essentially herding cats. They had left the safety of harbor but were not behaving like they had. They were still trying to get organized at 8 a.m., when, five minutes later, Hänert struck. *U-550*'s torpedo burst a hole in the side of the largest and richest target, the *Pan Pennsylvania*. The torpedo disabled the tanker's steering equipment, causing a 30-degree list, and she gradually settled by the stern. Though she may have looked doomed, the tanker remained afloat for days.

Captain Delmar Melum Leidy of the *Pan Pennsylvania* tried but failed to cut the engines off. Gasoline began to pour from the tanker, and "men abandoned ship in boats, life rafts, and some dove in water." One result of such situations is panic, even though "fires were reported in the boiler room ... there was no other fire. Although the ship settled slightly, there was no indication that the *Pan Pennsylvania* would sink." When men tried frantically to launch two boats without waiting for the tanker to stop moving, they hoisted one overboard, only for it to be immediately swamped. This effectively removed the lifeboat as an escape for fifty-six survivors, indirectly leading to the deaths of twenty-five men.[18] Leidy managed to calm the men struggling to launch the second boat before they, too, killed themselves.

Fifteen minutes after the attack, at 8.20 a.m., he also managed to shut off the engine. The survivors then abandoned ship in the remaining pair of boats and three rafts. Unbeknown to them, *U-550* and its men were actually hiding in the Sonar shadow created by their ship. After a few hours in the boats, the *Pan Pennsylvania*'s survivors were rescued by U.S.S. *Joyce* and U.S.S. *Peterson*. Awkwardly, by that time, the *Joyce* also had thirteen of the German attackers on board, including the commander. Both the tanker and the U-boat had lost many men.

The Allied counterattack was swift and decisive. Destroyer escorts U.S.S. *Joyce*, U.S.S. *Gandy*, and U.S.S. *Peterson* managed by depth charges to force *U-550* to the surface at 9.58 a.m.[19] All of their guns were trained on, and fired upon, the sub's conning tower and decks as the Germans rushed to escape, despite their having set off a white smoke flare as a signal of surrender. Four minutes later, the *Gandy* rammed the sub some 30 feet from the stern, while keeping up a stream of fire on the conning tower. A minute later, at 10.03 a.m., Hänert and his men officially surrendered. Due to the natural intensity of battle, feelings on both sides were very high, and opinions vary as to timing. The U.S. Navy concedes that "some tracer shells hit the *Pan Pennsylvania* and set afire her cargo." This illustrates the proximity of *U-550* to its victim and the dangers of friendly fire.

According to interviews of *U-550*'s engineer, Hugo Renzmann, scuttling charges were set in *U-550*, and "an explosion was heard in the submarine, evidently a scuttling charge."[20] Whether that is the case, all men escaped from below and the sub sank, as Renzmann assured—aside from one dead sailor in the conning tower, the engineer filled a tank with just enough air:

> [He did this] to keep it afloat a few more precious minutes while the men evacuate. Finally, he manually opened the water vents to sink the sub. It was his last duty. The

> *Ubootwaffe* required scuttling a U-boat as the final act of the engineer before leaving the vessel.[21]

Renzmann's assertion that he was the last to leave became more relevant due to the number of German bodies found afloat in the months ahead.

Then "*Peterson* came in for the kill. She fired two [depth charges] with shallow settings from her K-guns. Shortly after these explosions, the sub went down, stern first." At 10.05 a.m. (two minutes after surrender), the Germans were ordered to abandon ship. Twenty-five minutes later, *U-550* sank stern-first. "The crew abandoned ship except for those lying on the sub deck, killed or wounded by gunfire" from the destroyers. Photographs clearly show some German sailors sitting near the conning tower and floating nearby in individual inner tube-like rafts.[22]

In an improvised and irrefutably daring maneuver, at 10.45 a.m., the *Joyce*'s commander, Captain Robert Wilcox, went into the heart of the action, banged alongside the submarine, and managed in a very narrow time window to retrieve thirteen German sailors. The rescued included Hänert and Dr. Friedrich Torge, with a Red Cross arm-band and pockets filled with a schnapps flask and a bar of butter he grabbed. Wilcox's move is all the more impressive given the hair-trigger responses of men on the *Gandy* (which rammed *U-550*, thus damaging itself) and the *Peterson*.

It was a highly volatile battle where men on the destroyers were having trouble controlling their fire in the face of surrender signals. Aboard the sub, Dr. Torge said "panic ruled" in the final moments, and even the *Pan Pennsylvania*'s Captain Leidy only managed to put down more fatal runs for the boats by force of will. In other words, Wilcox ran the same risk of his ship being hit by friendly fire as the ricocheting shell, which set the *Pan Pennsylvania* ablaze. In the event, the Germans opened fire on the *Joyce* during his rescue, Wilcox had instructed the *Peterson* and the *Gandy* to open fire on the U-boat men, even if doing so put the *Joyce* and her sailors at risk of friendly fire.[23]

One of the Germans rescued died that day. Seven Germans were buried at sea or in the U.S.:

1. Machinist Heinrich Wenz was buried at sea, 11 a.m. on April 17 from U.S.S. *Joyce*.
2. At 9.51 p.m., on May 5, the first *U-550* body to be found off New England, that of seventeen-year-old Siegfried Zube, was discovered by U.S.C.G. *CGR 3082* and retrieved by U.S.S. *SC 985*. After an autopsy in Brooklyn, he was buried in the Long Island National Cemetery.
3. At 5.30 p.m. on May 11, Wilhelm Flade was discovered by U.S.C.G. *CGR 1989*, taken to Tompkinsville, Staten Island by U.S.S. *SC 1338*, and later buried next to Zube as unknown.

The surrendered officers and crew of *U-550* following sinking of the *Pan Penn* and the ramming and attack by three U.S. Navy destroyers await their fate. In a reversal of many scenarios earlier in the war, the forty-three surviving German sailors in the water are about to be abandoned to their deaths; their corpses and equipment will wash ashore in New England for the next three months. (*uscg.mil/history/uscghist/U550.asp, Public domain, Courtesy of Mark Munro, soundunderwatersurvey.com/ wrecks/u-550/ the-sinking-of-the-u-550*)

4. At 1.40 p.m. on May 16, U.S.S. *SC 630* found Machinist's Mate Günther Heder's body. It was later buried in Newport Historical Cemetery with a military ceremony.
5. At 6.40 p.m. on May 21, U.S.C.G. *CGR 3080* found unnamed German corpse south of Montauk and U.S.S. *PC 985* then took over the "malodorous cadaver," burying it at sea 7 a.m. on May 22.
6. At 5.20 p.m. on May 27, Carl Ludwig Jahnke's body was spotted from the air by U.S. Navy airship K 26, which vectored H.M.C.S. *St. Boniface,* J 332. The Canadians, who were escorting convoy HX 293 northward, retrieved the cadaver near Block Island. Jahnke's body was rolled in weighted canvas and buried at sea that evening.
7. At 7.38 a.m. on July 7, U.S.C.G. *CGR 3091* discovered a seventh body from *U-550* 100 miles southeast of Newport and buried him at sea. Identity being sought.[24]

Of forty-three Germans left alive in the water (one died on the conning tower), thirty-seven were never found, dead or alive. Seventy-five years later, U-boat historian Axel Niestlé, who knew him, wrote that Hänert "never stopped thinking about his men who lost their lives with U 550."[25]

Seventy men died that day and in the ensuing weeks; twenty-five from *Pan Pennsylvania* and a total of forty-five, not including those killed by aircraft off Iceland earlier, from *U-550*. They left a trail of tears which no doubt went on to further traumatize the hundreds of naval, coast guard and civilian servicemen who had to handle the Germans' bodies. The dozens of vessels, ports, and personnel utilized, with items and bodies found over three months, include the following:

April 30: *Pan Pennsylvania*'s empty motor-lifeboat picked up by Coast Guard Reserve off New Jersey

May 1: CGR retrieved life raft off the New Jersey and New York coasts

May 4: CGR retrieved "large life raft." Allied ships used wooden rafts, Germans "life rafts"

May 5: Siegfried Zube's body found by CGR off New York, buried LI National Cemetery

May 6: German escape-lung retrieved, likely that of Siegfried Zube

May 11: Wilhelm Flade found by CGR off New York, buried Long Island as "Unknown."

May 12: search for a suspected German life raft called off by blimps southeast of New York

May 16: Günther Heder found by U.S.S. Navy sub-chaser, buried in Newport

May 21: Body 5 (identity as yet unknown) found by CGR off Montauk, buried at sea

This image shows just behind the conning tower of *U-550* after it had surrendered and been fired on and rammed, but just before it sank and the forty-three floating "dead men walking" from *U-550* as they drift away forever from the doomed *U-550*. The destroyers have picked

May 22: Body 5 personal effects, clothes, notebooks, watches, given to naval intelligence, D.C.

May 25: German rubber life raft found close to Rhode Island shore (Buoy Able), Newport

May 27: Carl Ludwig Jahnke found by U.S. Navy airship and H.M.C.S. *St. Boniface*, buried at sea

June 13: CGR found one-man raft, $C0_2$ tube, cup, drogue, German labels, 80 miles off Montauk

July 7: Body 7 (identity as yet unknown), found by CGR, "German sailor," buried at sea.[26]

Fifty-nine Germans left Europe on *U-550*, and eleven returned to Ireland as PoWs three months later. Two were shot by planes off Iceland, one died on the *Joyce*, and forty-four died in the waters of New England, either during or after the battle. Of the men left in the water, six are accounted for and four named: Heder buried in Newport, Zube and Flade in Long Island, and Jahnke at sea. The names of the last two are not yet known, leaving the other thirty-seven named, but not found.[27]

Klaus Hänert's destruction of *Pan Pennsylvania* caused the loss of his *U-550* and provoked a counterattack by the U.S. Navy's *Gandy*, the *Joyce* and the *Peterson*. Several Allied vessels, including U.S.C.G.C. *General Greene*, were sent to sink the *Pan Pennsylvania*, but failed. Then it was bombed by planes and sunk on April 18. A flotilla of small-to-large craft located, transported, and buried the six German bodies found off the coast: H.M.C.S. *St. Boniface*, blimp K 26, *CGR 3091*, *CGR 3080*, U.S.S. *PC 985*, U.S.S. *PC 630*, *CGR 3082*, U.S.S. *SC 1338*,

their dozen survivors and are heading away. The cadavers of the men seen floating and floundering in the waters off Nantucket in this image taken midday on April 16, 1944, floated up along the northeast coast for three months. (*U.S. Navy, NARA, Public domain*)

CGR 1989, and others. At least twenty vessels and aircraft—not counting the sub, the inflatable life rafts, and the *Pan Pennsylvania* motorboat—were involved.

There were many macabre details, most of them, thankfully for the families of the dead, forgotten in naval intelligence files. Yet there was also speculation, or rumor, promulgated in part by the U.S. Navy, about "the apparent ... successful attempts made by certain men to escape from compartments in the vicinity of torpedo tubes or escape hatches." The inference is that since many Allied boats trafficked the area around the floundering *Pan Pennsylvania* before it sank without seeing any of the forty-four German sailors in life rafts, the bodies which floated up for months, from April 16 to July 7, must have been from sailors who remained alive in *U-550*, then somehow escaped using apparatus, ultimately floating, dead, toward shore. To bolster this theory, the Navy cited the "somewhat gruesome sequel" provided by the bodies of young sailors Flade and Zube. Regarding Zube, the following was noted:

> The body showed no injuries except burns on the head and face, probably from diesel oil; that the victim had died prior to submersion, as though he had been on a raft. Blood in the body was still fluid ... it was estimated that he had died only five days before being picked up.[28]

The presence of inflatable life-rings designed to help submariners make it to the surface even when passed out (called escape lungs) suggests the Germans used them to float from a submerged U-boat; however, the tube's primary purpose, put to use by *U-550* sailors, was to help keep them afloat while they awaited rescue—to keep their head above water if they dozed. Sadly, after analyzing his autopsy reports so carefully, the correct paperwork was removed from Siegfried's body, so that now he rests as a mere "Unknown." Recently, experts who have studied which hatches were open when *U-550* sank, by diving on the wreck, and who interviewed the submarine's senior-most engineer (Hugo Renzmann, who swore the U-boat was empty after he set the charges and ran up top), concluded that forty-four German sailors went up the conning tower and into the North Atlantic. They were then abandoned when the destroyers left to fulfill their mission of protecting the convoy.[29]

During this time, there were numerous "life jackets" found by Coast Guard and other beach patrols, and usually these would either say the manufacturer, whether U.S. or German, and the ship or person's name. Yet many were generic and of unknown origin. Then on June 15, 1944, "a state of non-invasion [was] declared for the Eastern Sea Frontier" as well as the U.S. Army's Eastern Defense Command. One result was that beach patrols, including those with dogs, were canceled. That brought to a close a detailed catalog of explosions heard offshore, rowing boats without lights, detritus from flour sacks to mattresses, pillows, sailors' caps, parcels of mail, and myriad other items washed up during war, including numerous rafts.[30]

Grave of Machinist's Mate Günther Heder from *U-550* lost April 1944 in Newport. His cadaver was retrieved by the U.S. Navy and his remains interred with military honors. Evidently, someone looks after the grave and that of the "Unknown sailor" from *U-853* buried nearby. (*Author's collection*)

Coastal defense had changed a lot since the landing of saboteurs on Amagansett in the spring of 1942. By the summer of 1943, there were many cases of people being prevented from photographing the beach, couples such as an unnamed "Colonel and a girl," found together on dark beaches, and even a doctor, named Ellis, who was shot "through the right arm above the elbow," at the Point O'Woods Long Beach Station at 3.07 a.m. on August 13, because he "would not halt," when asked to do so by a beach patrolman manning Post 297. A more typical event was the discovery of another "life jacket, button type," found a few hours later. The following day, a message found in a bottle beseeched the Coast Guard to voyage from Napeague to Faulkner's Island to rescue a crew under "Capt. White," because "all boats have been sunk by German sub."

Hänert was born in 1918 and lived until 2003 and age eighty-four. He joined the German Navy in the Olympia Crew of 1936, moving to the destroyer *Z6 Theodor Riedel*, until June 1940.[31] After a stint ashore, he joined the destroyer *Z15 Erich Stienbrinck,* up to December 1941. After joining U-boats in 1942, Hänert served as 2nd Watch Officer under ace Merten on *U-68* to July 1942. During a patrol to the Caribbean, they sank seven ships of over 50,000 tons. Hänert continued with Merten for two more patrols. After work-up and further training, he commissioned *U-550* in July 1943, then applied more training in the Baltic for six months. The *Pan Pennsylvania* was the only ship which Hänert sank, and he received no decorations. He was held as PoW until 1947. In 2012, a team of adventurers and historians lead by an attorney from New Jersey named Joe Mazraani discovered the wreck of *U-550* about 70 miles south of Nantucket.[32]

The 11,017-ton, T-3-type tanker *Pan Pennsylvania* was completed in Norfolk in 1943. It joined Convoy CU 21 in New York on April 15 bound for Barry, Wales. Her cargo was 140,000 barrels of eighty-octane gasoline as well as some warplanes on deck.[33] There were twenty-eight merchant ships in the convoy, all protected by "*Escort Division 21.5*, consisting of Coast Guard-manned destroyer escorts U.S.S. *Poole* (flagship), U.S.S. *Kirkpatrick*, U.S.S. *Harveson*, U.S.S. *Peterson*, U.S.S. *Joyce* ... reinforced by one Navy destroyer, U.S.S. *Gandy.*"

Fifteen minutes after being struck by a torpedo from *U-550*, the tanker came to a stop, and fifty-six of her men made it into the two remaining lifeboats and three rafts. The *Pan Pennsylvania's* survivors were picked up by U.S.S. *Peterson* and U.S.S. *Joyce*, which also had thirteen of their German attackers. The destroyer escorts quickly rejoined the convoy and headed east. They were taken to Londonderry, landing on April 26.

The *Pan Pennsylvania* continued to drift, ablaze from friendly fire. Ultimately several vessels fired into her, including U.S.C.G.C. *General Greene*, U.S.S. *Hazel*, U.S.C.G.C. *Harriette Lane*, U.S.S. *Sagamore*, U.S.S. *SC 1338*, and U.S.S. *Rescue*, all of which failed to sink the ship as she lay on its side. Two days later, airplanes bombed and sank the *Pan Pennsylvania*. Her wreck, along with that of *U-550* was

Twelve *U-550* survivors, including their commander, land in Londonderry, Northern Ireland on April 26, 1944, ten days after the battle around the *Pan Penn*. Forty-seven of their shipmates have died, including Wenz buried at sea from U.S.S. *Joyce*. (*U.S. Navy photo, Public domain, Courtesy of Mark Munro*)

discovered southeast of Nantucket, her massive propellers draped in generations of fishing nets.[34] Two weeks after she was abandoned, the *Pan Pennsylvania* empty motor lifeboat was discovered and retrieved by the Coast Guard Reserve off New Jersey.[35] Given the proximity to deep-water salvage equipment in Newport, New York, Boston, or Norfolk, as well as major ship-repair yards in the latter three ports, the *Pan Pennsylvania* almost certainly could have been salvaged, but for having been set alight by friendly fire, and even then she might have been salved. Four of her sisters were also sunk by U-boats: the *Pan Massachusetts*, the *Pan York*, the *Pan Norway* and the *Pan New York*.[36]

16

Three Boats and the Diminutive Fishing Schooner *Lark*

Kapitänleutnant Heinz Bielfeld brought *U-1222* into New England from May 21–24, 1944, starting southwest of Cape Sable then back-tracking the same way. She operated off Nova Scotia without success, attacking the tanker *Bulkoil* on May 22 south of Halifax, which provoked a counterattack by H.M.C.S. *Agassiz* and the Flower-class corvette H.M.C.S. *Norsyd*. On June 13, *U-1222* was ordered back to France. Due to the uncertainty of whether the bases would be captured by Allied land forces, Bielfeld kept Bergen as an option. The patrol began on April 16 in Marviken and ended when the U-boat was sunk on July 11, 1944. A British RAF Sunderland from Squadron 201 P0, under pilot I. B. F. Walters sank the boat south of Lorient with all fifty-six hands. After its *Schnorchel* was sighted and its stern broke the surface, three depth charges destroyed *U-1222*.

Bielfeld was born in Tientsin, China (then a German colony) in 1916 and was a member of the Crew of 1934. After work in aircraft weapons and coastal flying groups, he was made supernumerary watch officer aboard *U-97* in October 1940. Then he transferred to *U-151* up to August 1941 before taking command of *U-703* in October 1942. Bielfeld served on *U-1222* for seven patrols and sank three merchant ships of 18,315 tons and a warship of 1,870 tons. In December 1943, he received the German Cross in Gold. This was his and the boat's only patrol, with no ships sunk or damaged.[1]

Kapitänleutnant Volker Simmermacher brought *U-107* into New England for three days between June 12–14, 1944, rounding Cape Sable until the 13th, then southeast and away on the 14th. *U-107* attacked and damaged the American fishing sailboat *Lark* at 8.30 a.m. on the 13th on the Baccaro Bank, 50 miles west of Cape Roseway. The *Lark* was a 148-ton vessel owned by F. J. O'Hara Brothers of Boston. Her captain was James L. Abbott, responsible for twenty-seven men on board. After a torpedo missed, Simmermacher fired a warning shot over the

Lark's bows, which brought their diesel engine to a halt. The men abandoned ship in five fishing dories, except for Captain Abbott and the ship's cook, who remained aboard. Eventually, the U-boat left, crew reboarded, and the fishermen returned to shore as minor celebrities.

This patrol began in Lorient on May 10, 1944, and ended there on July 23 with the *Lark* the only vessel damaged. *U-107* was the first of the new *Schnorchel*-fitted boats to reach the Americas. She was ordered back to base in July but instructed to keep enough fuel to make for Bergen.[2] *U-107* was under "major overhaul" in Lorient from January 9 to April 30. On May 13, two sailors passed out and "nearly the entire crew had poisoning symptom" from carbon monoxide as a result of a crash-dive gone wrong. On June 10, their Naxos device detected an aircraft and so the submarine dove.

On June 13, other seaborne German U-boat commanders Lauterbach-Emden in *U-539*, Krankenhagen in *U-530*, Tillessen in *U-516*, Hellriegel in *U-543*, Niemeyer in *U-547*, and Bielfeld in *U-1222* were ordered from North American or North Atlantic waters to Bergen. On June 16, *U-107*'s men saw four fishing vessels, and on the 17th, they pursued a sound bearing on an Allied ship which then disappeared. They avoided destroyers and aircraft off Halifax on the way back to France. There were fears of a persistent oil trace from both sides of the sub up to June 22. They pursued a flashing light on June 24 and on July 11 pursued another sound bearing. On the 13th, *U-107* gave up attacking the ship *Irish Ash*. After dodging planes that dropped flares on July 23, the sailors gratefully joined their escort convoy and tied up to Keroman Bunker in Lorient.

Volker Simmermacher was born in 1919 in Strasbourg and lived until the age of eighty. His career total was three ships damaged for 15,570 tons, including the U.S.S. *Rapidan* damaged by mines in September 1943. He received no decorations. A member of the Crew of 1937a, he served as a watch officer aboard the battleship *Scharnhorst* to May 1941, then entered U-boat training. He was 1st Watch Officer of *U-107* under Harald Gelhaus from November 1941 to June 1943. He then took over command of *U-107* until August 1944. Finally, he worked up *U-3013*, commanding her from November 1944 until the capitulation.

The fishing schooner *Lark* was built in 1922 in Newcastle, Maine. It was 148 tons and owned by the O'Hara family with a dynasty of design, construction, ownership, and management of fishing vessels in the Gulf of Maine, Boston, and beyond. On February 1, 1942, Captain Parsons reported to the U.S. Navy in Boston that *Lark* had been approached by a man with a "foreign, guttural voice," on a 5,000-ton, Great Lakes-type freighter asking to buy fish from dories and fishing schooners. They were turned away and sailed south. The ship turned out to be Portuguese.[3] The *Lark* also reported the suspicious incident on arrival in Provincetown on January 31 from 60 miles off the cape, where they had been fishing.

At the time she was attacked off the Nova Scotian fishing banks in 1944, her captain was James L. Abbott, aged thirty-five, of Dorchester, Massachusetts and

Fishing vessel *Lark* having been shot up *U-107* under Volker Simmermacher in the Gulf of Maine on June 13, 1944, and survived—in Boston as part of a rare press conference staged by the U.S. Navy. (*NARA, U.S. Navy, Public domain, original in collection*)

her cook was Daniel Maloney, aged seventy-four. The *Lark* was an unarmed line-trawler equipped with a handful of dories which were stacked together on deck. These were operated by teams of rugged fishermen operating each small boat independently, equipped with barrels filled with lines with hooks spaced along them. It was grueling work, with dories periodically being separated from mother-vessels in the fog and rough seas, with tragic results.[4]

Her crew consisted of twenty-five men, of whom fourteen were American, eleven Canadian and Portuguese. They left Boston on June 5, 1944, for the fishing grounds off Nova Scotia. On the morning of June 13, the *Lark* was laden with 105,000 pounds of mixed ground-fish and was moving from the La Havre Banks to the fishing grounds off Seal Island, then planning to return to Boston. She was not sailing due to lack of wind, so was instead propelled by the diesel. Less than an hour before dawn, the *Lark* was 32 miles southeast of Cape Sable Lighthouse. The schooner's course was northwest, and she was making 8 knots over smooth seas with clear visibility. She held a straight course—no zigzagging; there was a bit of residual light from a waning moon, and the wind was a slight 5 knots from the west-southwest, over their left shoulder.

The schooner's motor alerted Simmermacher in *U-107* nearby to her presence, as at 5.55 a.m., under cover of darkness he fired a torpedo at her. It missed. Not one to give up easily, Simmermacher tried again at 6.15 a.m., only to have his second projectile also go to waste, though then usual end-run detonation was not reported. The misses were the result of the low draft, or small underwater target of the only partially full schooner, as compared with larger ships a submarine would usually encounter.

The *Lark* was provided with, and carried, a "confidential fisherman observer kit" as well as an observer nominated by the U.S. Navy. A detailed report describing the submarine—conning tower, condition and color of paint, location and relative strength of guns, configuration of bow—was later submitted to the U.S. Navy. *U-107* would have targeted the *Lark* based on such boats being equipped with radios to send in U-boat sightings to shore. This activity naturally made fishing boats the enemies of U-boats, which were just as capable as shore stations of hearing radio transmissions.

At 6.30 a.m., fifteen minutes after the second torpedo attack, Simmermacher brought *U-107* to the surface off the starboard flank of the *Lark* and fired a single warning shot. Engines were stopped and no evasive or countermeasures were taken. Immediately, twenty-three fishermen (all except Captain Abbott and Cook Maloney) abandoned ship in "good order" in five small dories. For the next forty minutes, the U-boat gunners rained fire on the wooden schooner with their 3.7-cm and 2-cm guns. Missiles of various sizes from these fusillades struck the hull, sails, pilot-house, rigging, and fishing dories stacked on deck. Abbott and Maloney stayed below, and neither was injured. *U-107* fired from roughly 600 feet away, circled the *Lark* while firing, left the scene briefly, then returned.

After the sun rose at 7.10 a.m., Simmermacher decided he had had enough of, or at least expended enough effort on, the little *Lark*. He took *U-107* close to the fishing dories as well as the schooner without hailing anyone. At 7.12 a.m., the sub submerged and headed off in a southeasterly direction, toward deep water.

By 10.15 a.m., the men in the five dories were all back on board their ship. Abbott and Maloney re-started the diesel to help retrieve them. On the way back to Boston, at 1.57 p.m. Abbott radioed to shore that his vessel had been attacked, circled and fired upon by a surfaced *U*-boat. This report, sent six-and-a-half hours after the first warning shot, was logged and passed to the commander of the Eastern Sea Frontier (Rear-Admiral Andrews) in New York. There were at least five shell-hits on the schooner which damaged the pilot house, the hull above the waterline, and both the main and riding sails. The *Lark* arrived back in Boston at 4.32 a.m. on June 15.

The attack on the *Lark* was difficult to hide, inasmuch as the battered schooner tied up at a public wharf in Boston, twenty-seven men were involved, and all survived to tell their tales. Rather than try to hide it, the U.S. Navy notified and coordinated their public relations officer, who liaised with the press. One story, titled "Victim Reveals Presence of Sub off Northern U.S.," was published by the *Washington Daily News* that very day and was retained in their Navy's file on the casualty, along with dozens of detailed photos and captions describing the damage. The Navy were careful to point out to the public that it was the first time in two years that enemy subs had been sighted on the northeast fishing banks. Given the myriad sightings of (and attacks on) U-boats in New England, fishing banks included, by Allied aircraft and ships, all members of the military in the U.S., Canada, U.K., and Germany knew the claims of June 15 to be falsehoods. The public only learned the following after the war:

> More than 500 fishermen in the First Naval District served commendably as confidential observers during the war and were issued certificates of appreciation for their services [which] greatly aided in combatting the submarine menace in the Atlantic. By using short-wave radios, these observers reported the locations of submarines, and convoys thus were routed away from the areas where the U-boats were operating.

The government went on to claim that fishermen sallied from thirty-two ports from Block Island to the Canadian border. The frontier's observation officer was Captain Vincent Astor (U.S.N.R.), who ferried *U-117* back to the U.S. after Navy service in Europe in World War I, used his yacht *Nourmahal* to spy on Japan, then Chase Bank to spy on the U.S.SR for his friend FDR, and pioneered placement of radios on fishing boats, including aboard Hemingway's *Pilar*. The commodore of the New York Yacht Club between 1928 and 1930, he was awarded six naval medals and commendations for duty in both world wars.[5]

Oberleutnant zur See Hans-Werner Offermann brought *U-518* on a four-day incursion into New England from September 16–19, 1944, coming up from the Carolinas. Off Hatteras in early September the boat withstood several intensive searches by vessels and aircraft. Starting south of Montauk *U-518* headed east on its way to Norway, providing weather reporting duties on the return voyage. The patrol began in Lorient on July 15 and ended in Kristiansand on October 24. On August 9, Allied convoy-escorts attacked *U-518* in mid-Atlantic.[6] During this patrol, *U-518* damaged the U.S.-flagged Liberty ship *George Ade* which later sank in a hurricane on September 13, 1944. *U-518* rode out the same hurricane which sank the U.S.S. *Warrington*, a destroyer, northeast of the Bahamas and several other Allied vessels. During the attack on the *George Ade*, the merchant ship's naval gunners put up a counterattack supported by the minesweeper U.S.S. *Project* and together they drove *U-518* away.

On the voyage to the Americas, Offermann was awarded the German Cross in Gold via radio on July 9. The boat deployed at least ten *Thetis* decoy-devices along its way, until July 22. Liberator bombers attacked *U-518* with three bombs, forcing a crash-dive and perforating ballast tanks with several bullets north of the Azores on the 29th. As their Wanze detection device informed the Germans of incoming aircraft they often crash-dived. On August 1, a Liberator caused another crash-dive. Starting with a four-hour test, the boat began to use the new *Schnorchel* device.

Offermann was told to conserve fuel in order to reach Bergen if necessary and to improvise if "objective area no longer seems worthwhile." That evening a search-light from above bore down on them and they crash-dived once more. On August 12, Offermann decided to focus on "Cape Fear and Cape Lookout, as well as the Cape Hatteras-to-Mona [Passage] Route." Headquarters confirmed his freedom to maneuver. On August 15, they sent the following marked "officer only" to all U-boats: "defense situation off Bordeaux is very intensified. Therefore, all boats, if not otherwise ordered, after exhausting combat power, no longer return to France, but to Norway."[7]

Clearly, the Germans had problems bigger then refueling, such as where home was. Next, the Naxos device pre-warned sailors of Allied attacks, enabling them to crash-dive and escape. Offermann expressed concern about humming noises. On August 26, they detected a sound-bearing which quickly faded, and two days later crossed the flight-path between New York and Bermuda, after crash-diving to avoid aircraft with lights. On August 31 in glass-flat or "duck pond" conditions, they tracked a convoy under escort, followed by two depth charges off Hatteras. Up to September 9, there were many crash-dives to avoid planes, periscope-depth and then full-surfacing operations, and *Schnorchel* voyages. Then Offermann watched a U.S. submarine of the S 42-type escorted by a destroyer passing by.

On September 12, Offermann was instructed to destroy *Kriegsmarine* orders, and on the 16th Offermann clarified that *U-518* was not a surfaced U-boat reported by the Americans as sighted from the air, then pursued a sound bearing. On the 18th, the U-boat was being boosted 20 miles a day in the Gulf Stream, and the following day passed up on attacking a neutral steamer. On the 28th, Offermann believed his boat was being tracked by an Allied search-group—most likely he was not being paranoid; they really were after him. On October 4, they switched to Ireland Circuit radio frequency, and on the 13th, *U-518* was ordered to proceed for Kristiansand South. On the 20th, they met with *U-534* under Nollau on the surface to join a convoy to Flekke Fjord. From October 21–23, she was made-fast to a vessel named *Fahrsund*, then sailed for Kristiansand with *U-534* and *U-714* under Schwebcke.

Offermann's superiors summarized that "the patrol cannot be considered satisfactory," pointing out that "the bad listening conditions had an unfavorable effect on the timely detection of targets in the course of the patrol. The *Kommandant* was reproached for not recognizing this and going to periscope depth much more often. Do not rely on listening gear." By contrast, the commander's summary focused on balancing meal times with battery charging. The 1944 Great Atlantic Hurricane appears to have only grazed *U-518* off Hatteras from September 13–14 as Offermann reported Force Five conditions and high swells. The Force Ten hurricane destroyed or grounded six U.S. Navy and U.S.C.G. vessels, killing more than 300 servicemen, and sinking U.S.S. *Warrington* offshore.[8]

Offermann was born in 1921 on the Danube River and was a member of the Crew of X/39. He was 1st Watch Officer of *U-129* from October 1941 to September 1943, then he trained with the 20th U-Boat Flotilla to 1944.[9] Overall, Offermann performed three patrols, damaged one ship and sank another. He received the German Cross in Gold as well as the Iron Cross 1st and Iron Cross 2nd Class and perished at age twenty-three. Destroyer escorts U.S.S. *Carter* and U.S.S. *Neal A. Scott* sank *U-518* with all hands in mid-Atlantic just before war's end, on April 22, 1945.

17

The Third Saboteur Landing off Bar Harbor, Maine, and the *Cornwallis*

Kapitänleutnant Hans Hilbig brought *U-1230* on a comparatively successful twenty-six-day patrol to New England from November 26 to December 20, 1944, landing two German agents on the coast of Maine near Bar Harbor, then sinking the Canadian ship *Cornwallis*. *U-1230*'s patrol can be considered successful when compared with his colleagues who had recently been harassed by Allied anti-submarine activities in the area or been sunk *en route* back to base. *U-518*, which left September 19, 1944, exited two months before.

On October 26, the convoy-escort U.S.S. *Bluebird*, IX 172, protecting an Army barge (the *Arnold William Ellis*) dropped a depth charge on a shoal of fish, thinking it was a U-boat, 30 miles east of Portland.[1] This illustrates that U.S. forces were on alert in the inner Gulf of Maine. *U-1230* headed west from Cape Sable for three days until November 28. On the night of November 29–30, Hilbig navigated his boat deep into Maine waters, past Bar Harbor to the north coast of Frenchman's Bay.[2]. After landing the two agents ashore, *U-1230* sank the *Cornwallis* at 4 a.m. on December 3 some 10 miles southwest of Mount Desert Rock. The attack was devastating on the 5,458-ton ship, which had already survived being torpedoed by *U-514* in port at Barbados over two years befoere.[3]

Hilbig then took *U-1230* southeast to Nantucket, attempting to intercept shipping passing the lightship *Nantucket* for some time. Between December 6 and 16, the U-boat remained on station out to 100 miles southeast. On the 17th, *U-1230* was back off Provincetown, then headed south and then east of Cape Sable on December 19–20.

After leaving Kiel on September 26 just ahead of an air raid, this patrol began in Horten, in Oslofjord, on October 8, 1944, and ended in Kristiansand on February 13, 1945.[4] It took fifty-one days for the U-boat to deposit two agents on Hancock Point, Maine. Hans Hilbig was born in 1917 and lived until 2004 and the age of eighty-six. A member of the Crew of 1936, he was until March 1943 seconded to the Luftwaffe.[5] The following month he joined the 27th U-boat Flotilla, then in October 1943 the 23rd U-Boat Flotilla. He commanded *U-1230* from January 26, 1944, until the surrender. He sank one ship and received no decorations.

William C. (Bill) Colepaugh grew up on a summer resort in Niantic, Connecticut, 1 mile west of the submarine base in New London. Enthralled from a young age by a Germanic grandmother who told him tales of German militancy, he resented wealthy summer visitors to the camp which his family managed year-round, then suffered a series of failed stints with an academy, university, the naval reserve, and merchant marine. Remarkably, he was accepted for sabotage school in Germany after arriving unannounced in Lisbon.

Despite having no introduction or no *bona fides*, he was soon being overseen by Admiral Canaris' *Abwehr* and trained by *SS Obersturmbannführer* Otto Skorzeny. His disenfranchisement with the United States was hardened in a military-style prep-school from which he was expelled, and in early 1941, he dropped out of the Massachusetts Institute of Technology. The U.S. Naval Reserve ejected him "for the good of the service" in June 1943.[6] Before and during the war, he ingratiated himself with sailors on German ships in Boston, including the captain of the *Pauline Friederich*.[7] This led to his approaching the German consulate in Boston and convincing them of his fealty to the cause of Nazism.

In 1941, he signed aboard the ship *Reynolds* in Canada (sunk of east Africa by Poske in *U-504* on October 31, 1942), worked aboard the Swedish freighter *Scania* (searched by *U-564* under Suhren on August 3, 1942, sunk by Dierksen of *U-176* on December 13, 1942, or the other *Scania*, hit by *U-82* under Rollman and sunk by *U-202*, September 11, 1941), and as a wiper on the U.S.-flagged tanker *William G. Warden* to and from South America in 1942. Colepaugh shipped out on the ship *Gripsholm*, on charter to the U.S. Department of State to deport Japanese and Germans and return with British and others who had married Americans. The ship was still manned by neutral Swedes. Despite the FBI being informed that the ship "was carrying individuals who were to be repatriated to Germany," and Colepaugh having a tail, or government observers assigned to him, he arrived in Lisbon (neutral, known for diplomatic intrigue and as a place where the likes of the Duke and Duchess of Windsor mingled freely with German spies) in mid-February 1944.

Clearly equipped with a persuasive personality, Colepaugh quickly convinced German emissaries in Lisbon of his genuine determination to join their side and infiltrate or attack the U.S. for Germany. They believed him, sent him to Germany, put him up in hotels where he was carefully observed without his knowing it, then approved him for an *Abwehr* camp in the Netherlands which provided special training for terrorists and traitors. *Abwehr*, literally meaning defense, provided German high-command with counterintelligence, sabotage, and espionage services.

In June 1944, Colepaugh was assigned to Erich Gimpel, a German in his mid-thirties who had lived in Peru, was highly trained in radios, and had just completed an assignment as a spy in Spain. Following training at a Security Service terrorist camp at The Hague, the pair made their way to Berlin for more training, then to Kiel, dressed in civilian clothes that they and other turn-coats had worn in the U.S. They arrived in the Baltic port on September 22 and spent two days aboard a German liner named the *Milwaukee*.[8] The two formed the nucleus of Operation *Elster* (Magpie in English).

U-1230's commander was twenty-seven years old—the same age as Colepaugh. A former Luftwaffe officer, Hilbig was meticulously prepared, a skill which would serve his passengers well. Like Deecke in *U-584* who deposited saboteurs in Florida, Hilbig had a brother in the U-boat arm: Kurt Hilbig commanded both *U-993* and *U-3526*.[9] He welcomed the two spies aboard with the understanding that attacks on merchant ships would be left for after the insertion and should not imperil the sabotage mission. After evading an aerial-bombardment of Kiel on September 24, *U-1230* joined a convoy on September 26 bound for Oslo, then lay over at the naval base in Horten. They trained for almost a week, leaving Oslofjord, then Kristiansand on October 8.

U-1230 needed to head north along the Norwegian coast for days in order to escape British bombers and naval ships. After sustaining an airborne attack and a lengthy voyage of fifty-one days, she entered Massachusetts Bay, where at first, they were unable to obtain navigational references off Cape Sable. Despite the fog, they did identify Mount Desert Light, and on November 20, they headed toward shore vectoring their location from commercial radio stations in Bangor, Portland, and Boston. They also enjoyed listening to American jazz. Though they saw a Liberty ship making its way toward St. John's, they refrained from sinking it.[10]

Intense moisture in the submarine during the patrol resulted in battery cases leaking, welds coming loose, and essential depth-sounding equipment such as echo sounders and hydrophones no longer operating in synchronicity. This required almost a week of repairs, with some of the welding having to be done at night on deck. They were also carefully monitoring moon phases, tides, vessel traffic, and radio traffic in anticipation of a night-time assault. Radioman Horst Haslau said *U-1230* spent most of its time near Schoodic Point at the eastern entrance to the bay, and that while Colepaugh was "acting exceptionally nervous and frightened," Gimpel was "very cool and confident, [and] helped repair our broken depth-meter in time."

While lying on the bottom for several days awaiting the attack, numerous vessels, including lobster boats, passed close by. They surfaced each night and finally, on the night of November 29 headed inland toward Bar Harbor and Hancock Point, on the northeast side of Frenchman's Bay. By 4 p.m., they passed Great Duck and Baker Island, then submerged, using the *Schnorchel*. In an extraordinary feat of seamanship, given the foggy conditions, contrary tides, and winter weather, and notwithstanding that they hit a buoy at 7 p.m., with the chains loudly scraping along the hull, *U-1230* passed east of Bar Harbor using the Mt. Desert Narrows between Iron Bound, Long Porcupine, and Jordan islands. Despite the travails, *U-1230* arrived off the mainland at Hancock Point a few hours ahead of schedule, at 10.30 p.m.

Two men—said by former intelligence operative Richard Gay to have been named Fritz and Konrad—rowed the saboteurs ashore.[11] The only men with those first names aboard *U-1230*, per German naval records, were Seaman's Apprentice (*Matrosenobergefreiter*) Konrad Heutger and Machinist's Mate Fritz Horstmann (*Maschinenmaat*). While it makes sense to send a junior sailor who was handy with small boats and accustomed to working on deck, sending a member of the engine-room staff like Horstmann would not seem logical given that Hilbig had a pool of sailors from the deck department to draw from, and the dinghy was not motorized, thus obviating the need for a mechanically minded person.

One story goes that two sailors insisted in stepping a token foot ashore to give a Hitler salute in America, so that they could later tell shipmates and family.[12] A more colorful version has them rowing back to the sub to get a sausage to mollify a dog barking onshore. In reality, the seventy or so summer vacation houses were empty in the off-season, as verified by Deputy Sheriff Dana Hodgkins, and the little row-boat made it back and forth to the sub (once) in less than half an hour. Since the sailors assumed that the saboteurs would all be caught and killed, Germans who had final contact with them believed themselves somehow special.

The turnaround time was, characteristically for Hilbig, extremely efficient: only twenty minutes from the launch of the dinghy to retrieval, stowage, and reversal of *U-1230* toward the sea.[13] Compared to the more than six hours required of *U-202* off Amagansett, and four hours for *U-213* to deposit Langbein in St. Martin's, Canada, earlier in the war, Hilbig's efficiency is notable. U.S. Naval officers who interviewed witnesses surmised simply that "two unarmed members of the ship's company rowed the two agents ashore, then returned to the U-boat."[14]

Colepaugh and Gimpel left a heavy machine used for decrypting messages back on the U-boat, even though it was integral to their mission. The entire effort hinged on the men setting up radio sets with which to exchange messages with Germany, then building and distributing new sets among Nazi sympathizers within the U.S. They pulled a suitcase and briefcase up a steep embankment in increasingly falling snow. Conspicuously without hats, they headed south, first on a simple track and then on a road.

In short order, the spies were seen by Harvard Hodgkins, a seventeen-year-old high school student and scout leader returning from a dance whose father Dana was the deputy sheriff. Then Mary Forni a twenty-nine-year-old mother and homemaker who was the Hodgkins' neighbor and the wife of the tax collector, also saw them from her car. Forni was going home from cards at her friend Margaret's when she observed Gimpel and Colepaugh coming the other way up West Shore Road toward Route 1, and that their footprints emerged from a logging trail that led to the ocean. She later noted:

> They stood out like sore thumbs because they were so overdressed ... These strange fellows you couldn't help but notice [with] their expensive-looking top-coats, fedoras, and attaché case ...they didn't have that Down East [coastal Maine] look. It was much like Wall Street. I described the sighting to my husband, Dante. He told me not to be so nosy.[15]

Yet neither witness made a formal report until Mrs. Forni and Harvard's mother, Mrs. Hodgkins exchanged observations the following day, at which point her husband Deputy Sheriff Hodgkins was alerted. By the time he checked over seventy mostly vacant buildings for signs of anomalies, *U-1230* had sunk the *Cornwallis* nearby, and the FBI were already in pursuit of potential terrorists.[16]

Within twelve hours, Colepaugh and Gimpel had boarded a taxi to the rail-line from the state capital in Augusta and boarded a bigger train from Portland to Boston, all in extraordinary short order. Ironically, the cab driver picked up a load of U.S. Navy cadets immediately after dropping the spies in Augusta. In Boston, they lay low for a night. Gimpel narrowly escaped a close call when a clothier near South Station noted that his trench coat appeared to be of German manufacture, yet recent; Gimpel explained away that he bought it in Spain and escaped entrapment, though he never wore the coat again. From then onward, they slept in their new clothes in order to break them in. The next day, they boarded a train from Boston to New York City, where they were quickly able to blend in, particularly armed with $60,000 in cash and diamonds, moving from a hotel on 33rd Street to Beekman Place on East 50th Street.

The next few weeks together in New York were characterized by intrigue, distrust, boredom, indulgence, and betrayal between the two men. They bought some items to make radios, stashed other gear and luggage in several storage lockers and an apartment on the Upper East Side. Colepaugh, a thin but not unhandsome young man, began indulging in all-night drinking binges, often ending in the arms of women, some motivated by passion, others by his money. Gimpel was less indulgent, but no more productive. They both essentially lounged, but lounged together. It was Christmas season, and they were both homesick sad, lonely, and pathetic. On whatever impulse, Colepaugh stranded Gimpel while his partner was having a suit fitted, ran to their apartments, and stole their suitcases of cash. He left them at Grand Central Station; however, a suspicious Gimpel ingeniously managed to find them on a rack, acted as though he was Colepaugh, and retrieved them.

The day after Christmas, a nostalgic Colepaugh contacted a classmate from military academy who lived on Long Island. They spent several days carousing with men (his friend), women (Colepaugh), and consuming copious drinks over numerous games of cards between long naps. Finally, they called the FBI together, which duly sent agents to the friend's home. Soon, based on Colepaugh's credibility, several agents convened on the home, and after long interviews, they set up a sting to entrap Gimpel in New York. He was quickly caught at a newsagent's in midtown Manhattan he was known to frequent, after Colepaugh described in granular detail how Gimpel would always reach into his inner coat-pocket with his right hand to retrieve his money clip.

Like most of the Dasch spy ring, Colepaugh and Gimpel were quickly tried and sentenced to death on February 14, 1945, by a military court convened at Fort Jay on Governor's Island, New York Harbor. By an amazing series of coincidences, FDR died on April 12, prompting ninety days of national mourning to July 12. By the time President Truman re-appraised their sentence on June 23, the German military had surrendered, and some in U.S. leadership no longer felt that the two men's deaths were warranted. Gimpel served his imprisonment for seventeen years in the U.S. until 1955 (in Leavenworth, Kansas, Atlanta, Georgia, and Alcatraz in San Francisco Bay), and Colepaugh (in Pennsylvania) until 1960. The American then transferred the furniture-building skills learned in prison to establish a successful business and reputation as a married, altruistic Rotarian and Boy Scout supporter in King of Prussia, outside Philadelphia.

After retiring to Florida, Colepaugh's true identity and betrayal of the U.S. became known, and a friend penned a book about him entitled *American Nazi*. He lived until 2005, suffering from Alzheimer's toward the end. The founder of Sharkhunters, a controversial U-boat enthusiast organization with members either side of the Atlantic and both sides of the war stated that Gimpel was a long-time member of Sharkhunters and they hosted him in Chicago in 1991 and 1993. In 1958, Colepaugh and Gimpel's activities were immortalized in the film *Spion für Deutschland* (*Spy for Germany*). Erich Gimpel moved to Brazil and lived beyond age ninety-eight, his reputation for charming the ladies still intact. He is said by Sharkhunters founder Harry Cooper to have returned to the U.S. several times, though exactly how many times, how and where he landed, is not known.

In 1984, erstwhile radio operator Horst Haslau also parlayed his war skills to obtain work with electronics manufacturer RCA in Indiana. During his sojourn in the U.S., he returned to Hancock Point:

> The *Ellsworth* [Maine] *American* published photos of America's one-time enemy wearing a John Deere cap and sitting in the Ellsworth Holiday Inn, holding a bottle of beer. The brand was Beck's the same German beer that was stocked on *U-1230*. Haslau said ... each crew member received one bottle for Christmas.[17]

This happened after the *Cornwallis* was sunk. Haslau became a U.S. citizen, befriended Mary Forni, and on passing away in 1999 had his ashes scattered over Frenchman's Bay.[18]

The *Cornwallis* was a steamship of 5,458 tons built by J. Coughlan and Sons of Vancouver in the service of the Canadian government whose original name was the *Canadian Transporter*. In 1932, she was transferred to Canadian National Steamships of Montreal and renamed *Cornwallis*. The ship was 400 feet long by 53 feet wide by 29 feet deep, with a single steam engine by John G. Kincaid of Greenock. Generating 370 hp, the power plant propelled her steel hull at 11 knots. On her final voyage, the *Cornwallis* was under command of Captain Emerson Horace Robinson, aged thirty-six, supported by First Mate Roy Littlewood Couves, aged twenty-six, and Chief Engineer Philbert Harry Dine. The head of the Royal Canadian Navy Volunteer Reserve unit was Leading Seaman Edward James Maughan. None of these men would survive the subsequent attack.

The *Cornwallis* had been struck and damaged by *U-514* under Auffermann in Carlisle Bay, Barbados twenty-six months before (in September 1942). First beached, then repaired in Trinidad and Mobile, she resumed service in August 1943.[19] There were a total of forty-eight persons on board the *Cornwallis* when she loaded a final cargo of sugar in bags and puncheons of molasses in Barbados in November 1944. Those onboard included seven gunners and one British "DBS"—distressed British seaman, a poor sod who was already shipwrecked and on the way to a safe haven, probably debilitated from working by virtue of PTSD. The ship carried no deck cargo, though often consignments of rum were included with cargoes of molasses, from which rum is partially derived.

After leaving Barbados on November 20, the *Cornwallis*'s routing instructions called for the ship to discharge in St. John, New Brunswick. Captain Robinson took her through the Cape Cod Canal and thereafter along Massachusetts, New Hampshire, and Maine heading for Fundy. With the Canadian ensign fluttering from the mainmast, all aboard were Canadian, except for one Dane. There was a 4-inch gun aft, a 12-lb gun in the forecastle, two Oerlikon machine guns aft, and a pair of machine guns on the bridge, none of which would be fired. Her speed was about 9.5 knots. On Sunday, December 3, the *Cornwallis* found itself between Mt. Desert Rock and the rugged Maine coast at Matinicus Rock, sailing into Hilbig's crosshairs just as *U-1230* was finally free to attack following her spy-insertion mission. The ship was heading northeast and no longer zigzagging. Conditions were clear, the seas smooth over a strong current, and there was a full yet waning moon. No other vessels, including *U-1230*, were sighted by the *Cornwallis*'s men.

The *Cornwallis* had her running lights (bright green and red lights on either side, white lights on the bow, bridge, and stern) turned on, which is unusual for wartime. Furthermore, a "dim white light on foremast" attracting further attention to the ship. Canadian mariner James (Jim) Vincent Bonnar minced no words regarding the effect of those lights. He told interviewer Ian Douglas Baird that "the reason the running lights were on was because the skipper was young and inexperienced, and he was concerned about being visible to local fishing vessels. That consideration cost him and all but five crew their lives."[20] Baird is the great-nephew of William Quilty, who along with friends Bern MacDougall and Jake Hoder from North Sydney were killed that day.

The Canadian sailors must have felt excited to be so close to home. Whatever complacency they may have been feeling was shattered just after 6 a.m. by an explosion up forward by the number one cargo hold on the starboard, or seaward side. The cover of the foremost hatch was blown skyward. There was a smell of cordite, but no fire. It took less than ten minutes for the ship to sink by the bow into the frigid December waters. By then, she was listing drastically to starboard.

Since there were only five survivors out of forty-eight, and all of them were far aft, or astern, when the ship was hit, the men that made it were unsure whether an SSS signal was sent; however, Yarmouth's radio station received a "submarine sighted on surface report" at 6.05 a.m. listing "off Desert Rock" as the location, which presumably the *Cornwallis*'s radio operators had been able to transmit before they died. The five witnesses were situated in their crew accommodation aft when the standby watch called all hands on deck. They tried to lower the lifeboat from starboard amidships, but it was caught on the metal davits and "smashed." As the ship rapidly sank to 300 feet, these men—two able-bodied seamen, two deck-hands, and a fireman—swam, or were washed, into the water. They managed to make it to life rafts, which floated free when the *Cornwallis* sank. One of these fortunate was crewman Jim Bonnar, and he was photographed with three of his compatriots shortly after their recovery.

Later that morning, aircraft *JR 4* out of Brunswick, Maine, sighted the rafts and vectored the fishing boat *Ivy M.* and one other to them. The *Ivy M.* took three men on board, and the other fishing boat took two from three rafts which they found 10 miles from Mt. Desert Rock, halfway between it and Long Island. At 11.30 a.m., a fishing vessel, possibly the *Notre Dame*, "reported sighting barrels and bodies 8 miles west-northwest of Mt. Desert Rock."[21] By 1.32 p.m., Naval Air Station Brunswick's planes confirmed sighting men on a pair of rafts 20 miles south of Mt. Desert—the island. U.S.C.G. *Snohomish* recovered four bodies, and as it became dark requested instructions from the U.S. Coast Guard in Rockland as to how to proceed.

After they rescued six of the merchant sailors, the fishermen transferred them to the naval crash-boat U.S.S. *26597* out of Southwest Harbor, by 6 p.m. One of the men died from exposure *en route* to shore, the others were taken landed in Rockland at 10 p.m. Fishermen also had the macabre task of recovering at least five bodies, since initially "air and surface craft searched the area of Mt. Desert Rock with negative results," on the intelligence of the SSS signal received in Yarmouth. Part of the confusion stemmed from the significant difference and distances between the very large island named Mt. Desert, on which Bar Harbor and many towns sit, and the comparatively tiny Mt. Desert Rock, which

Rare photograph of the few surviving members of the *Cornwallis*, sunk with great speed in freezing conditions by Hans Hilbig in *U-1230* on September 11, 1942. Forty-three officers and men died, some say because the captain left the lights on for fishermen to see and the men relaxed their guard, being so close to their Canadian homes. (*Courtesy of Michelle Bonnar, sister to James V. Bonnar, third from left, posted at uboat.net/allies/merchants/crews/person/75992*)

houses just a lighthouse with less than a handful of keepers. Naval authorities rationalized that the *Cornwallis* was unlikely to have been mined because of the rarity of commercial shipping transiting the route in question, water depth, and currents too strong for most moored mines.

Soren Christensen of Skagen Denmark was treated for shock and exposure at the coast guard dispensary in Rockland, as were John Buffett, of Cape Breton, James Bonnar, Deck Boy Albert Lasaga from Sandy Point, Newfoundland, and Elmer Cossman, a fireman of Halifax. A cook named Ted was seen to drown, and the bodies of John James Murray and K. V. Huppe were brought ashore. A vigorous counteroffensive was launched, with U.S.S. *Mervine*, U.S.S. *Davison Tillman*, and U.S.S. *Quick* dispatched urgently to conduct anti-submarine sweeps southeast of where *Cornwallis* was sunk. Later, U.S.S. *Buckley*, U.S.S. *Reuben James*, U.S.S. *Scroggins*, and U.S.S. *Hubbard* were all ordered to the scene to hunt and destroy the U-boat. Even the aircraft carrier U.S.S. *Bogue,* CVE 9, was diverted with its destroyer escorts while *en route* from New York.

U-1230 survived not just the patrol and intense counteroffensive, but the war. It was scuttled off Great Britain on December 17, 1945, more than a year later. The U-boat was only commissioned in late January 1944. Unlike most of the men on the *Cornwallis*, Hilbig lived until the age of eighty-six. Historian and researcher John Alexander Brett of Maine has been planning a detailed side-scan survey of the *Cornwallis*, using a remote-operated vehicle, when weather and scheduling permits.[22] The loss of forty-three sailors, aged from seventeen to sixty-one, from tight-knit Canadian maritime communities was sorely felt, particularly as a dozen of them were teenagers. The notion that they perished at least in part as punishment for keeping their lights on to assure fishermen of a safe passage, makes the loss more poignant.

18

Last Gasps: Four U-boats and the *Atlantic States*, U.S.S. *Eagle 56*, and the *Black Point*

Oberleutnant zur See Peter Rogowsky in *U-866* patrolled New England for roughly five days in March 1945. As the U-boat was sunk off Halifax days later and U-boat skippers no longer reported daily positions, details of the patrol are limited.[1] *U-866* passed south of Cape Sable quite close between March 8 and 10, then headed southeast from Cape Cod, exiting in that direction. No ships were sunk. This patrol began in Bergen on February 6. On March 18, the U.S. Navy destroyer escorts U.S.S. *Menges*, U.S.S. *Mosley*, U.S.S. *Lowe*, and U.S.S. *Pride* caught the Germans east-northeast of Halifax and sent them all to the bottom. Fifty-five sailors perished, including Rogowsky, aged twenty-five.[2] Rogowsky was born in Berlin in 1919 and was a member of the Crew of 1938. He began U-boat training in February 1941 and was supernumerary watch-officer on *U-595* up to April 1942.[3] After a few months in staff roles, he became 2nd Watch Officer of *U-185*, then a watch officer of the submarine *UF-2* up to March 1943. He joined *U-552* as a watch officer in March 1943 before taking command of *U-866* in September 1944. He led three smaller patrols from Germany and within Norway before the final and fatal one. Rogowsky sank no ships and received no decorations.

Kapitänleutnant Irwin Manchen brought *U-879* on a seven-day patrol into New England from April 2–8, 1945, *en route* to being sunk off Hatteras on the 30th. During the passage, the men damaged *Atlantic States* off Cape Cod on April 5. This patrol began in Kristiansand on 11 February, and Manchen sent weather information between March 6 and 15. Wynn credits *U-879* for sinking the *Belgian Airman* on April 14, the *Swiftscout* on the 18th, and the tanker *Katy* on the 23rd, all near Hatteras. Two U-boats were lost off Hatteras at that time (*U-857* under Premauer as well), meaning that any of the ships might have been sunk by either commander. Which submarine will be credited with which attack remains one of history's mysteries—until divers ascertain the truth.[4]

Manchen was born in East Prussia in June 1918 and was a member of the Crew of 1938. He was a group officer at the Naval War College to June 1942, then took up U-boat training in the 23rd U-Boat Flotilla, then the 24th U-boat Flotilla. From February to April 1944, he worked-up *U-879*, then assumed formal command. Aside from two short positioning patrols, the one to New England, Canada, and Cape Hatteras was the longest. Manchen's only ship damaged was the *Atlantic States*, and he was decorated with the Iron Cross 2nd Class.

The steam-turbine tanker *Atlantic States* was built by Sun Shipbuilding in Chester, Pennsylvania in 1943. Ordered in January 1941, she was owned by Atlantic Refining Company of Philadelphia, which homeported her in nearby Wilmington. Weighing 8,537 tons, the ship could carry 19,200 tons of petroleum cargo. At 6.48 p.m. on the evening of April 5, 1945, in the waning days of World War II, the *Atlantic States* departed Boston under command of Edgar Leroy Lindenmuth, aged thirty-six, of Upper Darby, near Philadelphia. Lindenmuth had been in the U.S. Navy as well as the naval reserves. His was married to Arline, and they were parents to John Leroy and Far Mehle. The master held command over forty-five merchant mariners who hailed from across the United States, from St. John, North Dakota to Stifler, Oklahoma and Hooks, Texas to Netcong New Jersey. Louis and W. M. Montgomery both hailed from Captain Lindenmuth's home town, suggesting a connection to him and to each other. Twelve of the fifty-seven men on board were U.S. Navy gunners.[5]

The tanker discharged crude oil in Boston and was steaming southward with orders to round Cape Cod, rather than utilize the Cape Cod Canal, with water to ballast her lower in the water and provide more "bite" for the propeller and rudder. The draft forward was 23 feet forward and 20 feet aft. Her destination was the oil terminal at Las Piedras, Venezuela. At 8.32 p.m., 8 miles from Highland Light, a torpedo from *U-879* under Manchen, positioned to landward of the ship, found its mark in the starboard quarter, penetrating the engine room, and tearing off the propeller and the rudder. This severe degree of damage left the ship helpless.

There were four lookouts on duty plus the chief officer and helmsman in the bridge. Her heading was just south of east as the tanker surged forward at an impressive 14.5 knots. Degaussing "F," "M," and "Q" coils were engaged at various amps. A torpedo detector was also activated yet did not sound until after the attack and until power was lost. The radio was not in use.

The naval armed guard lookouts were in pairs on the poop-deck and the merchant-mariners were stationed on the bridge wings. Although the weather was clear, the winds were 30–40 knots, and the sea was riddled with whitecaps and choppy. It was dusk, with there were no other vessels in sight. Neither the torpedo nor the submarine's periscope were sighted. The torpedo embedded itself in the engine room. It left behind a strong scent of cordite from the firing mechanism, with engine room staff witnessing powdered smoke. The attack neither injured nor killed any of the ship's crew.

The *Atlantic States* immediately settled by the stern. With a hole 10 feet in diameter blown in her side, she was soon down an extra 10 feet by the stern, with over 30 feet of draft, less forward, as the bow rose. There was nothing in sight for the gunners to fire at, and the stability of their firing platform deteriorated by the moment. Captain Lindenmuth ensured that the confidential codes were thrown overboard in weighted boxes and bags. Men set about opening valves to level off the trim of the ship, putting more water in the bow in the hopes of salvaging the tanker by redistributing weight. At 10.40 p.m., roughly ten minutes after the attack, the master gave the order to abandon ship, which was undertaken by fifty-two of the men. Five men elected to remain on board: Lindenmuth, the chief officer, first radio operator, the chief armed guard officer, and an able-bodied seaman. The others disembarked in three lifeboats: six in the number two, eleven in the number three, and thirty-five in the number four boats. Despite the heavy seas, no one was injured.

The Navy noted that "master stated that he had ordered abandon ship because he feared further attack, and since all propulsive machinery was out, there was no need for the majority of the crew to remain on board." Due to the fierce weather and nighttime, these boats were not able to return to the *Atlantic States*, even though it did not sink. As could be expected from an attack so close to Boston when the Allies were finally controlling the North Atlantic, the response to the attack was swift and significant. U.S.S. *Pert*, U.S.S. *Action*, U.S.S. *Schenck*, U.S.S. *Mayrant*, U.S.S. *Cates*, U.S.S. *Satterlee*, U.S.S. *Lorain*, U.S.S. *Knoxville*, and the frigates *El Paso* and *Brunswick*, as well as numerous planes were sent over the area to cover 50 miles around the casualty, looking for a sign of the *U-879*. Other vessels, which contributed were the tugs *ATR 14*, and *ATR 89*, supported by the *Wandank*, ATO 26, *SC 1280*, and the U.S.C.G.C. *Nemesis*. At least sixteen vessels went to both aid and avenge survivors of the *Atlantic States*.

The strong wind rendered deployment of blimps inadvisable. A salvage tug was sent with an estimated arrival time of 1 a.m. on April 6. Meanwhile, U.S.S. *Mayrant* (veteran of the *Coimbra* rescue), and at least six other vessels, some of them frigates, and ill-suited for the job in such conditions, formed a protective screen around the tanker to prevent, or at least discourage, further attacks. The *El Paso*, the *Brunswick*, the *Lorain*, and the *Knoxville* were dispatched from Casco, and *Action* and *Pert* from Nantucket. Senior among them was the destroyer-escort U.S.S. *Richard S. Bull*, DE 402. There was confusion among the rescuers over whether the *Atlantic States* hit a mine or was struck by a torpedo. Having the answer to that question would impact the most appropriate military response.

The U.S. Navy ship with overall command of the operation was the harbor patrol vessel U.S.S. *Guinevere*, IX 67, commanded by Lieutenant Edward L. Bergin (U.S.N.R.). She was an auxiliary schooner built by George Lawley and Sons in Neponset in 1921 and owned by the Edgar Palmer family, who donated her to the U.S. Navy on March 24, 1942. She was commissioned in Brooklyn on just three weeks later, on June 16. The action report filed by Bergin shows that he first learned of the casualty at 11.30 p.m. on April 5 and headed for the location, though the one he was provided proved to be off by 12 miles. They were able to follow the activities around aircraft and the tanker, which was letting off flares sighted by Bergin and his men at 12.50 a.m. on the 6th. By then, the winds had risen to 40–45 knots, visibility was 10 miles, the seas were rough, and the temperature was 33 degrees Fahrenheit.

At 1.21 a.m., the men in U.S.S. *Guinevere* sighted the ship's lifeboats, and Bergin maneuvered the 195-foot long, 503-ton, 33-foot wide and 15-foot deep ship alongside lifeboat number four. Within four minutes, they managed to collect all thirty-five men without injury or death, quite a feat of seamanship. Then they cut the lifeboat loose. Seven minutes later, the naval ship was alongside number three lifeboat and retrieved eleven survivors in less than four minutes. By 2.05 a.m., the *Guinevere* was alongside boat number two and took on six additional survivors, without losing any of the men entrusted to the boats by Captain Lindenmuth, though there were "minor injuries only."

Ten minutes later, at 2.20 a.m., Bergin was placed in charge of the overall rescue and guard operations around the *Atlantic States*. At 2.43 a.m., they sighted the tanker "down by the stern listing to starboard, with 3 feet of free-board showing." They were 18 miles from Cape Cod. Two minutes later, Bergin ordered all small craft in the vicinity to "form a protective screen around torpedoed ship." Six minutes later, at 2.51 a.m., "ComCortDiv 35 arrived at scene of action and relieved U.S.S. *Guinevere* [Bergin] as Officer-in-Charge at scene."

The *Guinevere* was ordered to peel off and return the survivors to the warmth of shore at 4.40 a.m. Escorted by *SC 1280*, she did so starting seven minutes later. At 6.02 a.m., Lieutenant Bergin informed the command center of his estimated arrival time in Boston with the survivors, and that one of the salvage tugs had attached a line to the stricken tanker. He added, "no-one injured, and ship appears in fair condition." The *Guinevere* docked at U.S. Naval Frontier Base's Pier number one in East Boston and disembarked the cold and exhausted survivors ashore.

At 4.01 p.m., U.S.S. *Mayrant* was towing the *Atlantic States* at 3 knots. It was advised that this set-up be maintained as "tugs do not have power to handle job in this strong wind," adding, "boarding party reports tanker *Atlantic States* had large hole about 10 feet in diameter at and below water-line near stern. This undoubtedly must have been caused by a torpedo." At 5.16 p.m., six naval vessels, or a mixture thereof, were screening the tanker, but four of them were deemed "small and rather ineffective under present wind and sea conditions." It was suggested to release U.S.S. *Schenck* and to add two destroyers to reinforce the screen. By 5.08 p.m., a tug had the tanker in tow and by roughly 6 p.m. on the following day (April 7), the *Atlantic States* was berthed back in Boston, where ultimately, she was dry-docked, repaired, and returned to service. On May

22, 1945, Lieutenant Bergin was awarded a Letter of Commendation with the authority to wear the ribbon. The *Guinevere* was transferred to the U.S. Maritime Commission on April 25 for disposal and decommissioned on August 2, 1945, between VE Day and VJ Day.

U-879 was tracked down and sunk off Cape Hatteras three weeks later, on April 30, by depth charges from four U.S. Navy destroyers in Task Group 2.10, composed of U.S.S. *Natchez* and destroyer escorts U.S.S. *Coffmann*, U.S.S. *Thomas*, and U.S.S. *Bostwick*.[6] All fifty-two Germans were lost. *Atlantic States* traded under the ownership of Winco Tankers until February 1961 and was scrapped in Hong Kong after two decades of service. Born in 1908, Captain Lindenmuth lived until 1970. The report on this casualty by the U.S. Navy in Boston was signed by Lieutenant (junior grade) Barbara Conard, the only female officer to any of over 250 Survivor Statements relating to this series.[7]

Kapitänleutnant Rudolf Premauer brought *U-857* through New England *en route* from Horten, which he left on February 6 and April 30, 1945, via Sable and Montauk westbound between April 7 and 11, to their being sunk off Hatteras. While the dates may never be known (Premauer gave only ten positions during eighty-four days), this was the standard route taken by over seventy other U-boats.[8] Premauer and his men may have spent more time in the region, as the date of the boat's demise is uncertain.

U-857 is listed as "missing since April 1945 in the North Atlantic off the U.S. East Coast. No explanation exists for its loss. Fifty-nine dead (all hands lost)."[9] Dr. Axel Niestlé's report is similarly vague. Some sources say that it is possible that *U-857* was lost in the same attack as *U-879* off Hatteras, or that a U.S. Navy airship destroyed her with a homing torpedo, as claimed by the crew of an airship on April 18. In several publications, *U-857* is given credit for sinking the *Belgian Airman* (on the 14th), the *Swiftscout* (18th), and damaging the *Katy* (23rd); however, they might also have been sunk by *U-879* under Manchen, which was sunk off Hatteras on April 30. The evidence lies embedded on the seafloor in the form of the hulks of three merchantmen and two U-boats.

Premauer was born in 1919 in Stuttgart and died at twenty-five. A member of the Crew of 1937b, he began U-boat training in February 1941 and was 1st Watch Officer of *U-510* up to April 1943.[10] He trained in the 24th U-Boat Flotilla up to August 1943, then work-up for *U-857* began, and he commanded her until they were both sunk. Though he was believed at first to have been sunk off Boston in a destroyer-led attack on April 7, that target was a wreck or whale, and not a U-boat. Depending on whether he or Manchen are given credit, Premauer sank two ships and damaged a third on this patrol and received no decorations.

Oberleutnant zur See Helmut Frömsdorf, aged twenty-four, brought *U-853* into New England for an extensive patrol from April 20 to when the boat was sunk of Newport on May 6, 1945. The incursion began about 50 miles south of Cape Sable, heading west for Portland. Though the submarine's logbook was destroyed, and Frömsdorf wisely never transmitted his position, his basic movements can be determined from the attacks which he made.[11] On April 23, a few miles off Cape Elizabeth Light, Portland, *U-853* sank the U.S.S. *Eagle 56*, a patrol craft, from which there were only thirteen survivors. U.S.S. *Selfridge*, DD 357, counterattacked while trying desperately to save freezing survivors. Unsurprisingly, she did not destroy the U-boat. As *U-853* was sunk shortly thereafter, the U.S. Navy used the concomitant fog of war to pretend that the *Eagle 56* had been sunk by a boiler explosion. To the great relief of survivor's families, officials admitted their error in 2001.

Frömsdorf attacked again, twelve days later, after *Großadmiral* Dönitz issued an end hostilities order for U-boats to cease hostilities on May 4, however. Evidently, Frömsdorf either did not receive the order, or he disregarded it. In any event, on the evening of May 5 in fog, he struck the 5,353-ton American-flagged collier *Black Point*, laden with 7,759 tons of coal from Newport News to Weymouth, Massachusetts. There were forty-six men on board under the command of Captain Charles E. Prior.[12] A well-placed torpedo blew 40 feet of the stern off the ship, which quickly started to sink off the fishing port of Point Judith, which juts into Block Island Sound.

The audacious, even suicidal attack took place in Rhode Island waters less than 10 miles southwest of Newport, base to a large portion of the U.S. Navy's Atlantic fleet. Many of the merchant sailors got away in a pair of lifeboats and a raft, but a dozen men, one of them a naval armed guard, perished. Survivors were picked up by the Norwegian ship *Scandinavia* and the Yugoslav ship *Karmen*. Smaller crash-boats from Quonset Point took fifteen of the survivors to Newport.

U-853 was sighted by a merchant ship (possibly the *Scandinavia* or the *Karmen*) and reported to naval authorities, who responded by quickly organizing a task group to destroy the submarine in the shallow, hemmed-in waters. U.S.S. *Moberly* quickly arrived on scene, followed by U.S.S. *Atherton* and others. Some 5 miles east of Grove Point, Block Island, the *Atherton*'s commander, Lieutenant-Commander L. Iselin (a sculptor educated at Harvard), detected the U-boat and Iselin dropped depth charges and hedgehog bombs. Then the hunters lost contact with *U-853*, lying prone on the bottom. Three hours later, contact was regained and the *Atherton* dropped a series of hedgehogs which, in the opinion of analysts, "probably destroyed the boat."[13]

Unconvinced that the U-boat was destroyed, naval ships pummeled away at the last known position until, in daylight, they discovered parts of a wooden navigator's table and an officer's cap – most likely Frömsdorf's. Fifty-six men had perished at a time when half a dozen other German U-boats were motoring toward the U.S. East Coast to surrender in Portsmouth, Canso, Shelburne, or Lewes. Frömsdorf could have surrendered in Newport had he wished.

Frömsdorf was born in Silesia in March 1921 and was twenty-four when killed. The *Black Point* and the *Eagle 56* represented his total tonnage; about

5,780 tons. He received no decorations. A member of the Crew of IX/1939, he went through U-boat training in the 1st U-Boat Flotilla and 22nd U-boat Flotilla to May 1943. He was 1st Watch Officer of *U-853* from June 1943 to August 1944, during which he was acting-commander from June 17 to July 9, 1944, under Helmut Sommer.[14] This was because Sommer had been killed by two Wildcat aircraft from U.S.S. *Croatan*, CVE 25, which strafed the boat, killing two and injuring twelve. Frömsdorf took charge and evaded further attacks by Avenger aircraft from the carrier some 30 miles away. The boat survived. After serving in late 1944 under Günter Kuhnke, he became commander of *U-853* on September 1, 1944.

The U.S. Navy patrol craft U.S.S. *Eagle 56* was the fifty-sixth in a series of sixty *Eagle*-class submarine chasers commissioned during the final months of World War I. The U.S. government essentially recruited assembly line pioneer Henry Ford to mass-produce 100 of the craft. First, they turned out to be cranky, or unwieldly to steer and handle. Then the war ended, so they reduced the number to sixty. At its height, the factory employed 8,000 workers in the Detroit area. Many of the new boats were subsequently delivered to the U.S. East Coast via the Great Lakes, Erie Canal, and Hudson River to New York.[15]

The *Eagle 56* had its keel laid on March 25, 1919, and launched on August 15 that year. The U.S. Navy commissioned her into the fleet on October 26 and by July 1920, she was classified the *PE 56*. By the resumption of hostilities in 1939, only eighteen of the original sixty boats remained in service. The *Eagle 56* spent the early war patrolling off the Delaware Capes, and on February 28, 1942, she rescued survivors of U.S.S. *Jacob Jones*, DD 130, off Cape May after *U-578* under Rehwinkel sank it earlier that day. Other activities included rescuing merchant mariners, running aground on a submerged hulk, then training at a Sonar school in Key West. Then, in June 1944, she was assigned in support of Naval Air Station Brunswick.

On Monday, April 23, 1945, the *Eagle 56* was towing targets for Navy dive-bomber planes off Cape Elizabeth, near the entrance to Portland when it came into the crosshairs of German submarine *U-853*. The German high command had ordered dozens of aggressive attacks on North America in the hopes of securing a better peace settlement for themselves. *U-853* entered New England on April 20, Hitler's birthday. One of the sleuths who pieced together the loss of the *Eagle 56* reported:

> Harold Petersen, a second-class machinists mate, was below deck when the explosion occurred, sending him crashing head-first into a metal locker. He made for the ladders but stopped to carry an injured sailor who was too hurt to move. With water pouring in and dozens of sailors jostling to get to safety, Petersen lost the injured man off his back, then was confronted by a panicked sailor who said he couldn't swim. Petersen told the sailor, "'whether you can swim or not, get away from this ship.' So, we both

> went. He never came up." Petersen made it over-board, clinging to wreckage in the chilly waters until rescuers arrived about fifteen minutes later.

Thirteen men managed to survive after being picked up half an hour later by U.S.S. *Selfridge*, DD 357, with one man picked up by the lightship *Nantucket*, which happened to be off station.[16] Forty-nine perished. The *Selfridge* counterattacked with nine depth charges once she picked up twelve men. When her crew picked up a "sharp, well-defined Sonar contact," they dropped nine Mark IX-type Mod 2 depth charges.

While the real fighting raged at sea, ashore members of the U.S. Navy decided to obfuscate and outright deny the possibility that their ship had been sunk by an enemy submarine so close to shore, and the end of the war in Europe. One theory is that the cover-up began to protect a local commander from scrutiny over failure to act and any concomitant punishment, but it quickly snowballed. Why nearby dive bombers, for example, chose to limit their activity to practice runs and did not attack *U-853* before, during, and as it sank their shipmates beneath their noses has never been explained.

Although *U-853* was the only enemy submarine in the area, and Frömsdorf proved himself highly aggressive by attacking the *Black Point* a week or so later, also close to shore, the U.S. Navy denied until 2001 that a U-boat could have sunk the *Eagle 56*. They claimed instead that she suffered an internal boiler explosion.[17] This is notwithstanding that her boilers had recently been overhauled, and some survivors saw a periscope, the colors of *U-853*'s emblem, as well as a conning tower. During the Naval Board of Inquiry at Portland (which began the next week), nearly half of the surviving American sailors saw "a red and yellow emblem on the submarine's sail [conning tower]. These insignia match the markings of *U-853*: a red horse on a yellow shield."

A local paper reported that crewman John Breeze "only saw it momentarily. We didn't know what we'd hit or what had hit us." Despite the evidence, the senior naval establishment quickly concluded that the *Eagle 56* had suffered a sudden and inexplicable boiler explosion, although that equipment had been maintained and overhauled just weeks before, and none of the fifty-nine other sister ships in the series had experienced such a catastrophe.

> The Navy reclassified the sinking as a combat loss and recommended that Purple Hearts be awarded to its forty-nine dead and twelve survivors. This also makes it the Navy's biggest single combat loss in New England. In June 2001, at a special ceremony aboard the museum-ship USS *Salem*, CA 139, in Quincy, the Navy awarded the Purple Heart to the three survivors and next of kin of those lost.[18]

Furthermore, on the sixtieth anniversary of the disaster in 2005 at Fort Williams Park in Portland, a granite and bronze memorial marker was unveiled between the two pairs of binoculars overlooking the Portland Head Light honoring the sailors of the *Eagle 56,* thanks in part to the efforts of a group of enthusiasts known as the U.S.S. *Eagle 56* Search Team. The *Eagle 56* was the only U.S. Navy warship lost due to enemy action in New England since the War of 1812.

The coal-carrying steamship *Black Point* was built by New York Shipbuilding of Camden, New Jersey in 1918 as the *Fairmont* for Coastwise Transportation of Boston. The U.S. Navy acquired her for their Overseas Transportation Service and named her U.S.S. *Fairmont*, ID 2429. She was returned to Coastwise in 1919, then two years later sold to the Hawaiian Steamship Company of New York and renamed the *Nebraskan*. That lasted until 1927, when she was sold to C. H. Sprague of Boston, her owners until her demise eighteen years later, and renamed a Black Point. She was 5,401 tons, and could carry 8,000 tons of coal, which she was designed for. She was operated by the Sprague Steamship Company of Boston and was on time-charter to the U.S. War Shipping Administration (WSA).[19]

In early May 1945, as the war in Europe was waning to its very last days and Hitler was trapped in a bunker in Berlin, the *Black Point* set off from Newport News, Virginia for an unescorted voyage to Weymouth, south of Boston. The ship was laden to near capacity with 7,595 tons of coal. Captain Charles E. Prior had responsibility for forty-five other souls, of whom five were naval armed guards and the balance merchant mariners. The evening of May 5, 1945, found the *Black Point* rounding Point Judith to port and heading east along the southern shore of Rhode Island. She was roughly 4 miles from Point Judith and making 8 knots, not zigzagging. Though there was a heavy groundswell from the east, the weather was fair, winds about 15 knots from the southeast, and visibility 5 miles. By some accounts the conditions were foggy, and visibility less. There were two other freighters: a tanker and a tug towing two barges visible to the lookouts on the bridge of the twenty-seven-year-old collier.[20]

The story about the tug and its barges is worth reciting because it was only identified in May 2018, as one of its crew members lay in hospice, the last surviving eyewitness. The tug *Chaplain* was completed just weeks before in the yard of Ira S. Bushey and Sons in Brooklyn. It was steam-powered, with a Fairbanks-Morse engine of 1,000 hp. Her owners were a Bushey affiliate named the Spentonbush/Red Star Companies, or Spentonbush Fuel Transport Service. One of her deck-hands was Louis Alfred Coley, Jr., a nineteen-year-old waterman whose mother, Catherine Madden, was born and raised on a barge in Boston. His shipmates had just towed a laden collier from the Delaware up to Fall River and were on their way back with two empty hulks "light," in ballast and strung along behind them. Coley said that "the sub was right under, and along their tug, and used it as cover, traveling in their shadow. They didn't realize this until it was too late, and the ship had been hit." Then Coley watched as "the ship was being circled by the U-boat and saw the ship went down."[21]

Being practical men, as soon as the crew of the *Chaplain* realized they were in the middle of a U-boat battlefield, they got out of the vicinity, which would explain the absence of records about their presence. Perhaps because they fled, at first Coley was unwilling to share his story. When told that a book was being written about what he saw over seventy-five years before, his first question was whether the author "was a card-carrying Merchant Mariner?" When told he was, he said, "then it's alright," and approved the use of this account and photos. His daughter-in-law, Louise (Schadtle) Coley wrote, "it was the most he talked in weeks."[22]

The torpedo fired by Frömsdorf found its mark in the side of the *Black Point* on the starboard flank at 9.40 p.m. The lookouts never saw the wake of the torpedo, although one of the several ships in the area—the pilot and engineer of the *Karmen* and the crew on the *Chaplain*—claimed to have seen one. There was no time for avoidance. The concussion was so severe that glass broke, smoke and soot shot from the engine exhaust stack, and survivors smelled cordite. The engines were shut down right away.

Captain Prior felt the ship had hit something, not the other way around. He said the stern, or 40 feet aft of the number five hatch, simply disintegrated, and the main mast fell over aft. He felt that the Navy gunner who was killed must have been trapped in the gunner's shack located far aft. "About seven men were below aft, and I don't believe they had a chance of saving themselves." The chief engineer raced from the mess to the engine room, and in a minute or so, the water had risen there to 5 feet. The first assistant engineer was in the engine room and reported the "terrible explosion, followed by a terrific vibration, and at the same time the engine raced like hell." The chief officer said they were half a mile from Buoy Charlie and reported seeing a "great deal of heavy blue smoke coming from number five hatch." He described how the "gunner's shack and mount were completely gone." Two firemen were blown against a bulkhead.

The blow was clearly mortal. A dozen men were killed on or near the stern. At 9.55 p.m., the *Black Point*'s bow section capsized, with part of it remaining afloat. Sometime after 10.05 p.m., even the bow sank in roughly 100 feet of water. Some of the confidential signals went down with the ships; other were carried ashore by Captain Prior, who immediately ordered abandon ship. His instructions were carried out in an orderly manner. Thirty-four survivors found themselves in the cold New England night in two lifeboats and a raft. Fortunately for them, there were U.S. Navy facilities throughout nearby Narragansett Bay, and a Navy crash-boat from Quonset Point, in the West Passage, promptly set out and retrieved fifteen men from other rescue vessels, taking them to Newport. When witnesses first reported the casualty, they thought it was a tanker since the stern had been blown up, and it was difficult to identify. At 9.22 p.m., radio stations in Salem picked up a mayday. Nearby Fort Adams, where a naval listening station had been set up, detected explosions in the east and west Narragansett Bay sectors at

9.35 p.m.[23] At 9.40 p.m., numerous 83-foot PT-style boats were requested from Newport, and five minutes later, a radio station on Fishers Island at the entrance to Long Island Sound advised that the New London naval base was sending four destroyers as well as two mine-clearing vessels (*YMS 201* and *YMS 444*), which were 270 tons and 136 feet long.

The *Karmen* rescued seventeen men from a life raft and put them aboard a Coast Guard boat. Then the *Scandinavia* plucked two men to safety and deposited them aboard the same local vessel. The U.S.C.G.C. *83487* out of Point Judith then took all nineteen survivors from rescue ships back to port. Two of the men were injured. Other U.S. Coast Guard boats *36354, 38344, 36383, 36400*, and *38679* plus a rescue-vessel named the *Hornbeam* arrived on the scene. A PBY aircraft circled the area, a blimp, and, later on, the U.S.C.G. vessels *36466* and *83486*. After witnessing the bow of the ship capsize and sink at 10.05 p.m., they marked the location of the wreck with two DAN buoys.

Out of the dozen men who perished, eleven were merchant mariners, and one was a naval armed guard named Stephen Spetz, aged twenty-nine. Boatswain's Mate Lonnie Whitson Lloyd (U.S.N.R.), aged twenty-six, had already survived the loss of the *Expositor*, in which seven perished mid-Atlantic when Heine in *U-303* raided convoy ON 166 on February 22, 1943. All of those who died on the *Black Point* were American, except for a Finnish fireman and wiper named Reino Emil Lindstrom. The loss goes down in history as the final American vessel and the last ship sunk in U.S. waters by a U-boat.

The humble *Black Point* was avenged the following day during a sustained and savage counterattack by numerous destroyers who persistently tracked and ultimately pinned the submarine down, destroying it and blasting away until conclusory debris in the form of German sailors and officer's caps, an abandon-ship kit, rations, sou'wester raincoats, a mattress, parts of a navigation desk, and a rubber boat floated to the surface, convincing the attackers of their success. At one point, two U.S. Navy blimps sent to document the action reported rhythmic metallic banging, which was intermittent, drowned out by the destroyers, and stopped after their attacks, as though submariners where signaling to be located and somehow rescued.[24]

Among the U.S. Navy vessels that attacked *U-853* was the destroyer-escort U.S.S. *Atherton* and the patrol frigate U.S.S. *Moberly*. The counterattack involved two PBY aircraft, at least one blimp, the aforementioned Coast Guard and other patrol boats as well as destroyers *Breckenridge*, *Blakely*, *Semmes*, *Barney*, *Amick*, *Ericsson*, *Baldwin*, *Frankford*, *Newport*, *Booth*, *Restless*, *Action*, *Card* (the aircraft carrier), and *Nelson*. The effort was given its own codename: Operation Observant and known less formally as the Battle of Point Judith.[25]

Today, the *Black Point* lies in two parts, with the bow upside down, and about 50 feet of the stern section lying upright about half a mile away.[26] In

This U.S. Navy photo shows what was retrieved from the surface, as well possibly by Navy divers, in the hours and days after USS *Atherton* and other destroyers sank *U-853* with all hands in Block Island Sound in May 1945. The catalog includes the end of a wooden flagstaff, artificial lungs, captain's cap, pillow, inflatable life raft, mattress and pillow, and a towel. (*Alan Boyle, "How an Expedition to Study a Sunken Nazi U-boat Rescued a Reputation," Science Magazine, May 2015*)

contrast, the wreck of *U-853* is upright and mostly intact. It has been a popular dive site for many decades. In 1960, a group of artifact hunters under Burton Mason of Submarine Research Associates in Trumbull, Connecticut, removed human remains from *U-853*, then publicized an effort to raise the submarine for tourism.[27] Right away, German and U.S. governments, U.S. Navy admirals, and clergy intervened to prevent such desecration of war graves and the scavengers were forced to surrender the remains of a German sailor removed from the wreck. They were buried with military honors in Newport, attended by representatives from West Germany, the German Consul in Boston, and the U.S. Navy. Commander Iselin became a renowned sculptor in Camden, Maine.[28]

The *Chaplain* and her four-man crew enjoyed colorful careers. Louis Coley served in the Merchant Marine 1942–1945, and the U.S. Army 1954–1957, servicing radios aboard spy planes in the Cold War, then U.S. Naval Reserve 1964–1971.[29] In 1946, the *Chaplain* (179 tons, 95 feet long, and 25 feet wide) joined the fleet of another Bushey affiliate, Sheridan Towing Company and sailed as the *Margaret Sheridan*. From 1951 to 2004, her named remained the *Ocean King*, under the ownership of Red Star Towing and Transportation Company, then Amerada-Hess Corporation, in 1977, then Farrell Ocean Services, then McKeil Marine Company, Russell Tripp, Bay State Towing Company, and Constellation Tug Company of Boston, which renamed her the *Carina* up to 2009, when the vessel was sold, before Constellation was acquired by Foss Maritime or McAllister Towing. Sadly, she seems to have been little-used as her last U.S.-owner referred to her as the "old girl," and said her nickname was "Pond Prince." The historic workhorse is believed to be either in the sand-mining sector or laid up in the Bahamas under the names *Carina, Chaplain*, *Margaret Sheridan*, *Ocean King*, and back to *Carina*, yet repeated searches of various Bahamian waterfronts have not turned her up. She was also rumored to have been sold into the aggregate-barging business there, which is just a shade shy of the boneyard.[30]

Tugboat crewman Louis Albert Coley Jr. (1926–May 6, 2018), bringing in the tow on two ship hulks which have been converted to coal barges and are being towed "light," probably into Verrazano Narrows, New York, from Narragansett Bay, Fall River in in the early 1940s. (*Courtesy of Capt. Coley and his daughter-in-law Luise Schadtle Coley, emails, phone calls, May 2018*).

19

Eight Surrenders: *U-858*, *U-1228*, *U-805*, *U-873*, *U-234*, *U-977*, *U-889*, and *U-530*

Kapitänleutnant Thilo Bode patrolled New England in the Type IXC/40 boat *U-858* for four to five days in May 1945. Bode only provided his positions for two days, April 3 and 4, south of Iceland. They began in Horten on March 11 and on April 14, *U-858* was joined by *U-518*, *U-546*, *U-805*, *U-880*, and *U-1235* to form the wolfpack *Seewolf*. The boats, however, were blocked by U.S.S. *Block Island* and U.S.S. *Croatan*—aircraft carriers determined to prevent an attack by U-boat-towed V 2 rockets on American soil and try to strengthen Germany's bargaining hand in surrender negotiations. Of the five boats, only two (*U-858* and *U-805*) survived the dragnet, arriving off the U.S. coast by April 24.[1]

U-858 was southeast of Newfoundland on May 8 when it received the surrender order that day. Bode surfaced the next day and at 4.10 p.m. broadcast the boat-number, position, course, and speed to the Allies. The following day, *U-858* was intercepted by U.S.S. *Sutton*, DE 771, and U.S.S. *Neal A. Scott*, DE 769, which were actually searching for *U-1228*. After the two destroyer escorts left to continue their quest, *U-858* was joined by U.S.S. *Carter*, DE 112, and U.S.S. *Muir*, DE 770. Finally, U.S.S. *Pope*, DE 134 and U.S.S. *Pillsbury*, DE 133, assumed command of Bode and his men. On orders from the Commander-in-Chief, Atlantic, U.S.S. *Pillsbury* placed an armed guard aboard *U-858*, then guided its erstwhile enemy to the designated hand-over point off Cape May, where they arrived at 7 a.m. on May 14. *U-858* then voyaged to New England, arriving in New London on June 5, 1945.

Bode was born in 1918 in Bochum and lived until 2014 and the age ninety-five. A member of the Olympia Crew of 1936, he served in the Spanish Civil War aboard the destroyer *Z6 Theodor Riedel*, then in a naval flak detachment until June 1940. From September 1942 until March 1943, he served as 1st Watch Officer of *U-505* under Peter Zchech, who later committed suicide at age twenty-five while on patrol. After training in the 24th U-boat Flotilla, and a second stint as 1st Watch Officer on *U-505* to August 1943, he took command of *U-858* in September 1943 until the capitulation. He sank no ships and was awarded the U-boat War Badge of 1939, the Spanish Cross in Bronze without Swords, and the Iron Cross 1st Class.

In New London, officers and crew were interrogated, particularly with regards to rocket technology and its possible adaption by submarines. Several of the PoWs were kept at Camp Atterbury, Indiana. Its new captors kept the boat active up to its destruction in November 1947. *U-858* underwent a three-week refit at Thames Shipyard adjacent to the U.S. submarine base in Groton. Items repaired included escape-trunks and other survival equipment and lasted until October 23. After moving to Portsmouth, *U-858* voyaged to Key West, where it was used for torpedo-firing experiments. By late April 1946, she was back in New London for maintenance, including sound surveys, *Schnorchel* operations, diving trials, and other tests up to June 1946.

U-858 was cannibalized for parts starting on June 14. Her death warrant was issued on April 21, 1947, when the boat, along with *U-873*, was allocated for torpedo testing or sale for scrap. In mid-November, *U-858*, *U-530*, *U-234*, and *U-889* were towed from Portsmouth to the wide natural harbor at Provincetown by the rescue ship U.S.S. *Tringa*, ASR 16, and Navy-yard tug U.S.S. *YTB 230*. Over two days, several U.S. submarines took turns destroying their former foes. *U-858* was sunk by U.S.S. *Sirago* some 40 miles off Provincetown on November 21, 1947.[2]

Oberleutnant zur See Friedrich-Wilhelm Marienfeld brought *U-1228* through New England from May 14–17, 1945, to surrender at Portsmouth. Only four dates from this patrol are provided in the war diary. *U-1228* left Kristiansand on April 14 and received its surrender order on May 9. Once it surfaced and reported its position mid-Atlantic, the submarine was instructed to head for St. John's, Newfoundland. The U.S. Navy Commander-in-Chief, Atlantic ordered destroyer escorts *Sutton* and *Neal A. Scott* 350 miles east of Cape Race to the sub's last known position. After they happened upon *U-858* on May 10, they left it and arrived at *U-1228* the next day. The weather, fog, icebergs, and heavy seas were too boisterous to safely effectuate the transfer of a boarding party on the 12th. They bypassed St. John's and instead made for a newly designated surrender point at Casco Bay. On May 15, after the *Sutton* was dispatched elsewhere, the *Scott* was ordered to escort *U-1228* to the Examination Anchorage off Portsmouth, where they arrived at 6 a.m. on May 17.[3]

Marienfeld was born in 1920, was twenty-five at surrender, and lived until 1973 and age fifty-three. A member of the Crew of 1938, he began naval service aboard the destroyer *Z7 Hermann Schoemann,* until August 1940. He then commanded the artillery lighter *Adventura* to October before joining U-boats late that year. Marienfeld served as 2nd Watch Officer of *U-205* from May 1941 to April 1942, then commanded *U-4* from June 1942 to January 1943, without patroling.[4] Marienfeld commanded *U-1228* from December 1943 to surrender, during which he sank the corvette H.M.C.S. *Shawinigan*, K 136, in the Cabot Strait. All ninety-one officers and men aboard were killed. Marienfeld received no decorations.

After surrender, *U-1228* was not allocated for any express purpose and therefore was declared as surplus to Allied requirements in November 1945. Initially, on June 23, she was earmarked to be scavenged for parts, then destroyed. This was confirmed by Portsmouth on September 19 using the term "cannibalization." There were several reasons for her condemnation, among them, it would take more than three months to work *U-1228* back up to seagoing state to be tested or paraded. Also, the similar sub, *U-858*, had already been selected in her place, and finally *U-1228*'s parts were needed (and indeed used) to supply *U-530* and *U-977* on their Victory Loan Bond tours of the U.S. and Caribbean starting that November.

The Tripartite Naval Commission (TNC) stemming from the Potsdam Agreement required all unallocated Axis submarines to be sunk by mid-February 1946. United States officials clearly took this mandate seriously, as urgent messages were sent to Portsmouth on December 11, 1945, in which the Chief of Naval Operations ordered her sunk "in open sea, depth not less than 100 meters," or over 350 feet. This was followed on January 8, 1946 with the authorization for crews to strip the sub of anything "other than not destroying the watertight integrity of the ship." She was towed out of Portsmouth on February 4 by U.S.S. *Penguin*, ASR 12, then *U-1228* was sunk by the submarine U.S.S. *Sirago*, S.S. 485, on February 5, 1946, some 37 miles northeast of Provincetown.[5] With cameras rolling for training purposes, the *Sirago*'s initial torpedo missed the German, passing beneath it. However, the second struck her aft, making *U-1228* heel over to starboard. Although the third also passed too deep, a fourth projectile broke the U-boat's back, and it sank immediately.

Korvettenkapitän Richard Bernadelli brought *U-805* into New England to surrender at Portsmouth on May 15, 1945. We know that no positions were given, as none are given in her war patrol diary kept on shore. *U-805*'s patrol began in Bergen on March 17, 1945, followed on April 14 by the boat joining five other submarines to form the *Seewolf* patrol line and draw escort hunter-killer groups away from the United Kingdom and English Channel. They were unsuccessful, and all but two of the U-boats were sunk by, among others, units supporting the carrier U.S.S. *Croatan*.

On April 18 and 19, U.S. Navy aircraft based in Terceira, Azores, found *U-805* on the surface twice; however, both times Bernadelli submerged and escaped. The escort-carrier U.S.S. *Mission Bay* was supporting the hunt from 50 miles away. On the night of April 20–21, the destroyer U.S.S. *Mosely* located the sub and attacked for two hours, again without result. Only *U-805* and *U-858* out of six survived, and by the 24th, they motored west, with Bernadelli heading to patrol off Halifax. Once the surrender order was received on May 8, *U-805* was the first to send out its surrender message at 3.10 a.m. on May 9. Confusion then reigned as the U-boat headed for the Azores, and the Allies sent ships from Newfoundland.

Crewmen aboard U.S.S. *Otter* and U.S.S. *Varian* obtained a visual on *U-805* on the morning of May 12 and were able to get a team of U.S. Navy sailors aboard her. Together, the Germans and their captors voyaged to the appointed surrender point in Casco Bay, arriving at 8 a.m. on May 15. Following surrender protocols, *U-805* was handed over to U.S. Coast Guard cutter *Argo* (which had helped save thirty men from the *Norness* to Newport in January 1942) for delivery to the Portsmouth Navy Yard.[6]

As the first German U-boat to arrive in Portsmouth, *U-805* created quite a sensation among the Navy, civilians, and press corps assembled there. This is due to the truism that U-boats were more than a physical asset; they were also a tool for inflicting psychological fear as well. U.S. Navy veteran Charlie Gray described the surrender process in Portsmouth:

> The Navy tug U.S.S. *Dekanisora*, with dozens of members of the press, met the sub off the Isles of Shoals. A large patch of green water, dyed with chemicals, was the spot marked for the rendezvous. Three German officers with "surly, expressionless faces" were seen on deck and a near-accident occurred when the U-boat cut across in front of the press tug, missing by about fifteen feet and angering the tug's captain. The official surrender took place at Kitt's Rock Buoy, one mile out from Whaleback Lighthouse, at the entrance to the harbor at 4.25 p.m. After the ship arrived at the Navy yard in Kittery and publicity photos were taken, twenty-seven crewmen and four officers were removed to the naval prison by bus.[7]

The German sailors were interviewed by naval intelligence about guided bombs, ballistic missiles, and jet planes. Gray interviewed a German lieutenant named Albert Finster who blamed the U.K. for the war and for ruining Hamburg (his hometown) via air raids.

By the end of 1945, the Allies had no requirement for the Type IXC/40 *U-805*. Per a Tripartite Naval Commission memo dated September 25 in Trinidad, she was considered, along with *U-1228*, to be in the "worst condition," of the subs in U.S. hands, and was projected to take more than three months to repair. The steady series of demotions leading to condemnation mirrors that of *U-1228*. Neither sub was ever formally allocated to the U.S. Navy by the commission. That meant they had to be destroyed on or before February 15, 1946; they were the only ones with that status in U.S. waters.

Ultimately, *U-805* was sunk by U.S.S. *Sirago* on February 8, 1946, some 40 miles northeast of Provincetown.[8] On February 4, a Navy yard tug brought *U-805* to Lower Portsmouth Harbor. U.S.S. *Sirago* left New London on the same day, heading for Provincetown. Between 3.18 p.m. and 10.58 p.m. on the 5th, the submarine rescue-vessel U.S.S. *Penguin*, ASR 12, set off with *U-805* in tow for Provincetown, but was ordered back, and so returned to the Portsmouth. Finally, at 6.37 p.m. on February 7, the U.S.S. *Penguin* with *U-805* in tow, set off for the execution site, following which the German and American submarines made the rendezvous.[9] At 8.46 a.m. on the 8th, *U-805* was cast off. At 9.59 a.m., the *Sirago* missed with a torpedo that passed beneath the U-boat. The same happened with the second torpedo. A third projectile struck home at 10.29 a.m., breaking the U-boat's back. A fourth torpedo was redundant, inasmuch as it passed over the spot where *U-805* had been, parting empty water.

Bernadelli was born in 1908 and lived until 1986 and the age of seventy-seven. Though he sank no ships during his career, he earned the Iron Cross 1st and Iron Cross 2nd Class as well as the Fleet War Badge.[10] A member of the Crew of 1932, he was initially a watch officer on the heavy cruiser *Admiral Hipper* up to March 1943, when he joined U-boats. After training in the 23rd U-boat Flotilla up to December 1943, he worked up *U-805* and commissioned her. Bernadelli commanded *U-805* from February 1944 until the capitulation. Detained as a PoW in the U.S., he is believed to have spent time at Fort Devens and was freed on March 7, 1946.

Kapitänleutnant Friedrich (Fritz) Steinhoff's *U-873* was escorted into New England by the U.S. Navy to enable her surrender at Portsmouth on May 17, 1945, two days after *U-805* under Bernadelli had done so. *U-873* sailed from Kristiansand on March 30 and was proceeding to an assigned operations area in the Caribbean Sea. On May 9, her crew gave themselves the option of surrendering in Gibraltar and the U.S., deciding to motor southwest to the Americas while Steinhoff decided. Then on the 11th, they surfaced, sent their position, and were instructed to make for Bermuda, even though they had originally been closer to the Azores.

The following day, U.S.S. *Vance* broke off from escorting convoy UGS 90 to escort *U-873* to Cape May. After a diversion toward Casco Bay, they altered course once again, and were sent to anchor in Portsmouth's Lower Harbor. The 1,600-mile passage from the Azores took place in heavy seas and lasted five-and-a-half days before the U-boat reached Portsmouth on May 16.[11] Early that morning, U.S.S. *Vance* was met in Portsmouth by U.S.C.G.C. *Argo*, with a particularly scrappy skipper, who descended on the duo from Kittery, just upstream. There was a clash of cultures between the German officers, whose demeanor the shoreside and tug personnel in Portsmouth took umbrage with.

At 1.41 p.m., the U.S.C.G.C. *Argo* called out from reduced commission in Chelsea, Massachusetts for over a year and came alongside *U-873* at Buoy Charlie to assist in mooring. Two minutes later, an armed guard from the base was placed aboard to replace prize crew. A few minutes after that, the submarine was secured to a Navy buoy, and by 3.05 p.m. *U-873* was berthed alongside at

Friedrich (Fritz) Steinhoff (right, light brown leather jacket) surrendering *U-873* in Portsmouth on May 16, 1945. They are about to step ashore from U.S.S. *Vance* in the U.S. for the first time and, according to one witness, call a press conference. He was dead by his own hand within days and buried in Massachusetts. His brother became a decorated scientist for the U.S. atomic program in the Cold War. (*U.S. Navy photo, public domain, c/o Joseph W. Haberkern, III, desausa.org/images2/uss_vance_capture/uss_vance_de_387_uboat_10.htm*)

the U.S. Navy base.[12] In an unusual twist for a captive, "Fritz Steinhoff, captain of the 305-foot U-boat 873, now already in harbor, announced that he would give a press conference soon."[13]

Steinhoff was born in 1909 and a member of the Crew of 1935. Before the war, he had been a seagoing officer in the commercial merchant marine, like his latter-day victims. At the time of surrender, he was thirty-five. From December 1939, he was a commander of the 4th Minesweeping Flotilla, and then of a coastal-defense group in Bergen to March 1941. From July to October 1941, Steinhoff served as watch officer aboard *U-96*, then in the 26th U-boat Flotilla's commander's course. He began workup for *U-511* in November and took over the boat in December 1941 for one year. From February 1943 to January 1944, he was on the staff of the 7th U-boat Flotilla, then began work-up for *U-873* in January 1944. Steinhoff sank two ships for 21,999 tons and damaged another for 8,773 tons. He was decorated with the Iron Cross 1st and Iron Cross 2nd Class, and the U-boat War Badge of 1939.[14]

Steinhoff and other officers were roughly interrogated, and then, contrary to the Geneva Conventions, were sent to the common jail in Boston, being goaded, ridiculed, and having trash thrown at them as they were marched through the streets.

> Steinhoff was interrogated at the Navy Yard on missile-launching equipment on U-boats. He had taken part in the submerged rocket-launching trials at Peenemunde in June 1942. This was in *U-511*. His brother was a scientist in rocket-development with the Luftwaffe. Ernst-August Wilhelm Steinhoff immigrated to the U.S. in November 1945 to assist American scientists with rocketry, was awarded by the U.S. government in 1958, and is in the International Space Hall of Fame.[15]

A few days after surrendering, Steinhoff committed suicide at Charles Street Jail in downtown Boston. He received the same sort of rough treatment as meted out to the men from *U-546* on the same subject, and probably by the same American interrogation team. Deeply angry and humiliated, the commanding officer smashed the glass on his watch, or sunglasses, which his captors had permitted him to keep. Then he cut his right wrist.[16]

The naval surgeon assigned to the U-boat, Dr. Karl Steinke, could not save him, so Steinhoff was taken to Massachusetts General Hospital, across the street. The suicide is said to have occurred in the morning, yet there is no time of death provided on the death certificate, which is rife with errors: it is dated May 19, 1946 (which is the wrong year), and says Steinhoff was a submarine captain but in the German Army, and about four words of text under cause of death are crossed over and illegible.[17]

It is understood that Steinhoff died either while being transported (his arrival was delayed) or that doctors on arrival allowed him to bleed to death on the operating table or gurney due to his having so recently been an enemy combatting, notwithstanding the Hippocratic Oath, whether intentionally or through negligence. Medical examiner W. J. Brickley ascribed the death simply to an "incised wound, right wrist." This clearly preventable incident cost the United States a valuable source of intelligence on submarine and sea-surface-to-shore ballistic missiles that were heavily employed during the Cold War.[18]

The handling of *U-873*'s people was so chaotic, shameful, and embarrassing that the highest naval official in the U.S., Admiral Ernest King, diverted his staff's attention to writing an investigative report condemning, among others, Jack Alberti. This was while operations against Japan were at their highest. The report was entitled, tellingly, "Irregularities Connected with the Handling of Surrendered German Submarines and Prisoners of War at the Navy Yard, Portsmouth—Investigation of." The report exposed captured subs, not yet stripped by intelligence personnel, left unguarded, emblems ripped from German uniforms while they were still being worn, then given to ordinary seamen, looting of subs as well as their personnel's belongings, and U.S. Navy sailors found asleep in various parts of German submarines, possibly as a result of raiding liquor cabinets therein.[19] Despite the scathing report, no U.S. officers were actually punished.

Throughout one report, phrases such as "flagrant disregard for orders," citations to the Geneva Conventions, "reprehensible" behavior, "supine attitude," and "dereliction of duty" by the Commandant of the base down, as well as drunkenness of sailors consistently appear. Private First-Class Solomon "Sol" Leventhal, described as a "husky marine," was offered the chance by civilian interrogator Alberti to hit Steinhoff in the head in his cell, and did so.[20]

Steinhoff is buried at Fort Devens, Worcester County, inland with nearly twenty other Axis soldiers, both German and Italian.[21] The list of notorious white-collar criminals (Madoff's minions) and terrorists (Boston Marathon bomber) who have served there since is extensive.[22] His crew was sent to Fort Meade, Maryland, and Camp McCain in Mississippi. *U-873* was given minor repairs and then utilized for limited trials up to early 1946. In March 1948, she was sold for scrap to Interstate Metals Corporation in New York. Extensive efforts along the New York and New Jersey waterfront as well as in contemporary business archives did not reveal details of her exact fate, the yard which broke her up, or the identity of the company or persons behind Interstate Metals (as in whether it was in fact a shell or straw company)—not even if she was cut up in the U.S., by whom or when.[23]

The fourth U-boat to arrive at Portsmouth was the Type-XB boat *U-234*, under *Kapitänleutnant* Johann-Heinrich Fehler, who reported its position mid-Atlantic on May 12, 1945. The patrol began in Kristiansand on April 16 then *U-234* passed between the Faroes and Iceland.[24] Fehler refused to believe, or countermanded, the May 4 "end hostilities" message. Once the men on *U-234* learned of the surrender, the two Japanese officers on board who were returning to Japan left a note on Fehler's table instructing him not to resuscitate them and wished the Germans well. After a polite wait, the Germans entered to find one of the Japanese men still alive; however, it was too late for him. Both suicides were buried at sea.[25]

A number of U.S. and Canadian warships were ordered to intercept *U-234* east of Flemish Cap, a seamount 50 miles east of St. John's. Fehler is known to have received the surrender order in the central North Atlantic on May 10, yet he defied the order and remained on a southerly heading for two days. After confirming that Steinhoff in *U-873* had surrendered, Fehler transmitted his position once on the 12th and headed for the U.S. coast. *U-234* finally confirmed its whereabouts two days later, and was intercepted that night by U.S.S. *Sutton*, which guided it toward the surrender rendezvous at Casco Bay during the night. A handover was effectuated at sea the following morning.

On the 15th, *U-234* was boarded by U.S. sailors including an armed guard. While the U.S. Navy crew was taking over, a sailor clumsily fired a German pistol inside the submarine, and the bullet hit another U.S. sailor in the lower back or buttocks. The sailor was taken off, with his fate variously reported as dead and fully recovered. Then subs and escort were ordered to motor toward the examination anchorage off Portsmouth, and motor past Casco Bay. The small convoy was amplified with the addition of two destroyer escorts; U.S.S. *Carter*, DE 112, and U.S.S. *Muir*, DE 770. The four arrived off Portsmouth on May 19.

As they neared Portsmouth, the prisoners were transferred to U.S.C.G.C. *Argo*, under command of Lieutenant Winslow, who took over at 8.51 a.m. His attitude toward the Germans was much harsher than the convivial camaraderie shown the Germans by the *Sutton*'s officers and men.[26] At 9.23 a.m., Winslow secured the submarine to a buoy in the lower harbor. They proceeded to the Portsmouth Navy Yard at around 11 a.m. A crowd was waiting, and so was a photogenic Winslow, a press-hungry, Joe-McCarthy-of-a-cutter-captain. Apparently to impress the swarm of reporters, Winslow had a visible argument with Fehler, who muttered that his men were being treated as gangsters. It worked. As the prisoners were disembarking in Portsmouth, Winslow yelled after Fehler 'That's what you are [gangsters]. Get the hell off my ship!' as he pointed to the gangway."[27]

Thus, the U.S. commander became a darling of the press despite such unorthodox conduct and the fact they had only been transferred ashore on his vessel for roughly three hours.[28] Parading prisoners for the purpose of public shaming contravenes the Geneva Conventions, to which the United States was and is an original signatory. By that point, such protocols were being largely ignored at Portsmouth, as noted in a later report and reprimand by the U.S. Navy.[29] The behavior seems more jarring when compared with the generally helpful provision of assistance given by U-boat commanders toward survivors in lifeboats off New England.

The major factors are the need to remember that the Germans could afford to be humanitarian after destroying Allied ships and killing many or even all of the crew, and secondly, the U.S. Navy and the U.S. public were not receiving reports of what was actually playing out offshore New England, with U-boat kindness rather than killings toward men in the water: they were receiving a very different, savage propaganda feed, and that information no doubt influenced their reaction toward the sailors. Being besieged by a fleet of enemy submarines for years was stressful for coastal residents, and some vented.

As the naval war began in New England, so it ended: with the real focus on defeating Japan. *U-234*'s supply mission to Japan and the cargo and personnel is unique, including as it did:

> Twelve passengers ... a German general, four German naval officers, civilian engineers and scientists and the two Japanese naval officers.... General Ulrich Kessler of the Luftwaffe, who was to take over Luftwaffe liaison duties in Tokyo; Kay Nieschling, a Naval Fleet Judge-Advocate was to rid the German diplomatic corps in Japan of the remnants of the Richard Sorge spy ring; Dr. Heinz

> Schlicke, a specialist in radar, infra-red, and countermeasures and director of the Naval Test-Fields in Kiel, and August Bringewalde, who was in charge of Me 262 production at Messerschmitt aircraft, and a close confidant of Willi Messerschmitt. He was accompanied by a colleague named Franz Ruf, who specialized in industrial machinery manufacturing.[30]

The Japanese passengers were Lieutenant-Commander Hideo Tomonaga of the Imperial Japanese Navy, a naval architect and submarine designer who had come to Germany in 1943 on the Japanese submarine I-29, and Lieutenant-Commander Shoji Genzo, an aircraft specialist and former naval *attaché*, returning to Japan.[31]

Fehler and other officers and men were taken to the Charles Street Jail in downtown Boston, like Steinhoff and his men from *U-873*. Again, interrogation was considered harsh, in part because of the valuable cargo and the high-ranking officers in board. The Messerschmitt engineers, for example, were intended to enable the Japanese to mass-produce Me 262 jet fighters to the detriment of U.S. and Allied forces. The unusual cargo included "drawings, arms, medical supplies, instruments, lead, mercury, caffeine, steels, optical glass and brass ... [half a] short-ton of uranium oxide stored in gold-lined cylinders," according to the inventory found on board *U-234* on May 19, 1945.[32] Despite rumor, there were no actual planes or plane parts aboard the submarine.

Fehler was born in 1910 in Berlin and a member of the Crew of 1936. Thirty-one when he surrendered, he lived until 1993 and the age eighty-two. Fehler served aboard the highly successful German merchant raider *Atlantis* under Bernard Rogge from December 1939 to December 1941, then joined Naval High Command North to March 1942. The next year, he was a group officer at the naval college, then joined U-boats in March 1943. He went through the commander's course in the 24th U-boat Flotilla. After workup from December 1943, he took command of *U-234* from March 1944 until the surrender.[33] Fehler was decorated with the Iron Cross 1st and Iron Cross 2nd Class as well as the Merchant Raider Badge (for leadership aboard the *Atlantis*) and the German Cross in Gold.

"News of *U-234*'s surrender with her high-ranking German passengers made it a major news event. Reporters swarmed over the Navy Yard and went to sea in a small boat for a look at the submarine."[34] The U.S. Navy explicitly forbade the press corps from interviewing *U-234* officers, men, and passengers specifically. This decision was based on signals intelligence intercepted from Germany on May 13 and is the only such injunction on a U-boat in New England. Fehler and his men were transferred among various PoW camps, including Fort Devens, Fort Hunt, Virginia, and Fort Meade, before returning to Europe, first to Brussels.[35] They were released during 1947.[36]

U-234 was of particular interest to her captors because she had been converted from a mine-laying U-boat into a transportation vessel between fall 1944 and spring 1945. Right away, in June 1945, it was recommended that *U-234* be "cleaned, inspected, and tested as necessary for underway operations, but only minimum preservative measures were to be taken." The Tripartite Naval Commission recommended that *U-234* receive a month of repairs. Starting on September 7, she was dry-docked in Portsmouth for ten days initially, yet remained there until mid-January 1946.

On January 17, 1946, *U-234* voyaged from Portsmouth to New London where on February 25, she performed sound surveys, followed a week or so later by diving trials, and the following week more tests for a sub-sea sound lab up to March 25 when it performed magnetic-ranging experiments. A week later, on April 2, *U-234* was returned to Portsmouth, where she was "placed out of service" on April 11. On May 28, the U.S. Navy requested to be advised when *U-234* and five other U-boats would be "ready for disposal." Cannibalization of her parts for other subs and uses continued steadily for over five months, until September 27, 1946, when the Chief of Naval Operation's declared *U-234* "ready for disposal" at Portsmouth.

In November 1947, more than fourteen months after she was considered stripped and ready for disposal, *U-234* jogged into Massachusetts Bay like a horse being led obediently to the knackers. First *U-234* and three other U-boats (*U-530*, *U-858*, and *U-889*) were towed to Provincetown by U.S.S. *Tringa* and U.S.S. *YTB 230*, arriving by November 19. The next day, the submarine U.S.S. *Greenfish*, S.S. 351, torpedoed and sank *U-234* some 40 miles northeast of Provincetown. *U-889* met her fate at the same general location and on the same day, *U-530* and *U-858* the day later. The convoy that had been six vessels returned to Portsmouth, pared down to two doughty ships, leaving no doubt which side won the Battle of the Atlantic.

The Type VIIC *U-977* never patrolled New England; however, it was sunk by her captors off Cape Cod following the war. *U-977* arrived at the Groton submarine base in New London on October 12, 1945, from Argentina under command of the U.S. Navy and escorted by the tug U.S.S. *Cherokee*, essentially as a metal PoW. The last U-boat to surrender, *U-977* was taken by *Oberleutnant zur See* Heinz Schäffer to Mar Del Plata, Argentina against standing orders, arriving on August 17, 1945. It was a mad escape of 108 days from Kristiansand to South America submerged almost the entire three months. The audacious dash was undertaken by a brazen young commander who published a book entitled *U-Boat 977—66 Tage unter Wasser* (sixty-six days underwater) in 1952 to debunk the many rumors around the voyage, the most persistent of which is the notion that they carried the German Führer aboard.

U-977 left Kiel on April 13 and arrived in Horten on the 20th. After nine days they repositioned to Kristiansand between April 30 and May 2 before making the lunge for the South Atlantic three days before the first order for U-boats to surrender and six days before the formal surrender. After the surrender, but before the voyage to Argentina, Schäffer deposited sixteen men who did not want to go (most of them married) to join him ashore via dinghy in Holsenöy, near Bergen. After sixty-six days submerged using their *Schnorchel*, they glided to a stop near the neutral, Spanish Cape Verde Islands for a swim, without contacting anyone. From then on, they headed more humanely on the surface. Proving that absurd rumors were not limited to either side, "Schäffer said his main reason was a German propaganda broadcast by Goebbels, which claimed that the Allies' Morgenthau Plan would turn Germany into a 'goat pasture' and that all German men would be 'enslaved and sterilized.'"[37] Other factors were fears of forced-labor and delayed repatriation of Germans after World War I, and the hope that Argentina's large German community might provide them with a new start there.

The trip was very stressful on the men—when seas closed the flap on the *Schnorchel* then air pressure ratcheted up, hurting their eardrums and potentially causing their noses to bleed. Schäffer ensured all torpedoes were kept on board, despite taking up living space, to avoid accusations he fired on Allied ships. Born in Berlin, Schäffer was aged twenty-one during this patrol and lived until 1979 and age fifty-seven. A member of the Crew of XII/1939, he served aboard *U-561* for sea trials 1941 to May 1942, then was 1st Watch Officer of *U-445*, and then U-AA in the 23rd U-boat Flotilla to December 1943. From November 1943 to December 1944, he commanded *U-148*. Having sunk no ships, Schäffer earned the Iron Cross 1st and Iron Cross 2nd Class and the U-boat War Badge of 1939.

On arrival in Argentina, the commanders of *U-530* and *U-977*—the only U-boats in the South Atlantic at the time—were accused of having sunk the 1907-built Brazilian naval cruiser *Bahia* off St. Peter and Paul Rocks on July 4, 1945. What really happened was that gunners practicing on kites towed behind the ship were allowed, by the removal of guard rails, to fire too low and set off depth charges on the stern, sinking the ship in three minutes. During the next four days before rescue, over 330 Brazilian naval sailors perished on equatorial conditions, with only roughly thirty-five survivors. Embarrassed and looking for someone to blame, the Allies singled out Schäffer and Wermuth, notwithstanding that *U-977* still had all its torpedoes (they blamed mines as a possible culprit). The officers and crew of both *U-977* and *U-530* were interrogated in Argentina then sent to the U.S. as PoWs (despite being captured months after the war with Germany ended), then, briefly, to the U.K. Schäffer was the last to be released, in late 1946 or 1947, roughly when the submarine was disposed of off Cape Cod.

Once in U.S. hands and despite breakdowns off Brazil, *U-977* was delivered under its own power to New London, where it arrived with U.S.S. *Cherokee* and *U-530* on October 12, 1945. It was taken over by the U.S. Navy as war prize, then re-purposed to tour seven U.S. East Coast ports in November and December 1945. Escorted by U.S.S. *Baker*, the pair left New London on November 5 and toured from the Hudson to the Potomac rivers, returning to New England on

December 13. On January 9, 1946, *U-977* was ordered taken from New London to Boston, where she arrived on the 16th and berthed at the Boston Shipyard. She was then cannibalized and "declared out of service and to be retained for explosive tests." By August 1, she was deemed "ready for disposal."

Three-and-a-half months later, the submarine U.S.S. *Atule*, S.S. 403, AGSS 403, boarded journalists in New London and on November 12, 1946, made their way toward Boston. Based on the Tripartite Naval Commission agreement between the U.K., Russia, and the U.S., the *Atule* was assigned to sink *U-977* on November 13, 1946. *U-977* was duly towed east from Boston Navy Yard to Provincetown by the yard tug U.S.S. *ATR 64*. At 11.19 a.m., U.S.S. *Atule* attacked using a "standard, steam-type torpedo" of the Mk 23 variety. The destruction was filmed from its victim, other ships, and the air. *U-977* rests 40 miles northeast of Provincetown. The *Atule* was a young submarine, commissioned in June 1944 and decommissioned on September 8, 1947. She was later recommissioned and served from 1951 to 1973. Sold to the Peruvian Navy, the sub was rammed and sunk off Callao by a Japanese fishing vessel in August 1988.

U-889 was surrendered in Shelburne on May 13, 1945, and later delivered by the Royal Canadian Navy to the U.S. Navy in Portsmouth on January 12, 1946. On May 8, 1945, *Kapitänleutnant* Friedrich Braeucker was ordered to surrender, and complied promptly by surfacing. He then proceeded to the nearest Allied port with a black flag of surrender flying. Two days later, on May 10, a Royal Canadian Air Force plane came upon *U-889* motoring on the surface at 10 knots and vectored the Canadian escort force W 6 to intercept, which it did within an hour. At first, Braeucker and his men were ordered to Bay Bulls, Newfoundland, then, the following day, the sub was assigned to H.M.C.S. *Inch Arran* and H.M.C.S. *Buckingham*, which escorted *U-889* into Shelburne. There Braeucker formally handed his boat over, with the Royal Canadian Navy boarding *U-889* on May 13.

Braeucker was born in Munich in 1919 and was a member of the Crew of 1937a and lived to the age of ninety-one. This was his only patrol and he sank no ships. He began his career to 1943 in torpedo boats and was the recipient of the Iron Cross 1st and Iron Cross 2nd Class and the Fast-Boat War Badge.[38] *U-889* was taken to Halifax on May 23 and on June 26 was commissioned into the Royal Canadian Navy (later back-dated to May 14). The Canadians utilized her for trials, initially keeping her in excellent condition. However, by the time the boat was delivered, its batteries had worn down and she was "in a generally non-operational condition." The U.S. Navy already had a similar U-boat (*U-858*) to experiment with, with no need of another. Even though it was accepted on January 17, 1946, *U-889* was soon taken out of service and remained moored at Portsmouth "for use as a potential source of spares until the cannibalization action was completed by September of 1946, and *U-889* was then ready for disposal" by the 27th of that month.

U-1228 being sunk by U.S.S. *Sirago* off Provincetown in November, a few years after the war. (*Courtesy of Derek Waller*)

U-339 surrendering in Canada, May 1945; it would end up in U.S. hands and be sunk off Provincetown within two years. (*Courtesy of Derek Waller*)

On November 20, 1947, the submarine U.S.S. *Flying Fish*, S.S. 229, was assigned to destroy *U-889* some 40 miles northeast of Provincetown; U.S.S. *Tringa* and U.S.S. *YTB 230* towed the inert German submarine to her destruction. *U-889* sank atop several compatriots: *U-530*, *U-858*, and *U-234*, all within thirty-six hours of each other. The *Flying Fish* was built at Portsmouth and commissioned there in December 1941. She received twelve battle stars before being decommissioned in 1954, being scrapped the following year.

U-530 patrolled between Halifax and New York in late April and early May 1945. Rather than surrender, her commander Wernmuth turned for South America. Her final patrol began in Horten on March 3 with orders to patrol off Halifax. In fact, although the log was destroyed and no daily positions were given, "finding little there, he [its commander, *Oberleutnant* Otto Wermuth] headed south to New York waters. From May 4 to 7, *U-530* fired nine torpedoes at Allied shipping off New York, but they all missed or malfunctioned." *U-530* transited New England by passing Cape Sable on or about April 20 and passed south of Montauk on or about April 25.[39]

Wermuth disregarded the surrender orders of May 6–8, defiantly heading for Argentina using its *Schnorchel*. Some of the young ensigns on board did not like the idea, but most of them agreed to go. They jettisoned five torpedoes overboard, and after two months arrived off Mar del Plata, Argentina on July 10, 1945. Wermuth surrendered at sea, the men were interned, and *U-530* was allocated to the U.S. Navy. Wermuth was born in 1920 and was a member of the Crew of X/1939. Twenty-four at the time of surrender, he served aboard the destroyer *Z3 Max Schultz*, *U-37*, *U-103*, and finally as commander of *U-853* before *U-530*. Along with the officers and men of *U-977* (which arrived in Argentina from Norway that August), *U-530* was accused of having sunk the Brazilian cruiser *Bahia* off Brazil on July 4, 1945, and they were imprisoned and interrogated in Argentina, the U.S., and the U.K. before being released in late 1946.

U-530 was shifted from Mar del Plata to Buenos Aires on July 28–29. After six weeks there, on September 11, *U-530*, *U-977* and the ocean-going tug U.S.S. *Cherokee*, ATF 66, departed Rio Santiago Naval Base bound for New England. Between September 16 and 20, the convoy visited Rio de Janeiro, then Port of Spain, Trinidad. Both submarines were required to repair their engines *en route*. While in Trinidad between October 2 and 5, the Allied Tripartite Naval Commission inspected the U-boats. The three vessels arrived in New London on October 12, 1945.

Thereafter the sub was touted to the American public. She and the destroyer-escort U.S.S. *Thomas*, DE 102, headed from New London on November 5 voyaging as far at the Texas-Mexico border before returning on December 22. A few weeks later, the U.S. Navy ordained *U-530* "out of service and to be retained for explosive tests." Along with *U-977*, she proceeded to Boston Navy Yard, arriving 18 January and deemed "ready for disposal" on September 27, 1946.

U-530 remained in Boston being scavenged from, for nearly two years, until November 1947.

The submarine U.S.S. *Toro*, S.S. 422, AGSS 422, had been in commission for three years when it was assigned to sink *U-530*. Begun in May 1944 at Portsmouth, she was commissioned in December then laid up in New London until May 1947. On November 21, 1947, the *Toro* fired the *coup de grâce* that struck *U-530* amidships, breaking its back 40 miles northeast of Provincetown. She rests with compatriots *U-234*, *U-858*, and *U-889*. *U-530* was the last German submarine sunk in New England. None of the hulls of seven German U-boats (*U-1228*, *U-805*, *U-977*, *U-530*, *U-234*, *U-889*, or *U-858*) have been pin-pointed or photographed in the over seventy years since. That was undoubtedly the U.S. Navy's intent, as the water is simply too deep. An experienced diver and longtime veteran of the National Oceanic and Atmospheric Administration (NOAA) observed:

> The area is deep enough to not be a concern for shipping traffic. Therefore, it is not a priority. It is not really an issue to keep recreational divers away. Not really an issue for pollution. Not really an issue for treasure-hunters. Not really a political issue, as these were war prizes, and there are no human remains. So, it's just an area that is sort of off-the-grid.[40]

20

Thirteen French and Italian Allied Submarines and Five German Cold War U-boats

During World War II, a hybrid fleet of cooperating Free French and Allied Italian submarines provided training and anti-submarine vessels to Allied navies in the Americas, from the Caribbean, Florida Keys, and Bermuda. Thirteen of them visited New London, Portsmouth, and Casco Bay for repairs rather than live-action training. Beginning in September 1943, they remained for two years. Submarine historian Mark Jones observed that "The French and Italian submarines were excellent for training purposes. Of heavy hull-construction, they could out-dive the older American R- and S-boats."[1] This was a symbiotic arrangement, as the U.S. Navy needed submarines while their own fleet waged a highly effective campaign to strangle maritime Japan, making those units loaned to them by French and Italians very timely. "Foreign submarines were vital to the U.S. Navy's anti-submarine training at a time when they faced a great shortage of modern submarines."[2] Given the delicate political situation and shifting alliances, the vessels were manned by their own French and Italian officers and men.

The Italians provided eight submarines and began their operational duties as decoys for U.S. aircraft and vessels out of Naval Operating Base (NOB) Bermuda:

> Italian submarines were always sent to Portsmouth ... to keep French and Italian submarines refitting at different bases, given the animosity of French naval personnel toward Italy. There were usually one or two Italian submarines at Portsmouth between July 1944 and September 1945.[3]

Evidently, pre-existing prejudices were not limited to adversaries.

The delivery route for these submarines was under Allied escort from Gibraltar to Bermuda, then to Portsmouth or New London for overhaul and "working up"[4] for a period of weeks. The presence of foreign-built subs in New England was not without mishap. The French *Amazone* ran aground at the Montauk Torpedo Testing Range in Fort Pond Bay, opposite Connecticut, on October 14, 1944, after its anchor chain snapped in a blow. No one was injured, there was no serious damage, and it was later towed back to New London by the tug U.S.S. *Sagamore*.[5] On May 12, 1945, just as several German U-boats were heading to Maine and Portsmouth to surrender, the Italian submarine *Goffredo Mameli* collided with the minesweeper U.S.S. *Jubilant*, AM 255, at Casco Bay, again with neither damages nor injury.[6]

The thirteen French and Italian submarines sailed in New England for a total of forty-four months. Seven French submarines called in New London for repairs as follows: the *Archimede* starting January 1944, the *Amazone* from October 1943, the *Le Glorieux* from July 1944, the *Argo* from April 1944, the *La Perle* from June 1944 for two weeks, the *Casabianca* from March 1945, and the *Le Centaure* for a month starting in December 1944.[7] Their greatest utility was in training exercises off Bermuda or further south, so their turnarounds were expedited.

Six Italian submarines (*sommergibili* in Italian) visited New London, Portsmouth, Casco Bay, and Portland, most of them escorted via the Cape Cod Canal. The *Enrico Dandalo* spent five months in New London and Portsmouth from October 1944 to March 1945. The *Tito Speri* was in Portsmouth from July to September 1944, and the *Goffredo Mameli* was a total of eight months in Portsmouth, Casco Bay, and New London from August 1944 to May 1945. The *Marea* spent six months between Portsmouth and New London from July 1944 to June 1945. The *Vortice* was nearly eight months between Portland, Casco Bay, and New London from June 1944 to January 1945. Lastly, the *Onice* was repaired in New London and Portsmouth between January and May 1945.

Keeping and maintaining European submarines was not cheap for the U.S. Navy. One can imagine the dismay or ire of New England yard workers on learning that their Allies had to be kept in separate bases to prevent fights breaking out between them. Three submarines which crossed to Bermuda without ever going north to New England were the French *Antiope*, which sailed to Key West, and the Italians *Giovanni da Procida* and *Atropo*, which both sailed for Guantanamo, then as far as Chile, by March 1945. The author interviewed an Italian prince who, as a young cadet on the *Atropo,* was permitted to run ashore on an uninhabited Bahamian beach during the passage. At least five Italian submarines had earlier been on hostile patrols to the Bahamas and Caribbean as part of the *Betasom* flotilla in early-to-mid-1942, sinking many ships.[8] Overall, "though using U.S. submarines would have been simpler, the foreign boats satisfactorily completed the assignments and thus made a valuable contribution to winning the Battle of the Atlantic."[9]

Through posturing and negotiating, brazen sub-grabs, and back room dealings by groups like the Tripartite Naval Commission, the U.S., U.K., and Russia repeatedly sent their emissaries to haggle over what was left of the *Kriegsmarine*'s most effective weapons: U-boats. Their behavior portended the Cold War ethos of keeping enemies close; Russia had utilized her submarines in the Baltic to achieve the highest death-rate ever in one attack when their S-13 under Lieutenant-Commander Alexander Marinesko sank the *Wilhelm Gustloff* in January 1945, which killed nearly 10,000 people fleeing the Red Army as part of Operation Hannibal, during which roughly 1,000 vessels moved 1.2 million Germans and their dependents from what is now Poland to Germany in fifteen weeks between mid-January and early May 1945.[10]

In contrast to the heroics and intrigue surrounding the capture of *U-505*, *U-1407* was rather more ignominiously pulled from the seafloor and shipped across the Atlantic on the deck of a ship. *U-2513* and *U-3008* were also whisked serendipitously across the ocean by the U.S., leaving Stalin to query Churchill about why the U.K. and U.S. were withholding German U-boat reparations from the Soviet Union. Though this study is concerned with the invasion of New England by German U-boats in time of war and the following four U-boats fall outside that immediate net, they did call in New England, and some of them left their bones there. Since future generations will find these wrecks in New England and, logically, want to know how they arrived there if not in time of war, they merit inclusion.

As a result of high-seas capture and stricter security, the capture of *U-505* was an exceptional achievement of seamanship, bravery, and connivance. *U-505* is the most famous German U-boat to tour New England waters. On June 4, 1944, the submarine was captured intact west of Africa by the U.S. Navy Task Group 22.3 under Captain Daniel V. Gallery aboard the U.S.S. *Guadalcanal*, CVE 60. By June 19, *U-505* was towed to Bermuda, where it was renamed U.S.S. *Nemo* and carefully studied in deep secrecy. After VE Day, the U.S. government proudly announced the capture of *U-505* and starting on 23 May began showing it in Philadelphia. From July 7 to January 1946, the sub returned to New London roughly a dozen times and toured New Haven, Portland, Boston, New Bedford, and Portsmouth, mostly raising money for war bonds but also undergoing repairs. It was (barely) able to survive several efforts to "retain her for explosive tests," or scrap her. With tenacious determination, Gallery and his brother, a man of the cloth, managed to have *U-505* moved to Chicago via the Great Lakes, where it is a jewel in the crown of the Museum of Science.[11]

Operation *Regenbogen* (Rainbow) was a quasi-official effort by U-boat commanders to scuttle their boats in May 1945 rather than have their enemies capture or them: twenty-three were sunk dashing from Germany to Norway, about 218 were scuttled, and more than 150 surrendered. Dönitz, who insisted U-boat records be preserved out of a sense of pride in their accomplishments, was torn between his loyalty to the Navy and leading the country he now led through the minefield of surrender and retribution. *U-1406* and *U-1407* were abandoned on orders by their commanders, *Oberleutnant zur See* Werner Klug and *Oberleutnant zur See* Horst Heitz on May 5 in Cuxhaven.

Two days later, *Oberleutnant* Gerhard Grumpelt, a passenger on a motor escort boat serving as guard ship, berthed alongside the U-boats at New Fishery Haven (*Neuer Fischereihafen*) in Cuxhaven, on his own initiative and against orders by Allies and Axis alike, snuck on board, opened the main flooding valves, vents, and conning towers of boat boats, thus sinking them. Within a year, Grumpelt was found guilty of a war crime and sentenced to seven years in prison, of which he served five. The sub was raised by the U.S. military and shipped from Kiel on the deck of the U.S.-flagged transport ship *Shoemaker*, arriving in Portsmouth on October 11, 1945. When estimates to make the sub operational rose to a million dollars *U-1406* was sold to private scrap-dealers in New York on May 18, 1948, and was broken up between June and December 1948.[12]

U-2513 surrendered in Horten on May 9, 1945, left Oslo on June 3 and arrived Lisahally, Northern Ireland, on June 9. That August, U.S.S. *Brant* escorted the sub to New London, in tandem with *U-3008*, arriving on the 25th. *U-2513* was refitted and used for training. Decommissioned in July 1949, she was towed to Key West in 1951 where, in October it was sunk during rocket tests by the destroyer U.S.S. *Robert A. Owens*.[13]

U-3008 departed Germany on its final war patrol on May 3, 1945. On the 11th, while still in the Baltic, it surrendered, arriving in Kiel on the 21st. The sub returned to Wilhelmshaven on June 2 and on June 21 left Germany for Lisahally, arriving in Northern Ireland on the 27th. Along with *U-2513*, *U-3008* was secretly whisked across the Atlantic under close escort by U.S.S. *Brant* and arrived in New London on August 25, 1945. Later moved to Portsmouth, she was decommissioned there on June 18, 1948. *U-3008* was subjected to various naval tests for the next four years. Then, in May 1952, demolition teams scuttled her. *U-3008*'s unusual career was not over, as its hull was then salvaged in the mainland U.S., and it was towed to the U.S. Navy base in Roosevelt Roads, Puerto Rico. Afterward, it was sold to Loudes Iron and Metal Company in September 1955. What was left of *U-3008* was broken up in Puerto Rico in January 1956.[14]

U-1105 was commissioned in April 1944, and her only commander, *Oberleutnant zur See* Hans-Joachim Schwarz, surrendered the submarine to the Royal Navy at Loch Eriboll, Scotland on May 10, 1945, as instructed. As the submarine was sheathed in a novel coat of rubber, the Allies at least initially were very interested to study the rubber's repellant effects. However, by the time the U.S. Navy and Royal Navy experimented with *U-1105*'s sonar-absorbing sheathing, it had been too poorly degraded. The Royal Navy passed *U-1105* to the U.S. and, after a difficult winter crossing, she arrived in Portsmouth on January 2, 1946.

Unsure what to do with her, the U.S. Navy sent samples of the rubber to laboratories at the Massachusetts Institute of Technology (MIT); they moved the sub next to MIT on February 14 to facilitate study. The U-boat remained in Boston's Charlestown Navy Yard until December 18 when it was relocated to the Mine Warfare Test Station in the Chesapeake Bay at Solomons, Maryland. *U-1105* then spent as much time submerged in shallow bays as above air, as she was experimented with often by demolition teams. She sank on September 29, 1948, then finally on September 19, 1949, off Piney Point, on the Potomac River near Washington, D.C. In the summer of 1985, the wreck was rediscovered and is now a dive preserve.[15]

Conclusion

The story of German U-boats in New England in World War II is one of jarring contrasts. Amateurs in the tens of thousands led a low-technology, timber, sinew, and skill effort to man thousands of little wooden ramparts and protect the American coast with a Coastal Picket Patrol. Though they may have achieved nothing, that was essentially more than their Navy accomplished in the region at that early stage. For most of the participants, New England was merely an area of transit rather than a final destination. It was a final lap of a slow, immensely long global voyage from Calcutta and Sydney via Cape Town, Panama, and Trinidad. It connected the hub of New York with the Halifax convoys, sending arrows into the Canadian quiver from which they were launched toward the U.K., many of them never making it. It was the cerebral cortex of a complex global spine of supply-chain logistics moving the essential matériel and personnel continuously required by a planet-consuming war.

The ratio or average success-rate of submarines in New England (seventy-three with thirty-eight attacks, for 52 percent hit rate) was equal to that of Bermuda (143 patrols, eighty ships attacked for 56 percent), but half that of the much larger Bahamas area (where 112 U-boat patrols sank 130 ships for 116 percent). Cape Cod, Nantucket Shoals, the currents of the Bay of Fundy, fog, and terrible New England winters nor'easters made navigation for both sides especially difficult, though the Murmansk Run and others were arguably worse. The U.S. had a channel through Cape Cod which the enemy could not access, yet they did not always use it: the *Atlantic States* and many others simply bypassed it, and it was blocked for months until someone decided to simply blow up the impediment.

A study of this nature must by necessity alternate between the larger picture (the macro, the grandiose), and the minutiae of daily survival and of the attackers as well. Though pipelines and populations, power supplies and patriotism, censorship and sensitivity of bowels to certain foods are covered, as well as airborne attack, sub-sea escapes, and much in between, few aspects of this story are as intrinsically representive of the struggle between Allied and Axis sailors, and between both groups of (mostly) men and their environments, than the sagas of individual lifeboats. Lifeboats are a topic only very rarely considered nowadays, in the context of tragedies like the *Deepwater Horizon* blowout (eleven killed, Gulf of Mexico, April 20, 2010) or the loss of the steamer *El Faro* in Hurricane Joaquin (thirty-three killed, off Bahamas on October 1, 2015), or the case of José Salvador Alvarenga who drifted in a small open boat for thirteen months from El Salvadoran to the Marshall Islands, landing on January 30, 2014.

A lifeboat can be a microcosm of the greater world, and indeed the war also: men in them were quick to recognize and encourage talent, but just as quickly prone to disappointment or despair, depending on how their needs were met and the overall situation was framed for them by leaders. Alfred Hitchcock realized the potential for pathos and empathy even in such a minimalist, austere setting by collaborating with John Steinbeck and hiring Tallulah Bankhead to mix in a spectrum of Allied sailors with German submariners. In 1944, he aired *Lifeboat*, which became a classic.

Sometimes, though, prejudices seeped into the boats like the water they sought to keep out. In verified history, this showed itself in subtle ways, such as British masters complaining to U.S. officials in Guantanamo or New Orleans that there was insufficient segregation between officers and "men," meaning non-officers, or the sailors whose pay was cut when forces beyond their control sank it, yet they were still expected to kowtow to authority, and upon whom the captains relied on to row the boats at all hours. In Bermuda, where officers were provided with access to private homes where fresh vegetables were delivered to their windows, white sailors went to the sailors' home and West Indians and those of color to the African Methodist Church. Senior merchant officers and engineers and other "essential" VIPs were flown back to New York, while regular sailors had to risk another dangerous sea passage, something they understandably dreaded.[1] In recent years, commendable progress has been made on databases and books on West Indian merchant mariners and servicemen, as well as African-American sailors, though not, so far as is known, for sailors from West Africa, the sub-contintent, or China.

In Halifax, survivors were turned away from military bases for improper uniforms, West Indians (and a German shepherd) from the *Wawaloam* were denied lodging until Captain Kenedy set them straight. Racism was discernable in the way other sailors referred to West Africans on *Mattawin*, and it was shown toward Europeans as well. Third Officer Reginald Johnson, twenty, of the *Thursobank* describes the day after they were sunk (March 23, 1942) in his lifeboat:

> I had trouble with the Chinese ratings, who seemed to be under the impression that the white men were going to claim all the food, and they announced their intention of throwing overboard all the white men from the boat. The situation became dangerous for a time; although the Chinese did not appear to have arms concealed anywhere, we were considerably outnumbered. However, with diplomacy, I managed to restore order, although there remained an undercurrent of dissatisfaction amongst the Chinese during the whole time we were in the boat. I reported their behavior to the Naval authorities at Halifax, but I do not think that any kind of disciplinary action was taken against them.[2]

The most obvious reason for insurrection was sheer numbers: the Chinese were twenty-five in number, the British nine, or just over 25 percent. Another factor may have been that the average age of the Chinese crew, one of whom was sixty-four years, was thirty-seven years, whereas, the average age of the British crew was twenty-seven (one was only fifteen and their leader was only twenty as Captain Ellis only put Johnson in charge of his starboard boat temporarily, then ending up going down with the *Thursobank*). Johnson said he last saw Ellis shining a torch on the boat; he did not go back because he had been ordered away by Ellis, another torpedo then struck, sinking the ship, and it was blowing a gale at night.

The Chinese were not "just" trimmers, but had a broad skill set: ten out of thirty-nine were firemen and stokers, the others were helmsmen (five quartermasters), one was bosun, with others spread among deck, galley, and pantry departments. They were a self-sustaining unit and often shared quarters separate from Europeans.[3] The authorities probably did not want to punish any groups of Chinese insurrectionists because they needed merchant sailors at that time so badly and Chinese on the essential link from Venezuela's Lake Maracaibo to the refineries in Aruba and Curaçao had earlier gone on strike rather than all be sunk by a concerted attack on their shallow, hard-to-replace specialty fleet by U-boats.

Regarding whether to abandon a solid lifeboat for a larger ship more susceptible to torpedoing, Second Officer Thomas in the *Peisander*'s boat four off Nantucket in May 1942 said, "I enquired of the crew if they wanted to be transferred. They unanimously agreed to stay with me. The master of the *Baron Semple* seemed surprised by my decision ... The survivors in the second boat also declined to be rescued." After topping up, they took their leave after having a cup of tea, rather like Drake as the Armada arrived in England in July 1588. It is noteworthy that officers Thomas and Brown in boat four and Wilson in the *Peisander*'s boat six allowed the men to effectively vote on their fates, and that each boat was permitted its own autonomy. This suggests a high degree of informality and is in contrast with the naval command and control method of always having and recognizing a "SOPA" (senior officer present afloat), or similar—in other words, a single decision maker whose word is binding on all present. The men's behavior may also be influenced by the custom of severing sailor's pay and benefits from the moment their ship was sunk, giving the men a sense that they no longer had a duty to the employer after said employer abrogated their duty to employees.

Regarding the chain of command aboard lifeboats, in most accounts, First Officer Brown is listed as being in charge of boat four, but Thomas, by writing the crew "agreed to stay with me," indicates he believed he was in charge, despite being out ranked by Brown, the SOPA. This, also is not unusual a lifeboat's command structure was often organic, reflexive, and informal: some were run like a gym class, with constant watches posted, stints at the oars, and each person involved in assigned tasks, broken by group activities like singing or swimming. Others devolved into almost mutinous, animalistic behavior, with all variants in between, depending on the management style, or lack thereof, of the leaders.

It was not uncommon for more senior officers, perhaps injured, sick, or overwhelmed, to be overshadowed, either insidiously or not, by younger sailors in the lifeboat. There is a massive gulf between the skill set required to manage over 100 people on a huge steel ship and those to navigate a 25-foot wooden sailing vessel 300–500 miles toward land while keeping afloat, moving, alive, and in fair spirits. As a result, there were often small-boat handlers (water-men, fishermen, American Field Service volunteers, yachtsmen, tug, and barge men) who knew more about small-boat-handling than their officers, and it showed. How the commander reacted—with encouragement or resentment—could influence the outcome of the voyages.

Those that embraced and harnessed the skills tended to survive. We will never hear the accounts of those than perished for failing to but it is well-known that often groups of boats entered a storm together, with only the best-manned one emerging alive. In life-and-death scenarios, men relied on brawn and not gold braid to guide them out. Pragmatism went a long way: Captain Jack Lapoint of the *Potlatch* survived being tangled with his ship as it sank, popping to the surface incapacitated with internal bleeding, broken ribs, and concussion. He immediately handed command to the mate until he could recover days later. Other masters effectively handed over control while keeping up appearances and being sure to give credit to the "real" sailors after they survived.

Turning down a rescue ship may not be as unusual as thought at first blush. Examples of lifeboats snubbing or being snubbed by rescuers, from Cuba to Canada offshore, include:

Captain Knut Bringedahl of the *O. A. Knudsen* to the *E. P. Theriault*, Abaco Bahamas, March 7, 1942

Captain Finn Rusti of the *Grenanger* said no to the *Almenara*, off Virgin Islands, April 12 1942.

Captain Richard Hocken, the *Pipestone County*, saw wreckage and sailed on, April 19, 1942.

Captain Ralph Williams of the *Vineland* saw Allied ship, it sped away, April 23, 1942.

Captain George Hazeleaf, the *Plow City* avoided *Peisander* boats only to be sunk, May 22, 1942.

Captain Norman Smith, the *Liverpool Packet*; rescuers feared they were Germans, May 31, 1942.

Captain Jack Lapoint of the *Potlatch* was avoided by the *Tysa* boat under Roggeveen, July 5, 1942.

Captain Louis Kenedy of the *Wawaloam* left the *Irish Rose* for H.M.S. *Campanula*, August 11, 1942.

Sometimes, so many boats arrived from different ships at the same port in the same time frame: groups from four ships a day in Bermuda, and three a day at other times in 1942; half a dozen or more a week in Bermuda the spring of 1942; three a week in Nassau, March 1942; survivors from four ships in a week in Newport; and thousands of Allied sailors landed, held in Trinidad, Guantanamo, Halifax at any given time.

Authorities became understandably confused. Thus, the fate of the *Potlatch* was conflated with those of other survivors from the *Anglo-Canadian*, the *Thomas McKean*, the *Tysa*, the *Willimantic*, and other ships that landed in tiny St. Martin, Dutch West Indies at the same general time. The Dutch governor had to insist that survivors of the *Tysa*—though Dutch—remained on the French side until his overwhelmed officials could process them.

There were other oddities, such as the boat from the *Cardonia* under Captain Gus Darnell landing on Tortuga, Haiti on March 10, 1942, only to be mistaken by locals for German invaders (not the only time such mistake was made). When survivors of the *Tysa* arrived on remote Dog Island north of Anguilla, they described the lighthouse keeper as an "Indian" living in a shed with his "squaw." The British wisely reimbursed local craft in their Caribbean colonies for rescuing Allied sailors, and also rewarded cargo salvage. As a result, numerous local craft (an informal Coastal Picket fleet of their own) scoured the Bahamas, Turks and Caicos, and the Caribbean for flotsam as well as survivors. Their home-built wooden sailing craft had such colorful names as the *Go-On*, the *Sparrow*, the *Content S.*, the *Monarch of Nassau*, the *Ena K.*, the *Autogo*, the *Vergemere IV*, the *Emily Conway*, the *The Sisters*, the *Manita*, the *Betsy R.*, and the *Flirt*. The little Allied tug *Letitia Porter* was sunk twice, without every serving the cause: on May 13, 1942, by Werner Hartenstein in *U-156* when he sank the mother ship carrying the tug, the *Koenjit*, then by Ulrich Gräf in *U-69* who found her bobbing unmanned in the Atlantic and sank her on June 5, 1942.

Impoverished islanders were creative with what they found, and several lifeboats were donated by grateful survivors: in Bermuda, one became the *Ralph,* after Captain John Ralph of the Canadian schooner *Helen Forsey*, gave it to

Gilbert Lamb, fisherman of Bermuda who towed them ashore on September 18, 1942. Captain Charles Roberts of the British tanker *Athelqueen* donated a boat to residents of Hope Town, Abaco, Bahamas after being sunk by the Italian submarine *Enrico Tazzoli* in March 1942. It was renamed the *Queen* and put to work ferrying freight to and from deeper-raft mail boats at anchor for years. Visitors to the Porcupine Club in Nassau sat in the gig hastily abandoned by the SMS *Karlsruhe* off the Bahamas in World War I. Captain Granville Bethel of Cherokee Sound, Abaco, salvaged a World War II lifeboat (likely from the *O. A. Knudsen*), renamed her the *Beluga* for her round whale-like bottom, and ferried mail and freight to the otherwise isolated settlement at Crossing Rocks. By contrast, Captain Norman Smith wanted to give the lifeboat from his ship the *Liverpool Packet* to the lobstermen of Seal Island who rescued and repatriated he and his men—coincidentally, his neighbors and friends; however, the parsimonious owners would not permit it.[4] It was just as odd that Captain Danielsen of the *Torvanger* was not fitted the lifeboats from the *Mattawin* by Captain Sweeney in Halifax on June 4, 1942.

As it is jarring to some, the idea of refuting aid proffered to distressed mariners needs to be put in context. One must view the risk of failure over a few day's voyage to the nearby coast as against the risk of failure over a month-long voyage to South Africa through waters largely dominated by an unseen enemy which had already effectively struck them.

> Most survivors ... would unhesitatingly have swapped the privations of a lifeboat voyage for the, perhaps illusory, safety and relative comfort of the *Baron Semple*, and thanked their lucky stars for the opportunity ... People who had spent day after day fruitlessly scanning the empty horizon for a rescue ship ... or vainly searching the empty skies for non-existent reconnaissance aircraft, would have found the decision of the *Peisander*'s crew utterly incredible, although one or two senior officers whose boats were picked up close to land sometimes expressed regret at being robbed of the professional satisfaction of reaching safety entirely by their own efforts.[5]

In many other cases, the skippers and their men were either so traumatized by being sunk by U-boats, felt so confident on being so close to shore, or, on a practical level, did not feel the lifeboats, food, bunks, and equipment on the rescuing vessel would be enough for their men, that they turned down the chance to be taken ashore.

A number of rescuing ships, including the *Torvanger*, rescued so many men from U-boat sinkings that they canceled their own voyages to head to shore out of a combination of necessity to land the newcomers and to avoid attack, sadly this did not save her and she was ultimately sunk as well. Many others like the *Havsten*, the *Tropic Star*, (irony of ironies) the *Baron Semple* herself (by *U-848* under Siegfried Rollmann on November 2, 1943), and the *Plow City* were indeed sunk themselves. The *Polyphemus* and many others were sunk after having rescued survivors from the *Norland*, and the *Tropic Star* fought off a U-boat attack with survivors of the *Pipestone County* on board. It was an odd time to be a seaman, particularly when the enemy sank a ship one day, provided survivors of the same ship supplies a few days later, and the same submarine, or one under a colleague, then sank the same poor wretches a second time before they made landfall. No wonder that men broke under that kind of sustained pressure, over not knowing anything except you might be next, again and again.

While the myriad extraordinary instances of hardship, danger, and bravery on all sides in the battles off New England have not been the subject of banner film treatment, documentary programs have done well depicting discoveries, human-interest and historical stories behind them to an engaged public. It has not always been that way. The *Port Nicholson*, like *U-853* at the hands of promoters in Connecticut, was used to perpetuate a fraud. The discovery of a fictional treasure-lode of 1.7 million ounces of platinum in her cargo manifest made international news, generating a frenzy of interest, amplified after investors lost millions to a failed salvor whose associate simply invented and doctored paperwork.[6]

The same hoaxers, who were offended to learn their partners had wiretapped conversations and resented being raided by the FBI, claimed to have found *U-233* in New England, even though the location its loss far east of Canada was well-documented by the two U.S. Navy destroyers (U.S.S. *Baker* under Hoffman and U.S.S. *Thomas* under Kellogg), which rammed and sank her on July 5, 1944, rescuing twenty-nine Germans off Nova Scotia who conclusively identified the boat. *Kapitänleutnant* Hans Steen had taken *U-233* from Norway on May 27, 1944, and lost thirty-two men when it was sunk.[7]

Experts describe the same salvor's 1993 claims of locating *U-1226* some 4 miles off Cape Cod, over 2,000 miles from where it last reported equipment malfunction, as "extremely doubtful."[8] The same confidence artists asserted the sub was on a shoal 41 feet deep, yet *U-1226* was a Type IX/C40 boat with a beam of over 22 feet (leaving less than 20 feet over it if on its side), and if the sub was sunk upright, it would actually stick out of the water by roughly 7 feet, perhaps more depending on tide, waves, and shifting sands. *U-1226* was 200 miles south of Iceland on October 28, 1944, when the salvor claims the sub was sunk by planes from Hyannis. Yet there is no mention in relevant air diaries of that date of attack on any U-boat in that area, just regular target practice by VT 10 and others at NAAF Hyannis for "torpedo training."[9] In fact, the Eastern Sea Frontier *Enemy Action Diary* emphatically states "no sinkings, attacks, contacts or sightings reported" on October 28, 1944.[10]

U-1226 under *Kapitänleutnant* August-Wilhelm Claussen could not possibly have motored it from Horten to Cape Cod from September 30 to October 28, and even had the Germans made it that far, the sub's assigned patrol area was Canada, not New England. It seems likely that, just before the internet made debunking such claims in seconds a reality, these individuals went through the lists of unaccounted U-boats, chose one, and made outlandish claims about finding it within sight of popular beaches. Given these frauds, it is less surprising that families of Germans killed aboard U-boats are wary of Allied historians purporting to know the fates of their loved ones.

The surprising aspect of this individual's frauds are not that he attempted them but rather that anyone believed him ever. It speaks, perhaps, to our enduring fascination with the relics of war, projecting proximity on them. The fact is that there really are ten German U-boats sunk, from as few as 8 miles east of Block Island (*U-853*), 70 miles south-southeast (*U-550*), 160 miles east of Cape Cod (*U-215*), and 40 miles from Cape Cod (*U-1228*, *U-805*, *U-977*, *U-530*, *U-234*, *U-889*, and *U-858*). Why people felt the need to invent two U-boat losses, when ten exist, is unknown.

While U-boats sinking ships in winter were heartless acts performed out of duty, so was the abandonment of forty-four German sailors from *U-550* by U.S. destroyer escorts. The resultant cadavers created snares for patrol boats in ensuring months, with each requiring at least two vessels, plus the allocation of multiple air and surface assets to destroy the *Pan Pennsylvania*, initially set ablaze by the very ships sent to protect it. The hunt for bodies from that incident led this author to a mass grave of Italian PoWs been killed by German rocket then an Allied skipper who had to seal their hold off to save his ship.[11] Graves of German and Italian sailors stretch from Long Island to Newport, where a skull had been pilfered from a war grave, to central Massachusetts. The odyssey of a German commander from surrender to common jail to a gravesite at the same place where notorious white-collar criminals are kept is an odd one. The same commander's brother rose to become a decorated scientist for the U.S. post-war. The radio operator from *U-1230*, Horst Haslau, had his ashes scattered over Frenchman's Bay, Maine, a playground for old-monied yachtsmen.

At the outset of war, when shipwrecked merchant mariners and gunners landed in New England, they were cared for by grassroots local organizations including churches, high schools, nurse-volunteers for the Red Cross, fishermen, auxiliary police, auxiliary foot patrols, and remote, small and isolated teams operating lighthouses on rocks of the Maine coast or windswept coasts of Nantucket. Later, towns and states developed better systems for caring for, transporting and hospitalizing victims, but by that time, it was largely too late, since the Germans tended to strike hardest at weak targets and move to other zones when defenses were hardened, as they eventually were with the arrival of new ships after 1943.

The irony was that between being sunk by Germans and landed in the U.S., Allied survivors were more likely to be taken care of by random U-boats in the area, then rescued Allied naval ships, the majority of which had been sent to the Pacific or Europe. The U.S. Navy and Coast Guard usually only got involved once the lifeboats had covered the most perilous portion of their voyage and made it close to shore. Once ashore, details of ship names and care of the crew were rarely shared by the Navy; even after the war, some information was only released piecemeal and for propaganda purposes. In other words, the organizations which did the least to rescue these sailors either buried the details from the public altogether or released it with the goal of giving themselves the most credit. Fortunately for public readership, because the U.S. was not fire-bombed like Europe, and did not destroy its records, most of the original records survived and are available for study, for a fee.

Due to the population density of New England, there were myriad false submarine sightings. Yet when creditable women witnessed German terrorists landing on Long Island and in Maine and reported it, they were ignored until it was too late and saboteurs had already infiltrated. The U.S. Navy's initial policy was essentially "see something, say nothing"—a form of "father knows best." This came from the very top, with Admiral King endorsing the mushroom theory of crew management: keep them in the dark and feed them muck: "Don't tell them anything. When it's over, tell them who won," was his reply regarding "a public relations strategy for the U.S. Navy in World War II."[12]

The saboteurs who landed in New England, Long Island and Fundy were not just Nazi spies, but in one case were American, and in all cases Germans who had lived in America. Despite his crowing, FBI boss J. Edgar Hoover only caught the men because some turned others in: all of them either surrendered or were surrendered. Rather than attack America, they were distracted and enticed by its freedoms; the temptation to lead the good life not available to them in totalitarian Germany and war-torn Europe. They all buried the tools of mass-destruction and fled into the arms of family, friends, or fleeting companions.

The U.S. Navy left an impressive trove of German U-boats' bones both near the shore and off-shore, most of them sunk near one another off Provincetown, yet the sites of intentionally sunk U-boats have been largely ignored and deemed out of bounds.[13] The presence of German, French, and Italian submarines (even including U.S., Dutch, and other subs) in New England during and after the war blurred the line between friend and foe, war and peace. The U.S. utilized naval assets of countries which had, under various regimes, fought with Germans against it, and were, at times, of indeterminate loyalty. Italian PoWs in the U.S. were divided into loyal or hostile, the French into Free French and Vichy French, the Norwegians were occupied by Germany, yet their irreplaceable merchant marine fleet and royal government in the U.K. were Allies, and loyal Americans of Japanese heritage were rounded up and plunked into deserts. The situation was always fluid, with the U.S. submarine *Dorado* and the French *Surcouf* likely sunk by friendly fire, with hundreds of other collisions resulting from blackout conditions on ships and shore and in convoys, and friendly fire incidents we may never know the full extent of. As sub-sea-exploration improves, answers to long-kept secrets will be revealed.

After VE Day, U-boats came to U.S. ports carrying officers and equipment for the Pacific theater or transited New England for South America after being ordered to surrender. By disobeying direct orders, these mavericks extended the war, providing conspiracy theorists with a vessel with which to fill their hopes, fears, and aspirations. These craft were brought back to the U.S., shown off, and then all but one of them destroyed. *U-505*, which was saved, became the economic engine of the Chicago museum which saved it. Getting the boats from Europe, from the grasp of erstwhile ally the Soviet Union, the British, Canadians and anyone else, led the U.S. to take extreme measures which in other circumstances might be considered outright theft. Some of the submarines were sold to impossible-to-trace shell companies with names like Interstate Metals, begging the question: whence did they travel? Who covered their tracks, and why?[14] Those of us separated from events by so much time forget the eagerness people and governments were to put the war behind, embrace and engage a future.

There are myriad ironies in these pages. Despite constructing and repairing submarines in Groton, Connecticut, is largely overlooked, since Long Island blankets it. After U-boat sailors were processed through Portsmouth, the U.S. Navy focused their ire and grilling on U.S. base personnel, not the Germans, reprimanding them for misconduct. French and Italian submariners had to be kept apart in the U.S., so that they would not fight—each other, something their U.S. hosts found baffling. A coastwise infrastructure of watching stations, including chapel-tops and lonely outcrops of land, became the stuff of local lore, with remnants still extant, like the U-boat bunkers of France which were finished before they could be destroyed by aerial bombs.[15] Five years later, New England was infiltrated by terrorists again, from Boston west, using the airways. This means that of the three major foreign attacks in the United States, two have been from the air, yet the ocean-borne one took by far the highest toll (50 percent more than Pearl Harbor, 30 percent more than 9/11). Rarely, though, does one hear talk of defending U.S. shores from submarine attack. The U.S. were gifted an intact U-boat, *U-202* off Amagansett in June 1942, which basically lay itself on an altar at their feet while they ignored it for hours. Yet the public's fascination with the saboteurs, and not their means of delivery means that few know the real back-story.

On a macro level, if it were not for Hitler siphoning off U-boats for Norway and the Mediterranean, more U-boats would have attacked the U.S. in early 1942. So, the British counter-intelligence teams that kept the German dictator off balance, believing Norway and the Med were constantly under threat, indirectly helped spare more carnage in New England. The impact on Britain's supply chain would have been felt even more acutely if Dönitz had prevailed on Hitler to release more boats to the U.S. from January to May 1942 when the lights finally went off, and the Germans began hunting elsewhere. The British felt the effects of Operation Drumbeat and Operation *Neuland* so sharply that Churchill decried the vulnerabilities they created. Only the need to keep the U.S. as Allies, overlain with diplomacy, caused him to bite his tongue. Besides, the bed was partially Britain's making, since they had bled the U.S. of so many destroyers under the Lend-Lease pact, and with Gallipoli and Singapore and having fled captivity by the Boers despite giving his own recognizance as an officer, Churchill had skeletons of his own.

There is little doubt that Admiral King, was (at the least) disliked by his Allies. C. L. Sulzberger, publisher of *The New York Times*, wrote that King "made enemies among ... the British brass," while J. W. Stilwell said he "almost climbed over the table at" Field Marshal Alan (Colonel Shrapnel) Brooke at the 1943 Casablanca Conference for suggesting King favored the Pacific over the Atlantic.[16] By deciphering their action as well as in action, some basic observations can be made about the U.S. Navy's at this time. Their own documentary evidence indicates that they kept their citizens, partners, even (i.e. Key West minefield) their own sailors in the dark; ignored the advice of British and Canadian Allies who were in a position to fix the problem; let local politicians defy them by keeping navigation and coastal lights on until too late; undermined competent sector-leaders with administrative tasks and ill-trained support; allowed amateurs like the Coastal Picket and Hemingway to distract from core mission; relegated much of the rescue, as well as search and destroy, work to the U.S. Coast Guard; and dismissed destroyers overseas day one, with little result yet tremendous cost to home-front.

The cumulative effect of this behavior was to undermine the public's perception of, and confidence in, the Navy as a combat-ready force, sentiments readily visible in local op-ed pieces as well as coast guard and naval analyses.

Yet, despite the drubbing they received by both the German *U-Bootwaffe*, their Allies like the bellicose Churchill, and the U.S. press, the U.S. Navy clawed their way out by finally following British lessons-learned, *vis-à-vis*: convoy and escort, closely coordinated between sectors and Allied navies, surface and air; utilizing and coordinating airborne assets more effectively and aggressively, including rescue; allowing Canadians to convoy into New England, and accepting Royal Navy ASW craft; integrating, adapting British and Canadian air groups, Italian and French submarines; clearing the Cape Cod Canal by whatever means necessary (blowing up the clogging ship); adapting, then perfecting, ever-evolving, new anti-submarine technology, surface and air; building massive numbers of new war and merchant ships (destroyers, Liberties, tankers); and developing and perfecting floating airborne cities in mid-Atlantic known as hunter-killer groups whose mission was to remain on station until VE Day, constantly destroying U-boats.

The innovative hunter-killer groups are truly the lasting credit of the U.S. Navy and its Allies, and that, more than anything, ended the attacks on New England at a crippling scale. They eliminated the U-tankers then waited for the rest of them to surface like whales or turtles out of air, to be detected, swarmed, and sunk. Had the Germans managed to perfect *Schnorchel* sooner, or submarine-to-air rockets, they might have had the terror-like impact that V-1 and V-2 rockets had over the U.K. The thinking was not isolated: the Italians, with leading expertise in the field, planned to penetrate New York Harbor with mini-subs early in the war, the Japanese did attack Pearl Harbor first with mini-subs, then floated fire bombs to mainland U.S., and the Allies lost Joseph Kennedy Jr. (the ambassador's son and future president's brother) in a suicidal exploding aircraft launched from Britain toward Europe as part of Operation Aphrodite in August 1944.[17]

Although the U.S. Navy admitted suppressing the truth about the loss of U.S.S. *Eagle 56*, they have been less forthcoming about the cause of loss U.S.S. *Turner* and where all of the dead were taken, or why they did not warn their shipmates about the Key West minefield or why the *Coimbra* survivors were said to have been taken to New York yet were not. Considering that the Battle of the Atlantic, the longest battle in the deadliest conflict ever, had millions of moving parts, a single-digit list of the unaccounted may seem small, and it is. The historical record now has 649 survival stories about those who made it to New England. Every few years more wrecks are identified, mapped, and explored, allowing us to determine how both U-boats and their victims sank.[18]

So, as the British are fond of saying, "truth will out." New England's victims cover a wide spectrum, from diminutive trawlers, to large man-powered schooners, a patrol boat built by Henry Ford, a passenger ship, and workaday steamers. The rescuers are just as diverse, with one of the most heroic, the *General Greene* later arrested by its erstwhile colleagues carrying drugs in the Caribbean, and others (the *Mary J. Landry*) rotting away behind rural homes near the New England coast.

While it may be faulted for not acting on what it learned in World War I and then from 1939 to early 1942, the U.S. Navy did learn from captured U-boats, incorporating design improvements post-war. They took their expertise in aircraft-carrier warfare in the Pacific and applied it to hunter-killer groups and closing the air gap between Europe and Canada. They are not likely to allow enemy craft to patrol to the entrance of their bases and sink ships such as the *Black Point* and the *Eagle 56* going forward, nor to be close enough to shore to land teams of saboteurs and sew mines. The Cold War provided extensive sub-sea defense experience to all sides. That being said, submarines continue to invade U.S. waters, carrying (for now at least, and so far as is known) drugs.

The United States left its northeastern flank exposed to German U-boats early in 1942 due to a number of factors: having effectively traded key destroyers to the U.K. for air bases, warship and merchant-ship production lagged a year behind, leaving just World War I-era equipment, and the U.S. Navy and the nation rushed off its resources to the Pacific first. Thousands of men and women (1,238 in

Bahamas, 1,061 in Bermuda, and 492 in New England, for 2,791 killed in action) and hundreds of Allied ships (130 in Bahamas, eighty around Bermuda, thirty-eight in New England, for 248) were lost in these regions of the North Atlantic because of these strategic errors.[19]

Despite the region's myriad universities, the Naval War College, and other research nodes, it is perhaps not surprising that the story of German U-boats in New England in either war has not been told, or at least widely read. The lack of a single huge passenger-ship fatality, the failure of the mines laid off Boston to explode, the loss of saboteur and mine-laden U-boats, and the destruction of almost all the final wave of terror-boats in the April–May 1945 time frame mean that, to many, area is not considered a battlefield of World War II. Censorship then sealed under red tape the heroics off Nantucket and Mt. Desert Rock and Nauset. Until now, comprehensive analyses of U-boat activity along Connecticut, Rhode Island, Massachusetts, New Hampshire, and Maine (from the prism of the U-boats themselves) had not been tabulated, parsed, and presented for scrutiny in book form.

As a result of improvisation and a can-do attitude by hard-bitten fishermen and charitable women's organizations, 649 men and women—friendly sailors—were plucked from freezing seas and deposited safely ashore in New England. A vibrant infrastructure supported by strong community ties rooted in hundreds of years, permitted swift hospitalization, transport, and repatriation of sailors and soldiers, enabling them to rejoin their units as well as their families. In the unfortunate cases where men were retrieved too late, friend and foe alike were buried with dignity, though the casting off of three British cadavers from the *Coimbra* and the abandonment of forty-three living sailors of *U-550* mars that record.

The evidence of all this activity—not just steel-on-steel but the pathos and humanity shown by Art Holmans toward the still-warm body of his son Sandy—is all there. Despite Albrecht Achilles in *U-161*, Captain Jensen, and the U.S., British, and Canadian military's efforts to prevent Sandy's death, each loss must also be seen in a wider perspective. Each tragedy was part of a war so global and pervasive in its reach that most people simply put their personal lives on hold until it was over. Those fortunate to have been spared the fate of three percent of the world's population, or roughly 60 million soldiers and civilians to have died, limped home ready to face the future.

In the final analysis, it is not the thirty-eight ships that were lost in New England waters to German submarines in World War II so much as the more than 10,000 Allied ships which made it through those waters safely.[20] That is the lasting legacy of the mission carried out by Allied servicemen. Just as the Germans knew theirs was a deadly game for both sides, so too were many lives lost in the Allied merchant marine, as the U.S. emerged from political isolation and phased into full-scale war.

Despite a sputtering and painful start, New Englanders pulled together and put their backs and their resources to outpacing the juggernaut of U-boat destruction. By eventually placing more ships on the water than U-boats could sink, the U.S. ultimately managed to win the Battle of New England which raged within sight of Point Judith, even after most German subs had surrendered. The records showing the bright with the dark are now open for inspection and discussion, like the periscope of a forgotten foe, come to remind the United States of its vulnerable underbelly.

Postscript

As soon as World War II ended, the U.S. Navy began implementing a defense strategy based on the severe lessons learned from the German invasion, then preparing itself for the Cold War ahead. U-boats utilized the continental shelf to access New England and the Atlantic Americas. Days after bombing Hiroshima and Nagasaki, President Truman "proclaimed that the resources on the continental shelf contiguous to the United States belonged to the United States." Not surprisingly, given the carnage and their recently demonstrated military might, no nation objected to the enlargement of an exclusive zone by the victors. The proclamation was later enshrined in international law by the United Nations as the Convention on the Continental Shelf.[1]

APPENDIX I

Patrols and Fates of Ninety German, Italian, and French U-boats and Submarines

#	U-Boat	Commander	Entered Region	Exited Region	Days	Rank at time	Date of Birth	Date of Death
1	*U-123*	Reinhard Hardegen	12/01/1942	15/01/1942	4	*Kapitänleutnant*	18/03/1913	09/06/2018
2	*U-125*	Ulrich Folkers	12/01/1942	22/01/1942	11	*Kapitänleutnant*	06/03/1915	06/05/1943
3	*U-109*	Heinrich Bleichrodt	17/01/1942	01/02/1942	12	*Kapitänleutnant*	21/10/1909	09/01/1977
4	*U-130*	Ernst Kals	20/01/1942	24/01/1942	5	*Korvettenkapitän*	02/08/1905	01/11/1979
5	*U-654*	Ludwig Forster	24/01/1942	27/01/1942	4	*Oberleutnant zur See*	09/10/1915	22/08/1942
6	*U-106*	Hermann Rasch	26/01/1942	29/01/1942	4	*Oberleutnant zur See*	26/08/1914	10/06/1974
7	*U-103*	Werner Winter	28/01/1942	08/02/1942	9	*Kapitänleutnant*	26/03/1912	09/09/1972
8	*U-107*	Harald Gelhaus	30/01/1942	03/02/1942	5	*Oberleutnant zur See*	24/07/1915	02/12/1997
9	*U-108*	Klaus Scholtz	02/02/1942	06/02/1942	5	*Korvettenkapitän*	22/03/1908	01/05/1987

10	*U-578*	Ernst-August Rehwinkel	22/02/1942	25/02/1942	5	*Korvettenkapitän*	30/10/1901	06/08/1942
11	*U-96*	Heinrich Lehmann-Willenbrock	25/02/1942	05/03/1942	9	*Kapitänleutnant*	11/12/1911	18/04/1986
12	*U-94*	Otto Ites	05/03/1942	09/03/1942	5	*Oberleutnant zur See*	05/02/1918	02/02/1982
13	*U-404*	Otto von Bülow	06/03/1942	12/03/1942	6	*Kapitänleutnant*	16/10/1911	05/01/2006
14	*U-588*	Victor Vogel	10/03/1942	13/03/1942	4	*Kapitänleutnant*	22/11/1912	31/07/1942
15	*U-71*	Walter Flachsenberg	16/03/1942	01/04/1942	9	*Kapitänleutnant*	26/10/1908	03/11/1994
16	*U-373*	Paul-Karl Loeser	19/03/1942	30/03/1942	11	*Kapitänleutnant*	26/04/1915	02/01/1987
17	*U-552*	Erich Topp	25/03/1942	30/03/1942	6	*Korvettenkapitän*	02/07/1914	26/12/2005
18	*U-754*	Hans Oestermann	27/03/1942	30/03/1942	4	*Kapitänleutnant*	19/05/1913	31/07/1942
19	*U-571*	Helmut Möhlmann	29/03/1942	04/04/1942	5	*Kapitänleutnant*	25/06/1913	12/04/1977
20	*U-203*	Rolf Mützelburg	03/04/1942	06/04/1942	4	*Kapitänleutnant*	23/06/1913	11/09/1942
21	*U-85*	Eberhard Greger	08/04/1942	10/04/1942	3	*Oberleutnant zur See*	15/09/1915	14/04/1942
22	*U-84*	Horst Uphoff	08/04/1942	11/04/1942	6	*Oberleutnant zur See*	03/10/1916	07/08/1943
23	*U-654*	Ludwig Forster	10/04/1942	14/04/1942	7	*Oberleutnant zur See*	09/10/1915	22/08/1942
24	*U-136*	Heinrich Zimmermann	12/04/1942	06/05/1942	8	*Kapitänleutnant*	21/01/1907	11/07/1942
25	*U-402*	Siegfried Freiherr von Forstner	17/04/1942	20/04/1942	4	*Korvettenkapitän*	19/09/1910	13/10/1943
26	*U-752*	Karl-Ernst Schroeter	20/04/1942	06/05/1942	7	*Kapitänleutnant*	03/12/1912	23/05/1943
27	*U-576*	Hans-Dieter Heinicke	20/04/1942	02/05/1942	13	*Kapitänleutnant*	18/05/1913	15/07/1942
28	*U-566*	Dietrich Borchert	01/05/1942	23/05/1942	23	*Kapitänleutnant*	28/02/1909	21/12/1990

29	*U-582*	Werner Schulte	07/05/1942	10/05/1942	4	*Kapitänleutnant*	07/11/1912	05/10/1942
30	*U-593*	Gerd Kelbling	08/05/1942	21/05/1942	13	*Kapitänleutnant*	12/06/1915	09/06/2005
31	*U-455*	Hans-Heinrich Giessler	10/05/1942	20/05/1942	10	*Kapitänleutnant*	12/01/1911	
32	*U-588*	Victor Vogel	11/05/1942	28/05/1942	17	*Kapitänleutnant*	22/11/1912	31/07/1942
33	*U-213*	Amelung von Varendorff	12/05/1942	06/06/1942	25	*Oberleutnant zur See*	20/12/1913	31/07/1942
34	*U-135*	Friedrich-Hermann Praetorius	17/05/1942	23/05/1942	7	*Kapitänleutnant*	28/02/1904	16/04/1956
35	*U-432*	Heinz-Otto Schultze	19/05/1942	15/06/1942	27	*Kapitänleutnant*	13/09/1915	25/11/1943
36	*U-553*	Karl Thurmann	25/05/1942	07/06/1942	13	*Kapitänleutnant*	04/09/1909	20/01/1943
37	*U-404*	Otto von Bülow	26/05/1942	03/07/1942	8	*Kapitänleutnant*	16/10/1911	05/01/2006
38	*U-578*	Ernst-August Rehwinkel	27/05/1942	09/06/1942	14	*Korvettenkapitän*	30/10/1901	06/08/1942
39	*U-653*	Gerhard Feiler	04/06/1942	06/06/1942	3	*Kapitänleutnant*	06/09/1909	15/01/1990
40	*U-701*	Horst Degen	07/06/1942	10/06/1942	4	*Kapitänleutnant*	19/07/1913	29/01/1996
41	*U-87*	Joachim Berger	08/06/1942	22/06/1942	14	*Kapitänleutnant*	23/06/1913	04/03/1943
42	*U-373*	Paul-Karl Loeser	08/06/1942	10/06/1942	3	*Kapitänleutnant*	26/04/1915	02/01/1987
43	*U-202*	Hans-Heinz Linder	11/06/1942	16/06/1942	6	*Korvettenkapitän*	11/02/1913	10/09/1944
44	*U-332*	Johannes Liebe	12/06/1942	21/06/1942	11	*Kapitänleutnant*	08/07/1913	18/10/1982
45	*U-89*	Dietrich Lohmann	01/07/1942	03/08/1942	16	*Korvettenkapitän*	12/10/1909	12/05/1943
46	*U-215*	Fritz Hoeckner	02/07/1942	03/07/1942	2	*Korvettenkapitän*	22/12/1912	03/07/1942

47	*U-754*	Hans Oestermann	25/07/1942	28/07/1942	4	*Kapitänleutnant*	19/05/1913	31/07/1942
48	*U-458*	Kurt Diggins	26/07/1942	29/07/1942	4	*Kapitänleutnant*	17/10/1912	01/03/2007
49	*U-132*	Ernst Vogelsang	30/07/1942	01/08/1942	3	*Kapitänleutnant*	31/08/1911	04/11/1942
50	*U-86*	Walter Schug	10/08/1942	19/08/1942	9	*Kapitänleutnant*	22/10/1910	29/11/1943
51	*U-455*	Hans-Heinrich Giessler	26/09/1942	29/09/1942	4	*Kapitänleutnant*	12/01/1911	
52	*U-608*	Rolf Struckmeier	06/11/1942	15/11/1942	8	*Kapitänleutnant*	27/07/1916	
53	*U-183*	Heinrich Schäfer	13/11/1942	16/11/1942	4	*Fregattenkapitän*	30/01/1907	08/01/1944
54	*U-161*	Albrecht Achilles	06/04/1943	19/05/1943	33	*Kapitänleutnant*	25/01/1914	27/09/1943
55	*U-174*	Wolfgang Grandefeld	22/04/1943	15822	5	*Oberleutnant zur See*	6252	27/04/1943
56	*U-190*	Max Wintermeyer	31/05/1943	06/07/1943	14	*Kapitänleutnant*	02/02/1914	04/05/1990
57	*U-230*	Paul Siegmann	02/08/1943	04/08/1943	3	*Kapitänleutnant*	24/05/1913	29/06/1990
58	*U-566*	Hans Hornkohl	07/08/1943	10/08/1943	4	*Kapitänleutnant*	07/04/1917	
59	*U-869*	Helmut Neuerburg	01/02/1944	09/02/1944	8	*Kapitänleutnant*	25/08/1917	11/02/1945
60	*U-550*	Klaus Hänert	09/04/1944	16/04/1944	7	*Kapitänleutnant*	01/02/1918	01/01/2003
61	*U-1222*	Heinz Bielfeld	23/05/1944	25/05/1944	3	*Kapitänleutnant*	30/08/1916	11/07/1944
62	*U-107*	Volker Simmermacher	12/06/1944	13/06/1944	2	*Kapitänleutnant*	01/02/1919	27/08/1999
63	*U-518*	Hans-Werner Offermann	16/09/1944	19/09/1944	4	*Oberleutnant zur See*	02/07/1921	22/04/1945
64	*U-1230*	Hans Hilbig	25/11/1944	20/12/1944	26	*Kapitänleutnant*	05/07/1917	11/06/2004

65	*U-866*	Peter Rogowsky	08/03/1945	12/03/1945	5	*Oberleutnant zur See*	10/06/2019	18/03/1945
66	*U-879*	Erwin Manchen	02/04/1945	09/04/1945	8	*Kapitänleutnant*	18/06/1918	30/04/1945
67	*U-857*	Rudolf Premauer	07/04/1945	11/04/1945	5	*Kapitänleutnant*	08/05/1945	30/04/1945
68	*U-853*	Helmut Frömsdorf	20/04/1945	05/05/1945	16	*Oberleutnant zur See*	26/03/1921	06/05/1945
69	*U-858*	Thilo Bode	07/05/1945	12/05/1945	6	*Kapitänleutnant*	19/02/1918	03/01/2014
70	*U-1228*	Friedrich-Wilhelm Marienfeld	10/05/1945	13/05/1945	4	*Oberleutnant zur See*	01/03/1920	26/08/1973
71	*U-805*	Richard Bernardelli	10/05/1945	15/05/1945	6	*Korvettenkapitän*	22/11/1908	21/02/1986
72	*U-873*	Friedrich Steinhoff	12/05/1945	16/05/1945	4	*Kapitänleutnant*	14/07/1909	19/05/1945
73	*U-234*	Johann-Heinrich Fehler	14/05/1945	19/05/1945	6	*Kapitänleutnant*	20/09/1910	15/05/1993
74	*U-977*	Heinz Schäffer	12/10/1945	13/11/1946		*Oberleutnant zur See*	28/04/1921	15/01/1979
75	*U-889*	Friedrich Braeucker	12/01/1946	20/11/1947		*Kapitänleutnant*	13/07/1919	05/11/2000
76	*U-530*	Otto Wermuth	04/05/1945	21/11/1947		*Oberleutnant*	20/07/1920	2011

APPENDIX II

One Naval and Thirty-Eight Merchant Victims

#	NAME	DATE	U-BOAT	CARGO	TYPE
1	*Norness*	14/01/1942	*U-123*	12,222 tons Admiralty oil	Motor tanker
2	*Alexandra Hoegh*	21/01/1942	*U-130*	12,000 tons crude oil	Motor tanker
3	*Thirlby*	23/01/1942	*U-109*	7,600 tons maize	Steamship
4	*Cayrú*	09/03/1942	*U-94*	cotton, cacao, cotton, leather	Steamship
5	*Ranja*	17/03/1942	*U-71*	Petroleum	Motor tanker
6	*Thursobank*	22/03/1942	*U-373*	7,839 tons general cargo	Motor ship
7	*Hertford*	29/03/1942	*U-571*	12,013 tons meat etc.	Steamship
8	*Nemanja*	08/04/1942	*U-84*	7,207 tons sugar	Steamship
9	*Pipestone County*	21/04/1942	*U576*	4,970 tons bauxite ore	Steamship
10	*West Imboden*	21/04/1942	*U-752*	7,357 tons general cargo	Steamship
11	*Taborfjell*	30/04/1942	*U-576*	2,200 tons sugar in 16,200 sacks, 70 tons chrome ore	Steamship
12	*Fort Qu'Appelle*	17/05/1942	*U-135*	9,200 tons general cargo, 500 tons acetone	Steamship

	LEFT	DESTINATION	FLAG	TONS	ALL	KIA	LIVED	NEW ENG.	WHERE FIRST LANDED
	New York	Halifax	Panama	9,577	41	2	39	39	Newport
	Caripito, Venezuela	Halifax	Norway	8,248	28	0	28	0	Shelbourne, NS
	New York	Halifax	U.K.	4,887	45	3	42	0	Halifax
	Rio de Janeiro via Para	New York	Brazil	5,152	89	53	36	6	New London, CT
	Houston	Halifax	Norway	6,355	34	34	0	0	(all lost at sea)
	New York	Cape Town	U.K.	5,575	56	30	26	0	Halifax
	Sydney, Aust.	Halifax	U.K.	10,923	62	4	58	0	Liverpool & Halifax
	San Pedro de Macoris, DR	Halifax	Yugoslavia	5,226	47	13	34	0	Halifax
	Trinidad	Boston	U.S.	5,102	46	0	46	23	Boston
	Durban	Boston	U.S.	5,751	35	0	35	35	Portland ME
	New York	Montreal	Norway	1,339	20	17	3	0	St. Johns, NB
	Kingston, Jamaica	Halifax	U.K.	7,127	47	13	34	0	Shelbourne, NS

13	*Peisander*	17/05/1942	*U-653*	6,590 tons of wheat, 97 tons tungsten, and wool	Motor ship	
14	*Skottland*	17/05/1942	*U-588*	Lumber	Steamship	
15	*Fort Binger*	18/05/1942	*U-588*	Ballast	Steamship	
16	*Norland*	20/05/1942	*U-108*	Ballast	Motor tanker	
17	*Plow City*	22/05/1942	*U-588*	4,971 tons bauxite ore	Steamship	
18	*Margot*	23/05/1942	*U-588*	5,500 tons military stores incl. aircraft parts, tanks, explosives, general cargo	Steamship	
19	*Zurichmoor*	23/05/1942	*U-432*	Ballast	Steamship	
20	*Polyphemus*	25/05/1942	*U-578*	5,936 tons of wheat, 790 tons wool	Motor ship	
21	*Liverpool Packet*	31/05/1942	*U-432*	1,945 tons U.S. Govt. stores	Steamship	
22	*Berganger*	02/06/1942	*U-578*	48,000 bags coffee, 1,000 bales linters, 1,138 liters sunflower seeds, hides	Motor ship	
23	*Mattawin*	02/06/1942	*U-553*	7,000 tons military stores	Motor ship	
24	*Aeolus*	03/06/1942	*U-432*	Fish	Fishing vessel	
25	*Ben and Josephine*	03/06/1942	*U-432*	Fish	Fishing vessel	
26	*Malayan Prince*	09/06/1942	*U-432*	General cargo	Motor ship	
27	*Lark*	13/06/1942	*U-107*	50 tons fish	Fishing vessel	
28	*Cherokee*	16/06/1942	*U-87*	Ballast - 350 tons sand	Steam passenger ship	
29	*Port Nicholson*	16/06/1942	*U-87*	1,600 auto parts, 4,000 tons military stores	Steamship	

Newcastle, Aust.	Liverpool via Panama	U.K.	6,225	61	0	61	61	Nantucket
New York	Sydney, NS	Norway	2,117	24	1	23	23	Boston
Belfast	New York	U.K.	5,671	61	1	60	0	Yarmouth, NS
Glasgow	Corpus Christi	Norway	8,134	48	0	48	8	New Bedford & Nantucket
Trinidad	New York	U.S.	3,282	31	1	30	30	New London, CT
New York	Cape Town, Egypt via Trinidad	U.K.	4,545	45	1	44	0	New York
Halifax	St. Thomas, USVI	U.K.	4,455	45	45	0	0	(all lost at sea)
Sydney, Aust.	Halifax	Dutch	6,269	80	15	65	26	New Bedford & Nantucket
New York	Halifax	Canada	1,188	21	2	19	0	Seal I., Cape Sable
Santos, Brazil	Boston	Norway	6,826	47	4	43	13	New Bedford, MA
New York	Cape Town	U.K.	6,919	71	0	71	39	Cape Cod, Nantucket, Boston, New Bedford
Gloucester, MA	Sea Island, NS	U.S.	41	6	0	6	6	Mt. Desert, ME
Gloucester, MA	Sea Island, NS	U.S.	102	8	0	8	8	Mt. Desert, ME
New York	Halifax	U.K.	8,593	40	0	40	0	(slightly damaged)
Le Havre Banks, NS	Boston	U.S.	148	27	0	27	27	Boston
Halifax	Boston	U.S.	5,896	169	86	83	83	Provincetown & Boston
Halifax	New York	U.K.	8,402	91	6	85	85	Boston

30	*Moldanger*	27/06/1942	*U-404*	8,700 tons salted hides, tallow, wool, veg. oil	Motor ship
31	*Alexander Macomb*	03/07/1942	*U-215*	9,000 tons military cargo, tanks, planes, explosives	Steamship
32	*Lucille M.*	25/07/1942	*U-89*	Fish	Fishing vessel
33	*Angelus*	19/05/1943	*U-161*	Molasses	Schooner
34	*Pan Pennsylvania*	16/04/1944	*U-550*	140,000 bbls 80 octane gasoline, aircraft on deck	Steam tanker
35	*Cornwallis*	03/12/1944	*U-1230*	Bagged sugar, molasses in barrels	Steamship
36	*Atlantic States*	05/04/1945	*U-879*	Ballast	Steam tanker
37	*Eagle 56*	23/04/1945	*U-853*	(no cargo - military ship)	Patrol craft
38	*Black Point*	05/05/1945	*U-853*	7,759 tons coal	Steamship

Buenos Aires	New York	Norway	6,827	44	14	30	0	Cape May, NJ
New York	Woods Hole, MA	U.S.	7,191	66	10	56	31	Woods Hole, MA
Yarmouth, NS	Fishing grounds	Canada	54	11	0	11	0	Shelbourne, NS
Barbados	Halifax	Canada	255	10	8	2	2	Portland, ME
New York	Barry, Wales	U.S.	11,017	81	25	56	0	Londonberry, Ireland
Sandwich, MA	St. John, NB	Canada	5,458	48	43	5	5	Rockland, ME
Boston	Las Piedras, Venezuela	U.S.	8,537	57	0	57	52	Boston
Patrol	Patrol	U.S.	625	62	49	13	13	Portland, ME
Newport News, VA	Weymouth, MA	U.S.	5,353	46	12	34	34	Point Judith & Newport
			199,392	1850	492	1358	649	16 ports in New Eng.

APPENDIX III

Sixteen Ports Where 649 Survivors Landed

#	What Ports	Landed	From Which Ships	Rescue Vessels
1	Boston, Massachusetts	268	*Mattawin* (20 on 6/2/42), *Port Nicholson* (85 on 6/16/42), *Skottland* (23 on 5/17/42), *Atlantic States* (52 on 4/5/45), *Cherokee* (38 on 6/16/42), *Lark* (27 on 6/13/42), *Pipestone County* (23 on 4/25/42)	U.S.S. *Guinevere*, U.S.C.G.C. *Esconaba*, H.M.S. *Halifax*, H.M.S. *Montgomery*, H.M.C.S. *Nanaimo*, F/V *O. K. Service IV*, *Tropic Star*
2	Newport, Rhode Island	160 (+2 KIA)	*Black Point* (15 on 5/5/42), *Norness* (39 on 1/14/42), *Peisander* (61 on 5/26/42), *Polyphemus* (23 on 5/7/42), *Mattawin* (19 on 6/2/42), *Norland* (3 on 5/7/42)	U.S.N. crash boat, U.S.C.G.C. *General Greene*, F/V *Malvina* D., U.S.C.G.C. *Argo*
3	Nantucket Harbor, Massachusetts	90	*Polyphemus* (7 on 5/6/42), *Peisander* (61 on 5/25/42), *Norland* (3 on 5/6/42), *Mattawin* (19 on 6/8/42)	U.S.C.G.C. *General Greene*, *CGR 37*, U.S.C.G. *3828*
4	Provincetown, Massachusetts	62	*Mattawin* (20 on 6/2/42), *Cherokee* (42 on 6/16/42),	S.S. *Norlago*
5	Portland, Maine	50	*West Imboden* (35 on 4/21/42), U.S.S. *Eagle 56* (13 on 4/23/45), *Angelus* (2 on 4/5/43)	U.S.S. *Turner*, U.S.S. *Bristol*, *Nantucket Lightship*, U.S.S. *Selfridge*
6	Madaket, Massachusetts	43	*Peisander* (43 on 5/25/42)	U.S.C.G. *3828*, *CGR 37*

7	New Bedford, Massachusetts	36	*Norland* (3 on 6/3/42), *Berganger* (13 on 6/2/42), *Polyphemus* (11 on 6/3/42), Norness (9 on 1/14/42)	F/V *Hunting-Sanford*, F/V *Alpha Estelle*, S.S. *Torvanger*
8	New London, Connecticut	36 (+1 KIA)	*Plow City* (30 on 5/22/42) *Cayrú* (6 on 3/10/42, 1 KIA)	U.S.S. *Sapphire*, Pyc 2, U.S.S. *Amc 202*
9	Woods Hole, Massachusetts	23	*Alexander Macomb* (23 on 7/3/42)	H.M.S. *Le Tigre*, FY 243
10	Nauset, Massachusetts	20	*Mattawin* (20 on 6/2/42)	self-rescued, then U.S.C.G. trucks, etc.
11	Point Judith, Rhode Island	19	*Black Point* (19 on 5/5/45)	S.S. *Karmen,* S.S. *Scandinavia*
12	Gloucester, Massachusetts	14	*Ben and Josephine* (8 on 6/3/42), *Aeolus* (6 on 6/3/42)	self-rescued in boats
13	Mt. Desert Rock, Maine	14	*Ben and Josephine* (8 on 6/3/42), *Aeolus* (6 on 6/3/42)	self-rescued in boats
14	Southwest Harbor, Maine	14	*Ben and Josephine* (8 on 6/3/42), *Aeolus* (6 on 6/3/42)	self-rescued in boats
15	Rockland, Maine	5	*Cornwallis* (5 on 12/3/44)	F/V *Ivy M.*, F/V *Notre Dame*
16	Brighton, Massachusetts	3	*Mattawin* (1 on 6/2/42)	by vehicle, three to hospital
	Totals: 16 ports, 5 states	649	Duplication of survivor numbers when the were landed in one port, then moved to another.	Over twenty-eight rescue boats

APPENDIX IV

Burial Locations of Eight U-boat Sailors

#	Found	Buried	Name & U-Boat	Where Buried	Found by
1	16-Apr-44	18-Apr-44	Heinrich Wenz, *U-550*	at sea, by U.S.S. *Joyce*	U.S.S. *Joyce* 16-Apr-44, died/wounds, buried at sea
2	05-May-44	06-May-44	Siegfried Zube, *U-550*	Farmingdale, LI, NY	CGR *3082* & U.S.S. *SC 985*, Tompkinsville NY
3	11-May-44	12-May-44	Wilhelm Flade, *U-550*	Farmingdale, LI, NY	CGR *1989* & U.S.S. *SC 1338*, Tompkinsville NY
4	06-May-44	17-May-44	Günther Heder, *U-550*	Newport, RI	U.S.S. *SC 630*, 16 May 1944, Newport RI
5	21-May-44	21-May-44	Body 5, *U-550*	at sea, by U.S.S. *PC 985*	CGR *3080*, U.S.S. *PC 98*, clothes sent to Office of Naval Intelligence in Washington, D.C., via NY
6	27-May-44	01-Jun-44	Body 6, *U-550*	at sea, by H.M.C.S. *St. Boniface* Massachusetts Bay	Blimp *K 26* & H.M.C.S. *St. Boniface*, command of A/LCdr John de la Fosse Frewer, RCNVR, for Halifax 1 June
7	19-May-45	24-May-45	Friedrich Steinhoff, *U-873*	Fort Devens, MA	Prison guards, Charles Street Jail, Boston, following (or during) suicide
8	06-May-45	24-Oct-60	Body 1, *U-853*	Newport, RI	Divers, confiscated, buried with military honors.

APPENDIX V

Fates of Ten U-boats Lost During and After the War

Sub No.	Date Sunk	Sunk by what Allied vessel	Region Sunk	Lat. / Long. Sunk	Date POW	How Surrendered
U-215	03-Jul-42	H.M.S. *Le Tigre*	East of Boston	41°48'N / 66°38'W	KIA	never surrendered
U-550	16-Apr-44	U.S.S. *Gandy*, U.S.S. *Joyce*, U.S.S. *Peterson*	70 nm SE of Nantucket	40°09'N / 69°44'W	POW and KIA mix	surrendered in battle
U-853	06-May-45	U.S.S. *Atherton*, U.S.S. *Moberly*	Block Island Sound	41°13'N / 71°27'W	KIA	never surrendered
U-1228	05-Feb-46	U.S.S. *Sirago*, S.S. 485	37 nm NE of Provincetown MA, in Gulf of Maine (see U-234), 600' of water	42°32'N / 69°37'W (Niestle says 42°30'N / 69°38'W)	17-May-45	surrendered Portsmouth NH
U-805	08-Feb-46	U.S.S. *Sirago*, S.S. 485	45 nm NE of Provincetown and 45 nm E of Gloucester in 850'	42°32'N / 69°27'W	15-May-45	surrendered Portsmouth NH
U-977	13-Nov-46	U.S.S. *Atule*, S.S. 403	45 nm NE of Provincetown and 45 nm E of Gloucester in 850'	42°33'N / 69°43'W	17-Aug-45	surrendered Argentina, motored to Boston 13 Nov. 1945

U-530	28-Nov-47	U.S.S. *Toro*, S.S. 422	40 nm NE of Cape Cod	42°39'N / 69°32'W	10-Jul-45	was taken to Argentina in 1945, towed to Boston MA
U-234	19-Nov-47	U.S.S. *Greenfish*, S.S. 351	40 nm NE Provincetown MA, in Gulf of Maine (see U-1228, U-889, same position), 600 feet	42°37'N / 69°33'W	19-May-45	surrendered Portsmouth NH 19 May 1945
U-889	20-Nov-47	U.S.S. *Flying Fish*, S.S. 229	off Cape Cod - same position as U-234	42°37'N / 69°33'W	13-May-45	surrendered Shelburne NS, transferred to NH 10 Jan. 1946
U-858	21-Nov-47	U.S.S. *Sirago*, S.S. 485	c. 40 nm off Cape Cod	42°31'N / 69°34'W	14-May-45	surrendered Lewes Delaware

Endnotes

Introduction

1. Command Relations, *Eastern Sea Frontier*, April 8, 1942, (on or after); fold3.com/image/295271188?terms=task%20group%201%5C.5%20ESF; Gannon, *Operation Drumbeat: The Dramatic True Story of Germany's First U-Boat Attacks Along the American Coast in World War II* (1990), p. 161; en.wikipedia.org/wiki/Eastern_Sea_Frontier.
2. en.wikipedia.org/wiki/Ernest_King.
3. Mason, Uboatarchive.net/ESF/ESFWarDiaryDec41APP3, en.wikipedia. org/wiki/Eastern _Sea_Frontier.
4. Uboat.net/men/hassler.
5. Gannon (1990), *op. cit.*, p. 416.
6. en.wikipedia.org/wiki/Pan-American_Security_Zone.
7. en.wikipedia.org/wiki/First_engagement_of_neutral_United_States_in_World_War_II_before_the_attack_on_Pearl_Harbor.
8. Uboat.net/allies/merchants/ship/872.
9. Mozolak, *New York Ships to Foreign Ports, 1939–1945* (2000); Janda.org: "*Isla de Tenerife*, Spain steamship built 1921, 5,115 tons, arrived N.Y. December 13, 1941, detained, proceeded outbound NY January 13, 1942; Mason, Uboatarchive.net/U-125/KTB125-3; Brown, *U-boat Assault on America* (2017), p. 159.
10. Offley, *The Burning Shore* (2014), p. 115.
11. Wiberg, *U-Boats in the Bahamas* (2016), vessel index for the Allied ships *Gulfland*, *Gulfbelle*, and *Republic*: "The *Gulfland* drifted until she grounded on top of tanker wreck S.S. *Republic*, which had been sunk on February 21, 1942, by a torpedo. After a few days, the *Gulfland* broke free and drifted until she grounded again. She continued to burn for 52 days and was declared a total loss on January 13, 1944." Navylog.navymemorial.org/gulfland. Meanwhile, that same week, "on 5 January 1942 the *Afrika Korps* received 55 tanks and new supplies and Rommel started planning a counterattack. On 21 January Rommel launched the attack. Caught by surprise by the *Afrika Korps*, the Allies lost over 110 tanks and other heavy equipment. The Axis forces retook Benghazi on 29 January and Timimi on 3 February," en.wikipedia.org/wiki/Erwin_Rommel, The National Archives (TNA),

Kew, U.K., Admiralty files (ADM), Trade Division, TD/139/1284, April 20, 1942, "S.S. *Coimbra*, Report of an Interview with the Chief Officer, Mr. W. L. Pinder."

12. *United States Army in World War II: United States Army Forces in Northern Ireland, Chronology*, "1942: 26 Jan. Initial increment of Magnet Force docks at Dufferin.... 34th Division." history.army.mil/reference/ireland/IreChr.htm, British Admiralty *War Diary, Home Commands*, 20.1.1942, reads: "Shipping and Convoys—contd.... A.T. 10 My 0359/19 Details of personnel and cargo loaded are as follows... Operation 'Magnet.' *Strathaird* and *Chateau Thierry* carrying American Military Personnel for Northern Ireland sailed from New York with Convoy A.T.10 and American escort on 15/1. 2. Request you sail three destroyers to M.O.M.P. [rendezvous] in position and at a time to be signaled later. After meeting they will escort above-mentioned ships to Belfast. 3. Remainder of convoy and escort will be proceeding to Iceland.... 6. Commodore of convoy is James Davis in *Chateau Thierry* 7. Available ships of 15th M.S.F. should mine-sweep...." fold3.com/image/301992183, details of all ships in Convoy A.T. 10 which carried the 4,000+ first Magnet contingent, Hague, Holdoway, Cooper, convoyweb.org.uk/at/index.html ?at.php?convoy=12!~atmain, they add that U.S.S. *Delta*, *Munargo* and *Borinquen* called at Iceland *en route*, and the U.S.S. *Charles F. Hughes* escorted from January 15–16. Operation Magnet, comprised of Convoy A.T. 10 and U.S. Navy Task Group 15 altogether comprised thirty-six ships: one aircraft carrier (U.S.S. *Wasp*), one battleship (U.S.S. *Texas*), three cruisers (two heavy, one light), eighteen destroyers, six merchant ships, four armed troop carriers, and three naval cargo and support ships. Four did not complete the entire mission due to engine trouble (U.S.A.T. *American Legion*) or diversion to Canada or Iceland (U.S.S. *Mayrant* and U.S.S. *Rowan* peeled off for Newfoundland with S.S. *Coimbra* survivors, then the transports U.S.S. *Delta*, U.S.S. *Borinquen* and U.S.S. *Munargo* called at Iceland on January 25, 1942. The only British ship was H.M.T.S. *Strathaird*. From largest to smallest the U.S. Navy ships were heavy cruisers U.S.S. *Quincy* and U.S.S. *Wichita*, cruiser U.S.S. *Tuscaloosa*, aircraft carrier U.S.S. *Wasp*, battleship U.S.S. *Texas*, repair ship U.S.S. *Delta*, armed troop carriers U.S.S. *Munargo*, U.S.S. *Chateau Thierry*, and eighteen destroyers of different ages and classes: *Charles F. Hughes*, *Eberle*, *Grayson*, *Gwin*, *Hilary P. Jones*, *Ingraham*, *Lansdale*, *Livermore*, *Ludlow*, *Mayrant*, *Meredith*, *Monssen*, *Roe*, *Rowan*, *Stack*, *Sterett*, *Trippe*, and *Wainwright*. The non-passenger merchant ships were S.S. *Barnett*, S.S. *Duchess of Athol*, S.S. *Betelgeuse*, S.S. *Neville*, S.S. *Ehresmann*, and S.S. *Athena*. U.S.S. *Almaack* was an attack cargo ship in the U.S. Navy, and the troop transport named U.S.A.T. *American Legion*. Thirty-six vessels engaged at varying times in this single convoy of 4,000 persons, trimmed from the 14,000 envisioned for it. That equates to about 110 delivered persons carried per ship. RMS *Queen Mary*, by contrast, sailed unescorted Boston to Sydney at the same time (January 16, 1942) and carried 8,398 troops with 905 crew—more than twice as many people, one a single ship, and with not a single naval escort. Skylighters.org/troopships/1942.html lists a dozen troop carriers, some merchant ships. Uboat.net/boats/patrols/patrol_3798, U-boat attacks on January 26, 1942: uboat.net/allies/merchants/search. For those unaware of the massive vacuum it left behind, the delivery of Magnet's freshly uniformed and photogenic soldiers far overshadowed the losses it caused, directly and otherwise, to the Allied cause on terrestrial and waterborne battlefields at that time. There are myriad images of Milburn Henke, one of them at oldmagazinearticles.com/WW2_US_34th_Infantry_Division

13. Blair, *Hitler's U-Boat War: The Hunters, 1939–1942* (1996), pp. 465–466; en.wikipedia.org/wiki/January _1942#January_26,_1942_(Monday), Breakdown

of Convoy AT 10: "Infantry Division (det[achment] of 109th Medical Battalion [136th Medical Regiment], det of 109th Quartermaster Battalion, Company "A" of 109th Engineer Combat Battalion, det of Military Police Platoon); det of 112th Engineer Combat Battalion; 10th Station Hospital; det of 63rd Signal Battalion, History.army.mil /reference/ireland/IRECHR, Convoyweb.org.uk/at/index.html?at.php?convoy=10!~atmain, for the specific contents Task Force 5, as in: 34th Infantry Division (Advance Command Post of Headquarters Company; 133rd Infantry Regiment less 2nd and 3rd Battalions, 151st Field Artillery Battalion); details from Skylighters.org/troopships/1942, Uboat.net/boats/patrols/patrol_3798; U-boat attacks on January 26, 1942: uboat.net/allies/merchants/search.

14. Hague, Holdoway, Cooper, et al., convoyweb.org.uk/at/index, Ww2db.com/other.php?other_id=44.
15. Gannon (1990), *op. cit.*, pp. 239–240.
16. Blair (1996), *op. cit.*, pp. 465–466.
17. Churchill had two incentives: correct a past tragedy and avoid a present one, with the same result: regain and retain ANZAC's allegiance going forward. The troopships were the *Felix Roussel*, the *Empress of Asia*, the *City of Canterbury*, the *Plancius*, the *Devonshire*, and the *Dunera* in convoy DM2 bound Durban to Malaya and BM12, from Bombay to Malaya. The *Empress of Asia* was badly bombed. Conditions on board were so poor that G. R. Rubin named his book on the episode *Durban 1942: A British Troopship Revolt* (London: Hambledon Press, 1992).
18. Uboat.net/allies/merchants/ship/1251; Hague, Holdoway, Cooper, et al., convoyweb.org.uk.
19. Brown (2017), *op. cit.*, p. 161.
20. *Ibid.*, p. 175.
21. Parker, *Running the Gauntlet: An Oral History of Canadian Merchant Seamen in World War II* (1994), p. 61, Chap. 2: Operation Drumbeat. Parker is passionate about the subject matter, in part since he has sat down with hundreds of Canadian merchant and naval sailors who faced death afloat in World War II, many of them multiple times. He goes on to p. 63 citing "from Boston to Key West, two hundred ships went down within ten miles of land," and U-boats "left five hundred ships, 2.5 million tons, littering the Atlantic seaboard, virtually within sight of land," which this author has not verified, thus withholds from the main text. Brown (2017), *op. cit.*, p. 183.
22. Offley (2018), "U-Boat Attacks Of World War II: 6 Months of Secret Terror in the Atlantic," New England Historical Society, newenglandhistoricalsociety.com/u-boat-attacks-of-world-war-ii-6-months-of-secret-terror-in-the-atlantic.
23. *The New York Times*, "Sinkings Indicated, 'Some Recent Visitors Will Never Enjoy Return Trip,' Says Spokesman. Asks silence by us all," January 24, 1942.
24. *Ibid.*
25. *The New York Times*, "Navy Strikes 'Strong Blows,' As U-Boats Continue Attacks," January 21, 1942.
26. *Ibid.*
27. *The New York Times*, "Sinkings Indicated, 'Some Recent Visitors Will Never Enjoy Return Trip,' Says Spokesman. Asks silence by us all," January 24, 1942.
28. *Lowell Sun*, "Kill the Water Rats," editorial June 19, 1942 (Lowell, Massachusetts).
29. *The New York Times*, "New U-Boat Victim Confirmed by Navy," January 17, 1942.
30. Admiral Montgomery, attributed to Reynolds, C., *Famous American Admirals* (Annapolis: Naval Institute Press, 1978), pp. 223–224; en.wikipedia.org/wiki/Alfred_E._ Montgomery, details of *Coimbra* rescues: Records of the Office of the Chief of Naval Operations, *Records Relating to Naval Activity During World War II, WWII Action and Operational Reports*. U.S.S. *Rowan* Action Reports, January 1942,

NARA, RG 24, Box 1381 (*Rowan*), Project #968133 [all], (War Diaries, RG 24, A1353, Stack 470, Row 35, Compartment 13, Shelf 7, U.S.S. *Rowan Action Reports*), U.S.S. *Rowan War Diaries*, January 1942, NARA, RG 38, Box 8151 (*Rowan*), (*War Diaries*, RG 38, Boxes 1391–1391A, Stack 370, Row 46, Compartment 13, Shelf 2, U.S.S. *Rowan* (DD 405), January 15, 1942, *War Diaries*), U.S.S. *Rowan Deck Logs*, January 1942, NARA, D.C., RG 38, Box 8151 (*Rowan*), (War Diaries, RG 38, A1353, Stack 370, Row 45, Compartment 12, Shelf 2, U.S.S. *Rowan* (DD 405), January 15, 1942, *Deck Logs*), [Includes cover letter from E. A. Montgomery, Chief of Staff, U.S.S. *Ranger* (flagship) dated February 11, 1942, File No. A16-3], U.S.S. *Mayrant Action Reports*, January 1942, NARA, RG 38, Box 1195, (*Mayrant*), (*War Diaries*, RG 38, A1353, Stack 370, Row 46, Compartment 09, Shelf 2, U.S.S. *Mayrant, Action Reports*), U.S.S. *Mayrant Action Reports*, January 1942, NARA, RG 38, Box 1195 (*Mayrant*), (*War Diaries*, RG 38, A1351, Stack 370, Row 45, Compartment 9, Shelf 1, U.S.S. *Mayrant, Action Reports*), U.S.S. *Mayrant Deck Logs*, January 1942, NARA, D.C., RG 24, Box 8151 (*Mayrant*), Project #968133 (War Diaries, RG 38, A1353, Stack 470, Row 34, Compartment 9, Shelf 6, U.S.S. *Mayrant* (DD 402), January 15, 1942, *Deck Logs*), *The New York Times*, "New U-Boat Victim Confirmed by Navy," January 17, 1942, The National Archives (TNA), Kew, U.K., Admiralty files (ADM), Trade Division, TD/139/1284, April 20, 1942, "S.S. *Coimbra*, Report of an Interview with the Chief Officer, Mr. W. L. Pinder."

31. *The New York Times*, "New U-Boat Victim Confirmed by Navy," January 17, 1942.
32. Radigan, Navsource.org/archives/05/405, U.S.S. *Rowan Action Reports*, Jan. 1942, NARA, RG 24, Box 1381 (*Rowan*); *The New York Times*, "New U-Boat Victim Confirmed by Navy," January 17, 1942.
33. *Gulf Sea Frontier War Diary*, Key West, Florida, April 20–27, 1942; fold3.com/image/268728936, Warsailors.com/singleships/gunvor, florida-keys-vacation.com/U.S.S-*Sturtevant*, shipwreckexpo.com/fkluckenbach, list of 17 U.S.S. *Sturtevant* victims at maritimequest.com/daily_event_archive/2008/04_apr/26_uss_sturtevant_dd240
34. ww2pacific.com/orion, Wiberg, *U-Boats in the Bahamas* (2016): The U.S. threw eighteen ships and two air squadrons to *protect German ships from the British navy* in 1939: more than they would deploy against the Germans in January, 1942. The 1939 U.S. fleet engaged in this operation included flush-deck destroyers U.S.S. *Borie*, DD 215, U.S.S. *Broome*, DD 210, U.S.S. *Lawrence*, DD 250, U.S.S. *King*, DD 242, U.S.S. *Truxton*, DD 229, U.S.S. *Cole*, DD 155, U.S.S. *Greer*, DD 145, U.S.S. *Ellis*, DD 154, U.S.S. *Schenck*, DD 159, U.S.S. *Jouett*, DD 396, U.S.S. *Benham*, DD 397, U.S.S. *Lea*, DD 118, U.S.S. *Philip*, DD 76, U.S.S. *Upshur*, DD 144, U.S.S. *Wichita*, CA 45 (heavy cruiser), U.S.S. *Tuscaloosa*, CA 37 (heavy cruiser), U.S.S. *Vincennes* (CA 44) (heavy cruiser), and U.S.S. *Twiggs*, DD 127. U.S. Navy patrol plane squadrons VP 33 and VP 51, formed in the Caribbean on Dec. 8, 1939. All U.S. units were based in Guantanamo Bay or Roosevelt Roads, Puerto Rico. Historycentral.com/navy/cruiser/Wichita. At least five Royal Navy ships deployed included H.M.S. *Hyperion*, H.M.A.S. *Perth* (Australian), H.M.S. *Caradoc*, H.M.S. *Orion* (light cruiser), and H.M.S. *Patella* (Royal Fleet Auxiliary, replenishment tanker seen off Fort Lauderdale).
35. Kolbicz (Uboat.net merchant ships editor), in email to author Feb. 25, 2018: "The problem is how to define 'U.S. waters' in the first place. Looking at a German naval map from this area I searched for U-boat attacks within the following area:

1. All attacks within grid CA, DA, DB, DC, DK, DO
2. All attacks within grid CB and DD, if they happened west of 60th meridian west
3. All attacks within grid BA, but only those in the Gulf of Maine
4. All attacks within grid DL, except south of narrowest part of Yucatan Channel

5. All attacks within grid DM, but only those north of Cuba
6. All attacks within grid DN, except south of narrowest part, Windward Passage

This area covers the whole U.S. East Coast, Gulf of Mexico, Bahamas, Bermuda and is limited to the east by the 60th meridian west. Our database shows 339 U-boat attacks within this zone, resulting in the loss of 290 ships (1,573,389 GRT) and damage to 49 more (351,777 GRT): # of attacks per year, followed by month (# of ships sunk/damaged)

316 attacks in 1942: Jan (20/1), Feb (30/1), Mar (47/6), Apr (48/10), May (49/13), Jun (47/7), Jul (23/4), Aug (7/2), Sep (1/0)

17 attacks in 1943: Mar (1/0), Apr (4/0), May (4/0), Jun (1/0), Jul (1/1), Aug (1/1), Sep (0/1), Dec (2/0)

3 attacks in 1944: Apr (1/0), Sep (0/1), Dec (1/0)

3 attacks in 1945: Apr (2/0) May (1/0)

Roughly half of them were U.S. vessels (162), 73 were British or Canadian and 37 Norwegian. Twenty-one were from other European countries, 37 from Central American countries and 9 from South American countries. Only 9 of the ships sunk were commissioned warships: U.S.S. *Atik*, H.M.S. *Bedfordshire*, *Cythera*, *Gannet*, *Jacob Jones*, H.M.S. *Kingston Ceylonite*, *Eagle* PE-56, *Plymouth* and U.S.S. YP-389. The biggest ships sunk were *Amerikaland* (15,355 GRT), *Ulysses* (14,647 GRT) and *William Rockefeller* (14,054 GRT).

Your estimate of the casualties is on point: *these 339 U-boat attacks resulted in the loss of 4,999 lives* (2,366 were aboard U.S. flagged vessels). The most casualties occurred in the sinking of *Lady Hawkins* (251), *Atik* (141), *Jacob Jones* (138), *Tacoma Star* (97) and *Plymouth* (95). There were no casualties in 77 of the attacks. Of course, these statistics only include ships attacked by German U-boats, a few attacks by Italian submarines happened in the area defined above and there were other wartime losses like ships straying into Allied defensive minefields, accidental explosions or collisions and groundings due to the blackout restrictions." Brown asserts that up to July 1942 some 367 Allied ships were sunk in the Americas, with 5,000 sailors killed, which would be a considerable overestimate, given there were nearly three more years of war ahead, Brown, *U-Boat Assault on America* (2017).

36. Blair (1996), *op. cit.*, Vol. I, *Appendix 5*, p. 777 and Blair, *Hitler's U-boat War: The Hunted, 1942–1945* (1998), Vol. II, p. 727.
37. Uboat.net/allies/merchants/crews/
38. Wiberg (2016), *op. cit.*, Appendices.
39. en.wikipedia.org/wiki/Cape_Cod_Canal.
40. en.wikipedia.org/wiki/Big_Inch.
41. Fold3.com/image/302120509?terms=Nantucket.
42. Uboat.net/allies/merchants/crews.
43. Uboat.net/allies/merchants.
44. *Gisborne New Zealand Herald*, January 15, 2015, nzherald.co.nz/nz/news/article.cfm?c_id=1andobjectid=11386999, "German submarine's secret WWII ship-sinking mission to NZ," Mallmann Showell, *U-Boats of the Second World War: Their Longest Voyages* (2014).
45. Brown (2017), *op. cit.*, p. 155, for *U-123* and New York film episode, see Blair (1996), *op. cit.*, p. 461, "*Bundesarchiv Bild* 101 II-MW-4006-20 Foto: Tölle 1942 January—February."
46. en.wikipedia.org/wiki/Norwegian_heavy_water_sabotage.
47. Parker (1994), *op. cit.*, p. 122, Ralph Kelly interview, Wiberg (2016), *op. cit.*, Part II, *Vineland*, pp. 168–176, interviews with Karen Ort, her father, *Vineland* survivor Erlin Conrad, and Turks and Caicos islanders in several communities.

48. Kahn, *The Codebreakers: The Comprehensive History of Secret Communications from Ancient Times to the Internet* (1996) for iterations of German and Allied signals intelligence, encryption, for German Raiders, German-navy.de/kriegsmarine/ships/auxcruiser.
49. d'Adamo, Regiamarina.net/detail_text_with_list.asp?nid=99andlid=1andcid=4.
50. White, *U Boat Tankers 1941–45: Submarine Suppliers to Atlantic Wolfpacks* (1998), Uboat.net/types/milkcows.
51. U.S. Naval Institute Press, Usni.org/magazines/navalhistory/2013-11/navys-escort-carrier-offensive.
52. Sheffield, *The Battle of the Atlantic: The U-Boat Peril*, March 30, 2011, bbc.co.uk/history/worldwars/wwtwo/battle_atlantic_01.
53. Kornblum, "Sea Hunters find deadly *U-215*," *USA Today*, July 21, 2017, features U-boat historian Kurson and diver Fletcher of *Sea Hunters*, in 2017, Tim Mulligan, NARA expert, named his 2011 book *Neither Sharks Nor Wolves: The Men of Nazi Germany's U-Boat Arm 1939–1945*, and a 2006 documentary series is named *U-boats, Hitler's Sharks*. Wolves were another analogy to U-boats; wolfpacks, lone wolves, predators, stalkers, etc.
54. en.wikipedia.org/wiki/French_submarine_*Surcouf*; Kurson, *Shadow Divers: The True Adventure of Two Americans Who Risked Everything to Solve one of the Last Mysteries of World War II* (2005).
55. "There was a coastal convoy system in operation during WWI. This system was from Newfoundland down to Florida. There was also a convoy system operating in the Caribbean as far west as Galveston. [In] just two years of WWI, 1917–1918, [they developed] a complete convoy system covering the Caribbean, North and South Atlantic, North Sea, Mediterranean as well as the Russian route. Quite remarkable." Email from convoy historian Tony Cooper, February 20, 2018.
56. en.wikipedia.org/wiki/BX_convoys.
57. Ibiblio.org/hyperwar/USCG/V1-Escorts/index, en.wikipedia.org/wiki/History_of_the_United _States_Coast_Guard#World_War_II.
58. The loss of the *Wilhelm Gustloff* in 1945 cost the lives of some 9,400 evacuees fleeing the Russians, German *Steuben* lost 3,508 lost, also to a Soviet sub, the *Principe Umberto* in 1916 lost 1,926 in World War I, the *Sultana* in 1866, while repatriating men from the American Civil War, killed over 1,800, the Royal Navy's *Lancastria*'s loss caused some 4,000 killed when it was bombed by the *Luftwaffe* in 1940. Roughly 30,000 Japanese, Dutch, Javanese, American, and other prisoners and slave laborers were sunk and killed by U.S. submarines from "hell ships" going to Japan in World War II. en.wikipedia.org/wiki/List_of_maritime_disasters_in_World_War_II.
59. en.wikipedia.org/wiki/SS_*Léopoldville*_(1929).
60. This study aims to parse the track of every U-boat as well as French and Italian training submarines that came to New England in World War II. To narrow the field down, a wide net was cast, first looking at every by German U-boats globally which met the minimum days to reach New England and return (all Italian or hostile French or Japanese subs were quickly eliminated). Every Allied ship which reported attacks in the area was studied; fortunately, time has winnowed out most of the false sightings. Then ships whose men rescued the crews of other ships cast into the sea by U-boats in the region were checked for a nexus to New Enland. The one Achilles heal to this methodology (or blind spot) is where (as with the *Cayrú*) a vessel with no other nexus to New England, which was sunk far away, still, due to the vagaries of voyages by other ships, had its surviving crew landed in New England, often with little or no fanfare, thus falling outside this research. The best way to avoid being blind-sided was to contact multiple

subject-matter-experts in the Americas and Europe, then peruse the massive troves of news articles, the day-to-day war diaries of the U.S. and U.K. navies where such landings were reported and required. Towns like Newport kept their own tallies of those landed and publish them after the war when censorship was lifted. The author does not know the weave of a net fine enough to efficiently catch every instance, yet presumes some occurred and did not make it to the press. The merchant mariners, from officers to engine wipers were highly valued on all sides, and were quickly flung back to the front lines. Those unfit to do so were given their own acronym: DBS for Distressed British Seaman, with their own files under British Transport at The National Archives, File BT 381/3634, No. 168757. Many suffered symptoms of trauma and had to be allowed to remain ashore.

61. en.wikipedia.org/wiki/SM_U-53.
62. en.wikipedia.org/wiki/German_submarine_*Deutschland*.
63. Suhren and Brustat-Naval, *Ace of Aces: Memoirs of a U-Boat Rebel* (2006).
64. Klim, *Attack on Orleans* (2014); emails to author, March 2018; en.wikipedia.org/wiki/Attack_on_Orleans.
65. *The New York Times, Current History, The European War, Volume XVII* (New York: The New York Times Company, 1919); Brown (2017), *op. cit.*, p. 71.
66. Eastern Sea Frontier *War Diary*, Chapter 1, June 1942, *The Submarine Situation*, pp. 1–6, NARA, Fold3.com. *Kapitänleutnant* Horst Degen of *U-701*, and six of his crew who survived being sunk were also held in Fort Devens, from July 12, 1942, five days after they were sunk off Cape Hatteras; Mason, Uboatarchive.net/U-701A/U-701INT.
67. Jenness, *WWII Came Close to Nantucket*, May 21, 2015, *Yesterday's Island, Today's Nantucket*, yesterdaysisland.com/wwii-came-close-to-nantucket0520151234 and Jenness, *On this Day in Nantucket History* (2014).
68. Mooney, *Nantucket Only Yesterday* (2000), pp. 84–85. Mooney's father was police chief and his mother the head nurse on Nantucket, and he became an island attorney and historian (per interviews with Maurice Gibbs, eye-witness to events, when he and Robert were children).
69. In about 2000, the author was a yacht captain and called over at Nantucket for several days, where his older brother worked for Dennis and Wendy Metcalf at Nantucket Moorings. He was cycling along the coast and struck up a conversation with a young German family. An air vent from some underground tank near the beach was sticking up, so on a whim he told the German children that it was the periscope of a German U-boat that got lost in the war, and popped up under the island, and that ever since they had been fed and watered through that pipe. Though the parents were not amused, the children believed this story, and the seeds for telling this story were sewn.

Chapter 1

1. Mason, Uboatarchive.net/U-123/KTB123-7, *U-123* patrol seven diary.
2. Hickam, *Torpedo Junction* (1996), numerous references to *U-123* under Hardegen's famous first rattle of the drumbeat in January 1942. Also in Gannon, *Operation Drumbeat* (1990); Blair, *Hitler's U-boat War: The Hunters, 1939–1945* (1996) and *Hitler's U-Boat War: The Hunted, 1942–1945* (1998); Brown, *U-Boat Assault on America* (2017); Gentile, *The Fuhrer's U-Boats in American Waters* (2006); Offley, *The Burning Shore* (2014); and Hoyt, *U-Boats Offshore* (1985).
3. Mason, Uboatarchive.net/U-123/KTB123-7, *U-123* patrol seven diary.
4. Holm Lawson, Warsailors.com/singleships/norness. Where a Norwegian-flagged vessel is discussed, every detail has been verified by webmistress Siri Holm

Lawson. She grew up in a family dedicated to caring for Norwegian mariners in Brooklyn NY during and after World War II. Norway's depth of gratitude to her for her exacting detail on the website is such that the King personally recognized her contributions to the nation's history. If the subject or ship is at all Norwegian, Warsailors.com was consulted, and readers should also check it.

5. National Archives, *Survivor's Statements (1941–1942), Series: Papers of Vice Admiral Homer N. Wallin, compiled 1941–1974. Record Group 38: Records of the Office of the Chief of Naval Operations, 1875–2006 Entry P-13* (College Park: Textual Reference, Military, 1942–1945): the *Norness.*
6. Holm Lawson, Warsailors.com/singleships/norness.
7. Holm Lawson, Email, February 21, 2018: "In the book '*Tilbakeblikk,*' kindly sent to me by a 'warsailor' in Norway who was himself a gunner on Norwegian ships during the war, I've found some details in an article written by Able Seaman Peder Andersen which help clear up the confusion. In other words, it is the book that was sent to me by someone who was on Norwegian ships during the war (but he was not on *Norness* himself, the author was)."
8. Holm Lawson, Warsailors.com/singleships/norness.
9. Mason, Uboatarchive.net/U-125/KTB125-3, *U-125* patrol three diary.
10. Niestlé (2014), *op. cit.*; emails to author 2016–18.
11. Mason, Uboatarchive.net/U-130/KTB130-2, *U-130* patrol two diary.
12. Photo of the *Grand Marshal* in Provincetown in May 1936, provincetownhistoryproject.com/PDF/mun_000_1178a-scrapbook-4-subject-index.pdf. The caption is "United Fisheries, F/V *Grand Marshall* to be converted to dragging, '41 circa Larry Colby Photo (This vessel became Capt. Frank Rose's F/V *Spring Chicken*)." Thegloucesterilove.blogspot.capelleom/2009_06_01_archive. Posted by Ron Gilson on *The Gloucester I Love*, June 12, 2009. The *Grand Marshal* is to the right, photo June 7, 1941, before the *Alexandra Hoegh* rescue or the boat's renaming.
13. Mason, *Uboatarchive.net/U-587/KTB587-2, U-587* patrol two diary.
14. Holm Lawson, Warsailors.com/singleships/alexandrahoegh, the *Alexandra Hoegh.*
15. Dunne, *Thomas F. McManus and the American Fishing Schooners* (1970), citing *Grand Marshal.*
16. A Gloucester fisherman's history website, downtosea.com/1901-1925/strayfsh.
17. Holm Lawson, Warsailors.com/singleships/alexandrahoegh.
18. Uboat.net/allies/merchants/ships/1284, *The Allen Collection*, for images.
19. The National Archives (TNA), the *Thirlby*, TD/DEMS/139, ADM/199/2139 (London: Public Records Office, 1939–1945).
20. *Ibid.*
21. Mason, Uboatarchive.net/U-109/KTB109-4, *U-109* patrol four diary.

Chapter 2

1. Mason, Uboatarchive.net/U-654/KTB654-2, *U-654* patrol two diary.
2. Mason, Uboatarchive.net/U-106/KTB106-5, *U-106* patrol five diary.
3. Mason, Uboatarchive.net/U-103/KTB103-6, *U-103* patrol six diary.
4. Mason, Uboatarchive.net/U-107/KTB107-5, *U-107* patrol five diary.
5. fold3.com/image/270159996?terms=Nantucket.
6. Mason, Uboatarchive.net/U-108/KTB108-6, *U-108* patrol six diary.
7. Mason, Uboatarchive.net/U-578/KTB578-3, *U-578* patrol three diary.

Chapter 3

1. Brown, *U-Boat Assault on America* (2017), pp. 178–179.

2. Thompson, *The Navy Hunts the CGR 3070* (1944), pp. 2–3.
3. *Ibid.*, p. 3
4. en.wikipedia.org/wiki/SS_*Gulfamerica*: "Hardegen surfaced his boat to finish the stricken tanker. In doing so he realized that they were close to the highly illuminated and populated coast of Jacksonville, and that there was the risk that if he fired, shots that flew over the *Gulfamerica* could hit the shore, putting civilian lives at risk. He therefore navigated around the *Gulfamerica*, placing himself between the shore and the tanker, and ensuring that shots that missed would land in the sea. In doing so, he lost valuable time. The distress call was received, and *U-123* was later engaged by the destroyer U.S.S. *Dahlgren*. *U-123* was damaged, but able to make a narrow escape back to Europe. Hardegen survived the war, and returned to Jacksonville in 1990, where he was received as an honored guest. He would say of the occasion that 'The town was very friendly to me.'" Uboat.net/allies/merchants/ship/1523l, referenced in Gannon, *Operation Drumbeat* (1990). This attack is not to be confused with the *Gulftrade* sunk earlier by Hardegen to the north. Mayport is near Jacksonville, northeast Florida.
5. Parkinson, *Nowhere is Too Far* (1960), p. 154.
6. Coastguardmodeling.com/index.php/cg-history/world-war-ii/battle-of-the-north-atlantic/the-hooligan-navy.
7. Parkinso (1960), *op. cit.*, p. 154.
8. Mort, *The Hemingway Patrols* (2009).
9. Doane, C., July 1, 2015: *Lit Bits*: "*Hooligan Navy, Yachts on Sub Patrol*," wavetrain.net /lit-bits/677-hooligan-navy-sailing-yachts-on-sub-patrol-during-wwii, "One Corsair vessel, *Jay-Tee*, did however once come in actual physical contact with the enemy when a U-boat surfaced directly under it." Also "skipper Willard Lewis in his 38-foot cabin cruiser *Jay-Tee* was surprised when a U-boat began to surface directly beneath him, damaging the hull's planking."
10. Hickam (1996), pp. 229–230 (see Cremer's version for truth: the Germans make no mention of any boat: Cremer, *U-Boat Commander* (1984), pp. 74–76).
11. Mason, Uboatarchive.net/U-333/KTB333-2 (*U-333* diary, 5-6 May 1942: no mention of *Jay-Tee*); Cremer (1984), *op. cit.* (no mention of *Jay-Tee*).
12. Cremer (1984), *op. cit.*, p. 72.
13. *Ibid.*, p. 76
14. Rice, C., "The Submarine Chaser Training Center Downtown Miami's International Graduate School of Anti-Submarine Warfare During World War II," historymiamiarchives.org/pdfs/Tequesta2010-p5-58.pdf: "A U-boat surfaced alongside a Florida sport cruiser and its commander yelled in English to the pleasure boat's startled occupants that there was a war on and admonished them for their carefree attitude, "Get the hell out of here, you guys! Do you want to get hurt? Now scram!" Cited in Gleichauf, J. F., *Unsung Sailors: The Naval Armed Guard in World War II* (Annapolis: Naval Institute Press, 1990), p. 251; Hickam, *Torpedo Junction* (1996), pp. 213–216 and 229–230; Mellor, W. B., Jr., *Sank Same* (New York: Howell Soskin, 1944), pp. 161–163; Freitus, J. and A., *Florida: The War Years 1938–1945* (Stockton: Wind Canyon Publications, Inc., 1998), p. 70; Huettel, W. C., *U-Boats off Gulf Shore: A Short History of the German U-Boat Invasion in the Gulf of Mexico* (Hogtown Press, 1989), p. 7; Morison, *The Battle of the Atlantic, Vol. I* (1948), p. 130; and Gannon, *Operation Drumbeat* (1990), p. 354.
15. Thompson (1944), *op. cit.*, pp. vii and 32
16. De Quesada, *U.S. Coast Guard in World War II* (2010), p. 8.
17. Thompson (1944), *op. cit.*, p. vii; Larson, *Bravo-Zero* (2000), p. 20
18. Brown (2017), *op. cit.*, pp. 161 and 179. After over twenty crossings of the Gulf Stream in sail-boats as little as 39 feet, from New England and back, since 1989, the

author asserts that one does not easily just "dip into the Gulf Steam" to melt ice, and, logically, nor would doing that resolve the main issue: returning back to shore in the same icy conditions. Getting to and from the Gulf Stream from New England on a small sailing vessel in wintry weather is a voyage in itself, not a day-trip.

19. History of the *Irene Forsyte*, en.wikipedia.org/wiki/U.S.S_Irene_Forsyte_(IX-93).
20. *Ibid.*
21. Christy, G., "'Corsair Fleet': The Brave American Civilian Crews Who Took on WW2 Submarines to Protect the Coast," December 12, 2016, warhistoryonline.com/world-war-ii/when-a-ragtag-group-of-foolhardy-men-took-on-u-boats-with-sailing_ship-xl.
22. Interview, NY Yacht Club Commodore Henry (Harry) Anderson, Newport, Fall, 2017. He said that on return from fighting in the artillery with General Patton in Europe, several servicemen in Newport complained to him about the myriad wartime reports of U-boats off Castle Hill Light. In truth, they were just cormorants mistaken for periscopes. Mason email, Jan. 16, 2018: part of the "fog of war" effect borne in part of pressure and stress, *Montoro/Epperson Mission*, debunking a claim for B 25 bomber of 17th Bomber Group, 57th Bomb Wing from Columbia, South Carolina AAB, or 36th Street Airport, Miami believed to have sunk a U-boat off Florida between March and August 1942 (incident #310). Believed to be conjectural, certainly unconfirmed. No such U-boat was lost.
23. Christy, G., (2016) *op. cit.*, Uboat.net corroborates the account of *R. M. Parker Jr.*'s rescue; however, for CGR 355 to have recovered ordnance from *Benjamin Brewster*, in which twenty-five died, seems suicidal, as the ship grounded in 37 feet of water and "burned for nine days until the cargo was consumed. The structure above the water was reduced to a molten mass of metal by the intense heat and the tanker was a total loss. The wreck was salved in September 1951 and was broken up." Uboat.net/allies/merchants/ship/1917. Three crew and a naval guard were taken to Burrwood, Louisiana, on July 10, 1942, by a coast guard vessel, perhaps the author refers to that incident. A salient challenge about reading propaganda is trying to divine where the facts end and the fiction starts or *vice versa*. A good rule of thumb is: if any of it has been made up, assume that all it has been made up, or at least compromised.
24. *Ibid.*

Chapter 4

1. Mason, Uboatarchive.net/U-108/KTB108-6, *U-108* patrol six diary.
2. Holm Lawson, Warsailors.com/singleships/norland, see William Cohen's narrative.
3. National Archives, *Survivor's Statements (1941–1942), Series: Papers of Vice Admiral Homer N. Wallin, compiled 1941–1974. Record Group 38: Records of the Office of the Chief of Naval Operations, 1875–2006 Entry P-13* (College Park: Textual Reference, Military, 1942–1945): the *Norland.*
4. Holm Lawson, Warsailors.com, Cohen, letter of 7pp. recounting the *Norland* loss, survival, Warsailors.com/norships/wcohen1, p. 1.
5. *Ibid.*, p. 2.
6. National Archives, *Survivor's Statements (1941–1942)*: the *Norland*, Holm Lawson, *op. cit.*, p. 2.
7. Holm Lawson, *op. cit.*, p. 4
8. National Archives, *Survivor's Statements (1941–1942)*: the *Norland.*
9. Holm Lawson, Warsailors.com/singleships/norland.
10. Mason, Uboatarchive.net/U-578/KTB578-4, *U-578* patrol four diary, the *Polyphemus* attack, succeeded.

11. Mason, Uuboatarchive.net/U-578/KTB578-4, *U-578* patrol four diary, the *Berganger* attack, succeeded.
12. Mason, Uboatarchive.net/U-213/KTB213-2, *U-213* second patrol diary (the *Berganger* attack by *U-213*, failed eight hours in), Holm Lawson, Warsailors.com/singleships/berganger.
13. The *Mary J. Landry* was still fishing in 1957 when she ran over and sank another F/V, named *B and E*. leagle.com/decision/1960763281f2d4821674. Some 72 feet long and 16.5 feet wide, this stalwart vessel is believed to be afloat. Several calls to members of families believed to own or have owned her produced no definitive result.
14. Which the *Norland* men were in which the *Polyphemus* boat was diligently calculated by Rainer Kolbicz of Uboat.net using source materials, by Holm Lawson on Warsailors.com.
15. Mason, Uboatarchive.net/U-578/KTB578-4, *U-578* patrol four diary.
16. National Archives, *Survivor's Statements (1941–1942)*: the *Polyphemus*
17. *Survivors Landed by Port*, Appendix (below).
18. Mason, Uboatarchive.net/U-566/KTB566-5, *U-566* encounters the *Polyphemus*, the *Norland* men.
19. Holm Lawson, Warsailors.com/singleships/norland.
20. Mason, Uboatarchive.net/U-593/KTB593-2, *U-593* encounter with *Polyphemus* boat, Uboat.net/boats/patrols/u593.
21. United States Coast Guard, *The Coast Guard at War, Assistance XIV, Volume II* (1947), p. 164, National Archives, U.S. Coast Guard Log Books, U.S.C.G.C. *General Greene*, RG 26, Entry No. 159 D, Box/Item 54, Stack 12E1, Row 6, Compartment 16, Shelf 1, Box 54 (1942), *General Greene*.
22. Mooney, *Nantucket Only Yesterday* (2000), pp. 84–85. These were boat four and boat six from the *Peisander*, whose men stayed overnight at Nantucket, from May 24–25, 1942. All three *Peisander* boats eventually landed at Nantucket, but Captain Shaw's boat, Boat Two, did not land until late on the 5th.
23. *Survivors Landed by Port*, Appendix (below).
24. Nantucket, 1942 resources: Maurice Gibbs, eye-witness, President *Emeritus*, Nantucket Shipwreck and Lifesaving Museum, emails to author, April 27, 2018, Hoyt, *U-Boats Offshore* (1985) pp. 198–199, *Nantucket Inquirer and Mirror*, "Red Cross Notes," July 18, 1942, Nantucket Atheneum, free online archive, olivesoftware.com/Olive/APA/Nantucket/get/ image.ashx.png, Mooney (2000), p. 85, *The U.S. Coast Guard at War, Assistance, XIV*, Oct. 30, 1944, media.defense.gov/2017/ Jul/02/ 2001772332/-1/-1/0/USCGATWAR-ASSISTANCE.PDF, pp. 14–15 and 163–165, fold3.com/image/268360706?terms= general%20greene, *General Greene*, fold3.com/image/268360701?terms=peisander, references to *Peisander* in *Enemy Action Diary*, cgmix.uscg.mil/PSIX/PSIXSearch.aspx for old boat names, *Nantucket's Coast Guard Auxiliary*, fold3.com/image/267912101, *General Greene* back in patrol, fold3.com/image/268974962, *General Greene* arrived at Newport, fold3.com/image/267911868, fold3.com/image/267911860? terms=general%20 greene, Holm Lawson, photo showing actual *Norland* survivors, mixed in with those of the *Polyphemus* in a boat (they are almost home), c/o daughter of James Glover, p. 164, fold3.com/image/ 268360706?terms= general%20greene, Item 2, Uboat.net/allies/merchants/crews/ship1666 for crew list, Wrussellwebster.com/articles/madaket-millie-a-coast-guard-legend-on-nantucket, Madaket Millie biography, coast watcher and character, National Archives (TNA), Kew, U.K., Admiralty files (ADM), Trade Division, TD/139/1284, April 20, 1942, 2139 (London: Public Records Office, 1939–1945). All are cautioned to be vigilant due to the the ease of conflating so many lifeboats so close in time and geography.
25. National Archives, *Survivor's Statements (1941–1942)*: the *Norland*.

26. *Fitchburg Massachusetts Sentinel*, "Two More Ships Sunk in Atlantic, Navy Discloses," June 5, 1942.
27. Uboat.net/allies/merchants/crews/person/59957.
28. Various source materials on the *Norland*, the *Polyphemus* were drawn from U.K. and U.S. national archives (NARA and TNA), Holm Lawson/Warsailors, Uboat.net/Kolbicz analysis and correction. Mason, KTBs (U-boat war diaries), U.S.C.G. deck logs, local journalists, and U.S.C.G. officers, journalists in Newport, Red Cross volunteers, interviews with Maurice Gibbs, support from the Nantucket Historical Association, and Nantucket Atheneum. See endnotes in Chapter Nine, below for details of crews of the *Mattawin* and the *Peisander*.
29. *Newport* [Rhode Island] *Mercury*, "Red Cross Here Aided 130 Sub Survivors Here, Disaster Relief Committee Revealed. Outfitted Crews of Six Ships Torpedoed Off this Area by U-boats in 1942," September 28, 1945.
30. *Survivors Landed by Ports*, broken down by area and ship, Appendix (below).
31. Holm Lawson, Warsailors.com/singleships/berganger, National Archives, *Survivor's Statements (1941–1942)*: the *Berganger.*
32. Holm Lawson, *op. cit.*, National Archives, *Survivor's Statements*: *Berganger.*
33. *Ibid.*
34. Boat Database, boatdb.net, boatdb.net/boat/mary-j-landry-228042. In hurricane Carol in 1954, the *Mary J. Landry* was washed ashore under Skipper Restaurant in Fairhaven, opposite New Bedford, along with several other boats. southcoasttoday.com/article/19980830/ news/308309993
35. *Newport* [Rhode Island] *Mercury*, "Red Cross Here Aided 130 Sub Survivors Here, Disaster Relief Committee Revealed. Outfitted Crews of Six Ships Torpedoed Off this Area by U-boats in 1942," September 28, 1945.
36. Niestlé, *German U-boat Losses in World War Two* (2014).
37. Mason, Uboatarchive.net/U-96/KTB96-8, *U-96* patrol eight diary, Uboat.net/men/commanders.
38. *Ibid.*
39. Mason, Uboat.net/allies/merchants/ship/1414, *Cayrú*, sank off NY, landed New London.
40. Mason, Uboatarchive.net/U-404/KTB404-2, *U-404* patrol two diary, Uboat.net/men/commanders.
41. Mason, Uboatarchive.net/ESF/ESFWarDiaryMar42APP4, Eastern Sea Frontier *Enemy Action Diary*, March 1942, also at fold3.com.
42. Though initially found guilty and sentenced to thirty years, Claus von Bülow was acquitted by the Rhode Island Supreme Court. The trial became the basis of the film *Reversal of Fortune* in 1990. en.wikipedia.org/wiki/Claus_von_Bülow.

Chapter 5

1. Mason, Uboatarchive.net/U-588/KTB588-3, *U-588* patrol three diary.
2. Wynn, *U-Boat Operations of the Second World War* (1997), Vol. II, p. 59.
3. Mason, Uboatarchive.net/U-71/KTB71-5, *U-71* patrol five diary.
4. *Ibid.*
5. Wiberg, *U-Boats of Bermuda* (2017); Uboat.net/allies/merchants/ship/1459.
6. Wynn (1997), *op. cit.*, Vol. I, pp. 28 and 53.
7. Mason, Uboatarchive.net/U-71/KTB71-5, *U-71* patrol five diary.
8. Holm Lawson, Warsailors.com/singleships/*Ranja*, ship, people, movements; Hague, Holdoway, Cooper, et. al., convoyweb.uk.org: volunteer editor Tony Cooper provided detailed support, author visit.
9. National Archives, *Survivor's Statements (1941–1942)*: the *Ranja.*

10. Mason, Uboatarchive.net/U-373/KTB373-4, *U-373* patrol four diary.
11. The National Archives (TNA), *Thursobank*, TD/DEMS/139, ADM/199/2139 (London: Public Records Office, 1939–1945), Uboat.net/allies/merchants/ships/1463, wrecksite.eu/wreck.aspx?16857, Ship registry database at crwflags.com/fotw/flags/gb~hffl#fedrl, theshipslist.com/ships/lines/bank for history of Andrew Weir Line, Hague, Holdoway, Cooper, et. el., convoyweb.org.uk, *Thursobank*.
12. National Archives, *Survivor's Statements (1941–1942)*: the *Thursobank*.
13. Italian submarines (*sommergibili*), German–Italian joint flotilla named *BetaSom*, all covered in Regiamarina.net, by Cristiano D'Adamo, input to author by Platon Alexiades, 2010–18.
14. Holm Lawson, Warsailors.com/singleships/havsten, citing an article published in the Norwegian WWII circular *Krigsseileren* in 1998, by *Havsten*'s Second Mate Karl Niva. A guestbook entry for the *Havsten*'s pet cat reads in part "he was unable to tell his rescuers anything ... because he was a cat. He was found clinging to a small liferaft by the crew of the *Tazzoli*, and taken into the submarine. The crew made a great fuss of him during the remainder of their patrol, but when the submarine returned to her base at Bordeaux he went ashore and disappeared. I wonder how many cats now alive in Bordeaux can trace their ancestry back to this little war-weary vagabond? (from *Cdte*. Mario Rossetto, who was the *Tenente* (First Officer) of the *Tazzoli* at the time)." Regarding the head-count of *Thursobank*:

    Total on board the *Thursobank*: sixty-four before the attack (of which thirty-four survived, thirty killed): five Navy gunners; seven Army gunners; fourteen British/European merchant mariners; thirty-eight Chinese, or Asian, merchant mariners: total sixty-four on board.

    In lifeboat: one third officer, Reginald Johnson in charge; one third Engineer; one U.K. Apprentice (total three British merchant sailors); two Navy gunners; three Army gunners (total five gunners); twenty-six Chinese ratings: total thirty-four survivors.

    Killed, lost or missing (empty *Thursobank* boat found by U.S.S. *Greer*, April 27, 1942): three Naval gunners; four Army gunners (total seven gunners); eleven merchant sailors (including Capt. Ellis); twelve Chinese ratings (total twenty-three merchant sailors): total thirty killed or lost.

    Conclusion: There is a difference of three killed between the survivor's account (Johnson) which is consistent: sixty-one aboard, minus thirty-four known survivors, meaning twenty-seven K.I.A. However, the memorials state with equal clarity that thirty men were K.I.A. Ubootwaffe.net, as quoted in wrecksite.eu, asserts sixty-four persons were onboard, which resolves the issue, even though the original source materials are not clear.
15. Mason, Uboatarchive.net/U-552/KTB552-8; *U-552* patrol eight diary, Uboat.net, *U-552* pages; Niestlé, *German U-Boat Losses of World War Two* (2014).
16. U.S. Navy *Eastern Sea Frontier Diary*, in Fold3.com for relevant dates. Uboat.net for casualties by ship name and *U-552* patrol summary by vessels sunk.
17. Mason, Uboatarchive.net/U-754/KTB754-2, *U-754* patrol two diary, Uboat.net, *U-754*.
18. Mason, Uboatarchive.net/U-571/KTB571-4, *U-571* patrol four diary, Uboat.net, *U-571*.
19. The National Archives (TNA), *Hertford*, TD/DEMS/139, ADM/199/2139 (London: Public Records Office, 1939–1945).
20. National Archives, *Survivor's Statements (1941–1942)*: the *Hertford*
21. The National Archives (TNA), *Hertford*, TD/DEMS/139, ADM/199/2139 (London: Public Records Office, 1939–1945).
22. National Archives, *Survivor's Statements (1941–1942)*: the *Hertford*.
23. Uboat.net/allies/merchants/crews/ship1480, The National Archives (TNA), the *Hertford*, TD/DEMS/139, ADM/199/2139 (London: Public Records Office, 1939–1945).

24. Mason, Uboatarchive.net/U-203/KTB203-6, *U-203* patrol six diary, Uboat.net patrol and commander pages.
25. Uboat.net/boats/patrols/details.php?boat=85anddate=1942-04-08.
26. U.S.S. *Roper*'s commander, Lieutenant Hamilton W. Howe, was awarded the Navy Cross and became a rear admiral. In 2002, Helmut Schmoeckel, past skipper of *U-802*, "suggested ... that the failure of *Roper* to rescue the U-85 crew after they abandoned the submarine and *Roper*'s subsequent depth-charging of U-85 should be investigated. He never used the phrase war crime." However, the allegation, based on inaccuracies in another book on the topic, lead to rumors that Howe had somehow actually been reprimanded for the deaths of all the German sailors of *U-85*, which was obviously a lost intelligence-gathering as well as humanitarian opportunity. The killing of forty-six sailors on April 14, 1942, were most likely a result of the adrenaline of combat, the intensity to the U.S. sailors of having a U-boat in such proximity, and extreme zeal to destroy an enemy whose gruesome havoc the U.S. crew had witnessed first-hand for months. That, and lack of adequate fire control. En.wikipedia.org/wiki/U.S.S_*Roper*_(DD-147). That same week Canadian Mess Boy Ralph Kelly of the *Vineland* wrote that off Hatteras "there were a lot of bodies around. We seen bodies pretty near every day." Parker, *Running the Gauntlet, An Oral History of Canadian Merchant Seamen in World War II* (1994), p. 122.
27. Wynn (1997), *op. cit.*, Vol. I, pp. 63 and 65.
28. Mason, Uboatarchive.net/U-84/KTB84-4, U-84 patrol four diary, Uboat.net; Wynn (1997), *op. cit.*, Vol. I.
29. The author and U.S.N. pilot Thomas Rudolph Evert's son, Congressman Tim Petri of Wisconsin (retired), have been trying since 2016 to obtain official recognition for Evert and his crew, who were killed in an air duel with a German flying boat over Biscay months later.
30. Hague, Holdoway, Cooper, et. al., convoyweb.uk.org. The National Archives (TNA), *Nemanja*, TD/DEMS/139, ADM/199/2139 (London: Public Records Office, 1939–1945).
31. National Archives, *Survivor's Statements (1941–1942)*: the *Nemanja*.
32. Mason, Uboatarchive.net/U-654/KTB654-3, *U-654* patrol three diary, Uboat.net.
33. Uboat.net/allies/merchants/ship/1519 re: loss of the *Empire Prairie*.
34. Mason, Uboatarchive.net/U-136/KTB136-2, *U-136* patrol two diary; Uboat.net, *U-136* patrol two; Uboat.net/men/commanders/1403 (Zimmermann biography).
35. Wynn (1997), *op. cit.*, Busch, Röll, Brooks, *German U-boat Commanders of World War Two: A Biographical Dictionary* (1999); Uboat.net, *U-136*.
36. Niestlé (2014), *op. cit.*
37. Mason, Uboatarchive.net/U-402/KTB402-3, *U-402* patrol three diary, Uboat.net.
38. National Archives, *Survivor's Statements (1941–1942)*: the *Empire Dryden, Harpagon, Steel Maker*, and *City of Birmingham*.
39. Mason, Uboatarchive.net/U-402/KTB402-3, *U-402* patrol three diary; Wiberg, *U-Boats off Bermuda* (2017); Uboat.net/allies/merchants/ship/1878, fold3.com key-word *City of Birmingham*.
40. Wynn (1997), *op. cit.*, Vol. I, pp. 263–264, Mason, Uboatarchive.net/U-402/KTB402-3, U-402 patrol three diary.
41. Blair, *Hitler's U-boat War: The Hunted, 1942–1945* (1998).
42. Busch, Röll, Brooks, (1999) *op. cit.*, Uboat.net/men/forstner.

Chapter 6

1. Blair, *Hitler's U-boat War: The Hunted, 1942–1945* (1998); Mason, Uboatarchive.net/U-752/KTB752-5, *U-752* patrol five diary.

2. National Archives, *Survivor's Statements (1941–1942)*: the *West Imboden.*
3. Mason, Uboatarchive.net/U-752/KTB752-5, *U-752* patrol five diary; Uboat.net.
4. National Archives, *Survivor's Statements (1941–1942)*: *West Imboden.*
5. Mason, Uboatarchive.net/U-576/KTB576-4, *U-576* patrol four diary; Uboat.net *U-576* patrol, *Pipestone County* pages.
6. Eastern Sea Frontier *Enemy Action Diary*, *Tropic Star*, April 25, 1942, War Diaries, at fold3.com/image/268191967?terms=tropic%20star. The author scoured Newspaperarchive.com using work-arounds, keywords, dates, ship names, to obtain any article about *Pipestone County* or *Tropic Star* men's arrival in Boston to no avail. Wrecksite.eu, Uboat.net, uboatarchive.net, and the documents from NARA were also searched. *Diary of Headquarters, First and Fifth Naval District, NOB Norfolk VA*, May 7, 1942, at fold3.com/image/267939039?terms= pipestone%20county, keyword *Pipestone County*, Wiberg, *U-Boats off Bermuda* (2017). Librarians at the Boston Athenaeum, Boston Public Library, The *Boston Globe*, and New England Historical and Genealogical Society were consulted. By coincidence, an alert interviewing officer doubled his work-load by volunteering to interview not just *Tropic Star* but *Pipestone County* survivors too.
7. National Archives, *Survivor's Statements (1941–1942)*: the *Pipestone County.* There is a reference to a strong smell of diesel oil on the sea surface and a small red dot on the horizon. Careful study of all Allied casualties in position 25 degrees north by 62 degrees west, as given (*c.* 400 miles SSE of Bermuda), show no Allied victims sunk anywhere near that location and that time. Nor were there any German or Italian submarines. That leaves one possibility, namely that they passed through a debris field of earlier attacks, drifting jetsam.
8. Hague, Holdoway, Cooper, et. al., convoyweb.org.uk/port/index.
9. *U-576* was discovered off Hatteras in the fall of 2014, cnn.com/2014/10/21/us/north-carolina-u-boat-wreck/index.
10. Browning, *United States Merchant Marine Casualties of World War II* (2011), p.77; Mozolak, *New York Ships to Foreign Ports, 1939–1945* (2000); National Archives, *Survivor's Statements (1941–1942)*: the *Pipestone County.*
11. Browning (2011), *op. cit.*, p. 77.
12. Fold3.com, Eastern Sea Frontier *Enemy Action Diary*, National Archives, *Survivor's Statements (1941–1942)*: the *Pipestone County.*
13. *Ibid.*, Fold3.com, *op. cit.*
14. *Ibid.*
15. Högel, *U-boat Emblems of World War Two 1939–1945* (1999); Uboat.net/flotillas/7flo.
16. Jordan, *The World's Merchant Fleets 1939* (1999); National Archives, *Survivor's Statements (1941–1942)*: the *Pipestone County*, included in which are *Tropic Star* statements by Captain G. Anderson to Lieutenant Hebb (U.S.N.R.), entitled "First Naval District Intelligence Office, Boarding Report," April 25, 1942, Boston, Massachusetts, Ref (a) NN1-131 for *Tropic Star* and Ref (b) NN1-142 for *Pipestone County* interviews, several for each ship.
17. en.wikipedia.org/wiki/U.S.S_Calypso_(AG-35).
18. Holm Lawson, Warsailors.com/singleships/taborfjell.
19. National Archives, *Survivor's Statements (1941–1942)*: *Taborfjell;* Fold3.com, Eastern Sea Frontier, *Enemy Action Diaries*, 1942.
20. Holm Lawson, Warsailors.com/singleships/taborfjell, citing Arve Wiborg.

Chapter 7

1. Mason, Uboatarchive.net/U-566/KTB566-5, *U-566* patrol five diary.

2. Wynn, *U-Boat Operations of the Second World War* (1997), Vol. I, pp. 263–264; Busch, Röll, Brooks, *German U-boat Commanders of World War Two: A Biographical Dictionary* (1999); Uboat.net/men/commanders/108.
3. Niestlé, *German U-Boat Losses of World War Two* (2014), *U-566*.
4. Mason, Uboatarchive.net/U-582/KTB582-2, Uboat.net/boats/patrols/patrol_1496; Busch, Röll, Brooks (1999), *op. cit.*; Uboat.net/men/commanders/1150, Regiamarina.net, *Giuliani* patrol data.
5. Niestlé (2014), *op. cit.*, *U-582*.
6. Mason, Uboatarchive.net/U-593/KTB593-2, *U-593* patrol two diary.
7. Blair, *Hitler's U-Boat War: The Hunted, 1942–1945* (1998); Wynn (1997), *op. cit.*, Vol. I; Uboat.net/boats/ patrols/patrol_1594; Mason, Uboatarchive.net/U-593/KTB593-2, *U-593* patrol two diary.
8. Busch, Röll, Brooks (1999), *op. cit.*; Uboat.net/men/kelbling.
9. Mason, Uboatarchive.net/U-455/KTB455-3, *U-455* patrol three diary.
10. *Ibid.*; Wynn (1997), *op. cit.*.
11. Mason, Uboatarchive.net/U-588/KTB588-3, *U-588* patrol three diary; steamer *Egba* not to be confused with the *Egda*.
12. Mason, Uboatarchive.net/U-588/KTB588-3, *U-588* patrol three diary, attacks on *Skottland* and *Fort Bringer.*
13. National Archives, *Survivor's Statements (1941–1942)*: the *Margot.*
14. Holm Lawson, Warsailors.com/singleships/skottland; Jordan, *The World's Merchant Fleets 1939* (1999).
15. National Archives, *Survivor's Statements (1941–1942)*: the *Fort Binger, Plow City, Skottland, Margot;* Holm Lawson, *op. cit.*
16. Jordan (1999), *op. cit.*; Uboat.net/allies/merchants/ship/3583.
17. Uboat.net/allies/technical/uk_radars; Kahn, *The Codebreakers: The Comprehensive History of Secret Communication from Ancient Times to the Internet* (1996); Morison, S. E., *The Atlantic Battle Won, May 1943–May 1945: History of United States Naval Operations in World War II, Volume 10* (1948), Blair (1998), *op. cit.*
18. Jordan (1999), *op. cit.*; Uboat.net/allies/merchants/ship/1694.
19. National Archives, *Survivor's Statements (1941–1942)*: the *Plow City*
20. *Diary of U.S. Naval Air Station,* Floyd Bennett Field, New York, NY, May 22, 1942, fold3.com/image/267899103?terms=plow%20city.
21. Headquarters of the Commander, Montauk Section (1942), *Third Naval District Diary*, May 26, 1942, fold3.com/image/268360711?terms=plow%20city%20 sapphire.
22. Navy Department, Office of Public Information, History of U.S.S. *Sapphire* (PYc 2) (1946), fold3.com/image/302063422.
23. Headquarters of the Commander, Montauk, May 26, 1942, Fold3.com link.
24. Eastern Sea Frontier *Patrol Log,* Naval Operating Base Newport, though the *Sapphire* and *Plow City* men went to New London, not Newport. Shows that the *General Greene* men were resting in Newport at the time, not at Nantucket or the *Plow City*. Fold3.com, NOB Newport entry, 26 May 1942, Fold3.com/ image/268360711?terms=plow%20city%20sapphire.
25. *Ibid.*
26. Wikivisually.com/wiki/U.S.S_Sapphire_(PYc-2).
27. Mozolak, *New York Ships to Foreign Ports, 1939–1945* (2000); Jordan (1999), *op. cit.*
28. The National Archives (TNA), *Margot*, TD/DEMS/139, ADM/199/2139 (London: Public Records Office, 1939–1945).
29. National Archives, *Survivor's Statements (1941–1942)*: the *Margot.*

30. The National Archives (TNA), *Margot*, TD/DEMS/139, ADM/199/2139 (London: Public Records Office, 1939–1945).
31. National Archives, *Survivor's Statements (1941–1942)*: the *Margot*.
32. Mozolak (2000), *op. cit.*; Jordan (1999), *op. cit.*
33. Email from Edwards' great-nephew Kevin Dawe, Fort Macleod, Alberta, Canada, August, 2017, regarding *Margot*'s Bosun Reginald Lloyd Edwards' survival then death with Captain Collins on the *Empire Turnstone* later in the war off Iceland.
34. Niestlé (2014), *op. cit.*, *U-588*.

Chapter 8

1. Wynn, *U-Boat Operations of the Second World War* (1997), Vol. I, pp. 42 and 302, Vol. II, pp. 55 and 64; Uboat.net/men/varendorff; Busch, Röll, Brooks, *German U-boat Commanders of World War Two: A Biographical Dictionary* (1999).
2. Beeby, *Cargo of Lies: The True Story of a Nazi Double Agent in Canada* (1996) [e-book/Kindle format, *ergo*, page numbers not given].
3. Mason, Uboatarchive.net/U-213/KTB213-2, *U-213* patrol two diary.
4. *Ibid.*
5. *Ibid.*, Holm Lawson, Warsailors.com/riksarkivet/banaderos3.gif
6. Uboat.net/boats/u213, "The boat was slightly damaged by depth-charges from a destroyer after being surprised on the surface in foggy weather in the Gulf of Maine. (Sources: Ritschel)" "The source for this information is one of the books of the German naval author Herbert Ritschel. He self-published a series of fourteen books with the title *Kurzfassung Kriegstagebücher Deutscher U-Boote*, containing shortened versions of all available U-boat KTBs with comments from this own research." Email, Rainer Kolbicz of Uboat.net, May 1, 2018.
7. Beeby (1996), *op. cit.*
8. Mallmann Showell, *U-Boats at War: Landings on Hostile Shores* (2000), p. 34.
9. Beeby (1996), *op. cit.*
10. Mallmann Showell, *U-Boats of the Second World War: Their Longest Voyages* (2014)
11. *Ibid.*
12. Uboat.net/ops/agent_u213, Beeby (1996), *op. cit.*

Chapter 9

1. Mason, Uboatarchive.net/U-653/KTB653-3, *U-653* patrol three diary, *Peisander, Mattawin.*
2. Jordan, *The World's Merchant Fleets 1939* (1999); Uboat.net/allies/merchants/ship/1666.
3. *Singapore Free Press and Mercantile Advertiser*, December 20, 1937; ship movements.
4. National Archives, *Survivor's Statements (1941–1942)*: the *Peisander*
5. The National Archives (TNA), the *Peisander*, TD/DEMS/139, ADM/199/2139 (London: Public Records Office, 1939–1945).
6. National Archives, *Survivor's Statements (1941–1942)*: the *Plow City*
7. Mayes, S., Shipsnostalgia.com/archive/index.php?t-29448, blog post; Bennett and Bennett, *Survivors: British Merchant Seamen in the Second World War* (1999), p. 191, for the *Baron Semple*'s interactions with the *Peisander* men: cites Second Officer Thomas.
8. Stilgoe, *Lifeboat: A History of Courage, Cravenness, and Survival at Sea* (2003), p. 217, Bennett and Bennett (1999), *op. cit.*; *Safe at Last*, pp. 191–192, (Chap. 9, citing "OA 89/2A, Second Officer W. M. Thomas."); *Nantucket Inquirer and*

Mirror, "Red Cross Notes," July 18, 1942, online archive, digital.olivesoftware.com/Olive/APA/Nantucket/get/image.ashx.png, Massachusetts.

9. Stilgoe, *Lifeboat: A History of Courage, Cravenness, and Survival at Sea* (2003), pp. 216–218.
10. United States Coast Guard, *The Coast Guard at War, Assistance XIV, Vol. II*, (1947), p. 163.
11. *Nantucket Inquirer and Mirror,* "Red Cross Notes," July 18, 1942, Nantucket Athenaeum; *Newport* [Rhode Island] *Mercury and Weekly News*, September 28, 1945.
12. United States Coast Guard, the *Peisander* rescue by the *General Greene*, uscg.mil/history/webcutters/ GeneralGreene1927.asp.
13. United States Coast Guard (1947), *op. cit.*, p. 162.
14. U.S.C.G. *Quarterdeck Log*, "Association News," eyewitness account by Fireman-2nd-Class Eric J. Phillips, Jr. in the columns, Vol. I6, No. 2, pp. 12–15 coastguardcombatvets.org/2001-Summer.pdf.
15. *U.S. Coast Guard Auxiliary History*, for *Peisander*'s two other boats' rescue off Nantucket, history.auxpa.org/collections/textarticles/article0002.
16. United States Coast Guard (1947), *op. cit.*, p. 163.
17. *U.S. Coast Guard Log Books*, National Records and Archives Administration, Textual References, Record Group RG 26, Entry Number 159 D, Box Item 54, Stack 12E1, Row 6, Compartment 6, Shelf 1, Box 54 (1942) *General Greene*, *Deck Logs*, NOB Newport, May 1942, June 1942. Hoyt, *U-Boats Offshore* (1978), pp. 198–203, describing the *Great Nantucket U-boat Hunt* (chapter heading), begun November 5, 1942, after a plane's pilot thought he saw a U-boat. A dozen or so naval vessels, including *General Greene*, spent days bombing the wreck of the old lightship *Nantucket*, which had been run over at that spot by S.S. *Olympia* in 1937.
18. His Majesty's Stationary Office, *Supplement* to the *London Gazette*, London, 10 November, 1942.
19. Hague, Holdoway, Cooper, et. al., convoyweb.co.uk; Jordan (1999), *op. cit.*, Uboat.net/allies/merchants /ship/1735, for *Mattawin.*
20. *U.S. Coast Guard Log Books*, NARA, RG 26, *General Greene,* (1942), Mrad, American Field Service Archives (2017).
21. The National Archives (TNA), *Mattawin*, TD/DEMS/139, ADM/199/2139 (London: Public Records Office, 1939–1945).
22. National Archives, *Survivor's Statements (1941–1942)*: the *Mattawin*
23. Mrad, American Field Service Archives (2017), emails to author, April 18, 2017.
24. *Ibid*.; The-afs-archive.org, ourstory.info/library/4-ww2/AFSletters/AFSNB4.
25. Holm Lawson, Warsailors.com/singleships/torvanger, for *Mattawin* details; fold3.com/image/267942236; warsailors.com/singleships/berganger, for details of *Berganger* port boat rifled by Thurmann on June 3 before U.S.S. *Plunkett* found it.
26. Mrad, American Field Service Archives (2017), *op. cit.*
27 The National Archives (TNA), the *Mattawin*, TD/DEMS/139, ADM/199/2139 (London: Public Records Office, 1939–1945).
28 The National Archives (TNA), the *Mattawin*, TD/DEMS/139, ADM/199/2139 (London: Public Records Office, 1939–1945).
29 The-afs-archive.org, ourstory.info/library/4-ww2/AFSletters/AFSNB4, Mrad, E. A., Archives Fellow, American Field Service, NYC, emails April 18, 2017.
30. The Reserved: Survivors Only table at the Allied Seaman's Institute in Halifax was the setting of many photos of grateful young men; novascotia.ca/archives/eastcoastport /results.asp?Search= seaman%27s+club andLanguage=English, Mrad, American Field Service Archives (2017), *op. cit.*, Parker, *Running the Gauntlet, An Oral History of Canadian Merchant Seamen in World War II* (1994); Wiberg,

U-Boats in the Bahamas (2016), the *Vineland* Chapter, Erling Conrad image, *op. cit.*

31. Holm Lawson, Warsailors.com/singleships/torvanger, *Torvanger* page, *Mattawin* rescue.
32. *Nantucket Inquirer and Mirror,* "Red Cross Notes," July 18, 1942, Nantucket Athenaeum; *Newport Mercury and Weekly News*, Sept. 28, 1945; author email and phone exchanges with eyewitness Maurice Gibbs of Nantucket, March–April 2018. Mooney, R. F., Hoyt, *Nantucket Only Yesterday: An Island View of the Twentieth Century* (2000); E. P., *U-Boats Offshore: When Hitler Struck America* (1985)
33. Exhaustive searches did not confirm exactly how they were moved from Nauset to Boston: either through easily accessible Providence and from there to Boston via boat, or via road.
34. Davies, *The Trade Makers: Elder Dempster in West Africa, 1852–1972, 1973–1989* (2000), pp. 266–267; fold3.com/image/267911860?terms= general%20greene, fold3.com/image /267911868.
35. Bennett and Bennett, *Survivors: British Merchant Seamen in the Second World War* (1999), p. 198; *U.S. Coast Guard Log Books*, NARA, RG 26, *General Greene*, *Deck Logs*, May–June 1942 (1942).
36. Davies (2000), *op. cit.* pp. 266–267; *U.S. Coast Guard Log Books*, NARA, RG 26, *General Greene*, *Deck Logs*, NOB Newport, May 1942, June 1942. S/Y *Morning Star* (ex-*Dorello III*), and its charismatic, swashbuckling owners, Capt. and Mrs. William M. Pond, educators from Harvard, are a story unto themselves. They owned several other large classic yachts: the *Indra, Gulnare*, and *Polaris* (ex-*Irolita*), taking paying students throughout the Caribbean even during the U-boat war's height; Wiberg (2016), *op. cit.*, p. 239. The Ponds were an adventurous pair trading with Central America and the Caribbean, educating students on Florida's Gulf Coast, to the end of their lives.
37. Mrad, American Field Service Archives (2017).
38. Mason, Uboatarchive.net/U-135/KTB135-3, *U-135* patrol three diary, attack on *Fort Qu'Appelle.*
39. Hadley, *U-Boats Against Canada: German Submarines in Canadian Waters* (1990) p. 95, Mason, Uboatarchive.net/U-135/KTB135-3, *U-135* patrol three diary.
40. United States Coast Guard (1947), *op. cit.*, pp. 163–166; Fold3.com, regional, port-specific, and vessel-specific diaries.
41. Uboat.net/boats/patrols/patrol_3881, attack; Uboat.net/allies/merchants/ ship/3516.
42. Niestlé, *German U-Boat Losses of World War Two* (2014), *U-135*.
43. Jordan (1999), *op. cit.*; wrecksite.eu/wreck. aspx?15130; Uboat.net/allies/ merchants/ship/3516.
44. The National Archives (TNA), *Fort Qu'Appelle*, TD/DEMS/139, ADM/199/2139 (London: Public Records Office, 1939–1945).
45. National Archives, *Survivor's Statements (1941–1942),*: the *Fort Qu'Appelle*
46. Hadley, *U-Boats Against Canada: German Submarines in Canadian Waters* (1990) p. 95; Uboat.net/allies/warships/ship/2684l, image of H.M.C.S. *Melville.*
47. Terry Patrick Ferster, son of James Carney Ferster, wrote to author, to say his father passed in March 2017 (weeks earlier), at age ninety-six. James Carney Ferster's great-grandson Emmett will soon inherit the jacket, keeping the tradition alive. Email to author, March 18, 2017.

Chapter 10

1. Uboat.net, Merchant Ships, the *Zurichmoor, Liverpool Packet, Ben and Josephine,* and *Aeolus.*

2. Uboat.net, Merchant Ships, the *Kronprinsen* and the *Malayan Prince.*
3. Mason, Uboatarchive.net/U-432/KTB432-5, *U-432* patrol five diary.
4. Wynn, *U-Boat Operations of the Second World War* (1997), Vol. I; Mason, Uboatarchive .net/U-432/KTB432-5, *U-432* patrol five diary.
5. Kurowski, *Knights of the Wehrmacht: Knight's Cross Holders of the U-Boat Service* (2004), Niestlé, *German U-boat Losses of World War Two* (2014), *U-432*; Uboat.net/men/schultze_heinz-otto; Busch, Röll, Brooks, *German U-boat Commanders of World War Two: A Biographical Dictionary* (1999).
6. Uboat.net/allies/merchants/ships/1696, *Zurichmoor.*
7. *Marine Engineer and Naval Architect,* U.K., 1925 edition.
8. Hague, Holdoway, Cooper, et al., convoyweb.co.uk, Mozolak, *New York Ships to Foreign Ports, 1939–1945* (2000).
9. National Archives, *Survivor's Statements (1941–1942)*: the *Zurichmoor.*
10. In the absence of survivors who would have otherwise reported to the Trade Division and Admiralty at The National Archives (TNA) in Kew, researchers we rely on Schultze's war diary at Uboatarchive.net/U-432/KTB432-5, *U-432* patrol five.
11. Jordan, *The World's Merchant Fleets 1939* (1999); wrecksite.eu; Uboat.net/allies/merchants/ship/1724, the *Liverpool Packet.*
12. Mozolak, *New York Ships to Foreign Ports, 1939–1945* (2000); Hague, Holdoway, Cooper, convoyweb.co.uk.
13. Wiberg, *U-Boats in the Bahamas* (2016), Part II, *Vineland* chapter, pp. 165–176.
14. National Archives, *Survivor's Statements (1941–1942)*: the *Liverpool Packet.*
15. Article entitled "The *Liverpool Packet*, sunk by Nazi U-boat, surfaces in new documentary New Brunswick filmmaker Mike Burchill meets eyewitness to his father's WW II rescue on Seal Island." Tattrie, Jon, *CBC News*, posted online: October 22, 2016. Cbc.ca/news/ canada/nova-scotia/liverpool-packet-mike-burchill-land-and-sea-1.3815750, April 2018, emails to author, 2016 to May 2018.
16. Burchill, M., *Liverpool Packet* facebook.com/groups/585275441662121 (2018).
17. *Ibid.*, Watt, R. E., *Statement of Facts*; Richardson, *B ... was for Butter and Enemy Craft* (1976).
18. Wrecksite.eu/wreck.aspx?15480, Uboat.net/allies/merchants/ships/1724; Mason, Uboatarchive.net/U-432/KTB432-5, *U-432* patrol five diary.
19. National Archives, *Survivor's Statements (1941–1942)*: the *Liverpool Packet.*
20. Burchill, M. (2018), *op. cit.*
21. Mason, Uboatarchive.net/U-432/KTB432-5, *U-432* patrol five diary.
22. Burchill, M. (2018), *op. cit.*; emails to author, October 16, 2016–spring 2018.
23. *Ibid.*, Watt, R. E., *op. cit.*
24. *Ibid.*
25. Richardson (1976), *op. cit.*, p. 73.
26. Burchill, M. (2018), *op. cit.*; Watt, R. E., *op. cit.*
27. *Ibid.*
28. Richardson (1976), *op. cit.*, p.73.
29. *Gloucester* [Massachusetts] *Daily Times*, June 11, 1942: "The Sinking of the *Ben and Josephine* Account," goodmorninggloucester.wordpress.com/tag/captain-joe-ciaramitaro.
30. "*Report on Interrogation of Survivors from U-432, a 500-Ton U-Boat Sunk at about 1200 GMT on 11 March 1943*," at goodmorninggloucester.wordpress.com/2012/01/17/that-german-u-boat-that-torpedoed-our-grandfathers-fishing-boat-the-ben-and-josephine-heres-the-account-of-its-day-of-reckoning, citing Mason, Uboatarchive.net/U-432INT.

31. National Archives, *Survivor's Statements (1941–1942)*: the *Aeolus*.
32. National Archives, *Survivor's Statements (1941–1942)*: the *Ben and Josephine;* Mason, Uboatarchive.net/U-432/KTB432-4, *U-432* patrol four diary.
33. *Nantucket Inquirer and Mirror*, September 8, 1945, "Nantucket Fishermen Awarded Service Certificates," Nantucket Atheneum free digital library, digital. olivesoftware.com/ Olive/APA/ Nantucket/get/image.ashx.png.
34. Norwood, D. M., *Sou'west Harbor Newsletter*, February 2010.
35. *Ibid.*
36. The National Archives (TNA), the *Malayan Prince*, TD/DEMS/139, ADM/199/2139 (London: Public Records Office, 1939–1945).
37. National Archives, *Survivor's Statements (1941–1942)*: *Malayan Prince*
38. Niestlé (2014), *op. cit.*, *U-432*, emails to author from Mike Burchill to reach out to Schultze's relatives, resulting in no success.

Chapter 11

1. Mason, Uboatarchive.net/U-553/KTB553-7; *U-553* patrol seven diary.
2. Hadley, *U-Boats Against Canada: German Submarines in Canadian Waters* (1990); Mason, *op. cit.*
3. Eastern Sea Frontier *Enemy Action Diary*, June 1–2, 1942; fold3.com/image/ 267911587.
4. Mason, *op. cit.*
5. Holm Lawson, Warsailors.com, *Moldanger, Washington Express;* Uboat.net/men/ thurmann, Uboat.net/boats/patrols/patrol_1291.
6. Mason, *op. cit.*; Wynn, *U-Boat Operations of the Second World War* (1997), Vol. I, p. 266.
7. Wynn, *U-Boat Operations of the Second World War*, Vol. II (1997), p. 53; Uboat. net/boats/patrols/patrol_1291.
8. Niestlé, *German U-boat Losses of World War Two* (2014), *U-553*.
9. Uboat.net/allies/merchants/ship/1556, *Bris* sunk by Adalbert Schnee in *U-201*; Uboat.net/boats/patrols/patrol_583.
10. Mason, Uboatarchive.net/U-404/KTB404-3, *U-404* patrol three diary.
11. Mason, Uboatarchive.net, KTB 404-3, *U-404* patrol three diary.
12. Jordan, *The World's Merchant Fleets 1939* (1999); Wrecksite.eu/wreck. aspx?17001.
13. Bjørn Milde's postcard collection; Holm Lawson, Warsailors.com/singleships/ Moldanger, the *Washington Express*
14. National Archives, *Survivor's Statements (1941–1942)*: the *Moldanger*; Holm Lawson, Warsailors.com/singleships/Moldanger; Uboat.net/allies/ merchants/ ship/1857.
15. *Ibid.*
16. Wikipedia.org/wiki/HMCS_*Buctouche*.
17. Radigan, Navsource.org/archives/12/010495, data on deck logs, commanders.
18. Holm Lawson interpreted and collated copious Norwegian accounts and interviews to convey the survival saga of the seven Norwegian sailors, Dane Poul Andersen and Swede Holger Aronsen.
19. Holm Lawson, Warsailors.com/singleships/washingtonexpr, photos, Dag Midbøe, Neil Carlsen.
20. Archive.paulrucker.com/activism/tuskegee_experiment
21. *Handelsflåten i krig,* (A Merchant Seaman's Story), *De seilte for vår frihet, Utanför Spärren, Tusen Norske Skip*, and *Sjøforklaringer fra 2. Verdenskrig*; Holm Lawson, Warsailors.com.

22. Wiberg, *U-Boats off Bermuda* (2017), Wiberg, *Schooner and Yacht Casualties in Bahamas, Bermuda and New England in World War II* (2010), ericwiberg.com/category/presentations. The post-World-War-Two lecture circuit and article-writing fields were competitive. MGM Studios' William James Fadiman rejected playwright Earl Schenck's treatment entitled *Torpedoed* (*Wreck of the* Potlatch) in July 1943, chiefly because other Allies in rafts had by then outlasted the *Potlatch* men's month-long boat voyage (letter in author's private collection). Jules Souza of Westport, Massachusetts survived alone on a raft for thirty-three days off the U.S. coast after the *Alcoa Guide* was sunk by *U-123* under Hardegen in April 1942. Southcoasttoday.com/apps/pbcs.dll/article?AID=/20081127/NEWS/811270447/-1/rss18; Kelshall, *The U-Boat War in the Caribbean* (1994), emails to author, 2009–2012 via Jerome Lee, Chaguaramas, Trinidad.
23. Progress-is-fine.blogspot.com/2013/03/astounding-feats-of-survival-at-sea. Thirty of the forty-four *Moldanger* men were rescued in three batches over seven weeks, as follows: sixteen men, motorboat, Capt. Hansen, at sea eleven days, rescued H.M.C.S. *Buctouche*, Newport, July 8; six men, gig, Third Mate Thore Legland, at sea twenty days, rescued U.S.S. *PC 495*, Cape May, July 16; and nine men, two rafts under Carpenter Olav Brekke, at sea forty-eight days, *Washington Express*, New York, August 17, 1942.
24. Mason, Uboatarchive.net/U-701/KTB701-3, *U-701* patrol three diary.
25. Uboat.net/boats/patrols/patrol_2111, Wynn, *U-Boat Operations of the Second World War* (1997), Busch, Röll, Brooks, *German U-boat Commanders of World War Two: A Biographical Dictionary* (1999); Uboat.net/men/commanders/19, Degen.
26. Niestlé (2014), *op. cit.*, *U-701*.
27. Mason, Uboatarchive.net, KTB 701-3, *U-701* patrol three diary; Douban.com/note/311443885 (re-post on a website in Mandarin script, long since unavailable).
28. Mason, Uboatarchive.net/U-87/KTB87-3, *U-87* patrol three diary.
29. *Ibid.*
30. Mason, Uboatarchive.net/U-213/KTB213-2, *U-213* patrol two diary; von Varendorff's failed shots at the *Berganger.*
31. *Ibid.*
32. Eastern Sea Frontier *Enemy Action Diary*, 3 p.m., June 22, 1942; fold3.com.
33. The National Archives (TNA), the *Port Nicholson*, TD/DEMS/139, ADM/199/2139 (London: Public Records Office, 1939–1945); National Archives, *Survivor's Statements (1941–1942)*: the *Port Nicholson* and the *Cherokee.*
34. Mason, Uboatarchive.net, KTB 87-3, *U-87* patrol three diary.
35. Niestlé (2014), *op. cit.*, *U-87.*
36. The National Archives (TNA), the *Port Nicholson*, TD/DEMS/139, ADM/199/2139 (London: Public Records Office, 1939–1945), National Archives, *Survivor's Statements (1941–1942)*: the *Port Nicholson.*
37. National Archives, *Survivor's Statements (1941–1942)*: the *Cherokee;* Jordan (1999), *op. cit.*
38. Blandford, *The Clyde Line*, *Steamboat Bill*, sshsa.org, Fall (1974), pp. 131–140.
39. Baughman, *The Mallorys of Mystic: Six generations in American Maritime Enterprise* (Middletown: Wesleyan University Press, 1972), emails with author from Charles Mallory, 2009 to April 2018, various Mallory or Munson Line ships: Clara Mallory married a Munson.
40. *Fitchburg* [Massachusetts] *Sentinel*, "Officials Laud C. D. [Civil Defense] Volunteers for Rescue Job," June 25, 1942, p. 2.
41. *Ibid.*, for Soviet details, Commandant, 1st Naval District, cables entitled *Diplomatic Situation*, July 26, 1942, Item. 6, U.S.A, from researcher John Chamberlain of New Jersey, email to author June 5, 2018.

42. Mason, Uboatarchive.net/U-373/KTB373-5, *U-373* patrol five diary, for *U-373*'s mine-laying operation off New York.
43. *Ibid.*; Kahn, *The Codebreakers: The Comprehensive History of Secret Communication from Ancient Times to the Internet* (1996).
44. *Ibid.*
45. Busch, Röll, Brooks, *op. cit.* (1999); Uboat.net/men/commanders/744, Paul-Karl Loeser.

Chapter 12

1. Eastern Sea Frontier *Enemy Action Diary*, 3.15 a.m., June 13, 1942; fold3.com; Mason, Uboatarchive.net/ESF, Uboat.net/ops/agents1942.
2. Mason, Uboatarchive.net/U-202/KTB202-6, *U-202* KTB, patrol six diary, backbone of this chapter.
3. Wynn, *U-Boat Operations of the Second World War* (1997), Vol. I, p. 148.
4. Busch, Röll, Brooks, *German U-boat Commanders of World War Two: A Biographical Dictionary* (1999), p. 148; Uboat.net/men/commanders.
5. Waller, *U-505 in the U.S. Navy 1944 to 1954 (from Capture to Disposal to Display)*, September 3, 2011.
6. *The New York Times*, March 9, 2011, nytimes.com/2011/09/03/nyregion/john-cullen-coast-guardsman-who-detected-spies-dies-at-90, obituary of CG patrolman John Cullen.
7. Garrett, *A Story Goes with It, archipelago literary journal*, Vol. 8, No. 2, 2004 (Brooklyn: Archipelago Publishers, Inc., 2004), archipelago.org/vol8-2/garrett; Uboat.net/ops/agents1942.
8. *Ibid.*
9. Ardman, H., "World War II German Saboteurs Invade America in 1942," *World War II Magazine*, February 1997, historynet.com/world-war-ii-german-saboteurs-invade-america-in-1942, twelve pages.
10. Citinoa, R., "Saboteurs: The Nazi Raid on America (Book Review)," reviewing Dobbs, M., *Saboteurs: The Nazi Raid on America* (New York: Alfred A. Knopf, 2004), which covered Operation Pastorius, historynet.com/saboteurs-the-nazi-raid-on-america-book-review, June 12, 2006 (three pages), and Abella and Gordon, *Shadow Enemies: Hitler's Secret Terrorist Plot Against the United States* (2002), pp. 276–277.
11. Garrett (2004), *op. cit.*; Uboat.net/ops/agents1942.
12. Ardman (1997), *op. cit.*
13. Mallmann Showell, *U-Boats at War: Landings on Hostile Shores* (2000), p. 28, author visited the site in May 2018, verifying with beach patrol and visually that these facts were plausible. The dunes stretch at least half a mile and the beach itself is roughly a quarter-mile from surf to dunes.
14. Dasch, *Operation Pastorius: Eight Nazi Spies Against America* (1959); Uboat.net/ops/agents1942; Ardman (1997), *op. cit.*; Kahn, *The Codebreakers: The Comprehensive History of Secret Communication from Ancient Times to the Internet* (1996).
15. Mason, Uboatarchive.net, KTB, 202-6.
16. *Ibid.*
17. *Ibid.*
18. Mallmann Showell (2000), *op. cit.*, p. 30.
19. Abella and Gordon (2002), *op. cit.*, pp. 3–4.
20. Dasch (1959) *op. cit.*; Uboat.net/ ops/agents1942.
21. Abella and Gordon (2002), *op. cit.*, pp. 3–4; Ardman (1997), *op. cit.*; Uboat.net/ops/agents1942; Mallmann Showell (2000), *op. cit.*, p. 30.

22. *Ibid.*
23. Dasch (1959), *op. cit.*; Uboat.net/ops/agents1942.
24. Uboat.net/boats/patrols/patrol_1505, for Deecke's patrol to Florida, Uboat.net/boats/patrols/patrol_4129 for a summary of Linder's patrols and attacks in *U-202*.

Chapter 13

1. Mason, Uboatarchive.net/U-332/KTB332-4, *U-332* patrol four diary.
2. The *Laconia* order was issued by German U-Boat headquarters (*Befehlshaber der Unterseeboote*, BdU for short: *Großadmiral* Dönitz and staff) banning the aid transport of Allied—or any—sailors. It resulted from the September 1942 sinking of the British transport ship RMS *Laconia* off West Africa by Werner Hartenstien in *U-156*. When the Germans realized that *Laconia* was loaded with thousands of German and Italian prisoners of war, they vectored other German and Italian submarines and began a large rescue operation. In order not to be sunk during days-long transits with men staning on the submarine's casing, or deck, the Axis officers transmitted in the clear (uncoded) to request freedom of passage on humanitarian grounds. Nevertheless, suspicious American aircraft opened fire on the submarines and they rescue mission was aborted. en.wikipedia.org/wiki/Laconia_Order.
3. Wynn, *U-Boat Operations of the Second World War* (1997).
4. Mason, Uboatarchive.net/U-89/KTB89-2, *U-89* patrol two diary; for *Donovania* information, convoyweb.org.uk/movement/index.html?home.htm~movementmain; Mozolak, *New York Ships to Foreign Ports, 1939–1945* (2000).
5. *Ibid.*
6. National Archives, *Survivor's Statements (1941–1942)*: the *Lucille M.*
7. Wynn (1997), *op. cit.*; Uboat.net; Mason, Uboatarchive.net, KTB, 89-2, *U-89* patrol two diary; *Donovania* movements at convoyweb.org.uk /movement/index.html?home.htm~movementmain; Hague, Holdoway, Cooper, et al., convoyweb.co.uk.
8. National Archives, *Survivor's Statements (1941–1942)*: the *Lucille M.*
9. Mason, Uboatarchive.net/U-754/KTB754-3, *U-754* patrol three diary.
10. Kornblum, "Sea Hunters find deadly *U-215*," *USA Today*, July 21, 2004.
11. Busch, Röll, and Brooks, *German U-boat Commanders of World War Two: A Biographical Dictionary* (1999), p. 105.
12. Wynn, *U-Boat Operations of the Second World War*, Vol. II (1997), p. 151.
13. Mason, reconstructed the war diary exclusively for this patrol into English Uboatarchive.net, sent to author March 3, 2018.
14. National Archives, *Survivor's Statements (1941–1942)*: the *Alexander Macomb*
15. Busch, Röll, Brooks (1999) *op. cit.*; Uboat.net/man/commanders.
16. Niestlé, *German Submarine Losses in World War Two* (2014), *U-215*.
17. Högel, *U-Boat Emblems of World War Two 1939–1945* (1999).
18. Canadian diver Mike Fletcher emails to author, Fall 2017, and in-person conversations with Dr. James Delgado of searchinc.com in Bermuda April 2018, richiekohler.com/project-files/discovery-of-the-u-215/2, Council of American Maritime Museums.
19. Hague, Holdoway, Cooper, et. al., convoyweb.co.uk.
20. National Archives, *Survivor's Statements (1941–1942)*: the *Alexander Macomb*.
21. *Ibid.*
22. TV program about the *Alexander Macomb* made in Canada: imdb.com/title/tt1094123/
23. Mason, Uboatarchive.net/U-458/KTB458-1, *U-458* patrol one diary.

24. *Ibid.*
25. Hague, Holdoway, Cooper, et. al., convoyweb.co.uk; Wynn, *U-Boat Operations of the Second World War* (1997), Vol. I.
26. Mason, Uboatarchive.net, KTB, 458-1, *U-458* patrol one diary.
27. Wynn (1997), *op. cit.*, p. 68.
28. Kurowski, *Knights of the Wehrmacht: Knight's Cross Holders of the U-Boat Service* (2004); Busch, Röll, Brooks (1999), *op. cit.*
29. Hadley, *U-Boats Against Canada: German Submarines in Canadian Waters* (1990); Hickam, *Torpedo Junction* (1996).
30. Mason, Uboatarchive.net/U-132/KTB132-3, *U-132* patrol three diary,
31. Uboat.net/men/commanders/1306; Niestlé (2014), *op. cit.*, *U-132*.
32. Uboat.net/boats/patrols/patrol_3649 (*U-86*).
33. Niestlé (2014), *op. cit.*, *U-86*.
34. Mason, Uboatarchive.net/U-455/KTB455-4, *U-455* patrol four diary.
35. *Ibid.*
36. Uboat.net/men/commanders/358.
37. Mason, Uboatarchive.net/U-608/KTB608-2, *U-608* patrol two diary.
38. Busch, Röll, Brooks (1999) *op. cit.*; Uboat.net/men/commanders.
39. Mason, Uboatarchive.net/U-183/KTB183-1, *U-183* patrol one dairy.
40. Busch, Röll, Brooks (1999) *op. cit.*; Uboat.net/men/commanders; Niestlé (2014), *op. cit.*.

Chapter 14

1. Bercuson and Herwig, *Long Night of the Tankers* (2014), pp. xi and 96 (photo caption), Mason, Uboatarchive.net/U-161/KTB161-5, *U-161* patrol five diary. The rendezvous was for later in German naval grid BD 5, in the central North Atlantic. In contrast, on April 18, *U-129* was between Bahamas and Bermuda and *U-162* was east of New England, great distances and days from each other.
2. *Ibid.*
3. *Ibid.*
4. *Deck Logs* of U.S.S. *Turner*; fold3.com/image/302074126?terms=angelus%20 turner. There is a twenty-four-hour difference between the survivor's sworn account and the *Turner* deck logs. Certainly, the *Turner* is the correct source. At 2.46 p.m. on the 26th, U.S.S. *Turner* broadcast the rescue to colleagues.
5. Kurowski, *Knights of the Wehrmacht: Knight's Cross Holders of the U-Boat Service* (2004); Busch, Röll, and Brooks, *German U-boat Commanders of World War Two: A Biographical Dictionary* (1999), Uboat.net/men/achilles.
6. National Archives, *Survivor's Statements (1941–1942)*: the *Angelus*
7. Kyte, J., "Rescue of the Crew of SC 709," *Heritage Notes*, Number 3, January 1993, Louisbourg Heritage Society (Canada).
8. "Capt. Walter Boudreau's Story: Louisbourg Rescue, 1943, and The Sinking of the *Angelus*," *Cape Breton's Magazine*, Issue 64, p. 2 (1993), capebretonsmagazine. com/modules/ publisher/item.php?itemid=4444; Caplan, R., August 1, 1993. The four were later given commendations, though clearly Boudreau cannot recall then.
9. Census figures, map and basic information at en.wikipedia.org/wiki/Belleoram.
10. Canadian Government, 1935 Census of Newfoundland, Belleoram, Microfilm Reel M-8048, pp. 103–126 and 145; ngb.chebucto.org/C1935/35-belleoram-for.shtml.
11. "Capt. Walter Boudreau's Story: Louisbourg Rescue, 1943, and The Sinking of the *Angelus*," *Cape Breton's Magazine*, Issue 64, p. 2 (1993); Caplan, R., August 1, 1993.
12. Barbadian (Bajan) blog, commemorating the attacks of World War II: bajanthings. com/Cornwallis-torpedoing-carlisle-bay-1942-75th-anniversary.

13. Wiberg, *U-Boats in the Bahamas* (2016); Wiberg, *U-Boats off Bermuda* (2017), covers ships sunk on Barbados–Canadian Maritimes routes.
14. Kelshall, *The U-Boat War in the Caribbean* (1994)
15. Uboat.net/boats/u161; Uboat.net/men/achilles; Niestlé, *German U-boat Losses of World War Two* (2014), *op. cit., U-161.*
16. National Archives, *Survivor's Statements (1941–1942)*: the *Angelus.*
17. "Capt. Walter Boudreau's Story: Louisbourg Rescue, 1943, and The Sinking of the *Angelus*," *Cape Breton's Magazine*, Issue 64, p. 2 (1993); Caplan, R., August 1, 1993, covers rescue, voyage, Boudreau's sailing life after the *Angelus.*
18. *Ibid.*
19. *Ibid.*
20. *Ibid.*
21. *Ibid.*
22. *Deck Logs*, U.S.S. *Turner*, fold3.com/image/302074126?terms=angelus%20 turner.
23. Radigan, Navsource.org/archives/05/648, en.wikipedia.org/wiki/U.S.S_Turner_(DD-648)
24. *Angelus Voyage #2*, letter and *Statement of Facts* from survivors Holmans and Boudreau, by O. Johnson, Operations, Victory Transport Salvage Co. Ltd., Hamilton, May 31, 1943, five-page report, email to author February 4, 2018, Facebook message from Myrden's son Peter Doig, Halifax, April 24, 2017–2018.
25. Colledge and Warlow, *Ships of the Royal Navy: The Complete Record of all Fighting Ships of the Royal Navy* (2010), p. 64, shows that the firm bought RCMS *Calgary* in 1946.
26 *Angelus Voyage #2*, letter and *Statement of Facts* from survivors Holmans and Boudreau, by O. Johnson, Operations, Victory Transport Salvage Co. Ltd., Hamilton, May 31, 1943, five-page report, email to author February 4, 2018, Facebook message from Myrden's son Peter Doig, Halifax, April 24, 2017–2018.
27. Parsons, R., historian, atlanticwrecks.com/victims_belleoram.shtm.
28. Dr. Frederick Smith at Memorial University of Newfoundland emailed the author in an effort to establish a research beach-head in Belleoram. Fortunately, Boudreau gave local interviews.
29. "Capt. Walter Boudreau's Story: Louisbourg Rescue, 1943, and The Sinking of the *Angelus*," *Cape Breton's Magazine*, Issue 64, p. 2 (1993); Caplan, R., August 1, 1993.
30. Radigan, Navsource.org; en.wikipedia.org/wiki/U.S.S_Turner_(DD-648).
31. Mason, Uboatarchive.net/U-608/KTB608-2, for *U-608*, patrol two diary.
32. Foxnews.com/us/2016/11/20/wwii-mystery-are-missing-sailors-actually-in-ny-cemetery
33. Re: *Benjamin Contee*, "Many men confined in the holds of the ship died, and the initial search of the ship upon its return to Bone, Algeria, failed to recover every casualty. The remains of thirty-six Italians were found in the ship when it arrived in the United States, and the men are buried in one grave." U.S. Department of Interior National Register of Historic Places Registration Form, Long Island National Cemetery, 2016, nps.gov/nr/feature/places/pdfs/16000113.pdf.

Chapter 15

1. Hadley, *U-Boats Against Canada: German Submarines in Canadian Waters* (1990).
2. Busch, Röll, Brooks, *German U-boat Commanders of World War Two: A Biographical Dictionary* (1999); Uboat.net/man/commanders.
3. Mason, Uboatarchive.net/U-190/KTB190-2, *U-190* patrol two diary
4. *Ibid.*
5. Busch, Röll, Brooks (1999), *op. cit.*; Uboat.net/men/commanders.

6. Mason, Uboatarchive.net/U-230/KTB230-3, *U-230* patrol three diary.
7. Werner, *Iron Coffins: A Personal Account of The German U-boat Battles of World War II* (2002); email to author, November 2009, regarding *U-Boats in the Bahamas*, whether Germans went ashore (aside from terror missions, they did not: he was emphatic: too dangerous, no benefit, no proof).
8. Mason, Uboatarchive.net, KTB 230-3.
9. Busch, Röll, and Brooks (1999), *op. cit.*; Uboat.net/men/commanders.
10. Mason, Uboatarchive.net/U-566/KTB566-10, *U-566* patrol ten diary.
11. *Ibid.*
12. Historikorders.com/page47/page77; Cornish (Can/R. 102446 Sergeant, R.C.A.F., No. 179 Sqn.) was awarded the Distinguished Flying Medal for this mission and another in the Med. The citation reads "on the night of 25th October 1943, Sergeant Cornish located another enemy submarine and again pressed home his attack in the face of heavy enemy fire. His aircraft was hit in the tail plane. The precision and accuracy with which Sergeant Cornish delivered his attack damaged the enemy submarine to such an extent that it was unable to submerge," Busch, Röll, and Brooks (1999), *op. cit.*, p. 244, Uboat.net/men/commanders.
13. Niestlé, *German U-boat Losses of World War Two* (2014), *U-869*.
14. Kurson, *Shadow Divers* (2005); emails with author, 2010–2017.
15. Wynn, *U-Boat Operations of the Second World War* (1997); Uboat.net/boats/patrols/patrol_1265, patrol summary, vpnavy.com, Ritschel, *Kurzfassung Kriegstagebücher Deutscher…* (1970–).
16. Hague, Holdoway, Cooper, et al., convoyweb.co.uk; Eastern Sea Frontier, *Enemy Action Diary*, April 14–15, 1943; fold3.com.
17. *War Diary, Chapter II, Two Submarines Sunk (Red Fox and Red George)*, p. 6 (p. 279 on document), Eastern Sea Frontier, *Enemy Action Diary*, April 14–15, 1943, fold3.com.
18. National Archives, *Survivor's Statements (1941–1942)*: the *Pan Pennsylvania*
19. Busch, Röll, and Brooks (1999), *op. cit.*, p. 108; Uboat.net/men/commanders/401, Hänert.
20. Munro and Jackson, co-hosts at site on *U-550*'s loss at soundunderwatersurvey.com/wrecks/u-550/the-sinking-of-the-u-550.
21. Peffer, *Where Divers Dare: The Hunt for the Last U-Boat* (2016), p. 89; emails with author 2017–early 2018.
22. *War Diary, Chapter II, Two Submarines Sunk (Red Fox and Red George)*, p. 6 (p. 279 on document); Eastern Sea Frontier, *Enemy Action Diary*, April 14–15, 1943, p. 7 (p. 280); Eastern Sea Frontier, *Enemy Action Diary*, April 14–15, 1943; fold3.com; soundunderwatersurvey.com/wrecks/u-550/the-sinking-of-the-u-550, reference to U.S. Coast Guard reappraisal of the loss in June 2005; Uboat.net; Niestlé (2014), *op. cit.*, *U-550* (Niestlé knew Hänert personally); emails to author 2018.
23. Munro, detailed custom charts of U-boat locations on seafloor, emails, October 2015. Other images from public domain including side-scans, soundunderwatersurvey.com/wrecks/u-550, Pfeffer, *Where Divers Dare* (2016).
24. National Archives, *Survivor's Statements (1941–1942)*: the *Pan Pennsylvania;* Eastern Sea Frontier, *Enemy Action Diaries; Deck Logs*, U.S.C.G., History.USCG.Mil, Fold3.com, Canadian National Archives; author visits to several graveyards in 2015–18; the *Pan Pennsylvania* tab, Uboat.net/allies/merchants/ship/3236.
25. Niestlé, email to author, February 23, 2018.
26. Various, mostly Eastern Sea Frontier, *Enemy Action Diaries*, April 16–July 7, 1944, at Uboatarchive.net, fold3.com.
27. Captain John Stanford of Rhode Island generously provided a detailed map and photo of the gravesites, in 2015–2016. Author has since shared detailed

information with the Newport Visitors and Convention Bureau et al. While the propellers of *U-853* are protected behind tight military security on the nearby naval base (limited permission can be granted ahead of time), the graves are both accessible to the public. Heder and the Unknown Sailor from *U-853* are at the Island Cemetery Annex. This is a small enclosure bounded by: Van Zandt Avenue/South; Butler Street/East; Evarts Street/North; and Brandt Street/West. Heder has a headstone with German bunting situated centrally against the back fence, beneath a tree, findagrave.com/memorial/ 15037603/gunther-heder. The Unknown Sailor is memorialized with a stone set in the grass, first or second row from the lane, military appearance, in white marble. The GPS coordinates are roughly 41.30 × 71.19W. Though harder to find, it is along the west side, outer from roadway, a third of the way from back heading toward the street, on the right.

28. *War Diary, Chapter II, Two Submarines Sunk (Red Fox and Red George)*, p. 6 (p. 279 on document); Eastern Sea Frontier, *Enemy Action Diary*, April 14–15, 1943, p. 9 (p. 282).
29. Munro, soundunderwatersurvey, emails with author 2017–2018; Peffer (2016), *op. cit.*, p. 89.
30. Fold3.com, ESF, numerous U.S.C.G. and U.S. Navy diaries with granular detail, NARA, etc. (cited above), included Canadian National Archives, persistent searches of Newspaperarchive.com.
31. Busch, Röll, and Brooks (1999), *op. cit.*, p. 108; Uboat.net/men/commanders/401, Hänert.
32. Munro, soundunderwatersurvey.com (2018); Peffer (2016), *op. cit.*; Captain Eric Takakjian, when not at sea or running various boards, tugboats and dive sites, has been very generous with his time patience and guidance. He lay a wreath for victims of the Battle of Point Judith, RI, despite the bends, and has fed the author helpful emails right up to publication.
33. National Archives, *Survivor's Statements (1941–1942)*: the *Pan Pennsylvania.*
34. Munro, soundunderwatersurvey.com (2018).
35. U.S.C.G. *Coast Patrol Diary*, northeast coast of New Jersey, Jersey Shore, detailed catalog of items recovered from the surf, many of them personal and macabre—life jackets, mattresses, clothes, etc. April 1944, fold3.com, before the foot patrols with dogs and horses were abandoned. See also Appendices (below) and lists in the main text of Chapter Fifteen.
36. Uboat.net/allies/merchants/search.php, list of four *Pan* series of vessels sunk by U-boats World War II, with details of casualty.

Chapter 16

1. Uboat.net/boats/patrols/u1222, Uboat.net/men/commanders/81.
2. Mason, Uboatarchive.net/U-107/KTB107-12, *U-107* patrol twelve diary.
3. National Archives, *Survivor's Statements (1941–1942)*: FV *Lark*. This file is unique of all the others inasmuch as many photographs with captions detailing exactly where bullets and shells hit the shute, the deck, the dories, and houses on *Lark*, and an entire page addressing and including "Com 1 Public Relations Officer Cognizant," (p. 3, 151251, NCR 10554).
4. The *Washington Daily News*, June 15, 1944, "Victim Reveals Presence of Sub off Northern U.S.," essentially a First Naval District Press Release, including a press interview will all twenty-seven crew and a photo-shoot. The only detail they witheld was that the attack occurred "recently." For other details of the U.S. Navy response, see Mason, *op. cit.* Uboatarchive.net/ESF/ESFWarDiary Feb42APP4, Eastern Sea Frontier *Enemy Action Diary.*

5. *Nantucket Inquirer and Mirror*, September 8, 1945, "Nantucket Fishermen Awarded Service Certificates," digital archives at the Nantucket Atheneum.
6. Mason, Uboatarchive.net/U-518/KTB518-6, *U-518* patrol six diary.
7. *Ibid.*
8. en.wikipedia.org/wiki/1944_Great_Atlantic_hurricane; loss of U.S.S. *Warrington*, Capt. Dawes, R. A. Jr. (U.S.N.-Ret.) *The Dragons' Breath: Hurricane at Sea* (Annapolis: Naval Institute Press, 1996).
9. Busch, Röll, and Brooks, *German U-boat Commanders of World War Two: A Biographical Dictionary* (1999); Niestlé, *German U-Boat Losses of World War Two* (2014), *U-518*.

Chapter 17

1. Eastern Sea Frontier, *Enemy Action Diary*, typical daily note in fold3.com/image/292546449.
2. Busch, Röll, and Brooks, *German U-boat Commanders of World War Two: A Biographical Dictionary* (1999); Kurowski, *Knights of the Wehrmacht: Knight's Cross Holders of the U-Boat Service* (2004); Uboat.net/men/commanders/484.
3. Uboat.net/ops/agents1944, this 129-day mission was *U-1230*'s only patrol, and *Cornwallis* her only victim. For ship's earlier damage, repair, destruction: Uboat.net/allies/merchants/ship/3382.
4. Mallmann Showell, *U-Boats at War: Landings on Hostile Shores* (2000), p. 33; Chief of Naval Operations (CNO), U.S. Navy, *Report on the Interrogation of German Agents Gimpel and Colepaugh Landed on the Coast of Maine from U-1230, dated 13 January 1945* (1945), ibiblio.org/hyperwar/USN/rep/U-1230/index.
5. Mallmann Showell (2000), *op. cit.*, p. 33; Astor details, en.wikipedia.org/wiki/Vincent_Astor; emails with NYYC historian John Rousmaniere, librarian Vanessa Cameron, NYYC.org.
6. National Counterintelligence Center, *Counterintelligence in World War II*, "Colepaugh and Gimpel," fas.org/irp/ops/ci/docs/ci2/2ch1_a (Federation of American Scientists, link broken, May 2018).
7. Miller, *A True Story of an American Nazi Spy: William C. Colepaugh, A Biography* (2013), by a friend of Colepaugh's who was shocked to learn of his friend's past late in their lives, National Counterintelligence Center.
8. *Ibid.*; Rose, J., editor and historian, "On a Dark and Stormy November Night," *Friends of Wompatuck News* (FOW), friendsofwampatuck.org, Fall, 2008 (first published 1993).
9. Uboat.net/men/commanders/483. He outlived his brother Kurt by fifty-three years until 2004; Busch, Röll, and Brooks (1999), *op. cit.*
10. A variance between Wynn's account in *U-Boat Operations of the Second World War* (1997) and Uboat.net's is rare, yet one appears to exist in this instance. To avoid detection, Hilbig would not have radioed his position daily: Wynn (1997), p. 235.
11. Rose (2008), *op. cit.*; "Nazi U-boats plagued Maine coast during WWII," SoMeOldNews blog, *Surprising Southern Maine History*, Someoldnews.com/?p=954. This author does not find such tales to be creditable, or the matter itself militarily meaningful beyond bragging rights. Sassaman, R., and Whitman, P. (illustrator), "Nazi Spies Came Ashore," *America in WWII Magazine*, 310 Publishing LLC, americainwwii.com/articles/nazi-spies-come-ashore (2005), historisches-marinearchiv.de/ projekte/crewlisten/ww2/ eingabe.php?site=1andvar1=wert1andvar2=wert2, transcription of official *Kriegsmarine*

Crew Lists database compiled by Hubertus Weggelaar and Horst Schmeisser, per Kolbicz, Uboat.net.

12. Email from Ronald Jackson, nephew of one of the Germans said to have stepped ashore. The name could be narrowed from the crew roster and Gay's account to two persons: Seaman's Apprentice Konrad Heutger and Machinist's Mate Fritz Horstmann. Gay, R., co-author, *They Came to Destroy America: The FBI Goes to War Against Nazi Spies and Saboteurs During World War II* (Missoula: Pictorial Histories Publishing Co., 2003), in which Gay is described as a former U.S. intelligence officer. It would be good to have this detail confirmed in the main text of a book of this nature. Yet unnecessarily and ironically it remains—literally—a footnote. After initial contact on 17 November, 2017, on 26 January, 2018, with deadlines looming and his uncle going to an assisted-living facility, the nephew wrote: "I am unable to provide the names at this time. My uncle.... is quite a stubborn individual. In his mind he still believes the account contained within the letter to be a treasured family story and does not wish to share it with others at this time ... he believes he can write such an account on his own that may find its way to print someday, maybe even a movie, he said." End of story, taken to the grave, and by a history teacher.
13. Rose (2008), *op. cit.*; Mallmann Showell (2000), *op. cit.*, p. 33; Uboat.net/ops/agents1944.
14. Sassaman (2005), *op. cit.* While Colepaugh was being sentenced to death, Harvard Hodgkins, nine years his junior, was being feted by Governor Dewey in New York City and shown all the city's highlights, including meeting Joe Lewis and Babe Ruth, following which Maine Maritime Academy gave him a full scholarship; Colepaugh outlived him by nineteen years. Chief of Naval Operations (CNO), U.S. Navy, *Report on the Interrogation of German Agents Gimpel and Colepaugh Landed on the Coast of Maine from U-1230, dated 13 January 1945* (1945), ibiblio.org/hyperwar/USN/rep/U-1230/index; Rose (2008), *op. cit.*
15. Rose (2008), *op. cit.*, p. 1.
16. Gimpel published a book on the experience called *Agent 146* (New York: St. Martin's Press, 2003). Gay (2003), *op. cit.*; Sassaman (2005), *op. cit*, very thorough treatment, 1944–2004, cites Gay (2003). Though Gimpel and Colepaugh were the last agents, or spies landed in the U.S. by the Germans in World War II, there was another who tried. Oskar Mantel, age forty, was to be dropped off in Maine in August 1944, aboard *U-1229*. The boat was sunk and though eighteen died southeast of Newfoundland on August 20, forty-one men survived and were taken prisoner. Mantel survived and confessed his plan (he had lived in New York City for twelve years and snuck into Germany via Japan and Russia). See "A Would-Be Nazi James Bond," *America in WWII Magazine*, 310 Publishing LLC, americanwwii.com/articles/a-would-be-nazi-james-bond. Presciently, his year-long intelligence assignment in Paris consisted of "always laying up with the women." Interrogators were struck by the wads of U.S. cash he carried and his willingness to "sell out to save himself." This consistent characteristic hardly made those who arrived in the U.S. by U-Boat excellent spy material. Yet the Germans mostly sent damaged, flawed, and poorly prepared men on these missions, increasing, it would seem from the evidence, their likelihood of failure, "Nazi U-boats plagued Maine coast during WWII," SoMeOldNews blog; Uboat.net/boats/u1229; Niestlé, *German U-Boat Losses of World War Two* (2014), *U-1229*.
17 Sassaman (2005), *op. cit.*; Gimpel (2003), *op. cit.*; Haslau, H. E., "The Night German Spies Landed at Hancock Point," *The Ellsworth American*, August 24, 1995, and August 31, 1995, Ellsworth, Maine.
18. *Spion für Deutschland* (*Spies for Germany* film) (1956); en.wikipedia.org/wiki/Unternehmen_Elster; Sassaman (2005), *op. cit.*; Rose (2008) *op. cit.*

19. National Archives, *Survivor's Statements (1941–1942)*: the *Cornwallis*; Uboat.net/allies/merchants/ship/3382.
20. Baird, I., great-nephew of William Quilty of North Sydney, who was killed when the *Cornwallis* sank. Email to author, July 12, 2017.
21. Uboat.net credits the *Notre Dame* with the rescue; however, *Survivor Statements* say it was *Ivy M.* and the U.S. Navy crash-boat U.S.S. *26597* and "navy vessels." As it should not take many more than three vessels to rescue six men, others may have been retrieving bodies or looking in the wrong place. Uboat.net/allies/merchants/ship/3382. With water that cold, what matters is that some men survived, less so exactly how they and their rescuers managed to achieve that result.
22. Diver J. Brett wrote that weather for the 2017 diving and exploration season did not permit his team the opportunity to scan the wreck. Emails to author, April 24, 2017, February 2, 2018.

Chapter 18

1. Mason, Uboatarchive.net, Uboat.net piece the patrol together post-fact.
2. Niestlé, *German U-boat Losses of World War Two* (2014), *U-866*.
3. Busch, Röll, and Brooks, *German U-boat Commanders of World War Two: A Biographical Dictionary* (1999).
4. Wynn, *U-Boat Operations of the Second World War* (1997), Uboat.net contradict each other on this point. Both authors employ original source material and then triple-check each fact, so it is rare that they are not entirely in accord. If nothing else this illustrates all of our fallibility, which also demonstrates that seventy-five years after these actions, a more accurate interpretation can be drawn, and facts forced to the surface from original sources that no one may have yet bothered to winnow out.
5. National Archives, *Survivor's Statements (1941–1942)*: the *Atlantic States*.
6. Niestlé (2014), *op. cit.*, *U-879*.
7. National Archives, *Survivor's Statements (1941–1942)*: the *Atlantic States*.
8. Uboat.net/boats/patrols/patrol_2550, projected patrol of *U-857*.
9. Uboat.net; Niestlé (2014), *op. cit.*, crediting Coppock, R., at the Foreign Document Section of the U.K. Ministry of Defense, Naval Historical Branch in London, in April 1994; emails to author, May 2018.
10. Busch, Röll, and Brooks (1999), *op. cit.*; Uboat.net/men/commanders/943 (Premauer).
11. Wynn, *U-Boat Operations of the Second World War*, Vol. II (1997), pp. 173–174; Uboat.net/men/commanders/332, Frömsdorf
12. National Archives, *Survivor's Statements (1941–1942)*: the *Black Point*.
13. Wynn (1997), *op. cit.*, p. 173; Niestlé (2014), *op. cit.*, *U-853*.
14. Busch, Röll, and Brooks (1999), *op. cit.*; Uboat.net/men/commanders/332, Frömsdorf.
15. Morgan and Taylor, *U-boat Attack Logs: A Complete Record of Warship Sinkings from Original Sources 1939–1945* (2011). From a military point of view, this was a challenging battle to study and interpret, as the U.S. Navy pretended it wasn't a battle at all until many decades later.
16. Puleo, *Due to Enemy Action: The True World War II Story of the USS* Eagle 56 (2005); Morgan and Taylor, *U-boat Attack Logs: A Complete Record of Warship Sinkings from Original Sources 1939–1945* (2011).
17. *Ibid.*
18. *Ibid.*

19. National Archives, *Survivor's Statements (1941–1942)*: the *Black Point*.
20. Luise Schadtle Coley, emails to author, January–May 2018, wrote: "My father-in-law [Capt. Coley] worked on tugs for Sheridan Transport.... He was born in Boston [1926], then moved to Perth Amboy. He worked on tugs, New Jersey to Boston, Connecticut, and Rhode Island, beginning in 1942 right after high school. His mother's family were in Bridgeport, CT, and when going along the coast they would come and wave to his shipmate from shore. That's how his father 'saw' his mother for the first time; he was invited to his shipmate's home, and the rest is history."
21. Emails, instant messages, calls, Luise Coley to author April 19–May 7, 2018, and June 10, 2019.
22. *Ibid*. Captain Louis Coley "went to be with his sweetheart" on May 7, 2018, as this book went to press. The story identifying which tug and barges and crew witnessed the *Black Point* sinking were not known until a week before his death. He only released them on strict condition the recipient was "fellow seaman" and card-carrying mariner.
23. Fort Adams was designed and overseen by West Point graduate General Robert E. Lee before he led the South in the American Civil War. In its absence, the British used hulks to blockade the harbor, including (allegedly) the remains of Captain James Cook's *Endeavour*. The fort is a popular venue for spectating yacht races and large music festivals.
24. Lynch, *Kill and Be Killed? The U-853 Mystery* (2008), Vol. 112, #3, U.S. Naval Institute Press (2008), Usni.org/magazines/navalhistory/2008-06/kill-and-be-killed-u-853-mystery.
25. Fold3.com/image/296555717, Eastern Sea Frontier *Enemy Action Diaries*.
26. Wreckhunter.net/DataPages/blackpoint-dat.
27. Lynch (2008), *op. cit.*
28. New England Historical Society, Newenglandhistoricalsociety.com/flashback-photo-battle-point-judith.
29. Emails, messages, calls, Luise (Schadtle) Coley to author, April 19–May 7, 2018, and June 10, 2019.
30. Emails from various tugboats enthusiasts, including Dave Boone in Philadelphia, Capt. Conti Culuntino, Capt. Brian Fournier, Craig Symonette, Capt. Eric Takakjian, Compass Maritime, Bahamas Maritime Authority, Marcon International, Mr. Kendal Butler, Capt. Michael Oakes, Capt. Billy Braithwaite, Ronald Lightbourn, Bradford Marine, Ray D'Arville, Capt. Murray, and Marcus Mitchell of Overseas Salvage. Finally a Las Vegas Nevada corporation called Liberty Oil Refining & Associates, Inc., libertyoil.org, owned by Kermit Waters since 1979, they have two jack-up rigs, a support ship and the *Carina* looking for oil and gas in the Bahamas. Calls and emails by this author in early 2018 were not returned.

Chapter 19

1. Waller (2015–2018), Uboat.net/articles/82; emails, October 2015–January 2018, Waller, *The U-Boats That Surivived: The Whole Story* (2010); archeion.ca/derek-m-waller-fonds.
2. Niestlé, *German U-boat Losses in World War Two* (2014), *U-866*; Wynn, *U-Boat Operations of the Second World War* (1997), Vol. II, p. 175; Waller (2010), *op. cit.*; archeion.ca/derek-m-waller-fonds, email inputs, October 2015 to April 2018.
3. *Ibid.*
4. Busch, Röll, and Brooks, *German U-boat Commanders of World War Two: A Biographical Dictionary* (1999).

5. Waller (2010), *op. cit.*, archeion.ca/derek-m-waller-fonds; emails to author with factual amendments, January 15, 2018.
6. *Ibid.*
7. Gray, "Nazi U-Boats Surrender at Portsmouth," from Gray's 1945 contemporaneous pamphlet, *Surrender at Sea, A compilation of the stories of the surrender of the Nazi submarines.* "Source: Charlie Gray, *Surrender at Sea,* (pamphlet), published by WHEB and Colonial Cleaners, Portsmouth, NH, June 1945. Abridged by J. Dennis Robinson at SeacoastNH.com Original essay © SeacoastNH.com," seacoastnh.com/nazi-u-boats-surrender-at-portsmouth/?start=3.
8. Niestlé (2014), *op. cit., U-804.*
9. Waller (2010), *op. cit.*; archeion.ca/derek-m-waller-fonds; emails to author with factual amendments, January 15, 2018.
10. Uboat.net, citing Fernando Almeida, contributor.
11. Busch, Röll, Brooks (1999), *op. cit.*
12. *Deck Logs,* U.S.S. *Argo*, U.S.S. *Vance*, NARA in D.C., Waller, emails, January 2018.
13. Gray (1945), *op. cit.*
14. Rust, E., *Naval Officers Under Hitler: The Story of Crew 34* (2009); Busch, Röll, and Brooks (1999), *op. cit.*; Uboat.net/men/Steinhoff.
15. en.wikipedia.org/wiki/Ernst_Steinhoff.
16. Mason, Uboatarchive.net/U-873A/U-873PrisonerTransfer; Uboatarchive.net/U-873A/U-873FollowUp, detailed dossier of original source materials.
17. Mason, Uboatarchive.net/U-873A/U-873FollowUp.
18. Mason, Uboatarchive.net/U-873A/U-873NIGReport.
19. *Ibid.*
20. *Ibid.*
21. Fort Devens was considered a lighter-duty prison, as "the most visibly anti-Nazis, 3,300 total, were shipped to Fort Devens and Camp Campbell, Kentucky," Uboat.net/men/pow/ pow_in_ america_processing.
22. Recent prisoners include Ponzi-scheme-abbettor Peter Madoff, the surviving Boston Marathon bomber (after he ran over and helped kill his brother), disgraced politician Anthony Weiner (caught sexting multiple times), Rajat Gupta (white collar), John Gambino (organized crime), and other mobsters, tax evaders, and terrorists, en.wikipedia.org/wiki/Federal_Medical_ Center_Devens #Notable_ inmates.
23. Waller, *U-Boats That Surrendered: The Western Atlantic (U.S.A, Canada and Argentina) Story* (2010); Uboat.net/articles/821, emails October 2015–April 2018; Waller, *The U-Boats That Surivived: The Whole Story* (2010); archeion.ca/derek-m-waller-fondsm.
24. Wynn, *U-Boat Operations of the Second World War* (1997), Vol. I, p. 170; Waller, *The U-Boats That Surivived: The Whole Story* (2010); archeion.ca/derek-m-waller-fondsm.
25. Waller, *U-Boats That Surrendered: The Western Atlantic (U.S.A, Canada and Argentina) Story*, (2010); Uboat.net/articles/821, emails to author October 2015–April 2018; Waller, *The U-Boats That Surivived: The Whole Story* (2010); archeion.ca/derek-m-waller-fondsm.
26. Christy, G., "A U-Boat Captain and a U.S. Coast Guard Cutter's Captain Meet at the End of World War II" (2017): "*Argo* took over command of *U-234* on 19 May 1945. Fehler went on board *Argo* and offered a handshake to Commander Moffat, a U.S. Navy representative. Denied this, Fehler made a remark about how soon Germany would rise again, and perhaps then the Americans would surrender to him. This began an intense dislike between Fehler and his American captors," *War History Online* (2017), warhistoryonline.com/instant-articles/opposites-meet-end-world-war, December 5, 2017.
27. *Ibid.*

28. Scalia, *Germany's Last Mission to Japan: The Sinister Voyage of U-234* (2009).
29. Mason, Uboatarchive.net/U-873A/U-873PrisonerTransfer.
30. Uboat.net/forums/read.php?20,60184,60184, Forum post about Messerschmitt, May 12, 2001.
31. en.wikipedia.org/wiki/German_submarine_U-234, Scalia, *Germany's Last Mission to Japan: The Sinister Voyage of U-234* (2009).
32. Busch, Röll, and Brooks (1999), *op. cit.*, Uboat.net/men/commanders.
33. Scalia, *Germany's Last Mission to Japan: The Sinister Voyage of U-234* (2009).
34. Gray, *Surrender at Sea* (1945).
35. History can present rather odd stories. This one relates to a young German PoW given his freedom by a sympathetic American woman, from Uboat.net/men/pow/escapes_us_2: According to the FBI, Mrs. Fannie Welvaert was employed at Lovell General Hospital, Fort Devens, where she became acquainted with 22-year-old Horst Becker, a German prisoner detailed to the hospital from the nearby camp. In a collaborative effort, Becker escaped from Fort Devens on 13 September 1945, after which the couple moved in with Mrs. Welvaert's parents. Stranger yet, she was 45 and had three sons in the service of the U.S.! They were caught but not shot, probably as the Atlantic war was over.
36. Schäffer, *U-Boat 977: The True Story of The U-boat that Escaped to Argentina* (2017), *U-977, Geheimfahrt nach Südamerika* (Wiesbaden: Linen Verlag, 1950), English Edition *U-Boat 977* (London: William Kimber, 1952). The book has been published as short version paperback "*66 Tage unter Wasser: die geheimnisumwobene U-Boot-Fernfahrt nach Argentinien,*"(Rastatt: Erich Pabel Verlag, 1986), per *Deutsches U-Boot-Museum,* dubm.de/en/the-last-voyage.
37. *Bahia* events, see en.wikipedia.org/wiki/Brazilian_cruiser_Bahia#Loss, Waller, Radigan, Navsource.org/archives/08/08504, U-977 (citing Mohl); emails to author from both.
38. Waller, *U-Boats That Surrendered: The Western Atlantic (U.S.A, Canada and Argentina) Story* (2010); Waller, Uboat.net/articles/82l, emails to author October 2015–April 2018, Waller, *The U-Boats That Surivived: The Whole Story* (2010); archeion.ca/derek-m-waller-fonds, *U-889*; Uboat.net/articles/82l.
39. Photo credits to Derek Waller, Ron Reeves, Yves Hubert, and Joe Radigan, Navsource.org.
40. Barnette, *Encyclopedia of Florida Shipwrecks, Volume I: Atlantic Coast* (St. Petersburg: Association of Underwater Explorers, 2010), AUE founder in Florida, emails, Januaru 31–mid-March 2018. A long-time NOAA staffer, Barnette also helped the author with *U-boats in Bahamas* (2016).

Chapter 20

1. Jones, "Submarine Shortage Solved: French and Italian Submarines as U.S. Navy Targets in the Western Atlantic, 1943–1945" (2015), *The Submarine Review*, June 2015, p. 2, citing Roscoe, T., and Voge, R., *United States Submarine Operations in World War II* (Annapolis: Naval Institute Press, 1949), p. 249.
2. *Ibid.*
3. *Ibid.*, p. 8.
4. *Ibid.*, p. 9.
5. Fold3.com, WWII Diaries, fold3.com/image/292511096?terms=amazone, *COM NY GR ESF,* keywords *Amazone*. Essentially determined key-word searching in Fold3.com database.
6. Jones (2015), *op. cit.*, p. 1.
7. Waller (German boats) and Alexiades (Italian boats), worked closely with the author 2010–2018. Jones' essay on the rather obtuse topic of French and Italian

boats and dispersal (or diaspora) from the Mediterranean Sea to Chile via Gibraltar and Bermuda was also central.

8. Thanks to Captain Paul A. Aranha in the Bahamas for arranging an interview with Prince Don Nicolò Maria Pignatelli Aragon Cortès (born 1923), Seventeenth Prince of Noia, age ninety-five. He fondly retold how as a young cadet, the commander of the Italian submarine *Atropo* came so close to an uninhabited Bahama island *en route* to Guantanamo in late February 1945, that young Nicolò and other young sailors had a joyful run along the sandy beach.
9. Jones (2015), *op. cit.*, p. 12.
10. Prince, *Death in the Baltic: The WWII Sinking of the Wilhelm Gustloff* (New York: St. Martin's Griffin, 2014); emails to author, February 2018; for summaries of the world's deadliest maritime disasters, en.wikipedia.org/wiki/MV*Wilhelm_Gustloff*.
11. Waller, *U-505 in the U.S. Navy 1944 to 1954 (from Capture to Disposal to Display)*, (2016); emails to author October 2015–April 2018; Waller, *The U-Boats That Surivived: The Whole Story* (2010); archeion.ca/derek-m-waller-fonds.
12. Waller, *U-1406 and U-1407: Were they Scuttled, or did they Surrender?* (2010); emails to author October 2015–April 2018; Waller, *The U-Boats That Surivived: The Whole Story* (2010); archeion.ca/derek-m-waller-fonds, uboat.net/articles/80, U.K. PRO files ADM 228/8, WO 235/632 and WO 235/64. Re: Grumpelt's Court Martial, "Law Reports of Trials of War Criminals, Vol, 1, English Edition," HMSO, 1947; Waller, *U-Boats That Surrendered: The Western Atlantic (U.S.A, Canada and Argentina) Story* (2010); Uboat.net/articles/82l.
13. Waller (2016), *op. cit.*; emails to author October 2015–April 2018; Waller, *The U-Boats That Surivived: The Whole Story* (2010); archeion.ca/derek-m-waller-fonds.
14. Waller, *U-Boats That Surrendered: The Western Atlantic (U.S.A, Canada and Argentina) Story* (2010); Uboat.net/articles/82l; emails October 2015–April 2018; Waller, *The U-Boats That Surivived: The Whole Story* (2010); archeion.ca/derek-m-waller-fonds.
15. Waller, *U-Boats That Surrendered: The Western Atlantic (U.S.A, Canada and Argentina) Story* (2010); Waller, *U-1406 and U-1407: Were they Scuttled, or did they Surrender?* (2010); Uboat.net/articles/82l, emails October 2015–April 2018, Waller (2016), *op. cit.*; emails to author October 2015–April 2018; Waller, *The U-Boats That Surivived: The Whole Story* (2010); archeion.ca/derek-m-waller-fonds; Uboat.net/ boats/u1105, en.wikipedia.org/wiki/German_submarine_U-1105.

Conclusion

1. Wiberg, *U-Boats off Bermuda* (2017) and *U-Boats in Bahamas* (2016), ericwiberg.com.
2. The National Archives (TNA), *Thursobank*, TD/DEMS/139, ADM/199/2139 (London: Public Records Office, 1939–1945), National Archives, *Survivor's Statements (1941–1942)*: the *Thursobank* (only a three-page sketch); Uboat.net/allies/merchants/ crews/ship1463.
3. *Ibid.* (except for NARA citation).
4. Wiberg, *U-Boats in the Bahamas* (2016) and *U-Boats off Bermuda* (2017), Appendices and Conclusions.
5. Bennett and Bennett, *Survivors: British Merchant Seamen in the Second World War* (1999), p. 191; *Safe at Last*, Chapter 9., pp. 191–192 (citing "OA 89/2A, Second Officer W. M. Thomas"); for *Baron Semple* interactions with *Peisander*

men (no clarity as to definition of "OA"); Stilgoe, *Lifeboat: A History of Courage, Cravenness, and Survival at Sea* (2003), p. 217; Mayes, Shipsnostalgia .com/archive/index.php?t-29448 (blog post).

6. Trickey, E., "Hook, Line, and Sinker, Maine treasure hunter Greg Brooks found the world's richest shipwreck off the coast of Cape Cod. Or at least that's what he told investors," *Boston Magazine*, August 25, 2015, bostonmagazine.com/news/2015/08/25/greg-brooks-port-nicholson. In 2004–2005, this author boarded heavily armed salvage and research vessel *Sea Hunter* in East Boston for an hour-long tour throughout, as a means to groom him to become a bundler and gather investors for the project. Nothing developed from it. At the same time, and on a related search, under the Tobin Bridge in East Boston, the author toured one of the *Ivy Trawlers*, believed to be the former *Harvard*. Built as a steam trawler in 1926, 179 feet long, she patrolled the North Atlantic Fishery then in 1941 was converted by the U.S. Navy for war patrolling (*v.* U-boats presumably) as the *Bellefonte*, then returned to Woods Hole Oceanographic Institute in 1944, becoming *Albatross III* from 1948 to 1959. whoi.edu/page.do?pid=116836andtid=5763andcid=1551. The author boarded this or a sister ship in where the Andrew McArdle Bridge meets Nay Street at the Bang Corporation, behind the Mobil station. In May 2018, Google Earth shows the vessel still there, at the north end of the bridge near KandD Equipment Repair, rafted with five commercial craft of varying sizes and disrepair and a barge. This author is in contact with a crew member from that time.
7. Uboat.net/boats/u233.
8. Uboat.net/boats/u1226; Niestlé, *German U-Boat Losses in World War Two* (2014), pp. 133 and 232.
9. Fold3.com/image/287161140?terms=hyannis%20air.
10. Fold3.com/image/292546467.
11. Morbidly, there are remains of thirty-six Italian PoWs from the Liberty ship *Benjamin Contee* at the Long Island National Cemetery in Farmingdale, central Long Island, NY. After the airborne German torpedo breached the cargo hold it was sealed with men in it. The ship was patched in Algeria and Gibraltar, yet continued westward with temporary repairs. Not surprisingly, the *Benjamin Contee* was barely seaworthy enough to cross the North Atlantic in winter and fell out of the convoy around the Azores more than once. Following arrival and repairs in Brooklyn Navy Yard, it was designated as a block-ship or Mulberry, a sunken dock to enable the supply chain in Normandie after D-Day in June 1944.

    > The ship left for New York, where she arrived on 24 January 1944. Following a more accurate search [in Brooklyn Navy Yard], in the hold there were discovered bodies of thirty-six unidentifiable Italian prisoners, who were buried on February 16, 1944, in Long Island National Cemetery.

    They held a Roman Catholic ceremony on board. Keefer, *Italian Prisoners of War in America 1942–1946* (1992), p. 25; Shortridge, Bud, S.S. *Benjamin Contee*, archeosousmarine.net/Pdf/benjamin_ contee.pdf-France, December 17, 2010; *Smooth Log, Armed Guard Unit*, 17 December 1943 reads: "All hands present at Roman Catholic mass said by British Chaplain on No. #2 Hatch for the Italian prisoners killed by torpedoing. Delegations from nearby British warships present.... [to] guard against souvenir-hunting by workmen." Signed Scott Cooley, Jr., NARA, D.C., Record Group 24, Stack 470, Row 900, Compartment 2, Shelf 3, Box 84. The author literally stumbled on these graves while searching the cemetery, at night, illuminated by headlights in the fall of 2017, for the graves of Zube and Flade of *U-550*. Location is: 2040 Wellwood Ave, Wyandanch (East Farmingdale), Plot Section 2C, Site 7, per findagrave.com, volunteer Glenn, September 12, 2008, FindAGrave Memorial #29748953. Cem.va.gov for related historic documents.

12. en.wikiquote.org/wiki/Ernest_King.
13. Barnette, emails to author, January 31, 2018: "The area … [of U.S. Navy U-boat sinkings] is well beyond the jurisdiction of current National Marine Sanctuary or proposed NMS areas." Waller, *U-Boats That Surrendered: The Western Atlantic (U.S.A, Canada and Argentina) Story* (2010); Uboat.net/articles/82l; emails October 2015–April 2018.
14. *Ibid.*
15. Author graduated from St. George's School in Middletown, Rhode Island, overlooking all of southern Aquidneck Island outside Newport. The chapel tower, gifted by Nicholas Brown (founding family of Brown University) provides the highest viewing station in the region. Not only were lookouts posted there and at nearby Sachuest Point (so the story goes), but concrete fortifications from those days remain today. It is now a National Wildlife Refuge, fws.gov/refuge/sachuest_point, where "during World War II, the U.S. Navy used this site for a rifle range and communications center."
16. en.wikiquote.org/wiki/Ernest_King: "Ernest J. King, Chief of Naval Operations, was a spare, no-nonsense officer with a strong distaste for publicity, some enemies among the Army and British brass, and one of the sharpest strategic minds in Washington," C. L. Sulzberger, publisher of *The New York Times*, in *The American Heritage Picture History of World War II* (1966), p. 335. J. W. Stilwell later witnessed when British Field Marshal "Brooke got nasty, and King got good and sore. King almost climbed over the table at Brooke. God, he was mad. I wished he had socked him." Joseph Warren Stilwell, referring to an argument King had with Alan Brooke at the Casablanca Conference in 1943, in which Brooke accused King of favoring the Pacific war. Sourced from George C. Marshall: *Organizer of Victory 1943–1945* (1973), Forrest C. Pogue, p. 305.
17. en.wikipedia.org/wiki/Joseph_P._Kennedy_Jr., *Operation Anvil and Operation Aphrodite.*
18. Michel, Etkin, Gilbert, Urban, Waldron, and Blocksidge, *Potentially Polluting Wrecks in Marine Waters* (2005); Barnette, *Encyclopedia of Florida Shipwrecks, Volume I: Atlantic Coast* (2010); emails to author, early 2018; sanctuaries.noaa.gov/news/aug16/exploring-world-war-ii-battle-of-the-atlantic.
19. Wiberg, *U-Boats in the Bahamas* (2016) and *U-Boats off Bermuda* (2017), Appendices and Conclusions.
20. Based on extrapolations of convoy data at Hague, Holdoway, Cooper, et al., convoyweb.co.uk. Sometimes a project like this can seem like sitting on the side of a major highway counting what cars go by. This research trilogy has attempted to account for knowledge gaps between Cuba and Canada and World War II, with an emphasis on offshore attacks and the survival sagas which Allied sailors were forced to endure.

Postscript

1. en.wikipedia.org/wiki/Convention_on_the_Continental_Shelf; this set a new international standard for what at one time was simply the distance a cannon shot could reach from shore seaward.

Bibliography

Abella, A. and Gordon, S., *Shadow Enemies: Hitler's Secret Terrorist Plot Against the United States* (Guilford: The Lyons Press, 2002)

Barnette, M. C., *Encylopedia of Florida Shpwrecks, Volume I: Atlantic Coast* (High Springs: Association of Underwater Explorers [AUE], 2010)

Baughman, *The Mallorys of Mystic: Six generations in American Maritime Enterprise* (Middletown: Wesleyan University Press, 1972)

Beeby, D., *Cargo of Lies: The True Story of a Nazi Double Agent in Canada* (Toronto: University of Toronto Press, 1996)

Bennett, G. H. and Bennett, R., *Survivors: British Merchant Seamen in the Second World War* (London: Bloomsbury Academic, 2003)

Bercuson, D. J. and Herwig, H. H., *Long Night of the Tankers: Hitler's War Against Caribbean Oil* (Calgary: Beyond Boundaries, Canadian Defense and Strategic Studies Series, 2014)

Blair, C., *Hitler's U-Boat War: The Hunters, 1939–1942* (New York: Random House, 1996); *Hitler's U-Boat War: The Hunted, 1942–1945* (New York: Random House, 1998)

Brown, K., *U-Boat Assault on America, Why the U.S. Was Unprepared for War in the Atlantic* (Barnsley: Seaforth Publishing, Pen and Sword Books, Ltd., 2017)

Browning, R., *United States Merchant Marine Casualties of World War II* (Jefferson: McFarland and Company, Inc., Publishers, 2011)

Busch, R., Röll, H., and Brooks, G., *German U-boat Commanders of World War Two: A Biographical Dictionary* (Annapolis, Naval Institute Press, 1999)

Cremer, P., *U-Boat Commander* (Annapolis: Naval Institute Press, 1984)

Cressman, R., *The Official Chronology of the U.S. Navy in World War Two* (Washington: Naval Historical Center, Contemporary History Branch, 1999)

Dasch, G. J., *Operation Pastorius: Eight Nazi Spies Against America* (New York: Robert M. McBride Co., 1959)

Davies, P. N., *The Trade Makers: Elder Dempster in West Africa, 1852–1972, 1973–1989* (Liverpool: Liverpool University Press, 2000)

De Quesada, A., *U.S. Coast Guard in World War II* (Oxford: Osprey Publishing, 2010)

Dobbs, M., *Saboteurs: The Nazi Raid on America* (New York: Alfred A. Knopf, 2004)

Dunne, W. M. P., *Thomas F. McManus and the American Fishing Schooners: An Irish-American Success Story* (Mystic: Mystic Seaport Museum, 1970)

Edwards, B., *The Quiet Heroes: British Merchant Seamen at War 1939–1945* (Barnsley: Pen and Sword Military, 2003)

Gannon, M., *Operation Drumbeat: The Dramatic True Story of Germany's First U-Boat Attacks Along the American Coast in World War II* (New York: Harper Perennial, 1990)

Gay, R., Cohen, S., and DeNevi, D., *They Came to Destroy America: The FBI Goes to War Against Nazi Spies and Saboteurs During World War II* (Missoula: Pictorial Histories Publishing Co., 2003),

Gentile, G., *The Fuhrer's U-boats in American Waters* (Philadelphia: Bellerophon Bookworks, 2006)

Gimpel, E., *Agent 146: The True Story of a Nazi Spy in America* (New York: Thomas Dunne Books, 2013)

Gleichauf, J. F., *Unsung Sailors: The Naval Armed Guard in World War II* (Annapolis: Naval Institute Press, 1990)

Goebeler, H. and Vanzo, J., *Steel Boat, Iron Hearts: A U-boat Crewman's Life Aboard U-505* (New York: Savas Beatie LLC, 2008)

Gray, C., *Surrender at Sea* [pamphlet] (Portsmouth: WHEB, SeaCoastNH.com, 1945).

Hadley, M., *U-Boats Against Canada: German Submarines in Canadian Waters* (Montreal: McGill-Queen's University Press, 1990)

Hague, A., *The Allied Convoy System 1939–1945: Its Organization and Operation* (St. Catherine's: Vanwell Publishing Ltd., 2000), (also Cooper, A., Holdoway, M. (webmaster), convoyweb.org.uk)

HarperCollins, *Atlas of the Second World War* (Ann Arbor: Borders Press, 1999)

Hickam, H., *Torpedo Junction: The U-boat War off America's East Coast, 1942* (Annapolis: Naval Institute Press, 1996)

Hill, J., (ed.), *The Oxford Illustrated History of the Royal Navy* (Oxford: Oxford University Press, 1995)

Högel, G., *U-Boat Emblems of World War Two 1939–1945* (Atglen: Schiffer Military History, 1999)

Holm Lawson, S., *Norwegian Merchant Marine and Ships* (Sackets Harbor, Warsailors.com, 2013)

Hoyt, E. P., *U-Boats Offshore: When Hitler Struck America* (New York: Stein and Day, 1985)

Hulse, A., *This Blood Red Sea* (U.K.: secondworldwar.org.com, 2014)

Jenness, A., *On this Day in Nantucket History* (Stroud: The History Press, 2014)

Jordan, R., *The World's Merchant Fleets 1939* (Annapolis: Naval Institute Press, 1999)

Kahn, D., *The Codebreakers: The Comprehensive History of Secret Communication from Ancient Times to the Internet* (New York: Scribner, 1996)

Keefer, L., *Italian Prisoners of War in America 1942–1946* (New York: Praeger, 1992)

Kelshall, G., *The U-Boat War in the Caribbean* (Annapolis: Naval Institute Press, 1994)

Klim, J., *Attack on Orleans: The World War I Submarine Raid on Cape Cod* (Stroud: The History Press, 2014)

Kurowski, F., *Knights of the Wehrmacht: Knight's Cross Holders of the U-Boat Service* (Atglen: Schiffer Publishing Ltd., 2004)

Kurson, R., *Shadow Divers: The True Adventure of Two Americans Who Risked Everything to Solve one of the Last Mysteries of World War II* (New York: Random House, 2005)

Larson, C. K., *Bravo Zero: The Coast Guard Auxiliary in World War II* (Washington: National Historian, United States Coast Guard Auxiliary, uscgaux.info, 2000)

Lindbaek, L., Solum, N., *Norway's New Saga of the Sea* (New York: Exposition Press, 1969)

Mallmann Showell, J. P., *U-Boats at War: Landings on Hostile Shores* (Annapolis: Naval Institute Press, 2000); *U-Boats of the Second World War: Their Longest Voyages* (Stroud: Fonthill Media, 2017)

Mellor, William B., Jr., *Sank Same* (New York: Howell Soskin, 1944)

Miller, N., *The War at Sea* (New York: Scribner, 1995)

Miller, R. A., *A True Story of an American Nazi Spy, William C. Colepaugh, a Biography* (Atlanta: Trafford, 2013)

Mooney, R. F., *Nantucket Only Yesterday: An Island View of the Twentieth Century* (Nantucket: Wesco Publishing, 2000)

Morgan, D. and Taylor, B., *U-boat Attack Logs: A Complete Record of Warship Sinkings from Original Sources 1939–1945* (Barnsley: Seaforth Publishing, 2011)

Morison, S. E., *The Battle of the Atlantic, September 1939–1943: History of United States Naval Operations in World War II, Volume 1* (Boston: Little, Brown and Co., 1948); *The Atlantic Battle Won, May 1943–May 1945: History of United States Naval Operations in World War II, Volume 10* (Boston: Little, Brown and Co., 1948); *The Two-Ocean War: A Short History of the United States Navy in the Second World War* (Boston: Little, Brown and Co., 1963)

Mort, T., *The Hemingway Patrols: Ernest Hemingway and His Hunt for U-Boats* (New York: Scribner, 2009)

Mozolak, J., *New York Ships to Foreign Ports, 1939–1945* (New Jersey: janda.org/ships/2000)

National Archives [U.S.]: *Survivor's Statements (1941–1942), Series: Papers of Vice Admiral Homer N. Wallin, compiled 1941–1974. Record Group 38: Records of the Office of the Chief of Naval Operations, 1875–2006 Entry P-13* (College Park: Textual Reference, Military, 1942–1945)

Niestlé, A., *German U-boat Losses During World War Two* (London: Frontline Books, 2014)

Noli, J., *The Admiral's Wolf Pack* (Garden City: Doubleday and Co., 1974)

Offley, E., *The Burning Shore: How Hitler's U-Boats Brought World War II to America* (New York: Basic Books, 2014)

Parker, M., *Running the Gauntlet, An Oral History of Canadian Merchant Seamen in World War II* (Halifax: Nimbus Publishing Ltd., 1994)

Parkinson, J., *Nowhere is Too Far, The Annals of the Cruising Club of America* (New York: The Cruising Club of America, Inc., 1960)

Peffer, R., *Where Divers Dare: The Hunt for the Last U-Boat* (New York: Dutton Caliber, Penguin Group, 2016)

Prince, C., *Death in the Baltic: The WWII Sinking of the* Wilhelm Gustloff (New York: St. Martin's Griffin, 2014)

Puleo, S., *Due to Enemy Action: The True World War II Story of the USS Eagle 56*, (Guilford: Lyons Press, 2005)

Richardson, E., *B … was for Butter and Enemy Craft* (Halifax: Petheric Press, 1976)

Ritschel, H., *Kurzfassung Kriegstagebücher Deutscher U-Boote 1939–1945* (trans.: *Short versions of war diaries of German submarines*) (Möltenort: Privately published, *c.* 12 *Band*, or Volumes, 1970–)

Rohwer, J., *Axis Submarine Successes of World War Two: German, Italian and Japanese Submarine Successes, 1939–1945* (Annapolis: Naval Institute Press, 1999)

Roscoe, T. and Voge, R., *United States Submarine Operations in World War II* (Annapolis: Naval Institute Press, 1949)

Roskill, S., The *War at Sea* (London: Her Majesty's Stationers Offices, 1954–1961)

Rust, E. C., *Naval Officers Under Hitler, The Story of Crew 34* (Annapolis: Naval Institute Press, 2017)

Savas, T., (ed.), *Hunt and Kill: U-505 and the U-boat War in the Atlantic* (El Dorado Hills: Savas Beatie LLC, 2004)

Scalia, J., *Germany's Last Mission to Japan: The Sinister Voyage of U-234* (Annapolis: Naval Institute Press, 2009)

Schäffer, H., *U-Boat 977: The True Story of The U-boat that Escaped to Argentina* (Annapolis: Naval Institute Press, 2017)

Stilgoe, J. R., *Lifeboat: A History of Courage, Cravenness, and Survival at Sea* (Charlottesville: University of Charlottesville Press, 2003)

Suhren, T. and Brustat-Naval, F., *Teddy Suhren, Ace of Aces: Memoirs of a U-Boat Rebel* (Barnsley: Frontline Books, 2011).

Syrett, D., *The Defeat of the German U-boats: The Battle of the Atlantic* (Columbia: University of South Carolina Press, 1994)

The National Archives (TNA) [U.K.]: TD/DEMS/139, ADM/199/2139 (London: Public Records Office, 1939–1945), (Admiralty, Royal Navy Survivors Statements for British-flagged ships)

Thompson, L., *The Navy Hunts the CGR 3070* (Garden City: Doubleday, Doran and Co., Inc., 1944)

Tod, G., *The Last Sail Down East* (Barre: Barre Publishers, 1965)

United States Coast Guard, *The Coast Guard at War, Assistance XIV, Volume II* (Washington, D.C.: Historical Section, Public Information Division, U.S.C.G. Headquarters, 1947)

Vause, J., *Wolf, U-boat Commanders in World War Two* (Annapolis: Naval Institute Press, 1990)

Voge, R., *United States Submarine Operations in World War II* (Annapolis: Naval Institute Press, 1949)

Waller, D. M., *The U-Boats That Survived: The Whole Story* (Arundel, National Defense Headquarters [U.K.] Directorate of History and Heritage, 2010), archeion.ca/derek-m-waller-fonds, uboat.net/articles/

Werner, H., *Iron Coffins: A Personal Account of The German U-boat Battles of World War II* (Boston: Da Capo Press, 2002)

White, J., *U-Boat Tankers 1941–45: Submarine Suppliers to Atlantic Wolf Packs* (Annapolis: Naval Institute Press, 1998)

Wiberg, E., *U-Boats in the Bahamas* (New York: Bricktower Press, 2016); *U-Boats off Bermuda: Patrol Summaries and Merchant Ship Survivors Landed in Bermuda, 1940–1944* (Stroud: Fonthill Media, 2017)

Williams, A., *The Battle of the Atlantic: The Allies' Submarine Fight Against Hitler's Grey Wolves of the Sea* (New York: Basic Books, Perseus Books Group, 2003)

Wynn, K., *U-Boat Operations of the Second World War, Volumes I and II* (London: Caxton Editions, Chatham Publishing, 1997)

Afs.org
Americanancestors.org
Ancestry.com
Convoyweb.org.uk
Ericwiberg.com
Facebook.com
Findagrave.com
Fold3.com
History.uscg.mil
Janda.org/ships
Maritimedocumentation.us
Nantucketatheneum.org
Newspaperarchives.com
Regiamarina.net
Sshsa.org
Theshipslist.com
Uboatarchives.net
Uboat.net
Warsailors.com
Westmorelandresearch.org
Wrecksite.eu

Index

Vessels: